REVELATION

A MANUAL

of

SPIRITUAL WARFARE

REVELATION

A MANUAL

of

SPIRITUAL WARFARE

"These shall make war with the Lamb, and the Lamb shall overcome them: for he is Lord of lords, and King of kings: and they that are with him are called, and chosen, and faithful."

Revelation 17:14

EXPOSITORY SERMONS
ON THE BOOK OF REVELATION
~ VOL. 2 ~

Max Doner

REVELATION: A Manual of Spiritual Warfare
Expository Sermons on the Book of Revelation, Vol. 2

www.ReformedLighthousePress.com

ISBN: 979-8-9858473-1-4

Cover design: www.greatwriting.org
Book layout, design and preparation for publication:
www.greatwriting.org

Unless noted otherwise, Scripture quotations are taken from the King James (Authorized) Version

REFORMED
LIGHTHOUSE PRESS

Chapter Contents

Appendices

38

The Woman and the Dragon, Revelation 12:1–6

"[1] *And there appeared a great wonder in heaven; a woman clothed with the sun, and the moon under her feet, and upon her head a crown of twelve stars:* [2] *And she being with child cried, travailing in birth, and pained to be delivered.* [3] *And there appeared another wonder in heaven; and behold a great red dragon, having seven heads and ten horns, and seven crowns upon his heads.* [4] *And his tail drew the third part of the stars of heaven, and did cast them to the earth: and the dragon stood before the woman which was ready to be delivered, for to devour her child as soon as it was born.* [5] *And she brought forth a man child, who was to rule all nations with a rod of iron: and her child was caught up unto God, and to his throne.* [6] *And the woman fled into the wilderness, where she hath a place prepared of God, that they should feed her there a thousand two hundred and threescore days.*"

Chapter 12 is an important turning point in the book of Revelation for two reasons. First of all, it marks the beginning of the fourth parallel section of this book, which covers chapters 12 through 14. We have already seen the first three parallel sections when we looked at the seven churches, the seven seals, and the seven trumpets.

Each of these parallel sections describes the things that will characterize the age between the first and the second coming of Christ. Each of these parallel sections takes up a theme and explains the circumstances that will characterize the age regarding that theme. The warfare of the churches, the works of the wicked, and the wrath of the Lord were the themes of these first three parallel sections.

This fourth parallel section of the book of Revelation takes up the theme of the work of Satan and his helpers. We are introduced to all of them in this fourth parallel section in chapters 12 through 14.

Satan, who is also called the dragon, does not do his work all by himself. Just like God employs angelic and human agents to accomplish His work, in the same way Satan employs demonic and human agents to accomplish his work. The dragon employs the beast that rises up out of the sea, the beast that rises up out of the earth, Babylon the great whore, and all the people who take the mark of the beast. These are Satan's four helpers who carry out his work on earth and who oppose and persecute Christ and His people.

In this fourth parallel section, we see the vision of the woman giving birth to Christ in chapter 12. We see the vision of the dragon and the two beasts and those with the mark of the beast opposing the kingdom of Christ in chapter 13. Babylon the whore is briefly described early in chapter 14. Then we see the vision of the victory of Christ over the dragon and his helpers at His second coming in the last half of chapter 14.

Just like the three previous parallel sections, we are told what will occur and characterize the time frame between the first and second coming of Christ. Each of these parallel sections opens with the things that occur at the beginning of this age, and they close with the things that occur at the end of this age.

We see Jesus born at the beginning of chapter 12, we see His second coming at the end of chapter 14, and we see the work of Satan and his helpers that takes place throughout the time frame between those two events.

But there is a second reason why chapter 12 is a very important point in the book of Revelation. Not only does it introduce the fourth parallel section in this book, but it also begins the second half of the book of Revelation.

When we introduced the book, we looked at its outline and saw that it is divided into two major sections. In chapters 1 through 11, we have a description of the physical conflict between believers and unbelievers. The visible, physical, and personal warfare that occurs between Christians and non-Christians is prominently displayed as the people of Christ assault the kingdom of darkness with the light of the gospel, and as the people of Satan assault the kingdom of Christ with social and physical persecution and death.

The conflict and warfare described in these first eleven chapters is primarily horizontal. It mostly involves people in conflict with people. But the second half of the book of Revelation, from chapters 12 to 22, sets forth the spiritual conflict between Christ and Satan. In the last half of the book, the narrative moves from being primarily about the conflict between believers and unbelievers to primarily being about the conflict between Christ and Satan. It moves from describing the visible physical conflict between the saved and the lost to the invisible and spiritual conflict that takes place between Christ and Satan.

Understanding that behind all physical events is a higher spiritual conflict between Christ and Satan explains why things happen as they do in the physical realm. After all, why were all of Job's flocks stolen, all his servants and children killed, and his health destroyed? Why did his wife and friends turn on him? Those were visible physical things that could be seen as only caused by people and natural events. But the reason those things were occurring on earth is that behind this human conflict and sorrow there was a spiritual and unseen conflict between God and Satan in heaven. The conflict in the invisible realm was played out in the visible realm.

The physical conflict occurring between the church and the world in the first half of Revelation is the result of the spiritual conflict between Christ and Satan revealed in the second half of the book. Christ's conflict with Satan in chapters 12 to 22 explains why the conflicts in chapters 1 to 11 occur.

The point is this: the conflict between the church and the world is just the outworking of the war between Christ and Satan. I am sure that from time to time things happen in your life and circumstances that seem completely inexplicable to you. You ask, "Why did that happen? What is that about?" The answer is that what you are experiencing is the visible part of the story that would make sense if you only knew the invisible part of the story that is hidden from your eyes.

We will not know about the invisible things that explain the visible things we experience until we get to heaven. Until then, we have to trust God like Job did, and trust Him even when He does not explain or reveal the whole story to us. I must have the disposition of Job when he says: *"Though he slay me, yet will I trust him."* I know that whatever is happening to me here on earth has a deeper, larger, and spiritual explanation that I will not understand until I get to heaven. Until then, I simply have to trust Him, even though I cannot understand what He is doing.

We know that God is doing the right thing, and that is enough. *"Shall not the judge of all the earth do right?"* Will He ever do wrong? Will He ever do you wrong? He will not. God can be trusted because of His character, even when He cannot be understood by the things that are seen.

In Revelation 12, we see Satan attempting to destroy Christ at His birth. Having failed at that task, he then turns his efforts to destroying the church, which he also fails to do.

The book of Revelation is a record of Satan's failures. At every single point in this book, he is defeated.

The book of Revelation is also a record of Christ's triumphs. At every single point, He succeeds. This is a great encouragement to Christians. Our sufferings are temporal, but our triumph in Christ is eternal, and knowing that will help us endure to the end without losing hope and without losing faith. This chapter tells us how Christ protects us as His people from the assaults of Satan.

The Appearance of the Woman

The appearance of the woman is in verses 1 to 2. *"And there appeared a great wonder in heaven; a woman clothed with the sun, and the moon under her feet, and upon her head a crown of twelve stars:*
2 *And she being with child cried, travailing in birth, and pained to be delivered."*

As John's visions continue, he sees a great wonder in heaven. This wonder is in the form of a glorious and magnificent woman, who is dazzling and awe-inspiring in her person and appearance. This woman represents the true Israel of God, which consists of those saved both before and after the coming of Christ. Old Covenant Israel brought forth the Messiah, and New Covenant Israel bears witness to the Messiah, and both are represented by this woman. This woman is said to bring forth Messiah, and after Messiah is caught up to heaven, this woman continues to be on earth and witness to the Christ she brought forth.

Therefore, the woman represents the people of God of both the Old Covenant and New Covenant era. The woman represents Old Covenant Israel because it was out of Old Covenant Israel that Messiah was born. The woman also represents New Covenant Israel because she is persecuted by Satan as soon as Christ ascends to His throne, and she is persecuted as long as the New Covenant era goes on.

The woman therefore represents the whole body of the people of God, both of the Old and the New Covenants, because there is only one body of Christ, one church, one true group of God's elect that predates and postdates Christ's first coming; and collectively, they are the presence of the kingdom of God here on earth.

This woman is said to be clothed with the sun, with the moon under her feet, and upon her head is a crown of twelve stars. This is a reference to Old Covenant Israel as it is symbolized in the dream of Joseph recorded in Genesis 37. By this time, Jacob has had all twelve of his sons, and it says in verse 5, *"And Joseph dreamed a dream, and he told it [to] his brethren: and they hated him yet the more."*

Whenever you preach the word of God, people hate you for it. God gave Joseph divine revelation, and Joseph was telling the revelation, but his brothers did not like it. Nevertheless, he conveyed God's revelation to them, verse 6. *"And he said unto them, Hear, I pray you, this dream which I have dreamed: [7] For, behold, we were binding sheaves in the field, and, lo, my sheaf arose, and also stood upright; and, behold, your sheaves stood round about, and made obeisance to my sheaf. [8] And his brethren said to him, Shalt thou indeed reign over us? or shalt thou indeed have dominion over us? And they hated him yet the more for his dreams, and for his words."*

Now here is our passage: *"[9] And he dreamed yet another dream, and told it his brethren, and said, Behold, I have dreamed a dream more; and, behold, the sun and the moon and the eleven stars made obeisance to me. [10] And he told it to his father, and to his brethren: and his father rebuked him, and said unto him, What is this dream that thou hast dreamed? Shall I and thy mother and thy brethren indeed come to bow down ourselves to thee to the earth? [11] And his brethren envied him; but his father observed the saying."*

Without delving into the meaning and application of the dream itself, the sun, the moon, and stars represent the entire nation of Israel that existed at that point in history. There were Jacob and his wife, represented by the sun and the moon; and there were the twelve sons, the children of Jacob, who were represented by the twelve stars. The father, mother, and the twelve sons were the totality of the nation of Israel at that point in history and are represented by those symbols.

When Revelation 12:1 says, *"And there appeared a great wonder in heaven; a woman clothed with the sun, and the moon. . . [and] a crown of twelve stars,"* this is drawing from the imagery of Joseph's dream, and it is saying this woman represents the whole nation of Israel, just as the sun and the moon and the stars represented the whole nation of Israel as it existed in Genesis 37.

Notice verse 2. *"And she being with child cried, travailing in birth, and pained to be delivered."* Israel is pictured as travailing in birth to bring forth the Messiah who is Jesus Christ. Since Genesis 3:15, when the seed of the woman was promised to crush Satan and his works, the covenant community of the people of God has cried out in travail for the birth of this promised Savior.

Israel has groaned and cried for Christ to come and save her from her sins and save her from her enemies all throughout the centuries. We hear these birth cries in the voice of the prophets and in the voice of the psalmists as they travailed with God in prayer and supplications for Messiah to come.

Israel suffered and travailed under the persecutions of the surrounding nations as she persevered in maintaining her national identity in the face of vicious attacks while waiting for Messiah to be born.

We see men like Simeon in Luke 2:25, who *"was just and devout, waiting for the consolation of Israel."* He was waiting for the coming of Messiah and persevering under oppression by Rome until Messiah should be born. He exemplified the maternal desires and travails of the nation of Israel as they waited to see Messiah born among them. Ever since the promises of Genesis 3:15, Israel has been pregnant with hope and expectation of Messiah's birth; and finally, at the appointed time, Israel is going to bring forth the promised Messiah into this world.

The Appearance of the Dragon

The appearance of the dragon is in verses 3 and 4. *"And there appeared another wonder in heaven; and behold a great red dragon, having seven heads and ten horns, and seven crowns upon his heads.*
4 *And his tail drew the third part of the stars of heaven, and did cast them to the earth: and the dragon stood before the woman which was ready to be delivered, for to devour her child as soon as it was born."*

As John continued in his vision, another wonder appeared in heaven. In contrast to the glorious, beautiful woman of verses 1 to 2, there is the appearance of a horrible, evil, dreadful dragon. The woman of verses 1 to 2 represents the true Israel of God, but this dragon represents Satan himself.

The identification of this dragon as Satan is made plain in verse 9. *"And the great dragon was cast out, that old serpent, called the Devil, and Satan."* Clearly, the dragon is Satan, who is also called the serpent and the Devil. He has numerous names. Furthermore, Revelation 20:2 says regarding the angel that *"he laid hold on the dragon, that old serpent, which is the Devil, and Satan, and bound him a thousand years."*

Twice, these four labels: Satan, the Devil, the serpent, and the dragon are given to the same person. Throughout the book of Revelation, wherever the dragon appears, without exception he represents Satan himself.

It says of this dragon in verse 3 that he is red—he is the *"great red dragon."* He is red because red is the color of blood, and Satan is pictured as bathed in blood because he is a murderer of men's bodies and a murderer of men's souls. Jesus said of Satan in John 8:44 that *"he was a murderer from the beginning."* The red horse of the second seal in Revelation 6:4 symbolized war and killing, in which much blood is shed, and therefore the horse is red in color. We will see in Revelation 17 that the great harlot Babylon sits on a red beast, and she herself is clothed in red because she, too, produces death and slaughter and bloodshed. Here we have this nightmarish dragon bathed in blood.

But there is more to this description. It says in verse 3 that he has *"seven heads and ten horns, and seven crowns upon his heads."* This is symbolic language, a symbolic description of the nature of Satan. Seven is the number of completion. Ten is the number of perfection. The heads with their crowns represent dominion. The head of a nation is one who wears a crown on his head and has dominion over the nation. The horns represent power and strength. Horns are what animals use to express their power and strength in fighting and gaining dominion. Putting all this symbolism together, the meaning is simply this: Satan has complete dominion over the world as the god of this world, and Satan has perfect power and strength to accomplish all he is allowed to do.

Ephesians 2:2 says that Satan is the *"prince of the power of the air."* Ephesians 6:12 says that Satan is the ruler *"of the darkness of this world."* In John 14:30 Jesus called Satan *"the prince of this world."* Second Corinthians 4:4 says that Satan is *"the god of this world."*

Satan is the king of this world. He controls all of the unsaved. They do his will, carry out his agenda, and engage in war and slaughter and murder at his command.

All this symbolic language tells us Satan has complete dominion over the wicked and this fallen world and he has perfect power to accomplish all he is allowed to do. He has great authority and great strength: he has great authority, symbolized by seven crowned heads; and he has great strength, symbolized by ten horns.

Satan does not do his work alone. Notice verse 4: *"And his tail drew the third part of the stars of heaven, and did cast them to the earth."* When Satan originally fell in his initial rebellion and sin against God, he did not fall alone. By his seducing power, he dragged along with him a vast number of angels who joined in his rebellion and who fell along with him. By his influence, Satan caused these angels to fall from their high place in heaven so they were brought down to the lowest place on earth where they exist as demons to assist Satan in his evil works.

We see in verse 7 that *"there was war in heaven: Michael and his angels"* (the good angels) *"fought against the dragon; and the dragon fought and his angels"* (the demons). The dragon has evil angels in his service called demons. These are the stars spoken of that were brought down from heaven to earth. Many of them are bound in the pit until the Day of Judgment as 2 Peter 2:4 and Jude 1:6 state, but many of them are loose and able to do the will of Satan.

Three is the number of perfection and completion. Therefore, one third is the idea of imperfection and incompleteness. It is a diminution of the primary number three. Verse 4 says that *"his tail drew the third part of the stars of heaven."* In other words, he was not able to get all of the angels to fall, but only a lesser part (a minority of them) to fall. But even though only a minority of them fell, they still constitute a vast number of demons, ready to assist Satan in his evil works. If there are hundreds of millions of good angels as the Scriptures declare, then certainly there are many millions of fallen angels to assist Satan in his work. Thus, not only did Satan fall, but he also brought about the fall of (symbolically speaking) the third part of the angels that were in heaven.

This horrible dragon is said, in verse 4, to stand before the woman who *"was ready to be delivered"* in order *"to devour her child as soon as it was born."* If you are a woman who has had babies, you understand this. Here you are, lying on your back having a baby, and there is someone standing between your legs to receive the baby. Now imagine if that person standing there was ready to choke the life out of your child as soon as it was born, and you knew it. Furthermore, this evil person is all covered in blood and he has all his evil helpers standing around, and you are giving birth. The thought of it is horrifying. That is the picture presented here. Here is Satan, standing before the woman who is ready to be delivered, so he can devour her child as soon as it is born.

What is pictured in Revelation 12:4 is recorded in Matthew 2. This story is often preached at Christmas because that is when we celebrate the birth of Jesus. But as wonderful as the birth of Jesus is, there were horrible people who wanted to do horrible things in relationship to that birth.

Notice Matthew 2:1–18: "*Now when Jesus was born in Bethlehem of Judea in the days of Herod the king, behold, there came wise men from the east to Jerusalem, [2] Saying, Where is he that is born King of the Jews? for we have seen his star in the east, and are come to worship him.*" All well and good so far. But now notice verse 3: "*When Herod the king had heard these things, he was troubled,*" not rejoicing, but troubled, upset, mad, angry "*and all Jerusalem with him.*" There was turmoil.

"[4] *And when he had gathered all the chief priests and scribes of the people together, he demanded of them where Christ should be born. [5] And they said unto him, In Bethlehem of Judea: for thus it is written by the prophet, [6] And thou Bethlehem, in the land of Judah, art not the least among the princes of Judah: for out of thee shall come a Governor, that shall rule my people Israel. [7] Then Herod, when he had privily called the wise men, enquired of them diligently what time the star appeared. [8] And he sent them to Bethlehem, and said, Go and search diligently for the young child; and when ye have found him, bring me word again, that I may come and worship him also.*" Here you see Satan, the liar, speaking through his agent, Herod, saying, "I want to worship Him!" No, he wanted to choke the life out of Him.

"[9] *When they had heard the king, they departed; and, lo, the star, which they saw in the east, went before them, till it came and stood over where the young child was. [10] When they saw the star, they rejoiced with exceeding great joy. [11] And when they were come into the house, they saw the young child with Mary his mother, and fell down, and worshipped him: and when they had opened their treasures, they presented unto him gifts; gold, and frankincense, and myrrh."* That is all wonderful.

But now the evil arises, verse 12: *"And being warned of God in a dream that they should not return to Herod, they departed into their own country another way.* [13] *And when they were departed, behold, the angel of the Lord appeareth to Joseph in a dream, saying, Arise, and take the young child and his mother, and flee into Egypt, and be thou there until I bring thee word: for Herod will seek the young child to destroy him."* There is Satan in the person of his agent Herod at the birth of Messiah waiting to crush the life out of Him.

Verse 14 continues the narrative: *"When he arose, he took the young child and his mother by night, and departed into Egypt:* [15] *And was there until the death of Herod: that it might be fulfilled which was spoken of the Lord by the prophet, saying, Out of Egypt have I called my son.* [16] *Then Herod, when he saw that he was mocked of the wise men, was exceeding wroth, and sent forth, and slew all the children that were in Bethlehem, and in all the coasts thereof, from two years old and under, according to the time which he had diligently enquired of the wise men.* [17] *Then was fulfilled that which was spoken by Jeremiah the prophet, saying,* [18] *In Rama was there a voice heard, lamentation, and weeping, and great mourning, Rachel weeping for her children, and would not be comforted, because they are not."*

Satan, with all of his demonic and human helpers, sought to destroy Christ as soon as He was born, but they utterly failed. Satan wanted to destroy Christ in order to subvert Christ's work of destroying the works of the devil. But Satan, with all of his demons combined with Herod and all of his soldiers, could not destroy Christ at His birth.

We see how invisible satanic activity drove visible human actions, and this satanic activity provides the real explanation for human atrocities. I am sure the people in Bethlehem were thinking, "Why did the King send his soldiers to slaughter all the children that were under two years of age?" You cannot even fathom how people could do such horrible things. The answer is that Satan himself is behind unsaved humans, driving them to do the things they do.

Islam is the right hand of Satan, and that is why it is a religion of murder and slaughter. At this point in history, we look at ISIS and we see all the horrible things they are doing to people: burning them, crushing them, gunning them down, drowning them, and other unimaginable atrocities. You ask how people could do that to other people. The answer is the same way Herod could slaughter all of these infants. He was driven and empowered and directed by the great, red, blood-drenched Satan to do it.

Do not be amazed at the evil that happens on earth. Recognize it is simply the outworking of what Satan is doing and what God allows him to do as God is accomplishing His purposes here on earth. We need to understand that behind all unsaved people and the horrible things they do is a demonic power and a demonic direction that causes them, in conjunction with their own fallen and depraved desires, to carry out the will of the Evil One, or attempt to carry it out. But God thwarts their true intentions every time. Satan never succeeded in killing Jesus as an infant, even though he did bring about the deaths of many other infants.

The Appearance of the Man Child

The appearance of the man child is in verses 5 and 6. It says, *"And she brought forth a man child, who was to rule all nations with a rod of iron: and her child was caught up unto God, and to his throne.* [6] *And the woman fled into the wilderness, where she hath a place prepared of God, that they should feed her there a thousand two hundred and threescore days."*

In spite of Satan's best efforts, Israel brought forth the man child Jesus Christ. Here is a male descendant of David who will occupy the throne of David and who will reign over the house of Jacob forever.

Notice verse 5: *"And she brought forth a man child, who was to rule all nations with a rod of iron."* This concept of ruling with a rod of iron is drawn out of Psalm 2:9.

Psalm 2:1–12 states: *"Why do the heathen rage, and the people imagine a vain thing?* [2] *The kings of the earth set themselves, and the rulers take counsel together, against the* LORD*, and against his anointed, saying,* [3] *Let us break their bands asunder, and cast away their cords from us."* Here is Herod, striving to destroy Messiah and His rule and reign.

Verse 4: *"He that sitteth in the heavens shall laugh: the* LORD *shall have them in derision."* Satan, even though he stands before the woman to destroy the man child as soon as He is born, utterly fails. God laughs in his face. He is saying, "You are not going to succeed."

Verse 5: *"Then shall he speak unto them in his wrath, and vex them in his sore displeasure."* God speaks to Herod, Satan, and all who set themselves against God's Son, and expresses His wrath toward them and vexes them in His sore displeasure. He says in verse 6, *"Yet have I set my king upon my holy hill of Zion."* That king is Jesus Christ. He is the anointed one.

Now Jesus speaks prophetically in verse 7. *"I will declare the decree: the* LORD *hath said unto me, Thou art my Son; this day have I begotten thee.* [8] *Ask of me, and I shall give thee the heathen for thine inheritance, and the uttermost parts of the earth for thy possession."* Satan offered all the kingdoms of the earth to Jesus in the temptation in Matthew 4:8–9. God the Father says to Jesus, "No, I will give them to You," which is exactly what occurs in Revelation 11:15.

Here is our verse—verse 9: *"Thou shalt break them with a rod of iron; thou shalt dash them in pieces like a potter's vessel."* This is fulfilled in Revelation 12:5, which says that Jesus shall *"rule all nations with a rod of iron."*

Verse 10: *"Be wise now therefore, O ye kings: be instructed, ye judges of the earth."* Listen up, Herod and your crowd. "[11] *Serve the* LORD *with fear, and rejoice with trembling.* [12] *Kiss the Son"*; that is, kiss His feet in submission and humility and obedience, *"lest he be angry, and ye perish from the way, when his wrath is kindled but a little."* Remember, you rebels, He has an iron rod in His hand. *"Blessed are all they that put their trust in him."*

When it says Jesus is *"to rule all nations with a rod of iron,"* it is saying that Jesus was born to sit on the throne of David and rule with a rod of iron over all His enemies, who are Satan and his people and his demons. This is exactly what Jesus did during His life here on earth. No demon, no unsaved person, and no government was able to overcome Him. When He died, it was because He laid His life down, not because it was taken from Him, as He says in John 10:17–18.

Notice in verse 5 it says that *"she brought forth a man child."* There is His birth, the beginning of His earthly presence. It goes on to say: *"and her child was caught up unto God, and to his throne."* There is His ascension to heaven, the end of His earthly presence. We have these two bookends of His birth and His ascension. Everything that occurs in between them is described with this phrase: *"who was to rule all nations with a rod of iron."*

What did Jesus do during His life while He was here on earth? He began to rule all nations with a rod of iron. He began to subdue these rebellious kings and people. He began to subdue Satan and his demons. He began to exercise the rule of the throne of David. He ruled demons, cast them out, commanded them to depart, and they obeyed. He ruled Satan's people and subdued and conquered and converted them to His own kingdom. As for those who were not converted, He successfully resisted their efforts to destroy Him until He offered Himself up as a substitutionary sacrifice for sin.

We see this illustrated in Luke 4. Here we see King Jesus ruling with a rod of iron. Luke 4 opens with the temptation in the wilderness: "1 *And Jesus being full of the Holy Ghost returned from Jordan,*
and was led by the Spirit into the wilderness, 2 *Being forty days tempt-*
ed of the devil. And in those days he did eat nothing: and when they
were ended, he afterward hungered. 3 *And the devil said unto him, If*
thou be the Son of God, command this stone that it be made bread.
4 *And Jesus answered him, saying, It is written, That man shall not*
live by bread alone, but by every word of God.

"5 *And the devil, taking him up into an high mountain, shewed*
unto him all the kingdoms of the world in a moment of time. 6 *And*
the devil said unto him, All this power will I give thee, and the glory
of them: for that is delivered unto me; and to whomsoever I will I
give it. 7 *If thou therefore wilt worship me, all shall be thine.* 8 *And*
Jesus answered and said unto him, Get thee behind me, Satan: for it
is written, Thou shalt worship the Lord thy God, and him only shalt
thou serve.

"9 *And he brought him to Jerusalem, and set him on a pinnacle of*
the temple, and said unto him, If thou be the Son of God, cast thyself
down from hence: 10 *For it is written, He shall give his angels charge*
over thee, to keep thee: 11 *And in their hands they shall bear thee up,*
lest at any time thou dash thy foot against a stone. 12 *And Jesus an-*
swering said unto him, It is said, Thou shalt not tempt the Lord thy
God. 13 *And when the devil had ended all the temptation, he departed*
from him for a season."

Who won in this contest of temptation? Jesus did. He defeated the devil himself. Let us keep reading. Verse 14: "*And Jesus returned*
in the power of the Spirit into Galilee: and there went out a fame of
him through all the region round about. 15 *And he taught in their syn-*
agogues, being glorified of all.

"16 *And he came to Nazareth, where he had been brought up: and, as his custom was, he went into the synagogue on the sabbath day, and stood up for to read.* 17 *And there was delivered unto him the book of the prophet Isaiah. And when he had opened the book, he found the place where it was written,* 18 *The Spirit of the Lord is upon me, because he hath anointed me to preach the gospel to the poor; he hath sent me to heal the brokenhearted, to preach deliverance to the captives, and recovering of sight to the blind, to set at liberty them that are bruised,* 19 *To preach the acceptable year of the Lord.* 20 *And he closed the book, and he gave it again to the minister, and sat down. And the eyes of all them that were in the synagogue were fastened on him.*

"21 *And he began to say unto them, This day is this scripture fulfilled in your ears."* Jesus is saying, "This passage in Isaiah describes My present ministry, rule, and power." "22 *And all bare him witness, and wondered at the gracious words which proceeded out of his mouth. And they said, Is not this Joseph's son?* 23 *And he said unto them, Ye will surely say unto me this proverb, Physician, heal thyself: whatsoever we have heard done in Capernaum, do also here in thy country.* 24 *And he said, Verily I say unto you, No prophet is accepted in his own country.* 25 *But I tell you of a truth, many widows were in Israel in the days of Elias, when the heaven was shut up three years and six months, when great famine was throughout all the land;* 26 *But unto none of them was Elias sent, save unto Sarepta, a city of Sidon, unto a woman that was a widow.* 27 *And many lepers were in Israel in the time of Elishah the prophet; and none of them was cleansed, saving Naaman the Syrian.*

"28 *And all they in the synagogue, when they heard these things, were filled with wrath,* 29 *And rose up, and thrust him out of the city, and led him unto the brow of the hill whereon their city was built, that they might cast him down headlong."* They took Him to the top of a cliff, intending to throw Him off to kill Him. Here are Satan's people acting to devour Messiah, just like Herod attempted to do at His birth.

Notice verse 30: *"But he passing through the midst of them went his way,* 31 *And came down to Capernaum, a city of Galilee, and taught them on the sabbath days.* 32 *And they were astonished at his doctrine: for his word was with power."* He defeats Satan himself in verses 1 to 13, and now He defeats Satan's people in verses 14 to 30.

They could not cast him off the cliff. He overpowered them.

Let us keep reading. Verse 33: *"And in the synagogue there was a man, which had a spirit of an unclean devil, and cried out with a loud voice,* [34] *Saying, Let us alone; what have we to do with thee, thou Jesus of Nazareth? art thou come to destroy us? I know thee who thou art; the Holy One of God.* [35] *And Jesus rebuked him, saying, Hold thy peace, and come out of him. And when the devil had thrown him in the midst, he came out of him, and hurt him not.* [36] *And they were all amazed, and spake among themselves, saying, What a word is this! for with authority and power he commandeth the unclean spirits, and they come out.* [37] *And the fame of him went out into every place of the country round about."* Jesus now defeats Satan's demons.

In Luke 4, Jesus defeats Satan in verses 1 to 13, He defeats Satan's people in verses 14 to 30, and He defeats Satan's demons in verses 31 to 37. This is just a sample of the beginning of His rule on the throne of David, bearing His rod, and defeating Satan and his helpers, whether they are human or demonic. None of them can triumph over Him. He triumphs over all of them, and this sample of His triumph in Luke 4 describes the totality of His ministry. He systematically destroyed the works of the devil and the devil himself wherever He went and whatever He did. At the end of His earthly ministry, He triumphed over Satan as well, even when it appeared Satan had won. Satan stirred up his agents to cause the death of Jesus on the cross, but Jesus defeated Satan by defeating death, rising from the grave, and ascending into heaven.

From His birth to His ascension, Christ triumphed over Satan at every point, defeated Satan in every battle, and repeatedly struck him with His rod of iron, shattering all of his attempts to thwart His saving work and the plan of God.

In Revelation 12:5, the child is caught up to God and to His throne. This is the end of Jesus' earthly presence. What happens after that? Verse 6 tells us: *"And the woman"* (this is the same woman that brought Messiah to birth in verses 1–5) *"fled into the wilderness, where she hath a place prepared of God, that they should feed her there a thousand two hundred and threescore days."*

When Jesus ascended into heaven, the woman who gave Him birth—that is, the true Israel of God, the saved people of God—remained behind. He went up to heaven, but they did not. Acts 1 describes the disciples as being left behind, looking up, and watching

Jesus ascend. He is gone, but they are still on earth.

The old Israel of God, who gave Christ His birth, has now become the new Israel of God through the institution of the New Covenant. It has now become the New Covenant church that represents Christ on earth and who testifies to Christ on earth. Jesus said in Acts 1:8, *"ye shall be witnesses unto me both in Jerusalem, and in all Judea, and in Samaria, and unto the uttermost part of the earth."*

The dragon, having been defeated by Christ, turns all his wrath upon Christ's kingdom and citizens, and is determined to destroy them. But the woman (the church) finds a refuge from the wrath of the dragon, and that refuge is the wilderness. Notice verse 6: *"And the woman fled into the wilderness, where she hath a place prepared of God, that they should feed her there a thousand two hundred and threescore days."*

To understand verse 6, we have to reflect for a moment on the Old Testament. We have already seen how many of the temporal judgments God brought upon the wicked in the trumpet judgments paralleled and echoed the plagues God brought on Egypt through Moses. We have also seen how Egypt and Pharaoh prefigured Satan in the bondage, oppression, and persecution he inflicts on the people of God.

In the Old Testament, Pharaoh represents Satan, and Egypt represents the place of bondage. Moses comes and brings the ten plagues and liberates the children of Israel and leads them out of slavery and into the wilderness on their journey to the Promised Land. This imagery is brought wholesale over into the book of Revelation. What is fascinating is that Pharaoh is called a dragon in several places in the Scriptures.

In Psalm 74, David is recounting the history of Israel. Looking back retrospectively, he says in verse 12, *"For God is my King of old, working salvation in the midst of the earth."* He describes that salvation: "[13] *Thou didst divide the sea"* (the Red Sea), *"by thy strength: thou brakest the heads of the dragons in the waters."*

Who got their heads broken in the Red Sea? Pharaoh and his army. They were the dragons in the waters. Notice verse 14, *"Thou brakest the heads"* (plural) *"of leviathan"* (singular) *"in pieces, and gavest him to be meat to the people inhabiting the wilderness."* Pharaoh is called "leviathan," or the "dragon," and he is said to have "heads," plural, just like the multi-headed dragon of Revelation 12. The Hebrew word translated "leviathan" is sometimes translated "sea monster," but it also can be translated "dragon," as it is in Isaiah 27:1.

In Ezekiel 29 we see this same imagery of Pharaoh as the dragon being set forth. Ezekiel 29:1–3 says: *"In the tenth year, in the tenth month, in the twelfth day of the month, the word of the LORD came unto me, saying, [2] Son of man, set thy face against Pharaoh king of Egypt, and prophesy against him, and against all Egypt: [3] Speak, and say, Thus saith the Lord GOD; Behold, I am against thee, Pharaoh king of Egypt, the great dragon that lieth in the midst of his rivers, which hath said, My river is mine own, and I have made it for myself."* This river spoken of here is the Nile River, which the Egyptians worshiped as a god. Pharaoh here is called a dragon.

How did Israel escape the dragon Pharaoh? She went through the Red Sea, where the dragon was stopped, and then Israel was able to go into the wilderness. What was the wilderness? The wilderness was a place of refuge from the dragon. In the wilderness, God protected Israel and fed her, and Israel's adversary the dragon could not reach her there. Never again did Pharaoh show up in the wilderness to harass the people of God.

In Revelation 12:6, the imagery is of the church fleeing into the wilderness, and there God protects His church and provides for His church, just like He protected Israel in the wilderness and fed her manna throughout the time between her liberation from Egypt and her entrance into the Promised Land.

Moses is the picture of the delivering Messiah who delivers Israel from Pharaoh, who is the picture of the dragon. Moses brings them salvation from bondage in Egypt, a picture of our salvation from the bondage of sin. He leads them across the Red Sea and destroys Pharaoh from ever being able to harm the people of God again. He then leads them through the wilderness until they reach the Promised Land, which represents the new earth of Revelation 21–22. While they are in the wilderness, He protects them and provides for them. He delivers them from their enemies and gives them manna from heaven. In the same way, under the New Covenant, in the wilderness of this world, God protects His church from the dragon Satan, provides for His church with the bread of life, and preserves His church until He returns. The length of this period of protection is symbolized by the number one thousand two hundred and sixty days, which represents the church age.

In our studies in numerology and in chapter 11, we demonstrated that one thousand two hundred and sixty days, forty-two months, and three and a half years are all exact equivalents, and this symbolic number is used to describe the time period between the first and second coming of Christ. In Revelation 11:3–7, it was the time period of the church's witness to the world. In Revelation 12:6, the twelve hundred and sixty days begins at the ascension of Jesus. When will it end? When the woman, the New Covenant church, finally reaches the Promised Land, the New Earth, spoken of in chapters 21–22. That is when her time in the wilderness of this age will be finished.

It is fascinating to note that Numbers 33 records exactly forty-two camping places that Israel stayed in on her journey from Egypt to the Promised Land. These forty-two camping spots between Egypt and the Promised Land speak of the forty-two months, or one thousand two hundred and sixty days, that New Covenant Israel spends on her journey to the new Promised Land, which is the New Earth.

So clearly, the forty-two months, the three and a half years, the twelve hundred and sixty days all begin at liberation, at the first coming of Christ, and it ends at deliverance into the Promised Land of the new heaven and the new earth at the second coming of Christ.

Take note that verse 6, *"And the woman fled into the wilderness, where she hath a place prepared of God, that they should feed her there a thousand two hundred and threescore days,"* is going to be greatly expanded and explained in more detail in Revelation 12:13–17, which we will look at in a subsequent chapter.

What I want you to take away from this passage is that God has a plan and the devil has a plan; and though the devil does horrible things, his plans are always thwarted, but the plan of God is always successful. Though Satan has a kingdom, it is being systematically destroyed, dismantled, and defeated. Christ has a kingdom, and it is systematically being built and strengthened and expanded, until there is complete success on the part of Christ, and complete defeat on the part of Satan.

As you go through things in this life, and bad things happen to you, recognize that it is the Evil One at work. But he is on a leash, God has him under control, and he is not going to be able to do any permanent harm. He may cause you a lot of pain, but he cannot hurt you, because God is working all things together for your good; and in that good is your comfort, even in the midst of the pain of all the things that occur to you.

We must recognize that behind all human actions are spiritual heavenly actions, a playing out of this conflict between God and Satan. Do not be discouraged about the bad things that happen here on earth as though somehow God is not in control. When all those babies were slaughtered in Bethlehem, God was in control of that. When people are being slaughtered in the world today, God is in control of that. He allows it to go so far, and no further. We shake our heads and ask why. And God says, "Trust Me. I am doing the right thing." Wait until you see the end; and when you do, you will say, the judge of all the earth has done right. Blessed be His holy name.

39

Satan Cast Out of Heaven, Revelation 12:7–12

"[7] And there was war in heaven: Michael and his angels fought against the dragon; and the dragon fought and his angels,
[8] And prevailed not; neither was their place found any more in heaven. [9] And the great dragon was cast out, that old serpent, called the Devil, and Satan, which deceiveth the whole world: he was cast out into the earth, and his angels were cast out with him. [10] And I heard a loud voice saying in heaven, Now is come salvation, and strength, and the kingdom of our God, and the power of his Christ: for the accuser of our brethren is cast down, which accused them before our God day and night. [11] And they overcame him by the blood of the Lamb, and by the word of their testimony; and they loved not their lives unto the death. [12] Therefore rejoice, ye heavens, and ye that dwell in them. Woe to the inhabiters of the earth and of the sea! for the devil is come down unto you, having great wrath, because he knoweth that he hath but a short time."

Chapter 12 began the second half of the book of Revelation. In the second half of this book, we see the spiritual warfare between Christ and Satan that lies behind the scenes and explains why things on earth happen the way they do. Behind all physical and visible reality is an invisible and spiritual reality that drives and shapes all of human history and all visible events we see and experience.

When things happen to you, what you see and experience is not the whole story. There are unseen factors behind it. There is war between Christ and Satan going on that is being played out on the stage of human experience. The war of Satan against Christ and the triumph of Christ over Satan are what shape all the events that occur in this age.

As we looked at Revelation 12:1–6, we saw that Herod's slaughter of all the children under two years of age in Bethlehem was caused by Satan's effort to destroy Christ when He was born. It was not just a crazy king that went and killed a bunch of kids; rather, it was Satan attempting to destroy Christ, and this explains the viciousness of the human behavior that was experienced by those in Bethlehem. Revelation allows us to see behind the scenes and understand what is happening in this world and why it is taking place.

This war between Christ and Satan has been going on since the garden of Eden. In Genesis 3 we have the serpent (Satan) assaulting God's creation and the people God made in His image. We know that Adam and Eve fell. Creation was ruined and Satan became the god of this world. But in Genesis 3:15, God promised that a Savior would be born of the seed of the woman who would crush the serpent and destroy the works of the devil. In due time, the Savior promised in Genesis 3:15 was born, and Satan's efforts to destroy Him were defeated. Revelation 12:1–6 records that defeat.

By Christ's life, death, resurrection, and ascension, Satan's doom was sealed. In the triumph of Christ lies the defeat of Satan. We immediately begin to see the defeat of Satan implemented in our passage in Revelation 12:7–12 in which Satan is cast out of heaven. Christ triumphs over His enemy, and immediately the effects and the fruits of that triumph begin to be implemented.

The War Described

The war is described in verses 7 to 9: *"And there was war in heaven: Michael and his angels fought against the dragon; and the dragon fought and his angels,* [8] *And prevailed not; neither was their place found any more in heaven.* [9] *And the great dragon was cast out, that old serpent, called the Devil, and Satan, which deceiveth the whole world: he was cast out into the earth, and his angels were cast out with him."*

We saw in verses 1 to 6 that Christ fought the war with Satan on earth, and Christ won that war. Satan was defeated at every point from Christ's birth to Christ's ascension. The victory of Christ now becomes the basis for winning every subsequent battle that is fought with Satan, whether fought by angels or fought by believers.

Immediately upon Christ's victory over Satan on earth and His ascension into heaven, the fruits of that victory begin to be harvested by Michael the archangel. He immediately goes to war with Satan to implement and enforce the victory over Satan that Jesus has achieved by His life, death, and resurrection.

First of all, notice the combatants. The combatants are mentioned in verse 7. *"And there was war in heaven: Michael and his angels fought against the dragon; and the dragon fought and his angels."* The combatants are Michael and his angels, and Satan and his angels, otherwise known as demons.

Michael is first introduced to us in the book of Daniel where he has the special function of being the guardian angel and protector of the people of God. He protected Israel, and he protects the church as well. In the book of Jude, he is called the "archangel" Michael, and there it is recorded that he had a previous conflict with Satan over the burial of the body of Moses. But now we see Michael under the direction of Christ as the leader of the angels in their war with the dragon.

This dragon is identified for us in detail in verse 9. *"And the great dragon was cast out, that old serpent, called the Devil, and Satan, which deceiveth the whole world."* He is given four descriptive titles in this passage. He is called *"that old serpent."* This tells us that the dragon is the same evil spirit being as the serpent who tempted Eve in the garden of Eden. This serpent in the garden of Eden is none other than the dragon, the devil, and Satan; they are all the same person. This is the one whose head the seed of the woman will crush as promised in Genesis 3:15.

Not only is he called *"that old serpent,"* harkening back to the story of the garden of Eden; secondly, he is also called *"the Devil."* This name means "slanderer." One who slanders is one who tells negative lies about another person in order to make him look bad in the eyes of others. It is the opposite of flattery, where one tells positive lies about another person to make him look good in the eyes of others. In both cases, they are lying. They are both evil.

But in this particular case, the devil is lying in order to make others look bad. The devil lied to Eve about God, falsely accusing Him of withholding something good from Eve when He forbade her to eat of the tree of the knowledge of good and evil. The devil has been lying and slandering God and His people ever since through his human agents who are part of his kingdom. His goal is to make God and His people look as bad as possible in the eyes of the world.

The third term that is used here is *"Satan."* This name means "adversary"—that is, he is the one who sets himself against Christ and His people and does all he can to harm them. He opposes every effort the Christian makes to serve God. He attempts to thwart every act of ministry, obedience, and worship, and attacks all we do for the kingdom of God.

The fourth thing this dragon is called is the one who *"deceiveth the whole world"* in verse 9. The devil lies when he slanders God and men, but he also lies about truth, reality, and morality. Satan deceives the world into thinking there is no God, or else that God is like themselves, or that the Bible is a fable, or that money is happiness, and any endless number of other things.

Satan deceives the whole world with false religions and with false methods of salvation. The public schools and universities, the newspapers and the radio, the internet and Hollywood, the politicians and business leaders are all filled with his lies, and they actively promote his deceptions. He deceives the whole world. There is no place, no people, and no nation that is exempt from the deception of Satan. His deception is universal and pervasive.

It says in 2 Corinthians 4:4, *"The god of this world hath blinded the minds of them which believe not, lest the light of the glorious gospel. . .should shine unto them"* and they should be saved. Only Christians have been freed from Satan's deceptions and they are able to see through his lies because they have that veil of blindness torn away.

The good news of the gospel is that Christ has torn that blindness away, and now we see. We see the truth of God's word and we see the reality behind the events that occur. We see through the lies that are perpetrated in this world—lies that say you can live any way you want, you can believe anything you wish, you can act in any fashion you desire, and everything will be fine. Those are the lies of the devil.

Because the devil cannot deceive believers, he seeks to destroy them and causes his people to persecute and martyr them. This dragon is the essence of evil, one who strives to deceive as many people as he can so he can take as many of them as possible to hell.

Having seen the combatants in verse 7, who are Michael and his angels against Satan and his angels, notice secondly, the conflict. The conflict is described in verses 8 and 9 in which it is said of the dragon and his angels that they *"prevailed not; neither was their place found any more in heaven. [9] And the great dragon was cast out, that old serpent, called the Devil, and Satan, which deceiveth the whole world:*

he was cast out into the earth, and his angels were cast out with him."

The conflict revolved around whether Satan had any right to be in heaven or have access to the presence of God any longer. Prior to the time of Christ's ascension into heaven and the conflict recorded here, Satan did have access to heaven and God's presence and God's courtroom.

In the book of Job, we see occurring what Michael now puts a stop to. Job 1:1–12 says: "*There was a man in the land of Uz, whose name was Job; and that man was perfect and upright, and one that feared God, and eschewed evil.* [2] *And there were born unto him seven sons and three daughters.* [3] *His substance also was seven thousand sheep, and three thousand camels, and five hundred yoke of oxen, and five hundred she asses, and a very great household; so that this man was the greatest of all the men of the east.*

"[4] *And his sons went and feasted in their houses, every one his day; and sent and called for their three sisters to eat and to drink with them.* [5] *And it was so, when the days of their feasting were gone about, that Job sent and sanctified them, and rose up early in the morning, and offered burnt offerings according to the number of them all: for Job said, It may be that my sons have sinned, and cursed God in their hearts. Thus did Job continually.*

"[6] *Now there was a day when the sons of God came to present themselves before the LORD, and Satan came also among them.* [7] *And the Lord said unto Satan, Whence comest thou? Then Satan answered the Lord, and said, From going to and fro in the earth, and from walking up and down in it.* [8] *And the LORD said unto Satan, Hast thou considered my servant Job, that there is none like him in the earth, a perfect and an upright man, one that feareth God, and escheweth evil?* [9] *Then Satan answered the LORD, and said, Doth Job fear God for nought?* [10] *Hast not thou made an hedge about him, and about his house, and about all that he hath on every side? thou hast blessed the work of his hands, and his substance is increased in the land.* [11] *But put forth thine hand now, and touch all that he hath, and he will curse thee to thy face.* [12] *And the LORD said unto Satan, Behold, all that he hath is in thy power; only upon himself put not forth thine hand. So Satan went forth from the presence of the LORD."*

As a result of this conversation between God and Satan, all of Job's servants were slaughtered, all of his possessions were taken, and all of his children were killed. Notice Job 2:1–6, "*Again there was a day when the sons of God came to present themselves before the* L*ORD*, *and Satan came also among them to present himself before the* L*ORD*. [2] *And the* L*ORD said unto Satan, From whence comest thou? And Satan answered the* L*ORD, and said, From going to and fro in the earth, and from walking up and down in it.* [3] *And the* L*ORD said unto Satan, Hast thou considered my servant Job, that there is none like him in the earth, a perfect and an upright man, one that feareth God, and escheweth evil? and still he holdeth fast his integrity, although thou movedst me against him, to destroy him without cause.* [4] *And Satan answered the* L*ORD, and said, Skin for skin, yea, all that a man hath will he give for his life.* [5] *But put forth thine hand now, and touch his bone and his flesh, and he will curse thee to thy face.* [6] *And the* L*ORD said unto Satan, Behold, he is in thine hand; but save his life."*

Here we see that Satan had access to the throne of God, and we see that Satan as the accuser is accusing Job of mercenary and selfish motives in serving God. The accusation was this: Job does not serve God and worship Him because of who He is; he serves and worships Him only for what he can get out of Him. He values God's blessings, but he does not value God Himself. Satan says to God, "Take away Your blessings from Job, and he will curse you to Your face."

Satan is slandering Job, and we see him, by implication, slandering God for commending Job, when Job (according to Satan) is really only using God for his own benefit. As the accuser, he has access directly into the presence of God and to the throne room and courtroom of God.

Not only does Satan accuse believers of false motives and of being unfaithful to God; he also accuses them of sins and transgressions. Notice Zechariah 3:1–7. *"And he shewed me Joshua the high priest standing before the angel of the* L*ORD"* (the angel of the LORD is the pre-incarnate LORD Jesus Christ), *"and Satan standing at his right hand to resist him."* Satan is standing at the right hand of Joshua. "[2] *And the* L*ORD said unto Satan, The* L*ORD rebuke thee, O Satan; even the* L*ORD that hath chosen Jerusalem rebuke thee: is not this a brand plucked out of the fire?*

"[3] *Now Joshua was clothed with filthy garments, and stood before the angel.* [4] *And he answered and spake unto those that stood before him, saying, Take away the filthy garments from him. And unto him he said, Behold, I have caused thine iniquity to pass from thee, and I will clothe thee with change of raiment.* [5] *And I said, Let them set a fair mitre upon his head. So they set a fair mitre upon his head, and clothed him with garments. And the angel of the* L*ORD stood by.* [6] *And the angel of the* L*ORD protested unto Joshua, saying,* [7] *Thus saith the* L*ORD of hosts; If thou wilt walk in my ways, and if thou wilt keep my charge, then thou shalt also judge my house, and shalt also keep my courts, and I will give thee places to walk among these that stand by."*

Without going into all the details of the passage, here is Satan standing to accuse Joshua the high priest of his sins. Joshua the high priest is a sinner. He is clothed with filthy garments which are symbolic of his personal sinfulness. This is bad enough, but on top of that, Satan stands to accuse him. As the adversary, he accused Joshua to Christ thus: "How can You accept such a one as this? Why, look at his filthy sins! The imagination of his heart is evil. His speech is corrupt. His behavior is inconsistent, and his motives are selfish. Surely You would not want such a one as this in Your heaven!" Satan does his best to drive a wedge between the Savior and His people and to alienate them one from another, and make them suspicious and distrustful of each other. This is the work of the accuser of the Old Testament saints.

Prior to the ascension of Christ into heaven, Satan had access to the throne of God in heaven, and there he slandered the motives and behavior of the believers. He accused the Old Testament saints of their sins, and he accused God Himself of being unjust in forgiving their sins when those sins had not been properly atoned for. But now, things are going to change dramatically for Satan.

In Revelation 12:7–9 Michael and his angels go on the attack. They are now able to enforce the victory Christ has achieved for His people, and they make no delay in doing so. As soon as Christ ascends in victory and triumph over Satan, Satan and his demons are attacked. Michael initiates the attack, and they are defeated and cast out of heaven. Never again will Satan and his demons have a place in heaven or any access to heaven. Satan will no longer be able to accuse the believers before the throne of God. Satan and his demons are permanently driven out. They are cast down to the earth, which is now their sole place of habitation until they are cast into the lake of fire at the second coming.

We see in Revelation 12:7–9 that Satan's descent into damnation has begun. He has been cast down from heaven to the earth, where he has a short time to function in a greatly limited fashion, and then he will be cast down into hell forever where he will be tormented for all of eternity. Satan is defeated and Satan is on his way out. Christ has delivered us from the devil and all his works. First John 3:8 says, *"For this purpose the Son of God was manifested, that He might destroy the works of the devil."* Destroying those works is exactly what He has done on the cross, and it is what He continues to do as He implements the accomplishments of the cross in this world and in Satan's kingdom, until the works of the devil are completely destroyed forever.

This event recorded in Revelation 12:7–9 is what Jesus was prophetically speaking of when He said in Luke 10:18–19, *"I beheld Satan as lightning fall from heaven. [19] Behold, I give unto you power to tread on serpents and scorpions, and over all the power of the enemy: and nothing shall by any means hurt you."* Jesus had sent the seventy out. He said, among other things, that they should cast out demons. They came back and said, "Lord, the demons are subject to us!" Jesus said, prophetically looking forward to this event that occurred at His ascension, *"I beheld Satan as lightning fall from heaven."* Because of that fall, He then says, *"I give unto you power to tread on serpents and scorpions."*

Satan is the serpent, and the scorpions are the demons. Revelation 9 tells us that Satan's demons have the sting of scorpions in their tails. Jesus gives us power over Satan and his demons, and they cannot hurt the believers now. That is not to say they cannot inflict some degree of pain and suffering on us, but they cannot hurt us—that is, they cannot destroy our relationship with God, they cannot stop us from arriving at our destiny of heaven, and they cannot deprive us of eternal life.

This event of Satan falling from heaven to the earth described in Revelation 12:7–9 is not only prophetically spoken of by Jesus in Luke 10:18–19, but this event is also what Jesus was speaking of prophetically when He said in John 12:31, *"Now is the judgment of this world: now shall the prince of this world be cast out."* Thinking of His impending crucifixion, He is saying that as a result of that event, Satan will be judged and cast out of heaven. This event is what Jesus was speaking of when He said in John 16:11, *"The prince of this world is judged."*

Jesus repeatedly spoke of this event, and He was very clear about what He came to achieve and what the results would be. He was declaring in these three passages that He would defeat Satan's kingdom and Satan's power. He would cast Satan out of heaven forever, and He would end Satan's tyranny over His saints. He would destroy both the devil and his works, and He would rid us and Himself of Satan's presence forever. Satan would be cast down!

The Result Declared

The result declared is contained in verses 10 to 12. Notice verse 10: *"And I heard a loud voice saying in heaven, Now is come salvation, and strength, and the kingdom of our God, and the power of his Christ: for the accuser of our brethren is cast down, which accused them before our God day and night.* [11] *And they overcame him by the blood of the Lamb, and by the word of their testimony; and they loved not their lives unto the death.* [12] *Therefore rejoice, ye heavens, and ye that dwell in them. Woe to the inhabiters of the earth and of the sea! for the devil is come down unto you, having great wrath, because he knoweth that he hath but a short time."*

Immediately upon Satan being cast out of heaven, the results of the victory over Satan are declared. From heaven, a loud voice tells us the results of this victory. All Christ purchased and accomplished by His life, death, resurrection, and ascension is now going to be made manifest.

Notice the list in verse 10: *"Now is come salvation. . ."* Now the salvation of Christ is seen. Because of Christ's accomplishment of His work on the cross and His resurrection, ascension, and casting Satan out of heaven, it is now clear how the salvation from Satan and his work promised in Genesis 3:15 was going to be accomplished by the seed of the woman. Now we see, with crystal clarity, that it was by means of the substitutionary atonement of Christ for our sins that He wrought salvation in us. He bore our sins in His own body on the cross and satisfied the righteous wrath of God against our sins by bearing that wrath Himself. Jesus satisfied all the claims of the law against us by bearing the punishment it required of us.

Now this salvation will be seen in all its fullness and righteousness and justice and perfection. It is now on display for the whole world to see, and it will be seen throughout the whole world. Now it will come to every people and tongue and tribe and nation. Salvation has come in its full accomplishment. Salvation has come in its full revelation. Salvation has come to all peoples and nations of the earth.

Now the strength of Christ is seen. Notice the second thing on the list. It says, "*Now is come. . . strength.*" The word in the original language is "*dunamis.*" It is the word for power—the power Christ has to defeat the devil, the power Christ has to save His people, the power Christ has to build His kingdom, the power Christ has to preserve His saints, and the power Christ has to defeat and restrain the wicked. These and many other manifestations of the power of Christ are now clearly seen, and will continue to be seen, until the end of time.

Now the kingdom of God is seen. This is the third thing on the list: "*Now is come. . . the kingdom of our God.*" In Daniel 2:32–35, the kingdom of God was pictured as a stone that was cut out without hands that would smash and destroy the kingdoms of this world and grow to fill the whole earth. That stone came at Christ's first coming, and it is now growing and destroying the kingdoms of this world and establishing the kingdoms of our God and of His Christ, so that He shall reign forever and ever. Daniel 2:44 says, "*And in the days of these kings shall the God of heaven set up a kingdom, which shall never be destroyed: and . . . it shall break in pieces and consume all these kingdoms, and it shall stand for ever.*"

At the ascension of Christ and the casting out of Satan, the kingdom of God on earth was established, and it began its growth on the day of Pentecost in Acts 2, and it has now grown to fill the whole earth. The kingdoms of men have come and gone. But what has not come and gone is the kingdom of God. It started in Jerusalem, it spread to Judea and Samaria, and now it is in the uttermost parts of the earth. The kingdom of God has gone on without remission, without diminution, and without limit. Now it is pervasive throughout the entire world, while the kingdoms of this world have been rising and falling and are increasingly being crushed and destroyed by the gospel.

When you look at local situations, you can say, the devil has a stronghold here, and it seems like everything is under his control. But when you look at the big picture, Christianity is the dominant religion in the whole world, and it has continued to grow and spread steadily from eleven disciples in the upper room, to hundreds of millions throughout history, to billions of people today. No longer does Satan's kingdom dominate the world. Christ's kingdom dominates the world.

Now the authority of Christ is seen. Notice the fourth item in the list, in verse 10. It says, "*Now is come. . . the power of his Christ.*"

The word translated *"power"* in the original language is *"exousia,"* which is different than *"dunamis,"* the word that was translated "strength." This word is translated *"authority"* elsewhere in the Scriptures in many places. Not only has the power of Christ come to do the work, but the authority of Christ has also come to direct the work. Power without direction is destructive, and direction without power is meaningless.

Christ has both authority and power. We see in Matthew 28:18 that all authority in heaven and earth has now been given to Him. Now He is King of kings and Lord of lords. Now He rules with a rod of iron, and every knee must bow and every tongue must confess that Jesus Christ is Lord. All will acknowledge the authority of Christ now, or they will acknowledge it later, but mark it down, they will acknowledge it. Now we see the authority of Christ upon His ascension and upon the casting down of Satan. Now Jesus is Lord of the kingdoms of this world.

In the temptation, Satan offered Jesus the kingdoms of the world if Jesus would bow to him. Jesus said, in effect, "Absolutely not. I will obtain them by crushing your head and taking them from you." This is exactly what He did through His death, resurrection, and ascension.

All of these things—the salvation of Christ, the power of Christ, the kingdom of Christ, and the authority of Christ—are made manifest because the accuser of our brethren has been cast down, who accused them before our God day and night.

For 4,000 years, from the creation until Christ, Satan had accused those in heaven and those on earth as being unworthy to be forgiven of their sins or of being justified by God. Satan implied that God was unjust in forgiving people and bringing them to heaven because there was no adequate atonement made by them or for them that would provide a basis for their forgiveness. God was forgiving Old Testament saints and receiving them into heaven on the basis of Christ's as-of-yet unaccomplished atonement. God was forgiving them on credit. Satan was saying that no one was going to pay the bill.

God the Father was forgiving the Old Testament saints on the credit of the promise that Christ was going to atone for their sins at some point in the future. The plan for atonement was established before the foundation of the world. But now that Christ has provided atonement for all of the Old Testament saints, and now that God is seen to be righteous for having forgiven their sins, Satan's arguments and accusations are seen to be without substance or merit. He is therefore thrown out of the courtroom of heaven because he now has no basis for his case or his charges.

This is what earthly judges do in our day and age. If an attorney tries to bring a frivolous case against someone, the judge throws both him and his case out of the courtroom because there is no merit to it. This is precisely what has happened to Satan. The accuser of our brethren is now cast down because there is now no condemnation for those who are trusting in Christ and His atonement for their forgiveness and acceptance with God.

Romans 8:1 says: "*There is therefore now no condemnation to them which are in Christ Jesus.*" All the condemnation that Satan had been heaping upon the people of God for 4,000 years is now gone.

Romans 8:30–39 reassures us of the same truth: "*Moreover whom he*" (God the Father), "*did predestinate, them he also called: and whom he called, them he also justified: and whom he justified, them he also glorified.*" At the end of verse 30, the saints are seen in heaven as glorified people. Notice the next verse, verse 31: "*What shall we then say to these things? If God be for us, who can be against us?* 32 *He that spared not his own Son, but delivered him up for us all, how shall he not with him also freely give us all things?* 33 *Who shall lay any thing to the charge of God's elect? It is God that justifieth.* 34 *Who is he that condemneth? It is Christ that died, yea rather, that is risen again, who is even at the right hand of God, who also maketh intercession for us.* 35 *Who shall separate us from the love of Christ?*"

And notice verse 38: "*For I am persuaded, that neither death, nor life, nor angels, nor principalities, nor powers, . . .* 39 *. . .shall be able to separate us from the love of God, which is in Christ Jesus our Lord.*" When believers die and go to heaven, there is no one there to accuse them. God will not accuse us; Christ will not accuse us; They are for us, They justify us, and They make intercession for us. There is no counter-party now, no adversary to bring charges against us. It is like the prosecution has left the building, and the only ones left are the defense—and the defenders are God the Father who justifies, and God the Son who died for us and makes intercession on our behalf. That is why there is now no condemnation. None. When you get to heaven, all there will be are justification, acceptance, reward, and blessing. There is now no condemnation for those who are in Christ—absolutely none.

I want you to notice the antecedent of a personal pronoun here, so let us read verse 10: *"And I heard a loud voice saying in heaven, Now is come salvation, and strength, and the kingdom of our God, and the power of his Christ: for the accuser of our brethren"* (our brethren—that is, believers, are now in view). The accuser of our brethren *"is cast down, which accused them before our God day and night.* [11] *And they. . ."* What is the antecedent of the personal pronoun *"they"*? It is *"our brethren."* Verse 11 is now talking about believers. "[11]*And they,"* that is the brethren, *"overcame him by the blood of the Lamb, and by the word of their testimony; and they loved not their lives unto the death."*

The victory of Christ over Satan and the victory of Michael and his angels over Satan now provide the basis for the victory of the believers over Satan throughout this age. Believers, it says in verse 11, are overcomers. It says, *"And they overcame him."* Remember the letters to the seven churches in chapters 2 and 3? Again and again, promises were made to the overcomers. Every letter repeated the promise that "he that overcomes," will obtain all these blessings and rewards.

Verse 11 tells us what that overcoming is and how it is achieved. It is an overcoming of Satan and his lies, temptations, and persecutions that he brings to bear on us. He assaults us. He has been cast down to the earth, and now he is assaulting our persons because he has no ability to destroy our souls, since perfect atonement has been made for them.

Therefore, Satan now brings his assault against our persons and our bodies. It says, *"they overcame him,"* first of all, *"by the blood of the Lamb"*—that is, by faith in Christ and His substitutionary atonement. Satan comes along and says, "You are so terrible, there is no way God is ever going to accept you." We overcome that lie by faith in Christ and His shed blood. By faith in Christ, we are delivered out of the grasp of Satan. By faith in Christ, we are transferred out of the kingdom of darkness and into the kingdom of light. By faith in the blood of the Lamb, we are forgiven and justified and reconciled with God, and delivered out of the hand of Satan. Now we are held safely in the hand of Christ, which is held in the hand of God, as John 10:28–29 promises. Psalm 92:4 says: *"For thou, LORD, hast made me glad through thy work: I will triumph in the works of thy hands."*

Secondly, we overcome Satan *"by the word of [our] testimony."* That is, we overcome him by open, public, vocal confession of Christ before men, and Satan is thereby defeated in his effort to stop the preaching of the gospel and the spread of the kingdom. If Satan cannot keep you from being saved, he wants to keep you from speaking up.

By our testimony of Christ and His gospel and the saving effect it has wrought in us, we push back the kingdom of darkness. We push back the lies and the deceptions, and we set forth the truth and expand the borders of the kingdom of God through the preaching of the gospel. By the preaching of the gospel, we rout Satan, we put him to flight, and we push him back into retreat and defeat. That has been going on for the last 2,000 years as Christianity has pushed against the gates of hell. The gates of hell have not prevailed, the gospel has spread, and now billions of people have become saved.

Thirdly, we overcome Satan by not loving our lives to the point that we are willing to die for Christ before we would ever renounce Him: "*. . .and they loved not their lives unto the death.*" By enduring persecution to the point of martyrdom, we overcome Satan. Believers will give up their lives before they give up their faith.

In Revelation 2:10–11, Jesus says to the believers and the church at Smyrna, "*Fear none of those things which thou shalt suffer: behold, the devil shall cast some of you into prison, that ye may be tried; and ye shall have tribulation ten days: be thou faithful unto death, and I will give thee a crown of life.* [11] *He that hath an ear, let him hear what the Spirit saith unto the churches. He that overcometh shall not be hurt of the second death.*" What are they overcoming? They are overcoming the devil. They refuse to give in, they refuse to lie down, and they refuse to back away. When Satan brings his assaults, they stand up; and if it kills them, so be it. But they never back up, they never back down, they never give in, and they never compromise.

Jesus says, "Even if you are cast into prison, and some of you are put to death, be faithful to the point of death, and I will give you a crown of life, because you will have overcome Satan. I overcame Satan, Michael overcame Satan, and you believers are going to overcome Satan." When you resist the devil, he flees from you, and you defeat him.

Not all believers are called to suffer actual death at the hands of persecutors, but they all endure trials and temptations and persecutions that Satan brings to bear upon them, and they do not quit following Christ because of the incoming assaults they receive. Believers persevere in resisting the devil, and the devil must retreat and flee before them, because they will not yield to him.

In the Christian life, believers win and the devil loses. He loses at keeping us from trusting Christ, he loses at keeping us from speaking about Christ, and he loses at keeping us away from Christ. He loses at turning us against Christ by his persecutions. When persecutions come, we stand strong, and he loses. He does not drive a wedge between Christ and us. Believers overcome Satan and his kingdom when they refuse to yield to the pressure he puts on them to deny Christ and forsake Christ. They are faithful no matter what that pressure is, no matter how great it may be, and no matter how much it costs.

Verse 12 says, *"Therefore rejoice, ye heavens, and ye that dwell in them."* Heaven is a better place now. *"Woe to the inhabiters of the earth and of the sea! for the devil is come down unto you, having great wrath, because he knoweth that he hath but a short time."* Earth is now worse off.

Verse 12 tells us the conclusion of the matter when it uses the word *"therefore."* Therefore, because of this casting out of Satan from heaven, certain things follow. First of all, heaven is greatly improved now that Satan's evil presence has been removed from it. Proverbs 22:10 says, *"Cast out the scorner, and contention shall go out; yea, strife and reproach shall cease."*

For 4,000 years, Abel had to listen to Satan, but now he is gone. Conflict, strife, accusation, argumentation, and condemnation are all now gone, and all that is left is peace and unity and acceptance and approval. These things now reign in heaven without interruption and without contradiction. Heaven is now a place of perfect peace.

However, the second conclusion is that not only is heaven greatly improved, but earth is now greatly distressed. The time Satan spent up in heaven was time he was not down here on earth creating trouble. But now earth is the only place he is. Full of wrath over his defeat and full of anger over the short time he has left before he is cast into the lake of fire, Satan is determined to do all the damage on earth he can before his demise. He cannot destroy the souls of believers because they are preserved by Christ, but he can assault their bodies with persecutions, and that is exactly what he does.

The devil's fury against believers is described in verses 13 to 17 of this chapter, which we will soon examine in detail. But the result is that between the first and the second coming of Christ, great tribulation will occur on earth because of Satan's hostility against the believers. We saw that tribulation when we looked at the four horsemen—

the white horse of conquest, the red horse of war, the black horse of famine, and the pale horse of death. These four horsemen of Satan ride in this age, and they cause immense pain and death and sorrow.

The world wars we have experienced, the famines, the chaos in the nations—all of these are examples of the wrath of Satan being expressed because he has been cast down to the earth and because he has a short time left. All believers in this age will go through great tribulation created by Satan in his efforts to harm them. In Revelation 7, when John had the vision of all the saints standing before the throne, we saw that these saints represented the entire community of all the saved people of all of the ages. When the angel asked John where these people had come from, he said, *"These are they which came out of great tribulation."*

What is that great tribulation? It is the period between the first and the second coming of Christ when Satan has been cast to the earth and is now creating havoc. We see this havoc when we read about the persecution of Christians by all the Muslim nations, by North Korea and China, and by Russia. In our own nation, people are being persecuted and fined hundreds of thousands of dollars just because they do not want to provide services to sodomite counterfeit wedding ceremonies.

This is Satan's wrath being brought to bear against the saints, and though he may touch our bodies, he cannot touch our souls. The same Christ who defeated Satan on the cross will in due time defeat Satan on this earth as well. Michael still stands for us, and he still fights for us, and all the power that defeated the devil initially is still available to defeat him continuously. The same power that cast him out of heaven is the same power that is working to protect us from him now. Though God gives Satan a little time and space in our lives as He did in Job's life, Job was not destroyed by it; instead, Job was blessed by it.

Every reader of this book would want to be Job if he or she could. You are getting your chance now. What is happening to you is Satan's war with Christ being played out on the stage of our nation and our lives. We need to be like Job and say, "The Lord gives and the Lord takes away; blessed be the name of the Lord, because when I get to heaven, I will have the unsearchable riches of Christ, which will more than compensate me for any loss I experienced in this world at the hands of the Evil One and his servants."

We have all of the resources available to us that hurled the enemy down to the earth in the first place, and that same power is still working to protect us and is still working to defeat the devil. So understand this: in the time period we are living in between the first and second coming, Satan is condemned, Satan is defeated, and Satan is on his way to destruction. He is fighting a losing battle, he is in retreat, the kingdom of God is advancing, and we are triumphant. We may be triumphant as martyrs, but we will be triumphant, and in that lies our confidence. This is the good news of the book of Revelation. Christ wins and His people win, and Satan loses and his people lose. Therefore, do not fear their face.

When I look at those who persecute Christians, I feel sorry for them. They are on the losing side. They win their court cases and they think they have won. But what about *the* court case, the very last court case, the one on the Day of Judgment? That is the only case that matters as to whether you win or lose. We need to look past the physical events that are happening in front of us, and recognize that behind them there is spiritual warfare going on, and that we are winning, Christ is winning, and in the end, Satan and his people will be destroyed.

Therefore, do not lose heart. Do not be discouraged. When you see the awful things that are happening in our nation, do not despair, but recognize that this is part of the war, and we are going to win. Let us fight on in the confidence that the victory has already been accomplished. It is now being implemented by Christ and His people.

Do you suppose when Michael went to war with the dragon, he had any confidence about what the outcome would be? He knew for certain he was going to win. But did he have to fight? It says in verse 7, "*Michael and his angels fought. . .*" They did not just "let go and let God," did they? They got in there and fought tooth and nail, and that is what we have to do. We will get bloody in the process, but the outcome is certain.

Fight the good fight of faith. Stand for Christ, speak for Christ, go forth in boldness and confidence in Christ. Know for certain that you are going to win, Christ is going to win, and in the end, all those who opposed Him will be crushed by the Stone.

40

Satan Persecutes the Woman, Revelation 12:13–17

> "13 *And when the dragon saw that he was cast unto the earth,*
> *he persecuted the woman which brought forth the man child.*
> 14 *And to the woman were given two wings of a great eagle,*
> *that she might fly into the wilderness, into her place, where*
> *she is nourished for a time, and times, and half a time, from*
> *the face of the serpent.* 15 *And the serpent cast out of his*
> *mouth water as a flood after the woman, that he might cause*
> *her to be carried away of the flood.* 16 *And the earth helped*
> *the woman, and the earth opened her mouth, and swallowed*
> *up the flood which the dragon cast out of his mouth.* 17 *And*
> *the dragon was wroth with the woman, and went to make war*
> *with the remnant of her seed, which keep the commandments*
> *of God, and have the testimony of Jesus Christ."*

Revelation 12 opens the invisible spiritual world and reveals the spiritual conflict that lies behind and shapes everything we see and experience in the material world. What we see and experience in life always has a deeper unseen narrative behind it. That deeper unseen narrative is the war that is going on between Christ and Satan.

This war between Christ and Satan is what shapes and drives all the events that occur on earth. God created the world and mankind; and when it was finished, it was pure and good. But Satan, through his temptation of Eve, caused the fall of humanity into sin and brought them under the wrath of God. Satan ruined mankind and the world by getting Adam and Eve to rebel against God and reject His authority over them.

But God was not going to be defeated by Satan. God was not going to allow his destructive work to stand. In Genesis 3:15, God promised that He would raise up a Savior of mankind from the seed of the woman, and this Savior would destroy the devil and all his works.

In due time this promise was kept, the Savior was born, and His birth is the subject of Revelation 12. We saw in verses 1 to 6 that when the nation of Israel brought forth Jesus, Satan tried, through his human instrument King Herod, to destroy Christ. Satan was defeated in his effort to destroy Jesus. Instead, throughout the life of Jesus and especially in His death, resurrection, and ascension, Jesus defeated and overcame Satan at every single point.

By His life, death, resurrection, and ascension Christ defeated Satan, and thereby laid the groundwork for Michael and his angels to defeat Satan as described in verses 7 to 12. We saw Satan cast out of heaven, and his ability to accuse believers before the throne of God terminated. Because of the triumph of Christ over Satan, not only was the groundwork laid for the victory of the angels over Satan, but provision was also made for the victory of believers over Satan.

We saw in verse 11 that by their faith in Christ and His substitutionary atonement as the Lamb of God, by their relentless witness to Christ's saving grace and gospel, and by their willingness to forfeit their lives before they denied their Savior, believers now overcome and conquer Satan. They defeat his kingdom, and they do so by advancing the kingdom of Christ over the whole world. The borders of Satan's kingdom are continually pushed back as believers work to expand the kingdom of Christ around the globe.

But even though Christ and the angels have conquered Satan and cast him out of heaven, and the believers have overcome him, this does not mean that Satan gave up the fight or became passive. Satan has not sunk into some hopeless despair and surrendered the field; far from it. Satan is full of anger over his defeat at the hands of Christ. He is enraged that he has been cast out of heaven and down to earth where he awaits his final judgment.

Knowing he has but a short time left before he is cast into the lake of fire, Satan is determined to do all the damage he can before his final demise. He cannot destroy the souls of believers because they are preserved and protected by Jesus Christ. But he can assault their bodies with his persecutions, and their minds with his lies. By these means he attacks believers in this age.

The devil's fury against believers was introduced to us in verse 6. It says, *"And the woman"*—that is, the church, the covenant community of the people of God—*"fled into the wilderness, where she hath a place prepared of God, that they should feed her there a thousand two hundred and threescore days."* As we expounded verse 6 in chapter 38, we saw that the covenant community of the people of God was seen to flee into the wilderness—that is, into a place of protection from Satan, where God guides her, protects her, and provides for her. What was introduced in verse 6 is now expanded and explained in verses 13 through 17. Verses 13 through 17 are an exposition of verse 6; and in these verses, we discover the full meaning of verse 6.

The Motive for Satan's Persecution of Believers

The motive for Satan's persecution of believers is found in verse 13. It says, *"And when the dragon saw that he was cast unto the earth, he persecuted the woman which brought forth the man child."* Satan is now defeated. He was defeated at the cross, and his defeat was publicly declared when he was cast out of heaven. He has been utterly humiliated before the whole spiritual world: before God, before the good angels, and even before his own demons who share in his defeat.

He should be utterly humiliated and ashamed, but Satan knows no humility or shame. Out of his defeat arises a boiling anger, and out of this anger comes hatred and persecution against that which represents his defeat. Satan can no longer persecute Jesus as we saw him doing while Christ was on earth. Therefore, he now persecutes the woman who brought Him forth. Satan cannot attack the Head of the church, so he now persecutes the body of the church made up of the believers in Christ.

Perhaps an illustration would help. Satan is like a criminal who has been declared guilty by the judge, has been sentenced to death by the judge, and has been consigned to death row by the judge to await his just punishment. But instead of admitting his guilt and accepting the justice of his punishment, the criminal is filled with anger and rage at getting caught and being condemned; and as a result, because he cannot attack the judge directly, he puts out an order to kill the judge's family.

When Satan saw that he was cast out of heaven and cast down to the earth, he began a furious persecution of the covenant community that had given birth to Christ. *"The woman"* was Old Covenant Israel, of whom Christ was born, in verses 1–5. *"The woman"* then became New Covenant Israel at the Last Supper. It is New Covenant

Israel, here still called *"the woman"* in verse 6 and in verses 13–17, that now becomes the object of Satan's malevolence. The woman of verses 13 to 17 is New Covenant Israel, the church of the living God.

To illustrate what verse 13 is talking about, notice Acts 9:1–5. Here we see the malevolence, the hatred, the anger, and the persecution of Satan against the woman once he has been cast down to earth. His instrument in persecuting the woman is Saul of Tarsus. Satan is behind all that Saul is and does.

Revelation 12:13 says: *"And when the dragon saw that he was cast unto the earth, he persecuted the woman which brought forth the man child."* Here is what that looks like. Acts 9:1: *"And Saul, yet breathing out threatenings and slaughter against the disciples of the Lord, went unto the high priest,* [2] *And desired of him letters to Damascus to the synagogues, that if he found any of this way, whether they were men or women, he might bring them bound unto Jerusalem.* [3] *And as he journeyed, he came near Damascus: and suddenly there shined round about him a light from heaven:* [4] *And he fell to the earth, and heard a voice saying unto him, Saul, Saul, why persecutest thou me?* [5] *And he said, Who art thou, Lord? And the Lord said, I am Jesus whom thou persecutest."*

Satan attempts to strike at Christ by striking at His people. Someone may not be able to injure your head, but if he can stomp and crush your foot, that is ultimately an attack upon the head. Satan has been cast to the earth, and in a rage he attacks the woman. He attacks her through human instruments of threatening and slaughter and persecution. Jesus declares in verses 4–5 that Saul is really persecuting Him by persecuting His people, because they are one body.

The Protection from Satan's Persecution of Believers

The protection from Satan's persecution of believers is found in verse 14. *"And to the woman were given two wings of a great eagle, that she might fly into the wilderness, into her place, where she is nourished for a time, and times, and half a time, from the face of the serpent."*

Just like a judge would make provision for the safety and security of his family against the criminals he condemned, and just like the head makes provision for the safety and protection of the body against attacks, in the same way Christ makes provision for the safety and protection of His church. Christ looks after His church with a jealous concern for her well-being and protection.

Notice the symbolic visual imagery that is used to describe this protection. She is *"given two wings of a great eagle, that she might fly into the wilderness, into her place"* of nourishment and protection. When we expounded verse 6, we saw the same kind of symbolic imagery used there, when the place of her protection was described as *"the wilderness."* Verse 6 and verse 14 speak in exactly the same symbolic imagery, but verse 14 supplies additional details.

When Israel fled from Pharaoh, Israel found a refuge in the wilderness. Israel crossed the Red Sea, went into the wilderness, and there she found refuge from the dragon, Pharaoh. In Ezekiel 29:1–3, Pharaoh is called the dragon. He is a picture of Satan who is called the dragon. In the wilderness, God protected Israel and fed her, while Israel's adversary, Pharaoh the dragon, could not lay hands on her when she was there. In the wilderness, Israel was beyond Pharaoh's grasp, and Israel was safe from Pharaoh's assaults.

This is the imagery of verse 14. *"And to the woman were given two wings of a great eagle, that she might fly into the wilderness, into her place, where she is nourished. . .from the face of the serpent."* Christ provides His church with a metaphorical wilderness in which to live where she is safe from the assaults of Satan. The church flees into this wilderness, and there she finds a place of refuge from the face of the dragon. In the wilderness, God protects His people; and in the wilderness, God provides for His church.

The wilderness spoken of here is not a specific geographical place under the New Covenant. The wilderness spoken of in verses 6 and 14 is any place and every place in the world where the people of God can find refuge from Satan's persecuting people and from Satan's persecuting governments.

The people of God have always had places of refuge somewhere in the world to which they can flee from Satan's agents of persecution. God sees to it that they do. The wilderness that God provides for His people under the New Covenant may be as small as an individual home, a forest, or a cave where people can be shielded from Satan's persecuting agents. It may be something as large as an entire nation where people find protection from Satan's persecuting agents.

In Matthew 2, Christ is born, and Herod, Satan's agent of persecution, wants to destroy Him. What does God provide as a place of refuge, what wilderness does God guide Mary and Joseph and Jesus into so they are beyond the reach of the serpent?

Verse 13 says, "*And when they*" (the wise men) "*were departed, behold, the angel of the Lord appeareth to Joseph in a dream, saying, Arise, and take the young child and his mother, and flee into Egypt, and be thou there until I bring thee word: for Herod will seek the young child to destroy him.* [14] *When he arose, he took the young child and his mother by night, and departed into Egypt:* [15] *And was there until the death of Herod: that it might be fulfilled which was spoken of the Lord by the prophet, saying, Out of Egypt have I called my son.*"

The place of refuge that God provided for Joseph and Mary and Jesus, the wilderness into which they were able to flee from the face of the serpent in this situation, was Egypt.

Notice further verses 19 to 23: "*But when Herod was dead, behold, an angel of the Lord appeareth in a dream to Joseph in Egypt,* [20] *Saying, Arise, and take the young child and his mother, and go into the land of Israel: for they are dead which sought the young child's life.* [21] *And he arose, and took the young child and his mother, and came into the land of Israel.* [22] *But when he heard that Archelaus did reign in Judea in the room of his father Herod, he was afraid to go thither: notwithstanding, being warned of God in a dream, he turned aside into the parts of Galilee:* [23] *And he came and dwelt in a city called Nazareth: that it might be fulfilled which was spoken by the prophets, He shall be called a Nazarene.*" Now the wilderness that God has provided for Jesus away from the face of the serpent is a city. It is now the city of Nazareth.

We see Satan the dragon persecuting the people, and God providing a wilderness for them to flee into, in Acts 8:1–5: "*And Saul was consenting unto his death*"—that is, to the death of Stephen who had been stoned in the previous chapter. "*And at that time there was a great persecution against the church which was at Jerusalem.*" Satan has been cast to the earth and now he is persecuting the woman. "*And they were all scattered abroad throughout the regions of Judea and Samaria, except the apostles.*" They flee, and they flee into places that are beyond the reach of Satan's persecuting agents. The wilderness is now the regions of Judea and Samaria. That is why we read later in chapter 9 that Saul had to go all the way up to Damascus to find them because that was the place of refuge to which they had fled.

Verse 2: "*And devout men carried Stephen to his burial, and made great lamentation over him.* [3] *As for Saul, he made havoc of the church, entering into every house, and haling men and women committed them to prison.* [4]*Therefore they that were scattered abroad went every where preaching the word.* [5] *Then Philip went down to the city of Samaria, and preached Christ unto them."*

Whenever Satan has begun to persecute the church, God always provides a wilderness to flee into, to escape that persecution. Revelation 12:14 says that the woman was given two wings of a great eagle to facilitate her flight into the place of refuge from the persecuting dragon. This symbolic imagery of having an eagle's wings given in order to facilitate escape is rooted in several Old Testament passages.

Notice Exodus 19:1–4. Israel has left Egypt, Israel has proceeded through the wilderness, and Israel has now come to Mount Sinai. It says, *"In the third month, when the children of Israel were gone forth out of the land of Egypt"* (they escaped from Satan, from Pharaoh the dragon), *"the same day came they into the wilderness of Sinai."* There is their place of protection.

"[2] *For they were departed from Rephidim, and were come to the desert of Sinai, and had pitched in the wilderness; and there Israel camped before the mount.* [3] *And Moses went up unto God, and the* Lord *called unto him out of the mountain, saying, Thus shalt thou say to the house of Jacob, and tell the children of Israel;* [4] *Ye have seen what I did unto the Egyptians, and how I bare you on eagles' wings, and brought you unto myself."* God is saying that the way in which He protected Israel and provided for Israel and brought Israel safely to Mount Sinai was like being flown there on the wings of an eagle.

This same metaphor is repeated in Deuteronomy 32:9–13. Here Moses is recounting the same incident, but he uses more expansive language. *"For the* LORD*'s portion is his people; Jacob is the lot of his inheritance."* Imagine that. We are God's inheritance. Verse 10: *"He found him"* (Israel) *"in a desert land, and in the waste howling wilderness; he led him about, he instructed him, he kept him as the apple of his eye."* God protected Israel like you would protect the pupil of your eyeball from injury.

"[11] *As an eagle stirreth up her nest, fluttereth over her young, spreadeth abroad her wings, taketh them,"* (her young eagles, and) *"beareth them on her wings."* As the eagle flies with her young on her back, "[12] *So the* LORD *alone did lead him, and there was no strange god with him.* [13] *He made him"* (Israel) *"ride on the high places of the earth, that he might eat the increase of the fields; and he made him to suck honey out of the rock, and oil out of the flinty rock."* Moses goes on and describes the blessings that occurred in the wilderness when God bore Israel on His back like a giant eagle as He carried them to the Promised Land.

The well-known passage in Isaiah 40:28–31 says, "*Hast thou not known? hast thou not heard, that the everlasting God, the* LORD, *the Creator of the ends of the earth, fainteth not, neither is weary? there is no searching of his understanding.* [29] *He giveth power to the faint; and to them that have no might he increaseth strength.* [30] *Even the youths shall faint and be weary, and the young men shall utterly fall:* [31] *But they that wait upon the* LORD *shall renew their strength; they shall mount up with wings as eagles; they shall run, and not be weary; and they shall walk, and not faint.*"

The eagle's wings spoken of in Revelation 12:14 are a metaphor, a symbol of God's help and protection and power. God will protect and empower and guide His church to places of safety from Satan's persecuting people by His providences and His provision. The church will be supernaturally led out of places of danger, and led into places of safety in various places around the world.

For example, America was a place of refuge from the persecution of believers in England, Europe, and elsewhere. The pilgrims came across on the Mayflower to find a place of refuge. God bore them on the wings of eagles, enabling them to establish a colony. For centuries, America was a place of refuge, the wilderness into which God transported His people so they could find a place of protection from the face of the serpent.

Sadly, the serpent has arrived in America, and now our own government has become the serpent that is beginning to turn on us and persecute us. We may have to flee in order to find protection from the face of the serpent. But mark it down: God will always provide a place for His people to flee to. That is the promise of verse 14.

How long will this supernatural enablement to find protection from Satan and his people go on? According to verse 14, it will go on "*for a time, and times, and half a time*"—the symbolic three and a half years, elsewhere called forty-two months, elsewhere called twelve hundred and sixty days. Notice that the "*time, and times, and half a time*" of verse 14 is the same period as the "*thousand two hundred and threescore days*" (twelve hundred and sixty days) of verse

6, showing these two time periods are equivalent because they both speak of the supernatural protection the people of God will enjoy in "*the wilderness*" between the first and second coming of Christ.

Satan will persecute the church during the time between his being cast out of heaven at the ascension of Christ and the second coming of Christ. Nevertheless, Christ will supernaturally deliver the church out of his hand, just like He supernaturally delivered Israel out of Pharaoh's hand. Christ will protect His church, Christ will nourish His church, and Christ will preserve His church all throughout this age, and deliver her from Satan's efforts to destroy her. That is the promise of protection from Satan's persecution of believers contained in verse 14.

The Method of Satan's Persecution of Believers

The method of Satan's persecution of believers is described in verses 15 to 16. "*And the serpent cast out of his mouth water as a flood after the woman, that he might cause her to be carried away of the flood.*
[16] *And the earth helped the woman, and the earth opened her mouth and swallowed up the flood which the dragon cast out of his mouth.*"

Here we are told, in symbolic language, the method Satan uses to try to persecute the church. The church is protected by Christ from physical assaults by providing a place to flee those physical assaults. But Satan still attempts to attack the church by sending out a flood of assaults toward the people of God.

What is this "*flood*" of assaults that Satan launches against the people of God to overwhelm them? The picture here is that of a tidal wave. People are on the shore, and the ocean launches a giant volume of water that is designed to go inland and swallow them up.

Frequently in the Old Testament, the metaphor of a flood is used to describe an attacking army. The Assyrians came in like a flood to overwhelm the land of Israel. While the metaphor is frequently used this way, there is another way to understand this flood. Having seen that Jesus protects His church from the pouring forth of physical persecution in verses 13 and 14, this flood of verse 15 seems to be something different and something in addition to that physical persecution. Psalm 144 sheds light on what this flood of Revelation 12:15 is referring to.

Notice Psalm 144:7–8. The psalmist is praying to God and he says,

"Send thine hand from above; rid me, and deliver me out of great waters, from the hand of strange children; [8] *Whose mouth speaketh vanity, and their right hand is a right hand of falsehood."* David is saying these great waters—this flood of lies from the enemy—is being thrust upon him. They are overwhelming him. He is asking God to deliver him from this flood of falsehood, slander, and lies.

Satan tries to overwhelm and sink the church beneath a flood of lies. Humanistic philosophies, false religions, political delusions, economic enticements, pseudo-scientific theories like evolution, and a thousand other lies are hurled at the church by Satan.

Satan tells the church that the Bible has errors, that men are fundamentally good, that obtaining health and wealth and happiness are the chief goals of Christianity, and that social action is the mission of the church. He tells them that church attendance is dispensable, the Fourth Commandment is obsolete, man is sovereign, and morality is relative.

This flood of lies is designed to carry away the church from her faith, from her mission, and from her God. This flood is like a river of death that is in contrast with the river of life that proceeds out of the throne of God. This is Satan's counterfeit river. If Satan cannot destroy the church because she is protected (see verse 14) then his goal is to cripple the church with compromise and corruption so that it becomes weak and ineffective in its witness and worship (see verse 15).

The church in every generation has been plagued by this flood of lies from Satan. But once again, Christ does not leave His church defenseless. He anticipated this evil work on the part of Satan, and even before He left this earth, He prayed for our protection from this flood of lies. In John 17, Jesus prays for the protection of the woman, His bride, the church.

In John 17:11 Jesus says to the Father, *"And now I am no more in the world, but these are in the world, and I come to thee."* He is looking ahead to the time after the ascension when Satan is cast down to the earth and begins this fierce persecution and this flood of lies. Jesus says, *"Holy Father, keep through thine own name those whom thou hast given me."* "Protect them, Father. Protect their unity, that they may be one, even as We are one." He says, "[12] *While I was with them in the world, I kept them in thy name."* "I preserved them." *"Those that thou gavest me, I have kept, and none of them is lost, but the son of perdition; that the scripture might be fulfilled."*

No disciples were killed when Jesus was captured. He said, "Take Me; let these go." He protected them. Verse 13: *"And now come I to thee"* (speaking of His ascension); *"and these things I speak in the world, that they might have my joy fulfilled in themselves."* "I am going to be gone, but I want them to be joyful in spite of their hardships."

Verse 14: *"I have given them thy word; and the world hath hated them, because they are not of the world, even as I am not of the world."* Jesus' thoughts were like this: "I am going away, and I need to leave something to sustain My church. I need to feed them with manna." The manna He provided for them was God's word, the Bible. It is the manna upon which we feed. It sustains us in the midst of the world's hatred.

Here is our verse, verse 15: *"I pray not that thou shouldest take them out of the world, but that thou shouldest keep them from the evil [one]."* In the King James Version, it just says *"Keep them from the evil,"* period. Evil is an adjective, and it modifies a noun. Here the noun is implied, not directly stated. In Greek grammar, it is what we call the substantive use of the adjective. The New King James Version supplies the noun, *"evil one"*—that is, Satan. Jesus says, in effect, "Lord, I pray not that You would take them out of the world like You are going to take Me out, but I want You to protect them from the Evil One, from Satan." What is the protection He prays for? Here is the protection: "[17] *Sanctify them through thy truth: thy word is truth."* Truth is the protection against the flood of lies that the Evil One spews forth.

Revelation 12:16 says, *"And the earth helped the woman, and the earth opened her mouth, and swallowed up the flood which the dragon cast out of his mouth."* The metaphor is clear. Actual, literal, physical floods that we experience do not last forever because the ground absorbs the floodwaters, and they disappear into the ground. In the same way, Satan's lies do not stand for very long in the church before God raises up a man to declare the truth, and thereby swallow up the lie that Satan has propagated.

By way of illustration, God raised up Martin Luther and the Reformers during the Reformation to swallow up the lies of Romanism with the truth of biblical teaching on justification by faith alone and the authority of the Scriptures alone. Faith alone, Christ alone, Scripture alone, Grace alone, and the Glory of God alone—these were the truths that swallowed up the satanic lies of Romanism that had been flooding Christendom for a long time.

Cults come along, but God raises up theologians and scholars to expose and defuse their false teachings. False humanistic philosophies come along, and God raises up apologetic ministries that rebut and refute the deceptions of humanism. The point is, God always raises up the means to defeat and dissipate the flood of lies Satan floods the world with in every generation.

In Isaiah 59:19, it says, "*When the enemy shall come in like a flood, the Spirit of the Lord shall lift up a standard against him.*" The enemy came in like a flood in the form of Roman Catholicism, and the Spirit of the Lord raised up a standard of Martin Luther and the Reformers against it, they dissipated its lies, and the church was protected.

So it has been in every generation. Just as Aaron's rod swallowed up the rods of Pharaoh's magicians, so the truth of God's word will swallow up the lies propagated by Satan's people. Just as the earth literally opened up and swallowed Korah, Dathan, and Abiram when they sought to corrupt the church of the Old Testament, so the lake of fire will swallow up Satan and his servants in the Day of Judgment for all the corruption they tried to bring into the church. Metaphorically and literally, the earth opens up to swallow this flood of lies and those who propagate them, and thereby the church is protected. An open grave is the earth opening its mouth to swallow up Satan's servants who persecute the people of God.

The point is simply this: whatever Satan throws at the church to overwhelm it, God provides a means to subdue it, defuse it, and extinguish its strength and power. The church is protected from the lies, it is sanctified by the truth, and the church continues to go on. Satan is defeated, the flood of his lies is dissipated, and the church continues to maintain the truth century after century after century. It continues to go forward and to triumph.

Neither the persecutions directed at the body nor the flood of lies directed at the mind is able to destroy the church. Christ protects her by providing her with a place of refuge physically from the persecutors, and Christ protects her spiritually by providing her with the means to turn back the flood of lies that would corrupt her theology and practice.

The Ongoing Nature of Satan's Persecution of Believers

The ongoing nature of Satan's persecution of believers is in verse 17. *"And the dragon was wroth with the woman, and went to make war with the remnant of her seed, which keep the commandments of God, and have the testimony of Jesus Christ."*

The dragon is enraged at the woman (the church) because his efforts to destroy it either by persecution or by deception have failed. Satan failed in the first generation, the generation in which John was writing Revelation in AD 95, but Satan does not give up the effort. If he cannot destroy the church in one generation, he will try to do so in the next generation. If he cannot ruin the church in one century, he will attempt to do so in the following century.

Each generation of believers begets the next generation of believers, who are here called the *"seed"* or the offspring of the woman. How are the offspring of the woman identified? What marks their true paternity? Is it infant baptism? Are successive generations of the church to be identified by having been sprinkled with water as infants? Absolutely not. The true offspring of the true church are identified by their conduct, not by their genetics; they are identified by their character, and not by rituals like infant baptism.

Notice in verse 17, as each new generation of the church is born through regeneration by means of the new birth, it is marked by two characteristics. First of all, the people are marked by the fact that they *"keep the commandments of God."* You can baptize babies all day long, but if they do not keep the commandments of God, they are not the seed of the woman.

In Matthew 28:19–20, Jesus says that His disciples should go, therefore, and make disciples of all nations, and baptize *"them"*—that is, baptize the disciples, and teach *"them"* to observe all things whatever He had commanded them. How do you know when individuals have become disciples? They keep all the things Jesus has commanded of them, whatever they may be. They do not keep them perfectly, but they keep them comprehensively, and they keep them as the dominating characteristic of their life, all the days of their life. These are the overcomers.

This is the first characteristic of the children of the church: they *"keep the commandments of God."* The second characteristic is that they *"have the testimony of Jesus Christ"*—that is, they publicly confess their faith in Christ as their Lord and Savior before the world. They are not closet Christians. We read in the Gospels that many believed on Him, but, out of fear of the Pharisees, they did not confess Him lest they be put out of the synagogue. What kind of believers were those? They were false believers.

If you are going to be understood to be a true member of the church of Jesus Christ, you must publicly declare yourself to be a Christian—to be one who is trusting in Jesus Christ as Lord and Savior. You must be one who preaches the gospel with whatever capacity you possess in whatever opportunities God provides. It may be something as simple as a mother teaching her children to fear God, keep His commandments, repent of their sins, and seek Christ; or it may be something as great as an evangelistic preacher who has filled stadiums with people. But somehow, in some way, you have to stand up before a hostile world and say, "I am a Christian. I am trusting in Jesus Christ as my Lord and Savior, my life is sold out to Him, and yours needs to be as well." That is what the testimony of Jesus Christ looks like.

Those who have the testimony of Jesus Christ publicly confess their faith in Christ as their Lord and Savior before the world. They publicly testify that Jesus Christ has redeemed them from their sins. This is how the church is renewed on the earth, century after century. As people follow the teachings of Jesus and proclaim the gospel of Jesus, the next generation of people is born to Jesus via the new birth. They are born again, not of corruptible seed, but of incorruptible seed, by the word of God that lives and abides forever. As you bear testimony to that word by your life and witness, the next generation is born.

The church is constantly renewed, the church is constantly persecuted, and the church is constantly protected from the lethal assaults of Satan and from the flood of lies launched by Satan. Every generation has to fight this war, and every generation will win this war. The church has been winning the war against Satan for 2,000 years. Do you think this generation is going to lose it? We are not. We are still triumphing in and through Christ.

As the church is renewed on the earth century after century through being born from above by the regenerating work of the Holy Spirit, century after century Satan sends out his people to persecute them and sends out his lies to deceive them. But, century after century, Christ provides protection for His people, and He provides a repudiation of those lies; and by that means, Christ sustains His church and leads them into final triumph. What you are going through today is what the church has been going through for the last 2,000 years, and will continue to go through until Jesus returns.

When we introduced this book, we said it was a manual of spiritual warfare. When you properly understand the truths these symbolic metaphors are conveying, you can understand this warfare, and know exactly what to expect in your own spiritual warfare. There may come a day when you have to physically get up and go somewhere else to escape being killed by Satan's persecutors. The church has always done that. The church will always have to do that. Christ will always provide a place for His people to go.

You are stunned by the volume and the variety of lies that have come into the church, and how so many congregations have imbibed them. But what is amazing is how God always raises up extraordinary men in every generation to expose and rebut those lies and to confirm the church in her faith. Thank God for the spiritual giants God raises up to swallow up the lies of the Evil One, and to sanctify the church through the truth. The church has never fallen before physical persecutions or intellectual deceptions, and it never will.

Let us be about begetting the next generation through the words of our testimony, so they too can triumph over the Evil One who is already defeated, and who fails every time he attempts to destroy the church.

41

The Beast Out of the Sea, Revelation 13:1–10

> "[1] *And I stood upon the sand of the sea, and saw a beast rise up out of the sea, having seven heads and ten horns, and upon his horns ten crowns, and upon his heads the name of blasphemy.* [2] *And the beast which I saw was like unto a leopard, and his feet were as the feet of a bear, and his mouth as the mouth of a lion: and the dragon gave him his power, and his seat, and great authority.* [3] *And I saw one of his heads as it were wounded to death; and his deadly wound was healed: and all the world wondered after the beast.* [4] *And they worshipped the dragon which gave power unto the beast: and they worshipped the beast, saying, Who is like unto the beast? who is able to make war with him?* [5] *And there was given unto him a mouth speaking great things and blasphemies; and power was given unto him to continue forty and two months.* [6] *And he opened his mouth in blasphemy against God, to blaspheme his name, and his tabernacle, and them that dwell in heaven.* [7] *And it was given unto him to make war with the saints, and to overcome them: and power was given him over all kindreds, and tongues, and nations.* [8] *And all that dwell upon the earth shall worship him, whose names are not written in the book of life of the Lamb slain from the foundation of the world.* [9] *If any man have an ear, let him hear.* [10] *He that leadeth into captivity shall go into captivity: he that killeth with the sword must be killed with the sword. Here is the patience and the faith of the saints.*"

In this fourth parallel section of the book of Revelation, the conflict between Christ and Satan is set forth which explains why things happen in the visible realm the way they do.

In chapter 12, we saw the effort of Satan to destroy Christ when He was born and as He lived on the earth. Not only did Satan fail to destroy Christ, but Christ also defeated Satan at every point. Having failed at that task and being cast out of heaven as a result, we saw Satan's work in persecuting the church, both with physical persecution to try to destroy it, and with a flood of lies to try to deceive it. But Satan is a failure. He was overcome by Christ, he was overcome by Michael and the angels, and he was overcome by the believers.

However, Satan will never give up the fight until he is forced to. He has no intention of withdrawing from the field of conflict. Satan's goal is to do as much damage to the church as he can before he is cast into the lake of fire, and to take as many people to hell with him as he is able.

While we see Satan in chapter 12 as the leading figure in persecuting and deceiving the church, he does not work alone. He has his demons to assist him, who are fallen angels. They played a prominent role in the Gospels and are spoken of in some detail in Revelation 9 as the locusts with scorpion stings in their tails. The demons are mentioned briefly in Revelation 12:7–9 when the dragon and his angels were cast out of heaven.

In addition to the demons we are familiar with, Satan has many human helpers to aid and assist him in his evil work. In these next two chapters, we are introduced to all of Satan's human helpers. This fourth parallel section covering chapters 12 to 14 has Satan and his helpers as its theme. It describes how Satan and his helpers operate between the first and second coming of Jesus.

There is the beast that arises out of the sea, which represents and symbolizes the persecuting governments of the world. There is the beast that arises out of the earth, which represents and symbolizes the persecuting false religions of the world. There is the harlot Babylon, which represents and symbolizes the seducing power of the world with all of its materialism and sensuality and pleasures. And finally, there are those who take the mark of the beast—representing and symbolizing all the unsaved people who willingly have their thinking and actions directed by Satan.

To state it as simply as possible, Satan is assisted in his evil work by anti-Christian government, which is the beast out of the sea; by anti-Christian religion, which is the beast out of the earth; by anti-Christian society, which is Babylon; and by the anti-Christian populace, which is all those who have the mark of the beast. These are his four helpers.

All of these helpers of Satan are seen to be at work as soon as Christ ascends into heaven, and they continue to operate until He returns and destroys them all in His final judgment. The point is that we wrestle not against just flesh and blood, as Ephesians 6:12 says. It is not just people who are opposing us as we seek to love Christ and live for Christ. Driving these people and directing these people and empowering these people are the rulers of the darkness of this world, who exercise spiritual wickedness of the highest order. It is Satan himself who drives and directs his people to carry out their evil against Christians.

John is telling us in this section that there is more than meets the eye when you see governments persecuting, cults deceiving, the world seducing, and the people raging against God and His church. What is behind all of them is Satan himself. When he is destroyed, all his helpers will cease to function.

But until that time comes, we must intelligently understand who we are dealing with, what we may expect from them, and how we should go about engaging in spiritual warfare against them. Whether it is the persecuting governments of the world, whether it is the false religions of the world, whether it is the seduction and enticement of the world, or whether it is the mass of unsaved humanity who hate Christ and His people, we will understand how to deal with them as we understand that Satan is behind them and empowering them; and therefore, we can grasp why they do what they do, and how we may view and respond to them.

In the passage before us in Revelation 13:1–10, we are going to look at the first of Satan's helpers—the beast that rises out of the sea. In subsequent chapters, we will look at Satan's other helpers—the beast that arises out of the earth, those who have the mark of the beast, and Babylon.

The Appearance of the Beast

The appearance of the beast is mentioned in verses 1 to 2a. Notice verse 1: *"And I stood upon the sand of the sea, and saw a beast rise up out of the sea, having seven heads and ten horns, and upon his horns ten crowns, and upon his heads the name of blasphemy.* [2] *And the beast which I saw was like unto a leopard, and his feet were as the feet of a bear, and his mouth as the mouth of a lion."*

In these initial verses, John describes the appearance of this horrible beast that is going to assist Satan in accomplishing his evil work. We see that he arises out of the sea. We discovered in our study of Daniel 7 that when used symbolically, the sea represents the churning mass of unsaved humanity. The wicked are like the troubled sea that cannot rest, that casts up mire and dirt. This beast arises out of the mass of unsaved humanity—that is, out of the wicked population of the earth.

He then describes this beast as being similar in appearance to the description of the dragon that was set forth in Revelation 12:3. We see that the dragon in 12:3 and the beast in 13:1 both have seven heads and ten horns. The beast is similar to the dragon because the beast shares and reflects the dragon's evil character and power.

These seven heads of the beast represent dominion and rule because the head always exercises dominion and rule over the body. Seven is the number that symbolizes completion. Therefore, these seven heads represent the complete number of kingdoms that exercise dominion and rule on the earth between the first and second coming of Christ.

The beast also has ten horns and a crown upon each of those horns. We have seen in Daniel 7 and elsewhere that horns represent power and strength, and crowns represent rule and authority. Ten is the number that symbolizes perfection and totality. We see these kings that rule these successive kingdoms between the first and the second coming of Christ have the perfect amount of power and authority they need to carry out their evil agenda. That evil agenda is represented by the name written on the heads of this beast.

The name written on the heads of this beast, on all seven of the heads, is the same name—and it is the name of blasphemy. Notice verse 1: *"I . . . saw a beast rise up out of the sea, having seven heads and ten horns, and upon his horns ten crowns,"* (he has authority and power and rule) *"and upon his heads the name of blasphemy."* So the heads (plural) have the name of blasphemy (singular) on every one of his heads. Every one of the seven heads is characterized by blasphemy.

The point is, blasphemy against God is the characteristic that guides each kingdom and each nation (symbolically speaking, all seven of them, the complete number of them) that will arise between the first and second coming of Jesus. Every nation and all nations that have arisen from the time of Christ to the present moment have functioned in defiance of God, have set themselves up as rivals to the authority of God, and have persecuted the people of God.

In a word, the kingdoms of this world and this age are a constant expression of blasphemy against God's authority by their policies and their laws, and in the exercise of their dominion and power. Even so-called "Christian" nations have had laws and policies and rulers that were anything but Christian. Like America, nations may give passing acknowledgment to God in their founding documents, but in their laws and policies they immediately begin to act contrary to His will and His honor. Kings set themselves up as the final authority and assert their will, irrespective of God's laws. Their very act of ruling is an act of blasphemy because they do not acknowledge God's authority over their kingdom or over their persons. They demand that their citizens see them as the ultimate and final authority in their lives.

Verse 2 gives us certainty regarding the identity of this beast out of the sea, and certainty that these seven heads and ten horns represent the authority and the power of all the successive kings and kingdoms between the first and second coming of Jesus. Verse 2 tells us the identity of this beast out of the sea. *"And the beast which I saw was like unto a leopard, and his feet were as the feet of a bear, and his mouth as the mouth of a lion."*

John describes this beast as being like a leopard, a bear, and a lion in its various parts. In Daniel 7, we saw that various world empires were characterized by a lion, a bear, and a leopard.

Daniel 7:2–7: *"And, behold the four winds of the heavens strove upon the great sea.* [3] *And four great beasts came up from the sea, diverse one from another"* just like this beast in Revelation 13:1 came up out of the sea. *"*[4] *The first was like a lion, and had eagle's wings: I beheld till the wings thereof were plucked, and it was lifted up from the earth, and made stand upon the feet as a man, and a man's heart was given to it.* [5] *And behold another beast, a second, like to a bear, and it raised up itself on one side, and it had three ribs in the mouth of it between the teeth of it: and they said thus unto it, Arise, devour much flesh.* [6] *After this I beheld, and lo another, like a leopard, which had upon the back of it four wings of a fowl; the beast had also four heads; and dominion was given to it."* Here we have the lion, the bear, and the leopard represented. *"*[7] *After this I saw in the night visions, and behold a fourth beast, dreadful and terrible, and strong exceedingly; and it had great iron teeth: it devoured and brake in pieces, and stamped the residue with the feet of it: and it was diverse from all the beasts that were before it; and it had ten horns."*

What are these four beasts—the lion, the bear, the leopard, and the ten-horned beast? Daniel 7:17 says, *"These great beasts, which are four, are four kings, which shall arise out of the earth."* Daniel tells us these beasts symbolize kings and kingdoms. The four beasts which Daniel saw in his vision have all been combined into one beast in Revelation 13:2. The leopard, the bear, the lion, and the ten horns are now all one composite beast.

This composite beast of Revelation 13:1–2 represents every form of civil government that has existed between the first and second coming of Christ, all of whom persecute the church. It represents all of the successive anti-Christian governments of this age. The appearance of this beast tells us clearly what he represents. He represents the dominion, power, and cruelty of all the blasphemous kingdoms of this age that persecute Christians.

This beast represents the dominion and rule (the heads), and the power and strength (the horns) of all the blasphemous (the name written on each head) kingdoms (the horns are all crowned) of this age that persecute Christians. These beasts are vicious animals that crush and tear and devour and destroy. These are predatory animals designed to destroy prey. The people of God are the prey that this composite horrible beast is devouring.

The point is this: Human governments are not the friend of the church. We need not be surprised that every government Christians have lived under since the time of Christ to the present moment have persecuted believers in various ways and to various degrees.

Human governments are driven by Satan to blaspheme God and to persecute the church. That is the way it always has been and that is the way it always will be until Christ's own government is established on the new earth at His second coming. This is why we do not look for Christian utopias to arise out of human governments. This is why we have wicked rulers and wicked judges and wicked lawmakers and wicked presidents.

Remember this sobering truth: When you go to work for the government, you go to work for the beast. Beware lest you become an agent to enforce his blasphemy. When working for the government, if you cannot be a minister of God for good to do good as God would have you do, then get out of government employment. As the government becomes increasingly evil, it becomes increasingly difficult to work for the government and not become an agent of the evil and blasphemy of that government yourself.

The Power of the Beast

The power of the beast is set forth in verse 2b–3 which says: *"and the dragon gave him,"* (the beast) *"his power, and his seat [throne], and great authority.* [3] *And I saw one of his heads as it were wounded to death; and his deadly wound was healed: and all the world wondered after the beast."*

In verse 2b and 3, we are told the source from which civil governments derive their power and authority that enables them to accomplish the enormous evil they do against other nations and their own people in general, and against Christians and the church in particular. Have you ever wondered why governments engage in the wars and the destruction that they do? Have you ever wondered why governments oppress and plunder and destroy their own citizens? Have you ever wondered why governments attack the Christians among them—those who are their most peaceful and productive and harmless citizens? It is because the dragon is driving them and empowering them to do so.

The point that is being made in verse 2b is that Satan energizes the civil governments of this earth. The power and position and authority of civil governments is given to them by Satan, and from those governments the four horsemen ride, bringing conquest and war and famine and death and the martyrdom of Christians as described in the first five seals of Revelation 6.

Jesus said in John 10:10 that Satan came only to kill and steal and destroy. This work of killing and stealing and destroying is primarily done on this earth and in this age through civil governments. People are worried about citizens having guns because they might kill some other citizens. They should be far more worried about governments having guns because governments have killed infinitely more people in their wars and by their policies than criminals ever thought about killing on the streets. The great danger to world peace and to the lives of humanity is not somebody shooting somebody else on the street; it is governments waging wars and slaughtering millions.

If, as Revelation 11:15 says, *"The kingdoms of this world [will] become the kingdoms of our Lord, and of His Christ"* then, clearly, they are not the kingdoms of our Lord and of His Christ now; instead, they are representatives of Satan and his kingdom. Verse 2b is clear. The governments of the earth get their power, their position (their throne), and their great authority from the dragon. Civil government is empowered by Satan and derives its authority from him.

Notice verse 3. It says, *"And I saw one of his heads as it were wounded to death; and his deadly wound was healed: and all the world wondered after the beast."* What is on every one of the heads of this beast? It is blasphemy. When we are told that one of these heads is wounded, it was the blasphemous behavior of that head that was wounded.

The kingdoms of this age are not always and exclusively strong against the church. From time to time, the ability of a nation to blaspheme God and persecute Christians may be severely wounded, curtailed, and limited, even to the point where it seems that persecution against Christians will never return again in that nation. This is because *"one of his heads . . .were wounded to death."* When the head of civil government is wounded in its blasphemy against God, it seems like the nation is saying, "We are going to follow God, we are going to support Christianity, and we are not going to persecute the Christians anymore." Blasphemy against God by the civil government has seemingly been put to death.

It may seem that a nation has had its determination to persecute Christians put to death for good; but amazingly, it always eventually revives its strength and recovers its zeal to start persecuting the church once again. This is because *". . .his deadly wound [is] healed. . ."* Blasphemy may be quieted for a while, but it always rises back up and reasserts itself. The evil of civil governments persecuting the church is never dead, even though it may be dormant for a little while. Governments always recover their zeal for persecuting the church. The deadly wound to its efforts to blasphemously persecute the church is always eventually healed.

For example, in our present day the USSR severely persecuted the church for seventy years; and then in 1991, the Soviet Union fell apart and was dismantled. The nations that made up the union went their separate ways. Gorbachev resigned, and Yeltsin became the president of Russia. As a result of this, religious liberty was brought to Russia after seventy years of severe persecution against the church.

But after twenty-five years of religious liberty, in 2016, new anti-evangelism laws were passed that are very severe, and Russian persecution of Christians is coming back to life. The blasphemy of the Russian government was only dormant for a while. It was not eradicated. It never is. This is just an example of what has been happening for the last 2,000 years. The power of the beast is always present and always operating because its power comes from Satan. While Satan's persecuting power working through the beast may be curtailed by God for a little while, it always revives and reasserts itself again.

This practice of persecuting Christians is the dominant practice of the kingdoms of the world, with occasional periods of dormancy in that persecution, only to flare up again with renewed strength and vigor to persecute the church with just as much zeal as it previously exercised.

We have had a little period of dormancy of persecution of Christians in America, but now government persecution of Christians is rising and it is becoming rampant, to the point that the government is forcing Christian businessmen to participate in sodomite counterfeit weddings. It is forcing pregnancy clinics to engage in speech that promotes abortion in abortion clinics. It is forcing taxpayers to fund the murder of children in abortion clinics. It is attempting to silence the voice of the church in the political arena, with threats of oppressive taxation.

It is going to get worse. Blasphemy on the head of the United States of America is becoming stronger and stronger, recovering from the apparent death that it had for a while. Satan is tireless and Satan is relentless, and he will not allow his servant, the beast, to cease or diminish its work of persecuting Christians unless God forces him to do so, which He does from time to time, so that His church may have periods of rest and peace before engaging in the battle once again.

The Worship of the Beast

The worship of the beast is in verse 4. *"And they worshipped the dragon which gave power unto the beast: and they worshipped the beast, saying, Who is like unto the beast? who is able to make war with him?"*

Notice it says in the last phrase of verse 3, *"and all the world wondered after the beast."* The world is enamored with the beast. The world looks upon civil government with admiration, and it marvels at its power and its authority and its abilities. The world follows, with the most intense interest, every detail of what the governments of this world do. In fact, the world worships the power and might and authority of the civil government, and thereby the world worships the Evil One who stands behind it and who gives it its energies and its abilities.

Most people would deny that they worship government and its satanic power. But notice the two questions that the people of the world ask as they admire the beast in verse 4b. *"Who is like unto the beast? Who is able to make war with him?"* They are asking, "Who can be compared with the beast, and who can overcome the power of the beast?" Their answer is that nobody can!

In the mind of the world, civil government is the ultimate authority on earth, and civil government has the ultimate power on earth. In the mind of the world, there is nothing more authoritative and nothing more powerful in the universe than civil government. Whatever you view as the ultimate source of authority and the ultimate source of power is your god.

By definition, God is the highest source of authority and the highest source of power there is. The world looks at civil government and says that there is no greater authority, and there is no greater power than that of the beast—that of the civil government. The world sees civil government and its satanic power and authority as its god, because to the world, there is no higher authority and power than its government.

Why do you think people gravitate toward government and its power the way they do? Why do they worship it as the highest authority in their lives, and as the greatest power they know of, and talk about it incessantly? It is because government—and by way of extension, Satan—is their god.

As Christians, we want the government to leave us alone. We are not interested in running other people's lives through coercion, and we do not want to be coerced by other people. We just want to lead a quiet and peaceable life in all godliness and honesty.

But government is nothing but coercion. Government proceeds out of the barrel of a gun. Government is organized force. There is a reason why people call it "law en*force*ment," because they go around with a gun forcing people to do things. Make no mistake—government is the exercise of force upon other people. It controls people through the threat and exercise of violence.

If the government approves of something, by definition that makes it right in the mind of the world. If the government disapproves of it, that makes it wrong in the mind of the world. Like a god, government defines morality. Government determines right and wrong. Government determines good and evil. Government determines truth and lies. Government's determination of those things is accepted as the final authority, and government has the power to enforce those things with the ultimate strength that exists on the earth. Governments have nuclear weapons as the ultimate barrel of their gun. Who is able to make war against such power?

In the world's mind, if the government says something is legal, then by definition it is moral. If the government says something is illegal, then by definition it is immoral. End of story. Government is god. If government is worshiped as god, then by extension, the evil dragon who empowers it is worshiped as well. If you look to government as your ultimate source of authority and as the ultimate expression of power, then you are an idolater and a worshiper of Satan. This is what verse 4 teaches.

The Blasphemy of the Beast

The blasphemy of the beast is in verses 5 and 6. "*And there was given unto him a mouth speaking great things and blasphemies; and power was given unto him to continue forty and two months.*" That should be a giant clue about what this beast is and how long it operates; it operates for forty-two months, the entire time between the first and second coming of Christ; and therefore, it represents all of the civil governments during that entire time period. "[6] *And he opened his mouth in blasphemy against God, to blaspheme his name, and his tabernacle, and them that dwell in heaven.*"

Civil governments see themselves as the supreme power on earth, and are filled with the conceit that they are the ultimate authority on all matters. If there is any suggestion that someone else is a rival to the power of civil authority, or that someone else is superior in authority over the civil government, the civil government begins to attack that idea with ridicule, mockery, and insults.

The government comes along and says things like this: "Sex outside marriage is normal." "Transgenderism is legitimate." "Homosexuality is just an orientation." "Abortion is healthcare." "Evolution is how we all got here." "Islam is a religion of peace." When you start to speak out against those lies, blasphemies, and immoralities, you are attacked with ridicule, mockery, and insults from the government, its agents, and its worshipers. By ridiculing the God of the Bible, by mocking His laws, by scorning the idea of His existence, by slandering His character, and by reviling those who worship Him, civil governments of this world try to make it seem ridiculous to even think about being a Christian, or believing what the Bible says about God and His promises.

Civil government presents Christianity and its beliefs as evil and foolish and contrary to the peace and unity of the nation. Civil governments do their best to turn the popular opinion against Christians and against their God, and to try to stigmatize them as being stupid at best, and as enemies of the state at worst. We see this frequently in Islamic countries, where Christians are arrested and charged with undermining the state for their activities. Governments demand that its citizens have ultimate respect for them, and insist that they, the citizens, have no respect for the God of the Bible and those who worship Him.

Civil authorities have always engaged in a program of blasphemy against God and His church and His people. This has been going on since Caesar demanded that the Christians burn incense to him and say, "Caesar is lord." If they refused, they were cast to the lions. Such blasphemy and persecution extend to this very day. When Christians try to meet and have church, the world laughs and mocks and ridicules, and government agents come in and arrest and imprison and kill. How long will this satanically driven government rule of the nations of the earth last? Verse 5 says it will last forty-two months.

We have already explored in detail the meaning of this symbolic time figure. We have seen that three and a half years—the time, times and half a time; the twelve hundred and sixty days; and the forty-two months—all refer to the same time period of the second half of human history, the time between the first and second coming of Jesus.

All the time between Christ's ascension and Christ's second coming, there will be a succession of governments and kings, represented by this beast, exercising satanic authority and power, and whose rule is marked by blasphemy against God and by persecution of Christians.

President Obama's sarcastic remark about the "bitter clingers," referring to the people who cling to their guns and their Bibles, was one of mockery. That is the voice of Satan speaking through the beast, blaspheming God and His word and His people.

The Final Manifestation of the Beast

The final manifestation of the beast is in verses 7 to 10. *"And it was given unto him to make war with the saints, and to overcome them: and power was given him over all kindreds, and tongues, and nations.*
8 *And all that dwell upon the earth shall worship him, whose names are not written in the book of life of the Lamb slain from the foundation of the world.* 9 *If any man have an ear, let him hear.* 10 *He that leadeth into captivity shall go into captivity: he that killeth with the sword must be killed with the sword. Here is the patience and the faith of the saints."*

This long succession of satanically empowered and satanically inspired governments which stretches from the ascension of Christ to the second coming will be concluded by the most evil civil government of them all—the government of the Antichrist, the man of sin, which is spoken of in 2 Thessalonians 2:3–10.

The very last manifestation of this beast out of the sea is the beast that ascends out of the bottomless pit in Revelation 11:7, whom we identified as the Antichrist. This final beast is the one described in 2 Thessalonians 2:4 who opposes and exalts himself above all that is called God or that is worshiped, so that he as God sits in the temple of God, showing himself that he is God.

Revelation 13:7: *"And it was given unto him"*—that is, to this final beast—*"to make war with the saints, and to overcome them."* Antichrist is going to win. He is going to defeat the church. He will overcome them. *"And power was given him over all kindreds, and tongues, and nations."* This final beast, this last kingdom that appears on earth before the second coming of Jesus, is going to triumph over the church with a transnational coalition of nations forming a one-world government assisting him.

Revelation 13:7 says, *"And it was given unto him to make war with the saints, and to overcome them: and power was given him over all kindreds, and tongues, and nations."* In Revelation 11:7–10 it says, *"And when they"*—that is, the two witnesses—*"shall have finished their testimony, the beast that ascendeth out of the bottomless pit shall make war against them"*—that is, against the church—*"and shall overcome them, and kill them.* [8] *And their dead bodies shall lie in the street of the great city, which spiritually is called Sodom and Egypt, where also our Lord was crucified.* [9] *And they of the people and kindreds and tongues and nations"* (Antichrist's coalition) *"shall see their dead bodies three days and an half, and shall not suffer their dead bodies to be put in graves.* [10] *And they that dwell upon the earth shall rejoice over them, and make merry, and shall send gifts one to another; because these two prophets"*—that is, the church—which *"tormented them that dwelt on the earth,"* is now dead.

What is described in Revelation 11:7–10 is summarized in Revelation 13:7. Here is the final beast in Revelation 13:7, the beast out of the bottomless pit, with his transnational coalition of all kindreds and tongues and nations over which he rules.

Notice Revelation 13:8: *"And all that dwell upon the earth shall worship him,"* which is what he demanded in 2 Thessalonians 2:3–4 when he presented himself to the world as God, *"whose names are not written in the book of life of the Lamb slain from the foundation of the world."*

This final beast that arises after this long succession of beasts sets himself up as God in the temple of God, and demands and receives the worship of the whole earth with the exception of one group—and that is God's elect, those whose names are written in the Book of Life of the Lamb slain from the foundation of the world. This is the sole group that will not say that Caesar is lord. The Antichrist will not tolerate a group of people who will not worship him and his civil government as being God on earth.

Christians will refuse to worship the Antichrist, just like Christians throughout the ages have refused to worship any king that claimed divinity, or lived in defiance against God and His laws. That is why Christians are not ultimately loyal to the kingdoms of this world, because our citizenship is in heaven. From the first century to this day, Christians have steadfastly refused to say Caesar is lord, and they will continue to refuse to do so to the Antichrist himself at the end of this age.

The Antichrist will therefore mobilize the whole world in a united persecution of all the Christians across the globe, with the result that the visible and public witness of the church will be silenced, and all but a small remnant of believers will be slaughtered. If Christ did not return in time, there would be no Christians at all saved alive; but for the sake of the elect, Christ will return in time, and that small remnant will be physically saved from Antichrist's efforts to totally eradicate them from the earth.

John closes this section with a word of comfort in verses 9 and 10. In verse 9 he says, *"If any man have an ear, let him hear."* In other words, "Listen up, people, I am going to tell you something really important." He has just given us a large amount of bad news. We have had eight verses of really bad news. The only tiny piece of light in all that news is that from time to time the blasphemy of nations against Christ and Christians will be temporarily subdued for a little while, but it is going to come roaring back. The only good news is that in history we are going to have small periods of freedom from government persecution and blasphemy against Christians, but the bad news is, it is not going to last. It always comes back from apparent death.

Therefore, he says in verse 9, "Listen carefully, I am going to give you some comfort." Here is the comfort, verse 10: *"He that leadeth into captivity shall go into captivity: he that killeth with the sword must be killed with the sword. Here,"* out of this understanding arises *"the patience and the faith of the saints."*

John is saying that these beastlike governments that lead you into captivity—that is, who imprison you in jails—will be led captive into the prison of hell for all eternity. They put you in prison? God is going to put them in prison. The beastlike government that kills you with the sword will itself be killed with the sword. They came along and slaughtered you? God is going to slaughter them with the sword of His mouth. Revelation 19:15–21 says that when Jesus returns on His white horse, a sharp sword will come out of his mouth, and He will destroy them with His word and cast them into the lake of fire.

This is why you can be patient under the persecution of civil governments, and why this persecution should not weaken your faith or destroy it. These governments that assume Godlike authority and exercise persecuting power will themselves be destroyed by God, and all who carried out their wickedness will be cast into hell.

Therefore, if you work for the beast, or you are planning to work for the beast, beware lest you become an instrument of the blasphemy of the beast, and thereby become an object of the judgment that falls on the beast. It is possible that, in certain circumstances, Christians can work in civil government and serve God there. Thank God for all those who are able to do so. But understand that someday the beast may very well ask you to stop serving God and start blaspheming Him by your actions.

If you are a police officer and the government tells you to arrest Christians at a church for assembling together, are you going to serve the beast? Or are you going to turn on the beast and say that you will not be an instrument of its satanic policies, nor will you be an instrument to exercise its satanic power in blaspheming the people of God, the church of God, or the truth of God? The government passes evil laws, and a civil judge now has to perform counterfeit sodomite weddings, contrary to God's law. A gay couple comes in and demands that he performs their wedding. Is the judge going to serve the beast, or is he going to resign his position?

These examples illustrate what those who serve in the civil government often have to face. Recognize that it is better to give up your job and career in civil government than become an agent of the blasphemy of the beast in its persecution of Christians and in its violation of God's laws.

When you see the power of the beast and the authority it has to reach into every area of your life in order to persecute you and imprison you and kill you, do not lose your patience and faith when this happens. Justice will be done in the end, and you will be vindicated and rewarded for your loyalty to Christ. Your oppressors will reap what they have sown, and you will see them receive what they have done to you.

We must not confuse any civil government or nation with the kingdom of God. Even the American government is part of the seven-headed beast empowered by Satan. Thankfully, it has had a wounded head, and its blasphemy has been largely suppressed for almost two centuries. But now that blasphemy is coming to life. You have to be patient under the degeneration of the nation and the healing of the wound to its blasphemy. You may suffer from it, or be imprisoned or killed with the sword. But do not lose your patience or your faith. Wait on God and trust in God that He will deal with your persecutors, as they have dealt with you.

Have no delusions about the goodness of human government. Civil government is supposed to serve God and be a minister of God and uphold His standards as Romans 13 says, and when it does, we are to submit to it and obey its laws. But the majority of the time it serves Satan, who is the god of the beast. (See Appendix 4.) Do not put your trust in politicians and say that if a certain man gets elected, then everything is going to be okay. It is not going to be okay, because Satan is bigger than any number of elected officials, and he runs the beast.

Sometimes Christians can get into a position in civil government and function in their office to undermine the blasphemy and evil work of the beast. They can work to oppose its anti-Christian policies and laws. This is a commendable service to Christ. But they often pay a heavy price for doing so, because if they stand up for Christ in government service, the government will react with hostility. Maybe you can find a place in government employment where you can escape that, and if so, well and good. But beware. Be alert. Be forewarned that it is a dangerous thing to work for the beast.

May we never fall into the idolatry of trust and confidence in the civil authority. Let us trust and worship God alone, and obey God rather than men.

42

The Beast Out of the Earth, Revelation 13:11–18

> "11 *And I beheld another beast coming up out of the earth;*
> *and he had two horns like a lamb, and he spake as a dragon.*
> 12 *And he exerciseth all the power of the first beast before him,*
> *and causeth the earth and them which dwell therein to wor-*
> *ship the first beast, whose deadly wound was healed.* 13 *And he*
> *doeth great wonders, so that he maketh fire come down from*
> *heaven on the earth in the sight of men,* 14 *And deceiveth them*
> *that dwell on the earth by the means of those miracles which*
> *he had power to do in the sight of the beast; saying to them*
> *that dwell on the earth, that they should make an image to the*
> *beast, which had the wound by a sword, and did live.* 15 *And*
> *he had power to give life unto the image of the beast, that the*
> *image of the beast should both speak, and cause that as many*
> *as would not worship the image of the beast should be killed.*
> 16 *And he causeth all, both small and great, rich and poor, free*
> *and bond, to receive a mark in their right hand, or in their*
> *foreheads:* 17 *And that no man might buy or sell, save he that*
> *had the mark, or the name of the beast, or the number of*
> *his name.* 18 *Here is wisdom. Let him that hath understanding*
> *count the number of the beast: for it is the number of a man;*
> *and his number is Six hundred three score and six.*"

We are in the fourth parallel section of the book of Revelation, which consists of chapters 12, 13, and 14. The theme of this fourth parallel section is Satan and his helpers. Chapter 12 dealt largely with Satan himself; chapters 13 and 14 deal with Satan's helpers. Satan is the primary enemy of Christ and His people, but Satan does not do his evil work alone. Satan not only has the demons to assist him in his evil work; he has humans to assist him as well.

In the last chapter we looked at the first of Satan's human helpers, the beast that arises out of the sea. This beast that arises out of the sea represents and symbolizes the entire succession of kings and kingdoms that arise and rule between the first and second coming of Christ. This beast out of the sea represents all civil governments that defy the authority of Christ, blaspheme the name of Christ, and mock and martyr the followers of Christ.

This beast out of the sea does not represent just one government, but all governments between the first and second coming of Christ. This is proven by the fact that this multi-headed, multi-horned, multi-crowned beast continues for forty-two months.

We saw in 11:1–2 that forty-two months is the time the unsaved world will trample the New Covenant church under its feet. It is a symbolic period of time. Forty-two months represents the entire church age.

This same symbolic time period of forty-two months is the time period this beast out of the sea exists and functions. Therefore, the beast out of the sea is going to exist and operate the whole time between the first and second coming of Christ, just like the church is going to be trampled underfoot by the Gentile nations the whole time between the first and the second coming of Christ. Because the beast is a composite of the world rulers and the world empires spoken of in Daniel 7, this beast therefore represents a composite of all the kings and kingdoms that will exist between the first and the second coming of Christ.

The problem with all the kings and kingdoms that exist between the first and second coming of Christ is that they derive their power and their throne and their authority from Satan himself, as it says in the last part of verse 2. The kingdoms of this world are the agents of Satan and the helpers of Satan through their blasphemy of Christ and through their persecution of Christians. The hostility of civil governments toward biblical Christianity over the last 2,000 years has been well documented.

It is true that, on occasion, the strength and vigor of one civil government or another to persecute Christians seems to have almost been killed for a time. The beast has a deadly wound given to it. But soon that defect in its service to Satan is healed; it resumes the persecution of believers, and it does so with just as much vigor as it ever had before.

The final civil government of this age, the one-world government of the Antichrist that arises when Satan is loosed, will be so empowered by Satan and will be so effective in its persecution of Christians that the visible presence and the public witness of the church in this world will be silenced, and virtually all the Christians will be martyred by the sword, as we saw in verses 7 and 8.

But Christ will return and slay the beast and the dragon who gave him his power, and He will deliver His church from the beast forever. Never again will the church have to live under hostile, secular, satanically motivated civil governments as it has for the last 2,000 years. But as bad as the beast out of the sea is, and as evil and satanically driven as civil governments are, they are just one of the helpers of Satan on this earth.

In verses 11 to 18, we are introduced to two more helpers that Satan has. The first is the beast out of the earth mentioned in verse 11, and the second, those who take the mark of the beast mentioned in verses 16–18.

This second beast mentioned in chapter 13 is introduced to us in verse 11 where it says, *"And I beheld another beast"* (one different from the first beast) *"coming up out of the earth; and he had two horns like a lamb, and he spake as a dragon."* While this second beast is quite different from the first beast that arises out of the sea, he works in very close cooperation with him. There is great harmony between the servants of Satan as they work together in a coordinated assault on the kingdom of God.

We have seen that the beast out of the sea represents and symbolizes the persecuting governments of the world between the first and the second coming of Christ. Now we will see that this second beast that arises out of the earth represents and symbolizes the persecuting false religions of the world.

The false religions, in concert with civil governments, have been tremendous sources of persecution and martyrdom of the true church throughout the last 2,000 years. False religions, no less than civil governments, are the servants of Satan and are driven by his hatred of Christ and His people to persecute and martyr the true saints of God.

We saw how the false religion of the Pharisees and the Sadducees worked together with the civil government of Rome to crucify the Lord Jesus, and such alliances have been going on ever since. False religion hates the true religion and does all it can to stamp it out. The second beast, who works alongside the first beast, lives and labors with that beast to stamp out the kingdom of God and the people of God.

We need to understand that this second beast who works alongside the first beast lives and labors as long as the first beast does. False religion, no less than civil government, has been at work in persecuting the church for the last 2,000 years, and will continue to be at this work until Christ returns.

These two beasts do not just appear at the very end of the age in the end times. These two beasts have been functioning since Christ's first coming and will continue to function until His second coming. They will continue the entire symbolic period of forty-two months, that time frame between the first and second coming of Christ.

We have to understand who this second beast is just as we had to understand who the first beast was, in order that we might clearly understand who the enemy is, and how we are to wage spiritual warfare against him.

The Identity of the Beast

The identity of the beast is declared in verse 11. Notice, it says, *"And I beheld another beast coming up out of the earth; and he had two horns like a lamb, and he spake as a dragon."* This second beast is clearly different from the first beast mentioned in verses 1 to 10. This beast is different in origin, he is different in appearance, and he is different in function.

Notice, it says he arises *"out of the earth,"* whereas the first beast arose out of the sea. The second beast has two horns like a lamb, rather than the seven heads and the ten horns like the first beast has. However, even though this second beast has the appearance of a small innocent lamb when he speaks, he speaks with a voice like a dragon. Consider the meaning of this symbolism expressed in the appearance of this second beast.

As to his origin, this beast arises out of the earth. This speaks of its worldly origin—that is, it arises from beneath, it arises from below, from out of the earth. It does not come down from above out of heaven. This metaphor of coming from beneath and coming from above is utilized in James 3:14–17, where it says the wisdom that is from above is pure, peaceable, easily entreated, and full of mercy and good fruits. In contrast to this heavenly wisdom is a wisdom that comes from beneath, that is earthly, sensual, and devilish. It does not come down from above.

This earthly, sensual, devilish wisdom comes from beneath, it comes from the earth, and it comes from among fallen humanity whose tongue *"is set on fire of hell."* The wisdom of this world is inspired by Satan himself. It is earthly wisdom. It is contrary to the wisdom that is from above, and it is this satanic earthly wisdom that is set on fire of hell itself that the second beast employs in his evil work on the earth. This second beast is earthly, sensual, and devilish. He arises out of the earth.

As to his appearance, he has the appearance of a little lamb with two small horns coming out of his head. This beast comes across as something innocent, harmless, and benign. Who is threatened by what appears to be a small lamb with two cute little horns coming out of his head? But his appearance is deceitful. It is designed to make you let your guard down, to feel safe, and even have feelings of sympathy and affection toward this sweet little lamb. But its outward form and appearance are a lie. Within, this lamb is full of satanic evil, and when it speaks, it speaks with the voice and the message of the dragon; that is, it speaks with the voice and message of Satan himself.

So it is with false religion on this earth. The source of false religion is not from above. It does not descend down from God. False religion is from beneath, it is earthly, sensual, and devilish. Its doctrines are doctrines that arise from the earth, from earthly men, from earthly wisdom, and out of earthly motives. False religion presents itself as innocent and harmless and benign. It promises acceptance and approval and advantage to all who embrace it. It is designed to make you feel safe and secure, and to draw out your sympathy and acceptance. Its visible face is one of harmless innocence. Its image is that of comfort and affection. It appears harmless.

As to its function, it intentionally deceives people. In spite of the harmless image false religion projects, false religion speaks with the voice of the dragon. It is full of seductive lies, false promises, and comforting delusions. It issues intimidating threats, it teaches a heretical method of salvation, and it sets forth a humanly devised god. In a word, false religion is a viper's nest of lies and deceit, which are all designed to turn men away from the true God and to cause them to worship a false god. False religion is designed to cause men to worship Satan, and it is designed to take them straight to hell.

Jesus said in Matthew 7:15, "*Beware of false prophets, which come to you in sheep's clothing, but inwardly they are ravening wolves.*" Here we have what appears to be a lamb, but who inwardly speaks with the voice of the dragon. This second beast looks like a sheep, but inwardly he is a ravening wolf. He is the lie of Satan dressed up as the truth. His two horns make him representative of all the false prophets, just like the two witnesses of chapter 11 were representative of all the faithful witnesses of Christ. This, then, is the identity of this beast. He represents all the false religions of the world between the first and second coming of Christ.

The Activity of the Beast

The activity of the beast is stated in verses 12 to 15, "*And he exerciseth all the power of the first beast before him, and causeth the earth and them which dwell therein to worship the first beast, whose deadly wound was healed.* [13] *And he doeth great wonders, so that he maketh fire come down from heaven on the earth in the sight of men,* [14] *And deceiveth them that dwell on the earth by the means of those miracles which he had power to do in the sight of the beast; saying to them that dwell on the earth, that they should make an image to the beast, which had the wound by a sword, and did live.* [15] *And he had power to give life unto the image of the beast, that the image of the beast should both speak, and cause that as many as would not worship the image of the beast should be killed.*"

The horrific behavior described here is the activity of this sweet little lamb. He is really not a lamb at all, is he? He is a wolf in sheep's clothing. He is a lamb that speaks with the voice of the dragon. He is the delusion of false religion that presents itself as something warm and wonderful, but within it is full of destruction and death.

In Matthew 7:15, when Jesus says, "*Beware of false prophets, which come to you in sheep's clothing, but inwardly they are ravening wolves,*" He is leading us to believe that this beast out of the earth that looks like a sheep is really a false prophet, and that is exactly what the rest of the book of Revelation identifies this second beast as.

We have a counterfeit unholy trinity in Revelation 13 made up of the dragon, the beast out of the sea, and the beast out of the earth, all of whom oppose the triune God and His people.

It is important to note that this beast out of the earth is never called by this name again in the remainder of Revelation. This beast out of the earth is universally referred to as *"the false prophet"* in all the subsequent passages in which he is referenced in Revelation, thereby establishing his identity without a doubt. This beast out of the earth is declared to be the false prophet in three other passages in Revelation.

First, notice Revelation 16:13–14. Here the vials of God's wrath are being poured out. It says: *"And I saw three unclean spirits like frogs come out of the mouth of the dragon, and out of the mouth of the beast, and out of the mouth of the false prophet."* We have the dragon, who is Satan; we have the beast, which is the beast out of the sea, the first beast spoken of in Revelation 13:1–10; and then the second beast of Revelation 13:11 is here called *"the false prophet."*

Secondly, notice chapter 19. Here the identification is crystal clear. In Revelation 19, where Jesus speaks of His second coming, it says in verse 19, *"And I saw the beast, and the kings of the earth, and their armies, gathered together to make war against him that sat on the horse, and against his army."* The beast out of the sea—that is, Antichrist and the kings of the earth—are now gathered together to make war against Christ.

Notice verse 20: *"And the beast was taken"* (the beast out of the sea), *"and with him the false prophet."* Now notice the description of the false prophet: *"that wrought miracles before him"*—that is, before the beast—*"with which he deceived them that had received the mark of the beast, and them that worshipped his image. These both were cast alive into a lake of fire burning with brimstone."*

The exact same behavior is predicated of this false prophet in Revelation 19:20, which is predicated of the beast out of the earth in Revelation 13:12–17. Clearly, the false prophet and the beast out of the earth are the same, because they both do the same thing: they both work miracles before the beast out of the sea, they both deceive those on the earth, and they both cause them to receive the mark of the beast and worship the beast.

Thirdly, notice 20:10. After Jesus returns, it says in verse 10, *"And the devil"* (the dragon) *"that deceived them was cast into the lake of fire and brimstone, where the beast"* (the beast out of the sea) *"and the false prophet*" (the beast out of the earth) "*are and shall be tormented day and night for ever and ever.*" Satan, and all the people who helped him through civil government and false religions, are all going to be cast into the lake of fire. This false prophet represents and symbolizes all the false prophets and false teachers of all the false religions between the first and second coming of Christ.

The two beasts of Revelation 13 represent all anti-Christian governments and all anti-Christian religions that exist between the first and second coming. The final anti-Christian government will be the government of Antichrist, and the final anti-Christian religion will be the religion that is dedicated to the worship of the Antichrist as god on earth. But they symbolize all governments and all false religions leading up to that final government and that final false religion, because they both continue for the symbolic forty-two months, which is the entire period between the first and second coming of Christ.

These two beasts, which represent anti-Christian government and anti-Christian religion, work together in perfect harmony because they both serve the same master—and that is the dragon. The dragon gives the first beast its power, and the dragon gives the second beast its power. Anti-Christian government and anti-Christian religion work together in the sphere of religion and in the sphere of civil government to persecute and destroy the message and the witness of the church.

Notice how the false prophet serves the beast and tries to bring the whole earth to worship and serve the beast in Revelation 13:12–15. Notice verse 12: "*And he*" (the false prophet, this second beast) "*exerciseth all the power of the first beast before him, and causeth the earth and them which dwell therein to worship the first beast, whose deadly wound was healed.*" The false prophet has all the power and authority available to him that the beast from the sea has, because the false prophet, like the beast, derives his authority and his power from Satan himself. Anti-Christian religions have the same access to the power of Satan that anti-Christian governments have.

What does the false prophet use his power to accomplish? Verse 12 says he causes all the people of the earth to worship the first beast—that is, the beast out of the sea we were first introduced to in verse 1. The meaning of this is quite plain. The false religions of this age, along with their false teachings, are designed by Satan to turn the hearts of men to worship civil government as their god. False religions are in league with the dominant political power of their day and use their influence to create a loyalty to the state that supersedes all other loyalties. Once false religion turns people away from the worship of the true God, the only god left to worship is the state.

The false prophet symbolizes the role of false religion in causing mankind to worship at the altar of civil government as its ultimate authority, and as the definer of right and wrong, good and evil, and truth and error.

Jesus was sentenced to death by the Jewish Sanhedrin, which served the Roman government. The Roman government and the false Jewish religion worked together to persecute the church. The Sanhedrin sacrificed biblical truth on the altar of political preferment and worshiped Roman approval over the teachings of Christ, and taught the people to do the same. Its members taught the people to fear Rome over God.

In John 11:47–53, the Pharisees are in a great conundrum over what they were going to do with Jesus. Notice: "*Then gathered the chief priests and the Pharisees a council, and said, What do we? for this man*" (Jesus) "*doeth many miracles.* [48] *If we let him thus alone, all men will believe on him, and the Romans shall come and take away both our place and nation.* [49] *And one of them, named Caiaphas, being the high priest that same year, said unto them, Ye know nothing at all,* [50] *Nor consider that it is expedient for us, that one man should die for the people, and that the whole nation perish not.*" In other words: "Let us kill Jesus and save the nation from following Him as their supreme authority, and then Rome will like us. By this course of action, we will serve Rome, Rome will serve us, and we will have a symbiotic relationship of mutual support and loyalty. Otherwise, Rome will come and destroy our nation if it follows Jesus."

Verse 51: "*And this spake he not of himself: but being high priest that year, he prophesied that Jesus should die for that nation;* [52] *And not for that nation only, but that also he should gather together in one the children of God that were scattered abroad.* [53] *Then from that day forth they took counsel together for to put him to death.*" What we see here is satanic false religion working with satanic civil government to attack the Lord Jesus Christ.

In John 19:12, the Jewish chief priest cried out to Pilate saying, "*If thou let this man go, thou art not Caesar's friend: whosoever maketh himself a king speaketh against Caesar.*" By this statement, the false Jewish religious leaders showed that their loyalties lay with Caesar.

They further evidenced their loyalty to the civil government of Rome by turning the people away from Christ and toward Caesar as being the one in whom they should trust to find their security and safety.

Furthermore, the pagan Roman religion of the day demanded emperor worship. The Roman population was required to burn incense to Caesar as an act of worship and to declare, "Caesar is lord!" If they did, they were given approval, and they were able to live and function under the blessing of the Roman government. But if they did not, then the Roman cult of emperor worship, and the priests within it, would turn the Christians in to the Roman government and they would be thrown to the lions in the Coliseum. Pagan Roman religion also worked together with the wicked Roman civil government to persecute the believers.

Every religion and religious teacher that points men away from Christ and away from biblical truth inevitably points them toward a false god and a lie. That false god is ultimately representative of the power of Satan and his beast, which is anti-Christian civil government, wherever it rears its ugly head on earth. When religion fails to serve God, it always and inevitably winds up serving the civil government, and causing people to worship the power and the authority of the anti-Christian state. It is happening right now. It has been happening for a long time.

At the present time, the Russian Orthodox Church has worked with the Russian government and influenced it to pass an anti-evangelism law against all the Protestant churches. Now if Protestant churches evangelize, they will be fined. The false prophet is in bed with the beast.

We have seen it throughout history from Roman Catholicism. The Catholic Church influenced the governments of Spain and France during the Reformation to have the Inquisition and to murder the believers in Jesus Christ. We have seen liberal Christianity trying to encourage the populace to embrace government policy of counterfeit sodomite marriage in our own country. Nationalist Hinduism is killing Christians in India, and the government assists them by turning a blind eye to the attacks of their devotees on believers. Islam in numerous nations is in bed with Islamic governments, and together the religion of Islam and the governments of Islam attack and slaughter the Christians.

All false religions serve the civil governments under which they live, and cooperate with them in turning the people away from Christ and Christianity, and in turning them to worship and serve the state as the ultimate arbitrator of truth and error, right and wrong, and good and evil.

In Revelation 13:13–15, we have an extended description of some of the methods the false religions use to persuade people to worship the state and its leaders and cause them to be seen as the ultimate source of authority and power. They do great wonders, making fire come down from heaven on the earth. They deceive those that dwell on the earth by means of these miracles which they have the power to do. They make an image of the beast; they animate the beast; and they give it some sort of life and movement so it can speak. But having done all of these pseudo-miracles, if people still do not accept what they are teaching, it says at the end of verse 15 that they cause them to be put to death.

Plainly, false religions use various deceptions, trickeries, illusions, and threats to persuade and pressure people to yield allegiance to and worship the satanically empowered civil government.

Whether the things listed in verses 13–15—such as calling fire down from heaven, or animating a physical image with lifelike movement and speech—are literal or figurative is not of major interpretive significance. What is being conveyed is that whatever satanic powers false religions may display, whatever apparent miracles they are able to perform, and whatever punishments they are able to threaten and inflict on those who do not worship the god of the state, believers in Christ are not to fall for it. They are not to be convinced by these things, so as to follow the teachings of these false prophets.

Notice Deuteronomy 13:1–5: *"If there arise among you a prophet, or a dreamer of dreams, and giveth thee a sign or a wonder,* [2] *And the sign or the wonder come to pass, whereof he spake unto thee, saying, Let us go after other gods, which thou hast not known, and let us serve them."* Moses is telling us there are prophets who can actually do miracles, and who will attempt to use the persuasiveness and power of those miracles to try to talk the people of God into turning away from Jehovah, and serving a different God. Are we to look at the miracles they perform and say, "They can do miracles! They must be of God; therefore, we should listen to them."? Is that what we are supposed to do?

Notice verse 3: "*Thou shalt not hearken unto the words of that prophet, or that dreamer of dreams: for the LORD your God proveth you*" (He is putting you to the test), "*to know whether ye love the LORD your God with all your heart and with all your soul.* [4] *Ye shall walk after the LORD your God, and fear him, and keep his commandments, and obey his voice, and ye shall serve him, and cleave unto him.* [5] *And that prophet, or that dreamer of dreams, shall be put to death; because he hath spoken to turn you away from the LORD your God, which brought you out of the land of Egypt, and redeemed you out of the house of bondage, to thrust thee out of the way which the LORD thy God commanded thee to walk in. So shalt thou put the evil away from the midst of thee.*"

Even if somebody can do real miracles, if the message that attends those miracles is to turn us away from Jesus Christ to follow another God, we are to repudiate those miracles as being a legitimate authentication that this person is speaking for God. We are not to see miracles as authoritative if they are used to contradict biblical teaching and to lead us away from the worship of Christ.

Jesus warned about the prevalence of such signs and wonders, especially occurring in the end times. In Matthew 24:24 Jesus said, "*For there shall arise false Christs, and false prophets, and shall shew great signs and wonders; insomuch that, if it were possible, they shall deceive the very elect.*" Jesus was saying that there are going to be great signs and wonders, and people are going to look at them and think that those who do them are true spokesmen for God. Only the elect will not fall for the deception.

Listen carefully: Doctrine always trumps signs and miracles. In other words, what has the highest authority is not whether someone can do miracles, but whether his teaching is in harmony with what the Bible teaches. Even if somebody can raise people from the dead, if his doctrine is contrary to the Scripture, that resurrection is a work of Satan. It is not a work of God.

It often happens in our day that false doctrine is fraudulently authenticated by supposed miracles. We see this in the charismatic movement. The claim will be made that a certain person was healed or there was some spectacular answer to a prayer; and therefore, what is being taught is the truth. It says in Isaiah 8:20, "*To the law and to the testimony: if they speak not according to this word, it is because there is no light in them.*"

We are being warned that false prophets will be able to do miracles. But since they are using those miracles to lead you away from Christ and to worship the beast, reject those prophets as having any validity. Signs and miracles are only to be used to confirm biblical truth; and if they are used to contradict it, then they are to be dismissed as deceptions, and their practitioners are to be dismissed as deceivers.

The activity of this beast out of the earth, this false prophet that represents and symbolizes anti-Christian religion, is that of turning men away from Christ to put their trust in the satanic god of anti-Christian civil government.

The Mark of the Beast

The mark of the beast is described in verses 16 to 18: *"And he"* (the false prophet, the beast out of the earth) *"causeth all, both small and great, rich and poor, free and bond,"* (no one is exempted, he causes them all) *"to receive a mark in their right hand, or in their foreheads:*
[17] *And that no man might buy or sell, save he that had the mark, or the name of the beast, or the number of his name.* [18] *Here is wisdom. Let him that hath understanding count the number of the beast: for it is the number of a man; and his number is Six hundred threescore and six,"* or six hundred sixty-six.

If the beast out of the sea, the false god of anti-Christian civil government, has existed the entire time between the first and second coming of Christ; and if the beast out of the earth, the false prophet of anti-Christian religion, has existed the entire time between the first and second coming of Christ, then it follows that the mark of the beast has existed just as long. As long as the beast out of the sea exists, and as long as the false prophet causes people to worship that beast, that long has the false prophet been compelling people to take the mark of the beast.

In other words, the mark of the beast is not some end-time phenomenon that has yet to come, that consists of some kind of an implanted computer chip or a mark tattooed into your forehead or your hand. It is not that at all. The mark of the beast has been around as long as the beast has existed, and the beast has existed since the first coming of Jesus, and the beast will continue to exist and function until the second coming of Jesus.

The point is that the mark of the beast is not a literal, physical, visible mark. The mark of the beast is no more literal and physical and visible than the seal of God on the foreheads of the believers spoken of in Revelation 7:3–8 is visible and literal and physical.

When we previously considered that passage, we discovered that this seal is the invisible presence of the Holy Spirit in our lives. It is said to symbolically be in our foreheads because the seal of the Spirit determines how we think, and therefore the actions we take as a result of what we think. The work of the Spirit is at the forefront of our minds, and it controls all of our thinking, and has the highest place of prominence in our lives.

The last verse of Revelation 13 talks about the mark of the beast; and notice what the very next verse in 14:1 talks about: *"And I looked, and, lo, a Lamb stood on the mount Zion, and with him an hundred forty and four thousand, having his Father's name written in their foreheads."* The writing of the mark of the beast in the foreheads and in the hands of the people of 13:18 is parallel with and in direct opposition to the writing of the name of God in the forehead of the believers in 14:1.

Everybody has a mark. Some have the seal of God, and some have the mark of the beast, but everybody has one. They are invisible. They are not physical or visible or literal. The concept of something being on the head is that of something which guides the thoughts, and the concept of something being on the hand is that of something which guides the actions.

This symbolic idea of something on your head guiding your thoughts and something on your hand guiding your actions is a very old concept, first introduced in Exodus 13:9 and expanded in Deuteronomy 6. This is not something new that somebody thought up and nobody knew anything about until computer chips or barcodes were invented.

Notice Deuteronomy 6:4–9: *"Hear, O Israel: The LORD our God is one LORD:* [5] *And thou shalt love the LORD thy God with all thine heart, and with all thy soul, and with all thy might.* [6] *And these words, which I command thee this day, shall be in thine heart* [7] *And thou shalt teach them diligently unto thy children, and shalt talk of them when thou sittest in thine house, and when thou walkest by the way, and when thou liest down, and when thou risest up.* [8] *And thou shalt bind them for a sign upon thine hand, and they shall be as frontlets between thine eyes,* [9] *And thou shalt write them upon the posts of thy house, and on thy gates."*

The idea in this passage is not that they would literally take Bibles and tie them to their hand, tie them to their forehead, tie them to the doorposts of their house, and tie them to the gate in the fence that surrounds the house. The idea is that the word of God should guide the thoughts of our mind, it should guide the actions of our hands, it should guide what we do inside our house, and it should guide what we do when we go out of our gate and into the world. This is symbolic language to say that the word of God should inform all of our thinking and all of our actions, both inside our house and when we go out into the world.

In Revelation 13, what is the mark of the beast himself? We are told in verse 1, *"And I stood upon the sand of the sea, and saw a beast rise up out of the sea, having seven heads and ten horns, and upon his horns ten crowns, and upon his heads the name of blasphemy."* Blasphemy is the mark on the beast himself, and if we take the mark of the beast, we are taking to ourselves thoughts and actions that are blasphemous. We think blasphemous thoughts, we do blasphemous things—that is the mark of the beast. Blasphemy is what marked the beast out of the sea. It was written on his head.

The mark of the beast is the blasphemy of the beast that guides all the thoughts of the unsaved and guides all the actions of the unsaved. The unsaved think like the beast and the unsaved act like the beast, and therefore they bear the mark of the beast. To have the mark of the beast is to have the character of the beast; just like to have the seal of God is to have the character of God.

We use this kind of language all the time. We see some young genius rising up—someone with a brilliant IQ, tremendous sports ability, and great popularity. What do we say? We say, "That kid is marked for greatness." Do we mean by this that he has some sort of a tattoo on his forehead or his hand? No. We mean he has the characteristics that are going to lead him to greatness.

When we say someone has the mark of the beast, we are saying he has the characteristics of the beast. What characterizes the beast? Blasphemy against God in both thought and action. To receive the mark of the beast is to partake of the character of the beast. False religion and false prophets teach and compel and cause their followers to be characterized by blasphemous thoughts and by blasphemous actions, and thereby compel them to take the mark of the beast.

Islam teaches that you must think like Mohammad and act like

Mohammad. If you affirm that you will think like Mohammad and act like Mohammad, then you have just taken the mark of the beast. Mohammad was a satanically inspired, satanically driven, and satanically indwelt man who established both a government and a religion to serve that government. Nowhere is the beast out of the sea and the beast out of the earth more clearly manifested than in Islamic government and Islamic religion. You can see it in the thinking and the behavior of Muslims.

But this is no less true with liberal Christianity, or Roman Catholicism, or Eastern Orthodoxy, or any of the other cults and "isms" that pervert the gospel of Christ, and ultimately cause men to trust in men for their salvation rather than to trust in Christ for their salvation.

To gain more clarity about what this mark of the beast looks like and produces, notice Revelation 14:9–11. *"And the third angel followed them, saying with a loud voice, If any man worship the beast and his image, and receive his mark in his forehead, or in his hand,* [10] *The same shall drink of the wine of the wrath of God, which is poured out without mixture into the cup of his indignation; and he shall be tormented with fire and brimstone in the presence of the holy angels, and in the presence of the Lamb:* [11] *And the smoke of their torment ascendeth up for ever and ever: and they have no rest day nor night, who worship the beast and his image, and whosoever receiveth the mark of his name."*

This passage starts and ends with the same phrase. Verse 9, *"If any man worship the beast and his image, and receive his mark."* Verse 11, *"who worship the beast and his image, and . . . receiveth the mark."* Those who receive the mark of the beast, worship the image of the beast.

When you worship civil government as your ultimate source of authority and as the final expression of power in the universe, you have the mark of the beast. Everyone has a god—either the true God or a false god. The true God is Jesus Christ, and the false god is civil government, inspired and directed by Satan, and aided and abetted by false religion.

The question is this: where does your loyalty lie? If you are a Christian, your citizenship is in heaven, and your loyalty is with Christ. When civil government demands that you do something contrary to what Jesus Christ requires you to do, the only appropriate response is that you must obey God rather than men.

Revelation 13:17 says *"that no man might buy or sell, save he that had the mark, or the name of the beast, or the number of his name."* Unless we fit in with the thinking and the actions of anti-Christian civil government as supported by anti-Christian religion, then buying and selling—that is, engaging in commerce—is going to be extremely difficult, if not impossible.

When we examined Revelation 2:18–29 regarding the letter to the church at Thyatira, we saw that unless you belonged to a trade guild, you could not buy or sell the items of that trade. But in order to belong to the guild, you had to worship the god of the guild and bow before his image and participate in his worship feasts. The Christians refused to do so, which made it impossible for them to engage in the trade the guild represented.

The point is simply this: When governments demand that, in order to do business in their country, you have to engage in ungodly practices, then it stops you from being able to buy and sell as a business in that country. There are many examples of this even in America today.

In Oregon, a couple of sodomites came into Aaron and Melissa Klein's Sweet Cakes Bakery and wanted them to provide a cake for their sodomite wedding. Aaron and Melissa's response was along these lines: "No, we are not going to do that. We believe that homosexual marriage is a sin against God, and we are not going to participate in that by providing you with our services of making and decorating a cake customized for your wedding. It would be declaring our agreement with that wedding, and it would involve us in a participation in it that would be a sin against God." They were fined $135,000 by the government which they had to pay, and they were put out of business. They can no longer buy and sell because they will not worship the beast. They will not worship at the altar of civil government that requires them to treat homosexuality as moral and proper behavior.

Barronelle Stutzman, who visited our church, was a florist. Two homosexuals came in and wanted her to provide flower arrangements—an expression of her artistic ability—for their wedding. She told them she would not do that. She is now involved in a lawsuit in which, if she loses, she will lose her home and all of her possessions. She will be put out of business.

Wedding photographers, tee shirt makers, and those who have venues where they host weddings have all been sued and fined and put out of business because of their refusal to worship the beast and his image. Government contracts require employers to provide full benefits to same-sex sodomite couples and domestic partners. Government has forced adoption agencies to allow sodomites to adopt children. Some adoption services refused to be a party to that wickedness and were forced out of business.

Government forces businesses to pay for abortions in their healthcare coverage. College professors are denied tenure because they are Christians. Dr. Eric Walsh had to fight for his job in Georgia's Department of Heath because he was a lay minister who preached in his church. He was fired because government officials said the personal beliefs he expressed in his sermons were incompatible with his public service.

Rowan county clerk Kim Davis in the state of Kentucky did not want to issue marriage licenses to same-sex couples, because those marriage licenses had her name on them. She was put in jail for that.

The point is that, unless you worship at the altar of government's anti-Christian blasphemous policies, you are fined, you are harassed, you are run out of business, you are penalized, you are fired, and you are even jailed. You cannot buy and sell unless you participate in the wickedness of the beast.

Revelation 13:18 says, *"Here is wisdom. Let him that hath understanding count the number of the beast: for it is the number of a man; and his number is Six hundred three score and six,"* or six hundred sixty-six. The mark of the beast, the name of the beast, and the number of the beast are synonymous with each other and are made equivalent to each other in verses 17 and 18. The question is, what does this 666 stand for?

Our passage tells us 666 is the number of man. On what day of the week was man created? On the sixth day. Six is the number of man. Three is the number of perfection. The point is, man was made on the sixth day of creation, and here we have a triple repetition, which intensifies the idea of humanism, humanity, or mankind. Therefore, 666 simply stands for perfect humanism. It is a number that represents man intensified, at the maximum expression of his humanistic rebellion against God. It is a symbolic number, just like virtually all the numbers in the book of Revelation are symbolic. It was never meant to be a literal number. All that is being said here is that the beast and the false prophet and those who follow them are following the wisdom of this world and the wisdom of men, rather than following God and the wisdom of God.

The point is that when you live a life of humanistic wisdom and blasphemy in thought and deed, you will have the mark of the anti-Christian civil government on you, you will have the approval of the anti-Christian civil government given to you, and therefore you will be able to freely do business with the government's happy approval.

If you refuse the mark of the beast, the ultimate penalty is being put to death. Notice it says in 13:15, *"And he had power to give life unto the image of the beast, that the image of the beast should both speak, and cause that as many as would not worship the image of the beast should be killed."* This actually happens in some countries today. In North Korea, if you do not worship The Supreme Leader, you are put to death. There is a cult of Kim worship required in North Korea, and if you do not go to the meetings and participate in the praise of Kim, you go to prison where you are tortured to death.

In Islamic countries like Saudi Arabia, if you preach the gospel, you are put to death. It is the same in Pakistan and many other Islamic countries. Unless you worship the state through the religion of the state, you will be put to death. And while that is not universally happening all over the world right now, it is going to happen when Satan is finally loosed and Antichrist is finally established with his one-world coalition.

The point is that those who take the mark of the beast are helping the beast in his persecution of Christians. That is why they go to hell along with the beast because they are helping in the work of the beast.

We have talked about Satan and his helpers. Who are his helpers? The beast out of the sea, which symbolizes anti-Christian civil governments; the beast out of the earth (also known as the false prophet), which symbolizes anti-Christian false religions; and those who take the mark of the beast, who symbolize the anti-Christian populace.

We must stand against Satan and his helpers, and if necessary, be willing to be put to death. We must refuse to blaspheme God, either in our thoughts or actions, even if we suffer civil penalties, imprisonment, or death. We must not bow to the state religion that worships the state.

We are in a war. We have been in a war from the time of the first coming of Christ, and we will continue to be in it until His second coming. The war is going to get worse as time goes on and as we get closer to the end, when ultimately the church will have its public voice and its visible presence extinguished from the face of the earth, and there will be just a few believers left whom Christ will rescue when He returns.

The Antichrist along with his false prophet is going to virtually extinguish the church from the face of the earth. We saw that in Daniel 7:21, Revelation 11:7–10, and in Revelation 13:7–8, and we will see it again as we continue our study in this book.

May the Lord help us to stand strong and refuse the mark of the beast—that is, reject blasphemous thoughts and blasphemous actions that are against Christ and His people. Let us call to repentance all those who have the mark of the beast, and exhort them by faith in Christ to obtain the seal of God on their forehead.

43

The Lamb with the 144,000
Revelation 14:1–5

> “1 *And I looked, and, lo, a Lamb stood on the mount Zion,*
> *and with him an hundred forty and four thousand, having his*
> *Father’s name written in their foreheads.* 2 *And I heard a voice*
> *from heaven, as the voice of many waters, and as the voice*
> *of a great thunder: and I heard the voice of harpers harping*
> *with their harps:* 3 *And they sung as it were a new song before*
> *the throne, and before the four beasts, and the elders: and no*
> *man could learn that song but the hundred and forty and four*
> *thousand, which were redeemed from the earth.* 4 *These are*
> *they which were not defiled with women; for they are virgins.*
> *These are they which follow the Lamb whithersoever he goeth.*
> *These were redeemed from among men, being the firstfruits*
> *unto God and to the Lamb.* 5 *And in their mouth was found*
> *no guile: for they are without fault before the throne of God.*”

The theme of this fourth parallel section in Chapters 12 to 14 is that of Satan and his helpers.

In the last half of chapter 12 we saw the work of Satan in attacking the church with physical persecutions and with a flood of false teachings. But in chapter 13, we were introduced to three of Satan’s helpers.

Satan’s first helper is the beast out of the sea, which represents the whole succession of anti-Christian civil governments between the first and the second coming of Christ. These anti-Christian civil governments are marked by blasphemy against God in their laws and their activities. This beast of anti-Christian civil government persecutes believers throughout this age, and, in its final manifestation under the leadership of the Antichrist at the end of this age, will ultimately overcome the believers and remove their visible presence and public testimony from the face of the earth.

Satan's second helper is the beast out of the earth, which represents anti-Christian false religion, whatever form it may take. This beast out of the earth, who is called the false prophet in the remainder of this book, speaks Satan's lies and deceptions throughout the world. False religions turn people away from Christ, and through their deceptions cause them to look to civil government as the ultimate source of authority, and as the ultimate object of trust and worship. These anti-Christian false religions have always taught people to serve and worship the civil authority as the god that determines right and wrong, good and evil, and truth and falsehood. By this means, false religions lead their followers to receive the mark of the beast by getting them to participate in the character of the beast, the blasphemy of the beast, and the work of the beast in persecuting believers.

Satan's third helper consists of those who have the mark of the beast. They are those who participate with the beast in his rebellion against Christ and in his persecution of believers. We saw this mark of the beast is not some physical mark on the hand or the forehead; instead, it is the character of the beast guiding the thinking and actions of those who are loyal to him and look to him as their ultimate source of authority.

To have the mark of the beast is to share in the character of the beast, express the blasphemy of the beast, and do the work of the beast in persecuting believers. Those who do those things have his mark on their thinking, and they have his mark on their actions. People have been bearing the mark of the beast the whole time between the first and second coming of Christ, because everyone has a mark. You either have the seal of God, or you have the mark of the beast. Humanity is divided into two categories of people: the saved and the lost. Each of them is marked by manifesting the character, the thinking, and the actions of the one with whom they identify and worship.

These three helpers assist Satan in his evil work here on this earth. Believers in Christ, who do not worship at the footstool of anti-Christian government, who do not follow the teachings of anti-Christian religion, and who do not fit in with the values and practices of the anti-Christian populace, will suffer greatly for refusing to do so. They always have, and they always will.

The believers in Christ who refuse to take the mark of the beast—that is, they refuse to embrace and practice the blasphemy of the beast—find themselves economically oppressed and persecuted even to the point of death. This economic oppression and persecution to the point of death will become greatly intensified and will reach its fullest expression at the end of this age under the one-world government of the Antichrist. However, we are experiencing it to a significant degree even now, and have been through the centuries.

As we looked at the last half of chapter 12 and all of chapter 13, we saw the work of Satan and his helpers. We saw how powerful they are, how popular they are, and how successful they are. All of this could be very discouraging to contemplate and experience as we live under an anti-Christian government, supported by anti-Christian religion, and surrounded by an anti-Christian populace. But in order to combat that discouragement, God gives us chapter 14, where we see the blessed outcome of those who refuse to receive the mark of the beast—that is, those who refuse to share in the character, the thinking, and the conduct of the beast.

But in chapter 14, not only do we see the blessed outcome of those who refuse to receive the mark of the beast, but we also see the misery and the ruin of those who do take the mark—that is, those who do share in the character, the thinking, and the conduct of the beast.

Therefore, in chapter 14 we receive great encouragement. In verses 1 to 5, we see the blessedness of the redeemed. In verses 6 to 11, we see the misery and damnation of the reprobate when the three angels pronounce God's judgment on them. In verses 12 to 13, we see the encouragement of the suffering saints: *"Blessed are the dead which die in the Lord."* Finally, in verses 14 to 20, we see the second coming of Christ, the separation of the righteous from the wicked, and the wrath of God poured out on the wicked.

The whole point of chapter 14 is to strengthen the saints in their spiritual warfare on this earth by showing them the eternal outcome and destiny of the two sides after this life is over. In this life, it seems very plain that the wicked are winning and we are losing. But that is an illusion. It is a temporary situation, and chapter 14 is designed to take us behind time and into eternity and show us the ultimate outcome, where we see Satan and his helpers utterly defeated and destroyed, and Christ and those who serve Him vindicated and eternally blessed.

In this life, it appears that Satan and the two beasts and those who have the mark of the beast win. That is the message of chapter 13. But in the life to come, it is clear that Christ and His people win and their victory is eternal, while Satan and his helpers lose and their defeat is everlasting. They are forever condemned to eternal wrath and suffering. That is the message of chapter 14. It is this understanding and perspective that encourages the saint to persevere in his faithfulness to Christ, even in the midst of severe economic and physical and social persecution.

We progress from a chapter that was rather discouraging, to a chapter that is tremendously encouraging. Chapter 14 gives a long-range view of how the conflict described in chapters 12 and 13 will play out, and this long-range view provides encouragement and motivation to keep on being faithful and patient. Notice Revelation 14:12: *"Here is the patience of the saints: here are they that keep the commandments of God, and the faith of Jesus."* This verse tells us what chapter 14 is all about, and what it is designed to produce in the hearts of God's people.

The Vision of Heaven

The vision of heaven is in verse 1: *"And I looked, and, lo, a Lamb stood on the mount Zion, and with him an hundred forty and four thousand, having his Father's name written in their foreheads."* John now sees a new vision indicated by the phrase: *"And I looked."* The first thing John saw was a Lamb standing on Mount Zion.

Whenever the book of Revelation speaks of someone being *"a lamb,"* or being *"the lamb,"* it is always, and without exception, a reference to Jesus Christ. (The false prophet in the previous chapter was only said to have two horns *"like a lamb"*; he is not said to be a lamb.) We see this first in chapter 5 in the vision of the Lamb before the throne of God who is undeniably Jesus Christ. Twenty-five times in this book the word "lamb" is used to describe Jesus. John also uses this term to describe Jesus in John's Gospel when he said of Jesus in John 1:29, *"Behold the Lamb of God, which taketh away the sin of the world."* The reason this title is given to the Lord Jesus is rooted in the Old Testament. In the Old Testament, a lamb was the substitutionary sacrifice made on behalf of the sinner to atone for his sins, thereby averting the wrath of God against him. But no animal is the moral equivalent of a human; and therefore, animal sacrifices were wholly inadequate to be a suitable substitute for a human. The Old Testament sacrificial lamb was only meant to be an illustration and foreshadow of the perfect sacrifice that would actually take away the sin of the world.

Jesus was that perfect sacrifice who was able to fully and truly and finally atone for the sins of God's people. Jesus was the true Lamb of God who bore the just wrath of God that was due to us for our sins. By taking on Himself the punishment that was due to us for our sins, Jesus satisfied the demands of divine justice on our behalf, so that God could freely forgive us because the just punishment that was due for our sins was fully paid by Jesus Christ through His death on the cross. As it says in 1 Peter 1:18–19, we were redeemed with the precious blood of Christ, who was like a lamb without blemish or spot.

Whenever Jesus is portrayed as the Lamb in the book of Revelation, it is designed to remind us of His self-sacrifice for sinners, His substitutionary atonement on our behalf, and His saving work in delivering us from the wrath to come. When the name "lamb" comes to your mind, all of these concepts should arise in your thoughts: He sacrificed Himself for me! He was my substitute who died in my place, and through His saving work, He delivered me from the wrath to come! All of those ideas are wrapped up in this title of *"Lamb."*

This Lamb of God is the great manifestation of the love of God. God's love is shown in the giving of His Son to be the Lamb of God to redeem sinners when He sacrificed Him for us. Christ's love is shown in laying down His own life for sinners. He was willing to endure and undergo the wrath of God on our behalf because He loved us to that degree.

This selfless Savior, this loving Savior, this wonderful Savior is the one who John saw when he saw the Lamb standing on Mount Zion. The Lamb of God was the first thing John saw when he looked into heaven. The Lamb of God is the central thing that John saw when he looked into heaven. The Lamb of God is the best thing that John saw when he looked into heaven.

We have far too low and carnal views of heaven. We talk about the streets of gold and the gates of pearl. None of that means anything. When John sees heaven, what instantly draws his attention is the Lamb of God. The first thing, the central thing, and the best thing he sees in heaven is the Lamb of God, and that is where his focus rests. *"I looked, and, lo, a Lamb."*

When it says that the Lamb stood on Mount Zion, we need to understand that this Mount Zion is heaven itself. It is not some mountain somewhere on the earth, although Mount Zion is a name for the literal mountain the city of Jerusalem was built on. But as it is used here, it is not talking about the mountain that Jerusalem was built on; instead, it is used as a name of heaven itself. Psalm 125:1 says of Mount Zion that it cannot be removed, but abides forever. That cannot be said of any earthly mountain. They are all going to melt with fervent heat. They are going to be moved, and they are not going to abide forever.

Mount Zion in the Scripture is to be sure a literal mountain with a literal city, but very often that term is used of the eternal city of God; namely, of heaven itself. In Hebrews 12:22, Mount Zion is also called *"the heavenly Jerusalem."* The Mount Zion John is seeing in Revelation 14:1 is actually heaven because in verse 2 it says, *"And I heard a voice from heaven,"* showing that this whole vision is a vision of heaven itself.

As John sees Jesus standing in heaven, Jesus is not standing there alone. With the Lamb, John sees 144,000 with the Father's name written in their foreheads. Notice the last part of verse 1: *"And I looked, and, lo, a Lamb stood on the mount Zion, and with him an hundred forty and four thousand, having his Father's name written in their foreheads."*

We have seen this 144,000 before in Revelation 7 when we saw that 144,000 were sealed with the seal of God in their foreheads. As we studied that passage, we saw that this 144,000 represented and symbolized the whole body of believers who are chosen by God and saved by Christ. All of them have the seal of God, here called "the Father's name," in their foreheads, which symbolized the indwelling Spirit of God, who is declared to actually be the seal of God in Ephesians 1:13.

In Revelation 7, the 144,000 were seen as still living on earth, surrounded by enemies and undergoing great trials. But here they are seen enjoying the blessedness of heaven, freed from their enemies and delivered out of all of their trials. Although the dragon and his helpers attacked and assaulted the church on earth, and though Satan did all he could to make the believers unfaithful to Christ, not one of the 144,000 that were sealed on earth are absent in heaven. All those Christ has called and justified here on earth are without exception glorified and present in heaven. The dragon, the beast out of the sea, the beast out of the earth, and those who bear the mark of the beast all failed to pluck even one of Christ's sheep out of His hand. All those Christ saves, He sanctifies and preserves and infallibly brings to heaven, and not one of them is lost. Jesus will never allow Satan the triumph of taking one of His saints to hell with him.

What this means is that whatever trials or temptations or persecutions are brought to bear on you by the dragon and his helpers, you are eternally secure in the power and the grace of Christ, and you will never be lost by Him. He who keeps you now will keep you to the end. He who saves you now will safely deliver you into heaven, and there will not be one that is lost along the way.

The Music of Heaven

The music of heaven is in verses 2 and 3. *"And I heard a voice from heaven, as the voice of many waters, and as the voice of a great thunder: and I heard the voice of harpers harping with their harps:* [3] *And they sung as it were a new song before the throne, and before the four beasts, and the elders: and no man could learn that song but the hundred and forty and four thousand, which were redeemed from the earth."*

Having seen the inhabitants of heaven in verse 1, which are the Lamb with His bride, John now hears a glorious anthem being sung, a hymn of praise and thanksgiving and worship and joy. The sound of this song is majestic, it is thunderous, and it is lovely. This song is like the sound of many waters. It is majestic. If you have ever been to Niagara Falls and heard the roar of the falling waters, this is what it sounds like. If you have ever been in a lightning storm and heard and felt the thunderclap shaking your very body, this is what this song sounds like. It is thunderous. This song is like the sound of a harp. It is lovely. If you have ever heard a harp skillfully played, this is what it sounds like. It is beautifully melodious.

Verse 2 says that this song is like the voice of many waters, and the voice of a great thunder, and the voice of harpers harping on their harps. The sound of this song is majestic and thunderous and lovely. There is nothing quiet about this song, and there is nothing trivial in this song, and there is nothing defective in this song. It has the power of a mighty waterfall. It has the voice of a tremendous thunder. It has the beauty of a melodious harp. It is a perfectly sung hymn of praise for a perfect salvation that has been provided in a perfect way by a perfect God. This song is full of grandeur and beauty and excellence and spiritual purity. It is music fit for heaven, and it is the kind of music we should be striving to sing here on earth.

This song that is sung is said to be a *"new song."* Notice verse 3: *"and they sung as it were a new song."* It is a new song because it expresses a new experience for those who are singing it. The 144,000 had been redeemed from the earth and are now glorified together in heaven. They are in a new place. They are in a new condition. They have a new understanding of the wonder of their salvation, the happiness of their future, and the blessedness of their Savior. Heaven is a new experience for them, and it requires a new song out of them to express the new understanding they have, the new condition they are in, and the new experience they are having.

As we grow in our Christian experience and understanding, we also have to grow in our acquisition of new songs. This is so we can express new dimensions of worship and praise to the Father and the Son and the Holy Spirit for the new experiences and understandings we gain as we mature.

We are always going to be learning new songs as long as we are gaining new understanding of all that God has done for us. If a new hymn is introduced in church, embrace it as a new opportunity to offer new worship to God. It expresses a new dimension of truth that perhaps we have never known before or expressed in this fashion. Let us learn it, sing it, and offer to God one more brick in the palace of praise that He deserves for the glory of His name and the work He accomplished on our behalf.

Notice the audience to whom this hymn of praise is sung, verse 3. It says, *"and they sung as it were a new song before the throne, and before the four beasts, and the elders."* It says that this new song is sung before the throne, that is, before God; it is sung before the four beasts, which are the seraphim; and it is sung before the twenty-four elders, which is the entire church in heaven. The church—the redeemed people of God—are singing to each other in Psalms and hymns and spiritual songs. They love to praise God, and they love to hear others praise God too. Heaven loves to hear the praises of God, and God loves to hear His people's praise as they sing to Him and as they sing before Him. It is a glorious anthem and a glorious audience, and the sound of praise is that which saturates the whole atmosphere of heaven. Singing has always been a central part of the praise of the people of God here on earth, and it will forever be a central part of the praise of the people of God there in heaven. Christians are intrinsically and inherently and at their core a musical people.

If you do not view yourself as musically gifted, you need to work at it. It is your occupation now, and it will be your occupation forever. Embrace music and embrace singing. You will do better when you get to heaven, but do your best now to engage in it, embrace it, and sing out as an expression of your love to God, as a testimony to His angels, and as a declaration and witness before the whole church of what God has done for your soul, and who God is to you in your heart.

But the music of praise is the music of experience, and that is why it says in verse 3 that only the 144,000 sing this particular song, because they alone understand what it means to experience redemption from the earth. Look at verse 3 again: *"and they sung as it were a new song before the throne, and before the four beasts, and the elders: and no man could learn that song but the hundred and forty and four thousand,"* (now here is the qualification they have for singing this song) *"which were redeemed from the earth."* This music of praise is the music of experience, and that is why only the 144,000 can sing this particular song, because they alone understand what it means to experience redemption from the earth. Angels have not experienced such a thing, and therefore angels cannot join in singing about something they have never known or experienced themselves.

Notice it says of these 144,000 that they are redeemed. They are not redeemed from sin, as we would expect it to say, but rather they are redeemed *"from the earth."* Now to be sure, redemption is primarily about redemption from sin, and the Bible is full of statements about redemption from sin. But that is not the emphasis here. Here, the emphasis is on their deliverance out of a persecuting and fallen world that was ruled and run by Satan and his helpers. The context is that of the dragon, the beast out of the earth, the beast out of the sea, and those who take the mark of the beast crushing the people of God. Deliverance from them means to be delivered out of the world in which they exist and function.

This is further reinforced in verse 4b. *"These are they which follow the Lamb whithersoever he goeth. These were redeemed from among men."* It says in verse 3 that they are redeemed out of the earth, and in verse 4 it says they are redeemed from among men. Clearly, the emphasis here is that we were in the world, and now we are out of the world. One of the great promises and benefits of Christ's saving work is declared in Galatians 1:3–5 when it says, "*Grace be to you and peace from God the Father, and from our Lord Jesus Christ,* [4] *Who gave himself for our sins, that he might deliver us from this present evil world, according to the will of God and our Father:* [5]*To whom be glory for ever and ever. Amen.*" Jesus did not just come to save us from our sins; He also came to save us from this present evil world.

This present evil world has been described in Revelation 12 and 13. This present evil world is one that is run by Satan and ruled by Satan, who uses anti-Christian government and anti-Christian religion and an anti-Christian populace to abuse and persecute and kill Christians. This world is a physically, morally, and spiritually fallen cesspool of evil in which we are strangers and sojourners and pilgrims. This present evil world is dominated by those who hate God and by those who hate us. Therefore, we have an aversion to this world, and a desire to be delivered from this world and to depart from it and be with Christ, which is far better! The good news is that Christ shall deliver us from this present evil world. In heaven we will be freed from its corruption, oppression, and persecution. We will sing praise to God that we no longer have to live under an evil government and alongside an evil people who are driven by evil religious beliefs.

Angels, who never had to live in this world like we do, will never personally know what it is like to be delivered out of it. They will listen to our song of praise for our deliverance, but they will never be able to sing it themselves because they have never experienced it.

The good news is that all we do not like about this old world will be gone forever when we inhabit the new heaven and the new earth wherein dwells righteousness.

You have probably seen images and stories of people who had been delivered out of horribly oppressive regimes such as China, Russia, East Germany, and North Korea, and somehow, they made it to America. Photographs reveal that when they get off the plane, they often get down on their knees and kiss the ground. They rejoice in the fact that they are now in the land of freedom, and that they were delivered from the tyranny they were once under. That is a picture of how we are going to feel when we are delivered out of this world and brought into the free world of heaven. But instead of kissing the ground, we will be praising the Savior.

The Purity of Heaven

The purity of heaven is described in verses 4 to 5. Verse 4 says regarding the 144,000: "*These are they which were not defiled with women; for they are virgins. These are they which follow the Lamb whithersoever he goeth. These were redeemed from among men, being the firstfruits unto God and to the Lamb.* [5] *And in their mouth was found no guile: for they are without fault before the throne of God.*"

Verses 4 and 5 describe the purity of those who are in heaven, and it describes it with a series of statements. The first statement is that "*these are they which were not defiled with women; for they are virgins.*" We have to understand that this is a symbolic statement, not a literal one. There is nothing morally defiling about women, and there is nothing morally defiling about sexual relations within the covenant of marriage. There is no virtue in remaining a virgin throughout one's life here on this earth, as opposed to becoming married and thereby losing one's virginity. All of this is made very clear from the creation narrative itself, in which God created man and woman with all of their sexual functions. God performed the first wedding ceremony between them and commanded them to be fruitful and multiply and fill the earth, and when they engaged in that activity, God looked on it and said, "It is very good."

Nothing in this regard has changed since the fall. Hebrews 13:4 says that marriage is honorable in all, and the bed is undefiled. As far as physical virginity, and as far as sexual activity with women, these things are neither virtues nor are they defilements. They are simply normal conditions and activities humans find themselves in and find themselves doing as they obey the commandments of God.

What Revelation 14:4 is speaking of is spiritual unfaithfulness to the Savior to whom the bride of Christ is betrothed in this world.

In Ephesians 5, the church is called the bride of Christ. We are spiritually betrothed to Christ, and we will consummate that final spiritual union with Him when He returns in the marriage supper of the Lamb. Paul says to the Corinthian church in 2 Corinthians 11:2: "*For I am jealous over you with godly jealousy: for I have espoused you to one husband, that I may present you a chaste virgin to Christ.*" For the church to lose her spiritual virginity would be for her to give herself to another god besides Jesus Christ. It would be for her to commit spiritual adultery by worshiping and serving another god.

James 4:4 says, *"Ye adulterers and adulteresses, know ye not that the friendship of the world is enmity with God? whosoever therefore will be a friend of the world is the enemy of God."* We lose our spiritual virginity and we become spiritual adulterers when we serve and worship another god in the place of Jesus Christ. Therefore, when it says in Revelation 14:4 that *"these are they which were not defiled with women; for they are virgins,"* it means that they did not worship the beast and take his mark or follow the false prophet and his teaching.

The point is that those who wind up in heaven are those who were faithful to Christ here on earth. They did not go after the beast out of the sea, or the beast out of the earth, or those who took the mark of the beast. Once they embraced Christ as their Lord and Savior, they never left Him to go after another god. They did not have spiritual communion and spiritual intercourse with the false gods and the false religions of this world. They were, as the sixth beatitude says, pure in heart; and therefore, they see God. Apostates do not make it into heaven. Those who follow Christ for a while and then follow the world and forget about Christ are not among God's elect.

The emphasis in the book of Revelation is the same as the emphasis in the book of Hebrews, and it is this: We know you are suffering for following Christ. Stay faithful to the end. Do not go back to the world to get relief from the persecution of the world. Do not go back to the world to get the pleasures of the world. Do not go back to the world to get the approval of the world. Stay strong. Suffer even to the point of death, and Jesus will reward you with everlasting life for having been faithful to Him.

That is why the saints all through the centuries would rather die than deny Christ, because they recognized that to deny Him might gain them a little time here, but it would mean they would lose Him forever. But to stay true to Him, no matter what the pressure is, though causing us to have *"light affliction which is but for a moment"* now, will work a far more exceeding and eternal weight of glory in the end.

The second thing it says about those that are in heaven is not only are they spiritual virgins, but it also says of them in verse 4 that *"These are they which follow the Lamb whithersoever he goeth."* That is, these are they who recognized, and who still recognize, Jesus Christ as Lord. When you follow someone, that person is in charge and you are not. He is in control, and you are not. His will is your will, and where he leads, you follow. This is what it means to *"follow the Lamb withersoever he goeth."*

The disposition of those in heaven is that of *"Not my will, but thine, be done."* They have no desire to go anywhere or do anything except that which the Lamb directs them to do. His will is the only will they have, and like Saul they say: *"Lord, what wilt thou have me to do?"*

So it is with believers. Who are those in heaven? They are those who followed the Lamb wherever He led. Wherever the hand of Scripture led them is where they went, no matter how foolish those beliefs seemed to be to the world, or even to other professing Christians who have more concern for what inflates the ego of man than what accomplishes the will of God. On earth, these strove to observe all things whatsoever He commanded; and in heaven, His command drives all of their conduct. Their wills are fully surrendered to His.

The third thing that is said of those who are in heaven is that *"These were redeemed from among men, being the firstfruits unto God and to the Lamb."* Under Old Testament law, the first fruits were that part of the crop that was dedicated to God and belonged to God. When you have a garden, not everything gets ripe at the same moment. You have some produce that comes ripe first. Under Old Testament law, you were to pick all of those things that came ripe first, put them in a basket, take them to the temple, and give them to God. All that became ripe later belonged to the farmer who could do with it as he wished. God did not lay claim to anything other than the first fruits as being that which belonged to Him.

In the same way, God's elect people, the whole number of the redeemed out of the earth, are the part of humanity that belongs to God, symbolically represented as these 144,000. They, the first fruits out of the earth, belong entirely to God. The remainder of humanity that is left behind belongs to the devil, who can do with them as he wishes. God does not lay claim to the remainder of humanity as belonging to Him. All He lays claim to is the first fruits. All of God's elect belong to Him, and the rest He leaves to Satan to do with as he wills, to bear his mark, and to carry out his purposes.

The fourth thing that is said about these people who are in heaven is that *"in their mouth was found no guile."* Guile is lying. It could easily be translated, "And in their mouth were found no lies." Those in heaven are those who were not liars. They were not those who said that Christ was their Lord when that was really not the case. The point is that there are no false professors in heaven.

How many people have told you they are Christians, and later on you realize they are not? They used guile to deceive you into thinking they were fellow believers when they were not fellow believers at all. Not one of those people winds up in heaven. Only those who are sincere in their worship and submission to Christ are in heaven. They are honest in their profession. They mean what they say, and they live what they profess. That does not mean they lived perfect lives, but they did serve, obey, and follow Christ as the dominating characteristic of their lives.

They did not lie and say they loved Christ with all their heart and soul and mind and strength when actually they really loved the world and those who served it. These are those who followed Christ with integrity. They did not toss the name of Jesus off their tongue to give an aura of spirituality while they lived ungodly lives. They are those who were genuine and sincere in their hearts and in their profession of faith in Christ as Savior and Lord.

The fifth thing that is said about those who are in heaven is that *"they are without fault before the throne of God."* This means that Christ has fully cleansed them from all of their sins. As it says in Jude 1:24, Jesus has presented them *"faultless before the presence of his glory with exceeding joy."* Through the saving work of Christ, their sins have been removed and their righteousness has been provided, so that when God looks upon them, He finds no fault in them. They are *"holy and unblameable and unreprovable in His sight."* They are *"holy and without blame before Him."* When God looks on them, there is no *"spot or wrinkle"* of any kind; *"they are holy and without blemish."*

Jesus presents His elect faultless before His Father. They are perfect. No sin is on their record. Perfect righteousness is on their record. God looks upon them and declares them justified! There is no point of criticism, no point of complaint, no point of improvement needed. God says, "You are perfect. You are holy as your Father which is in heaven is holy." This is what Jesus does for us.

As you think about the awful oppression and reign of the dragon, the beast out of the sea, the beast out of the earth, and all those who follow them, keep bright and clear in your mind the outcome you are going to have, even though you are sorely oppressed economically and physically, and harshly persecuted for following Christ. The good news of the gospel is that we will be with the Lamb on Mount Zion. Did you notice how the passage opens with the Lamb in verse 1, and how it closes with perfect people in verse 5? The Lamb is the one who produces those perfect people who stand before the throne.

Anytime you start getting weary of this world and the struggles you go through, speak to yourself in words like these: "I need to persevere. I need to be faithful to Christ. I need to walk with Him, live for Him, trust Him, believe Him, follow Him, and be sincere and genuine. If I do, then this is where I will arrive. This is the song I will be singing. I will be redeemed out of this horrible earth and brought into the presence of the angels and the saints. I will spend my eternity singing praise to God and enjoying fellowship with the Lamb of God, who saved me from my sins and out of this evil world, and from the Evil One who wanted to destroy me."

44

The Message of Judgment on the Wicked, Revelation 14:6–13

> *"6 And I saw another angel fly in the midst of heaven, hav-*
> *ing the everlasting gospel to preach unto them that dwell on*
> *the earth, and to every nation, and kindred, and tongue, and*
> *people, 7 Saying with a loud voice, Fear God, and give glory*
> *to him; for the hour of his judgment is come: and worship*
> *him that made heaven, and earth, and the sea, and the foun-*
> *tains of waters. 8 And there followed another angel, saying,*
> *Babylon is fallen, is fallen, that great city, because she made*
> *all nations drink of the wine of the wrath of her fornication.*
> *9 And the third angel followed them, saying with a loud voice,*
> *If any man worship the beast and his image, and receive his*
> *mark in his forehead, or in his hand, 10 The same shall drink*
> *of the wine of the wrath of God, which is poured out with-*
> *out mixture into the cup of his indignation; and he shall be*
> *tormented with fire and brimstone in the presence of the holy*
> *angels, and in the presence of the Lamb: 11 And the smoke of*
> *their torment ascendeth up for ever and ever: and they have*
> *no rest day nor night, who worship the beast and his image,*
> *and whosoever receiveth the mark of his name. 12 Here is the*
> *patience of the saints: here are they that keep the command-*
> *ments of God, and the faith of Jesus. 13 And I heard a voice*
> *from heaven saying unto me, Write, Blessed are the dead which*
> *die in the Lord from henceforth: Yea, saith the Spirit, that they*
> *may rest from their labours; and their works do follow them."*

Spiritual warfare is the constant theme of this age, and spiritual warfare is the constant experience of every believer, and it will be until Jesus returns. As we have looked at Revelation 12, 13, and 14, we have seen a vivid description of the work of Satan and his helpers as they assault the people of God. The dragon, the beast out of the sea, the beast out of the earth, and all those who take the mark of the beast are arrayed against Christ and His people.

Satan, the anti-Christian governments, the anti-Christian religions, and the anti-Christian populace, all severely persecute the people of God, both economically and physically, even to the point of death.

But the short-term success of Satan and his helpers in this age will give way to their eternal failure and damnation under the wrath of God, and the short-term harm that the people of God experience in this age will give way to their eternal triumph and vindication under the smile and blessing of God.

While the last half of Revelation 12 and all of chapter 13 told us about the temporary success of Satan and his helpers in assaulting the people of God, chapter 14 tells us about the everlasting triumph the people of God will have over them.

While the persecutions of Satan and his agents are severe, they are not to be compared with the blessedness of the people of God in heaven described in 14:1–5. There we saw the vision of heaven in which Christ the Lamb of God stands in the midst of those He has redeemed. They enjoy His love and fellowship for all eternity.

We also heard the music of heaven as the redeemed thundered out beautiful melodies of praise to their Savior for delivering them from this present evil world. The saints have been redeemed out of a persecuting and fallen world that was ruled and run by Satan and his helpers, and their praise for that deliverance will never end.

We also saw the purity of heaven. Those in heaven are those who were faithful to Christ on earth, and they did not go after other gods. They were true to Christ. Because they were pure in heart, they now see God in heaven. They followed Christ wherever He led them, and His will was their will. They were genuine believers in Christ on earth, and were sincere in their confession of Christ as their Lord before men. Therefore, they are now without fault before the throne of God.

Jesus has made them holy and unblameable and unreproveable in God's sight by providing them with redemption and righteousness. Jesus kept them from falling on earth, and Jesus now presents them faultless before the presence of His Father in heaven with exceeding joy. Never again will sin mar the happiness of the believers in heaven, nor will sinful people ever disturb their joy. Those in heaven have come out of great tribulation, and they will never experience tribulation again. Heaven is a place of perfect purity; and therefore, heaven is a place of perfect peace.

All of this is a great encouragement to suffering saints who now suffer under the heel of Satan and his helpers. That struggle will soon be over, and when it is over, it is over forever. This is a tremendous comfort and encouragement to believers while they suffer the persecution of Satan and his helpers.

However, John is not done providing suffering saints with encouragement. This whole chapter is given over to the encouragement of the saints. Not only do we see the blessedness of the redeemed in verses 1 to 5, but we also see the misery of the reprobate in verses 6 to 11.

One of the great struggles Christians have is the apparent prosperity of the wicked in this world while believers suffer social, economic, and physical persecution. We look at the wicked and we see they are able to have it all and enjoy it all. We look at ourselves and our fellow believers, and we see suffering and deprivation and martyrdom.

John teaches us to look past the temporary joy of the wicked to their impending doom, and thereby avoid having any envy toward them, or any resentment that we do not enjoy the prosperity and the power they possess.

Psalm 37:1–3 warns us against this envy of the wicked when it says, *"Fret not thyself because of evildoers, neither be thou envious against the workers of iniquity. 2 For they shall soon be cut down like the grass, and wither as the green herb. 3 Trust in the* Lord, *and do good; so shalt thou dwell in the land, and verily thou shalt be fed."*

We see the phenomenal blessedness of the righteous in verses 1 to 5, and we also see the terrible distress that is brought upon the helpers of Satan in verses 6 through 11. The message is this: Your sufferings are not worthy to be compared with the glory that shall be revealed to you. The prosperity of the wicked means nothing in light of the suffering they will endure for eternity in the flames of hell.

Do not complain under your sufferings, and do not be envious of the prosperity of the wicked, because your sufferings will lead you to glory, and their prosperity will lead them to damnation. Therefore, your sufferings are a better state than their prosperity. We need to take heed and believe what we are told about the misery of the reprobate. Instead of fearing them and envying them, let us pity them and patiently endure their insults, knowing God will deal with them in due time.

In verses 6 to 13, three angels deliver three messages regarding the reprobate. These three messages become increasingly severe as each of them is delivered. Collectively, these three warnings and messages are a sobering and alarming warning to the wicked to turn from their wickedness. But sadly, that warning will go unheeded, the wrath of God will fall upon them, and they will be cast into hell. This will be the end of our persecutors. This will be the outcome of the dragon and his helpers.

In these warnings to the wicked, we see the comfort that will be brought to the believers as they contemplate what God promises He will do to the dragon and his helpers.

Before we begin the exposition of the passage, I want to make some preliminary comments about these three angels themselves. Notice verse 6: *"And I saw another angel fly in the midst of heaven, having the everlasting gospel to preach unto them that dwell on the earth,"* verse 7, *"saying with a loud voice,"* verse 8, *"And there followed another angel, saying, Babylon is fallen."* Verse 9, *"And the third angel followed them, saying with a loud voice. . ."* The picture here is that of three angels, one after the other, flying through the atmosphere and shouting down at the earth.

Once again, we need to be reminded that Revelation is a book of symbolic visual imagery. We emphasized this very strongly in our introductory chapters to this book. The pictures that Revelation presents to our eyes through its verbal descriptions are not to be taken literally. It is not going to be the case that a literal angel is going to literally fly through the atmosphere of the earth and address the people dwelling on the earth with an audible, spoken message shouted from above.

We have previously established that the word "angel" means "messenger." The pastors of the seven churches in Revelation 2 and 3 were called angels because they were the messengers of God to the churches—that is, they conveyed God's message to the people and represented God's mind on issues the churches faced.

Therefore, these three angels represent God's messengers, whoever they are, wherever they are, and whenever they happen to appear on the face of the earth. There are three of them because three is the number that represents perfection and completion and finality. Therefore, these three messengers are representative of the perfect, complete, and final number of messengers that will convey God's message on earth between the first and second coming of Christ.

As we look at the messages these messengers are conveying, these are not one-time proclamations made at a single point in history. These three messages are relevant to every generation. They are to be proclaimed in every century. They are needed throughout the whole earth. These symbolic messengers symbolically fly over the whole earth to proclaim the message they have to all the peoples of the earth. They disseminate their message to the whole world and disseminate it in every generation. Therefore, these three messengers represent all of the preachers of God's word who proclaim this message in every generation over the entire world.

The First Message of Warning

The first message of warning is contained in verses 6 and 7. *"And I saw another angel fly in the midst of heaven, having the everlasting gospel to preach unto them that dwell on the earth, and to every nation, and kindred, and tongue, and people,* [7] *Saying with a loud voice, Fear God, and give glory to him; for the hour of his judgment is come: and worship him that made heaven, and earth, and the sea, and the fountains of waters."*

It is important for us to note that these three messages are not primarily directed at believers in Christ. These three messages are directed to the unsaved, they are directed to the world, and they are primarily pronouncements of impending judgment that is going to fall on them for their wickedness. They are warnings directed to the lost.

First of all, notice the timeless universality of the message in verse 6: *"And I saw another angel fly in the midst of heaven, having the everlasting gospel to preach unto them that dwell on the earth."* Notice it is called *"the everlasting gospel."* In other words, this is a timeless message. It is a message that lasts forever. It is not a message that is temporary, that goes away, or one day will be invalid or obsolete. This is a message that is relevant to every generation. It is not just some end-time proclamation for some special people living at a particular point in history. This is the everlasting message that has been going on and will go on forever.

Notice to whom it is addressed. It says in verse 6 that it is *"unto them that dwell on the earth,"* and in case there is any misunderstanding about whom that includes, it says, *"and to every nation, and kindred, and tongue, and people."* It is called the everlasting gospel, and it is addressed to those who dwell on the earth—that is, every nation, kindred, tongue, and people. It is a timeless message—it is the everlasting gospel. It is a universal message—it is for every person. Here is a message that is always relevant to every class and category of person who lives on the earth in any place, at any point in time, in any situation.

Secondly, notice the threatening nature of the message. The threatening nature is in verse 7: *"Saying with a loud voice, Fear God, and give glory to him; for the hour of his judgment is come: and worship him that made heaven, and earth, and the sea, and the fountains of waters."* The core of this message in verse 7 is that *"the hour of His judgment is come."* Everything else that precedes and follows that supports and flows out of that core message: The hour of His judgment is come.

It is important for us to understand that the everlasting gospel not only contains the good news of salvation; the everlasting gospel also contains the bad news of condemnation and judgment for all those who break God's law, dishonor God's name, resist God's authority, withhold God's worship, and reject God's Son.

The gospel not only has good news; it also has bad news. The good news is that if you embrace the gospel, you will wind up like the people in verses 1 to 5. The bad news is if you reject the gospel, you will wind up like the people in verses 6 to 11.

The messengers of God proclaim to the wicked of this world that the hour of God's judgment is come. You will not escape it. You will face it as soon as you die; and therefore, in light of this coming judgment, fear God, give glory to Him, and worship Him. God made the heaven and the earth and the sea and the rivers. He is the creator of all, He is the controller of all, and therefore He is the judge of all. You stand before God the Judge. If you do not fear Him, if you will not glorify Him, if you refuse to worship Him, all that awaits you is His imminent judgment that can fall on you at any moment.

No one who dismisses the coming judgment of God will ever escape that judgment by doing so. You can say you do not believe there is going to be a judgment, but that does not make it go away. The world acts today like it did in the days of Noah, with people eating and drinking, marrying and giving in marriage, indifferent toward God, mocking God, complacent in their sin, and ignoring God's warnings of coming judgment.

The messengers of God call out to the whole earth in every generation, saying: "The hour of His judgment is here! Recognize God, respect God, reverence God, and repent to God." But what do they do? They follow the false prophets of their age: the beast out of the earth. Therefore, to them is reserved the wrath of God.

This is bad news for the wicked, but it is good news for the righteous who are severely persecuted by Satan and his helpers. The angel is telling persecuted believers that judgment will come for those who do not fear God and who therefore persecute them. But their persecutors will not escape. Judgment will come for them. It is so certain to come, that it can be said that it has already come.

The gospel comforts the believer by promising him that he is reconciled to God and that his persecutors will not escape the wrath of God. He will have justice. Satan and his helpers will be judged in the end. So certain is that judgment to come that it could be stated as though it has already come, and therefore the messenger says: *"the hour of his judgment is come."*

The Second Message of Warning

The second message of warning is contained in verse 8: *"And there followed another angel, saying, Babylon is fallen, is fallen, that great city, because she made all nations drink of the wine of the wrath of her fornication."* We have previously identified three helpers of Satan, and now in this verse we are introduced for the first time to the fourth helper of Satan, which is Babylon.

The dragon, who is Satan, has his helpers: the beast out of the sea, which represents anti-Christian government; the beast out of the earth, which represents anti-Christian religion; those who take the mark of the beast, which represent the anti-Christian populace; and now Babylon, which represents anti-Christian society.

The concept of Babylon as a symbol of evil is very important. In fact, it is so important that Revelation 17 and 18 are given over to an extended description of the nature of Babylon, the evil of Babylon, and the destruction of Babylon. Babylon was a literal city in the Old Testament. It was the seat of the Babylonian Empire. It is where Israel was taken when Nebuchadnezzar conquered and captured Jerusalem and brought her population into captivity for seventy years. The book of Daniel covers this time period, as does the book of Ezekiel.

That Old Testament city represented a society that was the antithesis of godliness. Every vice, every wickedness, and every evil was practiced openly and defiantly in Babylon, and whoever resisted it was persecuted and mocked and punished, as the Jews were who lived within that city. Socially, culturally, and economically, Babylon crushed the people of God. Babylon personified godless society. As a result, Babylon then became a universal symbol of the social, cultural, and economic systems of the world that are organized in opposition to God. All wicked societies are Babylon the Great. Babylon the Great is a metaphor for all anti-Christian societies.

Babylon, in John's day, was exemplified by Rome. Today, it is exemplified in virtually every society on earth. We see it especially exemplified in cities like Chicago, New York, San Francisco, and Las Vegas, which are brazen in their evil, shameless in their vice, and corrupt in their materialism. Babylon allures, Babylon seduces, and Babylon draws people away from God.

What is Babylon? It is nothing more and nothing less than "the world" that John speaks of in 1 John 2:15–17. *"Love not the world, neither the things that are in the world. If any man love the world, the love of the Father is not in him.* [16] *For all that is in the world, the lust of the flesh, and the lust of the eyes, and the pride of life, is not of the Father, but is of the world.* [17] *And the world passeth away, and the lust thereof: but he that doeth the will of God abideth for ever."*

Theologically speaking, in that passage you could take out the word "world" and insert the word "Babylon," because the terms are virtually equivalent. Babylon is simply anti-Christian society that seeks to seduce the believer into forsaking Christ for the pleasures of this world. Babylon is the harlot that the 144,000 of verses 1 to 5 did not commit fornication with. It says of those in heaven in verses 1 to 5 that they were virgins. What this means is that they were not defiled with this woman, with this harlot Babylon.

Christians maintain separation from anti-Christian society. They maintain their virginity with reference to having intercourse with anti-Christian society—that is, they do not indulge in its vices, they do not indulge in its sins, and they do not indulge in its corruptions. In a word, those in heaven rejected worldliness while they lived on earth.

Like the Jews in captivity, we may be in Babylon, but we are never of Babylon. We live separated lives from it.

Just as God destroyed Old Testament Babylon, God will destroy anti-Christian society in this world. Revelation 18 details His destruction of Babylon over the course of twenty-four verses. We have all of Revelation 18 summarized in one verse in Revelation 14:8, when it says, *"Babylon is fallen, is fallen, that great city, because she made all nations drink of the wine of the wrath of her fornication."* When it says, *"Babylon is fallen,"* here we have the use of what we call the prophetic aorist—something that is so certain to occur in the future that it is stated in the past tense as though it has already occurred.

In John's day, Babylon was Rome, and when he wrote this verse, Rome had not yet fallen and would not fall for another 200 years. But he could say, "It is fallen. It is done. It is over." John could see that God was going to destroy this worldly society, and its destruction was so certain, he could state it as though it had already happened.

The problem is that Babylon has been reinvented and reestablished by Satan over and over again throughout history. The ungodly lust after the sins of anti-Christian culture: the pride, the sensuality, the vice, and the materialism that it offers. The ungodly keep reestablishing new Babylons generation after generation. Worldliness was a problem in John's day; it has been a problem throughout the centuries, it is a problem now, and it will continue to be a problem until this world is destroyed by Christ at His second coming. When Jesus returns, we will have a new world wherein dwells righteousness, and Babylon will be no more.

God makes it clear that those who fornicate with the world, who have intercourse with its pride, its vice, its materialism, and its evil, will drink the cup of God's wrath. The worldling who plunges into the arms of Babylon will not be saved by Babylon from the wrath of God. All of the wealth, all of the support structures, all of the cultural enjoyments, and all of the social cohesion that takes place in Babylon will be destroyed by God. Where will those be who loved and served Babylon when that occurs?

When people do not trust in the true God, they trust in government, in society, in false religion, and all the support structures which that false god supplies. God is going to smash it all, and where will they be without their gods? Let us not be envious of what Babylon has to offer, nor of those who drink up its sinful pleasures. Their foot will slide in due time. Everything they value so much will eat their flesh with fire in the end, as James 5:1–3 threatens.

The message is this: Envy not the worldling. Do not desire the dainties Babylon offers you. Love not the world, because the world passes away with the lusts thereof, and their place will be found no more. Our comfort, as we look at the world and the anti-Christian society in which we live, is that it shall be destroyed, but those who do the will of God will abide forever.

The Third Message of Warning

The third message of warning is in verses 9 to 11. It says, "*And the third angel followed them, saying with a loud voice, If any man worship the beast and his image, and receive his mark in his forehead, or in his hand,* [10] *The same shall drink of the wine of the wrath of God, which is poured out without mixture into the cup of his indignation; and he shall be tormented with fire and brimstone in the presence of the holy angels, and in the presence of the Lamb:* [11] *And the smoke of their torment ascendeth up for ever and ever: and they have no rest day nor night, who worship the beast and his image, and whosoever receiveth the mark of his name.*"

Notice how each of these messages becomes increasingly severe as they are delivered. First, we had a general warning of impending judgment, and a call to repentance and reformation of life and attitude toward God in verses 6 and 7. Secondly, in verse 8 we had a specific declaration that the worldly society in which the wicked lived would be destroyed, all the vice and opulence they enjoyed would be eliminated, and they would be left with nothing but the wrath of God.

But now in verses 9 to 11 we see this third message which is the most severe of all. It is a straightforward promise that the wicked will burn in hell forever, tormented in fire and brimstone, tormented day and night, and tormented without rest and without remission for all eternity. There is no more dire a threat than this, and if such a threat as this does not move men to repentance, then nothing will. A greater negative motivation could not be supplied, because nothing more awful than this is conceivable that could ever happen to a human being. Hell is the worst thing that could ever happen to any human—worse than any other experience that humans have ever had, or could ever have.

Notice the people in view in verse 9: *"And the third angel followed them, saying with a loud voice, If any man worship the beast and his image, and receive his mark in his forehead, or in his hand."* Then notice the last half of verse 11: *"who worship the beast and his image, and whosoever receiveth the mark of his name."*

Verses 9 to 11 start and end with the same people. All those who worship the god of human government as the final and ultimate authority in their lives—all those whose thinking with their head and actions with their hands are directed by the blasphemy of the human authorities to defy God—are all going to be the objects of the undiluted wrath of God. Those who think and act according to the direction of anti-Christian civil government, in defiance of God and His laws and authority, will be cast into hell.

What is hell like? Notice the description. First of all, it says in verse 10 they will be tormented with fire and brimstone. Brimstone is sulfur that is on fire. The idea is that of a volcano that is exploding and putting out fire and burning rock. There are some who like to say that the fire in hell is not literal. I disagree with that. But for the sake of argument, let us grant that the fire is not literal, but symbolic.

We need to understand that when we have symbolism in the Bible, the reality is always greater than the symbol that represents it. We had animal sacrifices. They were symbols of the final sacrifice of Jesus. Was Jesus' sacrifice greater than any animal sacrifice that symbolized it? Many more examples could be produced showing that the reality any symbol represents is always greater than the symbol that represents it. So, if hell is not real fire, and it is just symbolized by real fire, then the reality of the suffering in hell is going to be something greater than being burned in real fire. The awfulness of hell is not mitigated by saying that the fire is symbolic. If it is symbolic, then the suffering that people in hell experience is greater than would be produced by burning in actual fire.

Secondly, it says they are tormented in the presence of the holy angels and the Lamb; that is, they must not only endure torment of body but torment of soul and spirit as well. Part of this torment is enduring the utter humiliation and the abject shame that comes upon them as they dwell in the sight and presence of those they fought against. They have to endure utter humiliation before Christ and the angels, and they have to endure the shame of their own moral defilement in the presence of the perfect holiness of Jesus and the angels.

At some stage in your job experience you may have done some really dirty, filthy, rotten job like cleaning septic tanks that covered you, not just with dirt, but filth. Ashamed to be seen, your first objective after work would be to clean yourself up before anyone saw you. Understand that the moral filth and defilement of those in hell is infinitely greater and more loathsome. They are going to have to spend eternity dressed in these filthy rags in the presence of a holy Jesus and the holy angels, and forever bear the shame of the evil they have done.

Thirdly, not only are they going to be tormented with fire and brimstone in the presence of the holy angels and the Lamb, but it says they are going to be in that condition forever and ever. That is, the punishment is endless because their guilt always exists. Their guilt is never cleansed, and therefore their punishment never ends.

Fourthly, it also says they have no rest from that torment, day or night. You go to work and work all day long, but you get to go home and rest at night. You get to sleep and get away from it all. Sometimes you take a vacation, and you get a reprieve. On occasion you have a really bad headache or some intense pain, but you can take painkillers and experience some relief.

There is none of that in hell. There is no reprieve, there is no rest, and there is no moment in which this suffering can be escaped. They have no rest day or night. Not only does it go on for eternity, but it goes on twenty-four hours a day. The torment is constant, the torment is unremitting, and the torment is unending. There is no reprieve, there is no escape, and there is no relief.

This is one of the clearest passages in all the Scriptures regarding the horror of hell. There is no universalism here. Jesus is not going to save everybody. There are going to be lots and lots of people, great multitudes of them, in hell. Furthermore, there is no annihilationism here. It is not the case that when you die, you go into nothingness, you lose consciousness, and you cease to exist.

There is no universalism, and there is no annihilationism; there is simply the worst imaginable suffering in body and soul that one can experience for all eternity, without remission, day and night, forever and ever, and without end. Who winds up in that condition? Everyone who has the mark of the beast. Who has the mark of the beast? Everyone that is unsaved.

Either you have the seal of God in your forehead or you have the mark of the beast. There are no other categories of people on this earth. We saw the mark of the beast has been going on as long as the beast has existed. This passage is not describing some grossly evil people who live during the tribulation. It is speaking about all unbelievers who have rejected God as their ultimate authority and embraced men as their ultimate authority, and thereby embraced Satan as their ultimate authority.

My exhortation to you is this: Flee from the wrath to come. This is what the wrath to come looks like. I have heard people say things like this: "I do not want to go to heaven. I want to go to hell because all my buddies are going to be there, and we are going to play cards together." Do not delude yourself. Think of yourself when you have been the sickest. You have had the flu, with a high temperature, physically weak, and you are throwing up. Do you feel like playing cards with your friends when you feel like that? You are so miserable, you just want to be left alone, and you just want it to be over.

But earthly sickness is nothing compared to the misery of hell, and it will never be over. There will not be any joy in hell. The Bible says there will be weeping and wailing and gnashing of teeth, in outer darkness, where the smoke of their torment ascends up forever and ever.

This is what Jesus came to save us from. This is why we love the Lord Jesus. Jesus experienced hell for sinners on the cross when God poured out His wrath on Him. He experienced God's wrath, not just for one person, but for all of His elect, a multitude which no man can number.

The degree of suffering of Jesus on the cross is incomprehensible to us, and yet what He did has fully paid the punishment for all of our sins so we might be delivered from hell. This is why we ought to love Him with all of our heart and soul and mind and strength, because this is what He saved us from.

It is critically important to understand that when people minimize the hell that Jesus saved us from, they minimize the value of His salvation and the significance of His suffering, and thus the worship and gratitude that is due to Him. Those who cast off the doctrine of hell cast off the value and worth of Jesus Christ and His sacrifice on behalf of His people. If hell does not exist, then why did Jesus need to die? If hell is a benign place, then why is the work of Christ in saving us from it of any real importance? To minimize the doctrine of hell is to minimize both the glory of Christ and the value of His saving work.

Repent. His judgment is come. All the worldly pleasures that seem to supply you with so much fulfillment are going to be destroyed and stripped away, and all that will be left is the naked exposure of your wicked person before God as He pours out His wrath upon you. The Bible says our God is a consuming fire; and under His eye, you will be tormented for eternity for your defiance and rebellion against Him if you do not repent of your sins, and if you do not believe in Jesus Christ as your Lord and Savior.

Flee from the wrath to come by fleeing to Christ. Cast yourself on Him and say, "Lord Jesus, I do repent of my rebellion against You, and I do plead with You to save me from my sins." The Bible says that if we come to Him, He will not cast us out. If we come to Him laboring and heavy-laden under our sins and guilt and shame and fears of damnation, He will take that burden from us, and He will give us forgiveness and redemption and reconciliation and approval.

Notice verse 12: *"Here is the patience of the saints: here are they that keep the commandments of God, and the faith of Jesus."* The fact that this never-ending punishment awaits those who persecute the church and who hate Christ should encourage the believers to patiently hold fast to their profession of Christ under every sort of affliction and trial.

When you see what the ungodly are headed toward, you can endure some persecution to avoid their outcomes. You can afford to be patient, waiting to be delivered into what is described in verses 1 to 5, knowing you are going to be delivered out from what is described in verses 9 to 11.

What does it say about the believers in verse 12? They keep the commandments of God, and they keep the faith of Jesus. They are righteous in their behavior, and they are steadfast in their loyalty. In other words, their faith produces fruit, and the fruit of their faith is that they keep the commandments of God. They keep faithful to Jesus, and they keep faith in Jesus until the end of their days.

The reason we can afford to be patient with being under the heel of the dragon and his helpers is because we know our outcome and we know theirs. We simply wait with patience until those outcomes actually occur.

Notice verse 13: *"And I heard a voice from heaven saying unto me,*

Write, Blessed are the dead which die in the Lord from henceforth." We just finished reading the description of the dead who die with the mark of the beast. But what is the result of those who die with the seal of God, who die in union with the Lord?

It says, "*Blessed are the dead which die in the Lord from henceforth*"; that is, from the point of their death onward, they are blessed. While they were here, they were undergoing the misery of the oppression described in chapters 12 and 13. They were under the heel of Satan and his helpers. But from the point of their death forward, all they know is unmixed blessedness for all eternity.

It says, "*Blessed are the dead which die in the Lord from henceforth: Yea, saith the Spirit, that they may rest from their labours; and their works do follow them.*" Even if the believers are put to death because they keep the commandments of God and the faith of Christ, they are assured of a blessed life after death. What does that blessedness consist of? It consists of rest and reward. They "*rest from their labours, and their works do follow them.*"

In severe contrast to the outcome of their persecutors described in verses 10 and 11, where there is no rest and there is no reward, here believers have both rest and reward. They are rewarded for being patient in this life and remaining obedient and faithful to Christ until the end, and they have eternal rest from any more spiritual warfare.

Revelation is teaching us to hang on, because the best is yet to come. And what about those who seem to have it so good now? Pity them. Call them to repentance. But know that often they ignore judgment, they love Babylon, and they have embraced the blasphemy of anti-Christian government, anti-Christian religion, anti-Christian society, and all their anti-Christian friends who share the mark of those who worship the dragon.

You have to live separated lives from them. You speak to them like an angel speaking from heaven. You, as it were, shout across the chasm and divide between your life and their lives, and you say to them, "Come over and be saved!" But if they will not, the day will come when hell will be their outcome.

You look at your outcome, verses 1 to 5; you look at their outcome, verses 6 to 11; and therefore you are patient, verse 12. You keep on being faithful and loyal and obedient, and you know that in the end, you will have rest and reward, verse 13. This is the encouragement we have in our spiritual warfare in our lives. May the Lord keep it front and center before you so that when you go out into Babylon, you see it for what it is—and as a result, you do not allow yourself to be drawn in by its anti-Christian charms.

45

The Reaping of the Righteous and the Wicked, Revelation 14:14–20

> "14 *And I looked, and behold a white cloud, and upon the*
> *cloud one sat like unto the Son of man, having on his head a*
> *golden crown, and in his hand a sharp sickle.* 15 *And another*
> *angel came out of the temple, crying with a loud voice to him*
> *that sat on the cloud, Thrust in thy sickle, and reap: for the*
> *time is come for thee to reap; for the harvest of the earth is*
> *ripe.* 16 *And he that sat on the cloud thrust in his sickle on the*
> *earth; and the earth was reaped.* 17 *And another angel came*
> *out of the temple which is in heaven, he also having a sharp*
> *sickle.* 18 *And another angel came out from the altar, which*
> *had power over fire; and cried with a loud cry to him that had*
> *the sharp sickle, saying, Thrust in thy sharp sickle, and gather*
> *the clusters of the vine of the earth; for her grapes are fully*
> *ripe.* 19 *And the angel thrust in his sickle into the earth, and*
> *gathered the vine of the earth, and cast it into the great wine-*
> *press of the wrath of God.* 20 *And the winepress was trodden*
> *without the city, and blood came out of the winepress, even*
> *unto the horse bridles, by the space of a thousand and six*
> *hundred furlongs."*

One of the great struggles believers have wrestled with through the ages is the prosperity and success of the wicked, while the people of God are oppressed and persecuted. This prosperity of the wicked and the oppression of the people of God seems to be plainly unjust. It appears that, in this world, evil is rewarded and righteousness is punished. We ask ourselves: Where is God in all of this?

Asaph struggled with this whole dilemma in Psalm 73. There he described the prosperity of the wicked and all the advantages they enjoyed in life. The wicked scorned and mocked God, and yet they were not troubled with difficulties, they enjoyed good health, and they had great material prosperity. They were esteemed in the eyes of men and were looked upon with approval, envy, and admiration by all around them.

But the believers know little of prosperity and are plagued with difficulties. They are persecuted by the world and they live in poverty. Their efforts to live godly lives are mocked, and their efforts to serve God seem to produce little or no results.

When Asaph observed this, and considered the contrast between the prosperity of the wicked and the difficulties experienced by the righteous, he became discouraged, confused, and disheartened. He wondered if it would be better to give up serving the Lord and just go join the world. What preserved him from taking that course of action was the thought of the long-term results of making that choice. He remembered that, in the long run, the humble believer will be received and rewarded by God, while the prosperous wicked will be cast down into destruction and hell.

The lesson Asaph learned and the lesson that we must learn is this: The believer must live with a consciousness of eternal outcomes far more than he does with a consciousness of his present circumstances. The believer must live more by faith than he does by feelings. The believer must live more by the promises than he does by his perceptions. The believer must live more for the Day of Judgment than he lives for the day he is presently in.

This lesson that Asaph struggled with, that you and I struggle with, and believers in every generation have struggled with, is powerfully addressed in Revelation 14. When we see the prosperity and success and power of anti-Christian government, anti-Christian religion, anti-Christian society, and the anti-Christian populace; and when we see the persecution and poverty and plight of Christians as they serve the Lord, it is very easy to wonder if we are on the wrong side, and if it is a vain thing to live for Christ.

Revelation 14 says to you with great forcefulness that when you look at the ultimate outcomes of the believers and the unbelievers in the end, and not just in the short term, it is the height of wisdom to serve the Lord, and it is the height of folly to rebel against Him like the dragon and his helpers have done.

The indescribable blessedness of those who serve the Lord is set forth in the clearest terms in 14:1–5, which we looked at previously.

The unspeakable wretchedness of those who rebel against the Lord is set forth in the most horrific terms in 14:6–11, which we also looked at previously.

Seeing the long-term blessedness of those who serve the Lord and the long-term unspeakable wretchedness of those who rebel against the Lord is the reason why we can afford to be patient under our present sufferings, and continue to keep the commandments of God and the faith of Jesus Christ. This is why we can endure persecution to the point of death, because those who die in the Lord will forever rest from their wearisome spiritual warfare, and they will forever rejoice in the work they did for the Lord.

Now the question arises: How did those in 14:1–5 wind up in heaven? How did those in 14:6–11 wind up in hell? The answer is found in our passage in verses 14 to 20.

There we have a description of the final judgment which will come at the end of the world, in which Christ will separate those who served Him from those who defied Him. Those who served Him will be brought into heaven as described in verses 1 to 5 of this chapter. Those who defied Christ and served Satan will be cast into hell as described in verses 6 to 11 of this chapter.

The final Day of Judgment will demonstrate the wisdom of resisting the temptation to trade temporal pleasures and the approval of men for deliverance from persecution for serving Christ. This final Day of Judgment will also demonstrate the folly of those who refused to serve Christ so they could enjoy the temporal praise and acceptance of man and the prosperity this world has to offer.

On the Day of Judgment, the downtrodden Christians will be vindicated and exalted and delivered by Christ, and the powerful and exalted and wealthy rebels against Christ will be condemned and shamed and cast into hell. The final Day of Judgment is what we live for.

This is why we repented of our sins and became saved in the first place, because there is a Day of Judgment coming. This is why we engaged in the difficulty of confessing Christ and serving Christ before the eyes of the world, because there is a Day of Judgment coming. This is why we endure persecution and rejection and mockery and scorn from the world without backing down or backing up, because there is a Day of Judgment coming. This is why we are content under poverty and difficulty and pain and sorrow, because there is a Day of

Judgment coming. This is why we are faithful to Christ even if it costs us our lives, because there is a Day of Judgment coming.

The coming Day of Judgment will right all of the wrongs done to us. It will be the day when God exercises His vengeance on the wicked, and it will be the day when He vindicates and rewards His faithful saints. Therefore, all we do, all we think, and all we say is done in light of the coming Day of Judgment and how it will be viewed by Christ. Every day, all throughout the day, we are living with the Day of Judgment on our minds, guiding and directing the choices we make, the words we say, and the thoughts we think.

The wicked think they have no one to answer to but themselves. But they are in for a very rude awakening when the God whose existence they denied is the very God they must now give an answer to, and they will have no answer that will justify what they have done. They will see on that day that all they did was utterly indefensible; and speechless, they will be cast into hell.

This is the message our passage is teaching us. We see now that we are brought once again to the end of the age in this fourth parallel section. The fourth parallel section started in chapter 12 with the birth of Christ. Now it ends with the second coming of Christ. Each of these parallel sections starts with Christ's first coming and ends with Christ's second coming.

Our passage in verses 14–20 contains two visions: The first is the harvest of grain in verses 14 to 16; the second is the harvest of the grapes of wrath in verses 17 to 20. The first vision describes the gathering of believers from off the earth who will live with Christ forever; the second vision describes the judgment of the unbelievers who will be crushed under the wrath of God and cast into hell.

Here we have the fulfillment of the prophecy of John the Baptist regarding Christ, who warned the Jews that the coming Messiah would bring judgment to the world. John the Baptist said of Jesus in Matthew 3:12, "*Whose fan is in his hand, and he will thoroughly purge his floor, and gather his wheat into the garner; but he will burn up the chaff with unquenchable fire.*" The gathering of His saints and the pouring out of His wrath on the wicked is prophesied by John the Baptist at Christ's first coming, and it is fulfilled in Revelation at Christ's second coming.

The Reaping of the Righteous into Heaven

The reaping of the righteous into heaven is spoken of in verses 14 to 16. Notice verse 14: *"And I looked, and behold a white cloud, and upon the cloud one sat like unto the Son of man, having on his head a golden crown, and in his hand a sharp sickle."*

In verse 14, John sees a vision of a white cloud, and one like the Son of man seated on that cloud. This is spoken of in Daniel 7:13–14, which is a description of the Lord Jesus coming in judgment. It says: *"I saw in the night visions, and, behold, one like the Son of man came with the clouds of heaven, and came to the Ancient of days, and they brought him near before him.* [14] *And there was given him dominion, and glory, and a kingdom, that all people, nations, and languages, should serve him: his dominion is an everlasting dominion, which shall not pass away, and his kingdom that which shall not be destroyed."*

Daniel 7:13 pictures the Lord Jesus as being like unto the Son of man and coming with the clouds of heaven. This is what John describes in Revelation 14:14. This title, *"the Son of man,"* is a reference to Jesus Christ Himself. He was introduced to us under this title in Revelation 1:13. It says, *"And in the midst of the seven candlesticks one like unto the Son of man, clothed with a garment down to the foot, and girt about the paps with a golden girdle.* [14] *His head and his hairs were white like wool, as white as snow; and his eyes were as a flame of fire;* [15] *And his feet like unto fine brass, as if they burned in a furnace; and his voice as the sound of many waters."* It goes on to describe the Lord Jesus in verse 18 as being the One who was alive, who died, and behold, He is alive forevermore, and has the keys of hell and death.

This person sitting on this cloud in Revelation 14:14, based on Daniel 7:13–14 and Revelation 1:13–18, is the Lord Jesus Christ. Therefore, the scene depicted in Revelation 14:14 is that of the last judgment in which Jesus will judge the world. Jesus is sitting on a cloud, which we previously identified as a symbol of judgment when we expounded Revelation 1:7 when it says, *"Behold, he comes with clouds."* Clouds are a symbol of God coming in judgment. It also says in verse 14 that Jesus has a crown on His head, which is a symbol of sovereignty and authority, and in particular with this crown, a symbol of triumph.

The golden crown and the white cloud symbolize that Jesus is coming in righteous and triumphant judgment. This is not the only place this coming is described. Matthew 24:30–31 says: *"And then shall appear the sign of the Son of man in heaven: and then shall all the tribes of the earth mourn, and they shall see the Son of man coming in the clouds of heaven with power and great glory.* [31] *And he shall send his angels with a great sound of a trumpet, and they shall gather together his elect from the four winds, from one end of heaven to the other."* Here we also see Jesus coming in righteous and triumphant judgment. At His second coming, Christ will gather His people to Himself as He comes in the clouds of heaven with power and great glory.

The second coming of Christ for His elect is symbolized by the harvesting of ripe grain. We see Him with a sickle, and He is reaping the grain of the earth. This is something that Jesus Himself spoke of in Mark 4:26–29. *"And he"* (Jesus), *"said, So is the kingdom of God, as if a man should cast seed into the ground;* [27] *And should sleep, and rise night and day, and the seed should spring and grow up, he knoweth not how.* [28] *For the earth bringeth forth fruit of herself; first the blade, then the ear, after that the full corn in the ear.* [29] *But when the fruit is brought forth, immediately he putteth in the sickle, because the harvest is come."* This imagery of harvesting grain with a sickle symbolizes Christ harvesting the souls of men at the end of the world on the Day of Judgment.

Revelation 14:15 says: *"And another angel came out of the temple, crying with a loud voice to him that sat on the cloud, Thrust in thy sickle, and reap: for the time is come for thee to reap; for the harvest of the earth is ripe."*

In verse 14 we have seen the Son of Man sitting on the cloud with a sickle in His hand, but He is not doing anything. He is just sitting there with a sickle. He is ready to do something, but He has not been given permission to do anything yet. In verse 15, an angel comes out of the temple. This is the first of three angels that are going to appear in this passage. We will keep track of these angels. We are going to call them the first angel, the second angel, and the third angel. This is the first angel.

This first angel comes out of the temple—that is, out of the presence of God the Father from the temple which is in heaven. He bears a message from the Father to the Son, and the message is this: It is now time to harvest the souls of earth because the harvest is fully ripe. In

Mark 13:32, Jesus said, regarding His second coming and the final judgment, *"But of that day and that hour knoweth no man, no, not the angels which are in heaven, neither the Son, but the Father."* Only the Father knows when the time of the final judgment and the second coming is supposed to occur. In His humanity, Christ does not know. The Father sends a messenger to the Son, telling Him that the time has arrived. It is time to return and reap the earth.

Some people think it strange that the Father would send an angel to convey the message to the Son, and not just say it directly to the Son. But remember that Jesus in His humanity was subject to the will of the Father and was subordinate to the Father. If it is not strange that the Father would send an angel to strengthen His Son in the garden of Gethsemane, then it should not seem strange that God would send an angel to inform His Son when it is time for His second coming and the final judgment. This is what occurs. The Father sends an angel to the Son to say to Him that it is time.

Notice verse 16: *"And he that sat on the cloud thrust in his sickle on the earth; and the earth was reaped."* This reaping of grain symbolizes Christ harvesting all the souls that belong to Him, and gathering all His elect out of the world. He is doing what John the Baptist said He would do: He is gathering His wheat into His garner—that is, He is gathering His children into His storehouse which is heaven.

The Reaping of the Wicked into Hell

The reaping of the wicked into hell is set forth in verses 17 to 20. Verse 17 says, *"And another angel came out of the temple which is in heaven, he also having a sharp sickle."* Here the second angel appears. The first angel conveyed a message to Christ. This second angel appears with a sharp sickle in his hand, prepared to reap at the commandment of God, and he is sitting there waiting.

It is interesting to note that, in this passage, Jesus Himself gathers the harvest of believers, which are symbolized as being grain. But God commissions an angel to gather the wicked for their judgment. Jesus said to the believers in John 14:1–3, *"Let not your heart be troubled: ye believe in God, believe also in me. [2] In my Father's house are many mansions: if it were not so, I would have told you. I go to prepare a place for you. [3] And if I go and prepare a place for you, I will come again, and receive you unto myself; that where I am, there ye may be also."*

An angel is sufficient to take control of the wicked and bring them to judgment by force. But in our passage, it is Jesus Himself who personally comes to gather His saints into His loving arms and bring them safely into His loving home.

Notice the parable of the wheat and the tares in Matthew 13:24–30: "*Another parable put he forth unto them, saying, The kingdom of heaven is likened unto a man which sowed good seed in his field:*
[25] *But while men slept, his enemy came and sowed tares among the wheat, and went his way.* [26] *But when the blade was sprung up, and brought forth fruit, then appeared the tares also.* [27] *So the servants of the householder came and said unto him, Sir, didst not thou sow good seed in thy field? from whence then hath it tares?* [28] *He said unto them, An enemy hath done this. The servants said unto him, Wilt thou then that we go and gather them up?* [29] *But he said, Nay; lest while ye gather up the tares, ye root up also the wheat with them.* [30] *Let both grow together until the harvest: and in the time of harvest I will say to the reapers, Gather ye together first the tares, and bind them in bundles to burn them: but gather the wheat into my barn.*"

The disciples wanted to know the meaning of the parable. It says in verse 36: "*Then Jesus sent the multitude away, and went into the house: and his disciples came unto him, saying, Declare unto us the parable of the tares of the field.* [37] *He answered and said unto them, He that soweth the good seed is the Son of man;* [38] *The field is the world; the good seed are the children of the kingdom; but the tares are the children of the wicked one;* [39] *The enemy that sowed them is the devil; the harvest is the end of the world; and the reapers are the angels.* [40] *As therefore the tares are gathered and burned in the fire; so shall it be in the end of this world.* [41] *The Son of man shall send forth his angels, and they shall gather out of his kingdom all things that offend, and them which do iniquity;* [42] *And shall cast them into a furnace of fire: there shall be wailing and gnashing of teeth.* [43] *Then shall the righteous shine forth as the sun in the kingdom of their Father. Who hath ears to hear, let him hear.*"

Notice that He sends an angel to gather the wicked and to cast them into hell. This is what is happening in our passage. An angel is being sent, and he is going to reap the wicked, and the wicked are going to be cast into hell.

Revelation 14:18 says, "*And another angel. . .*" Here is angel number three. The first angel speaks to Christ, the second angel appears with a sickle in his hand, and the third angel comes to say something to the second angel. Verse 18: *"And another angel came out from the altar, which had power over fire; and cried with a loud cry to him that had the sharp sickle, saying, Thrust in thy sharp sickle, and gather the clusters of the vine of the earth; for her grapes are fully ripe."*

A third angel comes from the altar of incense to the second angel. We were introduced to the altar of incense in 8:1–5, and we saw it was the place where the prayers of the saints for vengeance against their persecutors were offered. It is in the final judgment that these prayers for vengeance are going to be fully answered, and it is then that the persecuted believers will see justice executed on their enemies for their cruel treatment of the believers. This third angel comes from the altar of incense and he has *"power over fire,"* which means he has power over the fire that was offered on the altar of incense.

Revelation 8:3–5 says, *"And another angel came and stood at the altar, having a golden censer; and there was given unto him much incense, that he should offer it with the prayers of all saints upon the golden altar which was before the throne. [4] And the smoke of the incense, which came with the prayers of the saints, ascended up before God out of the angel's hand."* Now here is our verse: "[5] *And the angel took the censer, and filled it with fire of the altar, and cast it into the earth: and there were voices, and thunderings, and lightnings, and an earthquake."* Verse 5 heralded the beginning of the seven trumpets of judgment.

It is this same angel that is now appearing in Revelation 14:18. He is the angel from the altar that has power to cast the fire of the judgment of God down upon the earth. He says to the second angel that is standing there with a sickle in his hand, "It is time for you to reap." This third angel exercises the authority given to him by God to bring the fire of God's judgment down upon the wicked, and that is exactly what he is doing in verse 18 when he says, *"Thrust in thy sharp sickle, and gather the clusters of the vine of the earth; for her grapes are fully ripe."*

This third angel is bearing God's answer to the prayers of the saints for justice, and that answer is contained in the instructions he gives to this second angel. The metaphor here is of the harvest of grapes out of a vineyard, a different metaphor than previously which was the harvest of grain out of a field. This shows the qualitatively different nature between the saved and the lost. Grapes are not grain. The idea of a harvest of grapes as a symbol of judgment is used in the Old Testament. It is used in Isaiah 63:3–4 and in Joel 3:13.

The third angel commands the second angel to gather the grapes because they are fully ripe—that is, the wicked have attained to the full number of them that shall ever be, and they have accomplished the full degree of wickedness they will ever be allowed to carry out. In a word, the iniquity of the children of Satan is full, and the time for their judgment has come.

Notice verses 19 and 20: *"And the angel thrust in his sickle into the earth, and gathered the vine of the earth, and cast it into the great winepress of the wrath of God.* [20] *And the winepress was trodden without the city, and blood came out of the winepress, even unto the horse bridles, by the space of a thousand and six hundred furlongs."*

The second angel thrusts his sickle into the earth. He gathers all the grapes and casts them into the winepress of the wrath of God. There, they are crushed under the wrath of God. It specifically says this takes place outside of the city, *"the city"* being a metaphor for the church. When it takes place outside the city, it means outside the City of God, outside the New Jerusalem which is the church of God.

In other words, the wicked do not belong to the church, they are not in the church, and they are shut out of the church. They are shut out from the presence of God, they are shut out from the society of the redeemed, and never again will there be any mixture of the wheat and the tares living together.

This judgment is a terrible judgment. The imagery is that of being crushed in the same way that grapes are crushed in the winepress. The treading of the winepress represents the vengeance of God in crushing all of His enemies, and the red juice of the crushed grapes strongly suggests the shedding and flowing of blood.

So great is the number of the wicked, and so great is the degree of vengeance exercised on them, that the blood that flowed from the winepress is as deep as a horse's bridle is off the ground. That is about four feet off the ground. Our text says the blood extends 1,600 furlongs. The measurement described as a furlong is a translation of the Greek word *"stadia."* A stadia is about 660 feet, about an eighth of a mile. This pool of blood is about 200 miles long and wide. Therefore, the blood is said to be about four feet deep, 200 miles wide and 200 miles long.

If this measurement is taken literally, that is over 30 cubic miles of blood. There are over a trillion gallons in a cubic mile. That is over 30 trillion gallons of blood. That is tremendously more blood than all the humans in the world have put together. This is clearly not a literal number.

These measurements are symbolic. Blood to the horse's bridle is a symbolic way of speaking of a great military defeat because horses were used in military battle in that day. When they had great slaughter, blood was splattered everywhere, even on the horses. A soldier might say, "We slaughtered the enemy, and their blood was splattered all over our horses' bridles."

Sixteen hundred stadia is the number given. The number sixteen is four times four, or four squared. The number one hundred is ten times ten, or ten squared. Therefore, we have four squared times ten squared, i.e., we have 16 times 100, which equals 1,600, the number in our text.

We know that numbers are used symbolically, and the number four symbolizes the earth. Ten symbolizes perfection. These two numbers are multiplied. Whenever we have the multiplication of numbers that are used symbolically, we have an intensification of the symbolic concept they represent.

What is being said is that the whole earth (4x4) will be perfectly, completely, and totally (10x10) judged by God, and no place and no person will escape His wrath and vengeance. The message being conveyed by this symbolism is that God's judgment will be unspeakably dreadful (blood to the horse's bridle) and it will be totally complete. It will cover the four points of the earth to totality and perfection.

This completes the description of the final Day of Judgment. Revelation 14 is one of the most sobering chapters in the entire New Testament, as it not only describes the glory of the redeemed in verses 1 to 5, but also the horrors of hell in verses 6 to 11. It describes the nature of the last judgment in verses 14 to 20 in very shocking and terrifying terms. It reinforces what the Scriptures declare when they say, *"It is a fearful thing to fall into the hands of the living God."*

Therefore, repent of your rebellion and receive Christ as your Lord and Savior, in order that you may be part of the harvest of grain that the Lord Jesus reaps when He comes again and receives His people to Himself, and takes them to the place described in verses 1 to 5.

Do not be defiant and rebellious against Christ; do not be among the grapes of wrath which He will trample out in that day. All of the wicked will be crushed beneath His wrath. None will escape. All will be cast into the dreadful hell described in verses 10 and 11, in which they drink the wine of the wrath of God which is poured out without dilution into the cup of His indignation. All the wicked will be tormented with fire and brimstone in the presence of the holy angels and in the presence of the Lamb, and the smoke of their torment will ascend up forever and ever, and they will have no rest day or night.

Everyone who is not a Christian has the mark of the beast. Every one of them is a servant of the dragon and his helpers. They all think and act like Satan does. Every one of them will be cast into hell.

This chapter declares that there are two destinies that could not be more different, and there is a Day of Judgment that is going to decide those destinies. The message of the gospel is this: Repent of your sins and rebellion against God, and believe in Jesus Christ as your Lord and Savior, so that your destiny will be living on Mount Zion with the Lamb, instead of weeping and wailing and gnashing your teeth in the outer darkness of the endless torment of hell.

Choose your destiny by choosing Christ. When you choose Christ, you will find that He will come and reap you into His kingdom on that day, and so shall you ever be with the Lord.

May we prepare for the Day of Judgment. May we think every day and every moment of every day about the Day of Judgment; and may it be the controlling thought that guides all our words, all our choices, and all our actions, because it is coming. This is what it will look like. The question is: Will you be gathered as grapes, or will you be gathered as wheat? If you have never done so, may you repent now. May you receive Christ as Savior now.

46

The Prologue to the Seven Vials, Revelation 15:1–4

> "1 *And I saw another sign in heaven, great and marvellous, seven angels having the seven last plagues; for in them is filled up the wrath of God.* 2 *And I saw as it were a sea of glass mingled with fire: and them that had gotten the victory over the beast, and over his image, and over his mark, and over the number of his name, stand on the sea of glass, having the harps of God.* 3 *And they sing the song of Moses the servant of God, and the song of the Lamb, saying, Great and marvellous are thy works, Lord God Almighty; just and true are thy ways, thou King of saints.* 4 *Who shall not fear thee, O Lord, and glorify thy name? for thou only art holy: for all nations shall come and worship before thee; for thy judgments are made manifest.*"

Chapter 15 opens the fifth parallel section of the book of Revelation. This book is not written in a linear fashion. It is not a consecutive chronological sequence in which things later in the book occur after things written earlier in the book.

The book of Revelation is written in a cyclical fashion. It is made up of seven sections which are all parallel to each other, each of which takes us on a journey from the first coming of Christ to the second coming of Christ. These parallel sections are not identical to one another. They differ from one another in the themes they emphasize.

In chapters 1 through 3, we saw the theme of the spiritual warfare that would take place within the churches that exist between the first and second coming of Christ. This was the section that described the seven churches.

In chapters 4 through 7, we saw the theme of the works the wicked do both in the world and against the church between the first and second coming of Christ. This was the section that described the seven seals.

In chapters 8 through 11, we saw the theme of the temporal judgments of God that would fall on the wicked between the first and second coming of Christ. This was the section that described the seven trumpets.

In chapters 12 through 14, we saw the theme of the description of Satan and his helpers who work together to persecute the church between the first and second coming of Christ. We saw the dragon, who represents Satan, assisted by four helpers: anti-Christian government, represented by the beast out of the sea; anti-Christian religion, represented by the beast out of the earth; anti-Christian society, represented by the great city Babylon; and the anti-Christian populace, represented by those who have the mark of the beast.

In this fifth parallel section, which covers chapters 15 and 16, we see the theme of God's anger against the willfully defiant. This is the section that describes the seven vials of the wrath of God being poured out.

In the third parallel section, the seven trumpets of God's judgment sounded in chapters 8 through 11. The purpose of the trumpet judgments was to bring temporal, physical, and spiritual judgments on the wicked as a partial retribution for the evil they have done to the saints, in order to provide them with a powerful incentive to repent before the final wrath of God falls upon them.

The purpose of the trumpet judgments was partly punitive, in that there was a partial retribution for the evil they had done. But it was also rehabilitative, in that there was a powerful incentive for them to repent. The trumpets were a sample of God's wrath to come and a warning to flee from the far greater wrath that will follow if they do not repent.

What was the response unsaved people gave to the seven trumpet judgments? We read in 9:20–21 that after these trumpets sounded, the rest of the men who were not killed by these plagues *"repented not of the works of their hands, that they should not worship devils, and idols of gold, and silver, and brass, and stone, and of wood; which neither can see, nor hear, nor walk; [21]Neither repented they of their murders, nor of their sorceries, nor of their fornication, nor of their thefts."*

Even though these trumpet judgments were lesser judgments, and even though they contained a gracious element within them of calling men to repent so they might not experience the greater wrath yet to come, they still did not listen. Not only did they not repent, but they also hardened themselves further against God's trumpet judgments.

What happens when God brings lesser judgments as an incentive for men to repent, but instead they only harden their hearts further? God does not just walk away. God brings greater judgments that are far worse, and which ultimately result in the destruction of the unrepentant. The trumpets of warning sounded, and when the sound is ignored and defied, then the vials of God's wrath are poured out.

We have an illustration of this increasing pressure God brings upon the defiant in the life and history of Pharaoh in Egypt. When Moses first came to address Pharaoh, he said to him that he had to let God's people go and stop oppressing them and persecuting them. Moses brought some lesser judgments to emphasize his point and to induce Pharaoh to listen and respond with obedience to God's instructions. The initial judgments and signs Moses brought were quite small in terms of their negative impact. But when Pharaoh hardened his heart, there were greater judgments brought that were more intense and more destructive. But when Pharaoh hardened his heart against even those, the final destruction of Pharaoh was accomplished in the Red Sea.

God is not like some parents. Their children act up, and they say, "You stop that!" But the child rebels even further and the parents back off and walk away because they do not want to engage in the battle. God is not like that. When the sinner acts up, God brings pressure to bear. When the sinner throws himself on the floor and kicks and screams in rebellion, God brings even more pressure to bear. God always wins these battles. If humanity will not submit to God, humanity will be destroyed by God. God never loses a battle with any person.

We have the same pattern in the book of Revelation. We saw the lesser judgments brought in the seven trumpets. We will now see the greater judgments brought in the seven vials. Ultimately, we will see the final destruction accomplished in Revelation 20, when all of Satan's helpers who did not humble themselves under the seven trumpets and the seven vials are ultimately destroyed along with Satan in the lake of fire, just like Pharaoh and his helpers were destroyed in the Red Sea.

The way of the transgressor is hard. But as he continues to transgress, it gets harder and harder. A man may start out life, or a society may be formed, in rebellion against God. Initially, God brings His lesser judgments to bear on such people to show them the errors of their ways and to move them to repentance.

But if an individual or a society persists in wickedness, refuses to repent, and becomes hardened against God, God does not just walk away. God begins to pour out terrible judgments on them and brings severe expressions of His anger against such people. A world that will not repent will be broken. The anger of God against defiant rebels will be severe, and the anger of God against defiant rebels will destroy them. This is the message of the seven vials in this fifth parallel section.

As we have seen the wicked of the world refuse to repent under the warning of the seven trumpets, we will now see the world severely punished under the wrath of the seven vials. Every generation between the first and second coming of Christ has heard God's warnings, and refusing to repent and plunging even deeper into sin, has then experienced terrible expressions of God's anger and wrath upon it. Every unrepentant sinner eventually exhausts God's patience and brings God's final judgment on his life.

Chapter 15 can be broken into two parts. The first part in verses 1 to 4 is the prologue to the seven vials. Several of these parallel sections have prologues. We saw previously that Revelation 8:1–5 was a prologue to the seven trumpets.

The second half of chapter 15 involves a presentation of the seven vials in verses 5 to 8. We have the prologue to the seven vials in verses 1 to 4, we have the presentation of the seven vials in verses 5 to 8, and finally, we have the pouring out of the seven vials in chapter 16.

The Vision of the Angels

The vision of the angels is contained in verse 1. *"And I saw another sign in heaven, great and marvellous, seven angels having the seven last plagues; for in them is filled up the wrath of God."*

John sees another symbolic visual image in heaven that is very powerful and amazing to him. It is great and marvelous. He sees seven angels having the seven last plagues. A plague is a public calamity, something that affects entire populations, something that affects a whole society of people. There is nothing singular or private or individual about these plagues. They impact large masses of humanity.

Verse 1 says about them that *"in them is filled up the wrath of God."* That is, they are the fullest expression of the wrath of God that will be seen on this earth prior to the second coming.

When it says, *"in them is filled up the wrath of God,"* it is not saying this is all of the wrath of God we will ever see. After these seven vials of wrath are poured out, there is far more of the wrath of God that will be seen in the eternal state as people are cast into the lake of fire to suffer forever in the worst possible agonies that people can experience. Hell is a far worse expression of the wrath of God than any of these seven vials are or all of them put together.

When it says in these seven last plagues *"is filled up the wrath of God,"* what is being said is that in these seven plagues is filled up all the wrath of God against men that will be seen on this earth before the second coming. God promised He would not send another flood. He is going to limit the expressions of His wrath. This is the fullest expression of God's wrath in this age, and this is the worst God will do while this world exists. But after this world ends, He will do far worse in the final judgment.

Those assembled in heaven in verses 2–4 behold the wrath of God about to be poured out on mankind for their willful defiance against God. As they view the angels holding these seven vials, and knowing what is in them, are those in heaven horrified by what they see is about to happen? Are they dismayed that God is going to deal so harshly with the impenitent on the earth by means of these horrific vials of wrath? Does this expression of God's anger and the suffering it is going to cause humanity offend the sensibilities of those in heaven regarding how a loving and merciful God ought to act? It does not offend them in the slightest; in fact, this pouring out of God's wrath on the impenitent is the cause and basis of their praise and worship of God.

Many people say God is cruel because of all the suffering He allows on the earth. The glorified saints in heaven find no fault with God for the suffering He brings on humanity in His providences, and we on earth should find no fault with God either.

When we see the suffering of humanity, we should say to ourselves that this is far less than what humanity deserves for its sins, and there is even greater suffering for its sins in the future in hell. The only remedy and relief from this suffering is repentance from sin and faith in Jesus Christ as Lord and Savior.

We see those in heaven justifying God, praising God, and exalting God for His holiness, His justice, and His righteousness in bringing this degree of suffering to bear upon this kind of people for this kind of sin and rebellion.

The Description of the Saints

The description of the saints is in verse 2. In verse 2 it says, *"And I saw as it were a sea of glass mingled with fire: and them that had gotten the victory over the beast, and over his image, and over his mark, and over the number of his name, stand on the sea of glass, having the harps of God."*

We were introduced to this sea of glass in Revelation 4:6. There we saw that the sea of glass, or this glassy sea, represented the peacefulness and the purity that surrounds the throne of God. This perfectly calm sea symbolizes that all around the throne of God is pure and peaceful and tranquil. Around the throne of God there is no ripple of anxiety. There is no heaving of turmoil. There are no waves of conflict. There are no storms of rebellion.

The wicked are like the troubled sea, which cannot rest, and casts up mire and dirt. There is no peace to the wicked. A troubled violent sea is always a symbol of sin and corruption and evil and turmoil and anxiety. A perfectly calm sea is the opposite of that. A calm ocean with a glassy surface is a symbol of peace and purity and serenity.

However, it says in verse 2 that this sea of glass is mingled with fire. Fire, in the book of Revelation, is always a symbol of God's judgment, and it indicates that from the serenity of God's throne is going to proceed the fire of God's judgment on those who have the mark of the beast. This fire of God's judgment is not sent forth because the throne of God has been threatened, or because there is anxiety over whether Satan and his helpers might overthrow it. The throne is not threatened in the slightest. Everything is calm, everything is peaceful, and everything is serene.

But God's justice has been violated, God's holiness has been offended, and God's judgment and wrath have been provoked. This fire that shoots through this glassy sea symbolizes the sending forth of God's wrath against the impenitent. Purity, peace, and justice characterize the environment of the throne of God, and we see all of this in the sea of glass mingled with fire.

Standing on this sea of glass are the glorified believers in heaven. They are identified as those who have gotten the victory over the beast, over his image, and over his mark, which is the number of his name—that is, those in heaven were those who refused the mark of the beast. They would not accept or practice the blasphemy of the anti-Christian world.

In Revelation 13:1, the mark that was on the head of the beast was *"blasphemy."* Those who take the mark of the beast on their head and hands are those who think blasphemous thoughts with their heads, and who engage in blasphemous deeds with their hands. This mark has existed since the first coming of Christ and will continue to exist until the second coming of Christ. It is the characteristic of all of the unsaved.

But those in heaven were not of them. Those in heaven are those who never accepted or practiced the blasphemy of the anti-Christian world which was expressed by anti-Christian government, anti-Christian religion, anti-Christian society, and the anti-Christian populace. These in heaven around the throne are the believers in Christ who lived as strangers and pilgrims and sojourners in this world, but they were never of this world. They never thought the blasphemy of the world, and they never practiced the blasphemy of the world, and by this means they had gotten victory over the mark of the beast.

They were in the world, but they were never of the world. They worshiped God rather than men. They were theists, not humanists. They were servants of God, not blasphemers of God. They were separated from idolatry, not immersed in idolatry. They embraced biblical truth, and rejected satanic lies. They followed Christ, and defied Satan. They practiced holiness and rejected temptation. They were loyal to Christ, and turned their backs on the world.

All of this is what it means to obtain the victory over the beast, and over his name, and over his image, and over his mark. They would not think like evil men, and they would not act like evil men. This is how they refused to take the mark of the beast, the mark of humanism in their forehead or in their hand.

These in heaven who obtained the victory over the beast, and over his image, his mark, and the number of his name are standing on the sea of glass around the throne of God. But they are not just standing there. It says in verse 2 that they have harps that have been given to them by God, and they are singing a song of praise to God. This is not the first time we have seen this in the book of Revelation. We have saints singing with harps in 5:8–10, in 14:2–3, and now in 15:2–4. Musical instruments are used in the worship of God in the courts of heaven, and therefore it is proper to use them in the worship of God in the churches on earth.

The Worship of the Lord

The worship of the Lord is in verses 3 and 4. *"And they sing the song of Moses the servant of God, and the song of the Lamb, saying, Great and marvellous are thy works, Lord God Almighty; just and true are thy ways, thou King of saints.* [4] *Who shall not fear thee, O Lord, and glorify thy name? for thou only art holy: for all nations shall come and worship before thee; for thy judgments are made manifest."*

It says in verse 3 that *"they sing the song of Moses the servant of God, and the song of the Lamb,"* implying that these two songs are really one song, which is expressed in the words recorded in verses 3 and 4. We have a single song with an extended title telling us that this song reflects the victory of both Old Testament saints and New Testament saints over their enemies. This victory of Old Testament saints and New Testament saints over their enemies is one that has been wrought for them by God Himself.

Under Moses the servant of God, Israel was delivered from Pharaoh and his people, and Israel obtained the victory over Pharaoh and his people at the Red Sea. The realization of that victory caused them to burst into a hymn of worship and praise in Exodus 15:1–18.

Under Christ the Lamb of God, the church was delivered from the dragon and his people, and the church obtained the victory over the dragon and his people at the cross. The realization of that victory causes them to burst into a hymn of worship and praise in our passage.

The pattern in the Old Testament is repeated in the New Testament: God brings a great victory for the people of God over their enemies, and they burst into a hymn of praise. That was true with Pharaoh and his people, and it is equally true with the dragon and his people. Both Old Testament saints and New Testament saints triumphed over the dragon and his helpers, and obtained victory over them through the mighty works of the Lord; and upon the realization of that victory, they burst forth in praise with joy and enthusiasm.

The victory over Pharaoh and the Egyptians was a foreshadowing of the victory over the dragon and his people; and therefore, this triumphant song that the glorified church in heaven sings is called the song of Moses and the Lamb. It is a single song of the victory of the people of God over their enemies, wrought for them by God, to whom goes all the glory and praise.

Notice the lyrics of this hymn of praise and worship, and how the focus of those lyrics is on God Himself. It says, beginning in the middle of verse 3, *"Great and marvellous are thy works, Lord God Almighty; just and true are thy ways, thou King of saints.* [4] *Who shall not fear thee, O Lord, and glorify thy name? for thou only art holy: for all nations shall come and worship before thee; for thy judgments are made manifest."*

Do you see how the focus of the lyrics of this hymn of praise and worship is on God? True hymns of worship are not about us. They are not man-centered, and they do not have a lot of me, myself, and I in them. They are all about He, Him, and God. True hymns of worship are God-centered, God-focused, and God-glorifying.

Notice what this hymn of praise by the people of God tells us about their understanding of God. First of all, there is a declaration about the *"works"* and the *"ways"* of the Lord.

There is a declaration of the works of the Lord. It says in verse 3, *"Great and marvellous are thy works, Lord God Almighty."* When it says that God's works are great, what is being said is that God's works are large in their extent, and they are deep in their effect.

God does nothing on a small scale. His works encompass all of time, they encompass the entire universe, they encompass all of the circumstances of life, and they encompass all of the people who have ever lived or ever will live. Let me ask you: Is that great in its dimension? Great are the works of the Lord!

But not only are these works great, it also says they are marvelous. When you look at His works, you marvel at what is done, and you stand amazed and overwhelmed by what has been accomplished. God's works are marvelous in that they are wise beyond comprehension, they are complex beyond understanding, and they are wonderful beyond the power of description.

We look at what God does, and we can only marvel with wonder at the profoundness of what He achieves, and we stand speechless before it. It says in 2 Corinthians 9:15, *"Thanks be unto God for his unspeak-*

able gift." There are no words of human speech that are adequate to express the marvelous nature of God's work. His works are so great and so marvelous because He is the Lord God Almighty. Notice verse 3: *"Great and marvellous are thy works, Lord God Almighty."* There are no throwaway terms there. Every one of those three terms is significant. He is the Lord; that speaks of His absolute sovereignty. He is God; that speaks of His ultimate authority. He is Almighty; that speaks of His infinite power. His great and marvelous works point to His sovereignty, His authority, and His power.

When we see how great and marvelous the works are, we are compelled to say that Someone with tremendous sovereignty and authority and power must have done them. Because of His absolute sovereignty and ultimate authority and infinite power, He is able to do these great and marvelous works. The greatest and the most marvelous work that the Lord God Almighty has ever done is that of saving His people from their sins and giving them victory over Satan and his helpers.

Finally, verse 3 tells us that He is the *"King of saints."* That is, He is the ruler over every believer, and the master of every Christian. The saints in heaven knew nothing of receiving Jesus as their Savior, but not receiving Him as their Lord. Every believer is ruled by a king, and that king is the Lord Jesus Christ. The Christian has no will of his own; his only desire is to do the will of his King.

These in verse 2 who have received that salvation and who have seen the victory God achieved over all of their enemies are standing, as it were, by their own sea. They are giving God praise and worship just like the Israelites did as they stood by their sea and saw that God had thrown the horse and the rider into the sea. It is remarkable that the four horsemen of the apocalypse are symbolized as horsemen, just like Pharaoh's army were horsemen. They are all thrown into the sea of God's wrath and destroyed.

But not only do we see a declaration about the works of the Lord; we also see a declaration about the ways of the Lord. Notice the last phrase of verse 3: *"just and true are thy ways, thou King of saints."* This next phrase speaks not of what God does, but how He does it. It speaks of God's character and God's conduct as He carries out and achieves His great and marvelous works.

When it says He is just in the way He does His great and marvelous works, it means that God's ways are always righteous. He never does His works in a sinful or morally corrupt fashion. There is rectitude, there is virtue, and there is righteousness in all He does. He is never unjust in His works. He is holy in all He does, He is pure in all He accomplishes, and no one can point to anything God has done and properly say that it was not done in the right way, or that it was not the right thing to do.

Many people have done great and marvelous things humanly speaking, but they did them in a corrupt and wicked way. But everything God does, His greatest works, His most marvelous works, are all done righteously.

But it also says regarding the way in which He does things that not only are they just, they are also true. Notice verse 3: *"just and true are thy ways."* The word *"true"* here means "genuine." God is genuine and sincere in all that He does. In other words, He does not pretend to be one thing while He is really another. God deceives no one, God lies to no one, and God never breaks any promise He has made. We could put it in the common vernacular like this: With God, what you see is what you get. God is exactly what He represents Himself to be in His word.

God is not like the politicians of our day. God is true, and when God says, "I am doing this in order to achieve that," you may be assured He means what He says. It is the truth. He will never tell you later that He really did not mean it.

This is what the King of saints is like. He who rules us is righteous, genuine, transparent, sincere, and honest in all of His dealings and in all of His works. In all of them, He demonstrates absolute integrity.

Secondly, this hymn asks a rhetorical question in verse 4. *"Who shall not fear thee, O Lord, and glorify thy name?"* The rhetorical question is asked: "Who would be so foolish as to not fear and glorify the Lord, especially in light of who the Lord is?" In order that there be no doubt as to who the Lord is, they begin to speak about His characteristics.

First of all, God is said to be holy: *"for thou only art holy."* God is the only one who is holy, the only one without sin; and therefore, the only one who deserves to be held in reverence and be given worship. No sinful being is ever worthy of fear and worship, but a pure and holy God is infinitely deserving of worship and reverence.

Holiness provokes worship because God is the only perfectly pure being in the universe. He is unique. There is no one like Him, there is no one above Him, and there is no one who has the purity He possesses. Therefore, when the question is asked, *"Who shall not fear thee, O Lord, and glorify thy name?"* The answer is: "Everyone should fear You, and everyone should glorify Your name, because You are holy."

A second reason is provided. It says, *"for all nations shall come and worship before thee."* Here is another reason why people would be foolish to not fear and glorify the Lord, because eventually, everyone is going to do it anyway. Eventually, all nations will bow the knee and worship the Lord in the future; and therefore, they should begin to do so now.

In Psalm 86:8–9 it says: *"Among the gods there is none like unto thee, O Lord; neither are there any works like unto thy works."* "Because of who You are, and what You have done, there is no comparing You with anyone else in the universe." The psalmist goes on to say in verse 9, *"All nations whom thou hast made shall come and worship before thee, O Lord; and shall glorify thy name."* If all nations are going to come and worship the Lord in the future, then we need to come and worship the Lord right now, because there is no god like God, and there are no works like His works.

The third reason that is offered as to why we should fear the Lord and glorify His name is not only because He is holy, not only because everyone is going to universally worship Him ultimately anyway, but also because it says, *"for thy judgments are made manifest."*

In other words, even now, at the time this hymn was being sung, the judgments of God were being made manifest in the assembling of these seven angels with these seven vials that are about to be poured out. When you see the coming judgment of God and the pouring out of His wrath and His anger, who would be so foolish as to not fear the Lord and glorify Him, and thus avoid the outpouring of those plagues?

If the judgments are going to be so great on the earth now, and the suffering is going to be so intense in our present experience, then how much worse will they be in the future for those who refuse to fear and glorify the Lord? Now is the time to fear the Lord. Now is the time to glorify the Lord. By doing so now, we may escape the judgments of God's wrath that are ready to be poured out by these seven angels standing with these seven vials of the wrath of God.

As we come to the conclusion of this hymn of worship, notice that even though it is sung by those who had gotten the victory over the beast, there is not a word in this hymn about themselves or the way they overcame. The pronoun "I" is not in the hymn.

Those who triumph through Christ do not want any glory for themselves. They do not even want to talk about themselves. Those who triumph through Christ want to give all the glory to Him and draw the attention of the whole world to Him. Heaven is heavenly because all self-centeredness and self-importance and self-glorification are completely lost and forgotten and forsaken in the praise of the greatness of the glory of God.

Psalm 115:1 says, "*Not unto us, O Lord, not unto us, but unto thy name give glory, for thy mercy, and for thy truth's sake.*" I am not saying that it is never appropriate to talk about myself or what God has done in me. But it should always lead to the focus being placed not on me, but on God, and all He has achieved and the victory He has accomplished in overthrowing the rider and his horse, and in delivering His people from hell.

47

The Presentation of the Seven Vials, Revelation 15:5–8

> *"[5] And after that I looked, and, behold, the temple of the tabernacle of the testimony in heaven was opened: [6] And the seven angels came out of the temple, having the seven plagues, clothed in pure and white linen, and having their breasts girded with golden girdles. [7] And one of the four beasts gave unto the seven angels seven golden vials full of the wrath of God, who lived for ever and ever. [8] And the temple was filled with smoke from the glory of God, and from his power; and no man was able to enter into the temple, till the seven plagues of the seven angels were fulfilled."*

Revelation is rooted in the Old Testament and is saturated with allusions and references to Old Testament symbolism and events. As we have proceeded through the exposition of this book, we have repeatedly turned to the Old Testament to understand the meaning and interpretation of the various symbols and statements it contains.

In the last chapter, we saw the saints in heaven singing the song of Moses and the Lamb when they saw the seven vials of wrath about to be poured out on the wicked. God's judgments on Pharaoh and his people are indicative of God's judgments about to be poured out on the beast and his people. As we see God punish and defeat and destroy the enemies of the people of God in the Old Testament, we see a foreshadowing and example of how God will also punish and defeat and destroy the enemies of the people of God in the New Testament.

These seven vials of wrath that are about to be poured out are very similar to the ten plagues that Moses brought upon Pharaoh in Egypt. Just like the Egyptian plagues, these seven vials bring tremendous suffering on those who willfully defy God. Just like the

Egyptian plagues, they culminate in the destruction of the willfully defiant in the final plague that is brought to bear at the second coming of Jesus.

As we began our study of this fifth parallel section of this book, we saw in the last chapter the prologue to the seven vials. We observed the glorified church in heaven praising God for the judgments that were about to be poured out when the seven angels with the seven last plagues were presented before them. Sinless glorified saints not only have no problem when they see God impose suffering on the wicked of the earth, but they actually break out into praise to God because they see the justice of it.

It has been well said that if God does not judge the wicked of this age, He is going to owe an apology to Sodom and Gomorrah for pouring out His wrath on them in a previous age. The people in heaven recognize this principle. They recognize that justice must be served, sin must be punished, and rebels must be subdued; and therefore, when God sets out to bring His wrath to bear on the wicked of this age, the saints in heaven rejoice that justice is once again going to be upheld, and that the moral balance of the kingdom of God is going to be restored.

God said in Romans 12:19, *"Vengeance is mine; I will repay, saith the Lord."* Repaying is exactly what God is doing in pouring out the seven vials of wrath. God is exercising His justice, and it is the exercise of His justice that the saints in heaven are praising Him for. While they were on earth, these saints were severely persecuted by the beast and his people. These saints had gotten the victory over the beast by refusing to renounce Christ, even though the beast had relentlessly pressured them to do so even to the point of death. But now, they see God obtaining the justice for them that they never received while on earth, and they are filled with joy and thanksgiving and praise to God for finally getting the justice they were owed for the evil done to them for serving Christ.

Having heard the praise of the saints as they saw the seven angels come forth to exercise the vengeance of God, let us now observe the commission of these angels and the carrying out of this vengeance as we examine the remainder of chapter 15 and all of chapter 16.

Having seen the prologue to the seven vials in verses 1 to 4, we want to consider the presentation of the seven vials in verses 5 through 8, and then we will see the pouring out of the seven vials in chapter 16.

The Source of God's Judgment

The source of God's judgment is in verse 5. *"And after that I looked, and, behold, the temple of the tabernacle of the testimony in heaven was opened."* We were introduced to these seven angels having these seven last plagues in which is filled up the wrath of God in verse 1: *"And I saw another sign in heaven, great and marvellous, seven angels having the seven last plagues; for in them is filled up the wrath of God."*

But now in verses 5 to 8 we have a much fuller description of these angels and the vials of wrath that are presented to them. Verse 5 says, *"And after that I looked, and, behold, the temple of the tabernacle of the testimony in heaven was opened."* This phrase *"the temple of the tabernacle of the testimony"* is a very long, extended, and descriptive title, and we want to look at it in some detail.

Verse 5 speaks of the tabernacle. The tabernacle was the movable building that God instructed Moses to build in Exodus 25–27. In this tabernacle were two rooms. The first room was called the Holy Place, which contained the lampstand with seven lamps, the altar of incense, and the table of showbread.

The second room was called the Holy of Holies, and it contained the Ark of the Covenant. The Ark of the Covenant was a rectangular wooden box completely overlaid with gold that was about two feet wide, about three and a half feet long, and about two feet tall. On the top of this gold covered box was a lid covered with gold, and it was adorned at each end with two upright sculptures of angels. This lid was called the Mercy Seat. Once a year, on the Day of Atonement, this lid was sprinkled with the blood of a sacrificial animal by the high priest to make atonement for the sins of the people.

The instructions for making the ark are contained in Exodus 25:10–21. Prior to the giving of these instructions, the children of Israel had crossed the Red Sea, arrived at Mount Sinai, and were camped at its base. God appeared to them there and made the Old Covenant with them. In order to execute and carry out the Old Covenant, God gave instructions for the establishment of the tabernacle and everything that was within it, and all the services that were to be offered in relation to it.

It says in Exodus 25:10–21, *"And they shall make an ark of shittim wood: two cubits and a half shall be the length thereof, and a cubit and a half the breadth thereof, and a cubit and a half the height thereof.* [11] *And thou shalt overlay it with pure gold, within and without shalt thou overlay it, and shalt make upon it a crown of gold round about.* [12] *And thou shalt cast four rings of gold for it, and put them in the four corners thereof; and two rings shall be in the one side of it, and two rings in the other side of it.* [13] *And thou shalt make staves of shittim wood, and overlay them with gold.* [14] *And thou shalt put the staves into the rings by the sides of the ark, that the ark may be borne with them.* [15] *The staves shall be in the rings of the ark: they shall not be taken from it."* I want you to notice verse 16: *"And thou shalt put into the ark the testimony which I shall give thee."* Something called the testimony is going to be put inside the ark.

Verse 17: *"And thou shalt make a mercy seat of pure gold: two cubits and a half shall be the length thereof, and a cubit and a half the breadth thereof.* [18] *And thou shalt make two cherubims of gold, of beaten work shalt thou make them, in the two ends of the mercy seat.* [19] *And make one cherub on the one end, and the other cherub on the other end: even of the mercy seat shall ye make the cherubims on the two ends thereof.* [20] *And the cherubims shall stretch forth their wings on high, covering the mercy seat with their wings, and their faces shall look one to another; toward the mercy seat shall the faces of the cherubims be."* Here is our verse again, verse 21: *"And thou shalt put the mercy seat above upon the ark; and in the ark thou shalt put the testimony that I shall give thee."*

In these instructions, it specifically says in verses 16 and 21, "You must put into the ark the testimony which I shall give you." God was going to give something to Moses to place inside the ark, and that thing was called the testimony. As a result of the placing of this testimony inside the ark, the ark was then referred to as the ark of the testimony.

Notice Exodus 25:22. It says, *"And there I will meet with thee, and I will commune with thee from above the mercy seat, from between the two cherubims which are upon the ark of the testimony."* Again, because this item called the testimony is going to be put inside the ark, the ark is now going to be referred to as *"the ark of the testimony."*

The question is, what was this "testimony" that was placed inside of the ark? The Bible is very clear about what it is. In Exodus 31:18 it says, *"And he gave unto Moses, when he had made an end of communing with him upon mount Sinai, two tables of testimony, tables of stone, written with the finger of God."* The Ten Commandments were the testimony. It says in Exodus 32:15 that *"Moses turned, and went down from the mount, and the two tables of the testimony were in his hand."*

This testimony that was placed into the ark which was in the tabernacle was the Ten Commandments that were written on two tablets of stone which were given to Moses by God on Mount Sinai. The reason these Ten Commandments were called the testimony is that they gave testimony and witness of God's moral government over man. They were a witness of mankind's duty to obey God, and they were a witness of what it was that God required of man.

They testified to the fact that man had an obligation to obey God, and they testified as to what that obligation was. They testified to the fact that God had moral authority over man, and that man had a duty to answer to God for his moral behavior. These two tablets testified to all of those things, and thus they were called the Testimony.

Therefore, as you read the Bible elsewhere and see this phrase, "the testimony," realize that it is a reference to the Ten Commandments. For example, in Psalm 19:7, *"The law of the LORD is perfect, converting the soul: the testimony of the LORD is sure, making wise the simple."*

It goes on to say in Exodus 40:20, *"And [Moses] took and put the testimony into the ark. . .and put the mercy seat above upon the ark."* Moses took the lid off the ark, he put the two tablets of stone into the ark, and he put the lid back on.

As late as the time of Solomon's temple it says in 1 Kings 8:9 regarding the ark, *"There was nothing in the ark save the two tables of stone, which Moses put there at Horeb, when the LORD made a covenant with the children of Israel, when they came out of the land of Egypt."*

Because the ark contained the testimony, namely the Ten Commandments, it was called the ark of the testimony. Because the ark of the testimony was placed in the tabernacle, the tabernacle then became known as the tabernacle of the testimony, and it was called that in Numbers 10:11. Eventually, the tabernacle of the testimony was replaced with Solomon's temple made of stone, and thus the temple became known as the temple of the tabernacle of the testimony, which is the descriptive term that is used here in Revelation 15:5.

"And after that I looked, and, behold, the temple of the tabernacle

of the testimony in heaven was opened." Now you know what the temple of the tabernacle of the testimony is. The temple on earth was a pattern of the true temple that is in heaven which John saw in his vision, but the same descriptive terminology is applied to them both. The temple in heaven and the temple on earth are both known as the temple of the tabernacle of the testimony.

The reason for bringing forth the name *"the temple of the tabernacle of the testimony"* is twofold. First of all, because this tabernacle was built during the exodus, and the testimony of the Ten Commandments was given then, it reminds us of the exodus and everything involved in it, including the plagues that fell on Egypt that initiated the exodus. These Egyptian plagues foreshadow the plagues that are about to be poured out of the seven vials which are given to the angels.

There are tremendous parallels between the plagues poured out on Egypt and the plagues poured out in these seven vials in chapter 16. John is preparing us to see that the Old Testament foreshadows the pouring out of these vials in the New Testament.

But secondly, and far more importantly, this term *"the temple of the tabernacle of the testimony,"* reminds us of the Ten Commandments. They are the testimony that declares God's moral authority over men, and the consequences of defying that authority. Sin is the transgression of the Law of God, and it is sin that calls down God's wrath upon men.

The wrath of God about to be poured out in these seven vials must be understood as fitting punishments for the violation of the testimony God gave in the Ten Commandments. The wrath of God makes no sense apart from the Law of God; and therefore, the law is set forth in Revelation 15:5, so that we might understand the wrath that is poured out in Revelation 16:1–21, and why it was poured out. It was poured out for the violation of that law, and for no other reason. The temple of the tabernacle of the testimony becomes the source of the vials of wrath that are about to be poured out.

In Revelation 11:19 it says, *"And the temple of God was opened in heaven, and there was seen in his temple the ark of his testament"* (the ark that contained the Ten Commandments), *"and there were lightnings, and voices, and thunderings, and an earthquake, and great hail."*

Once again, the temple of the ark of the testimony is the source of the violent wrath of God against men. It is precisely because men have thrown off the moral authority of God and they have violated the moral laws of God that God's wrath falls upon man. Both in Revelation 11 and in Revelation 15 we see the heavenly temple that contains God's law is the source of the earthly judgments that are about to fall.

We need to understand that God takes His moral law summarized in the Ten Commandments very seriously, and so should we. Four observations tell us that God takes the Ten Commandments very seriously.

First of all, its violation brings down the worst possible expressions of God's wrath. Trumpets of judgments, vials of wrath, and the lake of fire are all imposed because of the violation of the Ten Commandments, and for this alone.

All suffering in this world is God's punishment for the violation of His moral law. The trumpets and vials of His wrath are just a sample of what is to come in the lake of fire. It will get much worse when men are cast into the lake of fire for all of eternity.

All of this pain and anguish is designed to cause us to recognize that because we are sinners, we are under God's wrath; and therefore, we need to flee from the wrath to come by fleeing to Christ and finding in Him forgiveness and redemption. As we find forgiveness and redemption in Him, we find deliverance from the wrath to come, and ultimately in heaven we are separated from it forever.

God takes His moral law summarized in the Ten Commandments very seriously. Its violation brings down the worst possible expressions of God's wrath.

Secondly, God is still punishing men for their transgressions of the Ten Commandments; so clearly, they have not passed away. False teachers assert that the law has passed away, we now have Christ, and therefore we are not under the law—rather we now just live by the law of love (whatever that is). But what do we see God doing during the New Testament era? We see Him punishing men for their violation of the testimony—namely, the Ten Commandments.

The Ten Commandments have not passed away, not one of them. All of them are still in force; all of them have been in force and will be in force forever. Therefore, we cannot say we do not have to live by the Ten Commandments anymore because they have passed away. God in heaven still has the Ten Commandments there, and He is still pouring out His vials of wrath in this age on people for their violation of them.

Thirdly, it is our violation of the Ten Commandments that Jesus saves us from when He saves us from our sins, and it is the keeping of the Ten Commandments that Jesus exhorts us to practice in our Christian lives. Far from the Ten Commandments having passed away, they are an essential part of the Christian life. When we want to know how we should show our love to God, He says, "If you love Me, keep My commandments, and among those are the Ten Commandments."

Fourthly, for all eternity, the Ten Commandments are the laws we will live by in heaven. In heaven, we are not going to lie to each other. We are not going to steal from each other. We are going to worship on the Sabbath every week. All of these laws are going to guide our moral behavior for all of eternity.

When John speaks about the temple of the tabernacle of the testimony, the testimony of the Ten Commandments is at the very heart of the tabernacle of the temple. It is on the basis of them that the strongest expressions of God's wrath are brought down. It is on the basis of them that God is still punishing men for their violations. It is on the basis of them that we live the Christian life. It is on the basis of them that we will be living for all of eternity. The source of God's judgment is the violation of the Ten Commandments.

The Agents of God's Judgment

The agents of God's judgment are described in verse 6. It says, *"And the seven angels came out of the temple, having the seven plagues, clothed in pure and white linen, and having their breasts girded with golden girdles."*

Out of the temple of God in heaven come seven angels who have the seven plagues. When it says they have the seven plagues, it is speaking prospectively, because they are not actually given the vials of God's wrath which contain the plagues until the next verse. These angels are commissioned to execute God's wrath on an unrepentant people and are sent forth from the very presence of God, from out of the temple where God dwells.

This sending of seven plagues upon those who willfully defy God is spoken of in the Old Testament in Leviticus 26:21 where God says, *"And if ye walk contrary unto me, and will not hearken unto me; I will bring seven times more plagues upon you according to your sins."* The twenty-sixth chapter of Leviticus is a warning of God's wrath and the woes He will send upon Israel for her rebellion and idolatry. Four times in Leviticus 26, God says He will bring a sevenfold judgment on Israel if the people continue to rebel against Him. That quadruple declaration of that sevenfold judgment is stated in Leviticus 26:18, 21, 24, and 28.

God threatens Israel with this sevenfold judgment four times if it engages in idolatry and rebellion against Him, and each of these sevenfold judgments becomes increasingly severe so that if Israel does not repent at the first sevenfold judgment, an increasingly severe set of additional sevenfold judgments is brought. This continues on, and if Israel still refuses to repent, then ultimately she will be destroyed as a nation and violently removed from the land.

This same pattern of increasingly severe sevenfold judgments is what God is imposing on the beast and those working with him in their persecution of Christians and in their defiance of God. First there were the seven trumpets. When men refused to repent at them, then they have seven vials of God's wrath that bring greater destruction upon them. This pattern of seven judgments coming with increasing severity, again and again, until Israel either repents or is destroyed, is the same pattern we see in Revelation.

It says in verse 6, of these angels, that they are clothed in pure and white linen and they have a golden band around their chests. This description of these angels being dressed in white with a golden band around their chest is almost identical to the description given of the Son of man in Revelation 1:13. The similarity of dress of these angels to that of Jesus indicates their closeness with Jesus, their identification with Jesus, and their purity before Jesus. They are the righteous servants of God, and with utmost purity of motive and conduct they carry out the will of God.

These angels that are commissioned to bring these plagues have come from the immediate presence of God, and they come with the full authority of God to carry out the dreadful judgments of God on rebellious humanity. These angels are clearly being sent out of the temple and are acting at the command of God. They are the agents of God's judgments.

The Instruments of God's Judgment

The instruments of God's judgment are mentioned in verse 7, *"And one of the four beasts gave unto the seven angels seven golden vials full of the wrath of God, who liveth for ever and ever."*

This beast in verse 7 is described as being *"one of the four beasts."* We were introduced to these four beasts or living beings in Revelation 4:6 and following. There we saw these beasts were seraphim. They were angels that had six wings who were also spoken of in Isaiah 6:1–7.

One of these four seraphim who were around the throne now gives these seven angels seven golden vials full of the wrath of God. The word *"vial"* is a translation of the Greek word *"phiale."* All other translations translate this word as "bowl." A vial is a deep and slender vessel, while a bowl is a wide and shallow vessel. But the shape of the vessel is not really relevant. What is relevant is what is in that vessel and what happens when that vessel is upended and poured out. Since we are using the King James Version, we are going to refer to them as "vials," though if you think of them as bowls, as is translated in the New King James Version, that is perfectly fine. But the idea is that it is a vessel that contains a substance, and this substance is poured out. The shape of the vessel and the name of the vessel is irrelevant to the interpretation of the passage.

Many vessels used in the Old Testament temple were made of gold. It is therefore fitting that these vials that come out of the temple of the tabernacle of the testimony are also made of gold, since they come from the very altar of the temple of God in heaven. In Revelation 5:8 and 8:3, we see golden vessels being used in the temple in heaven, and, in particular, at the altar of the temple in heaven, where the prayers of the saints for justice are offered.

These judgments are God's answer to the saints' prayers for vindication, and they are conveyed from the altar in heaven to the angels in golden vessels. These vessels contain the wrath of God who lives forever and ever. People can often escape the wrath of their enemies by outliving their enemies and thereby being freed from their wrath. But no one is ever going to outlive God or outlast God, and thereby escape the wrath of God. He lives forever and ever. His wrath will last forever. The objects of that wrath will never escape that wrath because they can never escape Him.

This wrath of the eternal God is dreadful in its degree, because we are told these golden vials are full of the wrath of God. They are full to the top. The whole amount is there. Nothing is left out and nothing is held back. It is poured out to its maximum degree and to its full amount. These vials are the instruments of God's judgments.

The Glory of God's Judgment

The glory of God's judgment is in verse 8, which says, *"And the temple was filled with smoke from the glory of God, and from his power; and no man was able to enter into the temple, till the seven plagues of the seven angels were fulfilled."*

In the Old Testament, when God manifested Himself to men, He often appeared in such glory that they could not come near Him or stand before Him. For example:

- In Exodus 40:35, it says that Moses was not able to enter into the tent of the meeting, because the glory of God filled the tabernacle.
- In 1 Kings 8:10–11, when the priests dedicated Solomon's temple, they were unable to stand and minister because the glory of the Lord had filled the temple.
- In Isaiah 6:4, Isaiah records that the foundations of the doorposts of heaven shook, and the house was filled with smoke when he saw his vision of the Lord sitting upon His throne.
- In Ezekiel 44:4, it says Ezekiel fell on his face before the vision of the temple filled with the glory of God.

In these vial judgments, God is manifesting His glory and His power to such an intense degree that no angel and no glorified saint can stand in His presence.

In 1 Timothy 6:16, it says that God dwells in the light which no man can approach unto. God can only be approached when He wills, and only by the means He has appointed. The unapproachability of God is the result of the awe-fullness of His presence when He fully manifests His glory and His power in this work of judgment. Until this work of judgment is finished, and the degree of the manifestation of His glory and power in the execution of that judgment has subsided, no man is able to be in the personal presence of God. No one can approach to stay His hand of judgment by way of intercession once that judgment is determined to be carried out.

Verse 8 tells us of the dreadful irreversibility of God's judgments once they are set in motion. No intercessor can now approach Him and say, "Please, stop!" At this point, God is all done showing mercy and patience and goodness to these people. For them, the day of grace is over, and wrath is all that is left to them. The door of the ark is shut. Now it is just a matter of time before the wrath of God falls on them and carries them all away.

This, then, is the presentation of the vials of judgment. What is the source of this judgment? It is the violation of the testimony, also referred to as the Ten Commandments and the Law of God.

Who are the agents of God's judgment? It is these holy angels that come from the very presence of God, with the commission of God, to execute the wrath of God.

What are the instruments of God's judgment? They are these golden vessels that come from the very altar of God, where the prayers of the saints for vindication and for vengeance for the wrongs done to them are offered to God. This is God's answer to those prayers. He is sending forth, straight from the altar, golden vessels filled with His wrath. The seraphim gives them to the angels, and the angels are prepared to pour them out.

What is the effect of this judgment? The glory of God so fills the temple that no man can come into the temple or approach God. The execution of His wrath has been set in motion, and it is irreversible.

The point we must take away from this is the significance and importance of the Law of God. All of this wrath and judgment is because men have sinned against God. The Bible says that sin is the transgression of the law, and God has given us that law in his Ten Commandments. When men break those laws, it brings the wrath of God against them. We see that wrath in the seven trumpets of warning, we see that wrath in the seven vials of anger; and ultimately, we see that wrath in the lake of fire consisting of permanent, eternal, and irreversible judgment. Why does all of this occur? It occurs because men have broken God's laws.

Therefore, take God's law seriously. Learn the Ten Commandments. Recognize them as God's will for your life. It is not that by living according to them you are going to become saved. No one is saved by keeping the Ten Commandments because no one has kept them. Jesus saved us from God's wrath for the violation of those Ten Commandments. But Jesus, having lived them perfectly and saved us from the penalties they require of us, now says to us, in effect, "Here is how I expect you to live in your personal lives as saved Christians. Live by the commandments of God."

It is precisely because of the violation of those commandments that all the suffering in this world exists, brought to us by Adam, and then perpetuated by ourselves in our own evil moral choices.

When you see this horrible wrath that is going to be poured out in these seven judgments, you will say, over and over again, "Thank You, Jesus. Thank You, Jesus. Thank You for saving me from my violations of Your holy law. You gave testimony of Your authority over me and my duty to you, and I defied that." You will say, "Father, I repent of that. Forgive me for my violation of Your commandments, and save me through Your Son from the penalty they require of me."

The Bible says that whoever shall call upon the name of the Lord will be saved. That is the good news of the gospel, and that is what we celebrate in the Lord's Supper. In the Lord's Supper, we celebrate Jesus saving us from the wrath of God for our breaking of His Ten Commandments. Thank God that a provision of salvation has been made. The degree of the wrath God pours out on sinners tells us something of the degree of the evil that is involved in breaking God's law, and thus the value and worth of the sacrifice Jesus made in saving us from it.

Let us rejoice that we have a Savior who fulfilled the law and saved us from the penalties of the law, so we might live according to the law by His grace as we walk with Him through this life. May we show our love to Christ by keeping His commandments.

48

The Pouring Out of the Seven Vials, Revelation 16:1–21

"1 *And I heard a great voice out of the temple saying to the seven angels, Go your ways, and pour out the vials of the wrath of God upon the earth.* 2 *And the first went, and poured out his vial upon the earth; and there fell a noisome and grievous sore upon the men which had the mark of the beast, and upon them which worshipped his image.* 3 *And the second angel poured out his vial upon the sea; and it became as the blood of a dead man: and every living soul died in the sea.* 4 *And the third angel poured out his vial upon the rivers and fountains of waters; and they became blood.* 5 *And I heard the angel of the waters say, Thou art righteous, O Lord, which art, and wast, and shalt be, because thou hast judged thus.* 6 *For they have shed the blood of saints and prophets, and thou hast given them blood to drink; for they are worthy.* 7 *And I heard another out of the altar say, Even so, Lord God Almighty, true and righteous are thy judgments.* 8 *And the fourth angel poured out his vial upon the sun; and power was given unto him to scorch men with fire.* 9 *And men were scorched with great heat, and blasphemed the name of God, which hath power over these plagues: and they repented not to give him glory.* 10 *And the fifth angel poured out his vial upon the seat of the beast; and his kingdom was full of darkness; and they gnawed their tongues for pain,* 11 *And blasphemed the God of heaven because of their pains and their sores, and repented not of their deeds.* 12 *And the sixth angel poured out his vial upon the great river Euphrates; and the water thereof was dried up, that the way of the kings of the east might be prepared.* 13 *And I saw three unclean spirits like frogs come out of the mouth of the dragon, and out of the mouth of the beast, and out of the mouth of the false prophet.* [14] *For they are the spirits of devils, working miracles, which go forth unto the kings of the earth and of the whole world, to gather them to the battle of that great day of God Almighty.* [15] *Behold, I come as a thief. Blessed is he that watcheth, and keepeth his garments, lest he walk naked, and they see his shame.* [16] *And he gathered them together into a place called in the Hebrew tongue Armageddon.* [17] *And the seventh angel poured out his vial into the air; and there came a great voice out of the temple of heaven, from the throne, saying, It is done.* [18] *And there were voices, and thunders, and lightnings; and there was a great earthquake, such as was not since men were upon the earth, so mighty an earthquake, and so great.* [19] *And the great city was divided into three parts, and the cities of the nations fell: and great Babylon came in remembrance before God, to give unto her the cup of the wine of the fierceness of his wrath.* [20] *And every island fled away, and the mountains were not found.* [21] *And there fell upon men a great hail out of heaven, every stone about the weight of a talent: and men blasphemed God because of the plague of the hail; for the plague thereof was exceeding great."*

We have seen that the theme of this fifth parallel section is God's anger against the willfully defiant. The anger and wrath of God against willfully defiant people in this age is symbolized by pouring out on them the seven vials full of wrath.

This fifth parallel section in chapters 15 and 16 is divided into three parts. We have seen the prologue to the seven vials in 15:1–4. We have seen the presentation of the seven vials in 15:5–8. In this chapter, we will see the pouring out of the seven vials in 16:1–21.

There are remarkable parallels between the Exodus plagues brought on Egypt by Moses, the seven trumpets of judgment in Revelation 8–11, and the seven vials of judgment in Revelation 16. The Exodus judgments on Egypt are a foreshadow and indicator of the kinds of judgment that will be brought on the wicked in this age, whether they are partially expressed in the warning of the trumpets, or whether they are fully expressed in the wrath of the vials.

Both the trumpet judgments and the vials of wrath present the plagues in the same order. Both present the plagues as first striking the earth, then the sea, then the inland waters, then the sun, then the realm of the wicked is stricken with darkness, then on the Euphrates River, then on the whole world in a final judgment. The tremendous similarity of the trumpets and the vials is a result of their both being based on the Exodus plagues.

But the contrast between the trumpet and the vial judgments is very clear as well. The trumpet judgments are partial and limited in their effect, while the vial judgments are more complete and total in their effect. The reason for this is the trumpet judgments were meant to call men to repentance, but the vial judgments are meant to bring God's wrath on men because they refused to repent. Since the trumpet warnings were ignored, the vial judgments are poured out upon their idolatry, their refusal to repent, and their persecution of the saints.

Both the trumpet judgments and the vial judgments are God's answer to the prayers of the saints for justice that were offered in Revelation 6:9–11 when the souls under the altar said, "Lord, how long before You bring vengeance on those who martyred us?" In 8:3–5, those prayers of the saints for vengeance were offered on the altar.

When God says, *"Vengeance is mine, I will repay,"* He is not speaking empty words. He obtains vengeance, not only for Himself and the offenses done to Him; He also obtains vengeance for His saints and the offenses and injustices done to them. These trumpet judgments, and now these vial judgments, are what God's vengeance looks like in this life, in this world, and on this side of the Day of Judgment.

It is clear that these plagues are directed against unbelieving humanity and are not directed at believers. We saw the trumpet judgments were not to be poured out on those who had the seal of God in their foreheads, and in the same way, the vial judgments now are specifically said to be poured out on those who have the mark of the beast and who worship his image.

Although believers may experience sufferings as an indirect result of these judgments on the wicked, those sufferings will not harm them, and they will all be worked together for their good by God. The very judgment that is meant to destroy the wicked will either sanctify the believer or else promote the believer to heaven, but they will never harm him.

These vial judgments in chapter 16 can be broken down into two groups. In the first five vials that are poured out on the earth, we have plagues that will occur over and over again, all throughout this age between the first and second coming of Christ. The first five vials are not one-time events; rather, they each represent categories of events that repeatedly occur as judgments on the wicked throughout this age.

The last two vial judgments represent judgments that will occur at the end of this age, when the Antichrist appears and the united nations of the world make their final assault on the church to eradicate it from the earth. But at that point, Jesus will return in power and glory to deliver His church from Antichrist and his transnational coalition.

We saw this same pattern with the seals, where the first five seals represented categories of behavior the wicked would carry out throughout this age over and over again. But the sixth seal represented the judgment of God that would occur at the end of the age. We saw this same pattern with the trumpets, in which the first six trumpets describe repetitive temporal judgments that will occur throughout this age, but the seventh trumpet represents the final judgment of God that would occur at the end of this age. In the same way, these first five vials describe things that will occur all throughout the age, but the last two describe what is going to occur at the end of the age.

The first five vial judgments occur in every century, in every generation, and all around the world. The only chronological aspect of these vial judgments is confined to the last two of them—the sixth and the seventh—which speak of the activity of Antichrist and the final judgment.

We would expect that at the end of each of these parallel sections we would be brought to the end of the age and to the second coming of Christ. That is exactly what we see once again at the end of this fifth parallel section: we are brought to the second coming of Christ. This is the fifth time in this book that we have journeyed through this age to the second coming of Christ.

The Wrath of God Poured Out throughout This Age

The wrath of God poured out throughout this age is in verses 1 through 11, which contain the first five vial judgments.

Verse 1 says, *"And I heard a great voice out of the temple saying to the seven angels, Go your ways, and pour out the vials of the wrath of God upon the earth."* Seven symbolizes completeness, and these seven angels with their seven vials of wrath represent the concept that God will completely judge the wicked, and that He will be complete in the judgment He brings on them. God will not fail to bring retribution against each of the wicked, and He will not fail to bring retribution upon them for all their deeds. Not one of them will escape His wrath, and no evil deed will go unpunished.

This loud voice from the temple is God's because at this point in John's vision nobody else is in the temple. Smoke filled the temple in chapter 15, and no person could be in the temple with God while He was expressing the glory of His wrath, His vengeance, and His justice. But now, out of the temple comes a voice, so it must be the voice of God. God Himself personally commands the angels to commence the execution of His wrath upon the wicked. It says in Isaiah 66:6, "*. . .a voice from the temple, a voice of the LORD that rendereth recompence to his enemies.*" This is exactly what we have in Revelation 16:1, a voice coming out of the temple rendering recompense to His enemies.

This concept of God's wrath being poured out is frequently used in the Old Testament. It is used to indicate God's judgment against Israel for breaking her covenant, and it is used to indicate God's judgment against the persecutors of the people of God.

Consider the language of pouring out in Psalm 69:24. It says, "*Pour out thine indignation upon them, and let thy wrathful anger take hold of them.*" In Psalm 79:6 it says, "*Pour out thy wrath upon the heathen that have not known thee, and upon the kingdoms that have not called upon thy name.*" In Jeremiah 7:20 it says, "*Therefore thus saith the Lord GOD; Behold, mine anger and my fury shall be poured out upon this place, upon man, and upon beast, and upon the trees of the field, and upon the fruit of the ground; and it shall burn, and shall not be quenched.*" In Jeremiah 10:25 it says, "*Pour out thy fury upon the heathen that know thee not, and upon the families that call not on thy name: for they have eaten up Jacob, and devoured him, and consumed him and have made his habitation desolate.*" Finally, Ezekiel 7:8 says, "*Now will I shortly pour out my fury upon thee, and accomplish mine anger upon thee: and I will judge thee according to thy ways, and will recompense thee for all thine abominations.*"

When this language of pouring out is used, it is the final and full expression of the irreversible wrath of God on those who willfully defy Him. Trumpets sound warnings; vials pour out wrath. What God threatened in the Old Testament He accomplished, and what He threatens in this age He will also accomplish.

The fact that God commanded in John's day that these vials be poured out makes it certain that these vial judgments are among those things that must shortly come to pass, as we are told in Revelation 1:1. These vial judgments began to be poured out in the first century, and they have been poured out in every subsequent century.

Notice the first vial of wrath in verse 2: *"And the first went, and poured out his vial upon the earth; and there fell a noisome and grievous sore upon the men which had the mark of the beast, and upon them which worshipped his image."* Notice this vial is poured out on a specific class of people—those who have the mark of the beast and worship his image. How long has the mark of the beast and the worship of the image of the beast been going on? Since the first century. Therefore, how long has this first vial been poured out? Since the first century.

Now as we said, these images set before us are symbolic. But the symbol does convey a physical reality, and these symbols described in these seven vials each contain indications as to what that physical reality is.

These first four vials of wrath involve God using nature as an instrument of His judgment upon wicked men. They are poured out on the earth, the sea, the inland waters, and the sun. Nature is the agent of the wrath of God, and God, as it were, arms creation with weapons in order to punish His enemies.

The first vial is poured out on the earth, with the result that ugly and painful sores broke out on men who had the mark of the beast and who worshiped his image. These unsaved men who worship humanistic civil authority as their god are stricken with loathsome and disgusting sores on their bodies as a result of their willful defiance of God.

This would encompass every kind of disease that strikes ungodly people as a result of their ungodly behavior. Sinful lifestyles are exceedingly unhealthy, and bring with them diseases and sicknesses and injuries that those who live according to the law of God do not experience.

For example, dementia and cirrhosis of the liver that are the result of drunkenness, sexually transmitted diseases, and the negative health effects of drug addiction are just a few examples of destructive diseases that God brings upon those who live in willful defiance of His laws. They are an expression of this first vial of wrath He has poured on those who have the mark of the beast because of their willful defiance of God.

On occasion an innocent believer will get HIV, for example, through a needle stick or something similar when giving someone health care. Certainly that happens. But as I said, those things are not designed for their injury; instead, they will work together for their good, to conform them to the character of Christ, to open otherwise closed doors for ministry, or to bring them to heaven through their death.

While it is true that believers do get ordinary diseases like cancer and various things that are universally distributed among the population, and while they do die from them, these diseases are not an act of God's judgment on them; rather, they are a means of deliverance for them, to deliver them out of this present evil world, and to deliver them into the blessed presence of God. Romans 8:28 says, "*We know that all things work together for good to them that love God, to them who are the called according to his purpose.*"

There are unique diseases that are poured out on the wicked because of their wicked sinful lifestyle choices, and these are the vials of God's wrath that fall upon them. Their diseases are meant as acts of judgment upon them, to bring an end to their wickedness, and to usher them into hell.

Every destructive and fatal disease that is brought to bear on the wicked by God is a result of God's wrath being poured out on them in this first vial. This first vial is like the judgment of Exodus 9:8–11, in which boils broke out upon all the Egyptians for their willful defiance of God, but which did not fall upon the Jewish people.

In Acts 12:20–23, when Herod gave his speech and the people said, "*It is the voice of a god,*" the angel of the Lord smote him because he did not give God the glory, and he was eaten by worms and died. This is an example of what the pouring out of this first vial would look like in terms of God's judgment on the physical health and bodies of men.

The second vial of wrath is spoken of in verse 3. It says, "*And the second angel poured out his vial upon the sea; and it became as the blood of a dead man: and every living soul died in the sea.*" This second vial of wrath is like the plague of Exodus 7:17–21 in which the Nile River was turned into blood and all the fish in it died.

Here the judgment is much more severe than that of the second trumpet judgment. The second trumpet judgment was only partial, in which only a third of the ocean was turned into blood, and only a third of the sea creatures died. But here, the whole ocean becomes blood like that of a dead man, and every single creature in the sea dies.

The symbolism that is conveyed here is horrible and shocking: an ocean of coagulated blood in which everything is dead. Here is represented every kind of maritime disaster through which men are killed and cast into hell by God. Sea battles, hurricanes, cyclones, typhoons, tidal waves, and shipwrecks have killed countless millions as a result of God's wrath against them.

The Red Sea swallowed up Pharaoh and his army, and the seas of the world have been instruments of God's judgment in swallowing up the wicked in a similar fashion countless times since, in order to kill them and cast them into hell. The seas of the world are mixed with the blood of millions and millions of people who have died upon it under the wrath of God in the exercise of His providence and His judgment against their wickedness.

The third vial of wrath is contained in verses 4 to 7. *"And the third angel poured out his vial upon the rivers and fountains of waters; and they became blood.* [5] *And I heard the angel of the waters say, Thou art righteous, O Lord, which art, and wast, and shalt be, because thou hast judged thus.* [6] *For they have shed the blood of saints and prophets, and thou hast given them blood to drink; for they are worthy.* [7] *And I heard another [angel] out of the altar say, Even so, Lord God Almighty, true and righteous are thy judgments."*

This plague, as with the previous one, is like the plague of Exodus 7:17–21 when Moses turned the Nile River into blood. However, instead of it affecting the ocean like the second vial, this third vial affects all the inland waters. Once again, we have a very severe intensification of the third trumpet judgment that also struck the inland waters. In the third trumpet, only a third part of the inland waters were affected, and they were made bitter with wormwood. But in this third vial judgment, all of the springs and rivers are turned to blood.

Inland waters are critical to human life. They are the source of our fresh drinking water, without which we would quickly die. They are the source of our food because without rain or irrigation, food production ends and famine begins. The inland waters are the means to achieve a thousand tasks in society, from cleaning to industrial production, without which economic collapse is absolutely certain. Water pollution, waterborne diseases, droughts, floods, and many other similar events are instruments in the hand of God to bring His judgments on the wicked and to cast them into hell.

In verse 5 it says, *"And I heard the angel of the waters say, Thou art righteous, O Lord, which art, and wast, and shalt be, because thou hast judged thus."* This angel of the waters is apparently an angel God has appointed to administer all of His inland waters on the earth, just like He appointed these seven angels to administer His wrath. We saw in chapter 7 that there were four angels standing on the four corners of the earth, holding the four winds of the earth. God does not directly run the world Himself; He appoints angels to manage various aspects of His creation and to carry out various activities He has ordained to be accomplished.

The angel of the waters sees this judgment on the waters he administers as an excellent example of the punishment fitting the crime. He speaks of God the eternal judge as being altogether righteous and just and proportionate in the punishment He imposes on the wicked for their persecution and martyrdom of the saints. He says, "Lord, You are righteous for judging these people in this fashion. You are the eternal God, and Your wrath is just."

In verse 6 it says, *"For they have shed the blood of saints and prophets, and thou hast given them blood to drink; for they are worthy."* In other words, the same injury they have brought upon the saints is the very injury that will be brought upon them. We see murderers slaughtering innocent people, and then they themselves become slaughtered. They have killed; and therefore, they must be killed and cast into hell. It is the punishment they have made themselves worthy of by their evil deeds.

This has been going on through the centuries, where the persecutors and the murderers of the people of God have themselves become persecuted and murdered because they made themselves worthy of reaping what they have sown.

In verse 7, we see another angel. It says in verse 7, *"And I heard another out of the altar say. . ."* We are not told who this *"another"* is, but the implication is that it is another angel. We have the angel of the waters, and we have the angel of the altar. This angel of the altar is mentioned in 8:3–5, and he is also mentioned in 14:18. This angel of the altar now concurs with the angel of the waters, and he also justifies God in His judgments that God exercises upon the wicked.

The point being made with the unified voice of these two angels is that all the people in heaven (as we saw in 15:2–4) and all the angels in heaven concur that God's justice and wrath against the willfully defiant is totally appropriate and entirely righteous. When those in heaven (whether they are glorified saints or angels) see God pouring out His wrath upon the earth, they respond with approval, agreement, and applause.

The fourth vial of wrath is contained in verse 8. It says, *"And the fourth angel poured out his vial upon the sun; and power was given unto him to scorch men with fire.* [9] *And men were scorched with great heat, and blasphemed the name of God, which hath power over these plagues: and they repented not to give him glory."*

Just like with the trumpet judgments, we have seen these first four vial judgments strike the earth, the seas, the inland waters, and the stellar heavens. In the fourth trumpet judgment, the sun was partially darkened; but here in the fourth vial judgment, the power of the sun is expanded and increased in order to smite the wicked of the earth by scorching and burning them.

This intensification of the sun may be a reference to solar flares, or it may be a reference to atmospheric conditions on the earth that cause temperatures to soar to such high levels that men die from heatstroke, dehydration, and sunstroke. The tremendous rise in melanoma skin cancers in the last century could very well be an aspect of this judgment.

The pouring out of God's wrath in the Old Testament is often figuratively expressed as being accompanied by fire. For example, in Jeremiah 7:20 it says, *"Therefore thus saith the Lord GOD; Behold, mine anger and my fury shall be poured out upon this place, upon man, and upon beast, and upon the trees of the field, and upon the fruit of the ground; and it shall burn, and shall not be quenched."* Here we see God pouring out His fire upon the natural creation.

In Ezekiel 22:21–22 God says, *"Yea, I will gather you, and blow upon you in the fire of my wrath, and ye shall be melted in the midst thereof.* [22] *As silver is melted in the midst of the furnace, so shall ye be melted in the midst thereof; and ye shall know that I the LORD have poured out my fury upon you."*

It may be that the sun, rather than literally bringing high temperatures, is a symbolic reference to the burning and melting power of God's wrath when He pours it out upon the wicked. Lending evidence to that idea, it says of the saints in Revelation 7:16, *"They shall hunger no more, neither thirst any more; neither shall the sun light on them, nor any heat."*

Since the fall of man, the sun has not been our friend. This is why people in the Middle East completely cover their bodies; they cannot bear the sun's rays striking and harming their skin. This is why the sun is often used as a symbol of judgment.

God's wrath, whether it is literal or judicial, does not bring them to repentance. In verse 9 it says that they *"blasphemed the name of God,"* and *"they repented not to give him glory."*

When the wicked receive punishment for their sin, rather than repenting and justifying God in bringing the punishments, they slander God as being evil for bringing pain into their lives. They will not give Him glory by admitting they are evil and that God is righteous in bringing these judgments upon them. Instead, they justify themselves and accuse God of evil for bringing this pain into their lives. It is like when children act up, and one of their parents righteously takes them aside and spanks them for the sin they committed, and in response the children say, "I hate you!"

That is exactly what the people of the earth are doing toward God. They commit great wickedness and therefore He brings punishment on them. But instead of humbly bowing down and saying, "I am sorry, I have done wrong, please forgive me," they shake their fist in the face of God and defy Him even more.

The fifth vial of God's wrath is in verses 10 and 11. *"And the fifth angel poured out his vial upon the seat of the beast; and his kingdom was full of darkness; and they gnawed their tongues for pain,* [11] *And blasphemed the God of heaven because of their pains and their sores, and repented not of their deeds."*

"The seat of the beast" is the throne of the beast, and we have seen that the beast represents anti-Christian civil government. In John's day, the beast was Rome. In our day, the beast is the civil government of whatever country a person lives in. Every nation has a civil government over it, and that government is the beast.

The point in this fifth vial of wrath is that anti-Christian governments are not allowed by God to rule in ease and comfort. God brings darkness and pain and epidemics upon wicked rulers and upon the people who support them. The throne of civil government suffers internal strife, coups, seditions, assassination of its leaders, economic depressions, wars, famines, rebellions, and endless problems in the administration of its rule. All of these things are the judgments of God upon the beast out of the sea.

All of this causes great emotional and personal anguish to wicked rulers and their people so they, as it were, are constantly chewing their tongues in pain over the fact that they cannot get their agenda achieved. Because of God's wrath, kingdoms are in turmoil, and they experience civil war and strife and division and lawlessness and disrespect for authority. All of this causes men to be filled with fear and anxiety and anger. Great health epidemics break out due to the judgments of the first vial, and healthcare systems are overwhelmed and people die from lack of medical attention because of their pains and their sores, as it says in verse 11.

Verse 11 says the result is that these willfully defiant people do not repent, but they blaspheme God even more and dig themselves into even deeper holes of ever greater wrath from God as the result of their ever-increasing blasphemy and rebellion. It says in verse 11, *"And [they] blasphemed the God of heaven because of their pains and their sores, and repented not of their deeds."*

We see that the god of civil government is a poor god at best. But multitudes still worship at the altar of human government and human authority, even though it is constantly wracked with the judgments of God upon it, and even with all the failings it has and the destructive effects it brings on the people it rules.

These first five plagues occur throughout this age, and both nature and human government become instruments of God to bring His wrath to bear against defiant humanity, and there is nowhere anybody can go to escape either of them. Everyone is subject to God's wrath administered through nature, and everyone is subject to God's wrath administered through corrupt, evil, and wicked civil governments. This is what those who worship the beast experience as the wrath of God upon them.

The Wrath of God Poured out at the End of This Age

The wrath of God poured out at the end of this age is contained in verses 12 to 21, and it encompasses these last two vial judgments, the sixth and the seventh. These next two vials of wrath bring us to the end of this age. They are the judgments of God on the Antichrist and his one-world government for attempting to eradicate the church.

The sixth vial of wrath is poured out in verse 12: *"And the sixth angel poured out his vial upon the great river Euphrates; and the water thereof was dried up, that the way of the kings of the east might be prepared."*

The river Euphrates was introduced to us in the trumpet judgments in Revelation 9:14, and there we saw that the river Euphrates symbolized the coming of war, because from across that river the enemies of the people of God came in order to assault and conquer them. Both Assyria and Babylon came across the Euphrates to execute God's judgment and wrath on Israel when the northern kingdom was taken away by Assyria and the southern kingdom was taken away by Babylon. Therefore, this river symbolizes war, and the kings of the East represent the enemies of the people of God coming to wage war against them.

Notice verse 13: *"And I saw three unclean spirits like frogs come out of the mouth of the dragon, and out of the mouth of the beast, and out of the mouth of the false prophet."* This gathering of the nations together to make war against the people of God is provoked by this unholy trinity made up of Satan the dragon, anti-Christian government the beast, and anti-Christian religion the false prophet, also known as the beast out of the earth in Revelation 13:11.

In verse 13, we have come to the time when Satan is loosed and goes out to deceive the nations and bring them together into a unified, one-world effort to destroy the Christian church from the face of the earth. Antichrist appears for his little season, for his three and a half days. What we have in verses 12 and 13 and following is the same time period that is described in Revelation 11:7–10 and in Revelation 20:7–9.

In Revelation 11:7–10 it says, *"And when they shall have finished their testimony"* that marks the end of the symbolic thousand years, i.e., the church age, *"the beast that ascendeth out of the bottomless pit shall make war against them, and shall overcome them, and kill them. [8] And their dead bodies shall lie in the street of the great city, which spiritually is called Sodom and Egypt, where also our Lord was crucified. [9] And they of the people and kindreds and tongues and nations"* (the transnational coalition) *"shall see their dead bodies three days and an half, and shall not suffer their dead bodies to be put in graves. [10] And they that dwell upon the earth shall rejoice over them, and make merry, and shall send gifts one to another; because these two prophets tormented them that dwelt on the earth.* [11] *And after three days and an half"* the second coming of Jesus and the resurrection and the rapture occur, the world is destroyed, and the final judgment is brought, as verses 12–19 state.

In Revelation 20:7–9 it says, *"And when the thousand years are expired, Satan shall be loosed out of his prison,* [8] *And shall go out to deceive the nations which are in the four quarters of the earth, Gog and Magog, to gather them together to battle: the number of whom is as the sand of the sea.* [9] *And they went up on the breadth of the earth, and compassed the camp of the saints about, and the beloved city: and fire came down from God out of heaven, and devoured them."* This is exactly what we are dealing with in this sixth and seventh vial judgment.

In Revelation 16:13 it says, *"I saw three unclean spirits like frogs come out of the mouth of the dragon, and out of the mouth of the beast, and out of the mouth of the false prophet."* These unclean spirits are demons. Verse 14 says, *"they are the spirits of devils."* In the Gospels, Jesus frequently referred to demons as unclean spirits. This term *"unclean spirits"* is used of demons in Matthew 12:43 and in several other passages.

These demons or unclean spirits are metaphorically said to be like frogs. Frogs were unclean animals and therefore an apt metaphor for demons, just as snakes are unclean animals and an apt metaphor for Satan. Pharaoh's magicians brought forth both serpents and frogs as a result of their occultic miracles before Pharaoh.

Verse 14 says, *"For they are the spirits of devils, working miracles, which go forth unto the kings of the earth and of the whole world, to gather them to the battle of that great day of God Almighty."* Through the persuasive power of demonic miracles, the Antichrist, aided by the false prophet, will convince the whole world to unite together to wage war on the people of God in order to destroy them from the face of the earth. When this transnational coalition gathers together because of the demonic persuasive power of the Antichrist and the false prophet, then we know the second coming of Christ is imminent.

Notice verse 15: *"Behold, I come as a thief. Blessed is he that watcheth, and keepeth his garments, lest he walk naked, and they see his shame."* When the kings of the earth are gathered together to the battle against the believers, then you can truthfully say that Jesus can come back at any moment. But until that happens, you cannot.

Presently, the second coming of Christ is not imminent. People say that He could come back any day. No, He cannot. The reason He cannot is that Antichrist has not arisen, and the transnational coalition of nations has not been gathered together in order to go to war against the church to eradicate it from the face of the earth. When you see that happening, this is when you see the tree budding as Matthew 24:32–33 tells us, and then you know the end is near. This is when the woman starts to have her birth pangs (1 Thessalonians 5:3) and you know the delivery is near—that is, the coming of Christ is near.

In verse 15, Jesus says, *"I come as a thief."* In other words, He says: "My coming will be a surprise to the wicked but you will know about it." That day will not take you unaware, it says in 1 Thessalonians 5:1–4, but it will take the Antichrist and his transnational coalition unaware. He says, "[15] *Behold, I come as a thief. Blessed is he that watcheth, and keepeth his garments."* These garments are a reference to the robe of righteousness Christ has given us.

When Christ returns, we do not want to be found naked—that is, without the robe of Christ's righteousness on us obtained through repentance and faith in Jesus. If all we have is the filthy rags of our own righteousness, then we have no righteousness at all with which to dwell in the presence of God and in which to be properly clothed for the wedding supper of the Lamb.

Notice verse 16: *"And he"* (Antichrist) *"gathered them together into a place called in the Hebrew tongue Armageddon."* This is the only place in the Bible where the term Armageddon appears, and it literally means "the mountain of Megiddo." Megiddo was a large plain, many miles wide and long, located in northern Israel. It was a place where Israel experienced a marvelous deliverance from her enemies by God during the days of the Judges under Barak and Deborah. Judges 4–5 contains the historical record of Deborah and Barak fighting against Sisera and the Canaanites who were oppressing Israel. In Judges 5:20, they sing their song of victory, and they proclaim that the heavens fought on behalf of the people of God.

This term Armageddon means "the mountain of Megiddo," but Megiddo is a plain. There is no mountain there. Therefore, Armageddon cannot be a particular place. In the Bible, mountains are symbols of strength. God's people saw God as their mountain, as the place they could flee to in order to find refuge and protection. Armageddon is a metaphorical term that makes an allusion to God fighting on behalf of His people when they were delivered from their superior enemy in Judges 4.

God is our mountain of strength and protection when we are attacked by a superior force. God is our Armageddon, our mountain of protection and strength. Therefore, the term Armageddon is a beacon of hope and a positive term to the believer. At this final effort of Antichrist to destroy the church, God will be the mountain of strength who delivers His people when He returns in power and glory.

We conclude then that Armageddon is a symbolic term designating any time and place where the strength of the Lord is revealed to save His people from their far superior enemies because He is their mountain of deliverance. Armageddon is wherever in the world the strength of the Lord is revealed in the deliverance of His people in the final battle against Antichrist and his transnational one-world coalition of governments that come together to wipe out the church. It is not necessarily going to happen in Northern Israel.

The seventh vial of God's wrath is in verse 17: *"And the seventh angel poured out his vial into the air; and there came a great voice out of the temple of heaven, from the throne, saying, It is done.* [18] *And there were voices, and thunders, and lightnings; and there was a great earthquake, such as was not since men were upon the earth, so mighty an earthquake, and so great.* [19] *And the great city was divided into three parts, and the cities of the nations fell: and great Babylon came in remembrance before God, to give unto her the cup of the wine of the fierceness of his wrath.* [20] *And every island fled away, and the mountains were not found.* [21] *And there fell upon men a great hail out of heaven, every stone about the weight of a talent: and men blasphemed God because of the plague of the hail; for the plague thereof was exceeding great."*

There is a very interesting phrase in verse 17, and that is the phrase, *"It is done."* It is the same phrase Jesus uttered on the cross when He said, *"It is finished."* In other words, just as Jesus finished the redemption of the elect, God is finishing and completing His program and purpose for this world. It is done. The end of the world and the completion of God's program and purpose have been achieved.

In verse 18, and in verses 20 to 21, we have a description of the cataclysmic destruction of the created world by the hand of God. It consists of voices, thunder, lightning, and a great and mighty earthquake larger than any that has ever occurred in the history of the earth. Islands and mountains are removed. Great hailstones fall. The hail that falls is about the weight of a talent, somewhere between forty and a hundred pounds. In Texas they occasionally have hailstones the size of a golf ball that flatten crops and destroy and wreck everything. If ordinary hail causes that kind of damage, imagine the damage of forty-pound hailstones! What is being conveyed by this symbolic language is that total destruction is going to occur.

This cataclysmic destruction of the world at the end is also described in four other passages.

It is described in Revelation 6:12–14 under the sixth seal. It says when he opened the sixth seal, "[12] . . . *lo, there was a great earthquake; and the sun became black as sackcloth of hair, and the moon became as blood;* [13] *And the stars of heaven fell unto the earth, even as a fig tree casteth her untimely figs, when she is shaken of a mighty wind.* [14] *And the heaven departed as a scroll when it is rolled together; and every mountain and island were moved out of their places.*"

It is described in Revelation 11:13 when it says, "*And the same hour was there a great earthquake, and the tenth part of the city fell, and in the earthquake were slain of men seven thousand: and the remnant were affrighted, and gave glory to the God of heaven.*"

It is described in Isaiah 28:15–17. "*Because ye have said, We have made a covenant with death, and with hell are we at agreement; when the overflowing scourge shall pass through, it shall not come unto us: for we have made lies our refuge, and under falsehood have we hid ourselves:* [16] *Therefore thus saith the Lord GOD, Behold, I lay in Zion for a foundation a stone, a tried stone, a precious corner stone, a sure foundation: he that believeth shall not make haste.* [17] *Judgment also will I lay to the line, and righteousness to the plummet: and the hail shall sweep away the refuge of lies, and the waters shall overflow the hiding place.*" In other words, as strong as this coalition of wickedness is, God is going to flatten it with the hail of His judgment, and His own Son is going to prevail.

It is described in Haggai 2:6–7. "*For thus saith the LORD of hosts; Yet once, it is a little while, and I will shake the heavens, and the earth, and the sea, and the dry land;* [7] *And I will shake all nations, and the desire of all nations shall come: and I will fill this house with glory, saith the LORD of hosts.*" It is plain that the language in Revelation

16:18, 20–21 is drawn directly out of these passages in Isaiah 28 and in Haggai 2.

But men will continue to blaspheme God to the bitter end: "*. . .and men blasphemed God because of the plague of the hail; for the plague thereof was exceeding great.*" Men will not repent even when faced with God's final judgment. How hardened must the fallen human heart be!

Notice Revelation 16:19. It says, *"And the great city was divided into three parts, and the cities of the nations fell: and great Babylon came in remembrance before God, to give unto her the cup of the wine of the fierceness of his wrath."*

When it speaks of Babylon being divided into three parts, three is the number of perfection and completion and finality. When the city is divided into three parts, it is saying that there is complete, perfect, and final destruction of Babylon which represents anti-Christian society, and thus the entire kingdom of Satan is completely and perfectly and finally destroyed at the second coming of Jesus. All the cities of the nations, collectively referred to as Babylon (the sum of all of anti-Christian society), are brought to final ruin. Here the fierceness of the wrath of God is fully displayed.

Once again, we are brought to the second coming of Christ at the end of the age for the fifth time in this book, thus demonstrating the cyclic nature of the book of Revelation. It is not a linear chronology, as the Futurists and the Dispensationalists would say; rather, it is a cyclic chronology, traveling over and over again the same journey from the first to the second coming of Christ, with each journey emphasizing a different theme. Here the theme being emphasized is the wrath of God against the willfully defiant. We see there comes a point in time when people do not listen to the warnings of God's trumpet judgments, that God pours out final destruction upon them.

What is clear from these vial judgments is that God's wrath is terrible, it is final, and it is inescapable, no matter where people flee or what they look to for refuge. It is a fearful thing to fall into the hands of the living God, and this is the message of Revelation 16.

We would do well to flee from the wrath to come by humbling ourselves before God, confessing our sins, and asking God for mercy to be shown to us, forgiveness to be given to us, and a robe of righteousness to be provided for us; so that when He comes, He will look on us and say, "There is one of Mine."

What we have in these vial judgments is as close to hell on earth as there will ever be before the second coming. May God cause us to flee from the wrath to come by fleeing to Christ and finding in Him forgiveness, shelter, and protection.

49

Babylon Rides the Beast, Revelation 17:1–6

> "[1] *And there came one of the seven angels which had the seven vials, and talked with me, saying unto me, Come hither; I will shew unto thee the judgment of the great whore that sitteth upon many waters:* [2] *With whom the kings of the earth have committed fornication, and the inhabitants of the earth have been made drunk with the wine of her fornication.* [3] *So he carried me away in the spirit into the wilderness: and I saw a woman sit upon a scarlet coloured beast, full of names of blasphemy, having seven heads and ten horns.* [4] *And the woman was arrayed in purple and scarlet colour, and decked with gold and precious stones and pearls, having a golden cup in her hand full of abominations and filthiness of her fornication:* [5] *And upon her forehead was a name written, MYSTERY, BABYLON THE GREAT, THE MOTHER OF HARLOTS AND ABOMINATIONS OF THE EARTH.* [6] *And I saw the woman drunken with the blood of the saints, and with the blood of the martyrs of Jesus: and when I saw her, I wondered with great admiration.*"

Revelation is divided into two halves. The first half consists of chapters 1 through 11, which describe the visible and physical conflict between the people of God and the children of Satan that takes place on earth. The second half of this book consists of chapters 12 to 22, which reveal the invisible and spiritual conflict between Christ and Satan, and which explain what is behind the physical visible conflict on earth, and why things happen the way they do.

Therefore, the second half of the book of Revelation introduced us to Satan and his helpers. We were introduced to Satan as the dragon in chapter 12, and we saw how he persecuted the church.

But Satan does not do his work alone. Satan is assisted in his work on earth by anti-Christian government, which is the beast out of the sea. He is assisted by anti-Christian religion, which is the false prophet. He is assisted by anti-Christian society, which is Babylon. Finally, he is assisted by the anti-Christian populace, which are those who think and act as the beast tells them to think and act, and therefore are said to have the mark of the beast in their forehead and in their hand.

Satan and his four helpers are a formidable force against the people of God. However, in this second half of Revelation we see Christ systematically destroying Satan's helpers, and ultimately and finally destroying Satan himself. This destruction of Satan and his helpers takes place at the end of this age when Christ returns, but this destruction is described over a series of chapters and over a series of parallel cycles.

For example, the destruction of the anti-Christian populace (those who have the mark of the beast) is described in the fourth parallel cycle of this book in 14:9–11 at the end of the age when the final judgment comes. The destruction of the anti-Christian society (called Babylon) at the end of this age is briefly spoken of in the fourth parallel cycle in 14:8. It is also briefly spoken of in the fifth parallel cycle in 16:19. But the destruction of Babylon is covered at great length in the sixth parallel section of this book in chapters 17 and 18.

Further on in the sixth parallel section at the end of chapter 19, when Christ returns, we see the destruction of anti-Christian government, called the beast, and the destruction of anti-Christian religion, called the false prophet. Finally, in the seventh parallel section of this book, we see the destruction of Satan himself in 20:10 when Christ returns at the end of this age.

By the time we get to the end of the book, Satan and all of his helpers are defeated and destroyed by Christ, and the people of God who were so severely hated and persecuted by them are delivered, vindicated, and exalted into the everlasting kingdom of God in the new heaven and the new earth. Satan is doing his best in this age to harm the church and the people of God, but at every point, he is unsuccessful in dismantling and destroying the people of God and the kingdom of God on earth.

But just because these various destructions of Satan and his helpers are described over the course of seven chapters and over the course of numerous parallel cycles, it does not mean that these destructions of Satan and his helpers are strung out over an extended period of time, nor does it mean that they are sequentially accomplished one after the other. The destruction of Satan and his helpers all occurs at the same time. These events all occur at the second coming of Christ. They all occur at the end of the age.

Until the end of the age, Satan and his four helpers are active and doing all they can to overthrow Christ's kingdom. But Satan and his helpers do not have smooth sailing in carrying out their plans. They are restrained in their work and punished for their efforts by Christ, and are made miserable through the trumpet judgments and the vial judgments that Christ brings upon them. This is the reason they never succeed in eradicating the church from the earth, though they try very hard to do so. In fact, they try to the point of self-destruction, but never achieve what they attempt to accomplish. Satan and his helpers do terrible things, but they fail to reach their goals, and they always go down to defeat.

We have just been brought to the second coming of Christ at the end of chapter 16, which concluded the fifth parallel section. Therefore, in chapter 17 we are beginning the sixth parallel section of this book, which extends from chapters 17 to 19. Chapter 17 takes us back to the beginning of this age, and it will bring us to the second coming of Christ at the end of chapter 19.

Each of these parallel sections we have previously looked at emphasized a different theme, and this section we are about to embark on is no different. The theme of this sixth parallel section is the defeat of Babylon, the beast, and the false prophet.

Satan has four helpers, and we have already seen the defeat of those who have the mark of the beast in 14:9–11. Here, in this sixth parallel section, we see the full description of the defeat of the remaining three helpers of Satan. The defeat of Babylon is given the largest treatment. It covers all of chapters 17 and 18. In 19:20, the defeat of the beast and the false prophet are declared.

Chapter 17 tells us about the nature of Babylon and its relationship to the beast; chapter 18 tells us about the destruction of Babylon; chapter 19 tells us about the second coming of Christ and the destruction of the beast and the false prophet. This is the outline of this sixth parallel section. It covers the destruction of Babylon and the beast and the false prophet.

The Character of Babylon

The character of Babylon is described in verses 1 to 2. *"And there came one of the seven angels which had the seven vials, and talked with me, saying unto me, Come hither; I will shew unto thee the judgment of the great whore that sitteth upon many waters: [2] With whom the kings of the earth have committed fornication, and the inhabitants of the earth have been made drunk with the wine of her fornication."*

John had just seen the vision of the seven angels pouring out the seven vials of God's wrath in chapter 16. Now, in chapter 17, one of those seven angels comes to John and invites him to view the judgment that God is going to exercise upon Babylon. In verse 1 he says, *"Come hither; I will shew unto thee the judgment of the great whore."* This chapter and the next are all about the work of God in bringing judgment upon Babylon.

Now the fact that this great whore that sits upon many waters is the same as Babylon itself and is a symbolic image of her is made plain in verse 5, where it says she bears the title on her forehead of Babylon the Great. Satan always has his counterfeits of what Christ is and what Christ has, and this case is no different. Babylon is called the great whore that commits fornication with the kings and the people of the earth, and it is the counterfeit of the bride of Christ who is the faithful wife of the Lamb of God. The bride of Christ stands in direct opposition to the harlot Babylon. The bride of Christ is pure and holy and good, while the harlot Babylon is filthy and defiled and evil.

The reason Babylon is called the great harlot is that just like a prostitute, anti-Christian society allures and seduces and draws people away from God. It draws people away from God through the enticements of ostentatious luxury, corrupt entertainment, sexual perversion, and mind-altering drugs. Babylon appeals to men's pride, to their lust for power, and to their desire to be worshiped by others. Babylon encompasses the whole of the corrupt culture of the world that appeals to the lust of the flesh, the lust of the eyes, and the pride of life.

In a word, Babylon is anti-Christian society in all of its vices, in all of its humanism, and in all of its blasphemies against God. Babylon says to the people of the world, "Come and fornicate with me. Taste of my pleasures, and indulge in my vices. I will give you a garden of delights, and you will find an intoxicating fulfillment of every desire you have, no matter how evil it may be. I offer it all." This, then, is the great harlot Babylon that seduces the people of the earth to yield themselves to evil and to turn away from God.

It says of the great harlot Babylon that she sits *"upon many waters."* Old Testament Babylon that captured Israel and brought her into captivity was a city that literally sat on many waters. The Euphrates River ran through the middle of the city, and there was an extensive system of canals within the city that distributed water, so Babylon was often called the City of Waters. Therefore, this spiritual, metaphorical Babylon, which represents anti-Christian society, is said to sit upon many waters.

We are not left in doubt as to what the reference to *"many waters"* means. Notice verse 15 of this same chapter: *"And he saith unto me, The waters which thou sawest, where the whore sitteth, are peoples, and multitudes, and nations, and tongues."* So this whore, this anti-Christian society, is based upon and made up of peoples, and multitudes, and nations, and tongues.

The collective culture of people who live in rebellion against God is what constitutes anti-Christian society. Wherever in the world unsaved people gather together to form a society, there is where Babylon exists, no matter the nationality, no matter the language, and no matter the race. Babylon is the collective cultural consensus of the anti-Christian society made up of all those who bear the mark of the beast, wherever they live throughout the world, and in whatever age they live. In a word, all wicked societies are Babylon the Great Harlot, wherever they may be distributed throughout the world.

Babylon is anti-Christian society that seeks to seduce the believer into forsaking Christ for the pleasures of this world. We see this in verse 2. Notice it says, regarding this harlot, *"With whom the kings of the earth have committed fornication, and the inhabitants of the earth have been made drunk with the wine of her fornication."*

The kings of the earth fornicate with Babylon; that is, they encourage and participate in what the godless societies of the world want and desire. This is because the kings of the earth derive their existence and their wealth and their power from the anti-Christian societies over which they rule.

If an anti-Christian populace wants wicked and sinful policies put in place, the politicians bow the knee to them and give them what they want, so the society will support them and keep them in power. Kings, who are supposed to provide godly moral leadership to the nation, instead participate in the vices of the nation themselves, and even encourage further evil, in order to win favor and gain the further extension of their rule and reign. The kings of the earth have intercourse with the pride and materialism and vice and evil of the people they rule, and are often the worst participants in those things themselves.

But not only do the kings of the earth commit fornication with the harlot Babylon; the people of the earth are intoxicated and made drunk with the wine of the wickedness evil societies pour out for them to drink. Every day through the television, the Internet, the newspapers and magazines, the radio, the government school system, and the entertainment industry the inhabitants of the earth are made drunk with anti-Christian attitudes and are encouraged to engage in anti-Christian behavior.

This is why, as Christians, we need to maintain separation from this anti-Christian society, in terms of not indulging in its sins and seductions and vices. We have to live in the midst of this anti-Christian Babylonian society, but just like Daniel, Shadrach, Meshach, and Abednego, we must refuse to bow to its idols, we must refuse to fear its power, and we must refuse to indulge in the sins and corruptions it offers us.

We must maintain our witness, our prayer life, and our godliness, even though it angers Babylon and provokes its hatred and persecution, and makes its people want to throw us into their lions' den. Like Pilgrim and Faithful in the book *The Pilgrim's Progress*, while we must walk through this world's Vanity Fair on our way to the Celestial City, we must not be a partaker of what it offers.

Notice Revelation 18:4–8: *"And I heard another voice from heaven, saying, Come out of her, my people, that ye be not partakers of her sins, and that ye receive not of her plagues.* [5] *For her sins have reached unto heaven, and God hath remembered her iniquities.* [6] *Reward her even as she rewarded you, and double unto her double according to her works: in the cup which she hath filled fill to her double.* [7] *How much she hath glorified herself, and lived deliciously, so much torment and sorrow give her: for she saith in her heart, I sit a queen, and am no widow, and shall see no sorrow.* [8] *Therefore shall her plagues come in one day, death, and mourning, and famine; and she shall be utterly burned with fire: for strong is the Lord God who judgeth her."*

God is telling us to come out of Babylon and not to participate in her sins. God is going to pour out His wrath upon anti-Christian society and all it stands for, practices, and promotes. We do well to heed the advice of Revelation 18:4: *"Come out of her, my people, that ye be not partakers of her sins, and that ye receive not of her plagues."* We do well to heed that advice and to keep ourselves unspotted from the world. Just as God destroyed Old Testament Babylon, God will also destroy the anti-Christian society in which we live today.

Do not be drawn into the sins of this age and the vanity and pride the world so powerfully encourages. Do not love the world. Do not become intoxicated with the material and the sensual pleasures that it offers. This world will pass away with the lusts thereof, but they that do the will of God will abide forever.

This is the character of Babylon. She represents anti-Christian seduction. She seduces the kings, she seduces the people, and she says to both kings and people, "Come and follow me and indulge in my vices and my sins, and you will find happiness and the fulfillment of all of your wicked desires." The vast majority of people around the globe and through the centuries have bought into the seduction of the harlot—and as a result, Babylon has existed from the time of Christ to the present moment and will continue to exist until Christ returns, for Babylon is nothing more than anti-Christian society that constitutes the kingdom of Satan.

And while we have to physically live in the midst of anti-Christian society, we should not mentally live in the center of the city of Babylon. It says of the church in Revelation 12 that she fled to the wilderness. Remember the account of Abraham and Lot? Who went to the city? Who stayed out in the wilderness? Abraham, the man of God, stayed in the wilderness, and would not go into Sodom and participate in its lifestyle. Sadly, Lot went and lived in it, and Lot was ruined as a result.

Metaphorically speaking, we have to live in the wilderness, and not participate in the sins of the city. We have to be separate from it, and we have to come out from among those sins and live in a wilderness of isolation from the pleasure-mad wickedness of the city Babylon.

The Appearance of Babylon

The appearance of Babylon is in verses 3 to 6. *"So he carried me away in the spirit into the wilderness: and I saw a woman sit upon a scarlet coloured beast, full of names of blasphemy, having seven heads and ten horns.* [4] *And the woman was arrayed in purple and scarlet colour, and decked with gold and precious stones and pearls, having a golden cup in her hand full of abominations and filthiness of her fornication:* [5] *And upon her forehead was a name written, MYSTERY, BABYLON THE GREAT, THE MOTHER OF HARLOTS AND ABOMINATIONS OF THE EARTH.* [6] *And I saw the woman drunken with the blood of the saints, and with the blood of the martyrs of Jesus: and when I saw her, I wondered with great admiration."*

The angel gave a verbal description of the harlot Babylon in verses 1 to 2, and now John has a visual depiction of the harlot Babylon in verses 3 to 6. We move from a verbal to a visual description, but the message is still the same. John is carried away, it says in verse 3, *"in the spirit into the wilderness."* In chapter 12, the church fled into the wilderness to escape the persecution of the dragon. Therefore, it is not surprising that John would see the beast and Babylon in the wilderness, chasing and persecuting the church who had fled there to escape. What did John see in the wilderness? He saw Babylon the harlot sitting upon the beast. Babylon rides the beast, like a human rides a horse.

The identity of this beast in verse 3 is clear from the description of it. Notice, it says, *"I saw a woman sit upon a scarlet coloured beast, full of names of blasphemy, having seven heads and ten horns."* The beast is said to be scarlet or red in color. The dragon representing Satan was also said to be red in color in Revelation 12:3. Red is the color of blood, and both the dragon and the beast are red because they are drenched in the blood of the Christians they have slaughtered. Revelation 13:1–2 says that the dragon empowers the beast to do this work of slaughter, and that slaughter is explicitly described in 13:7.

Furthermore, the beast in Revelation 13:1 has seven heads and ten horns, just like this beast has. Finally, the beast of 13:1 has the name of blasphemy on his head, just like this beast has. Therefore, we conclude that the beast of 17:3 is the same as the beast out of the sea in 13:1–8. This beast is anti-Christian government, which is Satan's most powerful helper.

Verse 3 tells us about the relationship between Babylon and the beast, between anti-Christian society and anti-Christian government. The relationship between Babylon and the beast is that anti-Christian society rides upon anti-Christian government. Anti-Christian society rides the beast, and anti-Christian society rules the beast.

Notice Revelation 17:18. It says, *"And the woman which thou sawest is that great city"*—that is, Babylon. Now notice what it says about Babylon—*"which reigneth over the kings of the earth."* When you have a horse and a rider, who is in control? The rider controls the horse. Here we see this woman riding the beast. We are explicitly told in verse 18 that the great city Babylon rules over the kings of the earth.

Even though kings ostensibly rule over the people, the people are the ones who provide the king with his authority and his tenure, and it is a historical fact that popular revolt will take down any king. Therefore, we see the harlot Babylon riding the beast, to indicate that the beast serves the interests of the harlot Babylon, and the beast follows the direction of the anti-Christian society over which it rules.

However, at the end of this age, we will see the Antichrist and his transnational coalition of kings destroy the harlot Babylon. Anti-Christian government will rise up and destroy the anti-Christian society at the end of time. How that is going to work will be explained when we expound 17:16, which says of this transnational coalition of Anti-Christ and his ten horns, *"these shall hate the whore, and shall make her desolate and naked, and shall eat her flesh, and burn her with fire."*

But for now, all throughout this age, the harlot rides the beast and the harlot rules the beast. Government reflects the will of the people, and government serves the collective voice of the people. That is how governments rise to power, and that is how governments stay in power—by serving the people over whom they rule, and thereby gaining their popular support.

What does anti-Christian society look like? Verse 4 tells us. *"And the woman was arrayed in purple and scarlet colour, and decked with gold and precious stones and pearls, having a golden cup in her hand full of abominations and filthiness of her fornication."* This is what anti-Christian society looks like. Anti-Christian society looks wealthy and regal. Purple is the color of rulers. Anti-Christian society looks attractive and inviting and desirable. Gold and jewels and pearls speak of her wealth. The golden cup of her hand speaks of sensuous enticements.

This woman, this harlot Babylon, this anti-Christian society, looks splendid and attractive and inviting and glorious. She offers a beautiful cup to drink out of that conveys the impression that, because it is made out of gold, it must contain the finest of wine within it. But looks are deceiving. The cup is full of the abominations and the filthiness of her fornication.

Understand that the world presents itself as elevated and sophisticated and desirable and exciting. But all it has to offer is abominable filth and disgusting perversions that lead to misery and destruction. Evil often wears an attractive face and presents itself as exceedingly desirable, but its end is bitter and its fruits are poisonous.

Do not be deceived by external appearances and by initial impressions of what the world has to offer you. Sin is always deceitful, and even though it has a moment of pleasure, it always has a bitter ending.

Now what the harlot Babylon is by appearance in verse 4, she is by title in verse 5. Notice it says, *"and upon her forehead was a name written, MYSTERY, BABYLON THE GREAT, THE MOTHER OF HARLOTS AND ABOMINATIONS OF THE EARTH."* In Revelation, we have seen that a name on the forehead reveals the individual's character and his relationship either to God or to Satan. If you have the mark of the beast in your forehead, it represents the character you have and your relationship to Satan. If you have the seal of God in your forehead, it represents the character you have and your relationship with God. This harlot's name on her forehead reveals her evil character and her relationship with the beast.

The first word *"mystery"* is really not part of the title itself, but rather a declaration that something that has formerly been hidden is now going to be revealed by God. This is how the word "mystery" is used in the Bible. It is not used of something spooky or occultic. The word "mystery" is used to indicate that something previously concealed is now going to be revealed by God. This is something people could never have figured out on their own, but now they know it because God has revealed this hidden truth. For example, this is how the word "mystery" is used in Ephesians 3:3–5.

The mystery that is being uncovered and revealed is this title that describes the identity of this woman. Who is this woman? She is *"BABYLON THE GREAT"*—a claim of arrogant superiority and prideful self-glorification. "Look how great I am! I am Babylon the Great." This is what Nebuchadnezzar was saying in Daniel 4 when he said, "Is not this great Babylon that I have built for the glory of my name?" Modern-day society has the spirit of Nebuchadnezzar.

She is the shameless source of every perversion and every abomination on the earth. Notice, it says, *"BABYLON THE GREAT, THE MOTHER"*—that is, the source—*"OF HARLOTS AND ABOMINATIONS OF THE EARTH."* Anti-Christian society is the source of every kind of wickedness, and actively fosters and promotes every kind of vice. The world is proud of its wickedness, boldly advertises its wickedness, actively promotes its wickedness, and is utterly shameless in the declaration of its wickedness.

Jeremiah 3:3 speaks of hardened sinners having a whore's forehead, and who therefore refuse to be ashamed. This description fits the spirit of our culture that proudly promotes every perversion as a virtue, and every virtuous person as a bigot. Our culture shamelessly glorifies homosexuality, adultery, fornication, transgenderism, and sodomite marriage with no shame. Anyone who opposes those things is shamed by our culture. We have this whore, boldly and brazenly advertising herself to the world, offering the worst evils and being utterly shameless in enticing people to participate in them.

Now notice verse 6: *"And I saw the woman drunken with the blood of the saints, and with the blood of the martyrs of Jesus: and when I saw her, I wondered with great admiration."* Not only have the inhabitants of the earth been made drunk with the wine of the harlot's fornication; the harlot herself is also drunk. She is drunk with the blood of the saints and the martyrs of Jesus. Anti-Christian society knows very clearly who the Christians are, what they stand for, the message they preach, and the Christ they follow.

They are *"saints."* They live holy and separated lives. They are *"martyrs."* They bear witness to Jesus Christ, even to the point of death. The world knows who we are. They know the message we preach, and they know the Christ we worship and follow. They hate us for it.

Roman society reveled in seeing the blood of Christians spilled in the Coliseum, and they were drunken with amusement and entertainment and pleasure at the sight. The crowds roared as the blood spilled. They were drunken with the blood.

Roman society reveled in seeing the blood of Christians spilled in the Coliseum, and anti-Christian societies ever since have rejoiced in shedding the blood of believers. The wicked find it intoxicating to see believers martyred. It is party time for them when they can kill Christians. Revelation 11:10 makes that clear. Islam has been doing it for 1,400 years. Atheist nations have been doing it. Self-serving kings have been doing it. It has been going on since the time of Christ.

Christians have been martyred throughout this age, and they will especially be martyred when Satan is loosed and the Antichrist arises at the end of this age. Then the blood of Christians will flow, and anti-Christian society, it says in Revelation 11:10, will rejoice and its members will send presents to one another over the slaughter of the church.

As John beholds this vision, he is overwhelmed and amazed at the power and success of the harlot Babylon. He had just been told in verse 1 that he was going to be shown the judgment of the great whore, but all he has seen so far is her glory and her success. So he stands, verse 6 says, dumbfounded, amazed, and overwhelmed by what he sees.

At this stage in God's plan, we too stand amazed at the success of Satan and the accomplishments of the world in its fight against God. It seems like the world has won. It seems like the world has nothing but popularity, power, success, acclaim, and applause, while the Christians are a downtrodden, despised, and persecuted minority.

But the angel is now poised to show John the rest of the story. Then, this apparent success will be seen for the failure it is. In verse 7 it says, *"And the angel said unto me, Wherefore didst thou marvel? I will tell thee the mystery of the woman, and of the beast that carrieth her,"* and then he goes on to describe her utter destruction in the following verses.

We, like John, have to look past the present and into the future. When we understand the destruction that Babylon the great harlot will experience in the future, we will not be so intimidated and discouraged by her apparent success in the present, as she rides the beast and revels in the destruction of the saints, and as she promotes her wickedness in the world.

The story does not stop at verse 6. That is not the end of the story. The story stops at Revelation 22:21. We need to remember that, and be encouraged by understanding that as we find ourselves overwhelmed by the power of Babylon, and as we live in the midst of this crooked and corrupt culture, it will be defeated and destroyed. Our task is to maintain separation from the wickedness of it, and to walk through it as pilgrims and strangers and sojourners, and recognize that in the end, as it says in 18:8, *"her plagues [shall] come in one day, death, and mourning, and famine; and she shall be utterly burned with fire: for strong is the Lord God who judgeth her."*

There is coming a day when God is going to say, "That is enough!" He is going to rise in judgment and utterly destroy the pride and arrogance and perversion of our culture and society. When He does, the saints will shine as the stars of heaven, and we will be exalted and vindicated and conducted into the new heavens and the new earth, into a perfect society, one that is the antithesis of everything Babylon was. We shall live in that perfect New Jerusalem forever and ever, and Babylon will be forever gone. She will be cast into the lake of fire.

Do not be attracted to and impressed by the glitter and the glamour and the pleasures that the world is currently offering you as it entices you with deceptive invitations. *"Keep [yourself] unspotted from the world."* Babylon says, "Come away from Christ. Come lie with me. Come indulge yourself in my pleasures."

Turn away from that harlot. Be the faithful bride of Jesus Christ, so that, when He comes, He will find you to be a virgin, not having had intercourse with this world. If you are found faithful to Him, you will be conducted into the marriage supper of the Lamb to be with Him forever.

50

The Judgment of the Beast, Revelation 17:7–8

> "[7] *And the angel said unto me, Wherefore didst thou marvel? I will tell thee the mystery of the woman, and of the beast that carrieth her, which hath the seven heads and ten horns.* [8] *The beast that thou sawest was, and is not; and shall ascend out of the bottomless pit, and go into perdition: and they that dwell on the earth shall wonder, whose names were not written in the book of life from the foundation of the world, when they behold the beast that was, and is not, and yet is.*"

We enter into what is arguably the most difficult passage in the entire book of Revelation to interpret. In verses 7 through 18 the big picture is pretty clear, but the difficulty lies in the details and the complex language and the density of ideas contained within that language. There is a lot of meaning in every word and every phrase. Each verse is loaded with information.

To properly grasp what is being conveyed in this section not only requires sustained and focused attention, but it also requires careful analysis of the symbolic language and figures that are used. In a word, there is some hard mental work ahead of you if you are going to avoid being lost and confused in the language of this particular passage.

In the previous chapter, we looked at verses 1 to 6 in which the angel told John he was going to show him God's judgment on the harlot Babylon, which represents anti-Christian society. But initially, the angel gave John a sight of the prosperity, success, power, and seductiveness of this harlot Babylon. The angel revealed the close relationship between the harlot Babylon and the beast.

Anti-Christian society (the harlot Babylon) and anti-Christian government (the beast) work very closely together in order to promote the blasphemy of God, the persecution of Christians, and the practice of every possible abomination. Both government and society are intoxicated with the murder of Christians and with the practice of every kind of perversion of morality, both in thought and in deed.

As John sees the strength, prosperity, and success of this evil cooperation between the harlot Babylon and the beast, he is overwhelmed and amazed. John has been told in verse 1 of this chapter that he is going to be shown the judgment of the great whore, but all he has seen thus far is her glory and her success. Therefore, at the end of verse 6, John is dumbfounded with amazement.

We stand today where John stood at the end of verse 6. All we have seen for the last 2,000 years is the prosperity, success, power, and perversion of the harlot Babylon. Anti-Christian society and anti-Christian government have been working closely together to successfully seduce the world away from Christ for the last 2,000 years.

It says in Jeremiah 51:7, "*Babylon hath been a golden cup in the* L*ORD's hand, that made all the earth drunken: the nations have drunken of her wine; therefore the nations are mad.*" The whole world is insane in its rebellion against God as a result of the work of the harlot Babylon. We are dumbfounded and overwhelmed by the success of the anti-Christian forces in the world, and we doubt if there will ever be any way the forces of evil will someday be defeated.

But notice verse 7: "*And the angel said unto me, Wherefore didst thou marvel? I will tell thee the mystery of the woman, and of the beast that carrieth her, which hath the seven heads and ten horns.*" After seeing the prosperity and success of the harlot Babylon in union with the beast, the angel tells John not to marvel at the power and success of anti-Christian government and anti-Christian society. The harlot Babylon and the beast are both going to be defeated by Jesus Christ. He then proceeds to explain the demise and destruction of Babylon and the beast in the remainder of chapter 17 and 18.

Notice Revelation 17:14. It says, "*These*"—that is, the harlot and the beast—"*shall make war with the Lamb, and the Lamb shall overcome them: for he is Lord of lords, and King of kings: and they that are with him are called, and chosen, and faithful.*" Revelation 17:14 is the key verse of the book of Revelation. In this one verse we see the summary of the message of the entire book. Satan and his helpers are going to make war with Christ; Christ is going to make war with them and defeat them and triumph over them; and in His triumph is the triumph of His people who are called, and chosen, and faithful.

This is the message: The harlot and the beast make war against Christ and His people, and Christ is going to defeat the harlot and the beast and vindicate His people. Both anti-Christian government and anti-Christian society will be crushed under the heel of Christ.

The Summary of the Judgment of the Beast

The summary of the judgment of the beast is contained in verse 8a. Verse 8 says, *"The beast that thou sawest was, and is not; and shall ascend out of the bottomless pit, and go into perdition: and they that dwell on the earth shall wonder, whose names were not written in the book of life from the foundation of the world, when they behold the beast that was, and is not, and yet is."*

Although the angel has told John he is going to show him the judgment of the harlot Babylon in verse 1, he must first explain the judgment of the beast on which the harlot is riding.

The career of the beast in verse 8a is traced from start to finish with four points: 1) the beast *"was"*; 2) the beast *"is not"*; 3) the beast *"shall ascend out of the bottomless pit"*; 4) the beast *"will go into perdition."*

Those four phrases summarize the total existence of the beast, and we want to understand these four phrases and their meaning, but to do so will require our focused attention on the details of each point.

The beast, as we have said many times, represents and symbolizes anti-Christian government. That has been established already. Such anti-Christian governments have existed from the beginning of the formation of human societies. Their beast-like character was made clear in Daniel 7 when Daniel likens the Babylonian empire to a lion, the Medo-Persian empire to a bear, the Grecian empire to a leopard, and the Roman empire to a nameless, strong, terrible, and dreadful beast that has teeth of iron. Daniel describes these four world empires as being four great beasts in Daniel 7:3

The dragon, who symbolizes Satan in the book of Revelation, has always been the energizing power behind each of these kingdoms. In fact, Satan is the energizing power behind all human governments on earth, wherever they have been located, and whenever they have existed. All human governments are manifestations of the beast, and all of them are energized and empowered by Satan. We read in Revelation 13:2 that the dragon gives the beast his power, his throne, and his authority.

Prior to the first coming of Christ, Satan was at liberty to do much of what he pleased among the kingdoms of the world during the 4,000 years from creation to Christ. Those kingdoms constituted his kingdom, and he gave them their power and their direction, and that is what gave them their predatory nature, symbolized in the predatory beasts that represented each of them.

And while these satanically empowered kingdoms succeeded one another in history, one thing was a constant among them all: they were always striving to suppress and destroy the kingdom of God and the people of God on earth.

However, even though Satan was largely free to act as he wished among the governments of the earth from the fall to the first coming of Christ, he was still under the restraint and sovereign control of God to the degree that he could not extinguish the kingdom of God on earth.

Nevertheless, Satan was able to keep the kingdom of God on earth very small so that at one point in time prior to the flood, the kingdom of God consisted of only eight people on the earth who subsequently got into the ark.

After the flood, Satan was able to continue to keep the kingdom of God exceedingly small, confining it to a small number of people in a tiny piece of land in the Middle East. The kingdom of God was the nation of Israel in the land of Israel—at its height just a few million people, occupying one ten-thousandth of the habitable land area of the earth.

Excluding Antarctica and adding up all of the habitable landmasses of the earth, there are 52 million square miles. The land of Israel is only 8,000 square miles. Israel is approximately one ten-thousandth of the habitable land on the face of the earth. That is how big the kingdom of God was at its maximum size between the fall and the first coming of Christ. The whole rest of the world, outside of tiny Israel, was under the darkness of Satan's rule for 4,000 years.

However, when Christ came, there was a dramatic change. Satan, who previously was free to do virtually what he pleased among the kingdoms of the world, was bound and chained by Christ at His first coming, as Matthew 12:24–29 states. No longer was Satan able to deceive the nations and their anti-Christian civil governments as he was in the past.

At His first coming, Jesus bound Satan, and Jesus invaded Satan's kingdom, taking whatever He wanted and whomever He wanted out of his kingdom of darkness and bringing them into His own kingdom of light. This has continued without remission for the last 2,000 years. Christ so sharply curtailed Satan's liberty and ability to deceive the beastly governments of the earth that it was as though Satan had departed from the scene. It was as though Satan had been removed from the world stage and was bound and buried in a pit. And of course, that is exactly what the Bible tells us happened.

Revelation 20:1–3 says: *"And I saw an angel come down from heaven, having the key of the bottomless pit and a great chain in his hand.*
2And he laid hold on the dragon, that old serpent, which is the Devil, and Satan, and bound him a thousand years, 3And cast him into the bottomless pit, and shut him up, and set a seal upon him, that he should deceive the nations no more, till the thousand years should be fulfilled: and after that he must be loosed a little season."

John is describing what occurred at the cross when Jesus bound the strong man. This thousand-year period is a symbolic number that describes the time between the binding and loosing of Satan. For the last 2,000 years, Satan has been bound and buried with reference to his ability to deceive the governments of the world in the way he used to be able to do prior to the first coming of Christ.

The result of the binding of Satan and the reduction of his power to deceive the nations is that the governments he was the energizing power behind have also had their power reduced. If Satan is energizing the nations of the world, and Satan becomes bound, what impact does that have on the nations of the world? The energizing power he was giving to them to suppress the kingdom of God has been dramatically reduced and restrained.

Because Satan has been bound in the pit, and therefore cannot deceive and empower the human governments of the world as he did before the first coming of Christ, human governments of the world have been weak and unable to suppress the kingdom of God and the people of God like they once did. They are weak like the mixture of iron and clay is weak. The result has been an explosion of the kingdom of God across the globe to the degree that Christianity has become the dominant religion in the whole world. No longer is the kingdom of God a couple of million people confined to a country barely a hundred miles long and forty miles wide. Now the kingdom of God covers the whole earth, and numbers in the billions of people.

However, at the end of this age, Satan will be loosed from his pit as Revelation 20:3 says, *"he must be loosed for a little season."* Satan will experience a resurrection of his power and influence over the nations, with the result that the anti-Christian governments will receive a tremendous infusion of power and energy from Satan which they have not had since the first coming of Christ. Anti-Christian governments will suddenly have a revival of anti-Christian fervor that only existed between the fall and the first coming, and has not existed for the last 2,000 years to the degree it did before the first coming of Christ.

Once again, the beast will strive to suppress and eradicate the kingdom of God as it did before the first coming. In Noah's day, the beast reduced the kingdom to eight people! They are going to try to do the same thing again. Because of the revived power of Satan after he has been loosed, human governments will have a renewed power of persecution, only experienced by the people of God before the first coming. Therefore, we see that the activity of anti-Christian governments—that is, the activity of the beast—mirrors and parallels the activity of Satan himself, because Satan is the one who gives the beast his authority, his throne, and his power. Therefore, as it goes with Satan, so it goes with the beast.

What do we see, then, with Satan? He was alive from the fall to Christ's first coming. Then he went through a kind of a death and a burial when he was bound and plunged into the bottomless pit, beginning at the resurrection of Christ and continuing to this very day. But at some point in the future, he will have a resurrection from the pit and a return to power at the end of this age. Satan will be loosed and there will be, as it were, a second coming of Satan in which he has his previous power and ability and activity restored to him.

Take careful note of this point: What happens to Satan happens to the beast he empowers. The careers of the dragon and the beast run parallel to each other because the one is dependent upon the other. As goes the one, so goes the other; as goes Satan, so goes the beast. What we see happening with Satan is exactly what happens to the beast.

Before the first coming of Christ, the beast had full power and authority and motivation and liberty to oppress the kingdom of God, and was very successful at it. After the first coming of Christ, the beast lost life and power and ability to effectively stop the spread of the kingdom of God. The beast became weak, like the feet of Daniel's image that were made part of iron and part of clay; they could not get it together to effectively suppress the kingdom of God as they had done for the previous 4,000 years. The beast could not have the unity of purpose and singleness of mind and constancy of strength to stop the two witnesses of Revelation 11, who represent the church. He could not stop them from completing their mission of evangelizing the whole world and all of God's elect. Not until their testimony is finished is Satan released and his power restored to energize anti-Christian governments.

When all the work of evangelism is done and all of the elect are saved, Satan will be loosed; and as a result, the final manifestation of the beast will arise, which is the Antichrist and his transnational worldwide coalition and kingdom. The beast will revive. He will have a new infusion of power to persecute the people of God. The final beast, the Antichrist, the beast that arises out of the bottomless pit, will suddenly come to life with a unified powerful zeal to crush the kingdom of God.

What can we say historically about the beast? We can say regarding the beast, he *"was."* From the fall to the first coming of Christ, the beast had full power and full function to oppress the kingdom of God, and he did.

And then we can say regarding the career of the beast, he *"is not."* From the first coming of Christ to this present moment, in every century for the last 2,000 years, we can say of the beast that Christ has so bound Satan, the source of the beast's energy, that it is as though the beast has ceased to function in any meaningful manner to stop the spread of the gospel and the kingdom of God.

Have there been bits and pieces of persecution against the church? Have there been some short-term efforts, lasting a few decades, to try to extinguish the church in this or that location or country? Certainly there have been. There still are. But for all intents and purposes, the beast has been absent from mounting any concerted or meaningful effort to stop or reverse the spread of Christianity across the world and into every nation of the earth. We can say that for the last 2,000 years, even up to this very present moment, we can say right now, the beast *"is not."*

However, the day is coming when the beast will come roaring back to life. It will be like a resurrection. The beast will *"ascend out of the bottomless pit."* We identified the beast out of the bottomless pit in Revelation 11:7 as the Antichrist and his worldwide coalition of nations that will unify with him to seek to kill the church from off the face of the earth. Because Satan is loosed, Antichrist and his kingdom will arise.

Antichrist and his kingdom are the final manifestation of the beast. Antichrist and his kingdom are the beast out of the bottomless pit of 17:8, as well as the beast out of the bottomless pit of Revelation 11:7. Previously we said there were three beasts—the beast out of the sea, anti-Christian government; the beast out of the earth, otherwise known as the false prophet; and the beast out of the bottomless pit, which is Antichrist and his kingdom.

The final manifestation of the beast will come roaring back to life with a new power that Satan infuses into it because now Satan is finally free to energize and empower the nations like he has not been free to do since the first coming of Christ. The visible manifestation of this exercise of the resurgent power of Satan will be the rise of Antichrist and his transnational, worldwide coalition of all the kingdoms of the earth, united together in their determination to reduce the church to nothing, and they will be largely successful in doing that.

Recall the two bodies of the witnesses of Revelation 11 lying in the streets, and the world rejoicing in the triumph they had obtained over the church. They even sent presents to each other. It was party time because the church had been wiped off the earth in terms of her public testimony and her visible presence. There was a remnant left, and there always will be, but it will be a small remnant. Antichrist's goal is to eradicate the church from the earth and cause all of the earth to worship him as God.

But what will happen to the beast that arises out of the bottomless pit? Now we come to the fourth descriptor of the career of the beast contained in verse 8: He will *"go into perdition."* Antichrist and his kingdom will be cast into hell. Notice Revelation 19:19–20: *"And I saw the beast, and the kings of the earth, and their armies, gathered together to make war against him that sat on the horse, and against his army.* [20]*And the beast was taken, and with him the false prophet that wrought miracles before him, with which he deceived them that had received the mark of the beast, and them that worshipped his image. These both"* (the beast and false prophet) *"were cast alive into a lake of fire burning with brimstone."*

This same event of Christ driving the beast into perdition is also described in Daniel 7:11, 26. In verse 11 it says: *"I beheld then because of the voice of the great words which the horn spake."* (The horn is the Antichrist.) *"I beheld even till the beast was slain, and his body destroyed, and given to the burning flame."* That is the Antichrist going into perdition, the final beast and his kingdom. Notice verse 26: *". . . and they shall take away his dominion, to consume and to destroy it unto the end."* His dominion is going to be ruined, and he is going to be cast into the pit.

In Revelation 11 the same event is described. There we have the two witnesses who are preaching throughout the time between the first and second coming of Christ. It says of them in verse 7, *"And when they shall have finished their testimony,"* (nothing is going to happen until all the elect are saved, and when they are all saved, then) *"the beast that ascendeth out of the bottomless pit shall make war against them"*—that is, against the two witnesses who represent the church—*"and shall overcome them and kill them.* [8] *And their dead bodies shall lie in the street of the great city, which spiritually is called Sodom and Egypt, where also our Lord was crucified.* [9] *And they of the people and kindreds and tongues and nations"* (this is the worldwide coalition under Antichrist, the beast out of the bottomless pit) *"shall see their dead bodies three days and an half, and shall not suffer their dead bodies to be put in graves."* They will have complete disrespect for those they have slaughtered.

"[10] *And they that dwell upon the earth shall rejoice over them, and make merry, and shall send gifts one to another; because these two prophets tormented them that dwelt on the earth.* [11] *And after three days and an half the Spirit of life from God entered into them, and they stood upon their feet; and great fear fell upon them which saw them.* [12] *And they heard a great voice from heaven saying unto them, Come up hither"* (at the second coming, the rapture occurs; the believers go up to be with Christ to return in triumph with Him). *"And they ascended up to heaven in a cloud; and their enemies beheld them.* [13] *And the same hour was there a great earthquake, and the tenth part of the city fell, and in the earthquake were slain of men seven thousand: and the remnant were affrighted, and gave glory to the God of heaven.* [14] *The second woe is past; and, behold, the third woe cometh quickly.*

"[15] *And the seventh angel sounded; and there were great voices in heaven, saying, The kingdoms of this world are become the kingdoms of our Lord, and of his Christ; and he shall reign for ever and ever.*

[16] *And the four and twenty elders, which sat before God on their seats, fell upon their faces, and worshipped God,* [17] *Saying, We give thee thanks, O Lord God Almighty, which art, and wast, and art to come; because thou hast taken to thee thy great power, and hast reigned.* [18] *And the nations were angry, and thy wrath is come, and the time of the dead, that they should be judged, and that thou shouldest give reward unto thy servants the prophets, and to the saints, and them that fear thy name, small and great; and shouldest destroy them which destroy the earth.* [19] *And the temple of God was opened in heaven, and there was seen in his temple the ark of his testament: and there were lightnings, and voices, and thunderings, and an earthquake, and great hail."* Here is the beast going into perdition.

When the beast has his short-term success in largely wiping the church off the face of the earth, he does not then go on to triumph. He then goes on to hell and to defeat for all eternity. These shall make war with the Lamb, but the Lamb shall overcome them, for He is King of kings and Lord of lords.

Notice Revelation 20:7: "*And when the thousand years are expired, Satan shall be loosed out of his prison,* [8] *And shall go out to deceive the nations which are in the four quarters of the earth, Gog and Magog, to gather them together to battle: the number of whom is as the sand of the sea.* [9] *And they went up on the breadth of the earth, and compassed the camp of the saints about, and the beloved city: and fire came down from God out of heaven, and devoured them.* [10] *And the devil that deceived them was cast into the lake of fire and brimstone, where the beast and the false prophet are, and shall be tormented day and night for ever and ever.*"

When Satan is loosed, we are going to have anti-Christian civil government experiencing a resurrection of power under the leadership of the Antichrist, who is going to form a transnational coalition of all the nations of the world. Together, they are going to strive to wipe the church off the face of the earth. They will be largely successful, except for a small remnant, and as they go to finally destroy that small remnant, Christ will come and resurrect the dead in Christ, instantly glorify the few remaining believers, rapture them all up into heaven, and return and destroy Antichrist and all of his helpers, and cast them into the lake of fire. His people will be delivered, His judgment will be set, His kingdom will be established, and the new heavens and the new earth will be created. When the beast experiences his resurrection from the pit, he soon goes on to hell and defeat for all eternity.

In sharp contrast to this, when Christ experienced His resurrection, He went on to victory and to triumph. Notice Revelation 1:18. Jesus is speaking, and He says: *"I am he that liveth, and was dead; and, behold, I am alive for evermore, Amen; and have the keys of hell and of death."*

We could say of Christ that He *was*. For thirty-three years, He lived. And then we could say of Christ, He *was not*, for three days. He was dead in the grave. And then we could say of Christ, that He *ascended* out of the grave. This was His glorious resurrection. And then we could say of Christ, that *He triumphs* forevermore. He has the keys of hell and of death.

What do we see of the beast? He *was*, from the fall to Christ; he *is not*, from the resurrection to the loosing of Satan; he *shall ascend out of the bottomless pit* up to power after Satan is loosed; but after a very short rule, he goes down *into perdition*, into the lake of fire.

Christ defeats the beast of anti-Christian civil government and triumphs over it.

The Admiration of the Beast by the Wicked

The admiration of the beast by the wicked is in verse 8b. It says, *"and they that dwell on the earth shall wonder, whose names were not written in the book of life from the foundation of the world, when they behold the beast that was, and is not, and yet is."*

This second half of verse 8 describes the unsaved who are living on the earth during the time that the Antichrist appears.

When Satan is loosed at the end of this age and re-energizes the beast with unbridled zeal and power to wipe the church from the face of the earth, it will excite the enthusiasm and admiration of the unsaved. The unsaved *"that dwell on the earth"* will give blind loyalty and reverent worship to the Antichrist because he will be presenting himself as God on earth.

Notice 2 Thessalonians 2:1–15: *"Now we beseech you, brethren, by the coming of our Lord Jesus Christ, and by our gathering together unto him."* This is the second coming and the rapture. He is coming back, and we are going to be gathered together with Him.

He goes on to say: "[2] *That ye be not soon shaken in mind, or be troubled, neither by spirit, nor by word, nor by letter as from us, as that the day of Christ is at hand."* Paul is saying the second coming of Christ and the rapture are not imminent. They are not at hand. It cannot happen tomorrow.

He says, "[3] *Let no man deceive you by any means: for that day shall not come, except there come, a falling away first."* That is, there is going to be a great apostasy among the professing church before Christ comes. The reason for that apostasy is due to the coming of Antichrist at the head of the final manifestation of the re-energized beast. Verse 3 continues, *"and that man of sin be revealed, the son of perdition;* [4] *Who opposeth and exalteth himself above all that is called God, or that is worshipped; so that he as God sitteth in the temple of God, shewing himself that he is God."*

What is being described in Revelation 17:8b, when it says that *"they that dwell on the earth shall wonder, whose names were not written in the book of life from the foundation of the world, when they behold the beast,"* is the description of this falling away referenced in 2 Thessalonians 2:3. When they see the beast, they are going to say that this is not just another president or king; this is God on earth. They are going to be filled with wonder and admiration and awe at his appearance and presence.

The beast is going to demand that people worship him, and the false prophet is going to say to the people that they need to worship him, and those who will not worship him will be put to death. Those who love life more than they love Christ will apostatize and will worship the beast.

This great apostasy will occur because of the appearance of the man of sin, the Antichrist, setting himself up as God on earth so that the whole earth starts to worship him. The unsaved who dwell on the earth will not be able to see the deception they are under.

Notice verse 5: *"Remember ye not, that, when I was yet with you, I told you these things?* [6] *And now ye know what withholdeth"* (or restrains), *"that he might be revealed in his time."* The chain and the lock and the pit are restraining Satan now so that Satan might be revealed—that is, loosed—at the appropriate time. Until then, he is not going to be revealed, and the Antichrist is not going to appear.

Verse 7: *"For the mystery of iniquity doth already work"*: all the elements for this process are now set in place, *"only he who now [restrains, will continue to restrain] until he be taken out of the way."* Now who is the *"he"*? It is the angel of Revelation 20:1–3. It was the angel that had the chain and the lock, and he bound Satan and cast him into the pit, and restrains him there to this very day.

The *"what"* of verse 6, "Now you know *what* withholds," is the chain, the lock, and the pit. The *"who"* of verse 7, "You know *who* withholds," is the angel. It is when the angel finally stops restraining him that the apostasy and the appearance of Antichrist are going to occur, but not until then. Therefore, Paul says in effect, "Do not be worried, as though the second coming of Christ is imminent. It is not imminent. People have been writing you letters in my name; people have been saying the second coming of Christ is at hand; but that coming will not occur until Satan is loosed, Antichrist appears, and the great apostasy takes place."

But when the restraining angel and his chain are taken out of the way, verse 8, *"then shall that Wicked [one] be revealed."* This is Antichrist, the individual spoken of in verses 3 and 4, the man of sin. *"Then shall that Wicked [one] be revealed, whom the Lord shall consume with the spirit of his mouth, and shall destroy with the brightness of his coming:"* (just as in Revelation 19:20) "[9] *Even him, whose coming is after the working of Satan with all power and signs and lying wonders,* [10] *And with all deceivableness of unrighteousness in them that perish; because they received not the love of the truth, that they might be saved.* [11] *And for this cause God shall send them strong delusion, that they should believe a lie:* [12] *That they all might be damned who believed not the truth, but had pleasure in unrighteousness.*

"[13] *But we are bound to give thanks alway to God for you, brethren beloved of the Lord, because God hath from the beginning chosen you to salvation through sanctification of the Spirit and belief of the truth:* [14] *Whereunto he called you by our gospel, to the obtaining of the glory of our Lord Jesus Christ.* [15] *Therefore, brethren, stand fast."* Do not be deceived by the coming Antichrist and apostatize along with all the rest who loved the pleasures of unrighteousness more than they loved Christ. Stand fast in the faith, and stand strong for Christ.

The unsaved who dwell on the earth will not be able to see the deception they are under. They will be fully convinced by the false prophet to render worship to the man of sin—this Antichrist, who is the final beast on the earth. That these people who worship Antichrist are unsaved is clear from the fact that their names are not written in the book of life from the foundation of the world.

Notice Revelation 17:8. *"The beast that thou sawest was, and is not; and shall ascend out of the bottomless pit, and go into perdition: and they that dwell on the earth shall wonder,"* notice, *"whose names were not written in the book of life from the foundation of the world, when they behold the beast that was, and is not, and yet is."*

Notice, *"the beast that. . . is"* in the life history of those who dwell on the earth during the reign of the Antichrist. Notice the present tense. This group of people being spoken of in verse 8b is the group of people who dwell on the earth during the time of Antichrist, when the beast ascends up out of the bottomless pit. They behold and wonder at and worship the Antichrist with admiration and awe; and therefore, in the lives of this final generation, it can be said that from their frame of reference, that Antichrist *"is."*

So with reference to those in verse 8b who live during the time of Antichrist, from their time frame, they see that the beast *"was"* from the fall to Christ, they see the beast *"[was] not"* from Christ to the loosing of Satan, and they presently see that the beast now *"is,"* and they admire and wonder at his magnificence. Verse 8b speaks from the time frame of the reign of Antichrist. They and their beast will *"go into perdition"* in their near future, but that has not happened yet from the point of reference they are viewing the Antichrist from in verse 8b.

Verse 8b speaks of *"names [that] were not written in the book of life from the foundation of the world."* The book of life is the record of the names of all of God's elect who were chosen to be saved before the foundation of the world. Those who are saved have their names recorded there, and those whose names are absent from the book are those who are not, and will not, be saved. It is those whose names are not in the book of life who, though they may have professed to be Christians, will nevertheless follow and serve and worship the final manifestation of the beast and the person of Antichrist in the end times. This is the great falling away.

On the other hand, the elect are preserved by Christ from being deceived into worshiping the Antichrist. In Matthew 24:24, it says, *"For there shall arise false Christs, and false prophets, and shall shew great signs and wonders; insomuch that, if it were possible, they shall deceive the very elect."* But of course, it is not possible to deceive the elect. Christ sees to it that they cannot be deceived. He gives them eyes and discernment to see through the deception, and strength to reject it.

When this false Christ comes, this Antichrist, and this false prophet arises to empower him and lead people toward him, he is going to be so good, in terms of the deceivableness of unrighteousness and the miracles that he does, that if it were possible for the elect to be deceived, even they would be deceived. But it is not possible. Christ preserves His people, and no man can pluck them out of His hand.

Revelation 13:11–15 tells us that the false prophet will so deceive the non-elect with his power to do miracles, they will all worship the beast because of his deceptions. The result of this deception is that the beast, the Antichrist, and all who worship him, will make war against the people of God and against the Son of God. What will be the outcome of that war? *"These shall make war with the Lamb, and the Lamb shall overcome them."* Christ will triumph, and all those believers slaughtered by the Antichrist will return with Christ from heaven and share in Christ's triumph, and see vengeance exercised upon their enemies.

51

The History of the Beast, Revelation 17:9–14

"9 And here is the mind which hath wisdom. The seven heads are seven mountains, on which the woman sitteth. 10 And there are seven kings: five are fallen, and one is, and the other is not yet come; and when he cometh, he must continue a short space. 11 And the beast that was, and is not, even he is the eighth, and is of the seven, and goeth into perdition. 12 And the ten horns which thou sawest are ten kings, which have received no kingdom as yet; but receive power as kings one hour with the beast. 13 These have one mind, and shall give their power and strength unto the beast. 14 These shall make war with the Lamb, and the Lamb shall overcome them: for he is Lord of lords, and King of kings: and they that are with him are called, and chosen, and faithful."

Revelation is a book about spiritual warfare. It is about the war between Christ and Satan, and, by extension, between the servants of Christ and the servants of Satan. Although this conflict is long and protracted, the victory of Christ and His people over Satan and his people is absolutely certain; and furthermore, it is eternal.

This book gives us insight into the reason why things on earth occur the way they do.

On the one hand, it explains that the wars that occur, the plagues and famines that take place, the persecutions that are carried out, and the evil that is done are all the result of Satan's efforts to crush the people of God and to kill the kingdom of God upon the earth.

On the other hand, it explains that the perseverance of the people of God, the unstoppable spread of the gospel of Christ, the preservation of the church, and the triumph of Christians over the world and the flesh and the devil are all the result of Christ's purpose to build

His kingdom, to destroy the works of the devil, and to bring to pass His final judgment upon him.

We have seen the various aspects of this spiritual warfare in the previous chapters, but in the second half of Revelation, we are seeing the systematic destruction of Satan and his helpers by Christ in the triumphant exercise of His power at the end of this age. We have already seen the destruction of those who have the mark of the beast in chapter 14. In chapter 17 we are focused on the judgment of the great whore Babylon, who symbolizes anti-Christian society in all of its economic, social, cultural, and moral aspects.

In Revelation 17:1, the angel told John he was going to show him the judgment of the great whore Babylon, who rides on the back of the beast. The beast on which the whore rides symbolizes anti-Christian government, which has always assisted anti-Christian society in its rebellion against God and in its persecution of the saints. Anti-Christian government, which is the beast, provides anti-Christian society, which is the whore, with the power and the strength it needs to persecute the people of God.

When the homosexuals wanted to persecute Aaron and Melissa Klein of Sweet Cakes Bakery in Oregon for their refusal to bake a cake for a sodomite counterfeit wedding, whom did the homosexuals turn to for help? They turned to the beast, to our anti-Christian civil government, to enforce the persecution which the anti-Christian society wished to impose upon them. The beast fined Aaron and Melissa Klein $135,000 and ran them out of business, while the whore stood by and applauded with delight.

Since anti-Christian society derives its power from anti-Christian government to persecute the saints; and since this whore Babylon works so closely with the beast in this age; the angel proceeds to show us the history and the final judgment of the beast, before he tells us about the judgment of the great whore Babylon. In verses 7 to 18, the angel begins to tell us about God's judgment on the beast; that is, upon anti-Christian civil government.

In the last chapter, we looked at verses 7 and 8 and saw the summary of the judgment of the beast. We saw that between the fall and the first coming of Christ, Satan was free to empower anti-Christian government to persecute the people of God and to suppress the kingdom of God on earth; and as a result, the kingdom of God was tiny for the first 4,000 years of the earth's existence. But when Jesus came,

He bound Satan with reference to his ability to deceive the nations. Since the first coming of Christ to this very day, anti-Christian governments have been powerless to stop the spread of Christianity across the world and throughout the centuries. The kingdom of God is now huge and massive and worldwide.

But there will come a day when the final manifestation of the beast will arise because Satan will have been loosed to once again deceive the nations. Once Satan is unbound, the beast out of the bottomless pit, who is the Antichrist and his one-world government, will arise and will severely persecute the church to the point of destroying its visible presence and public witness, and only a small remnant will be left alive. But as the beast moves to destroy that small remnant, Jesus will return and deliver His people, destroy that wicked one with the sword of His mouth and the brightness of His coming, and cast him into perdition—that is, into the lake of fire.

Having seen the summary of the judgment of the beast in verses 7 to 8, in this chapter we will look at the history of the beast in verses 9 to 14. In symbolic language, John gives us the interpretation of what the beast with the seven heads and the ten horns represents. We must understand that both the numbers used and the terms employed in verses 9 to 14 are symbolic in nature. Efforts to literalize the numbers and terms contained in verses 9 to 14 leave the passage with as many different meanings as there are interpreters. Any literal interpretation of this passage must be rejected, and only a symbolic interpretation should be employed.

To properly grasp what is conveyed here is going to require our focused attention and thought, and it is going to require careful analysis of the symbolic language employed and the symbolic numbers that are used.

The Successive Beasts throughout History

The successive beasts throughout history are contained in verses 9 and 10. *"And here is the mind which hath wisdom. The seven heads are seven mountains, on which the woman sitteth.* [10] *And there are seven kings: five are fallen, and one is, and the other is not yet come; and when he cometh, he must continue a short space."*

While the term "beast" is used in the singular when referring to anti-Christian government, the concept of the beast is one that encompasses all of the anti-Christian governments from the beginning of time to the end of time. Over time, there has been a large number of successive anti-Christian governments, and they are all represented by this beast that has seven heads and ten horns.

Notice verse 7: *"And the angel said unto me, Wherefore didst thou marvel? I will tell thee the mystery of the woman, and of the beast that carrieth her, which hath the seven heads and ten horns."* In verse 7, John was promised by the angel that he would have the mystery of the beast with seven heads and ten horns explained to him. A summary explanation was given to John in verse 8 which we looked at in the previous chapter. But now, a more detailed and expanded explanation is going to be provided in verses 9 to 13. The Bible often does this. It gives us a summary, and then it gives us an expanded description based on that summary. This is what we have here. We have the summary in verse 8, and then we have the expanded description and explanation in verses 9 to 13.

Notice verse 9. *"And here is the mind which hath wisdom."* In other words, a wise person will understand the meaning of this symbolic beast, his seven heads, and his ten horns. The angel then declares in verse 9 that the seven heads represent seven mountains upon which the woman sits.

Some commentators think that these seven mountains are the seven literal hills upon which the city of Rome sat, and therefore the beast is Rome. However, if you take that view, which we do not, then you immediately run into unsolvable problems with trying to interpret verse 10, because no succession of Roman Caesars can be made to fit the five who have fallen, the one that is, and the other who is not yet come. There were far more than seven Caesars, and purely arbitrary choices must be made in the identification of those who are represented by these seven kings that are spoken of in verse 10. Therefore, we reject the notion that these seven mountains are the seven literal hills upon which the city of Rome was built.

There is a far more satisfactory interpretation of these seven mountains spoken of in verse 9, and that is to understand these seven mountains as seven kingdoms. In the Old Testament, a mountain is a symbol of strength, and from that, a strong kingdom was often referred to as a mountain.

For example, Jeremiah 51 details God's wrath against Babylon, the kingdom that took Israel captive in 586 BC. Among the many declarations of God's wrath against Babylon, in Jeremiah 51:25 God says of the Babylonian kingdom of Jeremiah's day, *"Behold, I am against thee, O destroying mountain, saith the LORD, which destroyest all the earth: and I will stretch out mine hand upon thee, and roll thee down from the rocks, and will make thee a burnt mountain."*

God calls the Old Testament literal kingdom of Babylon, a *"destroying mountain,"* thus referring to the kingdom as a mountain. Then He says that He is going to make you *"a burnt mountain."* In other words, "My fiery wrath is going to fall upon you."

In Ezekiel 35, the nation of Edom is referred to as *"Mount Seir"* repeatedly throughout that entire chapter. In Zechariah 4:7, God says of the King of Persia, who at that time was Artaxerxes the First, who had ordered a halt to the rebuilding of the temple: *"Who art thou, O great mountain? before Zerubbabel thou shalt become a plain."* God is speaking to Artaxerxes who ordered the building of the temple to stop. It is as if He says, "Though you are a great mountain, I am going to flatten you and level you with the ground."

This is just a sampling of the many times "mountain" is used to refer to kingdoms in the Old Testament. Therefore, this mention of seven mountains in Revelation 17 is not a reference to some specific geographical location, featuring seven actual geographical mountains; instead, it is a reference to seven kingdoms.

Furthermore, the number "seven" used here is also symbolic, as it is throughout the book of Revelation. When used symbolically, the number seven conveys the concept of completeness. Therefore, this statement that these seven heads are seven mountains means that these seven heads represent the complete number of kingdoms that have existed and will exist from the creation to the coming of Antichrist and his kingdom, which is the eighth and the final kingdom.

So these seven heads, which are seven mountains, represent all the anti-Christian governments of the world that have existed and will exist from creation to the time of Antichrist and his transnational one-world government, which is the eighth king and kingdom.

The last phrase in verse 9 tells us that the whore Babylon rides upon these kingdoms. The seven heads are seven mountains, which we have seen are seven kingdoms, all the kingdoms from creation to Antichrist, on which the woman sits. All throughout history, anti-Christian society, which is represented by this whore Babylon, has always ridden upon and ruled anti-Christian governments, and anti-Christian governments have always given their power to anti-Christian society.

The beast of anti-Christian government and the whore of anti-Christian society have always worked closely together to persecute and suppress the kingdom of God. From creation to Antichrist, we have had the beast, which is the succession of anti-Christian governments, and we have had the whore, which is anti-Christian society; and together, they have persecuted the people of God.

Notice verse 10: *"And there are seven kings: five are fallen, and one is, and the other is not yet come; and when he cometh, he must continue a short space."* Not only are there seven kingdoms, as verse 9 tells us, but there are also seven kings who rule those seven kingdoms. Every kingdom has a king. As we said, the number seven is symbolic in Revelation, and so are the following numbers that are employed to make up the division of these seven kings and kingdoms.

First, verse 10 tells us that five of these kings and kingdoms have fallen. These five kings and kingdoms represent all the kings and kingdoms that existed from creation until the time that John lived and wrote this book. From John's perspective, five had fallen.

The reason we assert that is because ten conveys the concept of totality, and therefore five represents less than the total number of kingdoms. It is a partial number of the total kings and kingdoms that will exist. If ten represents all the kings and the kingdoms that exist, then five represents part of them, the part that existed from creation until John's day. The five kings and kingdoms represent all the kings and kingdoms which had fallen and all of which no longer existed from creation until John's day in AD 95. Therefore, verse 10 says there are seven kings, but five are fallen.

Verse 10 goes on to tell us that one kingdom "*is.*" That is, one kingdom is currently and presently in existence. This is the sixth kingdom, which is the Roman Empire, the kingdom that John is currently living under and which exiled him to the island of Patmos. So the beast took the form of the Roman Empire in John's day, and that expression of the beast "*is*" in John's time frame.

Six symbolizes the concept of man; the concept of humanism because man was created on the sixth day. Rome was focused on the worship of a man, namely the worship of Caesar as God. Rome was therefore the quintessential humanistic empire, and thus appropriately labeled the sixth kingdom. But Rome also eventually fell.

Verse 10 goes on to mention a seventh king and kingdom yet to come, after John's day. Notice verse 10: *"And there are seven kings: five are fallen"* (these are the kings from creation to John), *"and one is"* (the one that existed in John's day, the Roman Empire), *"and the other"* (the seventh), *"is not yet come; and when he cometh, he must continue a short space."*

Verse 10 mentions a seventh king and kingdom yet to come after John's day, and this seventh kingdom lasts for *"a short space."* This seventh kingdom is the feet of Nebuchadnezzar's image in Daniel 2. In Daniel 2:41–43 is the description of the feet of Nebuchadnezzar's image that are made of part iron and part clay. This is this seventh kingdom.

This seventh king and kingdom represented by these feet of clay and iron represents all the fragmented kingdoms of the world that will exist from the fall of the Roman Empire, which is the sixth kingdom, to the appearance of Antichrist and his kingdom, which is the eighth.

This seventh kingdom that represents the collective fragmented kingdoms that exist from the fall of Rome to the appearance of Antichrist must continue, it says, *"a short space."* Now "short" is a relative term. Compared to a century, a decade can be said to be a short time. Compared to the 4,000-plus years between the time of creation and the end of the Roman Empire, the subsequent period of under 2,000 years since the fall of the Roman Empire can be said, in comparison, to be a short space.

So these seven kingdoms of verses 9 to 10 represent the complete number of all the kingdoms of the earth between the creation and the appearance of the Antichrist because seven is the number that symbolizes completion. The larger part of these kingdoms has fallen before John's day. These are represented by the five kings and kingdoms. One kingdom, the sixth, existed in John's day. When Revelation was written, it could be said of the Roman Empire, it *"is."*

One kingdom, the seventh, has yet to come after John's timeframe, and that kingdom is the collective and yet fragmented kingdoms that will exist between the fall of Rome and the rise of the Antichrist, and are represented by the feet of Daniel's image. The span of this final collective kingdom will be something less than the previous six put together because relative to their collective time span, the seventh kingdom will continue for a *"short space."*

If we have gone 4,000 years from creation to the fall of Rome, then it seems apparent we will not go another 4,000 years since the fall of Rome before the end comes. This conclusion may be wrong. The *"short space"* could be a short space relative to something other than the six kingdoms. It could be a short space relative to eternity. But it seems, in the context, the short space is in relationship to the other kingdoms, and that is why we drew the conclusion we did.

By way of summary, in verses 9 to 10 we have the description of the successive manifestations of the beast throughout history. These seven kingdoms describe the beast throughout human history up until the appearance of Antichrist.

The Final Beast at the End of History

The final beast at the end of history is described in verses 11 to 13. Verse 11: *"And the beast that was, and is not, even he is the eighth, and is of the seven, and goeth into perdition."*

In verse 11, we are introduced to the eighth beast. He is the final beast, because there are none who come after him. The number eight symbolizes salvation, and this final anti-Christian ruler offers a false salvation and is a fraudulent savior. He is the Antichrist; he is the counterfeit Christ. Verse 11 brings us to the final expression of the beast; the one who ascends out of the bottomless pit; the one who will go into perdition as we were previously told in verse 8.

This Antichrist and his kingdom is said in verse 11 to be *"of the seven."* This means that he stands in continuity with all the previous anti-Christian kingdoms that have existed on the earth, he shares their evil character, and he shares their same energizing power, which is the power of Satan. Therefore, he is *"of"* the seven in the sense that he stands in continuity with them in terms of sharing their evil character and their satanically given power.

This final manifestation of the beast, which is Antichrist and his kingdom, is an extension of all the previous kingdoms of the earth which collectively have made up the kingdom of Satan. Satan's kingdom is made up of all the anti-Christian governments and anti-Christian societies of this world. They all stand in continuity with each other as they unfold over the process of time. They are all of a single piece because together they make up the kingdom of darkness.

However, this final manifestation of the beast—the eighth—is by far the worst. The kingdom of Antichrist and his worldwide coalition of nations will far surpass any evil that has ever been done in any of the previous kingdoms on earth. At the end of time, Satan is loosed to do his worst, and he will do his worst through this final anti-Christian government, and the result will be, as Matthew 24:21 says, *"great tribulation, such as was not since the beginning of the world to this time, no, nor ever shall be."*

Verse 12 provides us with further detail about this worldwide transnational coalition of kings and kingdoms that Antichrist will bring together in order to launch his final assault upon the kingdom of God. Verse 12 says, *"And the ten horns"* (up until this time, we have been dealing with the seven heads, but now we come to the ten horns) *"which thou sawest are ten kings, which have received no kingdom as yet; but receive power as kings one hour with the beast."*

This beast is said not only to have seven heads, which are seven kingdoms as we have seen, but the beast also is said to have ten horns. Horns, like mountains, are symbols of strength and power, and therefore these ten horns represent ten kings. Ten is the number that symbolizes perfection and totality. There will be a perfect unity of all of the kings of the earth that will exist in the future at the time when Antichrist appears. In John's day, these ten kings had not yet appeared, and *"have received no kingdoms as [of] yet."* But they will receive power as kings in the future when the final manifestation of the beast arises which is the Antichrist. When Antichrist arises, then they shall *"receive power as kings one hour with the beast."*

When Antichrist arises, other kings will arise across the world as well, and these kings will yield their power and loyalty to Antichrist, submit to him, and serve his evil agenda. These ten kings—that is, the complete number of kings on the earth—"[13] *have one mind, and shall give their power and strength unto the beast,"* who, in this case, is the Antichrist, the beast out of the bottomless pit.

The whole world—all the kings and kingdoms of the earth—will finally unite with one mind and submit themselves to and serve the agenda of the Antichrist with one heart. All of their resources will be devoted to him and to his cause, and the desire of globalists to have a one-world government under one monarch will finally be realized. This coalition of the Antichrist and all the kingdoms of the world working together with one mind will last, it says in verse 12, *"one hour."*

This *"one hour"* is obviously a figurative term, one that is the same time period denoted by the "three and a half days" of Revelation 11:9–11. In that passage, Antichrist arises out of the pit, he persecutes the church, and their dead bodies lie in the streets. His one-world coalition and he rejoice together. They have party time, and they send presents to each other for three and a half days, which is a very small length of time in proportion to the three and a half years that the two witnesses spread the gospel through the whole world. This "one hour" is a figurative term for a short period of time that is equivalent to the short period of time denoted by the symbolic term of *"three and a half days"* in Revelation 11:9–11, and the *"little season"* of Revelation 20:3.

This time period in which Antichrist and his one-world government obtain unity together and obtain victory over the church is a very small period of time in proportion to the time between the first and the second coming of Christ, when the church expanded over the whole earth.

A *"short space"* is the time between the fall of the Roman Empire and the appearance of Antichrist. In relationship to that short space, we have the *"one hour,"* which is the time when Antichrist and his transnational worldwide coalition of kingdoms that work together will exist and triumph. For only as it were an hour the eighth king and his kingdom will exist and triumph.

And then verse 14 occurs: *"These"* (Antichrist and his transnational worldwide coalition of kings and kingdoms) *"shall make war with the Lamb, and the Lamb shall overcome them: for he is Lord of lords, and King of kings: and they that are with him are called, and chosen, and faithful."* Antichrist and his worldwide transnational coalition of supporters will make war against the church and largely destroy it. This is their hour of triumph. When Christ returns to rescue the small surviving remnant, this final manifestation of the beast, this Antichrist will make war with Christ Himself. But Christ will destroy the beast and all who assist him, and they will be cast into the lake of fire forever. Verse 14 is the key verse of Revelation, the verse that summarizes its entire message.

In Revelation 19:11–21, we have the glorious second coming of Christ described. It says in verse 19, *"And I saw the beast, and the kings of the earth, and their armies, gathered together to make war against him that sat on the horse, and against his army."* The whole world with all of its military power will be united for one purpose—and that is to destroy Christ when He returns.

What is the outcome of the battle? Verse 20: *"And the beast was taken, and with him the false prophet that wrought miracles before him, with which he deceived them that had received the mark of the beast, and them that worshipped his image. These both were cast alive into a lake of fire burning with brimstone.* [21] *And the remnant were slain with the sword of him that sat upon the horse, which sword proceeded out of his mouth: and all the fowls were filled with their flesh."*

Even when all the nations of the earth are united under one leader to fight against Christ, and even when they have all the military power of the whole world arrayed against Him, they will not prevail for an instant. Christ will destroy them with the sword of His word and with the brightness of His coming. When the devil does his worst, and when the devil exercises the maximum power he possesses to fight against Christ and His people, he utterly fails.

Christ is Lord of lords, and Christ is King of kings, and no one can stay His hand or resist His power or escape His wrath. When the kingdom of Satan is at the peak of its power, and when Satan has the whole world on his side and all of the kingdoms of earth unified in his service—when he has all of their resources at his disposal with all of their weapons—he will still go down to defeat at the hands of one Man, and that is the Man Christ Jesus.

We see things happening in the world today and we think the forces of evil are really powerful! But we have not begun to see the degree of evil that people under the Antichrist are capable of. Yet even when they are at the very peak of their power, Christ destroys them with the sword of His mouth and with the brightness of His coming. And if Christ has that level of power over them then, He certainly has them under His control now, and they can do nothing without His permission. What a great comfort to persecuted believers as they suffer Satan's assaults now!

Notice Revelation 17:17: *"For God hath put in their hearts to fulfill his will, and to agree, and give their kingdom unto the beast, until the words of God shall be fulfilled."* Who is in control—the Antichrist or God? Notice: God puts it in their hearts to fulfill His will. He controls them. They do not control Him, and they certainly do not control His people. No one can touch us without going through God and obtaining His permission first.

The encouragement of this passage is that when Satan does his worst, he goes down to defeat. He is doing something less than his worst today. Christ certainly has him under control now, if He is going to have him under control then. Therefore, we do not need to fear the forces of evil. The King of kings and the Lord of lords knows His enemies, He knows what they are doing, and He has them under His control. Everything they do to fight against Him is simply a further accomplishment of His purposes through them.

Therefore, we can view the future with optimism and courage and joy, knowing that God is working out His plan through the evil of Satan and his helpers to bring glory to Himself, to bring salvation to His people, and to bring them into the new earth.

The Scripture says to us dozens of times, "Fear not!" Jesus will triumph, and we will triumph in Him, for those that are with Him are called and chosen and faithful. The reason why we are with Him is because He chose us, He called us, and therefore we faithfully follow Him. When we follow Him, we know that, in the end, we will be found on His side and we will share His triumph. We will see all of our enemies cast into the lake of fire, and they will never torment us again.

Over and over again we see in Revelation that Christ and His people triumph, and Satan and his people go down to defeat. Do not envy them, do not fear them, and do not think they have something you do not. Recognize them for who they are—a defeated people serving a defeated king who is going to go down to his ultimate defeat in the end.

This is the encouragement we have, the promise we are given, the future we anticipate, and the hope we look forward to. Let us keep that vision bright before our eyes, and when the evil seems so strong, recognize that there is a God in heaven still, and evil is coming to an end.

52

The Destruction of Babylon, Revelation 17:15–18

> “15 *And he saith unto me, The waters which thou sawest, where the whore sitteth, are peoples, and multitudes, and nations, and tongues.* 16 *And the ten horns which thou sawest upon the beast, these shall hate the whore, and shall make her desolate and naked, and shall eat her flesh, and burn her with fire.* 17 *For God hath put in their hearts to fulfill his will, and to agree, and give their kingdom unto the beast, until the words of God shall be fulfilled.* 18 *And the woman which thou sawest is that great city, which reigneth over the kings of the earth.*”

In Revelation 17 we have been looking at the symbolic figure of the great harlot Babylon, who represents anti-Christian society in all of its economic, social, and cultural aspects.

We have also been looking at the symbolic figure of the beast, who has seven heads and ten horns, and who represents anti-Christian civil government, with all of its authority and power.

The harlot and the beast are Satan’s greatest helpers. The harlot seduces the world to follow Satan, and the beast pressures the world to follow Satan. Individually, each of them has tremendous power, but working together, their power is overwhelming. Working together is what the harlot and the beast have done since the beginning of creation up to almost the very end of time. The closeness of the cooperation between these two helpers of Satan is indicated by the symbolic image of the harlot riding the beast like a person would ride a horse. The rider gives the horse direction, and the horse gives the rider power and strength, and they become as one as they work together.

The harlot rides and rules the beast, and the beast gives his power and strength to the harlot. This horse and rider almost become a single organism, sharing the same mind and the same motive and the same passion as they pursue Satan's evil agenda together. But all of Satan's helpers, just like Satan himself, are doomed to defeat. They all fall under the wrath of God.

In Revelation 17:1, the angel promised John that he would show him the judgment of the great whore Babylon. But that also necessarily includes the judgment of the beast upon which she rides, because they are so closely allied with each other. Therefore, the angel begins with a description of the beast in verses 7 to 13 of this chapter.

We were given a summary of the history of the beast and the destruction of the beast in verse 8, but in verses 9 to 13, we are taken back and given a far more detailed history of the beast through the ages. However, the special attention of that section was focused on the final manifestation of the beast, which is the Antichrist and his kingdom. In verses 11 to 13, we saw that the last kingdom on earth, this eighth kingdom, will be that of the Antichrist and his worldwide coalition of all the nations of the earth, symbolically represented by these ten kings.

All the kings of the earth will submit themselves and their kingdoms to the Antichrist, place themselves under his authority, devote their resources to him, and carry out his will. They will make war against the church and destroy its visible presence and public witness, and when Christ returns to rescue the small remnant of His church that is left, Antichrist and his kingdom will make war with Christ Himself. Christ will overcome and destroy Antichrist and his kingdom, and will cast them into the lake of fire. That is the description of the judgment of the beast upon which the whore Babylon rides.

But what of the judgment of Babylon itself, which the angel promised to show John in 17:1? We have finally come to that judgment in 17:15–18, in all of chapter 18, and into the first part of chapter 19. In that extended section, we have the description of the judgment of the great harlot Babylon. Having seen the judgment of the beast, we will now see the judgment of the great whore that the angel promised to show us back in 17:1.

The Identity of Babylon

The identity of Babylon is spoken of in verse 15 and in verse 18. Notice verse 15: *"And he saith unto me, The waters which thou sawest, where the whore sitteth, are peoples, and multitudes, and nations, and tongues."* Now verse 18: *"And the woman which thou sawest is that great city, which reigneth over the kings of the earth."*

After declaring Christ's victory over the beast in verse 14, the angel now directs John's attention back to the great whore that sits upon many waters, who was initially described in verse 1. *"And there came one of the seven angels which had the seven vials, and talked with me, saying unto me, Come hither; I will shew unto thee the judgment of the great whore that sitteth upon many waters."*

Verse 1 says that the harlot Babylon sits upon many waters, and we are told in verse 15 what those waters symbolize. *"And he saith unto me, The waters which thou sawest, where the whore sitteth, are peoples, and multitudes, and nations, and tongues."* This inclusive, universalistic formula of peoples, multitudes, nations, and tongues is used throughout the book of Revelation with slight variations to designate the people who make up the anti-Christian society which constitutes Babylon.

Notice Revelation 11:7. It says, regarding the two witnesses bearing testimony to the gospel throughout this age, *"And when they shall have finished their testimony, the beast that ascendeth out of the bottomless pit shall make war against them, and shall overcome them, and kill them. [8] And their dead bodies shall lie in the street of the great city, which spiritually is called Sodom and Egypt, where also our Lord was crucified."*

Now notice verse 9: *"And they of the people and kindreds and tongues and nations shall see their dead bodies three days and an half, and shall not suffer their dead bodies to be put in graves. [10] And they that dwell upon the earth shall rejoice over them, and make merry, and shall send gifts one to another; because these two prophets tormented them that dwelt on the earth."* A slight variation of this universalistic phrase of peoples, multitudes, nations, and tongues is used of the anti-Christian society over which Antichrist rules.

We see the same terminology used in 13:7–8. In chapter 13, we have the beast that rises up out of the sea, which is anti-Christian government, and notice what it says: *"And it was given unto him"* (this final manifestation of this beast, the Antichrist) *"to make war with the saints, and to overcome them: and power was given him over all kindreds, and tongues, and nations. [8] And all that dwell upon the earth shall worship him, whose names are not written in the book of life of the Lamb slain from the foundation of the world."*

We see the same formula being used in 14:6 when it says, *"And I saw another angel fly in the midst of heaven, having the everlasting gospel to preach unto them that dwell on the earth, and to every nation, and kindred, and tongue, and people,* [7] *Saying with a loud voice, Fear God, and give glory to him; for the hour of his judgment is come."* The angel is addressing the lost multitudes of the earth and proclaiming that judgment has arrived.

Repeatedly, this inclusive universalistic formula of peoples, multitudes, nations, and tongues is used throughout Revelation to designate the people who constitute Babylon and who make up anti-Christian society, because it is *"out of"* every kindred, tongue, people, and nation that the elect are saved and redeemed by the blood of Christ, so that once they are saved, they are no longer identified by those terms.

For example, Revelation 5:9 says, regarding the saints in heaven, *"And they sung a new song, saying, Thou art worthy to take the book, and to open the seals thereof: for thou wast slain, and hast redeemed us to God by thy blood out of every kindred, and tongue, and people, and nation;* [10] *And hast made us unto our God kings and priests."*

When you are saved, you no longer are part of *"every kindred, and tongue, and people, and nation."* In Christ, there is neither Jew nor Gentile, there is neither bond nor free, there is neither rich nor poor, there is neither Asian nor American, there is neither black nor white. All of those distinctions disappear. We are the bride of Christ, we are the body of Christ, and we are the temple of God. We are a single people who are the children of God, and all those other distinctions cease to exist.

Therefore, when those terms are used, they are used of the unsaved mass of humanity, living in rebellion against God, out of which we were saved, and of which we are no longer a part. This phrase in 17:15 that speaks of *"peoples, and multitudes, and nations, and tongues"* represents the people of the earth who live in rebellion against God, and who together constitute anti-Christian society in its economic, social, and cultural aspects.

Negatively, the reason Babylon represents anti-Christian society in its economic, social, and cultural aspects is that the beast out of the sea represents anti-Christian government, and the beast out of the earth, otherwise known as the false prophet, represents anti-Christian religion. Babylon has to represent something besides those, and therefore it does not include those. Positively, what it does include is plainly described in chapters 17 and 18, and these chapters describe the economic, social, and cultural practices of a decadent society.

Wherever in the world unsaved people gather together to form a society, there is where Babylon exists, no matter the nationality, language, or ethnicity. In a word, all wicked societies throughout the world and throughout time are Babylon the harlot.

This metaphor of many waters to represent many nations is also used in the Old Testament. Isaiah 17:12–13 says, "*Woe to the multitude of many people, which make a noise like the noise of the seas; and to the rushing of nations, that make a rushing like the rushing of mighty waters!* [13] *The nations shall rush like the rushing of many waters: but God shall rebuke them, and they shall flee far off, and shall be chased as the chaff of the mountains before the wind, and like a rolling thing before the whirlwind.*" This metaphor of many waters representing the many nations of the earth is not something new or unique to John. This is a metaphor that has been frequently used in the Old Testament.

Literal Old Testament Babylon which took Israel captive in 586 BC had as its capital the city of Babylon, and the Euphrates River flowed through the center of it. From this river, a whole system of canals carried its waters throughout the city of Babylon, so that in Jeremiah 51:13 Babylon is said to be the city that "*dwelleth upon many waters.*"

Furthermore, Old Testament Babylon was a tremendous persecutor of the people of God, and therefore the title "Babylon" is a fitting metaphor for the anti-Christian societies of humanity that seduce and persecute the people of God. Old Testament Babylon that dwelled upon many waters became the symbol of all cultures and societies throughout the world and across time that seduce and persecute the people of God.

In Revelation 17:18 it says, "*And the woman which thou sawest*" (this is the harlot Babylon) "*is that great city, which reigneth over the kings of the earth.*" Here we have further information about Babylon. She is called "*that great city.*" This term "*great city*" is used repeatedly to describe Babylon.

It was called the great city, not because it was great in the sense that it was something to be admired. Babylon was great in the sense of being large and powerful and prosperous and successful in the ruthless pursuit of its evil agenda.

Because of the cyclical structure of the book of Revelation, we see the same themes addressed over and over again. Revelation 11:7–9 says, *"And when they shall have finished their testimony, the beast that ascendeth out of the bottomless pit"* (Antichrist) *"shall make war against them"* (against the church), *"and shall overcome them, and kill them.* [8] *And their dead bodies shall lie in the street of the great city."* Whenever you read this phrase "the great city" in Revelation, it is always speaking about Babylon. (The only exception is Revelation 21:10, but the textual support for the word "great" (applying to the word "city") in that passage is very weak, and it should probably be omitted.)

Notice verse 8. It says that *"their dead bodies shall lie in the street of the great city,"* (Babylon) *"which spiritually is called Sodom and Egypt, where also our Lord was crucified."* It is important for us to notice that chapter 11 speaks of two cities. In verse 2, it talks about *"the holy city."* We saw, when we studied this passage, that the holy city represented the church.

But in verse 8, we read about *"the great city,"* which represents anti-Christian society. It is called Sodom, representing the immorality of that society. It is called Egypt, representing the bondage of that society. Finally, it is called Jerusalem, representing the apostasy of that society. What was Sodom noted for? Its sexual immorality. What was Egypt noted for? The bondage the people experienced under the enslavement of Pharaoh. What was Jerusalem noted for? Apostate religion that crucified the Lord of Glory. Therefore, immorality, enslavement, and apostasy are what characterize Babylon.

This great city is a city of sexual immorality, slavery to Satan, and religious apostates who hate Christ and His people, and who rejoice when Christians are slaughtered. This is the nature and character of Babylon.

The second thing we learn about Babylon in Revelation 17:18 is that she rules over the kings of the earth. Notice verse 18: *"And the woman which thou sawest is that great city, which reigneth over the kings of the earth."*

The beast of anti-Christian government has always had to bow to and serve the harlot Babylon. Anti-Christian societies are the source out of which anti-Christian governments arise (Daniel 7:2–3, Revelation 13:1), and governments must serve the societies that formed them, or else the society will rise up and replace the government.

It has always been this way. Societies will not tolerate the beast ruling them; they must rule the beast, and they always do. Certainly the beast exercises some rule over them, but if it gets too obnoxious, they rise up and throw it off. All governments recognize that to some degree they have to pander to and please the populace they rule, or their rule will be destroyed. All through history, we see that when dictators get too arrogant, too cocky, and too oppressive, they wind up losing their heads.

So the harlot Babylon rides and rules the beast, and the beast uses its power to serve the harlot. This has been the case from the creation to the Antichrist. But we are going to see now that in the days of the Antichrist, at the end of this age, Babylon will be thrown off by the beast and will be crushed by the beast. No longer will anti-Christian government serve anti-Christian society; anti-Christian government will turn on anti-Christian society and destroy it.

The Destruction of Babylon

The destruction of Babylon is in verses 16 and 17. *"And the ten horns which thou sawest upon the beast, these shall hate the whore, and shall make her desolate and naked, and shall eat her flesh, and burn her with fire.* [17] *For God hath put in their hearts to fulfill his will, and to agree, and give their kingdom unto the beast, until the words of God shall be fulfilled."*

Once again, we have the same development of the explanation regarding the destruction of the harlot Babylon as we previously had regarding the description of the destruction of the beast. The destruction of the beast was summarized in verse 8, and then a much more detailed explanation was given in verses 9 to 14. There was a summary, and then the expansion and explanation. This same structure is true with the description of the destruction of Babylon.

The destruction of Babylon is summarized in verses 16 and 17. But then a much more detailed and extended explanation of that destruction will be given in 18:1–24.

Verse 16 tells us again about the ten horns of the beast, which were explained previously in verses 12 and 13. *"And the ten horns which thou sawest are ten kings, which have received no kingdom as yet; but receive power as kings one hour with the beast.* [13] *These have one mind, and shall give their power and strength unto the beast."* Verse 16: *"And the ten horns which thou sawest upon the beast, these shall hate the whore, and shall make her desolate and naked, and shall eat her flesh, and burn her with fire."*

When we studied verses 12 to 13, we saw that these ten horns represented ten kings. Ten is the number that symbolizes perfection and totality. Therefore, when the Antichrist arises, there will be a perfect unity of the totality of the kings on the earth, and all of them will yield their power and loyalty to the Antichrist and will serve him and his evil agenda with one mind and one heart. All of their resources will be devoted to him and to his cause. This coalition of Antichrist and all the nations of the earth will first form, and then in a surprising act of amazing folly and self-destruction, they will turn on and destroy one of Satan's helpers, the one who had been their own ally—namely, Babylon the seducing harlot.

The unified anti-Christian government of the world will turn on and destroy the economic, social, and cultural aspects of anti-Christian society, and thereby not only destroy it, but also impoverish itself. For some reason not revealed to us, the governments of the world will grow suspicious of the economic powers of the world, will see them as a threat, and will preemptively move to crush the economic, social, and cultural centers of power and influence so that the commerce of the world is virtually brought to an end. Anti-Christian society will be decimated and destroyed at the core of its strength, which is its economic power. The symbolic language in verse 16 is very graphic. The whore will be made desolate and naked, her flesh will be eaten, and she will be burned with fire. She will be stripped, consumed, and destroyed.

This same graphic language is used to describe God's coming judgments on faithless Israel in Ezekiel 16 and 23. We know what happened to Israel when Babylon came and decimated it and destroyed Jewish society. This same language and imagery that was used to describe God's judgment on Israel and the destruction of her society is now applied to the destruction of the Babylonian harlot and the society it represents. What Old Testament Babylon did to Israel and Jewish society is now done to the Babylonian anti-Christian society of the New Testament era at the end of this age after Antichrist arises.

The political power of the world turns against the economic power of the world, and, in a self-destructive civil war, destroys all the centers of commerce and banking and finance so that economic activity virtually grinds to a standstill. In chapter 18, we will see that the kings of the earth will mourn and regret the havoc they have wrought on the economic foundation of society, because they wound up impoverishing themselves in the process of crushing what they suspected was their rival and their enemy.

This one-world government crushed the society and people it exercised power over, but it wound up harming itself fatally in the process. In the perennial power struggle between the economic powers of the world and the political powers of the world, in the final days of this earth, the political powers will destroy the economic powers, and anti-Christian society will crumble into poverty and ruin. The horse will throw off its rider; the beast will throw off the rule and control of Babylon. This is the sign of the end of Satan's kingdom.

In Mark 3:24 Jesus said, *"And if a kingdom be divided against itself, that kingdom cannot stand.* [25] *And if a house be divided against itself, that house cannot stand.* [26] *And if Satan rise up against himself, and be divided, he cannot stand, but hath an end."* Jesus tells us that if the kingdom of Satan turns on itself and starts a process of mutual destruction, then Satan's kingdom *"cannot stand,"* but will come to *"an end."*

The wicked are not just one big happy family. They are filled with suspicion, jealousy, envy, and fear; and as a result, they often attack each other. That is the case here, with catastrophic results for both the victor and the vanquished. This is a Pyrrhic victory, in which in order to win the battle, you have to destroy yourself in the process.

Why does the beast destroy the harlot? As to the particular provocation that motivated the kingdom of Antichrist to attack the harlot, we are not told. But we do know what the ultimate cause of it was. Revelation 17:17 tells us: *"For God hath put [it] in their hearts."* That is, God has put it in the hearts of these kings *"to fulfill his will, and to agree, and give their kingdom unto the beast, until the words of God shall be fulfilled."* Verse 17 tells us plainly that the wicked are never out of God's control, and His sovereignty directs their choices so they wind up serving His purposes, even though in their minds they are striving to work directly against His purposes.

In Proverbs 21:1 it says, *"The king's heart is in the hand of the LORD, as the rivers of water: he turneth it whithersoever he will."* This is exactly what happens. It is God who put it in the hearts of the Antichrist and his supporting kings and kingdoms to turn on anti-Christian society, especially in its economic dimension, and crush it. They do not think they are serving God. They think they are doing what they want to do and what is in their best interests. The point is that God overrules and controls all political events to defeat His enemies, to save His people, and to glorify His name.

Notice Isaiah 10. The Assyrian king thought he was doing what he wanted to do when he came and conquered and captured Israel. But notice what God has to say about this event when the Assyrian came and took away the Northern kingdom. God says in verse 5: *"O Assyrian, the rod of mine anger, and the staff in their hand is mine indignation."* In other words, God is saying the Assyrian is a tool in His hand.

God says in verse 6: *"I will send him against an hypocritical nation, and against the people of my wrath will I give him a charge, to take the spoil, and to take the prey, and to tread them down like the mire of the streets."* Now notice verse 7: *"Howbeit he meaneth [it] not so, neither doth his heart think so."* God is in effect saying: "He does not think he is serving Me. He does not think he is an instrument in My hand. He does not mean to serve Me. He does not have a clue about Me."

The King of Assyria is doing what the King of Assyria wants to do, and in his mind, there is no consciousness that God is in control of what he does. And yet God says very clearly in verses 5 and 6, "I am in control of him. He is an instrument in My hand, verse 7, but he does not see it. He does not comprehend it." *"Howbeit he meaneth [it] not so, neither doth his heart think so; but it is in his heart. . ."* This is what he is conscious of, that he is going *"to destroy and cut off nations not a few."* But while he is out doing his will, he is really doing God's will, because nobody does anything without God being in control of it.

Now notice verse 12: *"Wherefore it shall come to pass, that when the Lord hath performed his whole work upon mount Zion and on Jerusalem"* (through this Assyrian king), *"I will punish the fruit of the stout heart of the king of Assyria, and the glory of his high looks."* In other words, God is saying, "Once I am done using the king of Assyria to punish Israel, I am going to turn around and punish the king of Assyria for his arrogance and his pride in thinking that he was the one who triumphed and conquered."

In the same way, God is going to use Antichrist and his one-world coalition to do His will, and, when He is done, He carries out their destruction. He allows Babylon to exercise all of her economic and cultural and social evil until He is done using her for His purposes, and then He brings about her destruction.

The point is this: Those who are not God's willing servants, always wind up being God's unwitting agents and serving His purposes after all, whether they thought they were or not; but in unwittingly serving His purposes, they receive no reward for doing so, as His willing servants do.

We see that God is in control; we see His purposes are being accomplished, we see the wicked destroying themselves, and we see our persecutors falling under the wrath of God. The wicked self-destruct, and the wicked always self-destruct, because sin can never provide a foundation for unity or strength or success.

What does Satan build his kingdom on? Sin. What does Antichrist build his kingdom on? Sin. What does the harlot build her society on? Sin. Sin is like a foundation of sand, and when the wind and the waves come, it always collapses. That is true in an individual's life when he builds his life on sin. It is also true in a nation's life, in a culture's life, and in the life of any religious system. When these systems are built on sin, they always collapse. The only kingdom that is never going to collapse is the kingdom of God, because it is built on a Rock, who is Jesus Christ.

That is why you need to build your individual life on Jesus Christ and be God's willing servant, and receive His reward of blessing and protection and salvation, instead of being His unwitting agent, thinking you are fighting against Him and triumphing over Him, while actually fulfilling His plans and purposes; and then when He is done achieving those through you, He destroys you. This is the God of the Bible, this is the God of history, and this is the God of the future.

What God did with Assyria, God will do with Babylon. God will cause instruments to rise up to destroy that which He wants to have destroyed, and He will provide instruments to save that which He wants to save. Therefore, as we look at the political events in this world as they unfold, we are not in any fear or terror or dread as to what is going to happen, because what is going to happen is exactly what God has purposed to happen. This does not mean that politicians are doing what is right or good. It only means that what they do serves the purposes of God in working all things together for the good of His people.

In God's sovereignty is our comfort and confidence that things are not out of control. Everything is unfolding according to plan, and that plan is being exercised by a good God who loves His people. He will protect them and guide them and guard them until that great day when He vindicates them and glorifies them before the whole world. The beast that persecuted us and the harlot that seduced us will be destroyed, and we will stand in victory over them both by the grace of God and through the redemption provided by Jesus Christ.

Let us face the future with confidence, with optimism, and with courage, and fight the good fight of faith today, knowing the battlefield has been designed for our victory.

53

Come Out of Babylon, Revelation 18:1–8

"[1] *And after these things I saw another angel come down from heaven, having great power; and the earth was lightened with his glory.* [2] *And he cried mightily with a strong voice, saying, Babylon the great is fallen, is fallen, and is become the habitation of devils, and the hold of every foul spirit, and a cage of every unclean and hateful bird.* [3] *For all nations have drunk of the wine of the wrath of her fornication, and the kings of the earth have committed fornication with her, and the merchants of the earth are waxed rich through the abundance of her delicacies.* [4] *And I heard another voice from heaven, saying, Come out of her, my people, that ye be not partakers of her sins, and that ye receive not of her plagues.* [5] *For her sins have reached unto heaven, and God hath remembered her iniquities.* [6] *Reward her even as she rewarded you, and double unto her double according to her works: in the cup which she hath filled fill to her double.* [7] *How much she hath glorified herself, and lived deliciously, so much torment and sorrow give her: for she saith in her heart, I sit a queen, and am no widow, and shall see no sorrow.* [8] *Therefore shall her plagues come in one day, death, and mourning, and famine; and she shall be utterly burned with fire: for strong is the Lord God who judgeth her.*"

In chapter 17, we saw a brief summary of the future destruction of Babylon in verses 15 to 18. We saw that the final manifestation of the beast (the Antichrist and his worldwide kingdom) is going to turn on Babylon and destroy it.

Very near the conclusion of this age, just before the second coming of Christ, anti-Christian government will turn on anti-Christian society and destroy it. Anti-Christian society, symbolically represented by Babylon the harlot, will be completely decimated. God will put it into the hearts of Satan's helpers to turn on each other and destroy one another.

But having seen a summary of the destruction of Babylon in chapter 17, we now have an extended description of the destruction of Babylon in chapter 18. Here, we are given considerably more detail about the nature of Babylon, about the evil of Babylon, and about the downfall of Babylon.

Chapter 18 can be divided into three sections. First of all, there is the exhortation to the saints to separate themselves from Babylon in verses 1 to 8. Secondly, there is the anguish of the ungodly over the fall of Babylon in verses 9 to 19. Thirdly, there is the rejoicing of the believers over the destruction of Babylon in verses 20 to 24. We will look at each of these three sections in turn as we come to them. In this chapter, we want to look at the first of these sections in verses 1 through 8, in which the saints are exhorted to separate themselves from Babylon.

Babylon represents anti-Christian society in its economic, social, and cultural aspects. Nowhere is this more clearly seen than in this chapter. However, the major emphasis at the core of the concept of Babylon is the economic aspect of anti-Christian society.

The major driver and the central concern of anti-Christian society is the worship of material wealth. The god of materialism and the worship of self-indulgent luxury as the highest goal and as the greatest good lie at the very heart of Babylon.

In the Sermon on the Mount, Jesus addresses this issue of materialism and the worship of material wealth. Notice Matthew 6:19–34: *"Lay not up for yourselves treasures upon earth, where moth and rust doth corrupt, and where thieves break through and steal:* [20] *But lay up for yourselves treasures in heaven, where neither moth nor rust doth corrupt, and where thieves do not break through nor steal:* [21] *For where your treasure is, there will your heart be also.* [22] *The light of the body is the eye: if therefore thine eye be single, thy whole body shall be full of light.* [23] *But if thine eye be evil, thy whole body shall be full of darkness. If therefore the light that is in thee be darkness, how great is that darkness!*

"[24] *No man can serve two masters: for either he will hate the one, and love the other; or else he will hold to the one, and despise the other. Ye cannot serve God and mammon.* [25] *Therefore I say unto you, Take no thought for your life, what ye shall eat, or what ye shall drink; nor yet for your body, what ye shall put on. Is not the life more than meat, and the body than raiment?* [26] *Behold the fowls of the air: for they sow not, neither do they reap, nor gather into barns; yet your heavenly Father feedeth them. Are ye not much better than they?* [27] *Which of you by taking thought can add one cubit unto his stature?* [28] *And why take ye thought for raiment? Consider the lilies of the field, how they grow; they toil not, neither do they spin:* [29] *And yet I say unto you, That even Solomon in all his glory was not arrayed like one of these.* [30] *Wherefore, if God so clothe the grass of the field, which to day is, and to morrow is cast into the oven, shall he not much more clothe you, O ye of little faith?* [31] *Therefore take no thought, saying, What shall we eat? or, What shall we drink? or, Wherewithal shall we be clothed?* [32] *(For after all these things do the Gentiles seek:) for your heavenly Father knoweth that ye have need of all these things.* [33] *But seek ye first the kingdom of God, and his righteousness; and all these things shall be added unto you.* [34] *Take therefore no thought for the morrow: for the morrow shall take thought for the things of itself. Sufficient unto the day is the evil thereof."*

Notice especially verse 24 in this reading: "*No man can serve two masters: for either he will hate the one, and love the other; or else he will hold to the one, and despise the other. Ye cannot serve God and [money].*"

Jesus had a great deal to say about money and materialism because money is the greatest idol of humanity, and it is the primary false god worshiped by mankind. It is the love of money that is the root of every kind of evil, and all the evil of Babylon rises out of that root, whether it is social evil or whether it is cultural evil.

Gross materialism has always been the central manifestation of Babylon in the past. Gross materialism is the central manifestation of Babylon today. Gross materialism will be the central manifestation of Babylon in the end. The world finds its fulfillment in things rather than in God, and the world loves materialistic self-indulgence more than it loves God. It worships the creation more than the Creator.

But this spirit of Babylon can also infect Christians as well. We see this in the church of Laodicea in Revelation 3:17 when it says, "*I am rich, and increased with goods, and have need of nothing.*" The church at Laodicea thought material gain was a sign of godliness, and material blessing meant that God was favorable toward them. But

Jesus corrects them and makes it clear they were in sin for their inordinate esteem of their material possessions, for their trust in them, and for the affection they had for them. The people of the church at Laodicea needed to repent of their esteem of their possessions, which caused them to value things more than they valued Christ.

If there is one point this passage in Revelation 18 makes clear, it is that this materialistic world with its obsessive attachment to luxury and pleasure will utterly perish, and all of those who sought and served wealth as their ultimate good will be cast into everlasting hell.

This passage teaches us that wealth is not the highest good, nor is wealth a permanent good. Wealth cannot save us from the wrath of God, and wealth will desert us in the hour of our greatest need. In a word, wealth is a very poor god. It is both too weak to meet our greatest need, and it is too temporary to provide us with any long-lasting security.

Christians have to earn and use money in this world. But it is imperative that we never compromise our values, our faith, or our witness for Christ in order to do so. If while faithfully living for Christ and serving Christ we become successful in business and we make a great deal of money, there is nothing wrong with that. Indeed, many of the godliest men in the Bible were very wealthy—men like Abraham and Job.

But wealth must be viewed for what it is. It is a gift of God that is a means to provide for the physical necessities of the body, a means to promote the gospel, and a means to help the poor. It is not to be used as a basis for pride and superiority over others, nor is it to be trusted in for our security.

Wealth is neither good nor bad in and of itself. It is our attitude toward it and our use of it that can either be a manifestation of evil or a means of bringing glory to God. As redeemed and yet fallen people, it is easy for us to adopt the attitude of the world toward wealth. That was the problem with the church at Laodicea.

We live in a very wealthy place here in America. We see the riches of the ungodly, we see the luxury in which they live, we see the pleasure they are able to purchase, and it is easy for us to envy that and to wish we had what they have, and start to compromise in order to obtain it. We can become utterly compromised in our moral conduct and abandon our obedience to Christ when we covet what the rich have, and set ourselves on a course to obtain it.

Notice 1 Timothy 6:1–19: "*Let as many servants as are under the yoke count their own masters worthy of all honour, that the name of God and his doctrine be not blasphemed.* [2] *And they that have believing masters, let them not despise them, because they are brethren; but rather do them service, because they are faithful and beloved, partakers of the benefit. These things teach and exhort.*"

This chapter opens with a description of economic disparity. Our passage describes servants who are poor and masters who are rich. Paul speaks about the issue of economics in the remainder of the passage. He is going to talk about the issue of money and wealth, and what our attitude should and should not be toward it, especially in a context of economic disparity.

Notice verses 3–18: "*If any man teach otherwise, and consent not to wholesome words, even the words of our Lord Jesus Christ, and to the doctrine which is according to godliness;* [4] *He is proud, knowing nothing, but doting about questions and strifes of words, whereof cometh envy, strife, railings, evil surmisings,* [5] *Perverse disputings of men of corrupt minds, and destitute of the truth,*" (now notice) "*supposing that gain is godliness: from such withdraw thyself.* [6] *But godliness with contentment is great gain.* [7] *For we brought nothing into this world, and it is certain we can carry nothing out.* [8] *And having food and raiment let us be therewith content.* [9] *But they that will be rich fall into temptation and a snare, and into many foolish and hurtful lusts, which drown men in destruction and perdition.* [10] *For the love of money is the root of all evil: which while some coveted after, they have erred from the faith, and pierced themselves through with many sorrows.*

"[11] *But thou, O man of God, flee these things; and follow after righteousness, godliness, faith, love, patience, meekness.* [12] *Fight the good fight of faith, lay hold on eternal life, whereunto thou art also called, and hast professed a good profession before many witnesses.* [13] *I give thee charge in the sight of God, who quickeneth all things, and before Christ Jesus, who before Pontius Pilate witnessed a good confession;* [14] *That thou keep this commandment without spot, unrebukeable, until the appearing of our Lord Jesus Christ:* [15] *Which in his times he shall shew, who is the blessed and only Potentate, the King of kings, and Lord of lords;* [16] *Who only hath immortality, dwelling in the light which no man can approach unto; whom no man hath seen, nor can see: to whom be honour and power everlasting. Amen.*

"[17] Charge them that are rich in this world, that they be not high-minded, nor trust in uncertain riches, but in the living God, who giveth us richly all things to enjoy; [18] That they do good, that they be rich in good works, ready to distribute, willing to communicate; [19] Laying up in store for themselves a good foundation against the time to come, that they may lay hold on eternal life."

Paul addresses the fact that people worship money instead of worshiping the Lord Jesus Christ, who is the only Potentate, the King of kings, and the Lord of lords. The point Paul is making is that a servant is not worse off because he is poor, and a master is not better off because he is rich. The true wealth of godliness with contentment is what really matters, and anyone in any socioeconomic status can have that kind of wealth. If we have food and clothing in the material realm, we have enough to be content.

Our great concern in life is not to gain more wealth. Our great concern is to obtain greater righteousness, godliness, faith, love, patience, and meekness as it says in verse 11. It is those things that constitute true wealth, and it is those things we should give our lives to pursuing. Money is subordinate to that, incidental to that, and is simply a means to enable us to pursue those goals.

The message of our passage in Revelation 18:1–8 is simply this: Come out of Babylon. Step away from the mad materialism of our age. Cast off the infatuation with luxury and reject any offers for the acquisition of wealth that would require you to compromise your Christian principles. God's wrath will fall upon those who idolize wealth. Do not be among them, and thereby escape the judgment that the worshipers of wealth will receive for their idolatry.

The Announcement of the Fall of Babylon

The announcement of the fall of Babylon is in verses 1–3. It says in verse 1: *"And after these things I saw another angel come down from heaven, having great power; and the earth was lightened with his glory."*

When it says in verse 1, *"And after these things,"* what it means is that this is the next vision in the sequence of visions. Throughout the book of Revelation, the phrase, *"and after these things,"* refers to the order in which the visions came to John, not the order of the events portrayed in the visions. That is, the phrase *"after these things,"* does not mean that the events recorded in chapter 18 occur chronologically after the events in chapter 17. This phrase, *"after these things,"* only means that after John received the vision of chapter 17, he received the vision in chapter 18 next. This is the way this phrase is always used in the book of Revelation, and it is used this way many times.

What did John see in this vision? He saw a mighty and glorious angel, and this angel made a very powerful and loud declaration. Notice verse 2. *"And he cried mightily with a strong voice, saying, Babylon the great is fallen, is fallen, and is become the habitation of devils, and the hold of every foul spirit, and a cage of every unclean and hateful bird."* The glory of this angel and the loudness of his voice is designed to grab the attention of believers who are in danger of falling under Babylon's spell and yielding to Babylon's seduction. The angel makes it clear to us that Babylon is doomed to destruction; and therefore, it is the height of folly to listen to her voice and join in her idolatry.

Allow me to illustrate. If you knew a business was certain to fail in the future, would you buy stock in it? And since you know Babylon is certain to fall under the wrath of God, should you participate in its worship of wealth? Notice that in verse 2, so certain is the fall of Babylon in the future, the angel proclaims its fall as having already occurred. Babylon has not yet fallen even to this very day, but it is going to fall. The angel states it as though it has already occurred. This is what we call the prophetic aorist, in which something is so certain to occur in the future, that it can be stated in the present as though it is already a past event.

The fall of Babylon is so great that it is compared to a completely destroyed and deserted city, into the wreckage of which the unclean animals and even the demons have moved to take up residence. Notice he says, *"Babylon the great is fallen, is fallen, and is become the habitation of devils, and the hold of every foul spirit, and a cage of every unclean and hateful bird."*

The closest analogy we see in our day are the ghost towns of bombed-out cities that are destroyed in the violence of modern warfare. You may have seen photographs of cities destroyed during war. Only the hulks and the rubble of bombed and burned-out buildings remain, and rats and birds are the main inhabitants of those structures. This is the destiny of the economy of this world in the end times, and all the wealth it contained. The greatness of Babylon is no protection for it when God is determined to destroy it.

Once again, we see that Old Testament Babylon is a very clear picture and foreshadowing of this New Testament Babylon spoken of in Revelation. In Isaiah 13:19–22, it says of Old Testament Babylon: *"And Babylon, the glory of kingdoms, the beauty of the Chaldees' excellency, shall be as when God overthrew Sodom and Gomorrah.* [20] *It shall never be inhabited, neither shall it be dwelt in from generation to generation: neither shall the Arabian pitch tent there; neither shall the shepherds make their fold there.* [21] *But wild beasts of the desert shall lie there; and their houses shall be full of doleful creatures; and owls shall dwell there, and satyrs shall dance there.* [22] *And the wild beasts of the islands shall cry in their desolate houses, and dragons in their pleasant palaces: and her time is near to come, and her days shall not be prolonged."* The same language is brought directly over into Revelation 18 and applied to the Babylon of our day.

In Revelation 18:3, the angel goes on to identify the cause of the destruction of Babylon: *"For all nations have drunk of the wine of the wrath of her fornication, and the kings of the earth have committed fornication with her, and the merchants of the earth are waxed rich through the abundance of her delicacies."*

Verse 3 is a declaration of the cause of the destruction of Babylon. Babylon is destroyed because she seduced the kings and the nations and the merchants to commit fornication with her. This fornication is a spiritual fornication. This fornication is that of forsaking the true God and engaging in the worship of another god—namely the god of money and material wealth, expressed in the mad pursuit of luxury as mankind's greatest good and greatest fulfillment.

God says in the First Commandment, *"I am the* Lord *thy God, which have brought thee out of the land of Egypt, out of the house of bondage. Thou shalt have no other gods before me."* It is the violation of this commandment that brings the wrath of God to bear on anti-Christian society and all who participate in her idolatry.

When you sacrifice loyalty to God in order to obtain economic advancement, when you sacrifice obedience to God in order to obtain economic security, when you sacrifice Christian principles in order to obtain material wealth, then you have committed fornication with Babylon. In a word, you have sold your soul for a mess of pottage.

Kings and nations and merchants will violate any principle of morality if it means they can multiply their wealth. Money becomes the justification for every behavior, no matter how wicked; and money is the goal of every policy, no matter how evil. The idolatry of wealth and all it can purchase is what constitutes the fornication of Babylon. It is serving money rather than God. Remember this: Behind the façade of luxury and wealth lies the certainty of the impending judgment of Almighty God.

The Admonition to Believers Regarding Babylon

The admonition to believers is in verses 4 to 5. Notice verse 4: *"And I heard another voice from heaven, saying, Come out of her, my people, that ye be not partakers of her sins, and that ye receive not of her plagues."*

Verse 4 tells us that a different voice from heaven now speaks, different from the angel that spoke in verses 1 to 3. This voice seems to be the voice of God Himself because when He addresses the believers, He calls them *"my people."* The message God gives to His people is this: "Come out of Babylon. Do not partake of her sins. Only by this means will you avoid participating in her judgment." This is the message of God to His people.

Clearly, Christians must engage in economic activity. They are instructed elsewhere in Scriptures to work hard to earn money and to store up and accumulate wealth. Christians should be economically self-sufficient through labor, through frugality, through saving, and through investment. God requires those things of us; in fact, the goal is to acquire sufficient wealth so we can not only meet our own needs throughout our entire lives, but so we have enough to be able to give to the poor who are unable to meet their own needs.

Christians are not called to withdraw from economic activity and the society in which they live. "Come out of Babylon" does not mean you should stop all your economic activity, take a vow of poverty, and live as a beggar in the streets. What it does mean is that Christians must refuse to compromise with any demands the world makes upon them to violate any Christian principle in order to be employed, do business, or acquire wealth.

Christians must refuse any line of work, and Christians must refuse any working conditions, that would involve them in disobedience to Christ. Here is the principle in a nutshell. Anything that would involve Christians in the compromise of any of the Ten Commandments must be rejected and withdrawn from, no matter how lucrative it might be, and no matter how great their need for money is. God will provide for His people without involving them in sin in order to do it.

Notice verse 5: *"For her sins have reached unto heaven, and God hath remembered her iniquities."* The iniquity of this world's economic systems and this world's economic activity is not small. It is gigantic. The economic, social, and cultural sins of anti-Christian society is without measure. Metaphorically speaking, if all of the sins of Babylon were stacked up, they would reach to the edge of the universe.

Verse 5 says, *"Her sins have reached unto heaven."* The sins of Babylon are uncountable in their number, and they are infinite in their evil. The economic crimes that have been performed and the violation of God's principles and commandments that have been committed are beyond counting. But God has not overlooked or forgotten even one of those sins. Not one act of economic wickedness has gone unnoticed by God, and every act of economic wickedness is going to be requited by God. *"Her sins have reached unto heaven, and God has remembered her iniquities."*

It may seem that fortunes are made by wicked commerce arising out of idolatrous motives in order that men may indulge in ostentatious self-serving luxury, and God has done nothing about it. Governments and individuals have stolen trillions of dollars from those who have rightly earned it, through both outright theft and through unjust and wicked taxation. Do not be deceived or think that because God has not acted yet to punish those sins, God will not act at all.

Fear God, and observe His ways, knowing that though He is patient with the wicked, their foot will slip in due time; and at the appointed hour, every sin will be remembered, and every idolatry will be punished. Those who have stolen from others and those who have compromised moral principles to get more wealth will all face their sins in the wrath of God on the Day of Judgment.

The rich man was clothed in purple and fine linen, and he fared sumptuously every day; but soon enough he found himself in hell, a beggar for a drop of water. What happened to the rich man in his time, is going to happen to the entire world economic system at the end of time. Babylon will be brought to judgment for her wickedness, and all who participated in that economic wickedness will be brought to judgment as well.

The admonition to believers, both now and throughout this age, is this: Do not participate in Babylon's sins. Live separated lives—lives that refuse to practice or participate in Babylon's sins. Refuse the temptations of sinful materialism, and reject materialism as a motivating factor in your life. Instead, seek first the kingdom of God and His righteousness, and all you need in the material realm will be given to you by God.

The Awfulness of the Judgment upon Babylon

The awfulness of the judgment upon Babylon is found in verses 6 to 8. The promise that Babylon would receive her plagues in verse 4 is now fulfilled in very explicit terms in verses 6 to 8. Notice verse 6: *"Reward her even as she rewarded you, and double unto her double according to her works: in the cup which she hath filled fill to her double."* Here, in verse 6, God says that Babylon will reap what she has sown. As Babylon has persecuted and punished the believers for refusing to participate in her sins, so let Babylon be persecuted and punished by God for committing those sins. God's justice is certain, and God's justice is exact.

God's justice will be a mirror image of the sin that was committed. This is the meaning of the threefold use of the word *"double"* in verse 6. Three times it says, "Give her double for her sins." This does not mean to give Babylon twice as much for her sins as she has committed, as though God would punish Babylon twice as much as her sins actually deserved. This is not what the passage means. If God punished people twice as much as their sins actually deserved, He would be unjust. What it means when it says to give her double for her sins, is that what is given back to Babylon is to be an exact double, an exact mirror image, of what Babylon gave out.

When you look in the mirror, what do you see? You see a double of yourself. What is being said is this: Give back to them exactly the same as they gave out to others. This is simply the law of an eye for an eye, and a tooth for a tooth. Nothing more and nothing less is just. You do not take out two eyes for one eye, and you do not take a finger for an eye. You take an eye for an eye. God gives an exact double to the wicked of what they gave to the believers.

Notice verse 7: *"How much she hath glorified herself, and lived deliciously, so much torment and sorrow give her."* This first phrase in verse 7 confirms what we said about the meaning of the word "double" in verse 6. However much she glorified herself and lived in self-indulgent luxury, give her that exact same amount of torment and sorrow.

Babylon's sin is that of pride and self-indulgence. She should have cultivated humility and servanthood toward others, but she did not. The spirit of Babylon is this: "How can I pamper myself and exalt my name among men?" The spirit of Christianity is this: "How can I serve others and exalt the name of Christ among men?"

The spirit of Babylon is that stated in the second half of verse 7: *"for she saith in her heart, I sit a queen, and am no widow, and shall see no sorrow."* "I am a queen. I sit on the throne. I am sovereign. I am secure. I am in control. I need to answer to no one. I will never regret my decisions and choices. I will never have any sorrow over my deeds or in my future. I am immune to judgment. I have it made." This describes the hubris and arrogance and self-confidence of those who worship wealth as their god and as their protection.

Verse 8: *"Therefore"*—because of that attitude—*"shall her plagues come in one day, death, and mourning, and famine; and she shall be utterly burned with fire: for strong is the Lord God who judgeth her."* Such arrogance as expressed in verse 7 will not go unpunished by God. Babylon will suddenly be destroyed, and that without remedy. Babylon will be destroyed in a day. Fullness of bread and abundance of pride will be replaced with death and mourning and famine and fire. Her destruction will be complete, and her destruction will be final. She will not be able with all of her resources and wealth to resist the judgment of God, for strong is the Lord God who judges her.

In light of the judgment of Babylon, how should we Christians view the subject of wealth? There is a great deal that could be said in reply, but I want to leave you with two thoughts.

First of all, remember that riches can never provide redemption, and therefore they should be of little concern to us. Consider the words of Psalm 49: *"Hear this, all ye people; give ear, all ye inhabitants of the world:* [2] *Both low and high, rich and poor, together.* [3] *My mouth shall speak of wisdom; and the meditation of my heart shall be of understanding.* [4] *I will incline mine ear to a parable: I will open my dark saying upon the harp.*

[5] *Wherefore should I fear in the days of evil, when the iniquity of my heels shall compass me about?* [6] *They that trust in their wealth,*

and boast themselves in the multitude of their riches; [7] *None of them can by any means redeem his brother, nor give to God a ransom for him:* [8] *(For the redemption of their soul is precious, and it ceaseth for ever:)* [9] *That he should still live for ever, and not see corruption.* [10] *For he seeth that wise men die, likewise the fool and the brutish person perish, and leave their wealth to others.* [11] *Their inward thought is, that their houses shall continue for ever, and their dwelling places to all generations; they call their lands after their own names.* [12] *Nevertheless man being in honour abideth not: he is like the beasts that perish.* [13] *This their way is their folly: yet their posterity approve their sayings. Selah.*

"[14] *Like sheep they are laid in the grave; death shall feed on them; and the upright shall have dominion over them in the morning; and their beauty shall consume in the grave from their dwelling.* [15] *But God will redeem my soul from the power of the grave: for he shall receive me. Selah.* [16] *Be not thou afraid when one is made rich, when the glory of his house is increased;* [17] *For when he dieth he shall carry nothing away: his glory shall not descend after him.* [18] *Though while he lived he blessed his soul: and men will praise thee, when thou doest well to thyself.* [19] *He shall go to the generation of his fathers; they shall never see light.* [20] *Man that is in honour, and understandeth not, is like the beasts that perish.*"

What David is saying is this: Money is meaningless. What matters is that God will redeem your soul from the power of the grave. But what wealth does He use to accomplish that? 1 Peter 1:18–19 says, "*Ye were not redeemed with corruptible things, as silver and gold, from your vain [manner of life] received by tradition from your fathers; But with the precious blood of Christ, as of a lamb without blemish and without spot.*"

The true riches are the redemption Christ provides, not the gold and silver the world holds forth as being the true riches. Recognize that riches can never provide redemption, and therefore they should be of little concern to us. If you have Christ, you have the only true and lasting wealth. You have "*the unsearchable riches of Christ,*" Ephesians 3:8.

Secondly, remember that the path of modest wealth is the safest path. In Proverbs 30:7–9, Agur says to God: "*Two things have I required of thee; deny me them not before I die:* [8] *Remove far from me vanity and lies: give me neither poverty nor riches; feed me with food convenient for me: [9] Lest I be full, and deny thee, and say, Who is the* LORD*? or lest I be poor, and steal, and take the name of my God in vain."*

Most of us are neither poor nor rich. We have modest wealth. We have food and clothing, we have a little money in savings, and we have a roof over our heads. God has provided well for us. That is the safe path. Those who determine to be rich pierce themselves through with many sorrows. They fall into many snares and hurtful lusts, which drown men in perdition. If individuals are so poor they have nothing (usually because they are slothful and lazy) and therefore do not have anything to eat, they wind up stealing, and taking the name of God in vain and cursing Him because He did not give them everything the wealthy have. Because of their envy and sloth, they petition the government to steal money from those who produce and give it to those who refuse to work.

Therefore, the path of moderate wealth is the safest path. Thank God you are not dirt poor, but also thank God you are not incredibly wealthy, because with great wealth comes great temptation. Not many mighty, not many noble, not many wise are in the kingdom. It is so easy with great wealth to fall into great sins because you have great opportunities to do it. One wise man has said this: "Poverty has slain its thousands, but prosperity its ten thousands."

We are likely to fall into terrible sins if we have enough money to have leisure and opportunity to do it. Be thankful you do not have that much wealth. You and I probably could not handle it, and if we had it, we would be ruined by it. We see in the majority of cases that those who do possess it are ruined by it.

Do not envy the wealthy. Do not indulge in the sins of Babylon to obtain the empty promise of Babylon, which is happiness through possessions. Happiness comes through a relationship with Jesus Christ and a clear conscience. If you have those things, you have the everlasting riches of Christ. Those are the true riches we want to aspire after and pursue.

Do you need to have a job and money? You do. The Bible makes that clear. But do not make them your god, and do not root your happiness in those things. Find your happiness in Christ and in the pursuit of righteousness and in seeking first the kingdom of God. As you do those things, your material needs will be taken care of. As soon as you die, you will not need any of those material things anyway. They are just temporary. They are here to get us through life. But when life is done with us, we are done with them. Therefore, let us not set our heart upon them. Let us set our hearts on Christ.

54

Two Responses to Babylon's Fall, Revelation 18:9–24

"[9] *And the kings of the earth, who have committed fornication and lived deliciously with her, shall bewail her, and lament for her, when they shall see the smoke of her burning,* [10] *Standing afar off for the fear of her torment, saying, Alas, alas, that great city Babylon, that mighty city! for in one hour is thy judgment come.* [11] *And the merchants of the earth shall weep and mourn over her; for no man buyeth their merchandise any more:* [12] *The merchandise of gold, and silver, and precious stones, and of pearls, and fine linen, and purple, and silk, and scarlet, and all thyine wood, and all manner vessels of ivory, and all manner vessels of most precious wood, and of brass, and iron, and marble,* [13] *And cinnamon, and odours, and ointments, and frankincense, and wine, and oil, and fine flour, and wheat, and beasts, and sheep, and horses, and chariots, and slaves, and souls of men.* [14] *And the fruits that thy soul lusted after are departed from thee, and all things which were dainty and goodly are departed from thee, and thou shalt find them no more at all.* [15] *The merchants of these things, which were made rich by her, shall stand afar off for the fear of her torment, weeping and wailing,* [16] *And saying, Alas, alas, that great city, that was clothed in fine linen, and purple, and scarlet, and decked with gold, and precious stones, and pearls!* [17] *For in one hour so great riches is come to nought. And every shipmaster, and all the company in ships, and sailors, and as many as trade by sea, stood afar off,* [18] *And cried when they saw the smoke of her burning, saying, What city is like unto this great city!* [19] *And they cast dust on their heads, and cried, weeping and wailing, saying, Alas, alas, that great city, wherein were made rich all that had ships in the sea by reason of her costliness! for in one hour is she made desolate.* [20] *Rejoice over her, thou heaven, and ye holy apostles and prophets; for God hath avenged you on her.* [21] *And a mighty angel took up a stone like a great millstone, and cast it into the sea, saying, Thus with violence shall that great city Babylon be thrown down, and shall be found no more at all.* [22] *And the voice of harpers, and musicians, and of pipers, and trumpeters, shall be heard no more at all in thee; and no craftsman, of whatsoever craft he be, shall be found any more in thee; and the sound of a millstone shall be heard no more at all in thee;* [23] *And the light of a candle shall shine no more at all in thee; and the voice of the bridegroom and of the bride shall be heard no more at all in thee: for thy merchants were the great men of the earth; for by thy sorceries were all nations deceived.* [24] *And in her was found the blood of prophets, and of saints, and of all that were slain upon the earth."*

Revelation declares and describes the spiritual warfare between Christ and Satan. It tells us that Christ will utterly defeat Satan and his helpers, and that defeat is set before us in chapters 17 and 18.

In chapter 17 we saw the defeat of the beast, which represents anti-Christian civil government, and we saw the defeat of Babylon, which represents anti-Christian society. Chapter 18 revisits and greatly expands the description of the defeat of Babylon that was summarized in 17:16.

In chapter 18 we are told a great deal about the character of Babylon, the evil of Babylon, and the downfall of Babylon. In the last chapter, we saw the exhortation given to the saints to separate themselves from Babylon in verses 1 to 8.

Babylon calls upon people to worship money and material wealth, and to make a god out of luxury and self-indulgence and prideful self-exaltation. Babylon calls upon people to compromise and sacrifice every principle of Christian morality and every point of Christian obedience in order to obtain wealth and the esteem of the society. The idolatry of wealth and all it can purchase is an act of spiritual fornication, and it is a violation of the First Commandment to have no god beside the God of the Scriptures.

Therefore, God calls His saints to come out of Babylon. What it means to come out of Babylon is for Christians to refuse to compromise with any demands the world makes on them to violate any Christian principle in order to be employed, in order to do business, or in order to acquire wealth. Anything that would involve them in the compromise of any of the Ten Commandments must be rejected and withdrawn from, no matter how lucrative it might be, and no matter how great their need for money. God will provide for His people without involving them in sin in order to do it. Only by carefully observing these principles can the Christian escape the wrath of God that falls upon Babylon and all who commit fornication with it.

Having seen the call to come out of Babylon in verses 1 to 8, we will now see the anguish of the ungodly over the fall of Babylon in verses 9 to 19, and the rejoicing of believers over the fall of Babylon in verses 20 to 24. Here are two radically different perspectives on the destruction of the very heart of anti-Christian society. The heart and soul of anti-Christian society is its economic activity, and everything within it revolves around its idolatry of wealth.

When the economic function of society is destroyed, when the money and the banking system collapse, and when commerce comes to a grinding halt, society will entirely cease to function. Death and mourning and famine follow, as Revelation 18:8 told us. Anti-Christian society is going to collapse under the wrath of God, and it is going to collapse at the hand of the beast.

When the beast destroys Babylon (which we saw in 17:16) by decimating its economic system (as we see in chapter 18), it will have effectively destroyed itself as well, because anti-Christian government cannot function for long if it does not have society's economic activity to provide it with tax revenue to pay its bills.

Even though Antichrist and his one-world coalition of governments somehow saw the economic powers of society to be a sufficient threat so they felt the need to destroy them, once they have destroyed them they recoil in horror over what they have done. They begin to mourn over the devastation they wrought to their own best interests for having destroyed Babylon. To obtain victory over their perceived enemy, they destroyed themselves in the process. When they finally realize this, they begin to mourn for having destroyed the Babylon they loved.

But for the believers it is an entirely different story. When the anti-Christian forces in this world that previously had been united in persecuting the church now turn on one another and destroy one another, this brings relief and joy to the believer, as he sees the justice of God visited upon the wicked for their persecution of believers.

In Revelation 11:9–10, we saw the wicked rejoicing as they saw the believers destroyed. But now it is the turn of the believers to rejoice in seeing the wicked destroyed by the Lord God visiting judgment on them.

But the difference is this: the victory of the world over the believers is only temporary. Symbolically it was represented by three and a half days. But the victory of believers over the wicked is everlasting, permanent, and eternal. Babylon will never rise again to persecute the church. At the end of this age, it will be destroyed forever. This is the broad outline of the section before us. Let us consider it together in further detail.

The Anguish of the Ungodly over the Fall of Babylon

The anguish of the ungodly over the fall of Babylon is recorded in verses 9 through 19. In this section, we see the despair and the self-pity of the kings, the merchants, and the shippers of merchandise over the tremendous economic loss they sustain when Babylon falls and her economic system is destroyed.

The destruction of Babylon and her economic system is foreshadowed in the Old Testament and described by the downfall of the city of Tyre in Ezekiel 26, 27, and 28. As you read those chapters, you notice the language of Revelation 18 is borrowed directly out of them, and is used in this chapter to describe the downfall of Babylon.

Tyre was an economic powerhouse in its day—a city that was renowned for trade and wealth and luxury. Tyre was actually a city that sat on an island just off the coast of Phoenicia in the Mediterranean Sea. Her trade was conducted by ships, and her merchants and her king were wealthy beyond imagination.

But Tyre was an exceedingly wicked city and society, and God pronounced His judgment on it with the same terminology that is applied to Babylon in Revelation 18. The downfall of Tyre and those who mourned over its destruction model the downfall and the lamentation of those who mourn over the final destruction of the world's economic system at the end of this age.

This anguish over the fall of Babylon is expressed by three groups of people. As these three groups see the destruction of their god of materialism and wealth and luxury, their whole world collapses, their hope is shattered, and their future is filled with despair. They weep and mourn, not for Babylon, but for themselves because of the tremendous personal loss they are experiencing. It is a very selfish weeping and mourning.

First of all, notice the anguish of the kings. The anguish of the kings is in verses 9 to 10. *"And the kings of the earth, who have committed fornication and lived deliciously with her"*—that is, with Babylon—*"shall bewail her, and lament for her, when they shall see the smoke of her burning,* [10] *Standing afar off for the fear of her torment, saying, Alas, alas, that great city Babylon, that mighty city! for in one hour is thy judgment come."*

The phrases *"the smoke of her burning"* and *"standing afar off for the fear of her torment"* are used repeatedly in this passage. They are used to symbolically convey the idea of the utter ruin of Babylon, and the horrified recoil of those who behold her ruin.

When you see the god you trusted in and placed all your hope and confidence in destroyed before your very eyes, it is a heart-crushing experience. The kings of the earth in concert with the Antichrist destroyed Babylon, but now they weep over what they have done with grief and regret.

It is like a jealous husband who kills his wife in a fit of anger because he suspects she has an interest in someone else, and after he has murdered her, realizes he has destroyed the most wonderful wife he could have ever had, and is now filled with grief and sorrow and regret.

So it is at the end of this age. For some reason, the kings of the earth who worship the god of materialism and all the luxury it can produce became suspicious of society's economic power. This moved them to destroy it, as we saw in 17:16. But now they regret what they have lost, and they realize the damage they did to themselves in the process.

The kings of the earth sold their souls for economic well-being and luxury. Now they have lost all they sold their souls to obtain. What makes it even more bitter is that they lost it by their own hand. The speed at which the economic power and the wealth of the world is dismantled is breathtaking. Verse 10 indicates that, symbolically speaking, it occurred in one hour—that is, it occurred in a very limited timeframe.

We can easily envision this when our own economic system in the United States was brought to a near-collapse in 1929 in the Great Depression, and in 2007 and 2008 in the Great Recession, both of which were due to perverse, government-imposed economic policies. Both the Great Depression and the Great Recession were a direct result of governmental blunders in the laws it passed and policies it implemented.

As the economic systems of the world become even more digitalized and interdependent and based on electronically generated currencies that have no real backing and are built on giant credit bubbles, it is easy to see how some government action could bring it all tumbling to the ground in a day. Multiple trillions of dollars of wealth could be destroyed in a short period of time by malicious government decisions, policies, laws, and actions.

This has happened on a limited scale before, and it is going to happen on a worldwide scale in the future. And when it does, the kings of the earth will lament over the destruction they caused to their own well-being, and, in that destruction, they will see the wrath of God brought to bear against them, for they say, *"in one hour thy judgment is come."*

Secondly, notice the anguish of the merchants in verses 11 to 16. These are the businessmen who are financially bankrupted by the collapse and the ruin of the world's economy. Their merchandise is now useless because the collapse of the monetary system makes it impossible for anyone to be able to purchase their goods.

Notice verses 11 through 13. *"And the merchants of the earth shall weep and mourn over her; for no man buyeth their merchandise any more:* [12] *The merchandise of gold, and silver, and precious stones, and of pearls, and fine linen, and purple, and silk, and scarlet, and all thyine wood, and all manner vessels of ivory, and all manner vessels of most precious wood, and of brass, and iron, and marble,* [13] *And cinnamon, and odours, and ointments, and frankincense, and wine, and oil, and fine flour, and wheat, and beasts, and sheep, and horses, and chariots, and slaves, and souls of men."*

Verses 12 to 13 provide a representative list of merchandise that can no longer be purchased in the Babylonian economic system. The trade goods in this list are selected because they represent the kind of luxury goods that the world lives for and idolizes and worships. Ostentatious jewelry, opulent apparel, extravagant decor, high cuisine, expensive transportation, and the use and abuse of servants—all these things come to an end.

Some commentators have noted that the first thing in this list is gold because it was valued the most highly, and the last thing on the list was the souls of men because they were valued the least. The priorities and values of Babylon are utterly inverted.

Because commerce is destroyed, access to luxury goods and the ability to purchase them has ended. Everyone is reduced to bare survival, and limited to the most basic goods that barely sustain life.

Notice verse 14: *"And the fruits that thy soul lusted after are departed from thee, and all things which were dainty and goodly are departed from thee, and thou shalt find them no more at all."* All those material possessions the world lusted after and idolized are now completely gone. Specialty items are no longer available.

Notice verse 15 through verse 17a. *"The merchants of these things, which were made rich by her, shall stand afar off for the fear of her torment, weeping and wailing,* [16] *And saying, Alas, alas, that great city, that was clothed in fine linen, and purple, and scarlet, and decked with gold, and precious stones, and pearls!* [17] *For in one hour so great riches is come to nought."*

The result of the destruction of the world's economic system is that the merchants that were enriched by it are brokenhearted at their losses, their bankruptcy, and their poverty. All they lived for and all they labored for is now gone, and it will never come back. They are utterly ruined, their god is dead, and their hope is destroyed. Riches have evaporated into thin air.

Thirdly, notice the anguish of the shippers. The anguish of the shippers is in verses 17b through verse 19. *"And every shipmaster, and all the company in ships, and sailors, and as many as trade by sea, stood afar off,* [18] *And cried when they saw the smoke of her burning, saying, What city is like unto this great city!* [19] *And they cast dust on their heads, and cried, weeping and wailing, saying, Alas, alas, that great city, wherein were made rich all that had ships in the sea by reason of her costliness! for in one hour is she made desolate."*

Here are represented all the suppliers of the merchants and the merchandise spoken of in verses 11 to 16. These shippers are the manufacturers and the suppliers of these goods, and they bring them into the city for the merchants to market and sell.

Ships were the primary instruments for conveying goods to the merchants from their source of manufacture in John's day. The point is that the manufacturers and shippers of the merchandise spoken of in verses 12 to 13 are also ruined in the fall of Babylon. Their cries of lamentation in verses 18 and 19 are not an expression of repentance, but cries of self-pity and sorrow over their economic ruin, because all they lived for is destroyed. They are brought from the pinnacle of wealth down to the pit of poverty. How are the mighty fallen!

Neither the kings nor the merchants nor the shippers are mourning and weeping over their sins. Instead, they weep and mourn out of self-pity and sorrow over the loss of their self-indulgent lifestyle for which they had sacrificed every moral principle, and even their own souls, to obtain.

However, the people represented in these verses are about to lose something far more important than their material wealth. They are about to lose their souls. And yet their obsession with their wealth and its loss makes them oblivious to the impending eternal judgment that is going to occur in a very short period of time when Jesus returns. They are so obsessed with the things of this life that they cannot even think about the life to come, and whether they are ready to face God or not. The issues of time completely block out the thought of eternity.

The warning of this section is very clear. Keep the things of this world in their proper place in your priorities, so that even if you were to lose every material possession you have, you would still continue to rejoice that you have a saved soul. You would still continue to rejoice that you have forgiveness of your sins. You would still continue to rejoice that you have fellowship with Jesus Christ. You would still continue to rejoice that you have the unsearchable riches of Christ. You would still continue to rejoice that you have eternal life. You would still continue to rejoice because those things are the things of true worth and permanent value.

That is why Jesus says in Matthew 6:19–21, *"Lay not up for yourselves treasures upon earth, where moth and rust doth corrupt, and where thieves break through and steal: [20]But lay up for yourselves treasures in heaven, where neither moth nor rust doth corrupt, and where thieves do not break through nor steal: [21]For where your treasure is, there will your heart be also."* If our treasure is in heaven, our hearts are in heaven; and if things in this life come or go, it is of small moment to one whose heart is in heaven, and whose wealth is laid up in Christ.

You can see by people's response to material things who their god is. When material things are our god, we live and die on their coming and their going. But when God is our God, money may come in or money may go out, but we recognize its temporary nature and its limited utility, and it affects us little either way. We understand that it is only useful to take care of the needs of our body until we get through this life. But the true riches are in Christ and in heaven and are laid up for our future there. That is where our heart is, and that is where our trust is. That is where our confidence is, and that is where our joy is. This is why we can say with Job, that whether the Lord gives wealth, or the Lord takes away wealth, *"blessed be the name of the* L*ORD."*

The Rejoicing of the Believers over the Fall of Babylon

The rejoicing of the believers over the fall of Babylon is contained in verses 20 to 24. Just as the believers in the Old Testament rejoiced over the fall of Old Testament Babylon in Jeremiah 51, so the New Testament believers will rejoice over the fall of the harlot Babylon at the end of this age. There are tremendous parallels between the language in Jeremiah 51 over the fall of Old Testament Babylon, and the language that is used in Revelation 18 over the fall of New Testament Babylon.

Here is a completely different reaction to the fall of Babylon than we have just seen. Verse 20: *"Rejoice over her, thou heaven, and ye holy apostles and prophets; for God hath avenged you on her."* This rejoicing is something that God calls upon us to do, and He says to those in heaven: "Rejoice!" He says to those on earth: "Rejoice!"

Who are those in heaven who are rejoicing at this point? Revelation 6 tells us who they are. In Revelation 6:9–11 it says, *"And when he had opened the fifth seal, I saw under the altar the souls of them that were slain for the word of God, and for the testimony which they held."* These are the martyrs that Babylon slaughtered. "[10] *And they cried with a loud voice, saying, How long, O Lord, holy and true, dost thou not judge and avenge our blood on them that dwell on the earth?* [11] *And white robes were given unto every one of them; and it was said unto them, that they should rest yet for a little season, until their fellowservants also and their brethren, that should be killed as they were, should be fulfilled."* After that, vengeance is going to come.

Well, it has come. The martyred saints in Revelation 6 who had been slaughtered through the ages by anti-Christian society, who were waiting for justice to be exercised on those who murdered them, are now having their prayers answered. God is turning to those martyrs in heaven and saying to them, "Rejoice!"

Not only is there part of the church in heaven, which is called the Church Triumphant, but there is also part of the church on earth, called the Church Militant; because for those in heaven, the battle is over, but for those on earth, the battle still rages. He says in verse 20, *"Rejoice over her, thou heaven"*—that is, the saints in chapter 6—*"and ye holy apostles and prophets"*—that is, those believers down on the earth who are still laboring for the Lord. They are the messengers of God's divine revelation here on earth. He says to both of these groups of people, *"God hath avenged you on her."* The reason for the rejoicing over the destruction of Babylon is that God has vindicated His saints and accomplished justice for them by punishing their persecutors.

Many Christians grow discouraged that the wicked seem to prosper so much and for so long. But in the end, their prosperity will do nothing to protect them from the wrath of God. In the end, the wicked will be judged and punished for the evil they have done, and the scales of justice will be balanced. Then the righteous will rejoice at the vindication of the justice of God and at the vindication of themselves as God justifies them and condemns the wicked who assaulted them.

The righteous do not delight in Babylon's suffering because they are sadistic, but because Babylon's suffering is the manifestation of God's justice, and it is God's justice they are rejoicing in. They are glad that God has defended the honor of His name. They are glad that God has defended the integrity of His law. They are glad that God has defended the truthfulness of the promises He has made, and that justice will prevail.

They rejoice because God has defended the honor of His name by not leaving sin unpunished and undealt with. They rejoice that God has demonstrated that His people were right all along in their belief and behavior, and that the false accusations and slanders lodged against them by the wicked were lies.

This rejoicing is rejoicing over the vindication of the believers and the vindication of the justice and the righteousness of God. Whatever pain and suffering the wicked endure, they have earned it for themselves by their works. The wages of sin is death. They are being paid what they have worked so hard to earn. God will not withhold their wages from them.

Now, notice verse 21: "*And a mighty angel took up a stone like a great millstone, and cast it into the sea, saying, Thus with violence shall that great city Babylon be thrown down, and shall be found no more at all.*" This imagery of a stone being cast into the sea as a symbol of God's judgment on Babylon is taken directly out of Jeremiah 51:60–64.

Jeremiah is prophesying of the downfall and destruction of Old Testament Babylon, who came under the leadership of Nebuchadnezzar and conquered Israel, captured her, and carried her away to be in exile in Babylon for seventy years.

Jeremiah 51:60–64, "*So Jeremiah wrote in a book all the evil that should come upon Babylon, even all these words that are written against Babylon.* [61] *And Jeremiah said to Seraiah, When thou comest to Babylon, and shalt see, and shalt read all these words;* [62] *Then shalt thou say, O Lord, thou hast spoken against this place, to cut it off, that none shall remain in it, neither man nor beast, but that it shall be desolate for ever.* [63] *And it shall be, when thou hast made an end of reading this book, that thou shalt bind a stone to it, and cast it into the midst of Euphrates:* [64] *And thou shalt say, Thus shall Babylon sink, and shall not rise from the evil that I will bring upon her: and they shall be weary.*"

Jeremiah wrote the judgments against Babylon in a book, and he told Seraiah his servant to go to Babylon, read what is in the book, and tie a rock to the book and throw it into the Euphrates River. The point is, just as when a stone is thrown into the water, it will never rise or be seen again; so, when Babylon falls, it will never rise or be seen again. What happened to Old Testament Babylon is going to happen to New Testament Babylon as well.

In Revelation 18, we have the imagery of the angel taking the millstone and throwing it into the sea, and this is symbolic of the fact that when God takes New Testament Babylon down and destroys it, it is not ever coming back.

Now notice verses 22 and 23a. It says, "*And the voice of harpers, and musicians, and of pipers, and trumpeters, shall be heard no more at all in thee; and no craftsman, of whatsoever craft he be, shall be found any more in thee; and the sound of a millstone shall be heard no more at all in thee;* [23] *And the light of a candle shall shine no more at all in thee; and the voice of the bridegroom and of the bride shall be heard no more at all in thee."*

The point of this extended description of all of the things that will cease to exist in Babylon is to show that there will be a complete collapse of the cultural, economic, and social functions of society when God's judgment falls upon it. For all intents and purposes, anti-Christian society will cease to function, and every aspect of life will grind to an absolute standstill. The judgment on Babylon will be complete.

This judgment falls upon Babylon for three reasons. First, it falls upon it because of its pride. Notice verse 23b. It says, "*for*" (or because) *"thy merchants were the great men of the earth."* When it says, *"thy merchants were the great men of the earth,"* the point is that those who were at the pinnacle of economic wealth sought glory for themselves as those to be admired and followed and worshiped. The world did admire and follow and worship them. They were thought of as the great men of the earth.

These great merchants—these phenomenally wealthy people of the earth—did not see themselves as stewards entrusted with God's wealth, who were supposed to use it for God's glory. Instead, those at the pinnacle of the wealth of the world said, with Nebuchadnezzar of old, *"Is not this great Babylon, that I have built. . .by the might of my power, and for the honour of my majesty?"*

As God looked at the pride that arose out of the economic excess of those who had overachieved in the accumulation of the wealth of this world, who saw their wealth as a commendation of themselves and an exaltation of their glory and as a means to draw people to worship and follow them, God brought judgment upon them.

God brought judgment on Babylon not only because of the pride that arose from its wealth, but secondly, God brought judgment on Babylon because of its sorceries. Verse 23, the last phrase: *"for by thy sorceries were all nations deceived."* The word *"sorceries"* refers to all of the deceptions and seductions that Babylon perpetrated in order to induce people to worship the god of material wealth.

Whatever it took to turn people away from the true God and to entice people to worship a false god, that is what Babylon did. She did it either through the seduction of godless, wicked entertainment, or through the promotion of perverted immorality, or through the engagement in satanic activity, or through the actual drugs of alcohol and opiates. Babylon used a variety of tools to seduce the people by her sorceries, and to cause the nations of the earth to worship the god of this world, who is Satan.

God brought judgment on Babylon not only because of her pride, not only because of her sorceries, but, thirdly, because of her persecution of Christians. Notice verse 24: *"And in her was found the blood of prophets, and of saints, and of all that were slain upon the earth."*

Anti-Christian society not only pursues evil as hard as it can, as much as it can, and as fast as it can, but it is also determined to destroy those who will not. Anti-Christian society has always relentlessly persecuted and martyred Christians because they alone stand as a reproach to its wickedness. This is why you see the hostility toward Christianity in our society.

We stand up and say, "This is wrong, and this is right. You need to stop doing this, and you need to start doing that, because this is how God says you should live." And when we raise our moral voice against the wickedness of our age, a vicious hostility rises up against us for taking a stand against the evil of our society.

As a result, when Christians speak out against Babylon, Babylon slaughters the Christians. It has been going on for centuries, it will continue to go on to the end, but it will be especially bad after Antichrist arises. All of the blood of all of the martyrs of all of the ages, from Abel till the end of time, will all be required of Babylon. She will be judged for all of the saints that have been persecuted and slaughtered.

Because of pride, because of seduction, and because of persecution, Babylon will be judged, and strong is the Lord God who judges her, as it says in verse 8 of this chapter.

In chapter 18, we see the sharpness of the contrast between the kingdom of God and the kingdom of Satan. We live lives that are separated from Babylon as verse 4 tells us to do. We are severely persecuted by Babylon as verse 24 tells us we will be. We rejoice at the fall of Babylon, as verse 20 instructs us to do.

On the other hand, the world plunges into the midst of Babylon and immerses itself in its mad worship of the god of wealth. The world practices all the sins of Babylon and traffics in all of the evil she offers as the means to obtain satisfaction and pleasure. The world therefore profoundly mourns the loss of Babylon.

There are only two camps to be in. The question is simply this: Do you stand against Babylon, or do you stand with Babylon? Do you live a life that is separated from her sins and her idolatries, or do you participate in her sins and her idolatries? What do you aspire after as you go through this life? To be like the Hollywood movie stars, or to be like our Puritan forefathers?

Remember this: the world passes away, and the lusts thereof, but he that does the will of God abides forever. Choose wisely. As verse 4 says, *"Come out of her, my people, that ye be not partakers of her sins, and that ye receive not of her plagues."*

We who are outside of Babylon, and are therefore persecuted by Babylon, wait for the destruction of Babylon. By faith we know that while Babylon is now riding the beast and possesses tremendous power, one day God will bring her down to destruction. We wait for that day because that will be the day of our vindication. Instead of people worshiping the 400 richest people in the world, they will be looking up to and admiring the godly people who lived righteous lives in this world.

May we be among that number, as we recognize that the wealth of this world is a pitiful substitute for the unsearchable riches of Jesus Christ. Let us esteem Him, pursue Him, and seek to acquire all of Him we can. Yes, we have to acquire a little material wealth along the way in order to survive so that we may follow Christ, but let us never confuse the temporal riches with the true riches.

55

The Marriage Supper of the Lamb, Revelation 19:1–10

"[1] *And after these things I heard a great voice of much people in heaven, saying, Alleluia; Salvation, and glory, and honour, and power, unto the Lord our God:* [2] *For true and righteous are his judgments: for he hath judged the great whore, which did corrupt the earth with her fornication, and hath avenged the blood of his servants at her hand.* [3] *And again they said, Alleluia. And her smoke rose up for ever and ever.* [4] *And the four and twenty elders and the four beasts fell down and worshipped God that sat on the throne, saying, Amen; Alleluia.* [5] *And a voice came out of the throne, saying, Praise our God, all ye his servants, and ye that fear him, both small and great.* [6] *And I heard as it were the voice of a great multitude, and as the voice of many waters, and as the voice of mighty thunderings, saying, Alleluia: for the Lord God omnipotent reigneth.* [7] *Let us be glad and rejoice, and give honour to him: for the marriage of the Lamb is come, and his wife hath made herself ready.* [8] *And to her was granted that she should be arrayed in fine linen, clean and white: for the fine linen is the righteousness of saints.* [9] *And he saith unto me, Write, Blessed are they which are called unto the marriage supper of the Lamb. And he saith unto me, These are the true sayings of God.* [10] *And I fell at his feet to worship him. And he said unto me, See thou do it not: I am thy fellowservant, and of thy brethren that have the testimony of Jesus: worship God: for the testimony of Jesus is the spirit of prophecy.*"

In the last chapter we saw a description of the destruction of Babylon, and we saw two opposite responses that were given to its destruction: the response of mourning, and the response of rejoicing.

When anti-Christian society is destroyed at the end of this age, the kings of the earth, the merchants, and the manufacturers and suppliers of goods will mourn and weep over the destruction of the world's economic system and the society that flows out of it. Because the world's economic system is destroyed, society collapses, and famine and death are the result. Therefore, there is a response of grief and sorrow by the wicked over the economic and personal loss they suffer when Babylon is destroyed.

But there is also a response of rejoicing when Babylon is destroyed. When anti-Christian society collapses at the end of this age, the believers both in heaven and on earth rejoice. They are finally delivered from Babylon's seduction and persecution, and they finally receive the justice and vindication they longed for. In 18:20 it says, *"Rejoice over her, thou heaven, and ye holy apostles and prophets; for God hath avenged you on her." "Rejoice"* is a command given by God to His people, a command they gladly obey, and a command they fully endorse.

In chapter 19, we see this glad obedience of the people of God in expressing joy and praise to God for the destruction of Babylon. God has said, *"Rejoice,"* and the people in chapter 19 respond with rejoicing over the destruction of the harlot Babylon.

The people of God always worship God in response to His mighty works. As we behold what God has done in creation, we respond in worship. As we behold what God has done in providence, we respond in worship. As we behold what God has done in redemption, we respond in worship. And as we behold what God has done in judgment, we also respond in worship. All of the works of God display the glory of God, and that is as true of His works of judgment as it is of His works of redemption and providence and creation.

In Revelation 19:1–10, we see the church worshiping the Lord their God for His mighty work of judgment on Babylon. Babylon is the great harlot who committed and enticed others to commit spiritual fornication—that is, to worship some other god beside the true God. Babylon used seduction to draw people away from God, or persecution to drive them away from God. Babylon betrayed God in every way she could.

In contrast to this harlot Babylon is the faithful bride of Jesus Christ, who never wavered in her love for Christ or in her loyalty to Christ. She maintained her virginity, in that she would not commit fornication with another god by worshiping the gods of Babylon. She saw herself as betrothed to Christ, and would not go after another, no matter what the enticements and no matter how great the pressure. The church, the bride of Christ, remained true to Christ.

We have these two women set in contrast with each another. We have the harlot Babylon, who is destroyed by Christ, and we have the church, who is married by Christ. The harlot is a symbol of spiritual fornication, but the church is a manifestation of spiritual faithfulness.

We see these two themes in these first ten verses of chapter 19. We have the theme of rejoicing over the judgment of the harlot Babylon, and the theme of rejoicing over the marriage of the bride of Christ. We will give our attention to these two themes as we look at Revelation 19:1–10.

The Rejoicing over the Judgment of the Harlot Babylon

The rejoicing over the judgment of the harlot Babylon is in verses 1–4. In chapter 18 we were instructed to rejoice over the destruction of the harlot Babylon, and here is the response to that instruction and the expression of that rejoicing.

Notice 19:1–4: *"And after these things I heard a great voice of much people in heaven, saying, Alleluia; Salvation, and glory, and honour, and power, unto the Lord our God:* [2] *For true and righteous are his judgments: for he hath judged the great whore, which did corrupt the earth with her fornication, and hath avenged the blood of his servants at her hand.* [3] *And again they said, Alleluia. And her smoke rose up for ever and ever.* [4] *And the four and twenty elders and the four beasts fell down and worshipped God that sat on the throne, saying, Amen; Alleluia."*

This section is the continuation and the conclusion of chapter 18, in which the saints are commanded to rejoice over the fall of Babylon. In these opening verses, we see this rejoicing being expressed by the people of God. After the vision of the fall of Babylon, John has another vision of the rejoicing of the believers and the worship they give to God for the exercise of His justice in requiting the sins of Babylon.

Notice verse 1: *"And after these things I heard a great voice of much people in heaven, saying, Alleluia; Salvation, and glory, and honour, and power, unto the Lord our God."* In this next vision that begins in

19:1, John now hears a multitude of people in heaven giving praise to God, and he records the content of their praise.

This praise to God opens with the word *"Alleluia."* This word means "Praise Jehovah." This term and title for God is taken from the Old Testament, which is no surprise since the book of Revelation is saturated with references and allusions to the Old Testament.

Having declared praise to Jehovah, the multitude of voices out of heaven now give a number of reasons for praising Jehovah, by ascribing to Him praise for what He has done, and for the attributes He possesses.

Having said, "Praise Jehovah," the people in heaven first of all praise God for providing them with *"Salvation."* God has saved them from their sins. God has saved them from His wrath. God has saved them from Satan and all his helpers, and in particular, his helper Babylon. No longer will God's people have to endure either the seduction of anti-Christian society or the persecution of anti-Christian society. God has saved them, and, because they recognize that, they loudly proclaim, "Praise Jehovah! Praise Him for His salvation!"

Secondly, they praise God for His *"glory."* God's glory is the blinding splendor of His majesty that brings all of creation to fall before Him in humility and fear and awe and worship. As they behold the purity of God's holiness, as they consider the outshining of His excellencies, and as they contemplate the infinite worth and value of His divine nature, they cry out with one voice, "Praise Jehovah! Praise Him for His glory!"

Thirdly, they praise Him for his *"honour."* They ascribe to Him honor, which is the esteem that is due to God. It is the respect that is given to one that is infinitely superior to us in every way. Whom do you honor? You honor those who are superior to you.

God is honored when He is shown reverence in our attitude toward Him. God is honored when we show humility in our conduct before Him. When we hold God in the highest regard, when we submit to His authority, when we speak glowingly of His accomplishments, we give Him honor. As the saints in heaven reflect on the honor that is due to God, they cry out with one voice, "Praise Jehovah! He is worthy of honor!"

Fourthly, they ascribe to God *"power."* This is an exaltation of the strength He has to defeat His foes, to deliver His children, and to accomplish all of His purposes, in spite of the opposition of the forces of Satan and his helpers that are arrayed against Him. Nothing is too hard for God, and no one can thwart God. His power is irresistible. None can stay His hand or stop Him from doing as He pleases. As the saints in heaven contemplate the power of God, they cry out with one voice, "Praise Jehovah! He possesses all power in heaven and on earth!"

This passage opens with tremendous praise that is thundered out by this multitude of voices in heaven, and they say, "Praise Jehovah for the salvation He provides, for the glory He possesses, for the honor He deserves, and for the power He exercises!"

Notice verse 2: *"For true and righteous are his judgments: for he hath judged the great whore, which did corrupt the earth with her fornication, and hath avenged the blood of his servants at her hand."*

The praise of God continues when the saints in heaven declare of God, "*. . .true and righteous are his judgments.*" It is the nature of all of God's judgments that they are true and they are righteous.

When God passes judgment on someone, it is always a true judgment. It never overstates or understates the true nature of the situation being judged or the true facts about what was done. The judgments of God are according to truth.

His judgments are also righteous judgments. The sentence He passes on those He judges is always proper and just. God does not pass too harsh of a sentence, nor does God pass too lenient of a sentence for what they have done. His punishments or His rewards are exactly proportionate to the behavior that is being judged by Him. The point is that there is perfect equity in God's judgments. As the saints in heaven reflect on the truth of God's judgments and the righteousness of God's judgments, they cry out with one voice, "Praise Jehovah! Alleluia! The Judge of all the earth will do right!"

But having made a general statement about the fact that God's judgments are true and right in every situation, in the latter part of verse 2, the saints in heaven now speak to the specific judgment that God has exercised on the great whore who corrupted the earth with her fornication, and who martyred the believers for their faithfulness to Christ. They say, "*. . .he hath judged the great whore, which did corrupt the earth with her fornication, and hath avenged the blood of his servants at her hand.*" That judgment was also a true and righteous judgment, just as all His judgments are.

God has avenged the believers for the temptations the harlot Babylon placed before them, and for the persecutions the harlot Babylon carried out against them. The believers see the truth of that judgment, and they see the righteousness of that judgment, and as they contemplate the specific judgment that God has brought to bear upon the great whore, they cry out once again, "Praise Jehovah!" That is their conclusion. Notice verse 3: *"And again they said, Alleluia. And her smoke rose up for ever and ever."*

As they see the smoke of the ruin of Babylon under the wrath of God, they recognize that this city is the object of God's eternal wrath, and it will never rise again. It will lie in smoldering ruins forever and ever, and the smoke of its ruin will rise without end for all eternity. It will never be rebuilt. Anti-Christian society will never be resurrected and restored for all eternity. It says in Psalm 19:9 that *"the judgments of the LORD are true and righteous altogether."*

Notice verse 4. *"And the four and twenty elders and the four beasts fell down and worshipped God that sat on the throne, saying, Amen; Alleluia."* In verse 4 we see the blending of the voices and the worship of all the believers in heaven, represented by the twenty-four elders; together with the angels, represented by the four beasts who are seraphim. Both the saints and the angels blend their voices and worship together to give honor to God who sits on the throne, and with one voice they say, *"Amen; Alleluia"*—Praise Jehovah!

The last phrase of verse 4 says, *"Amen; Alleluia."* Amen is a word of affirmation, approval, and agreement. When somebody prays a prayer, at the end of that prayer we say, "Amen." We are saying, in effect, "I affirm that prayer, I approve of that prayer, and I am in agreement with that prayer. I endorse what was just said or what was just done."

Both saints and angels affirm, approve, and agree with God's judgment on Babylon. When they see what God has done, they say with reference to what God has done, "Amen!" Then they say, "Praise Jehovah for what He has done!" Psalm 106:48 says, *"Blessed be the LORD God of Israel from everlasting to everlasting: and let all the people say, Amen. Praise ye the LORD."* This last phrase is lifted right out of Psalm 106:48 and placed here at the end of verse 4.

This then is the rejoicing over the judgment of the harlot Babylon. This is the praise that is given to God for the truth and righteousness of the judgment He exercised upon her, and the vindication and deliverance He provided His servants in her destruction.

The Rejoicing over the Marriage of the Bride of Christ

The rejoicing over the marriage of the bride of Christ is in verses 5 to 10. In verse 5, a new voice now speaks directly from the throne. *"And a voice came out of the throne, saying, Praise our God, all ye his servants, and ye that fear him, both small and great."* This exhortation is addressed to all those who fear God and serve God. Both of these behaviors universally characterize the people of God. Everyone who is in heaven is someone who fears God. This means the people there have a deep reverence for God and seek to please God in all they do because His approval is their greatest delight and His disapproval is their greatest dread.

But those in heaven are not only those who fear God; they are also those who serve God. They recognize that because they have been bought with a price, they do not belong to themselves; and therefore, they serve God with their body and with their spirit which are God's. Their chief concern in life is this: "What is the will of God for my life in each situation I am facing?" Their chief ambition in life is to serve God faithfully in every one of those circumstances. This is what it means to be a servant of God. As this voice in heaven calls out in verse 5 for praise, it calls out for a certain class and category of people to be doing the praising, and it is those who fear God and those who serve God.

How can those who will be in heaven be identified on earth? They are those who fear God and serve God in this life. No one will wind up in heaven who does not fear God and serve God in this life. Everyone in heaven shares these characteristics, because everyone in heaven was characterized by those things while they lived on earth. It is these inhabitants of heaven, who feared and served God while they were here on earth, whom the voice from the throne addresses with this exhortation: "Praise our God!"

Will you wind up in heaven? Well, do you fear God and serve God now? If not, then do not expect to be among those who fear and serve God for eternity. All those with saving faith both fear and serve God in this life, and this is how their saving faith is known and shown to be genuine.

When the voice from the throne in heaven addresses those in heaven who fear God and serve Him, verses 6–7 describe their response:

"And I heard as it were the voice of a great multitude, and as the voice of many waters, and as the voice of mighty thunderings, saying, Alleluia: for the Lord God omnipotent reigneth. [7] *Let us be glad and rejoice, and give honour to him: for the marriage of the Lamb is come, and his wife hath made herself ready."*

John takes special notice of the volume of the praise that is given to God, and he says the volume of the praise given to God is overwhelming in its loudness. The praise the saints give to God is likened to the sound of a great multitude speaking in unison. It is likened to the sound of a mighty waterfall crashing down on the rocks below with a mighty roar. It is likened to the sound of rolling thunder from a lightning storm that shakes the creation.

The volume of the praise is overwhelmingly loud because the enthusiasm of the praise is surpassingly great. The more excited people are, the louder they become in singing the praises of God. The multitude of the people in heaven, which no man can number, are all praising God at the top of their lungs with the totality of their enthusiasm as loudly as they possibly can.

What is the content of their worship? Verse 6: *"Alleluia: for the Lord God omnipotent reigneth."* This title speaks volumes about who God is and why He is praised. This name declares His sovereignty, that He is the *Lord* over all things and over all beings. This name declares His authority, that He is *God*, the highest authority in the universe, from whom there is no appeal. This name declares His power, that He is *omnipotent*, and nothing and no one can prevail against Him or overthrow His will.

As a result of His sovereignty, authority, and power, He reigns. The Lord God Omnipotent *"reigneth."* These people are saying that God is in charge, and not Satan or Babylon. The reason why we do not need to fear either the present or the future is because *"the Lord God omnipotent reigneth."* He will defeat our enemies, He will work all things together for our good, and He will bring us safely to heaven.

Notice verses 7 to 9: *"Let us be glad and rejoice, and give honour to him: for the marriage of the Lamb is come, and his wife hath made herself ready.* [8] *And to her was granted that she should be arrayed in fine linen, clean and white: for the fine linen is the righteousness of saints.* [9] *And he saith unto me, Write, Blessed are they which are called unto the marriage supper of the Lamb. And he saith unto me, These are the true sayings of God."*

Verses 7 to 9 declare the great cause for gladness and rejoicing and giving honor to God, which is that the marriage of the Lamb has come. At the end of this age, Christ will consummate His union with His people, and they will live with Him forever and ever. This spiritual marriage that is being spoken of here has its physical parallel and illustration in biblical Jewish marriages.

Biblical marriage customs indicate that the father seeks out and selects a bride for his son, just like Abraham did with Isaac. He makes arrangements for a marriage contract, the parties agree to it, and a betrothal is made between the bride and the groom. A betrothal is like our engagement, but it is far more binding. The betrothal in biblical times was a binding engagement that legally made the bride and groom a husband and a wife. A betrothal could only be broken by a formal divorce.

Recall that when Joseph found out that Mary, his betrothed wife, was pregnant before they had come together, he purposed to divorce her quietly, and not make her a public example of having violated her marriage covenant. Because of the betrothal, Joseph and Mary were legally married, but they had not started living together. They had not yet begun to cohabitate.

There was always a time period that elapsed between the betrothal and the actual consummation of the marriage. This time period allowed the bride to prepare herself and her wedding garment for the actual wedding. It also allowed the groom time to accumulate and pay the dowry to the father of the bride, and prepare a place for him and his bride to live. After an interval of time had passed, the day of the wedding was set, and a huge wedding feast was given. At the wedding feast, the betrothed couple were brought together to live with each other from that point forward in the same house, until death did them part.

This beautifully illustrates the marriage between Christ and His people. God the Father sought out a bride for His Son Jesus Christ. By divine sovereign election, He selected a people to be in union with His Son forever. He then gave this people to His Son as a manifestation of the love He had for Him. In due time, He betrothed us to His Son by effectually calling us into union with Christ. We were betrothed to Christ at our conversion when we were saved. We entered into a binding commitment to be married to Christ at our salvation. We were given the promise of the Spirit—that is, the Spirit's indwelling presence—as the token and guarantee of the consummation of the marriage in due time.

Paul says in 2 Corinthians 11:2, regarding the believers at Corinth, *"I have espoused [betrothed] you to one husband, that I may present you as a chaste virgin to Christ."* The believers at Corinth were betrothed to Christ. They were still virgins because the marriage had not yet been consummated, though it was concluded legally and contractually at their conversion. During this interval between betrothal and consummation, Christ is doing His part. Christ paid the dowry by His death on the cross. He paid the price for His bride with His own precious blood.

Furthermore, He has told us in John 14:1–3 that He must go away for a while in order to prepare a dwelling place for us. But if He goes away, He will come again to receive us to Himself, that where He is, there we may be also, in the mansions He has prepared for us. This is the time period we are in now—the time between the betrothal, which occurred at our salvation, and the wedding feast, when Christ returns to receive us into His home He is now preparing, the home where we will live with Him forever.

What are we, the bride, doing in this interval? We are making ourselves ready. We are preparing ourselves for the day when our husband returns to receive us into His everlasting home. After the great wedding feast, we will live with Him forever in the new heavens and the new earth, and dwell in the mansions He has gone to prepare for us.

Verse 7 says, *"Let us be glad and rejoice, and give honour to him: for the marriage of the Lamb is come, and his wife hath made herself ready."* Verse 7 describes the end of this age, when the betrothal period is over and the wedding supper of the Lamb has come, where we who were married to Christ at our conversion will be brought together with Christ to live with Him forever. All that was promised in our betrothal at our conversion, will now be provided at the wedding feast when He returns.

We have made ourselves ready for our wedding day by remaining faithful to Jesus Christ in the face of Babylon's persecutions and seductions while waiting for Him to return and deliver us. We have made ourselves ready by maintaining our testimony that Christ is our Lord, even though it cost us dearly to do so.

But while we are waiting, there are tremendous pressures upon us to abandon Christ and go after another lover. Christ has betrothed us to Himself. He has gone away to prepare a place for us, and while He is gone, we are exposed to temptations to unfaithfulness. We experience the temptations of the world—the lust of the eyes, the lust of the flesh, and the pride of life—that keep assaulting us to draw us away from Christ and into infidelity.

This problem we face is spoken of in Hebrews 3:12–14: *"Take heed, brethren, lest there be in any of you an evil heart of unbelief, in departing from the living God.* [13] *But exhort one another daily, while it is called Today; lest any of you be hardened through the deceitfulness of sin.* [14] *For we are made partakers of Christ, if we hold the beginning of our confidence stedfast unto the end."*

That is how we are making ourselves ready for the return of our husband. We are holding our confidence in Him steadfast until the end. In other words, getting ourselves ready means never forsaking Christ, never betraying our loyalty to Him, and never following after the gods of this world.

What is the result of being faithful and loyal to Christ before a hostile world during this waiting period? Notice verse 8: *"And to her was granted that she should be arrayed in fine linen, clean and white: for the fine linen is the righteousness of saints."* The result of faithfully confessing Christ before a hostile world and remaining loyal to Him until He returns is that we are given a robe of righteousness as recognition and reward for the faithfulness to Christ we maintained in His absence.

Christ gives us a wedding garment that admits us to the marriage supper of the Lamb because we maintained our virginity for Him. We did not commit spiritual fornication with the harlot Babylon by going after other gods while we were waiting for Him to return. We refused Babylon's seductions to worship other gods, we remained true to Christ, and He rewards us for our righteous acts of perseverance and faithfulness to Him by giving us a lovely wedding garment that marks us out as being His true bride, and as being the ones He will live with forever. The robe is the reward for our faithfulness in His absence.

Verse 9: *"And he saith unto me, Write, Blessed are they which are called unto the marriage supper of the Lamb. And he saith unto me, These are the true sayings of God."* To be called to participate in the wedding feast of the Lamb is the most blessed privilege one could ever experience, and the wonder of it overwhelms the mind. We are so awestruck at the contemplation of it that we ask, "Could it possibly be true, that Christ will return and receive me into His house to live with Him forever, with all of the spiritual intimacy that this metaphor conveys?" The angel assures John, and the angel assures us, *"These are the true sayings of God."* This is really going to happen, and this is exactly how it is going to be. Do not doubt it.

Now notice verse 10: *"And I fell at his feet to worship him. And he said unto me, See thou do it not: I am thy fellowservant, and of thy brethren that have the testimony of Jesus: worship God: for the testimony of Jesus is the spirit of prophecy."*

John is so overwhelmed at the vision he has seen, and the indescribable privilege it promises, and the immeasurable blessing that it conveys, that he falls down to worship and thank the one who brought him such wonderful news. But the angel immediately corrects him and tells him it is not the messenger that is to be worshiped. He says, "I am only a fellow servant with you and the other believers who possess and maintain a faithful testimony of Jesus Christ. Do not forget who I am. I am just a fellow servant alongside you and your fellow believers. You need to worship God."

When a pastor brings you the good news of the gospel, it is such good news that some might be moved to give him inordinate esteem for having brought that news. But the esteem needs to be given to the One who produced the news, not to the one who merely conveys it. This is what the angel is saying: Worship God. He produced this. I just told you about it.

It is the God who has provided all of this who is to be worshiped, not the messenger who simply tells what God has done. All true prophecy testifies of Jesus, all true prophecy focuses on Jesus, all true prophecy points men to Jesus, and it is Jesus who is to be worshiped—not the prophet who speaks of Him. It is the testimony of Jesus that is the essence of prophecy, and any time a prophet starts talking about himself instead of Jesus, he ceases to be a prophet of God.

Let us then take up the example of this passage, and praise God for what He has done in the world in His mighty acts of justice, and for what He has done in the church in His mighty acts of salvation.

If you ever wondered why Babylon exists, if you ever wondered why Babylon is so strong, and if you have ever wondered why Babylon is allowed to be so wicked, wonder no more. Babylon exists to prove who will remain faithful to Christ and who will not during the time between their profession of faith and their coming into the personal presence of Christ. Babylon exists in order to prove who His true bride is.

Instead of seeing that which persecutes us and causes us pain and seduces us as being an unnecessary evil, we need to see it as an instrument that God has placed in our lives to refine our character, to prove our faith, and to demonstrate our love and loyalty to Him.

The story is told about the husband and wife that were driving their car down the road, and on the sidewalk walking toward them was a beautiful young woman with a lovely shape, attractive clothing, and a beautiful face. As they went by, they both looked at the woman. After they passed, the wife turned to her husband and said, "When you look at a woman like that, are you attracted to her, and do you have a desire for her?" He replied to his wife, "When I see someone like that, it just gives me the opportunity to choose you all over again."

This is why God puts temptations and trials in front of us, because it gives us an opportunity to choose Him all over again. After many disciples had abandoned Christ, Jesus asked the apostles in John 6:67–69: *"Will ye also go away? [68]Then Simon Peter answered him, Lord, to whom shall we go? thou hast the words of eternal life. [69]And we believe and are sure that thou art that Christ, the son of the living God."*

As Babylon comes to us with its seductions and its persecutions, and through them puts enormous pressure on us to turn away from Christ, to be disloyal to Him, and to have intercourse with the gods of this world, we have an opportunity to say, "No! I am engaged and committed to Another! He has gone to a far country for a while, but He is coming back. And when He returns, He will find me to have been faithful to Him, and not to have gone out after another god."

How many professing Christians do you know who have made a profession of faith, persevered in it for a time, but when the temptations or persecutions of the world came upon them, went back into the world and abandoned their commitment to Christ? They will not receive a wedding garment on that day.

God is not aiming to make us comfortable in life or make life easy on us. Instead, God is providing us with endless opportunities to choose Christ over and over again, when the world repeatedly calls upon us to choose another to worship and follow.

An engaged man or woman remains true to their betrothed, no

matter how many others try to engage in flirting and seduction, and this is what we must do with Christ. Never forsake Him for another. If you are faithful to Him, when the wedding day comes, you will be welcomed into the wedding feast as one who is worthy of the One who was betrothed to you so long ago, and you will be welcomed into His everlasting home to live with Him forever.

The book of Revelation is speaking this message to us: "Yes, I know all about the spiritual battles you are facing. I have described them in these chapters. Here is why they take place, and here is what you will have if you remain faithful in confessing Christ and living for Christ throughout your life. Do not commit fornication with Babylon. Do not go after the gods of this world. Stay true to Christ, and, when He returns, you will be glad you did, and He will receive you into His everlasting home."

May the vision of this cause us to reject the temptation of the world to go after the gods it offers us—gods which are so cheap and tawdry and useless, which shall wind up in the smoking heap of the ruin of Babylon, and which will never be heard from again. Why would we ever go after a god like that? It would be the essence of foolishness. Let us be loyal and faithful to Christ alone.

56

The Second Coming of Christ, Revelation 19:11–21

"[11] *And I saw heaven opened, and behold a white horse; and he that sat upon him was called Faithful and True, and in righteousness he doth judge and make war.* [12] *His eyes were as a flame of fire, and on his head were many crowns; and he had a name written, that no man knew, but he himself.* [13] *And he was clothed with a vesture dipped in blood: and his name is called The Word of God.* [14] *And the armies which were in heaven followed him upon white horses, clothed in fine linen, white and clean.* [15] *And out of his mouth goeth a sharp sword, that with it he should smite the nations: and he shall rule them with a rod of iron: and he treadeth the winepress of the fierceness and wrath of Almighty God.* [16] *And he hath on his vesture and on his thigh a name written,* KING OF KINGS, AND LORD OF LORDS. [17] *And I saw an angel standing in the sun; and he cried with a loud voice, saying to all the fowls that fly in the midst of heaven, Come and gather yourselves together unto the supper of the great God;* [18] *That ye may eat the flesh of kings, and the flesh of captains, and the flesh of mighty men, and the flesh of horses, and of them that sit on them, and the flesh of all men, both free and bond, both small and great.* [19] *And I saw the beast, and the kings of the earth, and their armies, gathered together to make war against him that sat on the horse, and against his army.* [20] *And the beast was taken, and with him the false prophet that wrought miracles before him, with which he deceived them that had received the mark of the beast, and them that worshipped his image. These both were cast alive into a lake of fire burning with brimstone.* [21] *And the remnant were slain with the sword of him that sat upon the horse, which sword proceeded out of his mouth: and all the fowls were filled with their flesh.*"

In Revelation 12 and following, we have been introduced to Satan and his helpers. Satan was portrayed as the dragon in chapter 12, and his helpers are the beast out of the sea, representing anti-Christian government; the beast out of the earth, subsequently identified as the false prophet, representing anti-Christian religion; Babylon the great harlot, representing anti-Christian society; and all those who have the mark of the beast, representing the anti-Christian populace. These all make war against Christ and His people.

But in Revelation 12 and following, we also see that Christ destroys every one of Satan's helpers, and finally, Christ destroys Satan himself. Even though this destruction of Satan and his helpers takes place at the end of this age when Christ returns, John describes this destruction over a series of several chapters.

The destruction of those who have the mark of the beast is described in chapter 14. The destruction of Babylon is described in chapters 14, 16, 17, and 18. The destruction of the beast and the false prophet is described in chapter 19. Finally, the destruction of Satan is described in chapter 20. The end of this age is the end of Satan and all of his helpers. All of them will be destroyed when Christ returns.

We have noted on several occasions the cyclic nature of the book of Revelation. We have seen it is made up of seven parallel sections, and each traverses the time period between the first and second coming of Christ. Each of these sections has a different theme, and each of them emphasizes a different aspect of the spiritual warfare that will take place throughout this age.

However, what each of these parallel sections has in common is that each of them concludes with a description of the second coming of Christ. We can see the destruction of those who have the mark of the beast in chapter 14, because that chapter describes the second coming of Christ. We can see the destruction of Babylon in chapter 16 because that chapter describes the second coming of Christ. We can see the destruction of the beast and the false prophet in chapter 19 because that chapter describes the second coming of Christ. We can see the destruction of Satan in chapter 20 because that chapter describes the second coming of Christ.

Each of these parallel sections takes us from the first to the second coming of Christ, and at the end of each of these sections, we see the destruction of Christ's enemies and the vindication of His people.

As we progressed through each of these parallel sections, we have seen that the descriptions of the second coming of Christ have become more complete, giving greater detail about both the nature and the effect of the second coming. In the early parallel sections, the second coming was described in very limited terms. But as we have proceeded through the book, the descriptions of the second coming of Christ have become larger, more detailed, and more specific.

As we come to the conclusion of this sixth parallel section in 19:11–21, we have the fullest and the most complete description of the second coming of Christ we have had up to this point. The person of Christ in this passage is described in vivid symbolism and in great detail. The immediate and decisive victory He achieves over the beast and the false prophet is extensively set forth in dramatic terms.

Here is the most expanded description of Christ's defeat and judgment of the ungodly forces at the end of the world that is given anywhere in the book of Revelation. For the saints, the sight of the second coming is one of tremendous awe and joy as they observe it unfolding. But for the helpers of Satan, the second coming is a time of terror and defeat and destruction as they experience the wrath of God poured out upon them.

In this passage, we consider the destruction of the last two of Satan's helpers—the beast and the false prophet. We saw the destruction of those with the mark of the beast in chapter 14. We saw the destruction of Babylon in chapter 18. And now, in chapter 19, we see the destruction of the beast and the false prophet.

The Description of Christ and His Armies

The description of Christ and His armies is in verses 11 to 16. Notice verse 11. *"And I saw heaven opened, and behold a white horse; and he that sat upon him was called Faithful and True, and in righteousness he doth judge and make war."*

This phrase, *"And I saw heaven opened,"* has occurred throughout the book of Revelation, and it indicates the beginning of another vision. This vision introduces a scene of judgment in which Christ returns to the earth to vindicate His people and destroy His enemies. John sees Christ returning as a conquering warrior who has come to bring the wrath of God to bear upon the wicked of the earth, and to destroy anti-Christian government and anti-Christian religion.

It is important to remind ourselves again that Revelation is a book of symbolic visual imagery, and that much of what is said here is not to be taken literally. For example, the visual image of Christ astride a white horse does not mean that Christ will literally ride an actual horse from heaven down to earth. Literal horses do not fly through the void of space, nor do they fly through the atmosphere of the earth. But the symbolic imagery set forth in this visual picture does convey a literal message, and the literal message is this: Christ will return as a conquering King who is going to make war on His enemies, crush their rebellion against Him, and remove them out of His kingdom. John understood this imagery of a conquering king from the custom of his own day. In John's day, kings did go to war on actual horses; and therefore, it was a fitting symbol for John to use to convey the idea that Christ is a conquering King who is coming to defeat the enemies of His kingdom.

It says of Christ that he bears the descriptive titles of being one who was both faithful and true. Notice verse 11: *"And I saw heaven opened, and behold a white horse; and he that sat upon him was called Faithful and True."* These titles tell us something about Christ. Christ is one who is *"Faithful"* to His promises and His people, and Christ is one who is *"True"* to His promises and His people. Christ will be true to His word and faithful to His promises to judge the wicked and vindicate His disciples. Nothing that Christ has promised will fail, no one who trusted in Christ will be betrayed or abandoned, and everyone who has persecuted the people of God will be judged and punished.

Furthermore, in verse 11 it says in the latter part that *"in righteousness he doth judge and make war."* This world has always been filled with corrupt judges, and with wars that are motivated by greed, the lust for power, and the pursuit of self-glorification. But Christ is not a judge like the judges of this earth, and Christ does not wage war with the motives of those who wage war on this earth. When Christ passes judgment, it is always righteous judgment. When Christ initiates war, it is always righteous war, carried out in a righteous manner, in order to achieve a righteous purpose.

This is a great encouragement to believers in this present time in which it appears that lies and injustice have triumphed, and wars fought for evil reasons are pervasive across the globe. Christians are openly persecuted by these corrupt judges and through these evil wars, no matter where they live. In the face of this, we may be tempted to question the promises of God, the justice of God, and the faithfulness of God to His people and His word. But we must understand that many of God's promises are fulfilled in the end and not in the present. Therefore, we must live by faith until He returns, and then we will see those promises fulfilled. Christ's righteous judgment and Christ's righteous war will be the end of every unrighteous judgment and every unrighteous war forever. The Old Testament is full of promises and prophecies in this regard.

In Psalm 9:8 it says, *"And he shall judge the world in righteousness, he shall minister judgment to the people in uprightness."* Psalm 72:2 says, *"He shall judge thy people with righteousness, and thy poor with judgment."* Psalm 96:12–13 says, *"Let the field be joyful, and all that is therein: then shall all the trees of the wood rejoice [13] Before the LORD: for he cometh, for he cometh to judge the earth: he shall judge the world with righteousness, and the people with his truth."* Psalm 98:9 says, *"for [the LORD] cometh to judge the earth: with righteousness shall he judge the world, and the people with equity."* Isaiah 11:4–5 says, *"But with righteousness shall he judge the poor, and reprove with equity for the meek of the earth: and he shall smite the earth with the rod of his mouth, and with the breath of his lips shall he slay the wicked. [5] And righteousness shall be the girdle of his loins, and faithfulness the girdle of his reins."*

Over and over, the Old Testament promises Christ is going to come back, right all wrongs, vindicate His people, bring judgment on the wicked, and cause righteousness to reign in judgment and truth.

These titles of the returning Christ, that He is Faithful and True—and these descriptions of His activity, that in righteousness He judges and makes war—are a tremendous comfort to us when we struggle with all of the unfaithfulness and lies, and all the corrupt judgments and evil assaults we experience in this world. All of that is coming to an end and all of it will be rectified, and we will be delivered by the one who is faithful and is true. In righteousness He will judge, and in righteousness He will bring an end to all unrighteous attacks upon us.

Notice verse 12. *"His eyes were as a flame of fire, and on his head were many crowns; and he had a name written, that no man knew, but he himself."* Christ's eyes are as a flame of fire. We saw the same symbolism in 1:14 in John's initial vision of Jesus Christ. This metaphor of His eyes being as a flame of fire conveys the truth that nothing can be hidden or shielded from the eyes of Christ. His eyes burn down through every layer of deceit, in order to lay bare and expose the truth. His eyes see every action and thought and motive of men.

His eyes being like a flame of fire not only symbolizes His omniscient penetrating perception; this image also expresses His anger and indignation at the sin which His divine insight observes. These eyes see everything, they completely understand all they see, and they are angry at all the iniquities they observe. His eyes burn with indignation as He beholds the wickedness of Satan and evil men. Sometimes people say, "If looks could kill, I would be dead." When Jesus looks at His enemies with those eyes of fire, that look does kill.

Verse 12 goes on to say that *"on his head were many crowns."* In contrast to the false claim of sovereign rule that the dragon and the beast assert is the true sovereign authority that Christ possesses. Recall that both the dragon and the beast had a few crowns on their heads. But Christ's many crowns indicate that He exercises rule over all things, over all realms, and over all people. Whatever may exist, and no matter how many categories of things there are, Christ is ruler over each and every one of them. There is nothing over which Christ is not the crowned King. Whatever it may be, He wears the crown of authority over it. Nothing is exempt from His rule.

Jesus declared in Matthew 28:18 that all authority has been given Him in heaven and in earth, and these countless crowns symbolize His comprehensive and universal authority. No one can rebel against His authority and attempt to be an authority himself and ever succeed. We are told in 1 Corinthians 15:24–25 that Christ will put down all rule and all authority and all power, *"for he must reign, till he hath put all enemies under his feet."* These many crowns symbolize the comprehensiveness, the totality, and the infinitude of His rule over all things and over all people.

Verse 12 then goes on to say of Christ that *"He had a name written that no man knew but He Himself."* We know many names of Christ given in the Scriptures, each of which tells us something about the character, the nature, and the identity of Christ. But Christ also has a name which we know nothing about. The reason is there are aspects of His divine nature we can never comprehend. No man can understand Christ exhaustively. There are things about Christ that will always be a mystery to us and that we will never know.

Only the Son of God can understand the mystery of His own being. It would take one equal to Christ to fully comprehend Christ, and this is why it says in Matthew 11:27, *"and no man knoweth the Son, but the Father."* Only the Father fully knows the Son. There are aspects of the Son which are known only to Him and will never be known to us, because the finite creature can never fully comprehend his infinite Creator. Since Jesus is the express image of God, as Hebrews 1:3 says, then we would expect Him in His divine nature to be as inscrutable and as incomprehensible as God Himself is.

Therefore, He has a name that no man knows but He Himself. This tells us we can adore and worship God, even though we can never fully know or comprehend God.

Notice verse 13. *"And he was clothed with a vesture dipped in blood: and his name is called The Word of God."* First of all, verse 13 says that He is clothed in a vesture dipped in blood. This symbolic imagery is taken from the battlefield in which slaughter by the sword resulted in the blood of one's enemies splattering upon and ultimately soaking one's own garment. Here, the picture conveys the message that Christ's enemies will go down to defeat and death before Him, He will slay them all with the sword of His judgment, and none will escape His wrath. Therefore, His garments will be covered with the blood of those He has destroyed. Christ is symbolically pictured as the great warrior who seeks vengeance for His people, who comes to deliver them from their oppressors, and who brings great slaughter against the haters of Christ and the persecutors of His people.

The imagery in verse 13 is taken out of Isaiah. In Isaiah 63:1–2 there is a question-and-answer session going on. The question is asked, and then Christ gives the answer. Another question is asked, and Christ gives the answer again.

Notice Isaiah 63:1: *"Who is this that cometh from Edom, with dyed garments from Bozrah? this that is glorious in his apparel, travelling in the greatness of his strength?"* There is the first question; and here is Christ's answer: *"I that speak in righteousness, mighty to save."* That is who is coming.

The second question is in verse 2: *"Wherefore art thou red in thine apparel, and thy garments like him that treadeth in the winefat [the winepress]?"* Christ gives the answer in verse 3: *"I have trodden the winepress alone; and of the people there was none with me: for I will tread them in mine anger, and trample them in my fury; and their blood shall be sprinkled upon my garments, and I will stain all my raiment.* [4] *For the day of vengeance is in mine heart, and the year of my redeemed is come.*[5] *And I looked, and there was none to help; and I wondered that there was none to uphold: therefore mine own arm brought salvation unto me; and my fury, it upheld me.* [6] *And I will tread down the people in mine anger, and make them drunk in my fury, and I will bring down their strength to the earth."* This imagery of Isaiah 63:1–6 is placed into Revelation 19:13.

Revelation 19:13 not only says that He was clothed with a vesture dipped in blood; it also says that *"his name is called The Word of God."* Verse 13 identifies beyond any doubt who the one spoken of in this passage is when it says, *"his name is called The Word of God."*

John is writing Revelation, and John also wrote the Gospel of John. John said in John 1:1–3, *"In the beginning was the Word, and the Word was with God, and the Word was God.* [2] *The same was in the beginning with God.* [3] *All things were made by Him, and without him was not anything made that was made."* John goes on to say in verse 14, *"And the Word was made flesh, and dwelt among us, (and we beheld his glory, the glory as of the only begotten of the Father,) full of grace and truth."*

There is no question that this title, *"The Word of God,"* is a reference to Jesus Christ. Christ is the full expression of all that God has to say to mankind. Jesus is called The Word of God because Jesus is the sum and substance of God's communication to us. All that God has to say to us He has said through His Son and by His Son. In both His actions and His teachings, Christ has communicated the mind of God to man.

Many people have ignored the Word of God, and now the Word of God is going to bring judgment on them for doing so. Jesus made a very interesting statement in John 12:48. *"He that rejecteth me, and receiveth not my words, hath one that judgeth him: the word that I have spoken, the same shall judge him in the last day."*

When Jesus says, *"He that rejects me and receives not my words,"* He is saying that to reject Christ and to reject His word are one and the same thing. Jesus speaks the word of God, and Jesus is the Word of God, and both shall bring judgment upon those who have rebelled against them. The Word of God is coming. The very Word that the people of this earth have rejected is now going to come and bring judgment against them.

In verse 14, the people with Christ at His second coming are described. *"And the armies which were in heaven followed him upon white horses, clothed in fine linen, white and clean."* Here we are introduced to the armies from heaven that follow Christ as He triumphantly returns to earth. These armies are the whole company of Christ's redeemed people. At this point in time, all of the saved are with Christ. All of the dead whose souls were in heaven, and all of the living who were saved on the earth have now been either resurrected or transformed, they have all been taken up from earth to the side of Christ in the rapture, and they are now coming back with Christ in the heavens. We saw this event previously described in Revelation 11:11–12.

These people are spoken of in Revelation 14:4. *"These are they which were not defiled with women; for they are virgins. These are they which follow the Lamb whithersoever he goeth. These were redeemed from among men, being the firstfruits unto God and to the Lamb."* It is the nature of the people of God that they follow Christ wherever He goes. They will follow Him when He returns to the earth at His second coming.

Speaking of Antichrist and his coalition, it says in Revelation 17:14, *"These shall make war with the Lamb, and the Lamb shall overcome them: for he is Lord of lords, and King of kings: and they that are with him are called, and chosen, and faithful."* Revelation 17:14 describes in one verse, what is described in 19:11–21.

What Revelation 17:14 tells us is that when Christ comes to destroy the beast and the false prophet, those who are going to be with Him are the called, the chosen, and the faithful—that is, those who are redeemed from among men and who follow the Lamb wherever He goes. The bride of Christ in Revelation 19:8 was arrayed in fine linen, clean and white. In verse 14, the armies with Christ are clothed in fine linen, white and clean. Clearly, these armies that follow Christ are all of His saved people. The resurrection has occurred, the rapture has occurred, the marriage supper of the Lamb has occured, they are now all with Him, and they are all accompanying Him to the earth.

These saints do not fight alongside Christ as His helpers. Christ needs no helpers. He unilaterally achieves the defeat of our enemies by Himself. We saw in Isaiah 63 that He treads that winepress alone. It is Christ who has the blood on His garments. The saints have none. Their garments are white and clean. Furthermore, it is Christ who has the weapon of the sword. The saints have no weapon.

The saints are those whom Christ is defending and vindicating. The saints are there to bear witness to the deliverance Christ achieves on their behalf and to bear witness against their persecutors that Christ is bringing destruction upon. The saints follow Christ, and the saints observe Christ as Christ fights their battles for them by Himself.

Verse 15 states: *"And out of his mouth goeth a sharp sword, that with it he should smite the nations: and he shall rule them with a rod of iron: and he treadeth the winepress of the fierceness and wrath of Almighty God."* This verse contains three symbolic images: the sword out of the mouth, the rod of iron, and the winepress.

When it says, *"And out of his mouth goeth a sharp sword,"* this is figurative language, like virtually all the descriptions of physical objects in this passage are. The sword represents the word of God going forth out of His mouth in power and judgment. Jesus speaks, and His words smite the wicked with a power that destroys them.

The word of God that spoke the world into existence and had the power to create the universe is the same powerful word that is now used for the destruction of the wicked. Jesus has but to speak the word, and all the nations are smitten. It says in Isaiah 11:4, *"He shall smite the earth with the rod of his mouth, and with the breath of his lips shall he slay the wicked."*

If all God has to do is say, "Let there be light, let there be land, let there be stars and sun and moon," and they come into existence, do you suppose He can say, "Let them be destroyed," and they will be destroyed? The power of His word to create is the same power with which *"He shall smite the earth with the rod of his mouth, and with the breath of his lips shall he slay the wicked."*

Verse 15 goes on to say that *"He shall rule them"*—that is, the nations—*"with a rod of iron."* Psalm 2:9 says of Christ, regarding the nations, *"Thou shalt break them with a rod of iron; thou shalt dash them in pieces like a potter's vessel."* The imagery has now changed from smiting the nations with the sword of His mouth to striking a pottery vessel with a rod of iron. If you strike a pottery vessel with a steel rod, the pottery vessel shatters into a thousand pieces and is completely destroyed.

A third image is used in verse 15. It is that *"he treadeth the winepress of the fierceness and wrath of Almighty God."* The crushing of grapes in the winepress causes the juice to flow out of them. This is symbolic of Christ crushing the wicked under His wrath so their blood runs in the streets. This same language is used in Isaiah 63:1–6 which we read previously.

The language used in verse 15 tells us, in graphic symbols, the awfulness of the wrath of the returning Christ. There is a smiting with the sword of His mouth, there is a breaking with the rod of His anger, and there is a crushing in the winepress of His wrath. This is a terrible judgment that is coming on the wicked nations of the earth, and they will not escape. Verse 15 closes with the statement about *"the fierceness and wrath of Almighty God."*

Take note that what is described in this passage is the wrath of *"Almighty"* God; no one can resist His might or His power. All the wicked will be smitten, all the wicked will be broken, and all the wicked will be crushed beneath the wrath of Almighty God. Notice Jesus here is described as *"Almighty God,"* because He is the one doing the smiting, He is the one doing the breaking, and He is the one doing the crushing. Therefore, He is Almighty God.

Verse 16: *"And he hath on his vesture and on his thigh a name written, KING OF KINGS, AND LORD OF LORDS."* Verse 16 tells us a second name of Christ which we can know. Not only do we know Christ by the name *"The Word of God,"* as spoken in verse 13, but we also know Him by the name *"KING OF KINGS, AND LORD OF LORDS."*

The Antichrist saw himself as the ultimate and final lord and king of the earth, the one who ruled all other kings. He thought he was the king of all kings and the lord of all lords. As 2 Thessalonians 2:4 tells us, Antichrist declared himself to be God, and Antichrist demanded worship as God. In a word, 2 Thessalonians 2:4 tells us that Antichrist believed he was Lord of lords, and King of kings, he was God on earth, and men had to worship him as God. The whole ministry and activity of the false prophet was to persuade people to worship Antichrist as God on earth.

But as Christ is in name, so He is in reality. Christ is Lord of Antichrist, and Christ is King of Antichrist, and Christ is Lord and King of all those who follow Antichrist and help Antichrist, even though they had refused to acknowledge Christ as Lord.

This name *"KING OF KINGS, AND LORD OF LORDS"* that Christ possesses is written on the part of His garment that lies upon His thigh, plain for all to see, clear in the claim it conveys, and truthful in the declaration it makes. Jesus is Lord of lords, and King of kings, and it is the folly of the kings of the earth when they do not recognize that fact, and it is the wisdom of the kings of the earth when they do. When they do not recognize Jesus as King of kings and Lord of lords, and therefore as their King and their Lord, all that is left to them is the smiting, breaking, and crushing wrath of Almighty God.

The Destruction of the Beast and the False Prophet

The destruction of the beast and the false prophet is in verses 17 to 21. Notice, first of all, that when Christ appears, the destruction of the beast and the false prophet is imminent. Verses 17 to 18: "*And I saw an angel standing in the sun; and he cried with a loud voice, saying to all the fowls that fly in the midst of heaven, Come and gather yourselves together unto the supper of the great God;* [18] *That ye may eat the flesh of kings, and the flesh of captains, and the flesh of mighty men, and the flesh of horses, and of them that sit on them, and the flesh of all men, both free and bond, both small and great.*"

Immediately upon the appearance of Christ in the heavens, an angel announces the imminent destruction of the beast and the false prophet and all those who follow him, just like an angel announced the destruction of Babylon and all that inhabited it back in 18:1–2, which said: "*And after these things I saw another angel come down from heaven, having great power; and the earth was lightened with his glory.* [2] *And he cried mightily with a strong voice, saying, Babylon the great is fallen, is fallen, and is become the habitation of devils, and the hold of every foul spirit, and a cage of every unclean and hateful bird.*"

Previously, an angel appeared and announced the destruction of Babylon. Now, an angel appears and announces the destruction of the beast and the false prophet. The wicked nations, the Antichrist, and false religion have all had their little time of triumph and success, described in Revelation 11:9–11 as being three and a half days, in Revelation 17:12 as being an hour, and in Revelation 20:3 as being a little season.

These wicked nations, the Antichrist, and this false religion are going to have a time of triumph and success..But it is going to quickly come to an end. It is as when the Pharisees and the Sadducees triumphed over Christ and crucified Him. For three days they were winning. They were in the place of triumph. But then Christ came back to life and their triumph ended. In the same way, the Antichrist and the false prophet are going to have their little time of success and triumph. But Christ is going to come back, and their triumph will end.

It says in Job 20:5 that *"the triumphing of the wicked is short, and the joy of the hypocrite [is] but for a moment."* They see, too late, that their little time of triumph will translate into an eternity of suffering under the wrath of God in the lake of fire.

This glorious angel summons the scavenger birds of the earth, the flesh-eating vultures, to gather together to consume the slaughtered carcasses of those Christ has killed with the power of His word, the rod of His wrath, and the crushing force of His power. Verse 18 makes it clear that this judgment is universal, covering every category of person, and that it is worldwide, covering every location. People will not escape it, no matter their status in the kingdom of Antichrist. If they are great or small, if they are rich or poor, if they are here or there, it does not matter. They are all going to fall under the wrath of the returning Christ.

This supper of the vultures on the dead bodies of those whom Christ slays stands in sharp contrast to the supper of the Lamb in 19:7–9. It shows the exalted outcome of those who follow Christ. They are invited to the marriage supper of the Lamb. It also shows the shameful outcome of those who rebel against Him. They are the object of the supper of the vultures. The wicked become carrion for the vultures, while the righteous become the bride of Christ. A more dramatic contrast could not be made.

All of this is foreshadowed in the Old Testament in Ezekiel 39:7, 17–22. In verse 7 God says, *"So will I make my holy name known in the midst of my people Israel; and I will not let them pollute my holy name any more: and the heathen shall know that I am the* Lord, *the Holy One in Israel."* God has a message both to His people and to the heathen, and it is this: "I will make My holy name known through My judgment."

Now notice verses 17–22. *"And, thou son of man, thus saith the Lord* God; *Speak unto every feathered fowl, and to every beast of the field, Assemble yourselves, and come; gather yourselves on every side to my sacrifice that I do sacrifice for you, even a great sacrifice upon the mountains of Israel, that ye may eat flesh, and drink blood.* 18 *Ye shall eat the flesh of the mighty, and drink the blood of the princes of the earth, of rams, of lambs, and of goats, of bullocks, all of them fatlings of Bashan.* [19] *And ye shall eat fat till ye be full, and drink blood till ye be drunken, of my sacrifice which I have sacrificed for you.* [20] *Thus ye shall be filled at my table with horses and chariots, with mighty men, and with all men of war, saith the Lord GOD.* [21] *And I will set my glory among the heathen, and all the heathen shall see my judgment that I have executed, and my hand that I have laid upon them.* [22] *So the house of Israel shall know that I am the LORD their God from that day and forward."* This same imagery of the vultures feeding on the fallen is brought over into Revelation 19:17–18.

But not only do we see that when Christ appears, the destruction of the beast and the false prophet is imminent as the angel announces in verses 17 and 18; secondly, we also see that when Christ appears, the destruction of the beast and the false prophet is final. Notice verses 19–21.

Verse 19 says, *"And I saw the beast, and the kings of the earth, and their armies, gathered together to make war against him that sat on the horse, and against his army."* In verse 19 is the Battle of Armageddon that was previously spoken of in 16:16. There we saw that Antichrist and his transnational coalition of all the kings of the earth gather together to launch their final assault against the few remaining saints on the earth, but Christ returns to rescue them and to utterly crush Antichrist and his kingdom.

The Battle of Armageddon is the battle that takes place at the very end, when Antichrist has virtually wiped all Christians off the face of the earth. There is a small group left and he moves to wipe them out; Christ comes, they have a confrontation, and in the outcome, Antichrist and the false prophet and all who serve him are utterly annihilated and Christ's people are delivered.

In Revelation 19:19, Antichrist and his kingdom unite to make a final desperate stand against Christ as He returns. This is spoken of in Psalm 2:1–3 when it says: *"Why do the heathen rage, and the people imagine a vain thing?* [2]*The kings of the earth gather themselves together, against the LORD, and against his anointed, saying,* [3]*Let us break their bands asunder, and cast their cords from us."*

But, as Psalm 2 continues, He that sits in the heavens shall laugh: The Lord will have them in derision. He will speak to them in His wrath and vex them in His sore displeasure. He will smite them with a rod of iron.

Verse 20 says, *"And the beast was taken, and with him the false prophet that wrought miracles before him, with which he deceived them that had received the mark of the beast, and them that worshipped his image. These both were cast alive into a lake of fire burning with brimstone."* Verse 20 makes it clear this battle in verse 19 is immediately over before it hardly even begins. No description is given of the conflict because the mightiest army on earth is powerless in the face of Omnipotence.

In 2 Thessalonians 2:8, it says regarding this wicked one, that Christ will *"consume [him] with the spirit of his mouth, and shall destroy [him] with the brightness of His coming."* In a moment, it is all over. Like a spider thrown into the flame, they instantly wither before the power of the word of Christ and the brightness of the glory of Christ. Before they can lift a finger, they are destroyed. This is not like our wars, where one side wins a skirmish and then the other side wins a skirmish, and they go back and forth and eventually, after a couple of years, one side wins the war. This battle is not like that at all. This battle is instantly over.

Anti-Christian government represented by the beast and all who were loyal to the beast and participants with the beast are cast into the lake of fire. Anti-Christian religion represented by the false prophet and all who practiced it and promoted it are cast into the lake of fire. Anti-Christian government will cease to exist on the face of the earth; false religion will cease to exist on the face of the earth; and all who participated in them, promoted them, and were loyal to them, will all be cast into the lake of fire.

Verse 21 says, *"And the remnant were slain with the sword of him that sat upon the horse, which sword proceeded out of his mouth: and all the fowls were filled with their flesh."* Here is the remnant of the army of Antichrist, and they do not escape the wrath of God either. Everyone is mopped up, everyone is gathered together; they are all killed, and the destruction of the kingdom of Satan wrought by Christ is total, final, and complete. The birds of the air eat the bodies, their souls are cast into the lake of fire, and this world has come to its final end.

The lesson for us is this: We need to pay very careful attention to the names of Christ that are revealed to us.

1. We need to listen to Jesus, because He is the Word of God, as verse 13 says. God has not been silent. God has spoken. God has

spoken to us through His Son. Only a fool does not listen to the Word of God, because, if he does not, that Word will judge him one day.

2. We need to submit to Jesus, because He is the King of kings, and Lord of lords, as verse 16 says. These titles convey the truth that Jesus is the King, and therefore we need to listen to His words and submit to His rule. If we do, we will be in the armies that are coming back with Him, instead of the armies that are being destroyed by Him.

Who are these people in verse 14, the armies which were in heaven that follow Jesus upon white horses, clothed in fine linen, white and clean? They were those who recognized Jesus as the Word of God, and therefore they heard and heeded His message. They recognized that Jesus was King of kings, and therefore they submitted to His laws and followed His commandments.

The difference between being behind Christ and being defended by Him, and being in front of Christ and being destroyed by Him, is this: Did you own and acknowledge Jesus as your final source of instruction regarding all things, and as your ultimate authority in life? If you did, then He will be the Word you listen to and the King you submit to, and the blessing is that He will also be the Mighty Warrior who defends you and delivers you.

As we meditate on His names, let us join His army, and not the army of Antichrist and the false prophet. They live in defiance and rebellion against Christ, and because of it have their little time of joy and happiness, but as a result of it have an eternity of damnation in the lake of fire. May we choose wisely and recognize that while there are some things about Christ we cannot understand, what we can understand is that He has conveyed the words of God to us, and that He is the final authority over us. In light of that truth, let us believe Him, hear Him, and follow Him.

57

Satan Bound, Revelation 20:1–3

"1 *And I saw an angel come down from heaven, having the*
key of the bottomless pit and a great chain in his hand. 2 *And*
he laid hold on the dragon, that old serpent, which is the Dev-
il, and Satan, and bound him a thousand years, 3 *And cast*
him into the bottomless pit, and shut him up, and set a seal
upon him, that he should deceive the nations no more, till
the thousand years should be fulfilled: and after that he must
be loosed a little season. 4 *And I saw thrones, and they sat*
upon them, and judgment was given unto them: and I saw the
souls of them that were beheaded for the witness of Jesus,
and for the word of God, and which had not worshipped the
beast, neither his image, neither had received his mark upon
their foreheads, or in their hands; and they lived and reigned
with Christ a thousand years. 5 *But the rest of the dead lived*
not again until the thousand years were finished. This is the
first resurrection. 6 *Blessed and holy is he that hath part in the*
first resurrection: on such the second death hath no power,
but they shall be priests of God and of Christ, and shall reign
with him a thousand years. 7 *And when the thousand years are*
expired, Satan shall be loosed out of his prison, 8 *And shall go*
out to deceive the nations which are in the four quarters of the
earth, Gog and Magog, to gather them together to battle: the
number of whom is as the sand of the sea. 9 *And they went up*
on the breadth of the earth, and compassed the camp of the
saints about, and the beloved city: and fire came down from
God out of heaven, and devoured them. 10 *And the devil that*
deceived them was cast into the lake of fire and brimstone,
where the beast and the false prophet are, and shall be tor-
mented day and night for ever and ever."

In Revelation 20 we come to the seventh and final parallel section in the book of Revelation. Each of these seven parallel sections traverse the time period between the first and second coming of Christ. Each of them has a different theme, and each of them emphasizes a different aspect of the spiritual warfare that will take place throughout this age. Let us briefly review each of these parallel sections.

The first parallel section in chapters 1 to 3 described what spiritual warfare in the local church would look like between the first and second coming of Christ. There we looked at the seven churches.

The second parallel section in chapters 4 to 7 described God on His throne in heaven and the role He plays in the spiritual warfare we experience and the persecutions we endure between the first and second coming of Christ. There we looked at the seven seals.

The third parallel section in chapters 8 through 11 described the temporal physical and spiritual judgments God will bring on the wicked to punish them for their evil and to call them to repentance between the first and second coming of Christ. There we looked at the seven trumpets.

The fourth parallel section in chapters 12 to 14 described Satan and his helpers who work together to oppose and persecute Christ and His people between the first and second coming of Christ. There we were introduced to the dragon, the beast, the false prophet, Babylon, and those who have the mark of the beast.

The fifth parallel section in chapters 15 to 16 described God's anger and wrath poured out against the willfully defiant between the first and second coming of Christ. There we looked at the seven vials.

The sixth parallel section in chapters 17 to 19 described the character and the defeat of Babylon, the beast, and the false prophet between the first and second coming of Christ. This brings us to the seventh parallel section.

This seventh parallel section in chapters 20 to 22 describes the safety and protection the church enjoys between the first and second coming of Christ. The church enjoys this safety and protection because Satan is bound; and ultimately, after Satan is loosed for a little season, Satan will be destroyed at the second coming of Christ. This section closes with the description of the final judgment at the end of chapter 20, and the new heavens and the new earth in which the saints dwell forever in chapters 21 and 22.

In chapter 19, we came to the end of the sixth parallel section where we saw the second coming of Christ. What would we then expect as we move into the beginning of this seventh parallel section? We would expect to be taken right back to the first coming of Christ, and that is exactly what we find. Revelation 20:1–3 tells us about the binding of Satan that took place at the first coming of Christ. Satan remains bound for this entire age in which the New Covenant operates and the church evangelizes the whole world.

Right before the end of this age, Satan is loosed for a little season of time. He produces the great apostasy of the professing church, he raises up the Antichrist, and he inspires the formation of the world-wide transnational coalition of nations headed by the Antichrist which will persecute the church almost to the point of extinction. It is when the final effort is made to destroy the last of the Christians that Christ returns, saves His people from destruction, and casts Satan and all his helpers into the lake of fire. In Revelation 20, we traverse the time between the first and second coming of Christ.

Once again, it is important for us to understand that Revelation is not written in a chronologically linear fashion. It is written in a cyclic fashion. Therefore, the thousand-year period mentioned in chapter 20 does not occur chronologically after the second coming of Christ described in chapter 19, as the Pre-millennialists say it does.

The events in chapter 20 no more chronologically follow the events in chapter 19 than the events in chapter 12 chronologically follow the events in chapter 11. In 11:15–19, we had the description of the second coming of Christ, and then in 12:1–5, the theme went right back to the birth of Christ. Just as the events of chapter 12 do not chronologically follow the events of chapter 11, the events in chapter 20 do not chronologically follow the events of chapter 19.

The question then arises: How do we know when one cyclic section ends and another begins? It is very clear: each parallel section ends with the second coming of Christ and statements about the final judgment and the eternal state, and then the beginning of the next section starts with events back on earth that commence with the first coming of Christ and which are characteristic of the entire age. This is exactly what we see in chapter 19 and chapter 20.

Chapter 19 closes with a clear description of the second coming of Christ and the eternal state of the beast and false prophet in the lake of fire. Chapter 20 opens with a description of Satan being bound by Christ through His work on the cross at His first coming. Therefore, whatever this thousand-year period is, it does not occur after the second coming of Christ; instead, it occurs after the first coming of Christ.

Furthermore, it should be clear to anyone that the thousand years of Revelation 20:2–7 take place before and precede the second coming of Christ which is spoken of in Revelation 20:9, when Christ comes in flaming fire, taking vengeance on them that know not God and on them that obey not the gospel of our Lord Jesus Christ, as 2 Thessalonians 1:7–10 states. If the second coming is in verse 9, and it is, then clearly this millennium, this thousand-year period, takes place before that event. This millennium takes place between the first and the second coming of Christ.

We said at the very beginning that the central theme of this book was the victory of Christ and His church over Satan and his helpers. This was summarized in the key verse of the book, Revelation 17:14, when it says: *"These"* (speaking of Satan and his helpers) *"shall make war with the Lamb, and the Lamb shall overcome them: for he is Lord of lords, and King of kings: and they that are with him are called, and chosen, and faithful."*

This whole book is a description of spiritual warfare; of the battle between Christ and His people, and Satan and his helpers. The book is a chronicle of how Christ defeats Satan and all of his helpers, how Christ and His church are victorious, and how Satan and his helpers are all cast into the lake of fire. We see that this warfare takes place between the first and second coming of Jesus.

In chapter 12, we were introduced to Satan, who was called the dragon, and we were introduced to the dragon's four helpers—the beast, the false prophet, Babylon, and those who have the mark of the beast. As we have proceeded through chapters 12 to 19, we have seen the systematic destruction of each of these four helpers of Satan.

We saw the destruction of those who have the mark of the beast in chapter 14. We saw the destruction of Babylon in chapter 18. We saw the destruction of the beast and the false prophet in chapter 19. In chapter 20, we are going to see the destruction of Satan himself, that dragon, that old serpent, who is the devil.

Chapter 20 completes the victory of Christ over Satan and his helpers. When Satan is cast into the lake of fire, not a single enemy is left. Christ has totally vanquished Satan and his kingdom and his works and his helpers. It says in 1 John 3:8, *"For this purpose the Son of God was manifested, that he might destroy the works of the devil."* In the book of Revelation, this is exactly what we see Jesus doing: destroying the works of the devil.

This book promises and predicts that at the end of this age, Satan and the totality of his kingdom will be defeated and destroyed by Christ, cast into the lake of fire, and remain there for eternity, never to harm us again. And while this book also makes it clear that we will have much tribulation between now and then and that the spiritual warfare will be fierce, we need to persevere in our faith and in our faithfulness to Christ. The outcome for all those who do persevere is eternal triumph and blessedness in the kingdom of God forever. This book tells us that we are more than conquerors through Christ.

It is important for us to understand the structure of Revelation 20:1–10. First of all, in verses 1 to 3, we have a description of the millennial period on earth set forth, in which the topic of Satan's relationship to the nations of the earth during the thousand-year period is described. What is obvious in this passage is that Satan is bound.

Secondly, in verses 4 to 6, we have a description of the millennial period in heaven, in which the topic is the disembodied souls who are on thrones with Christ. Verses 1 to 3 and verses 4 to 6 run parallel with each other, the one referencing what is happening on earth and the other referencing what is happening in heaven, both of which are chronologically happening at the same time.

Thirdly, in verses 7 to 10, we have a description of the conclusion of the millennial period on earth at the end of this age, in which the topic is Satan's relationship to the nations of the earth during the little season that he is loosed to deceive the nations.

Therefore, you could read verses 1 to 3, skip verses 4 to 6, and pick up the reading at verses 7 to 10, and have a continuity of events as seen on earth. Let us do that. Verses 1 to 3, 7–10: *"And I saw an angel come down from heaven, having the key of the bottomless pit and a great chain in his hand.* [2] *And he laid hold on the dragon, that old serpent, which is the Devil, and Satan, and bound him a thousand years,* [3] *And cast him into the bottomless pit, and shut him up, and set a seal upon him, that he should deceive the nations no more, till the thousand years should be fulfilled: and after that he must be loosed a little season.* [7] *And when the thousand years are expired, Satan shall be loosed out of his prison,* [8] *And shall go out to deceive the nations which are in the four quarters of the earth, Gog and Magog, to gather them to-*

gether to battle: the number of whom is as the sand of the sea. [9] *And they went up on the breadth of the earth, and compassed the camp of the saints about, and the beloved city: and fire came down from God out of heaven, and devoured them.* [10] *And the devil that deceived them was cast into the lake of fire and brimstone, where the beast and the false prophet are, and shall be tormented day and night for ever and ever."*

Verses 1 to 3 says at the beginning of this New Covenant age, Satan is going to be bound. We will then have this thousand-year period of protection for the church during which Satan remains bound, after which Satan is going to be loosed, gather the nations together to attack the church, and when he has them almost destroyed, Jesus is going to come back. He is going to deliver the church by means of the rapture, destroy Satan and his people, execute the final judgment, send Satan and his people into the lake of fire, and send the believers into the new heaven and new earth.

During that thousand-year period occurring on earth, verses 4 to 6 describe what is going on in heaven. Notice he says in verse 4, *"And I saw thrones."* In the book of Revelation, the thrones of saints are never on the earth; they are always in heaven. The twenty-four elders sit on thrones in heaven. John says, *"And I saw thrones, and they sat upon them, and judgment was given unto them: and I saw the souls of them that were beheaded for the witness of Jesus."* Notice there are no bodies there; there are just souls—souls who are there because they had their heads cut off while they were alive on earth. Therefore, these are disembodied spirits.

These are the same group of spirits that are in the fifth seal in 6:9–11, who are under the altar of God and asking, "Lord, how long before You provide justice for us?" These are souls in heaven who were killed on earth during this thousand-year period. What are they doing in heaven? They are sitting on thrones and they are reigning. They were beheaded for the witness of Jesus and for the word of God. They *"had not worshipped the beast, neither his image, neither had received his mark upon their foreheads, or in their hands; and they lived and reigned with Christ a thousand years."* While this thousand-year period is happening on earth, during which Satan is bound, they are in heaven reigning with Christ during that same time period.

We can read verses 1 to 3 and skip to verses 7 to 10 and have a continuity of events as seen on earth. What happens in verses 4 to 6 occurs in heaven at the same time as the events in verses 1 to 3 and 7 to 10 are occurring, and are parallel with them, though they are occurring in a different realm.

In this chapter, we will consider together these first three verses that tell us about the binding of Satan, and in order to do so, we want to ask and answer three questions about the binding of Satan.

When Was Satan Bound?

The London Baptist Confession of Faith of 1689 says in chapter 1 and paragraph 9, "The infallible rule of interpretation of Scripture is the Scripture itself; and therefore when there is a question about the true and full sense of any Scripture. . .it must be searched by other places that speak more clearly." As we look at Revelation 20:1–3, we have to ask ourselves this question: Is there any other place in the Bible that speaks about the binding of Satan, or any other passages that might give us an idea about this event as to when it occurred and what it means? Thankfully, there are several passages we can look at that cast light on this passage.

The Bible speaks a great deal about Satan being bound, being defeated, and being overcome in both the Gospels and the epistles. We will look at several passages that use this same language of Satan's binding, defeat, and containment, and see what they have to say. These are ordinary prose passages we will be looking at. They do not use symbolic language like our passage does; and therefore, they will be normative in determining the meaning of the symbolic language our passage contains. Ordinary prose always trumps symbolic language in determining the meaning of the symbolic language.

First, notice the witness of the Gospels. The first passage is Matthew 12:22–29. "*Then was brought unto him*" (unto Jesus) "*one possessed with a devil, blind, and dumb: and he healed him, insomuch that the blind and dumb both spake and saw.* [23] *And all the people were amazed, and said, Is not this the son of David?*" (Is not this the true Messiah that the Old Testament promises?) "[24] *But when the Pharisees heard it, they said, This fellow doth not cast out devils, but by Beelzebub the prince of the devils*" (Beelzebub is another name for Satan.) "[25] *And Jesus knew their thoughts, and said unto them, Every kingdom divided against itself is brought to desolation; and every city or house divided against itself shall not stand:* [26] *And if*

Satan cast out Satan, he is divided against himself; how shall then his kingdom stand? [27] *And if I by Beelzebub cast out devils, by whom do your children cast them out? therefore they shall be your judges.* [28] *But if I cast out devils by the Spirit of God, then the kingdom of God is come unto you.* [29] *Or else"* (here is our passage) *"how can one enter into a strong man's house, and spoil his goods, except he first bind the strong man? and then he will spoil his house."*

Jesus is saying to the Pharisees, "Your explanation for the power I possess to cast out demons is illogical and self-contradictory, because if I am using Satan's power to cast out Satan's demons, then Satan is enabling Me to destroy his own kingdom." It would be like a military general calling on his artillery to bomb his infantry. You are not going to fight your own people and your own army, or else your kingdom is going to collapse. Jesus says in effect, "There is another explanation as to why I am able to cast out demons, and that is because I have bound the prince of demons, and therefore, I can ravage his kingdom."

Jesus has bound Satan to the degree and in the sense that He can now go into Satan's kingdom and do anything He wants and take anything He wants. Jesus is telling the Pharisees this: "My ability to cast out demons is because I have bound the master of demons, Satan himself. I can take Satan's people out of his kingdom of darkness and into My kingdom of light because I have bound him, and he cannot do anything to stop Me."

Here we have a clear statement about Jesus at His first advent binding Satan. The binding of Satan is associated with Christ's first coming and the establishment of His kingdom, which is the kingdom of God. It is interesting to note that the very word used in Revelation 20:2 for the binding of Satan is the same Greek word that is used in Matthew 12:29 for the binding of Satan.

Matthew 12:29 is a strong indication of when the binding of Satan took place. It took place at the first coming of Jesus while He was here on the earth. That is why He could cast out demons and take people who were in Satan's kingdom and bring them out of it and into His own kingdom. Because He had bound Satan, He could go in and pillage and plunder Satan's kingdom of his people, and take them to be His own people.

Notice Luke 10:17–19: In this passage, Jesus had sent the seventy out, and He told them to cast out demons and preach the gospel. They returned and they gave a report. It says: *"And the seventy returned again with joy, saying, Lord, even the devils [demons] are subject unto us through thy name.* [18] *And he said unto them, I beheld Satan as lightning fall from heaven.* [19] *Behold, I give unto you power to tread on serpents and scorpions, and over all the power of the enemy: and nothing shall by any means hurt you."*

Here we have the beginning of the downfall, the control, and the containment of Satan as a result of the first coming of Christ and His teaching and His works. Satan is falling from power. Jesus bound Satan in such a way that, not only could He ravage Satan's house, but His disciples could also ravage Satan's house. Once again, we see Jesus containing, controlling, and overpowering Satan and defeating his agenda and purposes. When does He do this? He does this at His first coming.

In verse 19, these serpents and scorpions are metaphors for Satan and his demons, the idea being that not only Jesus but also His disciples have power over the enemy and over his demons. The enemy can do nothing to harm or hurt the disciples as they go out and preach the gospel, nor can they stop the spread of the gospel.

In John 12:20–22, there were certain Greeks that came to worship at the feast who came to Philip and said, *"Sir, we would see Jesus."* The apostles bring the message to Jesus that Gentiles want to see Him. This has great significance to Jesus because it symbolizes the expansion of His kingdom to include all categories of people, and not just the Jews.

Notice what Jesus says in verses 31 and 32: *"Now is the judgment of this world: now shall the prince of this world be cast out.* [32] *And I, if I be lifted up from the earth, will draw all men unto me."* All men without distinction, be they Jew or Gentile, will be drawn to Him, and Jesus saw this foreshadowed in the coming of these Gentiles to speak with Him. This word "*cast out*" in verse 31 is the same root word as is found in Revelation 20:3 when it says that Satan was cast into the bottomless pit.

This casting out of Satan was the casting into the bottomless pit with all of its restraint. This concept of Satan being forcibly removed from his place of influence and control and being fallen and cast down and bound is found in several places in the Gospels. This terminology tells us that Satan was overcome, Satan was defeated, and Satan was bound at the first coming of Christ so Christ and His disciples could ravage his kingdom.

When it says that Satan was cast out and cast down, he was cast into the bottomless pit of Revelation 20:3, to a place on the earth where he is restrained from being able to deceive the nations.

Having seen passages from the Gospels that indicate when Satan was bound, secondly, let us consider passages from the epistles that indicate when Satan was bound.

Notice Colossians 2:13: *"And you, being dead in your sins and the uncircumcision of your flesh, hath he quickened together with him, having forgiven you all trespasses."* This is good news! All your trespasses are forgiven, no matter what kind they are, no matter how many they are, no matter how terrible they are: He has forgiven you all trespasses!

How did He do it? Verse 14 explains: *"Blotting out the handwriting of ordinances that was against us, which was contrary to us, and took it out of the way, nailing it to his cross."* Jesus took the bill that the law of God wrote out, that charged us with what we owed for our transgressions against it, and Jesus said, "I will pay that." He nailed it to His cross, and He paid every claim for punishment it made against us.

Now notice verse 15. Here is our verse: *"And having spoiled principalities and powers, he made a show of them openly, triumphing over them in it."* This word *"spoiled"* in verse 15 means disarmed. It means to be stripped of what one has. When warfare occurred and you defeated a soldier, you disarmed him by stripping off his sword and armor and shield, so he was left defenseless. To be *"spoiled"* is to be disarmed.

This phrase *"principalities and powers"* refers to Satan and his demons. As Paul is writing, he is looking back at the cross and writing about what happened at the cross. What happened at the cross was not only the forgiveness of our sins. What happened at the cross was the triumph over Satan. Jesus stripped him of all of his power. Jesus mocked him publicly and paraded him before the spiritual universe as a defeated foe.

This was the fulfillment of Genesis 3:15, in which the Son of the woman crushed the Serpent's head. What happened at the cross? Jesus disarmed Satan and his demons, publicly mocked them, and paraded them in disgrace as He triumphed over them.

Hebrews 2:14 says, *"Forasmuch then as the children"* (God's elect) *"are partakers of flesh and blood, he"* (Jesus) *"also himself likewise took part of the same; that through death he might destroy him that had the power of death, that is, the devil.*" When was the devil destroyed? When Jesus took part in our flesh and blood and died on the cross. By Christ's death on the cross, Satan's power of death was removed.

When it says that Satan was destroyed, it means he was defeated. His power over death was defeated and destroyed. It is not saying that Satan was destroyed in the sense that he was annihilated, as though he went away into nothingness. Jesus took away from Satan everything he had when He died on the cross. He defeated him. He took away his ultimate power over death, which means He took away all of Satan's lesser powers as well.

Notice 1 John 3:8. John says, once again looking back at the cross in verse 8, "*For this purpose the Son of God was manifested, that he might destroy the works of the devil.*" To destroy the works of the devil is what it means to destroy the devil.

Paul looks back on the first coming of Jesus and His work on the cross and says that Jesus disarmed Satan and publicly shamed him. The author of the book of Hebrews looks back on the cross and says that Satan's power over death was stripped from him. John looks back at the cross and says that Jesus was manifested to destroy the works of the devil. Did He succeed in destroying the works of the devil at His first coming? He absolutely succeeded. Once again, we see Jesus at His first coming destroying Satan's power and ability and freedom to do his work.

Notice Revelation 12:1–10, which we have studied before: "*And there appeared a great wonder in heaven; a woman clothed with the sun, and the moon under her feet, and upon her head a crown of twelve stars*"—this woman represented Israel—"[2] *And she being with child cried, travailing in birth, and pained to be delivered.*" She is pregnant with Christ; she is bringing forth Christ through the instrumentality of Mary.

Verse 3 reads: "*And there appeared another wonder in heaven; and behold a great red dragon, having seven heads and ten horns, and seven crowns upon his heads.* [4] *And his tail drew the third part of the stars of heaven, and did cast them to the earth: and the dragon stood before the woman which was ready to be delivered, for to devour her child as soon as it was born.*" The dragon is Satan, who carried out his work through Herod, who sought to kill Christ as soon as He was born.

"[5] *And she brought forth a man child"*—Jesus was in fact born; Herod did not succeed in destroying Jesus—*"who was to rule all nations with a rod of iron: and her child was caught up unto God, and to his throne."* His whole life: His birth, ministry, death, burial, resurrection, and ascension are all described in verse 5. Now consider verse 6. Here is what happens after the ascension of Jesus: "[6]*And the woman fled into the wilderness, where she hath a place prepared of God, that they should feed her there a thousand two hundred and threescore days.*

Upon the ascension of Jesus *"[7]there was war in heaven: Michael and his angels fought against the dragon; and the dragon fought and his angels, [8] And prevailed not; neither was their place found any more in heaven. [9] And the great dragon was cast out, that old serpent, called the Devil, and Satan, which deceiveth the whole world: he was cast out into the earth, and his angels were cast out with him. [10] And I heard a loud voice saying in heaven, Now is come salvation, and strength, and the kingdom of our God, and the power of his Christ: for the accuser of our brethren is cast down, which accused them before our God day and night."*

This is Satan falling like lightning from heaven; this is Satan being cast out and cast down. Where is he cast down into? He is cast down into this bottomless pit which is on the earth, in which he is contained and restrained and controlled so the disciples of Jesus can go into his house and take his people and bring them into the kingdom of Christ.

There is a great deal of evidence that Satan was defeated and cast down and bound by Christ at His first coming. There is no evidence in the Scripture that this took place at any other time, or that it has yet to occur at some time in the future.

Revelation 20:1–3 says, *"And I saw an angel come down from heaven, having the key of the bottomless pit and a great chain in his hand. [2] And he laid hold on the dragon, that old serpent, which is the Devil, and Satan, and bound him a thousand years, [3] And cast him into the bottomless pit, and shut him up, and set a seal upon him, that he should deceive the nations no more, till the thousand years should be fulfilled: and after that he must be loosed a little season."*

As we look at other clear passages that use this language and these symbols, it becomes quite obvious when Satan was bound. He was bound at the time of the cross by the work of Jesus at His first advent. This is not a binding that is going to take place at some point in the future after the second coming of Jesus, because the second coming of Jesus occurs in 20:9. This binding of Satan is something that has already taken place in the past at the first coming of Jesus.

Therefore, when did the thousand years begin? It began when Satan was bound. When was Satan bound? He was bound at the first coming of Jesus. If Satan was bound at the first coming of Jesus, then the millennium began at the first coming of Jesus. What does that mean? It means we are living in the millennium right now. The millennium is not something that begins in the future. It is something that began 2,000 years ago and has been going on up to this very point in time.

For How Long is Satan Bound?

The answer is very obvious. It says right in the text in Revelation 20:1–3 that he is going to be bound for a thousand years, and when the thousand years have passed, he is going to be loosed. The question we have to ask is this: Do we understand this thousand-year period literally or figuratively?

We know that apocalyptic literature is primarily symbolic. We also know that the usage of numbers in the book of Revelation is virtually always symbolic. And while certainly in this passage the angel is literal and Satan is literal, if we think about the rest of this symbolic picture, it quickly becomes obvious that the key is figurative, the lock it opens is figurative, the chain is figurative, and the pit is figurative. The reason they are figurative is because Satan is an immaterial spirit, and you cannot lock up an immaterial spirit with material objects. By definition, a spirit has an immaterial body, and material things cannot contain or constrain spirits. A spirit does not have a physical dimension that is limited by physical obstacles.

Therefore, if the key, the lock, the chain, and the pit are all symbolic, then by what rationale should we conclude that the prison sentence is literal? If the prison is symbolic, why would the prison sentence not also be symbolic?

Up to this point in our study of Revelation, we have seen that almost every number used is symbolic and not literal, and that the symbolic use of numbers is the norm, not the exception. We know that the number ten symbolizes and conveys the concept of perfection and totality, and one thousand is the cube of ten—ten times ten times ten equals one thousand. A thousand is simply perfection and totality raised to the third power. Any time a primary number is multiplied, it is an intensification of the idea of the symbolism of that number.

One thousand represents the perfect duration of time allotted by God to pass between the first and second coming of Christ. It is the total length of time for the church age. Just like the key and the lock and the chain and the pit are all symbolic of Satan being limited and contained by an act of God, the duration of a thousand years is also symbolic of how long that limitation and containment will last.

The number symbolizes an age-long but definitely limited period of time. One thousand was the largest number biblical authors had, and therefore, they use expressions such as thousands and thousands, or thousands times thousands, to indicate something larger than a thousand. The church age was a long period of time, so they used their largest number to symbolize that extended period of time.

This symbolic use of the number one thousand should not surprise us because it is used in a non-literal way elsewhere in the Scriptures. For example, in 2 Peter 3:8 it says *"that one day is with the Lord as a thousand years, and a thousand years as one day."* In Psalm 90:4 it says, *"For a thousand years in thy sight are but as yesterday when it is past, and as a watch in the night."*

The symbolic and non-literal use of the number one thousand occurs several times in the Bible, and we should not be surprised if it is used that way here. How long literally has Satan been bound? Up to this point in time, nearly two thousand literal years. In fact, in 2033 it will be two thousand literal years.

Some people did literalize this number one thousand, and therefore thought Satan would be loosed in AD 1033, and Jesus was going to come shortly thereafter. But it obviously did not happen, and the reason is because this number is not a literal number. It is a figurative number, which is why Jesus did not return at that time.

We have to remember that apocalyptic literature is primarily symbolic. All the elements of this prison are symbolic. Therefore, it stands to reason that the prison sentence is also symbolic.

When was Satan bound? At the time of Christ's first coming. For how long is Satan bound? For an age-long, but definitely limited period of time. The millennium actually ends when Satan is loosed. Less than a generation will then pass before the second coming occurs, as we are told in Matthew 24:34. This brings us to our third and final question.

Why Was Satan Bound?

First of all, we know that Satan is not bound to complete inactivity. For example, it says in 1 Peter 5:8, *"Be sober, be vigilant; because your adversary the devil, as a roaring lion, walketh about, seeking whom he may devour."* Clearly, Satan has mobility. He is able to walk about, and he is able to assault individual Christians and try to draw them into sin and away from Christ. Satan is free to tempt believers.

Furthermore, 2 Corinthians 4:3–4 says, *"But if our gospel be hid, it is hid to them that are lost:* [4] *In whom the god of this world hath blinded the minds of them which believe not, lest the light of the glorious gospel of Christ, who is the image of God, should shine unto them."* Satan is loose and operative regarding his ability to blind the mind of unbelieving people to the gospel.

Therefore, with reference to both believers and unbelievers, Satan is still operative and active. Clearly, Satan is not totally bound in every respect with reference to every possible activity he can engage in.

Secondly, we need to ask in what sense he is bound. It specifically says in verse 3 that he is bound so that he should deceive the nations no more, till the thousand years are ended. After that, he will be loosed.

His binding is in regard to the nations—that is, with respect to entire nations as a whole, and especially with respect to the function of their civil authorities. The result is that Satan is unable to deceive the nations of the earth into making a unified, intense, and prolonged effort to destroy Christianity in the world. This is why he was bound. The reason we know this is not only because it is stated in verse 3, but when we see Satan loosed from this restraint in verse 7, he promptly goes out to deceive and gather all the nations of the whole world into a unified transnational coalition to launch a murderous assault against the believers on the earth.

And while it is true that for the last 2,000 years individual nations have tried to destroy Christianity within their own borders, there has never been any kind of a coordinated, transnational, worldwide effort to do so, nor will there be until Satan is loosed. There always has been and there still are nations who tolerate and even protect Christians, and they have always had a place to which they could flee and find protection.

Furthermore, because Satan is bound, the two witnesses of Revelation 11:3–6, who represent the church and her missionary activity, cannot be stopped from spreading the gospel throughout the whole world. Like a mighty army, the church has expanded and spread its message into every nation on the earth, and Satan's kingdom has been plundered as hundreds of millions of Gentiles have been brought out of the kingdom of darkness and into the kingdom of light. Churches have been established across the globe, and Satan was restrained in the sense that he was powerless to stop it from happening. Satan is bound so that he cannot destroy the church as it functions as a mighty missionary army that is bringing the gospel to the nations.

We are living in a time of protection until, as it says in Revelation 11:7, our testimony to Christ and the gospel is finished, and the work of plundering Satan's kingdom of all of God's elect is completed. Only then will the thousand years be finished, and only then will Satan be loosed.

Jesus' ministry and death and resurrection marked the great turning point in Satan's domination of the world. From creation until Christ, Satan was free to deceive the nations, and the kingdom of God was confined to a tiny number of people because Satan was loose. But then Jesus came and bound him, and now the kingdom of God has expanded over the whole world because we have been protected from the kind of behavior Satan engaged in for the years between creation and the first coming of Christ.

Satan's control over the world has been broken, Satan has been stripped of his power, and he has been bound from being able to stop the light of the gospel from spreading over the whole earth. Jesus said in Matthew 24:14 that the gospel of the kingdom would be preached in the entire world for a witness to all nations, and then the end would come. Satan is powerless to prevent that from happening. Satan sits there bound, seeing his kingdom growing smaller and smaller as the kingdom of Christ grows larger and larger, and the evangelization of the world continually diminishes his control over it.

Before Christ came, the kingdom of God on earth was tiny. Now that Christ has come and bound Satan, the kingdom of God on earth is huge. This is why when the two witnesses preach in Revelation 11 and men try to hurt them, it says that "[5]*fire proceeds out of their mouth, and devours their enemies; and if any man will hurt them, he must in this manner be killed.* [6]*These have the power to shut heaven, that it rain not in the days of their prophecy: and have power over waters to turn them to blood, and to smite the earth with all plagues, as often as they will.*" They cannot be stopped until their ministry is finished. They defeat every effort to stop them. When the last elect person has been plundered out of the kingdom of Satan is when the thousand years will be over, it is when Satan will be loosed, and that is when the final end time will occur.

Satan was bound to prevent him from deceiving the nations of the earth into making a unified, intense, and prolonged effort to destroy Christianity in the world, and he was bound to prevent him from stopping the spread of the gospel throughout the whole world. We are living in a time of protection from the ravages of Satan until our work of evangelism is done and our testimony is finished. Let us be about that work with zeal and energy as we enjoy the protection of God in this age. Let us be thankful to God that we are living in a time when the work of Satan is greatly restrained.

58

The Millennium in Heaven, Revelation 20:4–6

> *"[4] And I saw thrones, and they sat upon them, and judgment was given unto them: and I saw the souls of them that were beheaded for the witness of Jesus, and for the word of God, and which had not worshipped the beast, neither his image, neither had received his mark upon their foreheads, or in their hands; and they lived and reigned with Christ a thousand years. [5] But the rest of the dead lived not again until the thousand years were finished. This is the first resurrection. [6] Blessed and holy is he that hath part in the first resurrection: on such the second death hath no power, but they shall be priests of God and of Christ, and shall reign with him a thousand years."*

Revelation 20 began the seventh and final parallel section of the book of Revelation. Each of the previous parallel sections of the book has traversed the time period between the first and second coming of Christ, and this last parallel section is no different.

Revelation 20:1–3 tells us about the event that took place at the first coming of Christ when Satan was bound by Christ at the cross and rendered powerless to deceive the nations. We then looked at what it meant for Satan to be bound.

First of all, it meant that Satan is unable to get all the nations of the earth to work together to persecute the church. The church enjoys a large degree of safety and protection from the persecution of civil governments in this age. Satan is unable to deceive the nations into making a unified, intense, and prolonged effort to destroy Christianity in the world. While it is true that for the last 2,000 years, individual nations have tried to wipe out Christianity within their own borders from time to time, there has never been any kind of a transnational worldwide effort to do so, nor will there be as long as Satan is bound so that he cannot deceive the nations into doing it.

Because Satan is bound, the church enjoys a large degree of safety and protection from the kind of persecution that would overwhelm it and eradicate it from the earth. Satan has been stripped of his power by Jesus Christ to persecute the church at that level.

Secondly, it meant that the church cannot be stopped from spreading the gospel throughout the whole world. The church is able to enter Satan's kingdom across the globe and penetrate into every nation, and bring hundreds of millions of people out of servitude to Satan and into the kingdom and service of Jesus.

In a word, Satan is so bound that the church can enter into his kingdom and plunder it at will, and Satan can do nothing to stop it. We can go into all the world and preach the gospel to every person, and Satan's hands are tied so that he is powerless to prevent it from occurring. This binding of Satan will continue until all of God's elect are saved.

This time period in which Satan is bound is called the Millennium, a symbolic thousand-year period in which the church is divinely protected from persecution and is successfully preaching the gospel message to all nations. This symbolic thousand-year period is an age-long and yet definitely limited period of time, during which we enjoy protection, and during which we engage in preaching the gospel to the whole world until our testimony is finished. When the last elect person has been saved, then our testimony will be finished. We do not know when the last elect person will be saved. It could occur today; it could occur many centuries into the future. But when the last elect person has been saved, then our testimony will be finished, and this millennial period of God's protection will be over.

As we live in this millennium of relative protection that is the result of the restraint of Satan, it does not mean that Satan is bound from engaging in any evil activity at all. Satan's restraint is partial, not complete; and Satan is still able to do a great deal of evil in this earth through his agents the beast, the false prophet, Babylon, and those who have the mark of the beast. The church is still severely persecuted, and it endures great suffering as believers bear witness for Jesus Christ.

It is Satan's goal to kill as many believers as possible, and throughout the last 2,000 years he has viciously slaughtered Christians without number. The slaughter of Christians is Satan's greatest victory in this age, but our passage today makes it clear that even Satan's greatest victory is a complete defeat because all those he kills immediately go to heaven to be with Jesus Christ.

In the last chapter, we explained the structure of Revelation 20 and saw that verses 1 to 3 were a description of the Millennium on earth, in which the topic was Satan's relationship to the nations during the Millennium, and we saw this relationship is one of being bound. We saw that verses 4 to 6 described the Millennium in heaven, in which the topic was the rule and reign of the saints in heaven who had been martyred by Satan and his agents in this age. We said that the events of verses 1 to 3 and the events of verses 4 to 6 run parallel with each other and occur during the same time period. The one set of events describes what is happening on earth, and the other set of events describes what is happening in heaven at the same time.

The point of allowing us to see what is happening in heaven while we are living through this millennial period on earth is to assure us that any death Satan and his people inflict on us now only results in victory and eternal life for us. The primary point of verses 4 to 6 is to demonstrate the victory of God's people who suffer Satan's attacks and martyrdom. They will receive a crown of glory for their faithfulness to Jesus Christ, and they will share in Christ's rule and reign until He returns. Second Timothy 2:12 tells us that if we endure suffering for Christ, we will also reign together with Christ. This passage in verses 4 to 6 is a picture of what that reign with Christ looks like.

Satan's effort to kill the believers never succeeds, because no sooner does he kill them than they immediately live again in heaven. Therefore during this millennial period, whether they live or die, there can be no defeat for believers, while at the same time there is nothing but defeat for Satan. That is the message of verses 4 to 6.

The Dwelling Place of the Martyrs

The first phrase in verse 4 says, *"And I saw thrones, and they sat upon them."* Now the question arises: Where are these thrones located? Are they located in heaven, or are they located on earth? The answer to that question is important because the location of the thrones will tell us the location of the souls that are sitting on them. It is important for us to take note that every time we see believers represented by the twenty-four elders sitting on thrones, those thrones are always, and without exception, in heaven. Let us take a quick survey through the book of Revelation.

Jesus says in 3:21, when making promises to the believers, *"To him that overcometh will I grant to sit with me in my throne, even as I also overcame, and am set down with my Father in his throne."* Where is the throne of Jesus? It is in heaven. Therefore, if we are sitting with Him in His throne, on thrones, then those thrones are going to be in heaven.

Notice 4:1–4. *"After this I looked, and, behold, a door was opened in heaven: and the first voice which I heard was as it were of a trumpet talking with me; which said, Come up hither, and I will shew thee things which must be hereafter."* Clearly, John is being taken up to heaven. "[2] *And immediately I was in the spirit: and, behold, a throne was set in heaven, and one sat on the throne.* [3] *And he that sat was to look upon like a jasper and a sardine stone: and there was a rainbow round about the throne, in sight like unto an emerald."* This is God the Father, sitting on His throne in heaven.

Now notice verse 4: *"And round about the throne were four and twenty seats and upon the seats I saw four and twenty elders sitting. . ."* What is interesting is that the word "seat" is the exact same Greek word that is translated "throne" in the first part of the verse. It is the Greek word *"thronos,"* and it should read, "[4]*And round about the throne were four and twenty thrones: and upon the thrones I saw four and twenty elders sitting, clothed in white raiment; and they had on their heads crowns of gold."* I do not know why the King James translated *"thronos"* as *"seats,"* when it is the exact same word for throne as the throne which God is sitting on. These twenty-four elders are not sitting on lawn chairs or wooden benches. They are enthroned. Twice in verse 4 it says that they were sitting upon thrones.

Notice 11:15–16. *"And the seventh angel sounded; and there were great voices in heaven, saying, The kingdoms of this world are become the kingdoms of our Lord, and of his Christ; and he shall reign for ever and ever.* [16] *And the four and twenty elders, which sat before God on their seats"*—once again, the Greek word is *thronos*, "throne"—and *"fell upon their faces, and worshipped God."* It should read: "[16] *And the four and twenty elders, which sat before God on their thrones."* These thrones are in heaven with God.

Notice 20:4. *"And I saw thrones"* (the exact same Greek word that was translated *"seats"* earlier), *"and they sat upon them."* Here, the same Greek word *"thronos"* is translated *"thrones,"* that was previously translated "seats." This inconsistency in the translation of *"thronos"* in the KJV could create misunderstanding for the English reader.

The point is this: the thrones upon which believers sit are located in heaven, and therefore these believers spoken of in Revelation 20:4–6 are also in heaven. We would expect that to be the case since immediately in verse 4, John tells us that those who sit on these thrones are the disembodied souls of men. The disembodied souls of men never remain on the earth. They always go immediately to either hell or to heaven. He says, *"I saw the souls of them that were beheaded for the witness of Jesus."* Their bodies have been beheaded, and therefore their souls are in heaven.

Of the forty-seven uses of the word *"thronos"* in the book of Revelation, it is used once of Satan's throne in 2:13, and it is used twice of the throne of the beast in 13:2 and 16:10. The remaining forty-four usages of the word *"thronos"* are all of thrones in heaven, either the throne of God or the throne of believers. The point is, any good and honorable throne is either in heaven or else in the new heavens and the new earth.

If these people are living and reigning with Christ for the thousand-year millennial age, we must ask: Where is Christ located during this thousand-year millennial church age? From what place is Christ reigning? He is reigning from heaven; and therefore, those who are reigning with Him are also reigning from heaven beside Him.

Therefore, the dispensational idea that somehow these saints are reigning from thrones on this fallen earth during some future millennial period is both unfounded and unscriptural. Instead, these saints are enjoying the purity and the blessedness of heaven in the immediate presence of Christ, as they behold His glory and participate in His rule from heaven. The dwelling place of the martyrs is in heaven.

Here then is Satan's defeat. By killing the saints on earth, he did not harm them. Instead, he promoted them to the glory of heaven, a place far better than anything they ever experienced on earth. In trying to harm the saints, Satan only brought about their increased blessing. He achieved the exact opposite of his goal. Only a fool fights Christ and His people and hopes to win, and Satan is the biggest fool of all.

The Justification of the Martyrs

It says in verse 4, *"And I saw thrones, and they sat upon them, and judgment was given unto them."* While believers are here on earth, the world passes judgment on them. They are scorned, mocked, condemned, and rejected by the world. They are viewed as wicked bigots and self-righteous hypocrites, the scum of the earth, and held in utter contempt by the unsaved. Society looks down on Christians and treats them with injustice, oppression, and scorn; but the sentence which society and the world pass on Christians is going to be overturned by God.

Notice it says in verse 4, *"And judgment was given unto them."* That is, a favorable judgment was given to them by God. The idea contained in that phrase is that judgment was passed for them instead of against them. They were given a favorable verdict by God. That this is the proper interpretation of that phrase is confirmed by Daniel 7:22 which describes the same event. It says, *". . .the Ancient of days came, and judgment was given to the saints of the most High."*

The world passes its judgment on us now, and its sentence is: "Condemned!" God will pass His judgment on His saints when they appear before Him at their death, and His sentence is: "Righteous!" What the saints in heaven experience is God vindicating them from the slanders, false judgments, and unjust sentence the world has passed on them. God vindicates His saints, God justifies His saints, and God exonerates His saints. God condemns and overturns the judgment of the world against them, and God acquits them and clears them of the accusations of evil men.

As Paul says in Romans 8:31, *"If God be for us, who can be against us?"* He goes on to say in Romans 8:33, *"Who shall lay anything to the charge of God's elect? It is God that justifieth."* If God is for us and if God justifies us, then we are eternally vindicated and liberated from all of the shame and contempt and slanderous judgment that the world has passed and placed upon us. The judgment of the world as to who we are and what we are will cling to us no more. It is gone forever. The accusations of the Evil One and his helpers are rendered meaningless and dismissed as being without any merit of any kind.

What did the world think of believers? What judgment did the world pass on the believers? Their judgment was: "Behead them!"

And what did God think of the believers? What judgment did He pass upon them? His judgment was: "Enthrone them!" God has a passionate concern for justice, and He will give justice to His people. Righteous judgment will be given to them.

The Identity of the Martyrs

Who are those sitting on these thrones in heaven and being justified by God? Verse 4 says, *"and I saw the souls of them that were beheaded."* Here are the saints of God who have proven the strength and genuineness of their faith by laying down their lives for Jesus Christ. I do not think this class of people mentioned here only consists of those who suffered a literal beheading while they were here on earth. After all, what about those who were burned at the stake? Are they excluded from this class of people because they died with their heads still attached to their bodies? What about those who were shot for their faith, or hung by the neck, or torn apart by lions? What of those who were starved to death in prison or beaten to death? Are they excluded because they died with their heads still attached to their bodies?

What of those who suffered the slow death of many decades of pouring out their lives and their health as a living sacrifice to Christ in faithful service to Christ, and who wore out their lives in serving Him and then died? Are they excluded because they died with their heads intact? Are not all of these saints martyrs for Christ?

Every Christian without exception is represented by those who are said to be beheaded for the witness of Jesus. Every Christian without exception is a martyr, because every Christian without exception lays down his life in one way or another for Jesus Christ, either in the quick death of beheading or in the long slow death of dying to self and laying down his life for Christ for a lifetime. Indeed, the word "martyr," a translation of the Greek word *"martus,"* means to be a witness, and is translated as the word "witness" twenty-nine times in the New Testament.

For example, Acts 1:8 says, *"But ye shall receive power, after that the Holy Ghost is come upon you: and ye shall be witnesses [martyrs] unto me both in Jerusalem, and in all Judea, and in Samaria, and unto the uttermost part of the earth."* Every Christian is a witness for Jesus Christ, every Christian pours out and lays down his life for Christ, and every Christian presents his body as a living sacrifice to Christ.

Therefore, every Christian is a martyr for Christ. This symbolic category of those who were beheaded for the witness of Jesus represents all Christians and every Christian, because all Christians are martyrs or witnesses, and all of them have laid down their lives for Christ in one way or another.

The Faithfulness of the Martyrs

Now in setting forth the faithfulness of these martyrs, John tells us that they were all marked by both positive and negative characteristics. Notice verse 4. It says, *"and I saw the souls of them that were beheaded"* (positively) *"for the witness of Jesus, and for the word of God, and"* (negatively) *"which had not worshipped the beast, neither his image, neither had received his mark upon their foreheads, or in their hands."*

Positively, these martyrs maintained their witness for Jesus. Even when threatened with beheading, they continued to confess Christ before men. They would not deny Christ, no matter the cost, and they openly confessed Christ, no matter the price. Whatever the price they had to pay to openly confess Christ, even if it meant the loss of their head, they were willing to pay it.

Furthermore, they defended the Word of God, taught the Word of God, and lived according to the Word of God. The Scriptures were their ultimate and final authority; and they would rather die than betray its teachings, deny its doctrines, or compromise its principles. They were beheaded for the witness of Jesus and they were beheaded for the Word of God. These are the two positive virtues that mark all believers in Jesus Christ: they openly maintain their witness of Jesus, and they live by and proclaim the Word of God.

Negatively, it says that the faithfulness of these martyrs was demonstrated by their refusal to worship the beast. They would not worship the civil government as God, or see the civil government as the ultimate source of authority, or see it as the final determiner of right and wrong. They would not think like anti-Christian government wanted them to think, or act like anti-Christian government demanded they act. They did not yield to its threats or its persecutions. Instead, they remained faithful to Jesus Christ. It was these faithful martyrs and witnesses who were justified by God and who were enthroned in heaven.

The Resurrection of the Martyrs

It says at the end of verse 4, *"and they"* (these martyrs) *"lived and reigned with Christ a thousand years."* Though they were killed for their faithfulness to Christ and His word, and though they were killed for their refusal to worship Satan through his agent the beast, they did not remain dead. Their bodies remained dead on the earth, but their souls were now more alive in heaven than they had ever been on earth. Their souls were made perfect and their souls were brought into perfect union with God; and as a result, it is said of them that they *"lived."* They were alive as they had never been alive before. They were filled with the perfect life that Adam had before the fall, but elevated to a level of permanent and perfect and eternal righteousness. This perfect new life their souls obtained at their death is declared to be *"the first resurrection,"* in verse 5.

Verse 5 says, *"(But the rest of the dead lived not again until the thousand years were finished.) This is the first resurrection."* Verse 6: *"Blessed and holy is he that hath part in the first resurrection: on such the second death hath no power, but they shall be priests of God and of Christ, and shall reign with him a thousand years."*

We must understand that the first sentence in verse 5 is a parenthetical statement. When it says, *"But the rest of the dead lived not again until the thousand years were finished,"* you could put parentheses around that sentence, and I did that above, though they are not there in the KJV translation. This first sentence is an aside. It is an interruption to the flow of thought that must be set aside for the moment and dealt with later, and we will deal with it shortly.

And so, setting aside the first sentence in verse 5 as a parenthetical statement, the flow of thought from verse 4 continues in the middle of verse 5 and then all the way through to the end of verse 6.

It would then read like this: "[4] *And I saw thrones, and they sat upon them, and judgment was given unto them: and I saw the souls of them that were beheaded for the witness of Jesus, and for the word of God, and which had not worshipped the beast, neither his image, neither had received his mark upon their foreheads, or in their hands; and they lived and reigned with Christ a thousand years.* [5]*. . .This is the first resurrection.* [6] *Blessed and holy is he that hath part in the first resurrection: on such the second death hath no power, but they shall be priests of God and of Christ, and shall reign with him a thousand years."*

All that is said of the believers in verse 4, and all that verse 4 says these believers experience, is called in verse 5 *"the first resurrection."*

The second half of verse 5 says, *"This is the first resurrection."* The word *"This"* refers back to all that was said in verse 4. This perfect new life that the martyrs received and is described in verse 4 is said in verse 5 to be the first resurrection. That is, everything that is said in verse 4 about the martyrs is the first phase of their resurrection. The second resurrection, or the second phase of their resurrection, will take place at the second coming when their dead bodies are raised and perfected and reunited with their already perfect souls that are in heaven as described in verse 4.

The blessedness of participating in the first resurrection of the soul being perfected and brought into perfect union with God in heaven upon one's death cannot be overstated. That blessedness is declared in verse 6. Notice, it says, *"Blessed and holy is he that hath part in the first resurrection: on such the second death hath no power, but they shall be priests of God and of Christ, and shall reign with him a thousand years."*

It says in verse 6, *"Blessed and holy is he that hath part in the first resurrection."* Who has part in the first resurrection? Those described in verse 4, the disembodied souls in heaven who are sitting on thrones, justified by God for their faithfulness to God while they were alive on earth. It says of them that they *"live,"* and this life they have in heaven as disembodied perfect souls in perfect union with God is said to be the first resurrection, and it is a blessed resurrection.

It says, *"Blessed and holy is he that hath part in the first resurrection"* in verse 6. Those who participate in the first resurrection, which is described in verse 4, are blessed for two reasons, one negative, and the other positive.

Negatively, it says in verse 6 they will never experience the second death. Notice verse 6: *"Blessed and holy is he that hath part in the first resurrection."* Here is the first aspect of their blessing, negatively, *"on such the second death hath no power."*

It is a wonderful thing to be delivered from the second death. What is the second death? The answer is contained in 20:13–15. *"And the sea gave up the dead which were in it; and death and hell delivered up the dead which were in them: and they were judged every man according to their works."* Now here it is, verse 14: *"And death and hell were cast into the lake of fire. This is the second death.* [15] *And whosoever was not found written in the book of life was cast into the lake of fire."*

Being cast into the lake of fire is the second death. Those who take part in the first resurrection, these souls described in verse 4, will never wind up in the lake of fire. In a word, the souls of believers in heaven can never run the risk of being cast into the lake of fire. They are forever delivered from that possibility. Once you get to heaven, you can never wind up in hell.

Positively, this blessedness of those in verse 4 who were said to have experienced the first resurrection consists in the fact that *"they shall be priests of God and of Christ, and shall reign with him a thousand years."* Believers in heaven minister as priests before the throne of God in giving Him worship. Believers in heaven reign with Christ in the kingdom of God by giving Him service. No more blessed position could ever be occupied than the position of being kings and priests before God, serving in the kingdom of God, all to the glory of God. Twice we are told, in verse 4 and verse 6, that this ministry of reigning with Christ will go on in heaven all throughout the millennial age—that is, the symbolic thousand-year church age.

But this millennial privilege of reigning with Christ will not cease at the end of the Millennium. Revelation 22:3–5 says this millennial reign that believers in heaven are engaged in now will be transformed into an eternal reign with Christ when the new heavens and the new earth are established, and we will have that status of priests and kings with Christ forever. He is making sure we know that this status and privilege is going to go on, and this blessedness is going to be experienced for the entire church age. As long as they are in heaven, they are kings and they are priests.

This is the blessedness of the believers when they die. They will never experience the second death, and they have this glorious privilege of being priests and kings with Christ and before the throne of God forever.

But what happens to the wicked dead during this thousand-year millennial period of the church age? This brings us back to the parenthetical first sentence in verse 5. *"But the rest of the dead lived not again until the thousand years were finished."* We said this sentence was parenthetical—that is, it interrupted the flow of thought. As we saw, if we set it aside, the flow of thought is uninterrupted from verse 4 to verse 5b and verse 6. It all flows as one topic. But we have this insertion of this first sentence in verse 5.

This parenthetical sentence tells us that the rest of the dead—that is, those whose souls do not go to heaven when they die—do not live again until the thousand years are finished. This death they experienced when they died during the church age is their first death. That is, when the wicked die in this age, their souls are not only separated from their bodies, but their souls are also finally and permanently and irrevocably separated from God. They are both physically dead and spiritually dead. Their souls are cast into hell, and they remain there in conscious torment for the entire millennial period. This is their first death.

It is only at the end of the millennial period when Christ returns that they are brought out of hell and reunited with their resurrected bodies; and therefore, since they are reunited with their resurrected bodies, they can be said to "live again." Verse 5: *"But the rest of the dead lived not again until the thousand years were finished."* The clear implication is that when the thousand years were finished, they did live again.

This "living again" at the end of the thousand-year period is described in Revelation 20:12–13. Notice verse 12: *"And I saw the dead, small and great, stand before God; and the books were opened: and another book was opened, which is the book of life: and the dead were judged out of those things which were written in the books, according to their works.* [13] *And the sea gave up the dead which were in it; and death and hell delivered up the dead which were in them: and they were judged every man according to their works."* Here they are resurrected out of hell, reunited with their bodies, and are standing before God on the Day of Judgment. Therefore, they can be said to be "alive again." But this life is very short. They are judged by Christ and are cast into the lake of fire and experience their second death, which is eternal separation from God and eternal pain and torment of body and soul forever in the lake of fire.

The righteous have a two-stage resurrection. First, their souls are raised to heaven and made perfect. That is the first resurrection. Then at the second coming of Christ, their bodies are raised and made perfect and reunited with their perfected souls, and that is the second resurrection. They then dwell forever in the new earth. Thus, the righteous have a first and a second resurrection.

But in contrast to the two-stage resurrection of the righteous, the wicked have a two-stage death. First, when they die physically, their souls are condemned to hell and experience torment there. That is their first death. Then, at the second coming of Christ, their bodies are raised and made suitable for eternal suffering, their corrupt souls are reunited with these bodies, and they are cast into the lake of fire. That is their second death.

When we see what occurs in heaven during the church age, it is a great encouragement to believers who suffer and lay down their lives for Christ, however they may lay them down. Those who suffer at the hands of the wicked and are finally killed by them go to heaven. But the wicked who killed them go to hell when they die. The wicked are condemned, though the world justified them; and the saints are vindicated, though the world condemned them.

What is being said in verses 4 to 6 is that Satan is always defeated and Satan's people are always defeated. But the saints always triumph, no matter the situation or circumstance they find themselves in. Even when Satan does his worst in this age we are living in, it always works out for our best and for his failure. For if we live, we get to live for Christ. And if we die, we get to be with Christ. We are in a no-lose situation. For them, they are in a no-win situation. The triumphing of the wicked is short, and the joy of the hypocrite is but for a moment, and then they are cast into hell along with the beast and the false prophet and Satan himself. They go into an eternity of suffering, while we go into an eternity of joy.

You need to think long and hard about whether you are going to experience the first and second resurrection, or the first and second death. The deciding factor between those two outcomes is this: Did you repent of your sins to Jesus Christ, receive Him as your Lord and Savior, and remain faithful to Him?

Or did you love the praise of men and the approval of the world so much, that you went the way of the world and worshiped the gods of the world and sought the pleasures of Babylon? On that great day, you will be called before the throne of God, and you will be judged according to your works, and your works will say that you lived a life of defiance and rebellion against the Lord Jesus Christ. When upon examination that record is established, you will be cast into the lake of fire forever.

But if you maintained the witness of Jesus and you followed the Word of God, and you refused to worship the gods of this world because you were worshiping Jesus Christ as God; then on that great day, judgment will be given in favor of you, you will be enthroned, and you will never run the risk of being in the lake of fire. You will forever be a priest and a king in the kingdom of God, to live in eternal happiness and bliss with the God who made you for Himself.

If you do not have a relationship with this God, you can never be happy in time or in eternity. If you would have a relationship with Him, then repent of your sins and believe in Jesus Christ as your Lord and Savior, and follow Him as His disciple. Those who are faithful to that commitment and to that life will be received into the everlasting habitations of the glory of heaven. May I meet you there in that great day, because you turned away from the gods of this world, and you followed the true and only God Jesus Christ.

59

Satan Loosed, Satan Destroyed, Revelation 20:7–10

> "[7] *And when the thousand years are expired, Satan shall be loosed out of his prison,* [8] *And shall go out to deceive the nations which are in the four quarters of the earth, Gog and Magog, to gather them together to battle: the number of whom is as the sand of the sea.* [9] *And they went up on the breadth of the earth, and compassed the camp of the saints about, and the beloved city: and fire came down from God out of heaven, and devoured them.* [10] *And the devil that deceived them was cast into the lake of fire and brimstone, where the beast and the false prophet are, and shall be tormented day and night for ever and ever.*"

Revelation 20 began the seventh and last parallel section in the book of Revelation. This last parallel section traverses the entire time period between the first and the second coming of Christ, just like the six previous parallel sections did.

Revelation 20:1–3 told us about the binding of Satan by Christ at His first coming. The result of this binding of Satan is that he is now unable to deceive the nations as he did in the past. He is unable to get the nations to work together to persecute the church, or to mount any kind of a transnational effort to destroy the church. Therefore, the church now enjoys a large degree of safety and protection from the persecution of civil governments in this age.

Furthermore, the result of the binding of Satan is that he is unable to stop the spread of the gospel around the world and unable to stop the penetration of the gospel into every nation. The church is able to enter Satan's kingdom and take all of God's elect out of it, and Satan can do nothing to stop it. Because Satan has been bound, he has been helpless to stop the conversion of hundreds of millions of people to faith in Jesus Christ during this age. The result, as Jesus said in Matthew 24:14, is that the gospel of the kingdom has been preached in all the world for a witness to all nations.

However, just because Satan has been bound so he cannot raise up a worldwide persecution against the church and cannot stop the worldwide spread of the church does not mean that he cannot still do a great deal of evil to the people of God. Therefore, as we looked at Revelation 20:4–6, we saw that during this age in which Satan is bound, there are still many who are beheaded for the witness of Jesus and for the word of God because they refuse to worship the false gods of this world.

But the encouragement to the believers in this age is this: when Satan persecutes and kills believers on the earth through his evil agents the Beast, the False Prophet, and Babylon, those same believers immediately go to heaven to rule and reign with Christ throughout this age. Satan's attacks on believers in this age accomplish nothing. It only increases their reward and blessedness because they are received by Christ and enthroned by Christ in the glory of heaven, where they rule and reign with Him until He returns.

This state of Satan being bound, and believers being protected from worldwide persecution so they can engage in a worldwide preaching of the gospel that plunders Satan's kingdom, is said to last for *"a thousand years."* We have seen that this number is symbolic and that it represents the totality of the time between the binding of Satan and the loosing of Satan. This symbolic millennial period has been going on for nearly 2,000 years thus far, and it will continue to go on as long as is needed for all of God's elect to become saved. But when the last elect person has been saved, then our testimony will be finished, and this millennial period of God's protection will be over.

When this millennial period ends, we are told that Satan will be released from the restraint he is currently under. We saw in Revelation 20:3, that when the thousand years is fulfilled, *"after that he must be loosed a little season."* When he is released from his present restraint, the end times will begin, which is that *"little season"* spoken of in verse 3. We do not know when the last elect person will be saved. That event could occur today, or it could occur many centuries into the future. But when it does occur, Satan will be loosed, and he and his helpers will viciously attack the Christian community with an overwhelming assault.

It is important for us to understand the sequence of events here, and to cast off commonly held but erroneous end-times thinking that is propagated by modern Dispensationalism. Many teach that the second coming of Christ is imminent and could occur at any moment, but this simply is not true. The second coming of Christ is not imminent. It cannot occur at any moment. The reason the second coming of Christ is not imminent and cannot occur at any moment is that several very clear and well-defined events must take place before Christ returns.

Before Christ returns, there will be the rise of Antichrist and his one-world government. There will be a widespread falling away from Christ by professing Christians and a large scale betrayal of true Christians by false Christians. The great transnational persecution of the church almost to the point of extinction is going to take place. False Christs and false prophets will be prevalent who will do signs and wonders in order to direct men to worship the Antichrist. There will be a shaking and crumbling of the universe itself. Only after these five events take place will the second coming occur.

Therefore, the second coming of Christ is not imminent. It is not something that could occur at any moment, as the Pre-tribulation rapture teachers would have us believe. All of these signs must come to pass first, and only after they do, will the second coming happen.

We have said that the second coming of Christ is not imminent, but what is imminent and what could occur at any moment is the salvation of the last elect person. Therefore, the loosing of Satan from the restraint he is currently under could happen today if the last elect person were to be saved today. Therefore, we need to always be ready for tremendous persecution to suddenly arise, and we need to always be ready to endure great suffering for Christ. We do not know when the last person will be saved. We do not know how much longer it will be before Satan is loosed. Therefore, we should be grateful for the time of protection we currently live in and do all we can now to spread the gospel and publicly bring glory to God, because the time may soon come when that is no longer possible.

Revelation 20:3 told us that at the end of this millennium of protection the church is currently enjoying, Satan would be released from the restraint on him for what is called a *"little season."* Verses 7 to 10 tell us what the result of that release will be. Satan will incite the nations to unify in an effort to destroy the church from the face of the earth. But before Satan and his helpers are able to complete that task, Jesus will return, He will rescue His saints, and He will cast Satan and all his helpers into the lake of fire.

In the previous chapters in the book of Revelation, the focus has been on Satan's helpers, on their evil work, and on their final defeat. But in chapter 20 the focus is on Satan himself, on his evil work, and on his final defeat. We saw the defeat of those with the mark of the beast in chapter 14. We saw the defeat of Babylon in chapter 18. We saw the defeat of the beast and the false prophet in chapter 19. Now in chapter 20 we are going to see the defeat of Satan.

In chapter 20 we have three major events occurring in relationship to Satan. First of all, Satan is bound; we saw that in verse 2. Then, Satan is loosed; we see that in verse 7. Finally, Satan is burned; we see that in verse 10 when he is cast into the lake of fire. The movement in chapter 20 is as follows: Satan bound, Satan loosed, and Satan burned. We are going to give our attention to this final event at the end of this age when Satan is loosed and then cast into the lake of fire.

The Loosing of Satan from His Bondage

The loosing of Satan from his bondage is in verse 7: *"And when the thousand years are expired, Satan shall be loosed out of his prison."*

We were told in verse 3 that at the end of this symbolic thousand-year period known as the Millennium, Satan would be loosed from his bondage for a *"little season,"* and verse 7 tells us about the fulfillment of that prediction. This little season is a very short period of time in relation to the thousand-year period during which the church enjoys protection from much of Satan's power.

We can gather an idea about just how short this little season is from other passages that speak about this same event. There are three other passages that speak of the length of this little season—two in the book of Revelation and one in the book of Matthew—and we want to look at each of them in turn. The first passage is Revelation 11:1–12:

"And there was given me a reed like unto a rod: and the angel stood, saying, Rise, and measure the temple of God, and the altar, and them that worship therein. 2 But the court which is without the temple leave out, and measure it not; for it is given unto the Gentiles: and the holy city shall they tread under foot forty and two months. 3 And I will give

power unto my two witnesses, and they shall prophesy a thousand two hundred and threescore days, clothed in sackcloth. [4] *These are the two olive trees, and the two candlesticks standing before the God of the earth.* [5] *And if any man will hurt them, fire proceedeth out of their mouth, and devoureth their enemies: and if any man will hurt them, he must in this manner be killed.* [6] *These have power to shut heaven, that it rain not in the days of their prophecy: and have power over waters to turn them to blood, and to smite the earth with all plagues, as often as they will.* [7] *And when they shall have finished their testimony, the beast that ascendeth out of the bottomless pit shall make war against them, and shall overcome them, and kill them.* [8] *And their dead bodies shall lie in the street of the great city, which spiritually is called Sodom and Egypt, where also our Lord was crucified.* [9] *And they of the people and kindreds and tongues and nations shall see their dead bodies three days and an half, and shall not suffer their dead bodies to be put in graves.* [10] *And they that dwell upon the earth shall rejoice over them, and make merry, and shall send gifts one to another; because these two prophets tormented them that dwelt on the earth.* [11] *And after three days and an half the Spirit of life from God entered into them, and they stood upon their feet; and great fear fell upon them which saw them.* [12] *And they heard a great voice from heaven saying unto them, Come up hither. And they ascended up to heaven in a cloud; and their enemies beheld them."* Then immediately upon the rapture of the saints up into heaven, we have the second coming with the sounding of the seventh trumpet.

When we explained this passage in chapters 32–34, we said that the one thousand two hundred and sixty days is the time in which the church bears witness throughout the world. The church is symbolically represented by these two witnesses.

During those symbolic one thousand two hundred and sixty days, the church is unstoppable in its witness and invincible in its progress, as verses 5 and 6 make clear. This long one thousand two hundred and sixty day period is followed by the rise of Antichrist, who is the beast that ascends out of the bottomless pit. It says in 11:7, *"And when they shall have finished their testimony"*—that is, when the last elect person is saved through the witness of the church—then *"the beast that ascendeth out of the bottomless pit shall make war against them."*

When Satan is loosed, Antichrist arises (this beast out of the bottomless pit), and a short symbolic three-and-a half-day period follows, mentioned in verses 9 and 11, in which the church is severely persecuted. We said that three and a half days was less than one-third of one percent of the one thousand two hundred and sixty days that symbolized the church age, in which the church was invincible in bearing witness to the whole world of the gospel of Jesus Christ.

The symbolic one thousand two hundred and sixty days of church witness to the world is equivalent to the symbolic one thousand years of Revelation 20; and the symbolic three and a half days of persecution of the church by Antichrist and his transnational coalition of nations is equivalent to the *"little season"* of Revelation 20:3.

However long the time is that Satan is bound and the church is invincible in its witness to the whole world, the little season that follows is extremely short in relationship to it and in comparison with it. It is just a few years. We have already enjoyed nearly 2,000 years of protection while Satan is bound, and one third of one percent of 2,000 years is only six years.

This passage is telling us that this *"little season,"* in relationship to the long season in which Satan is bound, is a very short *"little season."* The *"little season"* of Satan being loosed to raise up the Antichrist and form the transnational coalition of nations to attempt to destroy the church from the earth will be an extremely short period of time compared to the length of time the church has been powerful and victorious and successful in spreading its message and presence over the whole world.

The second passage is Revelation 17:12–14. It says, *"And the ten horns which thou sawest are ten kings, which have received no kingdom as yet; but receive power as kings one hour with the beast.* [13] *These have one mind, and shall give their power and strength unto the beast.* [14] *These shall make war with the Lamb, and the Lamb shall overcome them: for he is Lord of lords, and King of kings: and they that are with him are called, and chosen, and faithful."*

When we previously examined this passage, we saw these ten kings represent the transnational coalition that the Antichrist (here called the beast) is going to assemble through the power of Satan when Satan is loosed. The time period in which Satan empowers the Antichrist to raise up this transnational coalition of nations to war against the church and against Christ is said symbolically to be *"one hour,"* a term that speaks of a very short period of time in proportion to the time in which the church bears witness to the whole world. Here the symbolic "*one hour*" is equivalent to the "*little season*" of Revelation 20:3.

The third passage is Matthew 24. There is a detailed exposition of Matthew 24 in the appendix of this book that will demonstrate the accuracy of the explanation provided here.

Here, the disciples ask Jesus when His second coming will occur, and what signs will accompany it. We will start with verses 3 to 14, skip down to verse 24, and then to verses 29 to 30 to pick up the relevant passages.

Matthew 24:3–14: "*And as he*" (Jesus) "*sat upon the mount of Olives, the disciples came unto him privately, saying, Tell us, when shall these things be? and what shall be the sign of thy coming, and of the end of the world?* 4 *And Jesus answered and said unto them, Take heed that no man deceive you.* 5 *For many shall come in my name, saying, I am Christ; and shall deceive many.* 6 *And ye shall hear of wars and rumours of wars: see that ye be not troubled: for all these things must come to pass, but the end is not yet.* 7 *For nation shall rise against nation, and kingdom against kingdom: and there shall be famines, and pestilences, and earthquakes, in diverse places.* 8 *All these are the beginning of sorrows.*"

In verses 4–8, Jesus describes the normal characteristics of the church age that have been occurring for the last 2,000 years. But there is a transition with verse 9 that inaugurates the end times when Satan is loosed: "*Then shall they deliver you up to be afflicted, and shall kill you: and ye shall be hated of all nations for my name's sake.* 10 *And then shall many be offended, and shall betray one another, and shall hate one another.* 11 *And many false prophets shall rise, and shall deceive many.* 12 *And because iniquity shall abound, the love of many shall wax cold.* 13 *But he that shall endure unto the end, the same shall be saved.* 14 *And this gospel of the kingdom shall be preached in all the world for a witness unto all nations; and then shall the end come.*"

Skipping down to verse 24: "*For there shall arise false Christs, and false prophets, and shall shew great signs and wonders; insomuch that, if it were possible, they shall deceive the very elect.*" Now to verse 29: "*Immediately after the tribulation of those days shall the sun be darkened, and the moon shall not give her light, and the stars shall fall from heaven, and the powers of the heavens shall be shaken:* 30 *And then shall appear the sign of the Son of man in heaven: and then shall all the tribes of the earth mourn, and they shall see the Son of man coming in the clouds of heaven with power and great glory."*

The period in which Satan is loosed begins at verse 9; and in the subsequent verses, Jesus describes the events and the signs that will precede His coming. Firstly, the gospel will have been preached in all the world for a witness to all nations, and then the end will come. Secondly, believers will be hated by all nations, and the nations will seek to destroy and kill the people of God. Thirdly, there will be great apostasy of the professing church, and the true believers will be betrayed by the false believers. Fourthly, there will arise false prophets and false Christs, who will do signs and wonders so great that, if it were possible, even the elect would be deceived by them. Fifthly, there will be a great disruption of the created universe, in which the natural elements in the heavens will be shaken out of their places. Only after all of these things occur will Jesus return as described in verse 30.

Notice the commentary of Christ in verses 32–34 on the timeframe in which all of these events occur after Satan is loosed. *"Now learn a parable of the fig tree; When his branch is yet tender, and putteth forth leaves, ye know that summer is nigh."* In the spring, we see trees beginning to bud and bloom, and we say to ourselves that summer is on the way.

Verse 33: *"So likewise ye, when ye shall see all these things, know that it"* (the second coming of Christ) *"is near, even at the doors."* Here is our verse: *"[34] Verily I say unto you, This generation shall not pass, till all these things be fulfilled."* Jesus is saying that the generation that sees the things starting at verse 9, will not pass away until they see the event of verse 30—the second coming of Christ.

In other words, these symbolic terms of *"three days and a half"* from Revelation 11; *"one hour,"* from Revelation 17; and *"a little season,"* used in Revelation 20, will not last longer than one generation, because the generation that starts to see the things described beginning at verse 9, will not pass away until it sees the end of these things. The same generation that starts to see the fulfillment of these signs that begin with the loosing of Satan will not pass away until they see the coming of Christ. Since a generation in the Bible is forty years, this little season of Satan being loosed will last no longer than that, and probably significantly less than that.

The time between the loosing of Satan and the second coming of Christ will be very short. It will be just a few years, certainly less than one generation. Antichrist and his transnational coalition gathered together to slaughter the church from off the earth will have a very short reign. Jesus said, in Matthew 24:22, *"And except those days should be shortened, there should no flesh be saved"*—that is, every Christian would be destroyed, *"but for the elect's sake those days shall be shortened"*—that is, those days will only be for a short season, a little season.

To summarize: The three and a half days of Revelation 11:9–11, the one hour of Revelation 17:12, and the single generation of Matthew 24:34, are all equivalent to the little season of Revelation 20:3. Together, they convey the concept that the time that Satan is loosed, and therefore the time the reign of Antichrist and his one-world government will last, will only be a very few years and a very short time.

The Deception Practiced by Satan on the Nations

The deception practiced by Satan on the nations is described in Revelation 20:8–9a. It says in verse 8, speaking of Satan, *"And [he] shall go out to deceive the nations which are in the four quarters of the earth, Gog and Magog, to gather them together to battle: the number of whom is as the sand of the sea. [9] And they went up on the breadth of the earth, and compassed the camp of the saints about, and the beloved city."*

At this point in history, Satan's first goal will be to eradicate the church from the earth, and as soon as he is released from his restraint, he immediately employs his agents to accomplish that task. Satan raises up the Antichrist whom he personally indwells, and uses the false prophet (anti-Christian religion) to deceive the nations of the earth into joining the Antichrist in striving to kill every true Christian.

Jesus said in Matthew 24:11 (after Satan is loosed) that many false prophets would arise and deceive many. Jesus went on to say in Matthew 24:24 that these false prophets will show great signs and wonders that will deceive everyone except the elect.

This process of deceiving the nations into joining the Antichrist to make war against the church is described in Revelation 16:12–16. *"And the sixth angel poured out his vial upon the great river Euphrates; and the water thereof was dried up, that the way of the kings of the east might be prepared. [13] And I saw three unclean spirits like frogs come out of the mouth of the dragon, and out of the mouth of the beast, and out of the mouth of the false prophet.* [14] *For they are the spirits of devils, working miracles, which go forth unto the kings of the earth and of the whole world, to gather them to the battle of that great day of God Almighty.* [15] *Behold, I come as a thief. Blessed is he that watcheth, and keepeth his garments, lest he walk naked, and they see his shame.* [16] *And he gathered them together into a place called in the Hebrew tongue Armageddon."*

When we expounded this passage previously, we said that this sixth vial describes what happens during the little season of Satan's loosing. The removal of the river and the coming of the armies is a symbolic representation of the gathering of the nations under Antichrist to assault the church. But how was this gathering achieved and this unity accomplished in which all the nations of the earth come to serve Antichrist in his persecution of the church?

How this is accomplished is described in verse 14. It is through demonically empowered miracle working that all these false prophets, collectively referred to in verse 13 as "*the*" false prophet, deceive the nations into gathering together under the Antichrist, who is the last manifestation of the beast. These nations gather together under the Antichrist in order to carry out this final war against the church on earth, which is known as the Battle of Armageddon. Satan is going to deceive the nations into following the Antichrist through these false miracles done by the false prophets of anti-Christian religion.

In Revelation 20:8, we are also told that Satan, through his agents the Antichrist and the false prophet, is going to deceive the nations by means of the miracles of these false prophets. He is going to deceive the nations that are in the four quarters of the earth. The four quarters of the earth refers to the four points of the compass: north, south, east, and west.

The point is, this deception is going to be worldwide in its extent, and it is going to be worldwide in its effect. All nations throughout the entire world will be deceived into joining Satan and his Antichrist in a coordinated worldwide assault on the church in an effort to wipe it out completely. This worldwide transnational coalition of nations is collectively referred to in verse 8 as "*Gog and Magog.*"

These names Gog and Magog are taken from the prophecy in Ezekiel 38 and 39. In these two chapters, Gog is the name of a ruler, and Magog is the name of his people and kingdom over which he rules.

Ezekiel prophesies that Gog and his nation and people Magog will attack Israel. But God says that He will defeat them.

Historically, Gog and his people Magog were the enemies of the people of God. John takes these terms from Ezekiel and transfers them to the Antichrist and his people, who are the ultimate enemies of the people of God, and whom God Himself will destroy. Antichrist is referred to by the name Gog, and the coalition of nations serving him is referred to as Magog.

Verse 8 says that they are gathered together to battle, and they are so numerous that they are likened to the number of the grains of the sand of the seashore. That is a big army. This army consists of all of the people on the earth minus the believers. It will therefore be an army of several billion people. Notice verse 9a: *"And they"*—that is, Antichrist and his transnational coalition of all the nations and people on the earth—*"went up on the breadth of the earth, and compassed the camp of the saints about, and the beloved city."*

Verse 9a says of this great army of people that they will go up on the breadth of the earth and compass or surround the camp of the saints. A compass is a circle, and the idea is that they will encircle the camp of the saints and the beloved city.

Both of these terms, *"the camp of the saints"* and *"the beloved city,"* refer to the church, the people of God. The phrase, *"the camp of the saints"*, recalls the image of Israel during her pilgrimage and journey from Egypt to the Promised Land, when she camped in the wilderness. This image speaks of the fact that the church is made up of pilgrims who are on a journey from this world to the new earth, which is our Promised Land. We are aliens and strangers in this world; we are temporarily camped here, and we are traveling through this world because this world is not our home. We are on a journey, so we are the camp of the saints, camping our way through life until we finally get to our home, and camping our way through the centuries until we finally get to the new earth.

The image of "the beloved city" in verse 9, was also spoken of as "the holy city" in Revelation 11:2. It says, *"But the court which is without the temple leave out, and measure it not; for it is given unto the Gentiles: and the holy city shall they tread under foot forty and two months."* When we expounded that passage in chapter 32, we saw that the terms *"the holy city"* and *"the beloved city"* both referred to the same thing.

The symbolic concept of the holy city and the beloved city were fully developed and explained in Revelation 21:1–2, 9–10. Revelation 21:1–2 says, *"And I saw a new heaven and a new earth: for the first heaven and the first earth were passed away; and there was no more sea.* [2] *And I John saw the holy city, new Jerusalem, coming down from God out of heaven, prepared as a bride adorned for her husband."*

Verse 2 says the city is like a bride. This is explained in verses 9 and 10. *"And there came unto me one of the seven angels which had the seven vials full of the seven last plagues, and talked with me, saying, Come hither, I will shew thee the bride, the Lamb's wife.* [10] *And he carried me away in the spirit to a great and high mountain, and shewed me"*; and you would expect it to say, "he showed me a beautiful bride." But instead he says, He showed me *"that great city, the holy Jerusalem, descending out of heaven from God,* [11] *Having the glory of God."*

The holy city and the beloved city and the New Jerusalem are metaphors and symbolic pictures of the church, the bride of Christ. The holy city represents Christian society as it is lived out among the saints as they sojourn together through this world. It is a holy city that is the exact opposite of Babylon, which is the corrupt city that represents anti-Christian society as it functions in this world.

The church in this world is the holy city, the beloved city; but the wicked in this world is Babylon, the corrupt city, the anti-Christian society. We have Christian society, and we have anti-Christian society; we have the holy city, and we have Babylon. The Bible is a tale of two cities.

To summarize: these two terms in Revelation 20:9, *"the camp of the saints"* and *"the beloved city"* are symbolic terms that describe the church in her pilgrimage to the new earth, and the church in her society as she lives in a community of fellowship awaiting the coming of her Husband.

Clearly, the church is not in a single geographic locality at this point in history, because the gospel has been preached in the whole world, and only then does the end come. The church is scattered all across the face of the earth and it resides in every country. This is why the nations go up on the breadth of the earth, and surround the believers wherever they may be found, in an effort to destroy them wherever they may reside.

The assault of this transnational coalition of nations on the church wherever it is located on the earth is a unified, coordinated effort, as described in Revelation 11:7–10. It describes the assault on the camp of the saints in the beloved city. *"And when they"*—that is, the believers—*"shall have finished their testimony,"*—when they have preached the gospel to the whole world and all of the elect are saved, *"the beast that ascendeth out of the bottomless pit"*—that is, Antichrist indwelt by Satan—*"shall make war against them, and shall overcome them, and kill them."* The war will be successful. The church will be overcome; the church will be largely killed and destroyed. Only a small remnant will escape.

Verse 8: *"And their dead bodies shall lie in the street of the great city"*; notice, the great city is not the holy city. The great city is Babylon. Babylon represents anti-Christian society, wherever it is across the earth. Babylon is consistently called *"that great city"* throughout Revelation. When it speaks of the great city here, it is talking about Babylon. *"That great city which spiritually is called Sodom and Egypt, where also our Lord was crucified."*

"[9]And they of the people and kindreds and tongues and nations" is the transnational coalition—the whole unsaved world represented in verse 9a. Verse 9b says that they *"shall see their dead bodies three days and an half, and shall not suffer their dead bodies to be put in graves,"* which manifests the tremendous disrespect, dishonor, and scorn they pour out upon those they have slaughtered. *"[10] And they that dwell upon the earth shall rejoice over them, and make merry, and shall send gifts one to another; because these two prophets"* who represent the church in its witness and evangelism *"tormented them that dwelt on the earth."*

We have been tormenting the world for 2,000 years by preaching the gospel to unbelievers. They are tired of it. We have been telling them they are sinners living in defiance against God and on their way to hell. We tell them they need to repent, believe in Jesus Christ as their Lord and Savior, and live for His glory. And while the elect embrace the message, the rest of the world hates us for it, and they are finally going to get their opportunity to silence our voice once for all.

Notice also Revelation 13:6–7 which speaks of the final manifestation of the beast, who is the Antichrist. It says, *"And he opened his mouth in blasphemy against God, to blaspheme his name, and his tabernacle, and them that dwell in heaven. [7] And it was given unto him to make war with the saints, and to overcome them: and power was given him over all kindreds, and tongues, and nations."* There is the transnational coalition that makes war on the church and overcomes it.

This is the work that Satan deceives the nations into doing, and this is the work he gathers them together to accomplish. Operating through the apostate church, the united nations of the world will be deceived into working together to eradicate every Christian from the face of the earth. They will be largely successful in doing so, to the point that the public witness and the visible presence of the church will be removed from the earth, and only a tiny remnant scattered and in hiding will be left. When the last push is made to take them out, that is when Jesus returns.

The Destruction of Satan in the Lake of Fire

The destruction of Satan in the lake of fire is in verses 9b to 10. As they are surrounding the camp of the saints and are about to wipe out the last of them, it says, *"And fire came down from God out of heaven, and devoured them.* [10] *And the devil that deceived them was cast into the lake of fire and brimstone, where the beast and the false prophet are, and shall be tormented day and night for ever and ever."*

This worldwide transnational, coordinated effort to destroy the Christians from the face of the earth will be largely successful, to the point that the visible presence and the public witness of the church will be eliminated. The church will be slain and the church will be silenced except for a small remnant that have managed to flee and hide. When they are about to be discovered and destroyed as well, Christ will return to rescue them, by resurrecting the dead bodies of the martyred Christians, transforming the living believers and rapturing them all up to heaven, and then destroying Satan and all of his people.

As it becomes apparent to Antichrist, who is Gog, and to the nations that serve him, who are Magog, that Jesus is appearing in the heavens to rescue His people, Antichrist and his people will prepare themselves to fight against Christ Himself. By way of illustration, if an evil man is beating up another man's wife, and he has nearly killed her, but then the woman's husband shows up; the evil man will have to leave the wife he is beating and turn and fight the husband who has come to defend his wife. In the same way, Satan has virtually killed the bride of Christ on earth, but then the husband, Jesus, shows up, and now Antichrist has to turn and face the new Adversary who is coming to deliver His bride.

We see this in chapter 19. The second half of chapter 19 describes the second coming of Christ. Notice verse 12: "*His eyes were as a flame of fire, and on his head were many crowns.*" Verse 19: "*And I saw the beast, and the kings of the earth, and their armies, gathered together to make war against him that sat on the horse, and against his army.*" Now all the kings of the earth who make up this transnational coalition, together with Antichrist and the false prophet, turn and are going to make war against the returning husband, who is Christ.

We also see this in Revelation 17:12–14: "*And the ten horns which thou sawest are ten kings, which have received no kingdom as yet; but [will] receive power as kings one hour with the beast,*" "[13] *These have one mind, and shall give their power and strength unto the beast.*" Now here it is: "[14] *These shall make war with the Lamb, and the Lamb shall overcome them: for he is Lord of lords, and King of kings.*"

Notice 20:9–10. "*And they went up on the breadth of the earth, and compassed [surrounded] the camp of the saints about, and the beloved city: and fire came down from God out of heaven, and devoured them.* [10] *And the devil that deceived them was cast into the lake of fire and brimstone, where the beast and the false prophet are, and shall be tormented day and night for ever and ever.*"

When it says in verse 9b that fire came down from God out of heaven and destroyed them, this is a reference to 2 Thessalonians 1:7–10 which says, "*And to you who are troubled rest with us, when the Lord Jesus shall be revealed from heaven with his mighty angels.*" This is the second coming. Notice verse 8: "*In flaming fire taking vengeance on them that know not God, and that obey not the gospel of our Lord Jesus Christ:* [9] *Who shall be punished with everlasting destruction from the presence of the Lord, and from the glory of his power;* [10] *When he shall come to be glorified in his saints, and to be admired in all them that believe.*" When it says that fire came down from God out of heaven and devoured them, this is the fire. It is Jesus coming in flaming fire, taking vengeance on them that know not God and that obey not the gospel of the Lord Jesus.

This is further described in 2 Thessalonians 2. Notice verse 8. It says, "*And then shall that Wicked [one] be revealed,*" speaking of Antichrist, "*whom the Lord shall consume with the spirit of his mouth, and shall destroy with the brightness of his coming.*" Revelation tells us three times that His eyes are like a flame of fire.

When Jesus comes, He comes in flaming fire; and the brilliance of His glory with the anger of His justice flames out against the world and kills every single unsaved person on the face of the earth, because they are all that is left on the earth. When Jesus first appears, He resurrects the dead bodies of the saints that are in heaven, He transforms the bodies of the few remaining saints that are on earth, and He raptures them both up into heaven. All the saints are now with Him in glorified bodies, and then flaming fire falls on the wicked left on earth and it burns up every one of them. All of the unsaved people are put to death.

Revelation 19:20–21: *"And the beast was taken, and with him the false prophet that wrought miracles before him, with which he deceived them that had received the mark of the beast, and them that worshipped his image. These both were cast alive into a lake of fire burning with brimstone.* 21 *And the remnant were slain with the sword of him that sat upon the horse, which sword proceeded out of his mouth: and all the fowls were filled with their flesh."*

Jesus destroys the beast, He destroys the false prophet, and He destroys all those who have the mark of the beast. They are all dead in one blast of flaming fire. That is why there is no Battle of Armageddon. Antichrist and his people gather together to battle against the church, and they slaughter most of the church, and when they are just about to slaughter the rest, Jesus returns. But it is not a battle; it is a wipeout. It is not like Antichrist has a military assault and pushes Jesus back a little; and then Jesus has a military assault and pushes Antichrist back a little; and finally, after going back and forth in battle, Jesus wins. There is a blast of flaming fire, and it is over.

What is the result of this coming of Christ in flaming fire to exercise vengeance? Verse 10 tells us that Satan is burned. *"And the devil that deceived them was cast into the lake of fire and brimstone, where the beast and the false prophet are, and shall be tormented day and night for ever and ever."* He is cast into the lake of fire, where the beast and false prophet are, where he will never again be able to harm us for all eternity, and where he will be tormented day and night forever and ever.

This is the absolute and final end of Satan and his kingdom and his power. He will suffer forever for his sins against God and against us. He will be fully repaid and recompensed for all the evil he has done.

We will be fully delivered from his destructive work, and though he came to kill and to steal and to destroy, he will never do so again for all eternity. Satan is finished. His head, as Genesis 3:15 says, has been crushed. What he did in the garden has now been completely undone; his kingdom and his person have been destroyed; the garden is restored in the new earth; and it is as though Satan has never existed and never done a thing, so perfect and glorious is the restoration achieved by Christ.

It says in 1 John 3:8, *"For this purpose the Son of God was manifested, that he might destroy the works of the devil,"* and this is the ultimate and final destruction of the work of the devil. When Jesus returns, all those who have the mark of the beast, the false prophet, the Antichrist, and Satan himself are all cast into the lake of fire.

This final destruction is described in Isaiah 14:12–17. It says: *"How art thou fallen from heaven, O Lucifer, son of the morning! how art thou cut down to the ground, which didst weaken the nations!* [13] *For thou hast said in thine heart, I will ascend into heaven, I will exalt my throne above the stars of God: I will sit also upon the mount of the congregation, in the sides of the north:* [14] *I will ascend above the heights of the clouds; I will be like the most High."*

Verses 13 and 14 describe what Satan has always aspired to be and to do, and this is what he was attempting to do once he was loosed. But notice verses 15–17: *"Yet thou shalt be brought down to hell, to the sides of the pit.* [16] *They that see thee shall narrowly look upon thee, and consider thee, saying, Is this the man that made the earth to tremble, that did shake kingdoms;* [17] *That made the world as a wilderness, and destroyed the cities thereof; that opened not the house of his prisoners?"* Jesus opens the prison for all of His people as Isaiah 61:1 says, but Satan cannot open the prison that holds his people. Jesus is a powerful savior, but Satan is a pathetic failure.

This is the great, final, and climactic triumph of the Lord Jesus over Satan and his kingdom and all of his helpers. Throughout all eternity, we will not have to deal with any of them, for they are all eternally confined to the lake of fire.

The question I have to ask is this: Whom are you identified with? Are you identified with Satan, or with Christ? If you are identified with Satan, you will have his end. You will be cast into the lake of fire along with him. But if you are Christ's, if you have repented of your sins and believed in Him and served Him as Lord and Savior, He will deliver you into the new earth. Though the wicked may do us great injury, they can never permanently harm us. Christ will deliver us, and we will be with Him forever.

This is the glorious end of the story of Christ destroying all of His enemies. May God give us the courage to keep fighting the good fight of faith, to resist the devil who must flee from us, and not give in to his evil devices and his temptations, for we know his end. Let us not share in it by submitting to him; but rather, let us depart from it by resisting the devil and fighting against him.

60

The Day of Judgment, Revelation 20:11–15

> "[11] *And I saw a great white throne, and him that sat on it,*
> *from whose face the earth and the heaven fled away; and there*
> *was found no place for them.* [12] *And I saw the dead, small*
> *and great, stand before God; and the books were opened: and*
> *another book was opened, which is the book of life: and the*
> *dead were judged out of those things which were written in*
> *the books, according to their works.* [13] *And the sea gave up*
> *the dead which were in it; and death and hell delivered up the*
> *dead which were in them: and they were judged every man*
> *according to their works.* [14] *And death and hell were cast into*
> *the lake of fire. This is the second death.* [15] *And whosoever*
> *was not found written in the book of life was cast into the*
> *lake of fire.*"

The certainty of a final day of judgment for all humanity is a prominent teaching in the Scriptures. Hebrews 9:27 says, "*It is appointed unto men once to die, but after this the judgment.*" The Bible makes it clear in many passages that there will be a single, final day of judgment at the end of this age when Christ returns. It is important to understand that there is only one final judgment, at which every human who has ever lived will be judged. The Bible always speaks of the future judgment as a single event. It teaches us to look forward to the *Day* of Judgment, not the *Days* of Judgment. The Day of Judgment is always stated in the singular. It is never stated in the plural.

For example, Jesus said in Matthew 12:36 that "*every idle word that men shall speak, they shall give account thereof in the day of judgment.*" Paul says of God in Acts 17:31 that "*he hath appointed a day, in the which he will judge the world in righteousness.*" Numerous other passages use identical language, clearly showing that there is a single Day of Judgment, and there are no others.

The Bible is also clear that both believers and unbelievers will appear together before God at the same time to be judged all at once. This is taught in numerous passages. For example, in Matthew 25:31–46, in Romans 2:5–11, and in Revelation 11:17–18, both the saved and the unsaved appear together at the same time before Christ on the Day of Judgment.

All of these passages rebut the dispensational teaching that there will be three separate judgments. Dispensationalists say that there will be a judgment of believers at the rapture, to apportion rewards to each of them; and then seven years later at the second coming, there will be a judgment of the nations, to determine which of them are worthy to enter the millennial kingdom; and then finally, a thousand years after that at the end of the Millennium, there will be a judgment of all the unbelievers who ever lived.

This teaching of three separate judgments separated by periods of time is false, because Dispensationalists separate events over a long span of time that actually all occur closely together. The end of the Millennium, the rapture, and the second coming all occur in close proximity to each other at the end of this age. There cannot be three separate judgments for events that all occur in rapid succession. At the end of this age, there is one single judgment in which all men are judged, some of whom enter into eternal life in the new earth, and some of whom enter into eternal death in the lake of fire.

The purpose of this final judgment is to vindicate the justice of God, to vindicate the people of God, and to vanquish the enemies of God.

People often ask how God can be just when there is so much evil in the world. That charge would be valid if the evil in the world was never justly dealt with and punished in the end. But the final judgment is the vindication of God as being just because at the final judgment every wrong is properly punished, every evil receives its just recompense, and every good deed is properly rewarded.

God will perfectly balance the scales of justice on the last day, and the charge of God being unjust will be forever laid to rest. Just because we do not see perfect justice now does not mean that God is unjust, because He will bring perfect justice in the end on the Day of Judgment.

In this life, believers suffer a tremendous amount of persecution, scorn, hatred, and rejection. Society treats believers as being evil, and it views them with contempt. Believers suffer many injustices for the name of Christ and because of their loyalty to Him.

But Jesus promised to reward believers for their loyalty to Him. He said in Matthew 5:10–12, *"Blessed are they which are persecuted for righteousness' sake: for theirs is the kingdom of heaven.* [11] *Blessed are ye, when men shall revile you, and persecute you, and shall say all manner of evil against you falsely, for my sake.* [12] *Rejoice, and be exceeding glad: for great is your reward in heaven."*

The Day of Judgment is when Christ fulfills all those promises to believers and shows the wicked world that believers are indeed the blessed ones and the rewarded ones, and that the world's treatment and assessment of them was in fact completely unjust. On the Day of Judgment, Christ vindicates His people before the whole world, and He richly rewards His people for their service to Him before their eyes.

On the Day of Judgment, God will vanquish all of His enemies and punish them forever in the lake of fire for all the evil they have carried out against His name and His people. God has said, *"Vengeance is mine; I will repay, saith the Lord,"* and this is the day of repayment and vengeance. The Bible's description of the Day of Judgment tells us that it is a terrible thing to fall into the hands of an angry God, but it also tells us that it is a wonderful thing to be received into the arms of a loving God.

The difference between facing an angry God or a loving God on the Day of Judgment is the difference between rebelling against and rejecting Christ, or repenting of sin and receiving Christ as the Lord and Savior of your life.

The subject of the Day of Judgment is a very serious and sobering matter to contemplate. It demands our most focused thought and our most intense self-examination as to what our outcome will be on that day. There is nothing you will do in this life, and I mean absolutely nothing, that is more important than to be prepared to face God on the Day of Judgment. Nothing else matters besides that.

The Day of Judgment is real. We will all meet there. Our eternal destiny will be declared there, and there will be no appeal. What is described in Revelation 20:11–15 is exactly what we will see and experience; and therefore, we need to take it very, very seriously—more seriously than we have ever taken anything in our life.

The Time of the Final Judgment

The Bible, both in the Old Testament and the New Testament, tells us repeatedly that the final judgment takes place when Christ returns. We will look at one major passage in the Old Testament and one major passage in the New Testament in order to demonstrate this point.

First of all, notice the final judgment in the Old Testament described in Daniel 7. When we were explaining Revelation 11, we paused to examine Daniel 2 and Daniel 7. There, we talked about the flow and unfolding of human history.

Daniel 7:1–14 says, *"In the first year of Belshazzar king of Babylon Daniel had a dream and visions of his head upon his bed: then he wrote the dream, and told the sum of the matters.* [2] *Daniel spake and said, I saw in my vision by night, and, behold, the four winds of the heaven strove upon the great sea.* [3] *And four great beasts came up from the sea, diverse one from another.* [4] *The first was like a lion, and had eagle's wings: I beheld till the wings thereof were plucked, and it was lifted up from the earth, and made stand upon the feet as a man, and a man's heart was given to it.* [5] *And behold another beast, a second, like to a bear, and it raised up itself on one side, and it had three ribs in the mouth of it between the teeth of it: and they said thus unto it, Arise, devour much flesh.* [6] *After this I beheld, and lo another, like a leopard, which had upon the back of it four wings of a fowl; the beast had also four heads; and dominion was given to it.* [7] *After this I saw in the night visions, and behold a fourth beast, dreadful and terrible, and strong exceedingly; and it had great iron teeth: it devoured and brake in pieces, and stamped the residue with the feet of it: and it was diverse from all the beasts that were before it; and it had ten horns.* [8] *I considered the horns, and, behold, there came up among them another little horn, before whom there were three of the first horns plucked up by the roots: and, behold, in this horn were eyes like the eyes of man, and a mouth speaking great things.*

"[9] *I beheld till the thrones were cast down, and the Ancient of days did sit, whose garment was white as snow, and the hair of his head like the pure wool: his throne was like the fiery flame, and his wheels as burning fire.* [10] *A fiery stream issued and came forth from before him: thousand thousands ministered unto him, and ten thousand times ten thousand stood before him: the judgment was set, and the books were opened.* [11] *I beheld then because of the voice of the great words which the horn spake: I beheld even till the beast was slain, and his body destroyed, and given to the burning flame.* [12] *As concerning the rest of the beasts, they had their dominion taken away: yet their lives were prolonged for a season and time.* [13] *I saw in the night visions, and, behold, one like the Son of man came with the clouds of heaven, and came to the Ancient of days, and they brought him near before him.* [14] *And there was given him dominion, and glory, and a kingdom, that all people, nations, and languages, should serve him: his dominion is an everlasting dominion, which shall not pass away, and his kingdom that which shall not be destroyed."*

These four beasts symbolized the successive world empires that will arise on earth, from Daniel's day to the very end of time. These successive world empires will conclude with the reign of Antichrist, who is the "little horn" that comes up on the fourth beast that is described. When these world empires have run their course, concluding with the reign of the Antichrist, we read that the Ancient of Days comes in conjunction with Christ, here pictured as the Son of man in verses 13 and 14. When the Ancient of Days and the Son of man come at the end of the reign of Antichrist, the final judgment is set, and, as it says in verse 10, the books are opened.

In the expanded explanation the angel gives to Daniel in the remainder of the chapter in verses 19 to 27, the same sequence follows: Antichrist appears, and then God comes, and the final judgment commences, and the everlasting kingdom of God is established, which is the new heavens and the new earth.

Notice verses 19 to 22: *"Then I would know the truth of the fourth beast, which was diverse from all the others, exceeding dreadful, whose teeth were of iron, and his nails of brass; which devoured, brake in pieces, and stamped the residue with his feet;* [20] *And of the ten horns that were in his head, and of the other which came up, and before whom three fell; even of that horn that had eyes, and a mouth that spake very great things, whose look was more stout than his fellows."* That horn is the Antichrist. "[21] *I beheld, and the same horn made war with the saints,"* which is the final transnational persecution of the saints after Satan is loosed as described in Revelation 20:7–10, *"and the same horn made war with the saints, and prevailed against them"*—virtually wiping them off the face of the earth—"[22] *Until the Ancient of days came, and judgment was given to the saints of the most High"*; this is the second coming and the final judgment, *"and the time came that the saints possessed the kingdom"*; that is, the new heavens and the new earth. We see the age proceeds from Nebuchadnezzar to the rise of Antichrist. He virtually wipes the church off the face of the earth; then the final judgment comes; Antichrist is destroyed and cast into the lake of fire; and the saints possess the kingdom.

The same thing is described again in more detail in verses 23 to 27. *"Thus he said, The fourth beast shall be the fourth kingdom upon earth, which shall be diverse from all kingdoms, and shall devour the whole earth, and shall tread it down, and break it in pieces.* [24] *And the ten horns out of this kingdom are ten kings that shall arise: and another shall rise after them"* (the Antichrist); *"and he shall be diverse from the first, and he shall subdue three kings.* [25] *And he shall speak great words against the most High, and shall wear out the saints of the most High"* (this is the persecution in the end times), *"and think to change times and laws"* (Antichrist is going to throw away God's laws and establish the laws of Antichrist); *"and they"* (the saints) *"shall be given into his hand until a time and times and the dividing of time"*—that is, the three and a half days spoken of in Revelation 11:9–11, which is the period of Satan's loosing, when the saints are going to be given into the hand of the Antichrist.

Verse 26: *"But the judgment shall sit, and they shall take away his dominion, to consume and to destroy it unto the end."* That is the final judgment. "[27] *And the kingdom and dominion, and the greatness of the kingdom under the whole heaven, shall be given to the people of the saints of the most High, whose kingdom is an everlasting kingdom, and all dominions shall serve and obey him."* That is the new heavens and the new earth.

Here we see this sequence unfolding from Daniel's day to the very end of time. At the end of time, after the rise of Antichrist and his short period of success against the church, Christ and His Father come, the judgment is set, the books are opened, judgment is rendered, the wicked are cast into the lake of fire, and the righteous are conducted into the everlasting kingdom.

In Daniel 7:10, it says in the last phrase, *"the judgment was set, and the books"*—plural—*"were opened."* Here we have the books that record the works of men. Now notice Daniel 12:1–3: *"And at that time shall Michael stand up, the great prince which standeth for the children of thy people: and there shall be a time of trouble, such as never was since there was a nation even to that same time: and at that time thy people shall be delivered, every one that shall be found written in the book"* (singular). Verse 2 continues: *"And many of them that sleep in the dust of the earth shall awake, some to everlasting life, and some to shame and everlasting contempt.* [3] *And they that be wise shall shine as the brightness of the firmament; and they that turn many to righteousness as the stars for ever and ever."*

In Daniel 12:1, we see Michael rising and standing up for the people of God. This is a reference to Revelation 12:7–12 when Satan is cast out of heaven by Michael. He is cast down to the earth, and it says in verse 12, "*Woe to the inhabiters of the earth. . . .*" "You are going to have great trouble now that Satan is cast down to the earth, and he knows he has but a little time." This last 2,000 years has been a time period of tremendous tribulation for the people of God as they have sought to advance the kingdom of God across the world. But this tribulation caused by Satan will be immeasurably worse in the end times after Satan is loosed because Daniel says, regarding this period, that "*there shall be a time of trouble, such as never was since there was a nation even to that same time.*"

But at the end of that time it says, *"thy people shall be delivered"* (which will occur when Jesus returns) *"every one that shall be found written in the book."* Daniel then talks about the general resurrection, *"and many of them that sleep in the dust of the earth shall awake, some to everlasting life, and some to shame and everlasting contempt."* This is the final judgment and the final disposition of the people. Those who are written in the book shall be resurrected to life, and those who are not written in the book shall be resurrected to shame and everlasting contempt and will be cast into hell.

So we see the *books* in Daniel 7:10, and then we see the *book* in Daniel 12:1. We have the books of works, and then we have the book of life. Both of these books are spoken of in Revelation 20:12 at the final judgment.

Having seen the final judgment in the Old Testament described, notice secondly, the final judgment in the New Testament described in Matthew 24. (There is a detailed exposition of this chapter in the appendix).

Matthew 24 and 25 form a single unit of eschatological teaching that describes future events from the time of the first coming of Jesus to the time of the second coming of Jesus, the final judgment, and the eternal state.

Notice Matthew 24:3: *"And as he"* (Jesus) *"sat upon the mount of Olives, the disciples came unto him privately, saying, Tell us, when shall these things be? and what shall be the sign of thy coming, and of the end of the world?"* The question is: "When are You coming back, and when is the world going to end?" These questions imply those two things are going to happen at the same time.

Jesus then tells them the things that do not constitute the signs of His second coming and the end of the world in verses 4 to 8. These things in verses 4 to 8 are the things that are going to characterize the entire age from start to finish until the end times come. We are living in this period described by verses 4 to 8 right now.

But in verses 9 to 29, Jesus tells them the things that do constitute the signs of His coming and are signs of the end of the world. Once all of those signs recorded in verses 9 to 29 come to pass, the second coming takes place. Verse 30 says, after the signs of verses 9 to 29 occur, *"And then shall appear the sign of the Son of man in heaven: and then shall all the tribes of the earth mourn, and they shall see the Son of man coming in the clouds of heaven with power and great glory. 31 And he shall send his angels with a great sound of a trumpet, and they shall gather together his elect from the four winds, from one end of heaven to the other."*

Matthew 25:31 takes up the language of 24:30–31 and continues the description of what occurs after the second coming. "*When the Son of man shall come in his glory, and all the holy angels with him, then shall he sit upon the throne of his glory: 32 And before him shall be gathered all nations: and he shall separate them one from another, as a shepherd divideth his sheep from the goats: 33 And he shall set the sheep on his right hand, but the goats on the left.*" At this point the books are opened, and the record of the behavior of the people is read and declared.

Here is the record of the behavior of the sheep—those who are saved: "*34 Then shall the King say unto them on his right hand, Come, ye blessed of my Father, inherit the kingdom prepared for you from the foundation of the world: 35 For I was an hungred, and ye gave me meat: I was thirsty, and ye gave me drink: I was a stranger, and ye took me in: 36 Naked, and ye clothed me: I was sick, and ye visited me: I was in prison, and ye came unto me. 37 Then shall the righteous answer him, saying, Lord, when saw we thee an hungred, and fed thee? or thirsty, and gave thee drink? 38 When saw we thee a stranger, and took thee in? or naked, and clothed thee?* [39] *Or when saw we thee sick, or in prison, and came unto thee?* [40] *And the King shall answer and say unto them, Verily I say unto you, Inasmuch as ye have done it unto one of the least of these my brethren, ye have done it unto me."*

Here is the record of the behavior of the goats—those who are not saved: "[41] *Then shall he say also unto them on the left hand, Depart from me, ye cursed, into everlasting fire, prepared for the devil and his angels:* [42] *For I was an hungred, and ye gave me no meat: I was thirsty, and ye gave me no drink:* [43] *I was a stranger, and ye took me not in: naked, and ye clothed me not: sick, and in prison, and ye visited me not.* [44] *Then shall they also answer him, saying, Lord, when saw we thee an hungred, or athirst, or a stranger, or naked, or sick, or in prison, and did not minister unto thee?* [45] *Then shall he answer them, saying, Verily I say unto you, Inasmuch as ye did it not to one of the least of these, ye did it not to me.* [46] *And these shall go away into everlasting punishment: but the righteous into life eternal."*

The books are opened, the works are read, and based on the works that they did or did not do, their eternal destiny is declared and their disposition is made, either into the new heavens and the new earth or into the lake of fire. Once again, we see that the final judgment takes place at the second coming of Christ, and once again, just like in the book of Daniel, the righteous and the wicked appear before the Judge at the same time at the end of human history after the second coming of Christ, and they are all sent either into everlasting life or into everlasting punishment in the lake of fire. None of them is sent into some kind of a thousand-year millennial kingdom that follows the second coming, as the Dispensationalists would have us believe.

The pattern we saw in Daniel 7 and in Matthew 25 is the same pattern that occurs in Revelation 20. In Revelation 20, Satan is bound at the first coming of Christ in verses 1 to 3. Throughout this present age in which we live, Christians are martyred but taken immediately to heaven in verses 4 to 6.

At the end of this age, Satan is loosed, the Antichrist and the nations attempt to wipe the church off the face of the earth, and Jesus returns with flaming fire to rescue His church and destroy His enemies, in verses 7 to 10. And then immediately upon His second coming, the final judgment begins, in verses 11 to 15.

This exact same pattern repeats itself over and over again in the Scriptures. The small and the great stand before God, the books of men's works and the book of life are opened, and the judgment is rendered. All men are sent either into the lake of fire, verse 15: *"And whosoever was not found written in the book of life was cast into the lake of fire"*; or, they are sent into the new heavens and the new earth, 21:1–3*: "And I saw a new heaven and a new earth: for the first heaven and the first earth were passed away; and there was no more sea.* [2] *And I John saw the holy city, new Jerusalem, coming down from God out of heaven, prepared as a bride adorned for her husband.* [3] *And I heard a great voice out of heaven saying, Behold, the tabernacle of God is with men, and he will dwell with them, and they shall be his people, and God himself shall be with them, and be their God."*

The Bible is clear: there is this age that concludes with the second coming and the final judgment of all men, all at once, whether saved or lost; and then there is the age to come, in which men live forever either in the lake of fire or in the new earth with its new heavens. This is the chronology of time and eternity as to when the judgment occurs, who is there, and what happens when it takes place.

The Process of the Final Judgment

In verses 11–15, we are told what the process of the final judgment will be. First of all, notice the throne and its occupant. Verse 11: *"And I saw a great white throne, and him that sat on it."*

The throne of judgment is called *"a great white throne."* We saw in Matthew 25:31 that the throne of judgment was called *"the throne of his glory."* In Daniel 7:9, His throne was said to be like *"a fiery flame."* Each of these various terms that describe the nature of God's throne tells us something about that throne. It is a great throne, showing its overwhelming authority. It is a white throne, showing its absolute purity. It is a throne of glory, showing its tremendous magnificence. It is a throne like a fiery flame, showing its awesome fearfulness.

The throne of God has played a prominent role in the book of Revelation. The throne of God is described in Revelation chapters 1, 3, 4, 5, 6, 7, 8, 12, 14, 16, 19, 20, 21, and 22, and is often mentioned numerous times in each of those chapters.

The reason the throne of God is mentioned so often, and why it plays such a prominent role in the book of Revelation, is to show that God is in sovereign control of all the events of history, that all that occurs is under His direction and is done by His authority, and that every person is accountable to Him for all he or she does. The book of Revelation is filled with references to the throne of God to remind suffering saints as they progress through this age that God is in control of all and that He is sovereign over all.

This brings us great comfort as we are assaulted by the Wicked One and his servants. Even though people today do not acknowledge the existence of that throne, and they do not bow before the authority of that throne, one day, every one of them will appear before that throne and be judged by the One who sits upon it. You do not defy the throne of God and escape unscathed. The book of Revelation makes that abundantly clear.

The occupant of this throne is Christ Himself. Matthew 25:31 says it is *"the Son of man"* who sits on the throne of His glory, judging the people of the earth on the last day. Furthermore, Jesus said in John 5:22, *"For the Father judgeth no man, but hath committed all judgment unto the Son."*

Jesus goes on to say in John 5:25–27, *"Verily, verily, I say unto you, The hour is coming, and now is, when the dead shall hear the voice of the Son of God: and they that hear shall live.* [26] *For as the Father hath life in himself; so hath he given to the Son to have life in himself;* [27] *And hath given him authority to execute judgment also, because he is the Son of man."*

Acts 17:31 says that God *"hath appointed a day, in the which he will judge the world in righteousness by that man whom he hath ordained; whereof he hath given assurance unto all men, in that he hath raised him from the dead."*

Second Corinthians 5:10 says that *"we must all appear before the judgment seat of Christ; that every one may receive the things done in his body, according to that he hath done, whether it be good or bad."*

In 2 Timothy 4:1, Paul says to Timothy, *"I charge thee therefore before God, and the Lord Jesus Christ, who shall judge the [living] and the dead at his appearing and his kingdom;* [2] *Preach the word. . ."*

This same Jesus Christ the world condemned and crucified and mocked and rejected is the One they are going to have to answer to, and He is the One who is going to pass judgment on them. All men will have to face Jesus Christ as their judge and give an account to Him of how they dealt with Him. The question will be this: Did you honor Christ as God? Did you recognize Him as your Lord? Did you trust in Him as your Savior? Or: Did you reject His claims, ignore His authority, and despise His name? Your works will reveal the answer.

The time to submit to Jesus Christ is now, and thereby obtain His smile and favor on the Day of Judgment. As for those who will not submit to Christ now, their knees shall bow anyway, and their tongues shall confess that Christ is Lord, as they are being cast into the lake of fire.

Secondly, notice the objects of the judgment.

The first object of judgment is the earth and the heaven. Notice verse 11: *"And I saw a great white throne, and him that sat on it, from whose face the earth and the heaven fled away; and there was found no place for them."*

The natural creation became fallen when Adam fell, and therefore God's judgment must fall on it because of its corruption. Romans 8:19–21 tells us about the corruption of the natural creation that came upon it as a result of Adam's fall. A corrupt creation cannot stand before a holy God, and therefore it is symbolically said to flee from the face of God, where it is cast into a kind of hell, as described in 2 Peter 3.

In 2 Peter 3, the subject matter is the second coming of Christ. The day of His coming is called the day of the Lord. Notice verses 10 to 12. *"But the day of the Lord will come as a thief in the night; in the which the heavens shall pass away with a great noise, and the elements shall melt with fervent heat, the earth also and the works that are therein shall be burned up.* [11] *Seeing then that all these things shall be dissolved, what manner of persons ought ye to be in all holy conversation and godliness,* [12] *Looking for and hasting unto the coming of the day of God, wherein the heavens being on fire shall be dissolved, and the elements shall melt with fervent heat?"*

The result of this judgment on the old fallen corrupt creation is that it will go through a fiery hell of judgment, and then it will be re-made into a sinless, perfect new creation. Notice verse 13: *"Nevertheless we, according to his promise, look for new heavens and a new earth, wherein dwelleth righteousness."* Both Isaiah 51:6 and Hebrews 1:10–12 speak of this same event.

Because of sin, this world we live in now is a corrupt, ruined, and fallen world, with its natural disasters, its deadly diseases, its destructive animals, and its noxious plants. All of that will be done away with in the new heavens and the new earth. Eden will be restored, and every effect of the fall will be removed.

The second object of judgment is all of humanity, verses 12–13. *"And I saw the dead, small and great, stand before God; and the books were opened: and another book was opened,"* (notice *books*, plural; and *book*, singular) *"which is the book of life: and the dead were judged out of those things which were written in the books, according to their works.* [13] *And the sea gave up the dead which were in it; and death and hell delivered up the dead which were in them: and they were judged every man according to their works."*

Verses 12 and 13 speak of the resurrection of all the dead who have ever lived on the face of the earth. The dead, small and great, encompass the totality of all of humanity, from Adam to the last person born on earth. This phrase *"small and great"* is used to refer to all believers in Revelation 11:18, and it is also used to refer to all unbelievers in Revelation 19:18. The *"small and great"* encompass all the believers and all the unbelievers, in other words, all the people who have ever lived.

No one will be absent from the Day of Judgment, and no one will escape the Day of Judgment. There will be 100 percent attendance. It is not going be like some people today who choose to opt out of going to church on Sunday. Nobody will be able to say, "I do not want to go to the Day of Judgment today." Absence is not an option. You are coming to the Day of Judgment. The angels will see to that.

Whether the bodies of people were buried at sea, or whether they were buried on the land, whether their souls were in heaven or whether their souls were in hell, all of them are resurrected, all of them are reunited with their bodies, and all of them are assembled before this great throne and He who sits upon it.

As we saw in Daniel 7:10, we also see here that the books that contain the infallible record of every thought, word, and deed of every person that ever lived are now opened. Nothing anybody ever thought or said or did will ever be forgotten just because time has elapsed. Each person is judged according to the works he performed in his lifetime and what those works reveal about his attitude toward Jesus Christ, as to whether he had genuine faith in Christ as his Lord and Savior or not. Our works reveal our true beliefs, and our conduct reveals the God that we actually worship. What we believe determines what we do, and what we do reveals what we believe. Therefore, our works are an infallible indicator of our faith in Jesus Christ or our rejection of Jesus Christ.

We are not saved by our works. We are saved through repentance of sin and faith in Jesus Christ. We are saved by Him and by His works, not by ours. But when we are saved, we are also transformed, and that transformed life is the manifestation that true saving faith actually resides in us. Therefore, Jesus can look at what people did, and from it deduce what they believed.

This is why judgment is always and everywhere in the Scripture not according to profession, but according to works, because a person can profess to be one thing and then live an entirely different way. Not what you profess, but how you live, is what reveals who you really are. Our works are an infallible indicator of our faith in Jesus Christ or our rejection of Jesus Christ.

When Jesus is preaching the Sermon on the Mount, and He is drawing His sermon to a conclusion, He has this final word to leave with the people to whom He is preaching.

Notice Matthew 7:21–23: *"Not every one that saith unto me, Lord, Lord, shall enter into the kingdom of heaven; but he that doeth the will of my Father which is in heaven.* 22 *Many will say to me in that day, Lord, Lord, have we not prophesied in thy name? and in thy name have cast out devils? and in thy name done many wonderful works?* 23 *And then will I profess unto them, I never knew you: depart from me, ye that work iniquity."*

What was it that characterized their lives? They were workers of iniquity. Their lives were dominated by sin and controlled by sin, and they spent their lives serving sin, even though they went to church and talked about Jesus. He says in effect, "If I really am your Lord, and if you really believe that, then it is going to transform your behavior in such a way that you will do the things which I command you; and you will do the will of My Father who is in heaven." Jesus said in verse 20, *"By their fruits ye shall know them."*

Jesus goes on to say, regarding the final day of judgment in Matthew 7:24–27, *"Therefore whosoever heareth these sayings of mine, and doeth them, I will liken him unto a wise man, which built his house upon a rock:* 25 *And the rain descended, and the floods came, and the winds blew, and beat upon that house; and it fell not: for it was founded upon a rock.* 26 *And every one that heareth these sayings of mine, and doeth them not, shall be likened unto a foolish man, which built his house upon the sand:* 27 *And the rain descended, and the floods came, and the winds blew, and beat upon that house; and it fell: and great was the fall of it."* The difference between those two outcomes on the Day of Judgment is this: Were you a doer of the word, or not?

James tells us in James 1:22, *"But be ye doers of the word, and not hearers only, deceiving your own selves."* You actually have to do what the Bible says. When the Bible says, "Do not lie," you do not lie. When it says, "Do not steal," you do not steal. When it says, "Honor your father and mother," you actually honor your father and mother. When it says, "Remember the Sabbath Day to keep it holy," you keep it holy, and so on with the rest of the Ten Commandments, and with all the commandments of the New Testament as well. Jesus said that by their fruits you shall know them. On the Day of Judgment, He will know who everyone is, and whether they were servants of His or servants of Satan by the works that characterized their lives.

We also want to take note that just as we saw in Daniel 12:1 that there is a book that contains the name of every saved person, Revelation 20:12 says, *"And I saw the dead, small and great, stand before God; and the books were opened: and another book was opened, which is the book of life."*

We have already seen this book of life mentioned in Revelation 3:5, 13:8, and 17:8. We saw that this book contains the name of each of God's elect who were chosen before the foundation of the world. It is the book of the Lamb that was written from the foundation of the world.

Not only is a search made of the books of human works, but a search is also made of the book of life, which is the book that has the names of all of God's elect inscribed in it. What we find is all whose names are written in the book of life also demonstrated by their works recorded in the book of works that they were saved people. There is agreement between the book of works that shows their works of faith, and the book of life which lists of all of God's elect. Search is also made of this book of life on the Day of Judgment, and whoever's name is found in it is received into heaven, and whoever's name is not found in it is cast into the lake of fire. Our works will show that Christ really was our Lord in whom we believed, and our names written in the book of life will confirm that we were God's elect that He came to save. The record of the two books will match.

The lake of fire as a place of punishment is horrific to contemplate. Death and hell, it says in verse 14, are cast into the lake of fire. Neither death nor hell will have any function or place from this point forward. The separation of the soul and body, which is what death is, will never occur again for all eternity, for either the saved or the lost. Physical death will cease to occur. Nor will there ever be any need for a place to contain the disembodied souls of the lost, which is what hell is. Hell is a place to contain disembodied souls that are waiting for their final judgment.

There will be no place for disembodied spirits because such will never exist again. It is resurrected people, body and soul together, that will be cast into the lake of fire, and never will their bodies and souls be separated. Both death and hell are metaphorically cast into the lake of fire, because they will cease to exist.

This lake is called a *"lake of fire."* As Isaiah 33:14 says, it is a place of *"everlasting burnings."* This is declared to be the second death, the last death, the final death, and the eternal death, from which there is no deliverance forever. We have already seen this in our exposition of Revelation 14:9–11. *"And the third angel followed them, saying with a loud voice, If any man worship the beast and his image, and receive his mark in his forehead, or in his hand,* [10] *The same shall drink of the wine of the wrath of God, which is poured out without mixture into the cup of his indignation; and he shall be tormented with fire and brimstone in the presence of the holy angels, and in the presence of the Lamb:* [11] *And the smoke of their torment ascendeth up for ever and ever: and they have no rest day nor night, who worship the beast and his image, and whosoever receiveth the mark of his name."*

We read in Revelation 20:10: *"And the devil that deceived them was cast into the lake of fire and brimstone, where the beast and the false prophet are, and shall be tormented day and night for ever and ever."* Clearly, there is no annihilation of these souls that are cast into hell. Satan is cast into hell, and all those with the mark of the beast that participated in the work of the beast, the work of the false prophet, and in Babylon will be cast into hell. All of the lost, Satan, and all of his demons are all in the lake of fire together, where they are tormented day and night, forever and ever, and have no rest in body and soul for all eternity.

People dispute whether this fire is literal or not, and as we said in chapter 44; if it is literal, it is awful. But if it is symbolic, remember the reality portrayed by the symbol is always greater than the symbol itself, which means the reality is even worse. There is no escaping the awfulness of the torment and suffering and pain of hell by saying the fire is symbolic; because, if it is symbolic, it still represents a reality that corresponds to fire and all of its characteristics. Just as our resurrected bodies are suited to dwell for eternity in heaven, so the bodies of the resurrected lost are suited to be tormented in hell forever without being destroyed.

But what of those who are written in the book of life? Revelation 21–22 describes their outcome. They dwell in the new heaven and the new earth; and they dwell with Christ forever in eternal, perfect bliss and happiness, in which Eden is restored, sin is removed, and the devil is vanquished. They enjoy the immediate personal presence of Christ, who will fellowship with them and feed them and provide for them forever and ever.

So here are the two destinies. Mark it down—there are no other destinies. There is no third possibility. You do not get to sit this one out. Everyone is either going to wind up in the new heaven and the new earth, or in the lake of fire. There are no other alternatives.

The question I must ask is this: Where will you be? What do your words and your works indicate your outcome is going be? Do your words and works demonstrate a genuine faith in Jesus Christ, or do they show that you merely give lip service to Christ, while you live as you please, and live in a fashion the world approves of, because you participate in its sin and wickedness?

If you are not living a separated life from the world, then you are not living a saved life. The Bible tells us in James 2 that faith without works is dead. James issues this challenge: "Show me your faith by your works." This does not mean we have to be perfect people. What it does mean is that the dominating characteristic of our life needs to be that we follow and serve and obey Jesus Christ as Lord and Savior and that we faithfully confess Him before men and cling to Him as our God, and that we do so all the days of our life.

The disposition of the Christian is this: "Lord, what will You have me to do?" Not: "What do I want to do?" They tell all the kids at graduation, "You can be whatever you want to be! You can do whatever you want to do!" Well, what if someone wants to be a professional thief?

You cannot be whatever you want to be. You must be whatever God wants you to be, and you must do whatever God wants you to do. If that is the disposition and the direction of your life, then Jesus will say, "I see that you viewed Me as Lord, you trusted Me as Savior, and you demonstrated the reality of that by your effort to obey Me all the days of your life. Well done, good and faithful servant." No one who is not a demonstrated servant of Jesus Christ in his actions will ever be conducted into the new earth.

What are you doing to serve Jesus Christ? Is your life given over to the service of Jesus? If it is, then the works that you do in serving Him will bear a fine record on the Day of Judgment of the genuineness of your faith in Him.

Do not be confused in thinking those works are what save you. Those works are what demonstrate that you are saved and that you do love the Lord Jesus and you do believe in Him as your Savior. You are doing them not to earn something, but to display something. It is important that we maintain that distinction.

So we do not do good works to earn something; we do good works to display something, and that something is our love for the Lord Jesus Christ. He says, "If you love Me, keep My commandments." I keep His commandments, not to earn something, but to show something—and that is to show love for the One I really believe is Lord and Savior.

Let us prepare for the Day of Judgment by trusting in Christ alone for the forgiveness of our sins, and demonstrating the genuineness of that faith by living for Him in all we do and say and think. When you fail, get up and start living for Him again. Jesus is a Savior of sinners, not of perfect people. We need to recognize that, as Christians, we are going to fall and fail many times. It does not mean that we are going to go to hell because of that, provided that when we fall and fail, we confess our sins to Him. When we do, He is faithful and just to forgive us our sins, and to cleanse us from all unrighteousness. Then we get up and start following Him again.

Those are the kinds of works that demonstrate a genuine faith in Jesus. As we engage in works of obedience and repentance all the days of our life, we demonstrate that Jesus is our Savior and Lord.

61

The New Heaven and the New Earth, Revelation 21:1

> "[1] *And I saw a new heaven and a new earth: for the first heaven and the first earth were passed away; and there was no more sea.*"

One of the most important verses in the entire Bible is 1 John 3:8 which says, *"For this purpose the Son of God was manifested, that he might destroy the works of the devil."* The whole Bible, from start to finish, is a revelation and record of the Son of God destroying the works of the devil.

In the beginning, God created a perfect and glorious heaven and earth, and populated it with every kind of living creature. The pinnacle of God's creation was making man in His own image and after His own likeness. God looked upon everything He had made, *"and, behold, it was very good."* It was pure and pristine, it was holy and righteous, and it was perfect and beautiful. There was no death, no sorrow, and no pain.

But this paradise God made was invaded by Satan. He lied to Adam and Eve, he led them into committing sin against God, and as a result paradise was ruined. Mankind became subject to death and sorrow and pain, and was condemned to eternal wrath and punishment. The works of the devil ruined and wrecked and defiled the original creation of God, brought depravity and death upon humanity, and imposed a curse on the natural creation. But God was not about to surrender to Satan, and He was not going to allow his work to stand. Satan's triumph in the garden of Eden would not prevail.

Therefore, in Genesis 3:15 God declared war against Satan, and promised that the seed of the woman would come and crush the head of the serpent. Jesus Christ, who is the promised seed of the woman, was going to come and destroy Satan's work. He was going to reverse the curse on mankind and creation, restore the ruined paradise, and redeem mankind from sin and all of its consequences. In a word, everything Satan had done, Jesus was going to undo; all that Satan had achieved, Jesus was going to dismantle. Satan's work would be like it had never been done, so great was the destruction that was going to be brought upon it, and so great was the restoration that was going to be made from it by Jesus Christ.

As history has unfolded over the last 6,000 years, we have seen the seed of the woman come in the person of Jesus Christ. Through His coming, and through His life, death, resurrection, and ascension, Jesus defeated the devil, robbed him of his power and his people, and invaded and ruined his kingdom. For the last 2,000 years, Jesus has been systematically dismantling Satan's kingdom and has been systematically building the kingdom of God.

We have seen Christ's victory over Satan progressively described in the book of Revelation, and in chapter 20 we came to the climax and conclusion of Christ's work in destroying the work of the devil. In chapter 20, we have seen Satan and all his helpers cast into the lake of fire.

We have seen Christ triumphantly sitting on His great white throne of judgment. We have seen the vindication and deliverance of all Christ's people whose names are written in the Lamb's book of life. Now, in chapters 21 and 22, we will see the complete ruin and the full reversal of the work of Satan as the curse is completely removed and paradise is fully restored. Once again God dwells with men in the new earth. The garden of Eden is restored, the way to the tree of life is opened, and mankind's dominion over the earth is returned back to him. Perfect purity and permanent righteousness are now in the possession of every redeemed person, and never again can sin enter into the human experience. In the new heaven and the new earth, nothing is left of Satan's work. It is completely destroyed. Now everything is the work of God alone. Satan's work has been obliterated. God's work has been permanently established forever.

In the new heaven and the new earth, we see the perfection and completion of redemption and the permanent holiness and happiness of the people of God for eternity. The triumph of Christ over Satan is perfect and permanent, and, because of that triumph, we will have peace and joy forever and ever without limit and without end.

All of this has been set before us in these last two chapters. As chapter 21 now opens, we are introduced to the new dwelling place of the people of God, which is the new heaven and the new earth. Here is where we will dwell for eternity, and here is our future home, a place of perfect happiness and holiness.

The Renewal of the Heaven and the Earth

The renewal of the heaven and the earth is spoken of in verse 1a. *"And I saw a new heaven and a new earth: for the first heaven and the first earth were passed away."* In 20:11 we saw the heaven and the earth fleeing from the face of Christ as He sat on the great white throne of judgment. This fleeing away of heaven and earth from Christ was the result of the corruption and curse that had fallen on them as a result of Adam's fall. A corrupt creation would never be a suitable dwelling place for a perfect people, and were it left in its corruption, the victory of Christ over the work of Satan would be incomplete. Therefore, Christ purifies the heavens and the earth with fire by reducing them back to their smallest elements, from which He then rebuilds them into a new heaven and a new earth, in which dwells purity and righteousness.

When verse 1 says there is going to be a new heaven and a new earth, it does not mean they will be brand new, as though God created them out of nothing like He did the first time in Genesis 1. The Greek word that is translated "new" in verse 1, means "new in kind" or "new in quality." It does not mean "new" in the sense that it never existed before. It means that it now has a new quality about it.

This new earth and heaven will be the old earth and heaven reduced to their fundamental elements and then remade with new qualities. It will be similar to the resurrection of our bodies. Our bodies are corrupted by sin, and they are reduced to their fundamental elements in the grave. But then they are resurrected with new qualities and with freedom from all the effects of sin. It is still the same body we had before, but it is resurrected and imbued with new qualities. God does not make a brand-new body for us; rather, He takes our old body, reduces it to its fundamental elements, and then remakes it in the resurrection with new qualities.

So it is with the new heaven and the new earth. They have been corrupted by sin, and they will be reduced to their fundamental elements with a fervent heat. God will then reshape those elements into the new heaven and the new earth, with new qualities and with freedom from the curse and its effects that sin brought upon it. Therefore, the new heaven and the new earth will be the present heaven and the present earth cleansed and purified and remade in glorious perfection and free from all corruption. The old creation will not be annihilated; instead, it will be regenerated.

Two passages in the Bible make this point. The first is Hebrews 1:10–12 which says, *"And, Thou, Lord, in the beginning hast laid the foundation of the earth; and the heavens are the works of thine hands."* This speaks of Genesis 1. Verse 11: *"They shall perish"*—that is, the original creation is going to perish. *"But thou remainest; and they all shall wax old as doth a garment;* [12] *And as a vesture shalt thou fold them up, and they shall be changed: but thou art the same, and thy years shall not fail."*

The earth is being used up and worn out, and just like a worn-out garment, when it is finally too worn out to wear, it is folded up and put away. But the creation does not remain in that situation. The worn-out creation *"shall be changed"*; the word in the original means to be transformed. This original creation is going to wax old like a garment, and then it is going to be transformed. It is not going to be annihilated. It is going to be *"changed,"* not eliminated.

The second passage is Matthew 19:27–29 which says: *"Then answered Peter and said unto him, Behold, we have forsaken all, and followed thee; what shall we have therefore?* [28] *And Jesus said unto them, Verily I say unto you, That ye which have followed me, in the regeneration when the Son of man shall sit in the throne of his glory, ye also shall sit upon twelve thrones, judging the twelve tribes of Israel.* [29] *And every one that hath forsaken houses, or brethren, or sisters, or father, or mother, or wife, or children, or lands, for my name's sake, shall receive an hundredfold, and shall inherit everlasting life."*

Jesus calls the end of the world when He sits on His throne and gives rewards to His faithful servants *"the regeneration."* This word means to restore something to its pristine state; it means to renovate or to renew. There will be a transformation of the old heaven and earth into the new heaven and earth, here called a *"regeneration"*—in other words, a renovation and a renewal of the old heaven and earth.

Having looked at those two passages that state there is going to be a transformative and regenerative process that is going to occur to the heaven and the earth, notice how this process is described in both the Old Testament and in the New Testament. We will look at two passages in the Old Testament, and then two passages in the New Testament.

First, notice the two passages in the Old Testament. The whole idea of there being a new heaven and new earth is not something unique to the book of Revelation. It was spoken of in the Old Testament in several places.

God says in Isaiah 65:17–19, *"For, behold, I create new heavens and a new earth: and the former shall not be remembered, nor come into mind.* [18] *But be ye glad and rejoice for ever in that which I create: for, behold, I create Jerusalem a rejoicing, and her people a joy.* [19] *And I will rejoice in Jerusalem, and joy in my people: and the voice of weeping shall be no more heard in her, nor the voice of crying."*

God says to the children of Israel in Isaiah's day that, at some point in the future, He is going to make a new heaven and a new earth. What will characterize that new heaven and new earth is joy and gladness, and there will be no sorrow or crying. John borrowed that same language and used it in Revelation 21:1–4 to describe the new heaven and the new earth. In Isaiah 65, the emphasis is on the joy and the gladness that is going to be in the new heaven and the new earth, rather than in the sorrow and crying that are in the present heaven and the present earth.

Isaiah 66:22 says, *"For as the new heavens and the new earth, which I will make, shall remain before me, saith the* Lord, *so shall your seed and your name remain."* Here, the emphasis is on the permanence of the new heaven and the new earth, as opposed to the temporary nature of the present heaven and the present earth, which are going to wax old and be folded up like a garment and be changed.

The earth we are living on now and the heaven that is above us now have a limited lifespan. They are temporary. When Jesus Christ returns, they are going to be transformed into a new heaven and a new earth. Isaiah 65:17–19 tells us the new heaven and the new earth will be characterized by joy and gladness, rather than by sorrow and crying; and Isaiah 66:22 tells us that the new heaven and new earth are going to be characterized by permanence as opposed to temporariness.

Secondly, notice two passages in the New Testament. The first is Romans 8:18–23. In verse 18 it says, *"For I reckon that the sufferings of this present time are not worthy to be compared with the glory which shall be revealed in us."* There is the present time, and there is a future time. The present time is a time of suffering. The future time is a time of glory.

Verse 19: *"For the earnest expectation of the creature. . . ."* Here the King James Version renders the Greek word for "creation" with the word "creature." Each time you see the word "creature," it means "creation," because that is what the original Greek word means. That exact same Greek word is used four times in this passage. The first three times, the KJV translators render it "creature," "creature," and "creature," and the fourth time they translate it "creation." Why they did that is not clear. In the New King James Version, it is translated consistently as "creation" all four times, because it is the same Greek word. Therefore, when we quote it, we are going to substitute the word "creation" for "creature," because that is what the original Greek word means.

Verse 19: *"For the earnest expectation of the creation waiteth for the manifestation of the sons of God."* That is, the natural creation is waiting for something. It is waiting for there to be a public declaration of who the true sons of God are. There will come a day when it will be manifest who the sons of God are. The creation is waiting for that day.

Verse 20: *"For the creation was made subject to vanity"*—that is, the creation was brought into a state of futility. Why? Because the creation chose to be brought into that state? No. It says, *"not willingly, but by reason of him who hath subjected the same in hope."* In other words, God put the curse on the first creation and made it subject to futility, not because the creation chose that, but because God chose to impose that on the creation as a result of Adam's fall.

But at the same time, in the promise of the coming Redeemer, He also subjected that creation to the hope that it, too, would be redeemed. We must understand that when Christ died on the cross, He did not die just to redeem the elect from sin, He also died to redeem the natural creation from the curse brought on it by Adam's sin. This is why the creation has hope. He has *"subjected the same in hope."*

Verse 21: *"Because the creation itself also shall be delivered from the bondage of corruption into the glorious liberty of the children of God."* What do we know about the creation right now? It is in bondage to corruption. This world is corrupt. The heavens are corrupt. They are corrupt as a result of being under the curse, and that because of Adam's sin. But it shall be delivered from that corruption and curse, and it shall be delivered into the same liberty that the children of God have, which is freedom from the curse and the corruption of sin.

Verse 22: *"For we know that the whole creation groaneth and travaileth in pain together until now."* This world and this universe are groaning and travailing in pain because of being under the curse. Why do we have earthquakes and volcanoes and diseases? Why do we have all the natural disasters that occur, not only on the earth but in the universe as well? These things are the groaning of the creation because it is under the curse of God. The universe is not functioning the way God originally designed it to function. It is broken, corrupted, and defective; and as a result, it is waiting to be delivered from that brokenness and corruption, just as we are waiting to be delivered from our brokenness and our corruption.

Verse 23: *"And not only they"*—that is, not only the creation—*"but ourselves also, which have the firstfruits of the Spirit, even we ourselves groan within ourselves, waiting for the adoption, [that is], the redemption of our body."* Our bodies are going to be redeemed at the resurrection. That is when the sons of God are going to be manifest, and that is the same time the creation is delivered from the bondage of corruption also. That is when the creation shall realize the hope it has of being delivered from the effects of the curse and the fall. Creation is not annihilated; it is delivered from corruption into glorious liberty. That occurs when the true sons of God are made manifest on the Day of Judgment. Our resurrection and the earth's renovation will occur at the same time.

Therefore, the rapture, when we are resurrected, occurs at the same time the earth and heavens are renovated. The rapture and the appearance of the new heavens and the new earth are not separated by a thousand and seven years, as the Dispensationalists would have us believe. They say the rapture occurs, and then there is a seven-year tribulation, then Jesus comes back, then there is a thousand-year Millennium, and at the end of the thousand-year Millennium, the new heavens and the new earth are created.

Romans 8 makes it clear that the new heavens and the new earth, which is the renovation of this world and its deliverance from corruption, occurs at the same time the believers experience their deliverance from corruption in the resurrection and are manifested to be the sons of God. Therefore, there is just one final event at the end of this age—one in which Jesus returns, we are raptured up to be with Him, and return back to earth with Him. Immediately the great white throne judgment takes place, the renovation of the new heavens and the new earth is accomplished, and the eternal state begins.

There is this age we are in now, and there is the age to come, and they are divided by the second coming, the final judgment, and the renovation of the new heavens and the new earth. That is biblical eschatology. This scheme the Dispensationalists have invented that there are three separate events, one at the rapture, one seven years later at the second coming, and one a thousand years later at the end of the Millennium is completely unbiblical. Those three events all occur at the end of this age.

Notice 2 Peter 3:3–13. *"Knowing this first, that there shall come in the last days scoffers, walking after their own lusts,* [4]*And saying, Where is the promise of his coming? for since the fathers fell asleep, all things continue as they were from the beginning of the creation."* Clearly, the topic under discussion is the second coming of Jesus Christ.

Verse 5: *"For this they willingly are ignorant of, that by the word of God the heavens were of old, and the earth standing out of the water and in the water:* [6] *Whereby the world that then was, being overflowed with water, perished."* The scoffers are saying that Jesus has not come back in a long time; and therefore, He is not going to come back at all. Peter replies, making this point: It was a long time between the creation and the flood, and yet in the flood, God wiped out the entire world. Therefore, if He wiped it out once, that sets a precedent for Him wiping it out the second time.

However, He is not going to wipe it out the second time by water, like He did the first time, because He promised He would never do that again in the Noahic covenant. Verse 7 says, *"But the heavens and the earth, which are now, by the same word are kept in store, reserved unto fire against the day of judgment and perdition of ungodly men."* The world is going to be destroyed the second time by fire.

Verse 8: *"But, beloved, be not ignorant of this one thing, that one day is with the Lord as a thousand years, and a thousand years as one day.* [9] *The Lord is not slack concerning his promise, as some men count slackness; but is longsuffering to us-ward, not willing that any should perish, but that all should come to repentance."* In other words, what is delaying the second coming of Christ is that we are living in this symbolic thousand-year period in which God is saving His elect. When the last elect person is saved, the end times begin with the loosing of Satan. This is why the delay has gone on for 2,000 years now, because God has a lot of people to save.

When all that should not perish have come to repentance, then, as verse 10 says, *"the day of the Lord will come."* How will it come? *"As a thief in the night; in the which the heavens shall pass away with a great noise, and the elements shall melt with fervent heat, the earth also and the works that are therein shall be burned up."* What should our response be to this fact? *"[11] Seeing then that all these things shall be dissolved, what manner of persons ought ye to be in all holy conversation and godliness, [12] Looking for and hasting unto the coming of the day of God, wherein the heavens being on fire shall be dissolved, and the elements shall melt with fervent heat? [13] Nevertheless we, according to his promise, look for new heavens and a new earth, wherein dwelleth righteousness."*

Here, we see in detail the process of the renovation of the earth and the heaven described. In verse 7, it says that this earth is reserved unto fire. In verse 10, it says it is going to be subject to a fervent heat, and it is going to be burned up. In verse 12, it says it is going to be on fire, and there is going to be a fervent heat. Everything is going to be melted back to its basic elements. Out of this molten mass of elements, verse 13 says a new earth and a new heaven are forged. Therefore, when Revelation 21:1 says that the first heaven and the first earth were passed away, it means that they passed away in their present form, not that they ceased to exist.

Notice Revelation 21:1: *"And I saw a new heaven and a new earth: for the first heaven and the first earth were passed away."* We say of someone who died that he "passed away." We do not mean he was annihilated; we mean he is gone as to his past form, but we do expect to see him in a new form at the resurrection.

In the future, paradise will be restored in the new earth and heaven. The curse will be gone. The dragon, the beast, the false prophet, Babylon, and those who have the mark of the beast will be absent. The beauty and perfection of creation and nature will be restored.

Isaiah 11:1–9 speaks about the coming of Jesus: *"And there shall come forth a rod out of the stem of Jesse, and a Branch shall grow out of his roots: [2] And the spirit of the LORD shall rest upon him, the spir-*

it of wisdom and understanding, the spirit of counsel and might, the spirit of knowledge and of the fear of the Lord; [3] *And shall make him of quick understanding in the fear of the* Lord: *and he shall not judge after the sight of his eyes, neither reprove after the hearing of his ears:* [4] *But with righteousness shall he judge the poor, and reprove with equity for the meek of the earth: and he shall smite the earth with the rod of his mouth, and with the breath of his lips shall he slay the wicked."* We see the second coming of Jesus Christ, in which He exercises final judgment by smiting the wicked with the rod of His mouth and slaying the wicked with the breath of His lips; that is, He will smite them and slay them with the power of His spoken word. "[5] *And righteousness shall be the girdle of his loins, and faithfulness the girdle of his reins."* He will judge in righteousness and faithfulness.

Having described Christ and His second coming in judgment, when He smites the earth with the rod of His wrath and gives justice to the oppressed—that is, to the believers—notice verses 6 to 9. Here is the description of the new heavens and the new earth: "*The wolf also shall dwell with the lamb, and the leopard shall lie down with the kid; and the calf and the young lion and the fatling together; and a little child shall lead them.* [7] *And the cow and the bear shall feed; their young ones shall lie down together: and the lion shall eat straw like the ox.* [8] *And the sucking child shall play on the hole of the asp, and the weaned child shall put his hand on the cockatrice' den.* [9] *They shall not hurt nor destroy in all my holy mountain: for the earth shall be full of the knowledge of the* Lord, *as the waters cover the sea."* Here we have a beautiful description of the physical nature of the new earth, in which there is no more curse and no more conflict between mankind and creation, or between creation and itself.

Notice Isaiah 65:16–25. "*That he who blesseth himself in the earth shall bless himself in the God of truth; and he that sweareth in the earth shall swear by the God of truth; because the former troubles are forgotten, and because they are hid from mine eyes.* [17] *For, behold, I create new heavens and a new earth: and the former shall not be remembered, nor come into mind.* [18] *But be ye glad and rejoice for ever in that which I create: for, behold, I create Jerusalem a rejoicing, and her people a joy.* [19] *And I will rejoice in Jerusalem, and joy in my people: and the voice of weeping shall be no more heard in her, nor the voice of crying.* [20] *There shall be no more thence an infant of days, nor an old man that hath not filled his days: for the child shall die an hundred years old; but the sinner being an hundred years old shall be accursed.* [21] *And they shall build houses, and inhabit them; and they shall plant vineyards, and eat the fruit of them.* [22] *They shall not build, and another inhabit; they shall not plant, and another eat: for as the days of a tree are the days of my people, and mine elect shall long enjoy the work of their hands.* [23] *They shall not labour in vain, nor bring forth for trouble; for they are the seed of the blessed of the* LORD, *and their offspring with them.* [24] *And it shall come to pass, that before they call, I will answer; and while they are yet speaking, I will hear.* [25] *The wolf and the lamb shall feed together, and the lion shall eat straw like the bullock: and dust shall be the serpent's meat. They shall not hurt nor destroy in all my holy mountain, saith the* LORD."

In the Old Testament, New Covenant blessings are often symbolically described in Old Covenant terminology, language, and imagery. But the overall thrust of this section is that this is what the new earth is going to be like. There is not going to be any reproduction, but the Jews did not understand that. There is not going to be any death, but the Jews did not understand that. Therefore, He symbolically describes eternal longevity in these earthly and Old Covenant material terms.

But you can see, shining through this description that was adapted to the people of the day, the glory and the nature of the new earth. The beauty and perfection of creation and nature will be restored physically, emotionally, socially, intellectually, and spiritually. Everything will be perfect, everything will be peaceful, and everything will be pure. This is the description of the renewal of the heavens and the earth in the Old Testament.

The Absence of the Sea

Revelation 21:1 says, "*I saw a new heaven and a new earth: for the first heaven and the first earth were passed away; and there was no more sea.*" Verse 1 tells us that the new earth Christ will make has no more sea. Some take this literally and say that the new earth will have no oceans of water upon it. It is possible this is what it means.

However, it is very unlikely that this is the meaning of the phrase, "*and there was no more sea.*" When we look at the original creation, an entire day, the third day of creation, was devoted to the creation of the oceans, the dry land, and the plants. Another whole day, the fifth day of creation, was devoted to filling those oceans with life and the air with birds. The oceans were very significant in the original creation and were a big part of it, occupying two large parts of two days in the original six days of creation. When God looked upon it, He pronounced it all *"very good."* There was nothing bad about the oceans or anything He made in the oceans.

The sea is a large part of the revelation of the glory of God in creation. Scientists estimate that 25 percent of all species on the earth dwell in the ocean, and they have hardly begun to catalog them all. One has only to observe the intense beauty, the stunning variety, and the tremendous complexity of the life in the oceans to be powerfully moved to worship the wisdom and the power of God, and one has only to see the vast expanse of the oceans to be moved to worship the majesty of the greatness of God. It seems unlikely that such a tremendous revelation of the glory of God in the original creation would be done away with in the new creation. The oceans were part of the original unfallen earth, and it would seem they would be part of the new unfallen earth as well. We would not expect that God would abandon an entire category of His creative work in re-creating the heavens and the earth.

Furthermore, the physical oceans are presented as a good thing in the book of Revelation, out of which the worship of God arises. Notice Revelation 5:11–13. Here we have a picture of heaven with God the Father sitting on the throne and the Son with the Father. The praise begins to thunder forth. *"And I beheld, and I heard the voice of many angels round about the throne and the beasts and the elders: and the number of them was ten thousand times ten thousand, and thousands of thousands;* [12] *Saying with a loud voice, Worthy is the Lamb that was slain to receive power, and riches, and wisdom, and strength, and honour, and glory, and blessing.* [13] *And every creature which is in heaven, and on the earth, and under the earth, and such as are in the sea, and all that are in them, heard I saying, Blessing, and honour, and glory, and power, be unto him that sitteth upon the throne, and unto the Lamb for ever and ever."* Verse 13 says the sea and all that is in it is a source of the worship of God. Not only does the physical ocean not have a negative connotation in the book of Revelation, but it is also seen as a place out of which the praise of God arises.

Furthermore, notice Revelation 14:6–7: *"And I saw another angel fly in the midst of heaven, having the everlasting gospel to preach unto them that dwell on the earth, and to every nation, and kindred, and tongue, and people,* [7] *Saying with a loud voice, Fear God, and give glory to him; for the hour of his judgment is come: and worship him that made heaven, and earth, and the sea, and the fountains of waters."*

Verse 7 says we are to *"worship Him that made heaven, and earth, and the sea, and the fountains of waters."* Here the sea is said to be a provocation to worship God, just as the other three elements of creation are a provocation to worship God. We are explicitly told that in the eternal state there will be a new earth and heaven in Revelation 21:1, and in Revelation 22:1, that there will be a fountain of water.

Therefore, it stands to reason that there would be a new sea as well. If three of the elements listed in verse 7 are explicitly declared to be part of the new creation, it would seem that the fourth would be part of the new creation as well. If God is going to give us a new heaven, and if God is going to give us a new earth, and if God is going to give us a new fountain of water, then why would He not give us a new sea as well?

Now if all of this is true, and the new earth will in fact have oceans just like the first earth did, then why does Revelation 21:1 say that in the new heaven and the new earth there was no more sea? The reason is because the word "sea" has a symbolic meaning as well as a literal meaning. When the word "sea" is used symbolically, it represents the churning mass of godless humanity.

Isaiah 57:20 says, *"But the wicked are like the troubled sea, when it cannot rest, whose waters cast up mire and dirt."* Sin always produces turmoil, whether in the life of an individual, a family, a society, or a nation.

Daniel 7:1–3 says, *"In the first year of Belshazzar king of Babylon Daniel had a dream and visions of his head upon his bed: then he wrote the dream, and told the sum of the matters.* [2] *Daniel spake and said, I saw in my vision by night, and, behold, the four winds of the heaven strove upon the great sea."* The sea is whipped up into this maelstrom of turbulence by these winds. Verse 3: *"And four great beasts came up from the sea, diverse one from another."*

The sea is pictured as being whipped into a maelstrom by powerful winds so that the ocean is in tremendous turmoil like it would be in a hurricane. Out of this tumultuous mass of humanity symbolically pictured as a troubled sea, the kings and empires of the earth arise, symbolized by four vicious beasts: the lion, the bear, the leopard, and the beast with great iron teeth. The kingdoms of the world do not arise out of the literal ocean. The nations of the earth arise out of the masses of humanity, which are here pictured as an ocean.

We see the same symbolic usage of the sea in Revelation 13:1–2. *"And I stood upon the sand of the sea, and saw a beast rise up out of the sea"* (the same language Daniel uses, the beast rising up out of the sea) *"having seven heads and ten horns, and upon his horns ten crowns, and upon his heads the name of blasphemy.* [2] *And the beast which I saw was like unto a leopard, and his feet were as the feet of a bear, and his mouth as the mouth of a lion: and the dragon gave him his power, and his seat, and great authority."*

In Revelation 13:1–2, just as in Daniel 7, this composite beast represents the anti-Christian governments of this present age. It shares the characteristics of the anti-Christian governments Daniel spoke of because the same vicious beasts that are used to describe this beast in Revelation 13 are used to describe the kingdoms in Daniel's vision in Daniel 7.

Once again, the sea out of which this beast of anti-Christian government arises represents the churning mass of unsaved humanity, casting up its mire and dirt, creating anti-Christian governments that viciously oppress and attack the kingdom of God and the people of God. Out of the wicked populations of the earth, anti-Christian governments arise.

Finally, notice the explicit declaration of the symbolic meaning of the sea in Revelation 17:1. *"And there came one of the seven angels which had the seven vials, and talked with me, saying unto me, Come hither; I will shew unto thee the judgment of the great whore that sitteth upon many waters."* The question is: What are those waters? They are symbolic oceans. Notice that verse 15 gives the explanation: *"And he saith unto me, The waters which thou sawest, where the whore sitteth, are peoples, and multitudes, and nations, and tongues."* In verse 1, Babylon the harlot that represents anti-Christian society is said to sit upon—or have her support and foundation from—many waters, which is a reference to the oceans of the earth.

Verse 15 tells us that the water of the sea represents peoples, and multitudes, and nations, and tongues. In a word, the sea represents the whole fallen mass of unsaved humanity that makes up the anti-Christian society that Babylon symbolically represents and out of which anti-Christian governments arise.

Therefore, when Revelation 21:1 says that there is no more sea, this is the sea it is talking about. In the new heavens and earth, there will be no seething mass of unsaved humanity casting up the mire and dirt of sin and rebellion against God.

As we look out at our world today and at the news available to us, we see seething masses of people demonstrating and rioting. There is conflict in which this group is against that group, people are committing crimes against others, and the whole political morass is a seething caldron of a troubled ocean of humanity. They are all fighting with each other, and are all fighting against God. This is what is going to be absent from the new earth.

All of the unrest and turmoil and conflict that arose from the wicked storming against God is going to be eliminated. All the raging violence against the dominion of God will be done away with, as it says in Psalm 2: "[1] *Why do the heathen rage, and the people imagine a vain thing?* [2] *The kings of the earth set themselves, and the rulers take counsel together, against the* Lord, *and against his anointed, saying,* [3] *Let us break their bands asunder, and cast away their cords from us.*" This is the sea of humanity fighting against God, and it will be gone. All of its members will be cast into the lake of fire.

It says of God in Psalm 65:7 that He "*stilleth the noise of the seas, the noise of their waves, and the tumult of the people.*" To still the sea is to still the tumult of the people. When there is no more sea, there will be no more tumult of the people. The tumult of rebellion is gone. You will never find it in the new earth.

We read of the sovereign God subduing the wicked when He subdues the seas and their waves, pictured in Psalm 93:1–4. It says, "*The* Lord *reigneth, he is clothed with majesty; the* Lord *is clothed with strength, wherewith he hath girded himself: the world also is stablished, that it cannot be moved.* [2] *Thy throne is established of old: thou art from everlasting.*" Now notice: "[3] *The floods have lifted up, O* Lord, *the floods have lifted up their voice; the floods lift up their waves.* [4] *The* Lord *on high is mightier than the noise of many waters, yea, than the mighty waves of the sea.*"

These floods are the oceans that have lifted up their voice against God, and what is being asserted in Psalm 93 is that God is mightier than all the massive resistance that is generated and lifted up against

Him by the sea of wicked humanity, casting their waves of blasphemy and hatred against Him. He will take those waves and He will smash them. He will take those waters and He will remove them, because the Lord on high is mightier than the mighty waves of the sea. The sea of rebellious humanity has been eliminated from the new heavens and the new earth because it is completely incompatible with the character of the new creation.

This is what the new heavens and the new earth will be like. This is the dwelling place of the people of God. Revelation 21 describes the Father's house, which has many mansions that Jesus has gone to prepare for us, and that He will return to bring us to. In this place, there will be the presence of a perfect creation, and there will be the absence of any sinful people.

The question is this: Will you be there? Will you be in the new heaven and the new earth, where there is no more sea of wicked humanity? Or will you be in the lake of fire, where the sea of wicked humanity is?

The difference between being in the new heavens and the new earth, or being in the lake of fire, is the difference between whether you have repented of your sin and received Jesus Christ as your Lord and Savior, or whether you continue to persist in your sin and reject the authority of Christ over your life, and the saving grace He offers to everyone who calls upon Him. The Bible tells us in Romans 10:13: *"For whosoever shall call upon the name of the Lord shall be saved."*

Believe on the Lord Jesus Christ and you will be saved. Repent of your sins. Receive Christ as your Savior. Recognize Him as your Lord. Follow Him as your Master. Find from Him salvation and deliverance from all judgment, and He will bring you into this new heaven and this new earth that is perfectly peaceful, totally blessed, and entirely pure, where you will have eternal life, and where you will live forever. May God help us to be among those who are in the new heaven and the new earth, and not among those who are cast into the lake of fire.

62

The Blessedness of the People of God, Revelation 21:2–4

> "[2] *And I John saw the holy city, new Jerusalem, coming down from God out of heaven, prepared as a bride adorned for her husband.* [3] *And I heard a great voice out of heaven saying, Behold, the tabernacle of God is with men, and he will dwell with them, and they shall be his people, and God himself shall be with them, and be their God.* [4] *And God shall wipe away all tears from their eyes; and there shall be no more death, neither sorrow, nor crying, neither shall there be any more pain: for the former things are passed away.*"

The conclusion of the book of Revelation sets before us the glorious triumph of Christ over Satan and his works. Satan and those who served and followed him are forever punished in the lake of fire and are forever removed from Christ's kingdom and His people. Never again will Satan and his people be able to tempt us or persecute us.

But the conclusion of the book of Revelation not only sets before us the glorious triumph of Christ over Satan and all his works; it also sets before us the glorious future and dwelling place of the people of God. Christ provides us with a new heaven and new earth that is as pristine and pure and perfect as heaven and earth were before the fall of Adam.

In Revelation 21, paradise is restored, and the restless sea of humanity that lived in rebellion against God will never again inhabit the earth. This new heaven and new earth is the eternal home Christ has provided for those He has saved from their sins. It is a place of permanent purity and holiness, a place where sin can never enter again.

There we will have eternal life, eternal happiness, and eternal peace. There we will have perfect fellowship with God and perfect fellowship with one another. Sin can never again degrade and ruin our fellowship with God or with one another. This was the description of the dwelling place of the people of God we saw in the previous chapter.

Having seen the eternal dwelling place of the people of God as being the new heaven and the new earth in verse 1, we want to consider two more glorious truths. First of all, we want to consider the description of the people of God in verse 2. There they are described as a holy city and as a bride. Secondly, we want to consider together the blessedness of the people of God in verses 3 and 4. That blessedness consists in the presence of God being with them in verse 3, and in the absence of the curse being upon them in verse 4.

The glories of the home Christ has prepared for us and the blessedness of the life Christ has promised us are almost incomprehensible to our fallen minds. The contemplation of our eternal state fills us with wonder and awe and leaves us overwhelmed with amazement and gratitude as we read the verbal description that seems entirely inadequate to convey the full reality of all that God has prepared for those who love Him.

As we stand at the edge of the shore of a vast ocean of blessing that God has provided as our eternal inheritance, let us wade out as far as we can in our mental understanding, knowing that we can only grasp a tiny part of all God has laid up for His own dear children in the new heaven and the new earth. Our eternal destiny will be something in which the reality we experience will far surpass the expectations that were raised by the promises that are given. Heaven will not fall short of our expectations; instead, it will infinitely surpass them.

How often has someone told you about something, or promised you something, or sold you something, and said it will be this and it will do that for you, but after you received it you were disappointed? It was less than what you expected and less than you were promised.

God says, as it were, “Heaven is going to be like this, and it is going to provide that for you.” And when you get there, you are going to say, “I was not told the hundredth part of how wonderful it is! This so far exceeds my expectations that I cannot express how much more wonderful it is than I was ever led to believe by these descriptions contained in the Bible!”

The Description of the People of God

The description of the people of God is in verse 2. It says: *"And I John saw the holy city, new Jerusalem, coming down from God out of heaven, prepared as a bride adorned for her husband."*

Having seen the dwelling place of the people of God in verse 1, which is the new heaven and the new earth, John now begins to describe the inhabitants of that dwelling place in verse 2. John describes the inhabitants of the new heaven and the new earth with two metaphors: he describes them as the holy city, and he describes them as the bride of Christ.

First of all, John saw the holy city, the new Jerusalem. In the book of Revelation sharp contrasts are set forth between the kingdom of Satan and the kingdom of Christ. We have seen that there is a city in the kingdom of Satan, and this city is called Babylon. It is the city that is full of abominations and fornication and filthiness and blasphemy. It is the city that kills the Christians within its midst. This city Babylon represents anti-Christian society in all its wickedness wherever it appears in the world. This anti-Christian society, this Babylon, will be destroyed by Christ. We have seen this in chapters 17 and 18.

But in sharp contrast to Babylon is the city of the kingdom of God. The city of God is described first of all as the holy city. It is called the holy city because it is morally pure. Within it is no sinful practice or behavior. Within it righteousness rules, and Christlikeness characterizes the thoughts and words and behavior of every person within it. This holy city described in verse 2 represents Christian society as believers live together in righteousness and holiness.

Imagine living in a truly Christian city:

- a city where there is no need for police, courts, or jails;
- a city where there is no crime, fear, or violence;
- a city where there is no need for fences, locks, or alarms;
- a city where there is no discrimination between rich and poor or black and white;
- a city where there is no multiculturalism, no persecution, and no divisions;
- a city where there are no politicians, no regulatory agencies, and no oppressive laws;
- a city where everyone does the right thing all of the time in every circumstance;

- a city where everyone is patient, kind, understanding, and loving;
- a city where people care more about their neighbor than they care about themselves;
- a city where courtesy, selflessness, and serving others is the practice of every citizen;
- a city where there are no hospitals, doctors, or drugs;
- a city where there are no sirens, no screams for help, and no homeless people;
- a city where everyone is holy, happy, and God-centered;
- a city where the worship of God is the chief activity and delight of all the people.

Here in this heavenly society, people will live as God intended them to live before sin ever entered the human race. This is what the holy city looks like. But this city is not only called a holy city in verse 2, it is also called the new Jerusalem.

We are told repeatedly in the Old Testament that Jerusalem was God's chosen city. For example, in 2 Kings 21:7, God said: *"In Jerusalem, which I have chosen out of all tribes of Israel, will I put my name for ever."* Many similar passages with similar language tell us that Jerusalem was the special city of God. It was the city where His presence and His name dwelt, and it was the city where His temple was placed. Jerusalem was established as the city of God.

But sadly, Jerusalem failed to worship and glorify God as she should have. For example, in Isaiah 1:21–23 it says of Jerusalem, *"How is the faithful city become an harlot! it was full of judgment; righteousness lodged in it; but now murderers.* [22] *Thy silver is become dross, thy wine mixed with water:* [23] *Thy princes are rebellious, and companions of thieves: every one loveth gifts, and followeth after rewards: they judge not the fatherless neither doth the cause of the widow come unto them."*

Jerusalem failed to worship and glorify God as she should have, and her crowning failure was the rejection and crucifixion of her Messiah, Jesus Christ. As a result, Jerusalem was rejected by God. Jesus said regarding Jerusalem in Matthew 23:37–38, *"O Jerusalem, Jerusalem, thou that killest the prophets, and stonest them which are sent unto thee, how often would I have gathered thy children together, even as a hen gathereth her chickens under her wings, and ye would not!* [38] *Behold, your house is left unto you desolate."* We know this city and house were destroyed by God in AD 70.

Just as God rejected old Israel and created a new Israel with the New Covenant, so God rejected old Jerusalem and has made a new Jerusalem under the New Covenant. Paul makes this clear in Galatians 4:21–26. Paul says: *"Tell me, ye that desire to be under the law, do ye not hear the law?* [22] *For it is written, that Abraham had two sons, the one by a bondmaid, the other by a freewoman.* [23] *But he who was of the bondwoman was born after the flesh; but he of the freewoman was by promise."* (This referred to Hagar and Sarah, Ishmael and Isaac.) "[24] *Which things are an allegory: for these are the two covenants; the one from the mount Sinai, which gendereth to bondage, which is Hagar.* [25] *For this Hagar is mount Sinai in Arabia, and answereth to Jerusalem which now is, and is in bondage with her children.* [26] *But Jerusalem which is above is free, which is the mother of us all."*

Clearly, the Old Covenant concept of Jerusalem has passed away with the Old Covenant, and the Jerusalem which is above has replaced it. The Jerusalem which is above is the new Jerusalem, and the author of the book of Hebrews speaks of this new Jerusalem in Hebrews 12:22–24. He says to the believers, *"But ye are come unto mount Zion, and unto the city of the living God, the heavenly Jerusalem."* It is this heavenly Jerusalem that exists now in heaven that is said to come down from God out of heaven in Revelation 21:2.

Revelation 21:2 says, *"And I John saw the holy city, new Jerusalem, coming down from God out of heaven."* This is the Jerusalem Paul was speaking of in Galatians 4:26. This is the Jerusalem spoken of in Hebrews 12:22. It is this heavenly Jerusalem that exists now in heaven, that is said to come down from God out of heaven, and which will be the city of God on the new earth.

This is why as Christians we are not obsessed with the Jerusalem that is in Israel. We are obsessed with the Jerusalem that is in heaven. That is the holy city. And while the old Jerusalem failed to worship Jesus Christ, the new Jerusalem will certainly worship Christ, and it is this new Jerusalem made up of all the saved that God will own as His holy city, and the city where He will put His name forever.

In Isaiah 65:17–19 God says: *"For, behold, I create new heavens and a new earth: and the former shall not be remembered, nor come into mind.* [18] *But be ye glad and rejoice for ever in that which I create: for, behold, I create Jerusalem a rejoicing, and her people a joy.* [19] *And I will rejoice in Jerusalem, and joy in my people: and the voice of weeping shall be no more heard in her, nor the voice of crying."* This is the Jerusalem which is above, which will come down from heaven, and will be the city of the New Earth. Therefore, when God said He would put His name in Jerusalem forever, this is the Jerusalem He is speaking of.

When Jesus ascended to heaven, the new Jerusalem, the society of the saved, was established there. The new Jerusalem that is in heaven continues to grow, and one day it will come down to the earth, and that society of the new Jerusalem will inhabit the new earth, and this is the society in which we will live forever.

It is interesting to observe that the wicked city of Babylon rose up out of the sea of fallen humanity, but the holy city of Jerusalem comes down from God out of heaven. The difference in their origin is what explains the contrast in their character.

Notice that a second characteristic of the inhabitants of the new heaven and earth is declared. Verse 2 says, *"And I John saw the holy city, new Jerusalem, coming down from God out of heaven,"* (here is the second characteristic) *"prepared as a bride adorned for her husband."*

The idea that a city would also be personified as a woman is introduced to us in the Old Testament. For example, Old Testament Jerusalem was referred to as *"the virgin, the daughter of Zion,"* in Isaiah 37:22. The idea that a city would be personified as a woman was also introduced to us in Revelation 17, when the city of Babylon was also called *"the mother of harlots"* and *"the great whore."* But in sharp contrast to Babylon the harlot, we have Jerusalem the bride of Christ. A city being symbolized as a woman is common in the Scriptures, and it should come as no surprise to us here.

The symbolism of the church as the bride of Christ is well known and developed at length in Ephesians 5:22–33. Furthermore, we have seen the church symbolized as the bride of Christ attending the wedding supper of the Lamb in Revelation 19:7–9. Here in Revelation 21:2 and later in 21:9, the church is explicitly declared to be the bride of Christ.

Revelation 21:9 says, *"And there came unto me one of the seven angels which had the seven vials full of the seven last plagues, and talked with me, saying, Come hither, I will shew thee the bride, the Lamb's wife."* And what did he then show him? The new Jerusalem, the holy city, which is the society of all of the saved. Collectively we form not only the holy city, the new Jerusalem; we also form the bride of Christ.

Just as the city of new Jerusalem is designed to symbolize the purity and perfection of a Christian society, so the symbolism of the church as the bride of Christ is designed to convey the commitment Christ has to us, and the closeness Christ has with us. Marriage conveys the idea of commitment and closeness between a husband and wife.

The church is the single object of Christ's love; therefore, He will never forsake us for someone else. He is absolutely committed to us and to us alone. Furthermore, the church has the most intimate relationship with Christ, into which no one else can ever intrude. Christ has a heart-to-heart relationship with us. We are as secure in Christ and as close to Christ as a husband and wife would be in the perfect marriage.

In Isaiah 61:10 it says, *"I will greatly rejoice in the* L*ORD*, *my soul shall be joyful in my God; for he hath clothed me with the garments of salvation, he hath covered me with the robe of righteousness, as a bridegroom decketh himself with ornaments, and as a bride adorneth herself with her jewels."* The Old Testament speaks of this marriage between Christ and His people in which He clothes His bride with the garment of salvation and righteousness.

These two symbolic metaphors describe the inhabitants of the new earth in relationship to one another, and in relationship to Christ. The inhabitants of the new earth in relationship to one another are a holy city, a perfect Christian society in which perfect love prevails between all the people who live there. The inhabitants of the new earth in relationship to Christ are His bride, enjoying perfect security and perfect closeness, sharing a transcendent love for one another that will never end.

The Blessedness of the People of God

The blessedness of the people of God is spoken of in verses 3 and 4. *"And I heard a great voice out of heaven saying, Behold, the tabernacle of God is with men, and he will dwell with them, and they shall be his people, and God himself shall be with them, and be their God.*
[4] *And God shall wipe away all tears from their eyes; and there shall be no more death, neither sorrow, nor crying, neither shall there be any*

more pain: for the former things are passed away."

Verse 3 opens with a declaration that a great voice spoke out of heaven in order to convey the message of verses 3 and 4. The loudness of this voice and the heavenly origin of this voice are entirely fitting for the incredibly important announcement that is about to be made. This announcement summarizes the totality of the blessedness of the redeemed in two overwhelming statements: First of all, that God will dwell with His people, in verse 3; and secondly, that the curse and all of its effects will forever be removed, in verse 4.

First of all, consider that the blessedness of the people of God consists of God dwelling in the midst of them. It says in verse 3, *"And I heard a great voice out of heaven saying, Behold, the tabernacle of God is with men, and he will dwell with them, and they shall be his people, and God himself shall be with them, and be their God."*

When it says that the tabernacle of God is with men, the word *"tabernacle"* conveys neither the idea of a tent nor does it convey the idea of something that is temporary and transient which can be packed up and moved. Rather, the word *"tabernacle"* conveys the idea of a dwelling place where God's presence and God's glory is manifested among His people.

For example, in Leviticus 26:11–12 God says, *"And I will set my tabernacle among you: and my soul shall not abhor you. [12] And I will walk among you, and will be your God, and ye shall be my people."* God is saying that when He tabernacles among His people, He will not be offended at them, and His presence and His glory will be in their midst.

Notice Ezekiel 37:24–28. Ezekiel is talking about the future of the people of God, and he makes this very interesting statement in verse 24. *"And David my servant shall be king over them; and they all shall have one shepherd: they shall also walk in my judgments, and observe my statutes, and do them."*

Biblical chronology makes it clear that David had been dead for centuries when this was written. Yet here it says, *"David my servant shall be king over them; and they all shall have one shepherd."* The word "David" is used by way of metonymy—that is, by way of substitution of one thing for another. "David" is used for Jesus Christ, who is the son of David. Therefore, when it says, *"David my servant,"* we could read it, *"and Jesus, the son of David my servant, shall be king over them."*

It says, "[24] *And David [Jesus] my servant shall be king over them; and they all shall have one shepherd: they shall also walk in my judgments, and observe my statutes, and do them.* [25] *And they shall dwell in the land that I have given unto Jacob my servant, wherein your fathers have dwelt; and they shall dwell therein, even they, and their children, and their children's children for ever: and my servant David"* [Jesus] *"shall be their prince for ever."*

The land of Israel was never really *"the land"* God was ultimately promising. When Abraham went into the land of Israel, did he think that it was the land that God gave to him? He knew it was just the foreshadowing of the land. He was really looking for the city whose builder and maker was God, the new Jerusalem, as described in Hebrews 11:8–16. Abraham was looking for a heavenly country. When God said to Abraham that He was going to give him the land forever, did Israel have the land forever? Not at all. Israel had the land, and they lost it to Babylon; they had the land back again, and they lost it again to Rome. They lost it for 2,000 years, and now they have it back again. The land that is never lost is the new heaven and the new earth, of which the Middle Eastern land of Israel was just a picture. The land promised to Abraham was the new earth. Only the new earth is the land God's people will dwell in forever.

Verse 26: *"Moreover I will make a covenant of peace with them"* (the New Covenant); *"it shall be an everlasting covenant with them: and I will place them, and multiply them, and will set my sanctuary in the midst of them for evermore."* What sanctuary is that? Verse 27: *"My tabernacle also shall be with them: yea, I will be their God, and they shall be my people.* [28] *And the heathen shall know that I the* Lord *do sanctify Israel, when my sanctuary shall be in the midst of them for evermore."*

God is saying, "Through the ministry of My servant Jesus Christ, I am going to give you the land. I am going to make a new covenant with you, and I am going to tabernacle in the midst of you—that is, My presence and My glory will be in the midst of you forever in the land that I give you, which is the new earth."

When it says in Revelation 21:3 *"Behold, the tabernacle of God is with men, and he will dwell with them, and they shall be his people, and God himself shall be with them, and be their God,"* it is telling us that God will be a God who shows favor to us instead of wrath toward us; that God will have us as His own special people who will have permanent access to His immediate presence; and that God will have personal fellowship with us as His own dear children.

In other words, what is being promised in Ezekiel 37:24–28, and what is being promised in Revelation 21:3, is that God will be a Father to us, with all of the love and communication and provision and protection that a perfect father would give to his own beloved children. He will never leave us or forsake us. He will always be with us for all eternity.

God will never withdraw His presence from us. Never again will He place His wrath on us as he did on Adam after the fall. Instead, God will love us with an everlasting love, and with lovingkindness He will draw us to Himself forever. He will never abhor us or cast us away.

A very beautiful and touching description of this love God will have for us and express to us has already been given in Revelation 7:15–17 where it says of the saints: *"Therefore are they before the throne of God, and serve him day and night in his temple:"* (the new Jerusalem, the dwelling place of God, the tabernacle) *"and he that sitteth on the throne shall dwell among them."* This is what is stated in Revelation 21:3.

Verse 16: *"They shall hunger no more, neither thirst any more; neither shall the sun light on them, nor any heat.* [17] *For the Lamb which is in the midst of the throne shall feed them, and shall lead them unto living fountains of waters: and God shall wipe away all tears from their eyes."*

This is what it means when it says He will dwell with us, and He will be our God, and we will be His people. We will have the most intimate communion with Him, we will have His personal presence, we will have His fatherly care, and we will have His unending commitment that He will never leave us or forsake us for all eternity.

But the blessedness of the people of God not only consists of God dwelling in the midst of them; secondly, the blessedness of the people of God consists of freedom from the curse. Notice Revelation 21:4. It says, *"And God shall wipe away all tears from their eyes; and there shall be no more death, neither sorrow, nor crying, neither shall there be any more pain: for the former things are passed away."*

The new earth and the new heaven will be known by what is not there, as well as by what is there. We have seen in verses 1 to 3 what is there, and it is wonderful. We have a new heaven and a new earth; we have the holy city, the new Jerusalem; we are the bride of Christ; and God Himself will be our God and dwell in our midst, and we will be with Him forever.

But it is also wonderful because all the effects of sin and the curse that are so painful and difficult for us to bear now will be entirely absent then. The seething mass of unsaved humanity will be absent, as verse 1 made clear when it said there will be no more sea. We will be delivered from problems outside of ourselves that arise because of evil people around us and the wicked Babylon in which we now live. That sea of wicked people will be gone.

But there are also problems that arise from within ourselves. Because of the sinfulness and corruption we have within us, we are subject to death and sorrow and crying and pain. But the wonder of being redeemed by Christ—the wonder of residing in the new heaven and the new earth—is that we will never experience those things again.

Never again will you have to weep over the loss of a loved one. Never again will you have to suffer the agonizing loneliness that such a death brings upon you. Never again will you sorrow over the rejection and loss and persecution this world brings upon you. Never again will you suffer the emotional and physical pains that are the result of a broken body and a broken soul. In the new earth, everything that is good will be present; and thank God, everything that is bad will be absent. Death and sorrow and crying and pain will never be experienced ever again. Amazingly, all of this is promised to us in the Old Testament.

In Isaiah 25:8–9 it says, *"He will swallow up death in victory; and the Lord GOD will wipe away tears from off all faces; and the rebuke of his people shall he take away from off all the earth: for the LORD hath spoken it.* [9] *And it shall be said in that day, Lo, this is our God; we have waited for him, and he will save us: this is the LORD; we have waited for him, we will be glad and rejoice in his salvation."*

Isaiah 35:10 says: *"And the ransomed of the LORD shall return, and come to Zion with songs and everlasting joy upon their heads: they shall obtain joy and gladness, and sorrow and sighing shall flee away."* When the first heaven and the first earth pass away, death and sorrow and crying and pain will also pass away. And just as the first heaven and the first earth can never return, death and sorrow and crying and pain can never return either. Death is swallowed up in victory.

This then is the blessedness of the people of God. They have the presence of God, and they have the absence of the curse. The holy city and the bride will dwell in the presence of God, free from the curse for all eternity. God will have a perfect commitment to them and a perfect closeness with them so that all they experience is unending joy and peace and happiness in the glory of heaven.

These are the wonderful things that God has laid up for us. Human words are entirely inadequate to try to describe something that is supernaturally infinite, and that is why all that has been said to us is just a tiny part of all we are going to experience. A person would be a fool to miss out on this blessedness of living in this holy city, having this wonderful relationship with Jesus Christ, dwelling in the presence of God, and having the absence of all that is destructive and harmful.

This is what Christ promises us in the gospel. These are the everlasting riches of Christ. All we have to do to obtain them is repent of our sins and believe in and trust Jesus Christ as our Lord and Savior. Turn from following self and Satan and sin, and say to God, "God, I am done with that! I want to be a pure man, I want to be a pure woman, I want Christ to save me from my sins. O, Lord Jesus, save me! Be my Master; I will follow You. Be my Savior; I will trust You, and trust in nothing and no one but you to present me faultless before God's presence with exceeding joy."

Believe on the Lord Jesus Christ, and you will be saved. Whosoever shall call upon the name of the Lord will be saved. Call upon Him now. He will save you. If you do, the new heaven and the new earth will be your destiny.

63

The King of the People of God, Revelation 21:5–8

> *"[5] And he that sat upon the throne said, Behold, I make all things new. And he said unto me, Write: for these words are true and faithful. [6] And he said unto me, It is done. I am Alpha and Omega, the beginning and the end. I will give unto him that is athirst of the fountain of the water of life freely. [7] He that overcometh shall inherit all things; and I will be his God, and he shall be my son. [8] But the fearful, and unbelieving, and the abominable, and murderers, and whoremongers, and sorcerers, and idolaters, and all liars, shall have their part in the lake which burneth with fire and brimstone: which is the second death."*

Revelation 21 and 22 set before us the glorious future of the people of God. After Christ returns, He will bestow on us all He has promised us, and all He has promised us is described in the last two chapters of Revelation.

As we have begun a study of these last two chapters, we have seen the dwelling place of the people of God in verse 1, which consists of the new heaven and the new earth. This dwelling place will be paradise restored. What the heaven and the earth were before the fall when Eden was the dwelling place of mankind is what we shall have again. All the beauty and perfection of creation will be restored, and once again, everything will be very good, and no harm will ever again arise out of nature. Furthermore, Satan and his people will be gone forever, and only Christ and His people will live on the new earth. The restless sea of fallen humanity that lives in rebellion against God will never live among us again.

We not only saw the dwelling place of the people of God in verse 1, but we also saw the description of the people of God in verse 2, where they are said to be the holy city and the bride of Christ. The people of God are said to make up the holy city, the New Jerusalem, and these terms symbolize and represent the Christian society of the saints who live in perfect harmony and perfect holiness with one another. In the society of the saints, there will be no sinful practices, there will be no sinful attitudes, and there will be no sinful words. There is only righteousness in their behavior, there is only Christlikeness in their character, and there is only love in their attitude toward one another.

These people who inhabit the new earth are not only said to be a holy city, describing their Christian society; they are also said to be the bride of Christ, describing their delightful relationship with Jesus. This symbolic metaphor of the church being the bride of Christ is designed to convey the truth about the commitment Christ has to us, and the closeness Christ has with us. This symbolism conveys the transcendent love Christ has for His people, a love He will express to us forever, and a love we will return to Him who first loved us.

But there are still more riches to be seen in these opening verses of chapter 21. Not only did we see the dwelling place of the people of God in verse 1, and not only did we see the description of the people of God in verse 2, but we also saw the blessedness of the people of God in verses 3 and 4. This blessedness consisted of two things.

First, it consists in God dwelling with His people, as verse 3 declared. The blessedness of having God's presence with us and God's glory manifested to us is a blessedness that is beyond description. To have God's favor toward us, God's presence with us, and God's love shown to us is wonderful beyond words. God's fatherly care for us will meet every need we have to the fullest degree and at the deepest level.

Second, it consists in freedom from the curse, as we saw in verse 4. In the new earth, never again will we experience death or sorrow or crying or pain. Never again will there be human suffering of any kind. Never again will we hurt emotionally, and never again will we suffer physically. There will be no sadness, there will be no depression, and there will be no grief. All we will know on the new earth is joy and peace and pleasure and contentment.

So we see in verse 1 the dwelling place of the people of God; we see in verse 2 the description of the people of God; and we see in verses 3 and 4 the blessedness of the people of God. But as wonderful as those things are, God is not done unfolding the blessing that awaits us. God now reveals in verses 5 through 8 the King of the people of

God. That King and ruler, as we shall see, is none other than Jesus Christ Himself.

In verses 5 to 8, we are told of the one who is sitting upon the throne, what He has to say, and who the subjects of His kingdom are; and just as importantly, who they are not. We see the wonderful proclamations and the wonderful promises this King makes to His people, and in these statements from the enthroned Christ we find great hope and comfort and peace. Let us consider together the King of the people of God in verses 5 through 8.

The Identity of the King

Notice verse 5. *"And he that sat upon the throne said."* Verse 5 introduces us to the Person who is enthroned in this new earth. The throne He is sitting on is the same throne spoken of in Revelation 20:11: *"And I saw a great white throne, and him that sat on it, from whose face the earth and the heaven fled away; and there was found no place for them."*

This is the throne of judgment and power and authority. It is the throne from which rule will be exercised in the new heavens and the new earth for all eternity.

In verse 6, the occupant of the throne identifies Himself. He says: *"I am Alpha and Omega, the beginning and the end."* These two titles, *"Alpha and Omega,"* and *"the beginning and the end,"* were both first mentioned in Revelation 1.

Revelation 1:4–6 says: *"John to the seven churches which are in Asia: Grace be unto you, and peace, from him which is, and which was, and which is to come; and from the seven Spirits which are before his throne; [5] And from Jesus Christ, who is the faithful witness, and the first begotten of the dead, and the prince of the kings of the earth. Unto him that loved us, and washed us from our sins in his own blood, [6] And hath made us kings and priests unto God and his Father; to him be glory and dominion for ever and ever. Amen."*

The subject of verses 4 to 6 is Jesus Christ. He is the One who washed us in His blood from our sins. He is the one who made us kings and priests to God and his Father. Now notice verse 7. It says, *"Behold, he cometh with clouds"* (speaking of the second coming of Jesus); *"and every eye shall see him, and they also which pierced him: and all kindreds of the earth shall wail because of him. Even so, Amen."* Verse 7 makes it certain that the subject of verses 4 to 7 is Jesus Christ.

Now notice verse 8: *"I am Alpha and Omega, the beginning and the ending, saith the Lord, which is, and which was, and which is to come, the Almighty."* Here we move from speaking in the third person—that is, John speaking about Christ—to this individual speaking in the first person in verse 8: *"I am Alpha and Omega, the beginning and the ending, saith the Lord."* In verse 8, the same titles are used, *"Alpha and Omega," "the beginning and the ending,"* that are used in Revelation 21:6.

In Revelation 1:8, the person speaking there not only says of Himself that He is the Alpha and Omega, and the beginning and the ending; He also says of Himself that He is, and was, and is to come, and that He is the Almighty. This Lord that is speaking in verse 8 says, "I am the Alpha and the Omega, I am the beginning and the end, and in addition to that, I am eternal and I am omnipotent." But who is speaking in verse 8? Who bears these titles—Alpha and Omega, the beginning and the end, the one who is, and was, and is to come, the Almighty?

Notice verses 9 to 11: *"I John, who also am your brother, and companion in tribulation, and in the kingdom and patience of Jesus Christ, was in the isle that is called Patmos, for the word of God, and for the testimony of Jesus Christ.* [10] *I was in the Spirit on the Lord's day, and heard behind me a great voice, as of a trumpet,* [11] *Saying, I am Alpha and Omega, the first and the last: and, What thou seest, write in a book, and send it unto the seven churches which are in Asia; unto Ephesus, and unto Smyrna, and unto Pergamos, and unto Thyatira, and unto Sardis, and unto Philadelphia, and unto Laodicea."*

Here, this voice once again claims the title of Alpha and Omega; and it now adds a new third title, and that is *"the first and the last."* He says, "I am Alpha and Omega," (title number 1); He says, "I am the beginning and the end," (title number 2); and He says, "I am the first and the last," (title number 3).

But who does this voice belong to? Verses 12 to 13 says: *"And I turned to see the voice that spake with me. And being turned, I saw seven golden candlesticks;* [13] *And in the midst of the seven candlesticks one like unto the Son of man, clothed with a garment down to the foot, and girt about the [chest] with a golden [belt]."* This is the one who is doing the talking, the one like unto the Son of man. This voice and these titles belong to the Son of man, Jesus Christ. God the Father was never called the Son of man, and God the Holy Spirit was never called the Son of man. Only one person in the Godhead bears that title, and that is Jesus Christ.

Notice the further description of Jesus Christ, who is the Alpha and the Omega, the beginning and the ending, and the first and the last, in verses 14 to 18: *"His head and his hairs were white like wool, as white as snow; and his eyes were as a flame of fire;* [15] *And his feet like unto fine brass, as if they burned in a furnace; and his voice as the sound of many waters.* [16] *And he had in his right hand seven stars: and out of his mouth went a sharp two-edged sword: and his countenance was as the sun shineth in his strength.* [17] *And when I saw him, I fell at his feet as dead. And he laid his right hand upon me, saying unto me, Fear not; I am the first and the last:* [18] *I am he that liveth, and was dead; and, behold, I am alive for evermore, Amen; and have the keys of hell and of death."*

There can be no doubt whatsoever that it is the resurrected Christ who is speaking here as the Son of man, claiming to Himself the title of Alpha and Omega, beginning and ending, and first and last. The first and the last is also identified as the resurrected Christ, the one who lived, who died, and who lived again and is alive forevermore, and who has authority over hell and death so that death and hell must obey Him. We undeniably see that these titles belong to Christ. He speaks them, and He identifies Himself by them.

Notice Revelation 22:12–13. Jesus Christ is speaking here and He says, *"Behold, I come quickly; and my reward is with me to give every man according as his work shall be."* He is the one who is coming, and who gives men the reward for their works.

Now notice verse 13: *"I am Alpha and Omega, the beginning and the end, the first and the last."* All three titles that are used of Jesus Christ in Revelation 1 are also used of Jesus Christ in Revelation 22:13. Jesus says of Himself both in chapter 1 and in chapter 22, "I am Alpha and Omega, I am the beginning and the end, and I am the first and the last." All three of these titles belong to and are descriptive of Jesus Christ, and indisputably so.

Therefore, when we return back to our passage in Revelation 21:5–6, and we see the one sitting on the throne saying that He is *"Alpha and Omega, the beginning and the end"* in verse 6; then clearly, this person who is on this throne in verse 5 is Jesus Christ. Now here is the monumental point: This same person who says that He is the Alpha and the Omega, the beginning and the end, also says something else. Notice verse 5: *"And he that sat upon the throne said"*—verse 6—*"I am Alpha and Omega, the beginning and the end"*—verse 7—*"He that overcometh shall inherit all things; and I will be his God."*

The monumental point is that Jesus declares that He is our God in the clearest possible terms, thus proving His deity beyond any shadow of a doubt. Therefore, it is inexcusable that the Jehovah's Witnesses and so many other heretical cults who claim to believe in the Bible's authority and teaching would deny that Jesus Christ is God. The one sitting on the throne here is absolutely Jesus Christ, and Jesus Christ says, *"I will be his God, and he shall be my son."*

If you have ever wondered if the Bible definitively and absolutely and without question proves the deity of Christ, you have just heard the proof out of the mouth of Christ Himself. He says in verse 7, "I am God." Therefore, any statement the Bible contains about God is a statement that is applicable to Christ and is true about Christ.

Sometimes the Bible speaks of God as the Father, and what the Bible says about the Father as a Person is not necessarily true of the Son, because the Son and the Father are distinct Persons. But when the Bible speaks about God as God, as opposed to speaking about God as Father, then that statement is a statement that is applicable to Christ and is true about Christ. For example, when it says in Genesis 1:1, *"In the beginning God created the heavens and the earth,"* we see that Jesus was the one who created the heavens and the earth, and the New Testament bears that out clearly in three distinct places (John 1:3, Colossians 1:16, Hebrews 1:2). This is why it says in John 5:23, *"All men should honour the Son, even as they honour the Father. He that honoureth not the Son honoureth not the Father which hath sent him."*

The Son and the Father both deserve equal worship, equal praise, and equal honor because They are equal in Their essence, in Their attributes, and in Their deity. The Son is just as much God as the Father is God. This is why it says, *"All men should honour the Son, even as"* (just as much as, or in the same fashion as) *"they honour the Father."* If you think of Jesus as something less than the Father in terms of His attributes, His essence, and His deity, then you are a blasphemer, and you are not a Christian. The identity of the King of the people of God on the new earth is God the Son, Jesus Christ.

The Proclamations of the King

The King makes two proclamations from His throne. The first proclamation is made in verse 5: "*And he that sat upon the throne said, Behold, I make all things new.*" That is, there will be nothing that is left untransformed that was part of the first heaven and the first earth. We will not find in the new heavens and the new earth that some things are delivered from the effects of sin, while other things are still defiled as a result of sin.

For example, among your personal possessions, you have some brand-new things that are still in perfect condition, but you also have other things that are worn and rusted and show signs of decay. Not everything you have is brand new. But in the new heavens and the new earth, everything will be made brand new, and everything will be in pristine condition, without any effects of the curse upon it. The earth itself in all of its physical characteristics (the plants, the animals, the stellar heavens, and humanity itself) will be put back into brand-new condition, and it will remain in brand-new condition for all eternity because there will be no sin to cause its decay or degradation ever again. Nothing will grow old, nothing will wear out, and nothing will rot or decay or rust or break.

Matthew 6:19–20 makes it clear that in this sin-cursed earth "*moth and rust doth corrupt,*" but in the new earth, neither moth nor rust will ever corrupt anything again. He who upholds all things by the word of His power will uphold the newness of all things for all eternity, for when Jesus makes all things new, they stay that way forever. We have an inheritance that is incorruptible, and undefiled, and that does not fade away. It is reserved in heaven for us. All of the effects of sin on all of the things it touched will be totally eradicated to the point that it will be as though the effects of sin had never existed in the first place. This will especially be true of saved people. Every saved person will be made new. Their bodies will be renewed back to the condition Adam and Eve's bodies were in before the fall. Never again will the body be subject to sickness or aging or injury. They will have perfect physical health 100 percent of the time.

Their souls will also be renewed back into the image of God so they perfectly reflect God's moral character and God's communicable attributes. Never again will our flesh or our spirit find any attraction to any sin, or find any pleasure in it or any desire for it. All darkness of mind, all dullness of spirit, and all reluctance of the will regarding spiritual matters that we struggle so much against now will trouble us no more. We will be new people. The old things will pass away, and all things will become new. Our zeal for obedience and worship and praise and learning about the things of God will be limitless and endless. We will finally be pure in heart, in the fullest sense of that term.

As it says in Isaiah 43:18–19: *"Remember ye not the former things, neither consider the things of old.* [19] *Behold, I will do a new thing; now it shall spring forth; shall ye not know it? I will even make a way in the wilderness, and rivers in the desert."* Isaiah is saying that it is not going to be the way it used to be anymore. God will make all things new so that the character of all things is transformed. All obstacles are removed: there will be a way in the wilderness; and all blessings will flow forevermore: there will be rivers in the desert.

As we hear these things, we wonder: Could all of this really be true? Will God really do this wonderful work? Notice verse 5b: *"And he that sat upon the throne said, Behold, I make all things new. And he said unto me, Write: for these words are true and faithful."* Jesus is saying, "Yes, it is true. I will be faithful to that promise, and it will be true as I stated it. I will make all things new. This is really going to happen, and this is exactly how it will be, and I mean exactly what I say. Write that down." This then is the first proclamation: *"Behold, I make all things new."*

But there is a second proclamation the enthroned King makes in verse 6: *"And he said unto me, It is done."* When Jesus died on the cross, He said something slightly different. He said, *"It is finished."* What He meant when He said, *"It is finished,"* was that His mighty work of redemption had come to an end, because His purchase of it was completed.

That is not what Jesus is saying here when He says, *"It is done."* He employs different words in the original language. When He says, *"It is done,"* He is saying, "It has come to pass." He is not saying that it has come to an end, which is what He said on the cross. When He says, *"It is done,"* He is saying that all Jesus had promised to do, He has now brought to pass. When He is at the point in future history described in this passage after the New Heavens and Earth are created, He will have done all He promised, and brought to pass all He said He would achieve.

Jesus promised to destroy the works of the devil, and it has come to pass. It is done. The work of implementing all that He purchased on the cross has come to pass. It is done. The promise to fully save His elect from their sins has come to pass. It is done. The removal of the curse from the physical creation has come to pass. It is done. All Satan accomplished has now been completely undone and entirely reversed and totally overthrown. It has come to pass. The finished provision that Christ made on the cross to redeem us from our sins has now been fully implemented, and the plan of redemption has now been fully executed and completed. It is done.

It is like a divine building project. The blueprint of God's plan was made in eternity past. The financing for God's plan was provided at the cross by the payment of the precious blood of Christ. The completion of God's plan will be achieved when the new heavens and the new earth are finished and the resurrected saints inhabit it. The building of the kingdom of God will be done, and the final inspection will be passed.

Viewing the resurrected saints inhabiting the new heavens and the new earth, and viewing all of His elect gathered together in the place of His finished work, Jesus says, *"It is done."* The construction project is completed. All that was planned has now come to pass. The blueprint is now a reality. What Jesus starts, Jesus finishes, and what He purposed to do, He fully accomplished. Jesus counted the cost, paid the price, did the work, and finished the project He set out to achieve.

Jesus looks at the whole scope of history, and at all that He has achieved, and He says, *"It is done."* The plan has been fully executed. He sees what He has achieved, and He is fully satisfied. There is nothing left to do by way of implementing the promises and the plans of God. The application is simply this: All that Jesus has promised to us, He will fully perform for us, and He will not stop until it is done. Not one thing shall fail of all that the Lord has promised. All will come to pass. Isaiah 42:4 says of Jesus, *"He shall not fail nor be discouraged, till he have set judgment in the earth."* The book of God's decrees sealed with seven seals has been fully carried out.

The Subjects of the King

As we have considered this wonderful King and His wonderful kingdom, the thought naturally arises: Who will enter into this kingdom? Who will be the subjects of this King? Who will receive the blessings this King has to bestow? The answer to those questions is provided in verses 6, 7, and 8. Those who will be included in the kingdom of Christ are described in verses 6 and 7. Those who will be excluded from the kingdom of Christ are described in verse 8. We want to look at each of them in turn.

First, notice the citizens of the kingdom. The citizens of the kingdom have two essential characteristics. First of all, they are those who have acted on the gracious invitation of Christ. Notice verse 6: *"And he said unto me, It is done. I am Alpha and Omega, the beginning and the end."* Now here is the gracious invitation of Christ: *"I will give unto him that is athirst of the fountain of the water of life freely."*

This thirst spoken of in verse 6 is the intense longing for reconciliation with God and redemption from sin. Here is one who says, *"My soul thirsts for God, for the living God: when shall I come and appear before God?"* Here is one who recognizes that just as water is necessary for physical life, a relationship with God is necessary for eternal life. Here are those who *"hunger and thirst after righteousness."* When they heard the gospel, they understood that Jesus Christ was the fountain of life. They understood that Jesus made an open invitation during His ministry: *"If any man thirst, let him come unto me and drink. He that believeth on me, as the scripture hath said, out of his [innermost being] shall flow rivers of living water."* When one who thirsts for righteousness and for God believes in Jesus Christ, that thirst will be satisfied. He will never thirst again.

The water of eternal life is freely given to anyone who feels the thirst of being alienated from God, and who feels the need to be reconciled to God, and who believes in Jesus Christ as the one who can meet those needs and provide that reconciliation. Who is in the kingdom of God? Those who come to Christ for eternal life and who freely receive from Him the satisfaction their souls longed for, the satisfaction of being presented faultless before the presence of the Father.

This same offer is still open today. Jesus will give to him that is athirst of the fountain of the water of life freely. Notice in Revelation 22:17 the gracious invitation is repeated. It says, *"And the Spirit and the bride say, Come. And let him that heareth say, Come. And let him that is athirst come. And whosoever will, let him take the water of life freely."* The water of life is Jesus Christ. To receive Christ is to have the thirst for reconciliation with God fully quenched and satisfied.

This is the first characteristic of those who are citizens of the kingdom. They have felt the thirst of alienation from God. They have felt the thirst for righteousness that arises out of the guilt and the shame of sin. They have heard the gracious invitation of Christ to come unto Him. He said, "I will quench your thirst with My forgiveness, My redemption, and My reconciliation—indeed, with My very Person." They acted on that gracious invitation of Christ, and they obtained eternal life from Christ; and as a result, they will never thirst again.

But the second characteristic of those who are citizens of the kingdom is not only that they have acted on the gracious invitation of Christ, but they have also overcome the temptation to forsake Christ. Notice verse 7: *"He that overcometh shall inherit all things; and I will be his God, and he shall be my son."* There is no one in heaven who is not an overcomer.

When we studied the seven churches in chapters 2 and 3, we saw these seven churches were representative of the kind of spiritual warfare that churches would endure throughout this New Covenant age in which we are living. We saw that each of the letters closed with promises to the one who overcame the temptations that beset that church and the believers within it. At the end of every one of those letters, Jesus said, *"To him that overcometh"* I will grant the blessings and benefits of salvation.

Satan does everything he can to draw Christians away from Christ through temptation, or drive them away from Christ through persecution. Those who overcome the seduction of temptation to forsake Christ, and those who overcome the pressure of persecution to forsake Christ are those who prove the genuineness of their faith in Christ. They are the overcomers. To be an overcomer does not mean that you overcame every individual sin in your life so that you became sinless. To be an overcomer means that you overcame the pressure Satan applied to you through either temptation or persecution to forsake your faith in Christ and your faithfulness to Christ. In other words, to be an overcomer means you overcame the temptation to turn your back on Christ and walk away from Christ.

The faith that saves is a faith that also transforms; and that transformation of life and character is what enables believers to continue to follow Christ no matter the cost of doing so, and in the face of very powerful incentives to forsake Him. The overcomer overcomes Satan's efforts to draw him away from Christ. The overcomer perseveres in his battle against his own sin to the end of his life. The overcomer never quits. The overcomer never gives in. The overcomer never gives up.

Most importantly, the overcomer never changes sides. He remains faithful to Christ to the end. He overcomes Satan's efforts to either drag him away or drive him away from Jesus Christ. It is people who cling to Christ in this life, no matter the pressure, who inhabit the new heaven and the new earth in the next life. They believed in Christ and came to Christ to obtain everlasting life, they persevered in faith in Christ and in faithfulness to Christ to the end of their lives, and they overcame every temptation to forsake Him. It is the people who believe and overcome who are the citizens of the kingdom of Christ.

Having seen the citizens of the kingdom, notice secondly, the outcasts from the kingdom. The outcasts from the kingdom are mentioned in verse 8. *"But,"* in contrast to those who are in the kingdom, *"the fearful, and unbelieving, and the abominable, and murderers, and whoremongers, and sorcerers, and idolaters, and all liars, shall have their part in the lake which burneth with fire and brimstone: which is the second death."*

Who is not in the kingdom? Those who are excluded are those who were afraid of the cost of following Christ. They were *"the fearful"* who thought, "I am afraid if I speak up for Christ, I will lose my job; I am afraid if I speak up for Christ, people will laugh at me." There are many other bad things that can happen to you if you publicly confess Christ before men. People who are afraid to publicly confess Christ before men will never enter the kingdom of God.

The outcasts from the kingdom are those who refuse to believe in Christ as their only hope of salvation. Notice verse 8: *"But the. . . unbelieving."* These are those who would not believe in Christ as Savior while here on this earth. They would not believe in Him as God the Son who came to rule and reign in their lives and to save them from their sins. They would not believe the Son of God, the word of God, or the promises of God.

Those who are outcasts from the kingdom are those who practice moral abominations. It says in verse 8, *"But the. . . abominable."* This is a general word that encompasses all the things that God declares are an offense to Him. Many sins are listed in the Bible as being an abomination to God, and this term encompasses them all. These are those who practice moral abominations.

The outcasts from the kingdom are those who murdered others through homicide or through abortion. It says in verse 8, *"But . . .murderers."* There is a lot of murdering that has gone on in the history of the world. It started with Cain, and it has been going on ever since. Many Christians have been murdered because they followed Christ, as we have seen throughout this book. Millions have been murdered in unjust wars by evil governments. Many people wrongly think of abortion as something less than murder. Abortion is the murder of a human being, and those who practice these murders, defend these murders, and justify these murders will all be cast into hell.

The outcasts from the kingdom are they who practice sexual immorality of every kind. It says in verse 8, *"But. . . whoremongers."* God gave us sexuality, and it is a great blessing when it is exercised within the context of marriage. God says in Hebrews 13:4 that marriage is honorable in all, and the bed is undefiled. It is whoremongers and adulterers that God will judge. Those who persist in sexual immorality, who justify it, defend it, and go on in it, will never enter the kingdom of God.

The outcasts from the kingdom are those who practice witchcraft and sorcery. Notice verse 8, *"But. . .sorcerers."* This would include anyone who is involved in any kind of witchcraft in any way. This is Satanism at its core. Something supposedly as innocent as playing with Ouija boards and reading horoscopes, all the way to human sacrifices done on altars at midnight masses on Halloween in the worship of Satan is encompassed by this word. You do not practice any kind of witchcraft or sorcery, defend it, and continue on in it, and ever expect to enter the kingdom of God.

The outcasts from the kingdom are those who worship false gods and follow false religions. Verse 8 says, *"But. . .idolaters."* An idolater is anyone who worships anything other than the true God. The very first commandment is, *"I am the LORD thy God. . . Thou shalt have no other gods before me."* Those who worship the gods of men's imaginations, the gods of the false religions, and the gods of the cults will never enter the kingdom of God. There will not be one Muslim who worships Allah who will enter the kingdom of God. There will not be one Mormon who worships the false gods described by Joseph Smith that will enter the kingdom of God. There will not be one Jehovah's Witness who denies the deity of Christ who will enter the kingdom of God. They are all idolaters, and there are many more religions just like these who worship false gods. They defend that idolatry, they persist in that idolatry, and that idolatry defines their lives. They will not enter the kingdom of God.

Finally, the outcasts from the kingdom are all those who are liars. Verse 8 says, *"But. . .all liars."* Many people would never openly do things like murder, sorcery, whoremongering, and idolatry. But lying is very prevalent, and it is an especially great sin among those who profess faith in Christ. Those who live lives of deceit, dishonesty, and slander are those who have lived their lives as liars; and no person who lies, defends his lies, and goes on in the practice of lying will ever inherit the kingdom of God. Satan is the father of lies. Some defend lying by defending what they call "little white lies." A lie is what caused the fall of the human race in the garden of Eden. There are no little lies. Either tell the truth, the whole truth, and nothing but the truth, or do not speak.

In a word, as we take all of these characteristics and compress them together, they describe those who have the mark of the beast. This is what the mark of the beast looks like; it is those who live and act and think in this fashion. These are they who think like Satan in their minds, they act like Satan with their hands, and they follow Satan with their lives. They may deny that, but their works prove that Satan is their god. You only have one of two gods. Either Jesus Christ is your God, or Satan is your god, and there are no other gods.

People who practice and defend and continue on in the things that are mentioned in verse 8 as the dominating characteristic of their lives will never enter the kingdom of Christ. Rather, it says in verse 8, that they will be cast into *"the lake which burneth with fire and brimstone,"* where they will be justly tormented for their sins for all of eternity. This is the second and the final death from which there is no recovery. The outcasts from the kingdom are those who chose to spend their lives separated from God here on this earth, and this ensures that they will spend eternity separated from God in the lake of fire.

You do not ignore God, defy God, and rebel against God all your life, and then show up on the Day of Judgment and go into heaven. It does not work that way. You either believe in Christ, follow Christ, and serve Christ now, or you will never be with Him then. We are going to see this as we study 22:11, where it says, "He that is unjust in this life, let him continue to be unjust for eternity; and he which is filthy in this life, let him continue to be filthy for eternity; and he that is righteous in this life, let him continue to be righteous for eternity; and he that is holy in this life, let him continue to be holy for eternity." This is an interpretive reading of that verse, but this is exactly what it means.

Eternity is a continuation of what you have begun and practiced here. If you have lived a life of humility in following Christ now, as imperfect as it may be, and that has been the defining characteristic of your life, Jesus will own you and confess you as His and bring you into His kingdom.

The problem is not that you are a sinner. Christ came to save sinners. Sin is not the problem. It is unrepentance from sin and unbelief in Christ that is the problem. When you repent of your sins and believe in Christ as Savior and Lord, and then seek to follow and obey Him, even though your life is far from perfect, Christ will forgive you, Christ will receive you, and Christ will reward you in heaven as one who was faithful to Him and continued to follow Him all the days of your life. When you fell into sin, you confessed your sin, and He was faithful and just to forgive your sin, and to cleanse you from all unrighteousness. You then go on in renewed obedience. If you live your life that way, you will have a good outcome on the Day of Judgment.

We tend to labor under so much fear because in our hearts, we are closet legalists. We think things like, "I have not done good enough for God to accept me." Do you know what that is? It is salvation based on works. The real question is this: "Did Christ do good enough for God to accept you?" As far as you doing good enough, the issue is this: What is the disposition and direction of your life? Are you turning away from the sins in verse 8, or are you continuing in the sins of verse 8, justifying them, and going on in the practice of them without any sense of repentance or any sense that you need to turn from these things?

It is not about perfection; it is about direction. Are you going toward Christ, or are you going away from Christ? Those who went toward Him all their life will be with Him throughout all eternity. Those who went away from Him all their life will be away from Him for all eternity. Choose this day what your destiny will be by what you do now in relationship to Jesus. Turn from your sins and trust Christ as your Savior now.

Will you be invited into His kingdom or will you be cast out from it? The choice is up to you. Repent of your sins, believe in Jesus, confess Jesus, follow Jesus, and you will be invited into His glorious kingdom.

64

The New Jerusalem, Revelation 21:9–21

"9 *And there came unto me one of the seven angels which had the seven vials full of the seven last plagues, and talked with me, saying, Come hither, I will show thee the bride, the Lamb's wife.* 10 *And he carried me away in the spirit to a great and high mountain, and showed me that great city, the holy Jerusalem, descending out of heaven from God,* 11 *Having the glory of God: and her light was like unto a stone most precious, even like a jasper stone, clear as crystal;* 12 *And had a wall great and high, and had twelve gates, and at the gates twelve angels, and names written thereon, which are the names of the twelve tribes of the children of Israel:* 13 *On the east three gates; on the north three gates; on the south three gates; and on the west three gates.* 14 *And the wall of the city had twelve foundations, and in them the names of the twelve apostles of the Lamb.* 15 *And he that talked with me had a golden reed to measure the city, and the gates thereof, and the wall thereof.* 16 *And the city lieth foursquare, and the length is as large as the breadth: and he measured the city with the reed, twelve thousand furlongs. The length and the breadth and the height of it are equal.* 17 *And he measured the wall thereof, an hundred and forty and four cubits, according to the measure of a man, that is, of the angel.* 18 *And the building of the wall of it was of jasper: and the city was pure gold, like unto clear glass.* 19 *And the foundations of the wall of the city were garnished with all manner of precious stones. The first foundation was jasper; the second, sapphire; the third, a chalcedony; the fourth, an emerald;* 20 *The fifth, sardonyx; the sixth, sardius; the seventh, chrysolite; the eighth, beryl; the ninth, a topaz; the tenth, a chrysoprasus; the eleventh, a jacinth; the twelfth,*

> *an amethyst.* [21] *And the twelve gates were twelve pearls; every several gate was of one pearl: and the street of the city was pure gold, as it were transparent glass."*

As we have studied the book of Revelation, we have read a great deal about the city of Babylon, which represents anti-Christian society in all of its economic, social, and cultural aspects. Babylon is inhabited by all those with the mark of the beast. Babylon's religion is that of the false prophet. Babylon supports the beast of anti-Christian government. Babylon is the creation of the dragon who is Satan himself.

The totality of this city of Babylon is viewed as a harlot, the great whore who seeks to seduce all people into following Satan by means of temptation or persecution. We have seen that the dragon, the beast, those with the mark of the beast, the false prophet, and Babylon will all be defeated by Christ and cast into the lake of fire.

In contrast to this great harlot Babylon stands the bride of Christ, the new Jerusalem. The bride of Christ and the new Jerusalem are both terms that symbolize the church of God, the Christian society that inhabits the new earth.

We were first introduced to the symbolic image of the church being the bride of Christ in Revelation 19:7–9, where the emphasis was on the marriage supper of the Lamb. There we saw that Christ and His church, made up of all the resurrected believers of all the ages, are finally brought together in one place to be joined in permanent spiritual union for all eternity. Never again will the saints be separated from Christ, and never again will the saints be separated from one another.

The second mention of the church as the bride of Christ is in Revelation 21:2. In that passage, we saw the symbolism of the church being the bride of Christ joined together with the symbolism of the church being the holy city, the new Jerusalem. Notice 21:2: *"And I John saw the holy city, new Jerusalem, coming down from God out of heaven, prepared as a bride adorned for her husband."*

Both the symbolic terms, *"the holy city, new Jerusalem"* and the *"bride adorned for her husband,"* represent the church and describe the relationship believers will have with one another and with Christ. The symbolism of the holy city conveys the purity and the perfection of the Christian society that will exist on the new earth between believers. The symbolism of the bride conveys the irrevocable commitment that Christ has to His people, and the personal closeness that Christ has with His people.

In relationship to one another, believers are a holy city, a perfect Christian society, in which perfect love prevails among all who live together in that society. In relationship to Christ, believers are His bride who enjoy perfect security and personal closeness with Him, and who receive from Him and give to Him a perfect and transcendent love that will never end.

This concept of the church being both the new Jerusalem and the bride of Christ introduced in Revelation 21:2 is now greatly expanded in 21:9 through 22:5. Chapter 21 could have ended with verse 8, and that could have been the end of the book of Revelation. Everything that is going to be said about the church in the eternal state was said in those first eight verses.

Revelation 21:1–8 is a concise summary of the future blessings Christ has provided to His people in the new heavens and the new earth, but that concise summary is then followed by an expanded description of those blessings in 21:9 through 22:5. Each of the concepts set forth in 21:1–8 is taken up and expanded in the remainder of chapter 21 and on into chapter 22.

Therefore, as we proceed through the section ahead of us, we are going to be revisiting, at some length, concepts that were only mentioned in verses 1 to 8. In verses 1 to 8 we have the summary, but in verse 9 to 22:5, we have the expansion of that summary.

As John describes the bride, the Lamb's wife, pictured here as the holy city of Jerusalem, we must remind ourselves that we are dealing exclusively with symbolic visual imagery. It is important for us to understand that nothing about this new Jerusalem is to be taken literally. Every aspect of this city is a picture of the church, and no such literal city exists, or ever will exist. Every aspect of this city is a symbol of something else, and therefore we must do away with any notion that the physical descriptions given here will be a physical reality when we come into the new earth. In the new earth, there are no gates made of pearls, and there are no streets made of gold.

These are visual symbolic images that convey a message about the nature, the privilege, and the blessing the church will enjoy in the new earth as believers live with one another and with Christ for eternity.

So, in contrast to the ugly whore Babylon, now we are going to see the beautiful bride, the new Jerusalem.

The Appearance of the City

Notice verse 9. *"And there came unto me one of the seven angels which had the seven vials full of the seven last plagues, and talked with me, saying, Come hither, I will show thee the bride, the Lamb's wife."* This angel that comes to John appears to be the same angel that showed John the judgment of the harlot Babylon back in Revelation 17:1, because virtually identical language is used to describe him in 21:9 as was used to describe him in 17:1.

Notice Revelation 17:1. *"And there came one of the seven angels which had the seven vials, and talked with me, saying unto me, Come hither; I will show unto thee the judgment of the great whore that sitteth upon many waters."* Notice Revelation 21:9: *"And there came unto me one of the seven angels which had the seven vials full of the seven last plagues, and talked with me, saying, Come hither, I will show thee the bride, the Lamb's wife."* The reason for this same angel being introduced to us with the same language and phraseology is to draw our minds to a contrast between these two cities.

There was a book written by Charles Dickens called *The Tale of Two Cities*, about the cities of Paris and London during the time of the French Revolution. The Bible is a tale of two cities as well: the city of Satan, which is Babylon; and the city of God, which is the new Jerusalem. This contrast is immediately set up for us in the parallel language that is employed in 17:1 and 21:9.

This parallel introduction draws our minds to the contrast between these two cities. Babylon is the wicked city of the world that represents anti-Christian society. Jerusalem is the holy city of the kingdom of God that represents Christian society.

The point is, you cannot live in both Babylon and Jerusalem at the same time. To choose one city is to renounce the other city. As Christians, we reject the world and we choose the church. We reject wickedness and we choose holiness. We reject humanism and we choose Jesus Christ.

Just as in Revelation 21:2, so here also in verses 9 and 10, the concept of the church as the bride of Christ and the concept of the church as the holy Jerusalem are combined together. The angel tells John in verse 9 that he is going to show him the bride, the Lamb's wife. In order to do so, he shows him the city of the new Jerusalem in verse 10.

Notice verse 9: *"And there came unto me one of the seven angels which had the seven vials full of the seven last plagues, and talked with me, saying, Come hither, I will show thee the bride, the Lamb's wife."* Having just declared that he was going to show John the Lamb's bride and wife, we would expect that he would show John an image of a beautiful woman. But notice verse 10: *"And he carried me away in the spirit to a great and high mountain, and showed me"* not a beautiful woman, but *"that great city, the holy Jerusalem, descending out of heaven from God."* Therefore, the holy city is a symbolic picture of the symbolic picture of the church as the bride of Christ.

As the angel shows John the new Jerusalem, he is showing the nature of the church and the privileges and blessings the bride of Christ will enjoy as she dwells on the new earth in the personal presence of Jesus Christ.

Notice three points about the appearance of this city.

First of all, notice the glory of the city. The glory of the city is stated in verses 10 and 11. It says, *"And he carried me away in the spirit to a great and high mountain, and showed me that great city, the holy Jerusalem, descending out of heaven from God,* [11] *Having the glory of God: and her light was like unto a stone most precious, even like a jasper stone, clear as crystal.*

John is carried away to a *"great and high mountain"* to see the glory of the promised land of the new earth, just as Moses was brought to the top of mount Pisgah to see the glory of the promised land of Canaan. Both men were able to see the glorious provision God made for His people.

In verse 10, the church is said to be descending out of heaven from God, because all the resurrected and living saints were raptured up into heaven when Christ returned, and now they are descending down out of heaven into the new earth. What is being conveyed by this language is that the church has a heavenly origin. It comes down from above. The reason it has a heavenly origin is that from heaven her salvation was planned, from heaven her Savior was given, and from heaven the Spirit was sent. The church has a heavenly origin, and this is why, in verse 10, the city that represents her is said to descend from heaven.

But the church has more than her origins from God; she also reflects the glory of God as verse 11 says: *"having the glory of God."* That is a very profound and wonderful statement. The church has the glory of God. What is the glory of God? God's glory is His attributes.

His attributes express His glory and reveal His glory.

In the beginning, Adam and Eve were created in the image of God; and as a result, they perfectly reflected God's communicable attributes to the degree they were given the capacity to possess them. In the beginning, Adam and Eve had the glory of God. But Adam and Eve fell. The image of God in them became deeply disfigured, and the reflection of God's glorious attributes became clouded and darkened by human depravity. But in salvation, that glorious image of God is being progressively restored in us, first by regeneration, then by growth in Christlikeness, and ultimately by glorification at the resurrection.

At the second coming of Christ, the image of God in man will be fully and perfectly restored, and the church will shine forth with a perfect display of God's character and holiness which will make the church brilliant and glorious. The church will have the glory of God, because the church will have been restored to the perfect image of God in which she was originally made, and she will then manifest the communicable attributes of God to the fullest extent possible in her person and her conduct.

This glory the church has is the possession of likeness to Christ. First John 3:2 says we will be like Him when we see Him at His second coming. To be like Christ is to have the glory of God. Romans 8:29 says that we are predestinated to be conformed to the image of Christ. When we fully obtain that image, we will shine with the glory of God. This glory that will shine out of us is likened to the radiance of a brilliant, flawless diamond. This stone in verse 11 is called a jasper stone. *"Having the glory of God: and her light was like a stone most precious, even like a jasper stone, clear as crystal."*

This stone in verse 11 is called a jasper stone, but the Greek word translated "jasper" occurs only in the book of Revelation, and its meaning is somewhat uncertain. The stones that we know as jaspers in our day are opaque; they are not as clear as crystal. It seems, therefore, that this stone mentioned in verse 11 is more like a diamond than anything else since it is said to be as clear as crystal, and it is said to be *"most precious"*—that is, exceedingly valuable. Just as Moses' face shined with the glory of God when he came down from Sinai after meeting with God, so the church will shine with the brilliant reflected light of the glory of God, just like a diamond flashes back the light that is shined into it.

It is the hope of obtaining this glory that is repeatedly set before believers in the New Testament as an incentive to persevere in the faith, and as an inspiration to continue in faithfulness to Christ. It says in Romans 8:18, *"I reckon that the sufferings of this present time are not worthy to be compared with the glory which shall be revealed in us."* It is this glory described in Revelation 21:11 that Paul is promising will be revealed in us in Romans 8:18. It is the glory of perfect conformity to the character of Jesus Christ. As we look at the appearance of the city, the first thing we see is the glory of the city in verses 10 and 11.

But not only do we see the glory of the city; secondly, notice the wall and the gates of the city. Notice verse 12. It says the city *"had a wall great and high."* Historically, cities had walls for safety, security, and protection. What is it that provides the church with her safety and security and protection? It is the salvation that God has given us.

Notice Isaiah 60:14–22: *"The sons also of them that afflicted thee shall come bending unto thee; and all they that despised thee shall bow themselves down at the soles of thy feet; and they shall call thee, The city of the LORD, The Zion of the Holy One of Israel."* In the Day of Judgment, we are going to be vindicated before all of the wicked who persecuted us, and they are going to bow down to us and say, "You Christians, you are truly the city of God." Those who lorded it over us in this life will be bowing at our feet in the next life.

Verse 15 continues: *"Whereas thou hast been forsaken and hated, so that no man went through thee, I will make thee an eternal excellency, a joy of many generations.* [16] *Thou shalt also suck the milk of the Gentiles, and shalt suck the breast of kings: and thou shalt know that I the LORD am thy Saviour and thy Redeemer, the mighty One of Jacob.* [17] *For brass I will bring gold, and for iron I will bring silver, and for wood brass, and for stones iron: I will also make thy officers peace, and thine exactors righteousness."* Now here it is, verse 18: *"Violence shall no more be heard in thy land, wasting nor destruction within thy borders; but thou shalt call thy walls Salvation, and thy gates Praise.*

"[19] *The sun shall be no more thy light by day; neither for brightness shall the moon give light unto thee: but the LORD shall be unto thee an everlasting light, and thy God thy glory.* [20] *Thy sun shall no more go down; neither shall thy moon withdraw itself: for the LORD shall be thine everlasting light, and the days of thy mourning shall be ended.* [21] *Thy people also shall be all righteous: they shall inherit the land for ever, the branch of my planting, the work of my hands, that I may be*

glorified. [22] *A little one shall become a thousand, and a small one a strong nation: I the LORD will hasten it in his time."*

Isaiah gives us a prophetic declaration of the blessing and the dwelling place of the people of God in the new earth. He says regarding the walls that surround the city in the new earth, that these walls shall be called "Salvation." If you look ahead in Revelation 21 at the verses we have not yet expounded, you will recognize that whole phrases are lifted from this passage in Isaiah 60 and are used by John in Revelation 21.

This wall around the new Jerusalem represents the salvation that the church has received. This same truth is echoed in Isaiah 26:1–2: *"In that day shall this song be sung in the land of Judah; We have a strong city; salvation will God appoint for walls and bulwarks.* [2] *Open ye the gates, that the righteous nation which keepeth the truth may enter in."*

This imagery of our ultimate destiny being a glorious city is one that is rooted in the book of Isaiah, and the walls that surround this city are twice declared to be "salvation." God provided abundant opportunity for people to enter into the salvation He provided. This is why the city has twelve gates within its walls, and this is why they are all open and never shut because, at any time, anyone may come into the city through the gates and experience the salvation that all those within the city enjoy.

Notice Revelation 21:12–13. *"And had a wall great and high, and had twelve gates, and at the gates twelve angels, and names written thereon, which are the names of the twelve tribes of the children of Israel:* [13] *On the east three gates; on the north three gates; on the south three gates; and on the west three gates."*

Here we see this city not only has a wall, the city itself is also a square with a north, south, east, and west wall; and each of these walls has three gates, for a total of twelve gates. These gates are guarded by twelve angels, one of them at each gate, who control who goes into those gates. Entrance into God's city, the church, is not open to anyone who chooses to come in on any terms he pleases. Those gates only admit those to whom God gives the right.

Notice Revelation 21:27, *"And there shall in no wise enter into it any thing that defileth, neither whatsoever worketh abomination, or maketh a lie: but they which are written in the Lamb's book of life."* This is why the angels are at the gates: to guard who comes in. Certain people are absolutely kept out—namely, those who are described in verse 27. It is those who are believers in Jesus Christ and have the salvation of Christ that are allowed to enter in.

The angels ensure no unsaved people will ever be found within the church that dwells on the new earth. The angels are going to be sent, and they are going to gather the believers and the unbelievers and will bring them to the judgment. They are going to ensure that only the believers wind up in the new earth. Only those who are saved will enter through the gates and be counted as members of the church in God's eternal kingdom.

The significance of the names of the twelve tribes of Israel being inscribed on these gates is that Old Testament Israel was the means God used to prepare and provide a way to enter into the salvation that God has provided. It was through Israel that Jesus came, and therefore it was through Israel that the doors of salvation were open to the whole world. We see this in Revelation 12:1–2, in which we saw *"a great wonder in heaven; a woman clothed with the sun, and the moon under her feet, and upon her head a crown of twelve stars: [2] And she being with child cried, travailing in birth, and pained to be delivered."* The woman is Israel, and she brought forth Jesus Christ.

Israel was the means through which Messiah came into the world, and through whom salvation was provided to the world. It was through Israel that Jesus came, and therefore it was through Israel that the doors of salvation were opened to the whole world. This is the significance of the names of the twelve tribes being on the doors of the wall of Salvation.

This city is a four-sided city. We know that the number four conveys the concept of the entire world because it represents the four points of the compass—north, south, east, and west. The point is that through these twelve gates there has been abundant opportunity for the whole world to enter into the salvation Christ has provided and be brought together into the fellowship of the church, no matter where in the world they lived, or what direction they came from. Jesus Himself said in Luke 13:29, *"And they shall come from the east, and from the west, and from the north, and from the south, and shall sit down in the kingdom of God."*

The church in the new earth is made up of the saved from all over the earth who come to salvation through the means provided through Old Testament Israel, which is Jesus Christ. The gates of salvation have always been open to anyone from anywhere who will enter through them on God's terms, which is faith in God's Son as their Lord and Savior.

Having seen the glory of the city in verses 10 and 11, and the wall and the gates of the city in verses 12 to 13, notice thirdly, the foundation of the city in verse 14. *"And the wall of the city had twelve foundations, and in them the names of the twelve apostles of the Lamb."* Just as Old Testament Israel was the means through which God brought salvation to the church, the New Testament apostles were the means through which God provided the doctrinal foundation for the church.

Ephesians 2:19–22 says: *"Now therefore ye are no more strangers and foreigners, but fellowcitizens with the saints, and of the household of God;* [20] *And are built upon the foundation of the apostles and prophets, Jesus Christ himself being the chief corner stone;* [21] *In whom all the building fitly framed together groweth unto an holy temple in the Lord:* [22] *In whom ye also are builded together for an habitation of God through the Spirit."* It was the work and the writings of the apostles that took the church from being a few people in a small geographical spot to being a multitude which no man could number from all across the world and from every kindred, tongue, tribe, and nation. The apostles wrote the New Testament, which established the doctrinal foundation of the church by setting forth and preserving the record of the life and teachings of Jesus Christ. The apostles also spread the gospel from Jerusalem to Judea to Samaria and then in every direction to the uttermost parts of the earth, whether north, south, east, or west. The apostles brought the gospel to the Gentiles, and the apostles made the gospel a worldwide religion for all peoples, no matter where they lived.

In preserving the record of the life and teachings of Jesus Christ, and by spreading the gospel to the uttermost parts of the earth, the apostles were the foundation of the church. They brought the Lamb of God to the whole world in their writings and in their evangelism.

The fact that the names of the twelve tribes of Israel are on the gates, and the fact that the names of the twelve apostles are on the foundation stones, conveys the truth that the Old Testament and New Testament people are all one church, that Christ has one bride, and that there is a single salvation that unifies them all into one body. This city is the one that Abraham was seeking when it says of him in Hebrews 11:10 that *"he looked for a city that hath foundations, whose builder and maker is God."* The new earth is the actual Promised Land, of which Canaan was a foreshadow; and the new Jerusalem is the actual City of God, of which old Jerusalem was a foreshadow. The new Jerusalem in the new earth is where the full potential for a truly Christian society will finally be realized. This, then, is the appearance of the city: its glory, its wall, its gates, and its foundation.

The Measurement of the City

The measurement of the city is in verses 15 to 17. Verse 15 says, *"And he that talked with me had a golden reed to measure the city, and the gates thereof, and the wall thereof."* Here we are told the angel uses a golden measuring stick to measure the city.

We were introduced to this concept of measurement in Revelation 11:1–2, when the New Covenant temple, the church on this present earth, was measured. We learned that measuring has nothing to do with the actual dimensions of the object being measured because measurement in the book of Revelation is a symbolic act, not a literal one.

In Revelation 11, we saw that measurement was for the purpose of marking out for preservation the thing that was being measured. It is like putting a fence around your garden: you mark it out for preservation from being assaulted by the deer and the rabbits. There is this marking out, this measuring out of the church for protection that occurred in Revelation 11:1–2. Because the church on earth was marked out for protection and preservation by God, the church would never be destroyed from the earth by her enemies. God put a line of protection around her.

This same meaning regarding the act of measurement is also being conveyed by the measurement of the new Jerusalem in Revelation 21. By this measurement, God is saying that the new Jerusalem, the church that is on the new earth, will be preserved and protected by God for all eternity. In the new earth, God has measured and marked out His church as the special object of His care and protection, and nothing will ever again be able to attack or harm it.

To illustrate this point, notice Zechariah 2:1–13. *"I lifted up mine eyes again, and looked, and behold a man with a measuring line in his hand."* Some measuring is being done here. "[2] *Then said I, Whither goest thou? And he said unto me, To measure Jerusalem, to see what is the breadth thereof, and what is the length thereof.*" This is the same thing the angel is doing in Revelation 21.

"[3] *And, behold, the angel that talked with me went forth, and another angel went out to meet him,* [4] *And said unto him, Run, speak to this young man*" (to Zechariah,) "*saying, Jerusalem shall be inhabited as towns without walls for the multitude of men and cattle therein.*" In other words, Jerusalem is going to be so big, it will be impossible to contain it within literal walls. What do we have in heaven? "*A multitude which no man can number, of every kindred, tongue, tribe, and nation.*" Try to build a wall around that. But notice verse 5: "*For I, saith the LORD, will be unto her a wall of fire round about, and will be the glory in the midst of her.*" God says that He is going to provide the protection for the city—that He will be her wall.

"[6] *Ho, ho, come forth, and flee from the land of the north, saith the LORD: for I have spread you abroad as the four winds of the heaven, saith the LORD.* [7] *Deliver thyself, O Zion, that dwellest with the daughter of Babylon.*" Here we have our two cities, Jerusalem (Zion) and Babylon. "[8] *For thus saith the LORD of hosts; After the glory hath he sent me unto the nations which spoiled you: for he that toucheth you toucheth the apple of his eye.*" The pupil, the little dark spot in the middle of the eye and the most sensitive part of it, is called the apple of the eye. If somebody tries to poke you in the eye, you will do anything to protect it. God says that the new Jerusalem is the apple of His eye; He will protect it, He will be a wall of fire around it, and He will guard it as closely as men would protect the very center of their eyeball.

Verse 9: "*For, behold, I will shake mine hand upon them, and they shall be a spoil to their servants: and ye shall know that the LORD of hosts hath sent me.* [10] *Sing and rejoice, O daughter of Zion: for, lo, I come, and I will dwell in the midst of thee, saith the LORD.*" God is going to dwell in the midst of the new Jerusalem. He will be with us, and He will be our God, and we will be His people.

Verse 11: "*And many nations shall be joined to the LORD in that day,*" (from north, south, east, and west) "*and shall be my people: and I will dwell in the midst of thee, and thou shalt know that the LORD of hosts hath sent me unto thee.* [12] *And the LORD shall inherit Judah his portion in the holy land, and shall choose Jerusalem again.* [13] *Be silent, O all flesh, before the LORD: for he is raised up out of his holy habitation.*"

In verse 1, we see that a man is coming to measure. What is the result of this measurement? In verse 5 God says, in effect, "I am going to be a wall of fire of protection around My city." In verses 8 and 9 He says, "He who touches you is like one who touches the apple of My eye. I will shake My hand on your enemies, and they shall be a spoil, and you shall know that the Lord is the One who protects you." Then in verses 10 and 11 He says, "Sing and rejoice. I will come. I will dwell in the midst of you" (He says it twice), "and you shall know that the Lord of hosts has sent Me unto you."

Zechariah is speaking in chapter 2 about the events in Revelation 21 and 22 in relationship to the new Jerusalem and the protection God will give to it. The point is, because of this measurement and what it means about the protection of God, in the new earth the church will be absolutely secure.

Revelation 21:16–17 says, *"And the city lieth foursquare, and the length is as large as the breadth: and he measured the city with the reed, twelve thousand furlongs. The length and the breadth and the height of it are equal.* [17]*And he measured the wall thereof, an hundred and forty and four cubits, according to the measure of a man, that is, of the angel."* Here we are told that this city is a perfect cube. It has the same length and width and height in each dimension, and each of those dimensions is said to be twelve thousand furlongs.

What we have here is a symbolic shape and a symbolic dimension. The reason the city is pictured as a perfect cube is that the Holy of Holies in the Old Testament tabernacle where the glory and presence of God dwelt was also a perfect cube. The Holy of Holies in the Old Testament tabernacle was ten cubits wide, ten cubits long, and ten cubits high.

By describing the church as being a perfect cube like the Holy of Holies was, John is conveying that the perfect church on the new earth is going to be indwelt by the glory of God and the presence of God, just like the Old Testament tabernacle was indwelt by the presence of God and the glory of God in the Holy of Holies.

The significance of the church being pictured as a perfect cube is that God is going to dwell in our midst. The church is the new Holy of Holies. This is another reason why we read in Revelation 21:11 that the city has the glory of God, not only because we will reflect the glory of God in the restored image of God in us, but also because the very Person and glory of God Himself will dwell in our midst.

The reason the cube is said to be twelve thousand furlongs wide and long and tall is that twelve conveys the concept of the people of God, and ten conveys the concept of perfection and totality, multiplied by itself three times to intensify its meaning. Twelve times ten times ten times ten, which equals twelve thousand, conveys the idea that in the new earth dwells the perfect totality (ten times ten times ten) of all of the people of God (times twelve) from all of human history. Not one of them is missing.

The word "furlongs" in Greek is "stadia," from which we get our word stadium. A stadia is about an eighth of a mile, which is 660 feet. Twelve thousand stadia equals about one thousand five hundred miles if you were going to literalize this measurement. In the United States, one thousand five hundred miles is about the distance from the Canadian border to the Mexican border at the tip of Texas. One thousand five hundred miles is the distance from the Pacific Ocean to the Great Lakes. A square of one thousand five hundred miles by one thousand five hundred miles would cover 70 percent of the landmass of the continental United States.

These numbers are not meant to be taken literally, and I am not suggesting that they should be, but the size of these numbers conveys the vastness of the size of the church in the new earth. Revelation 7:9 says the church before the throne of God is a great multitude which no man can number, of all nations and kindreds and people and tongues. The point is that the church in the new earth is perfectly complete, it is vast in number, and the glory and presence of God dwells in the midst of it.

Notice verse 17: *"And he measured the wall thereof, an hundred and forty and four cubits, according to the measure of a man, that is, of the angel."* Verse 17 tells us this city is surrounded by a wall, and we have already seen that this wall is salvation, and the symbolic measurement that is given to this wall is one hundred forty-four, in this case, cubits.

Whether this measurement of one hundred forty-four cubits is a measurement of the height of the wall or the thickness of the wall does not matter, because both the wall and its measurement are symbolic. We have already seen in verse 12 that this wall represents salvation, and the number one hundred forty-four is twelve times twelve. Twelve conveys the concept of the people of God, and twelve times twelve is an intensification of that concept.

We have come across this number one hundred forty-four previously in the book of Revelation—in Revelation 7:4, and in Revelation 14:1–3—and we have seen that one hundred forty-four thousand represents the totality of the people of God. The point regarding this wall that has this measurement of one hundred forty-four is that all of the people of God are all encompassed within God's salvation represented by the wall. All of them are within God's saving purposes and God's saving work. We are surrounded with the wall of salvation, and none of us is outside of it. The perfect totality of all the people of God is within the wall of salvation.

The Material of the City

The material of the city is spoken of in verses 18 to 21. Verses 18 to 21 tell us the various building materials that are used in the construction of the new Jerusalem. *"And the building of the wall of it was of jasper: and the city was pure gold, like unto clear glass.* [19] *And the foundations of the wall of the city were garnished with all manner of precious stones. The first foundation was jasper; the second, sapphire; the third, a chalcedony; the fourth, an emerald;* [20] *The fifth, sardonyx; the sixth, sardius; the seventh, chrysolite; the eighth, beryl; the ninth, a topaz; the tenth, a chrysoprasus; the eleventh, a jacinth; the twelfth, an amethyst.* [21] *And the twelve gates were twelve pearls; every several gate was of one pearl: and the street of the city was pure gold, as it were transparent glass."*

What we have here is a list of building materials. The purpose of this list of these symbolic construction materials used to build this city is to convey a message about the value of the church, the beauty of the church, the permanence of the church, and the purity of the church. Gold and pearls and precious stones are items of great value, they are items of intense beauty, they are items of endless longevity, and they are items of flawless purity.

Verse 18 tells us the wall was made of jasper, which we saw in verse 11 is probably a diamond because it is clear as crystal, and it is the most valuable stone there is. The wall represents salvation, and that salvation is as valuable and beautiful and durable as diamond. The wall is not only the wall of salvation, but it is the most valuable, beautiful, and durable salvation that could possibly be provided. It is likened to a diamond.

It also says in verse 18 that the city itself was pure gold—that is, the whole city, the whole cube, was pure gold. The purity of the gold was so great that its purity was at the same level perfectly clear glass has. It is not that the gold is clear like glass, but the gold is pure like clear glass is pure.

Just as any imperfection in glass is easy to see, so any imperfection in the church would be easily seen. But there is no imperfection to be seen in the church in the new earth, just as there is no imperfection to be seen in clear glass. In Job 23:10 Job said about God, *"But he knoweth the way that I take: when he hath tried me, I shall come forth as gold."* That is why the city is said to be pure gold. We have been through the furnace of affliction, we have been through the furnace of sanctification and glorification, and when we come into heaven, we will be without any pollution or defect. We will be perfect.

The salvation of the church is exceedingly valuable. It is like diamond, and it is like gold. The purity of the church is absolutely perfect. It is as perfect as crystal clear glass.

In verses 19 to 20, we are further told that the twelve foundation stones, which represented the twelve apostles, are actually made out of precious gemstones, each gemstone being unique from the other, but all being equally valuable, equally beautiful, and equally permanent.

It is possible to assign numerous significances to these twelve stones from the Old Testament, and choosing among the possible significances of these twelve stones is difficult. However, the clearest passage that is the closest in parallel description is found in Isaiah 54:10–14.

Isaiah 54:10–14 says, *"For the mountains shall depart, and the hills be removed; but my kindness shall not depart from thee."* When are the mountains going to depart and the hills be removed? When this old heaven and earth are burned up. Verse 10 continues, *"Neither shall the covenant of my peace be removed, saith the LORD that hath mercy on thee."* The covenant of peace is the New Covenant. The New Covenant is never going away. Even after the heavens and the earth pass away, the New Covenant remains. It is eternal. Hebrews 13:20 tells us that it is the everlasting covenant.

Now verse 11: *"O thou afflicted, tossed with tempest, and not comforted."* That was their condition in Isaiah's time, and that is our condition now. He is talking to us—we who are tossed and afflicted with tempest, and not comforted. He says to us, *". . .behold, I will lay*

thy stones with fair colours, and lay thy foundations with sapphires.
12 *And I will make thy windows of agates, and thy gates of carbuncles,*
and all thy borders of pleasant stones. 13 *And all thy children shall*
be taught of the LORD*; and great shall be the peace of thy children.*
14 *In righteousness shalt thou be established: thou shalt be far from*
oppression; for thou shalt not fear: and from terror; for it shall not
come near thee."

The symbolism in Isaiah of God rebuilding Israel with precious stones was an indication that she would experience peace and righteousness and protection, the three things she was currently lacking. It was the apostles, through the preaching of the New Covenant, the covenant of peace spoken of here, who brought peace with God to the people, who brought righteousness before God to the people, and who brought protection from God to the people through their apostolic ministry.

All that is promised here—righteousness, peace, and protection—was brought to us by the apostles as they preached the covenant of peace that was established by God with His people at the Last Supper. Peace and righteousness and protection, which were proclaimed in the New Covenant by the apostles, were the precious and valuable and beautiful gemstones of truth that the apostles gave to the church. The apostles, as it were, scattered costly gemstones of truth wherever they went as they preached the gospel to the people. The truth the apostles proclaimed produced peace for those people, righteousness for those people, and protection for those people, not only in time, but also for all eternity.

The point is that the message of the apostles was exceedingly valuable—as valuable as gemstones. Are not righteousness and peace and protection as valuable as gemstones, especially peace with God, and righteousness before God, and protection being provided to you by God? Is that not exceedingly valuable? That is what the apostles brought us as they preached the covenant of peace. They scattered with both hands the unsearchable riches of Christ to all of those around them as they preached the gospel and provided the foundation of the church. The apostles built the church, as 1 Corinthians 3:12 says, with gold and silver and precious stones. This is the meaning of the foundations of the new Jerusalem being garnished with gemstones. The apostles brought us exceedingly valuable things through their ministry.

Notice verse 21. *"And the twelve gates were twelve pearls; every several gate was of one pearl: and the street of the city was pure gold, as it were transparent glass."* The gates in the wall of salvation are said to be twelve pearls, and these twelve pearls represent Jesus Christ Himself. Jesus spoke of Himself as the pearl of great price in the parable in Matthew 13:45–46.

Furthermore, Jesus said in John 10:9, *"I am the door"* (I am the gate); *"by me if any man enter in, he shall be saved."* If the walls represent salvation, then Jesus is the doorway into that salvation.

Jesus is said to be the pearl of great price, and these gates are made out of pearls of great price. These pearls are doors, and He is the door. Jesus is the one who brings salvation and opens the door to salvation to all peoples from the north and south and east and west.

Notice, in verse 21, that every gate is exactly the same, telling us there is only one way of salvation, and that is through Jesus Christ. No matter where you come from, whether the north, south, east, or west, you will have to enter through the exact same gate, the gate of Jesus Christ, who is the door and the pearl. The apostles differed from one another in gifts, and that is why they differ from one another in their gemstone designations. But Christ never differs from Himself, and salvation is the same for everyone, and that is why every gate is the same. Every gate is a pearl.

Having seen the gates and the wall in verse 21, notice also in verse 21 the street of the city. The street of the city is said to be *"pure gold,"* as pure as perfectly transparent glass is pure. Once again, this golden street represents and symbolizes Jesus Christ, because Jesus said of Himself in John 14:6, *"I am the way."* The Greek word for *"way"* is "*hodos,*" which means a road or a street. In other words, Jesus says, "I am the street you must walk on if you would come to God. I am the way, the truth, and the life, and no man comes to the Father except through Me. Every person must travel the road that I am in order to get to the Father."

Therefore, the gates are Christ and the streets are Christ because He is the pearl of great price, and He is the door into salvation, and He is the way upon which we must walk if we are to arrive at the destination of the Father and of heaven.

Each aspect of this city symbolizes some truth about the church. It is a passage that is very dense with symbolic imagery. This new Jerusalem symbolizes the glory and blessing and privilege that the church will enjoy in the new earth.

This new Jerusalem—this church—is made up of all of the saved of both the Old and the New Testaments. They constitute the bride of Christ. The glory and presence of God dwells in this church: it dwells in these people, with these people, and in the midst of these people. This church will be holy and pure and protected forever. What we have described in the imagery of this building is a perfect people, living on a perfect earth, in the presence of the perfect Trinity, for all of eternity.

Now I have to ask you: Are you in that church? Have you entered into salvation through Jesus Christ? Have you recognized that He is the only way into the city? You must go through Him and in the way in which He has directed if you are ever going to be a member of this blessed city. May the Lord cause you to repent of your sins and trust in Jesus Christ as your Lord and Savior from those sins, so that these gates might be such that when you approach them, the angel says, "Enter into the joy of your Lord."

65

The New Earth is the Temple of God, Revelation 21:22–27

"[22] *And I saw no temple therein: for the Lord God Almighty and the Lamb are the temple of it.* [23] *And the city had no need of the sun, neither of the moon, to shine in it: for the glory of God did lighten it, and the Lamb is the light thereof.* [24] *And the nations of them which are saved shall walk in the light of it: and the kings of the earth do bring their glory and honour into it.* [25] *And the gates of it shall not be shut at all by day: for there shall be no night there.* [26] *And they shall bring the glory and honour of the nations into it.* [27] *And there shall in no wise enter into it anything that defileth, neither whatsoever worketh abomination, or maketh a lie: but they which are written in the Lamb's book of life.*"

There is an old hymn by Jim Reeves with these words:

> This world is not my home, I'm just a-passing through.
> If heaven's not my home, then Lord what will I do?
> The angels beckon me from heaven's open door,
> And I can't feel at home in this world anymore.

This hymn and hundreds like it express the discontent Christians have with this life and this world, and the excitement and anticipation they have about the next life and the world to come.

Christians are fascinated with what life will be like in the eternal state, where there is not only no more death or sorrow or crying or pain, but where they will also experience the immediate presence of God and personal fellowship with Jesus. It is exciting beyond words to contemplate being in a world where sin and all of its effects are completely eradicated, and where being in the immediate personal presence of Christ is our daily experience.

This is why these last two chapters of the book of Revelation are so delightful to contemplate. They open a window into what eternal life will consist of and what it will look like. As we have proceeded through Revelation 21, we have seen where we are going to live, the blessings we will enjoy, and the deliverance we will have from the things that trouble us so much in this life.

Paradise restored and paradise perfected will be our home in the future. It is a glorious future to contemplate. This paradise will be inhabited by a perfect church made up of perfect believers in Christ, who are pictured and symbolized as the bride of Christ and as the holy city, the new Jerusalem.

In the previous chapter, we looked at the appearance of the city and saw that the new Jerusalem shined with the glory of God. It was surrounded by salvation that was brought to us through the twelve tribes of Israel. They were the instrument of God to bring forth the Messiah for our salvation.

That salvation encompassed people from every point on the globe: from the north, south, east, and west. It encompassed both Jews and Gentiles. It was proclaimed to the whole world by the apostles through their evangelistic efforts and writings. The apostles provided the foundation for the church through their ministries and by their authorship of the New Testament.

We not only saw the appearance of the city, but we also saw the measurement of the city. God has marked out His church for eternal protection. Furthermore, the church was symbolized as a perfect cube just like the Holy of Holies in the Old Covenant tabernacle; and just like the Holy of Holies was filled with the presence of God, the church will also be indwelt forever by the presence of God.

We saw that the church is vast in size, made up of a multitude which no man can number; and we saw that the church is perfectly complete, with not one believer missing from it.

Finally, having seen the appearance of the city and the measurement of the city, we considered the material of the city. As we looked at the construction materials used to build this city, we saw a message about the beauty of the church, the purity of the church, the value of the church, and the permanence of the church. These valuable and precious building materials tell us that the church is of great value, the church has intense beauty, the church has endless longevity, and the church has flawless purity.

All of this glory the church possesses and displays in her appearance and measurement and material is the result of the glorious person and work of Jesus Christ. As the pearl of great price, He provides a door of entrance into the kingdom of God; and as the street of gold, He provides the pathway to God.

But John is not done with his description of the new Jerusalem and the blessedness which the people of God are going to enjoy in the new earth. He now greatly expands and explains the chief blessing the redeemed will enjoy in the new earth, and that is the presence of God in our midst.

John told us that God would dwell among us in 21:3: *"And I heard a great voice out of heaven saying, Behold, the tabernacle of God is with men, and he will dwell with them, and they shall be his people, and God himself shall be with them, and be their God."* We saw in verse 16 that the church on the new earth is the eternal and final Holy of Holies. But now in verses 22 to 27, we see that God's presence fills the entire church, and no place exists where God's special personal presence is not found.

In verses 22–27, we will consider the glorious habitation of God in the new earth, and we will see the temple of God in which we will dwell for all eternity.

The Nature of the Temple

Verse 22 says regarding this new Jerusalem, this holy city: *"And I saw no temple therein: for the Lord God Almighty and the Lamb are the temple of it."*

In verse 22, John makes a remarkable statement when he says of the new earth that there is no temple in it. The reason this is such a remarkable statement is that the temple had always been the center of the religious life of the people of God, both in the Old Covenant community and also in the New Covenant community. It has always been the case for the people of God that the temple is a unique place, completely unlike any other place on earth. The temple is the place believers go in order to experience the special presence of God, because God manifests Himself in the temple in a way He does nowhere else on earth. Here on earth, when you want to draw near to God, you go to the temple.

During the Old Covenant period, believers went to the Jewish tabernacle or temple where the Holy of Holies was, and in the Holy of Holies dwelt the special presence of God. The temple is what believers traveled to when they wanted to draw near to God and be in the presence of God.

During the New Covenant period, the local churches are the temples of God, in which believers are both the living stones that make up that temple and the priests who minister within that temple.

The local church is where Christ manifests His special personal presence on earth, which He made clear when He said regarding the local church in Matthew 18:20 that *"where two or three are gathered together in my name, there am I in the midst of them."* We must take note that this was a promise made to the gathered local church, not to a group of Christians getting together on a Thursday night for a Bible study in somebody's home.

The special presence of God is now manifested in the New Covenant temple, which is the local church, in a way in which it is not manifested anywhere else. The church is what you travel to when you want to be close to God, be in the temple of God, and experience the special presence of God. Christ has promised to manifest His special personal presence to His church, which is something above and beyond His general indwelling presence that is with us all of the time.

But we see a progression here. Under the Old Covenant, the special presence of God was manifested in only one place on earth, and that was the Jewish temple. Under the New Covenant, the special presence of God is manifested in many places all around the earth, wherever a biblically functioning church gathers for its stated meetings. But in the new earth, the special presence of God will be manifested in every place, because the whole earth will be the temple of God. His special personal presence will be manifested to every believer at every moment, wherever he may be on the face of the new earth.

In the new earth, the special presence of God is everywhere. It is not limited to a particular location you need to travel to. You do not need to travel to the temple when you already live within the temple—that is, when you live within the special presence of God already. This is why the church in the new earth was symbolically described in verse 16 as a cube, the shape of the Holy of Holies, because the special presence of God—that is, His Shekinah glory—dwells in the midst of the church on the new earth like it did in the Old Testament Holy of

Holies. In the new earth, there is no place to go in order to become closer to God or in order to draw near to God, because God's omnipresence has now become His special personal presence. God's omnipresence and His special personal presence have now become one.

This is why verse 22 says there was no temple within the new Jerusalem because the new Jerusalem itself, and in its entirety, is the temple. The Lord God Almighty and the Lamb fill the new Jerusalem with the fullness of Their presence. There is no place you will be able to go to get more of God because all of God will be manifested everywhere in the new earth, all of the time.

Revelation 7:15 says of the believers in the new earth: *"Therefore are they before the throne of God, and serve him day and night in his temple: and he that sitteth on the throne shall dwell among them."* Revelation 3:12 says as a promise to the church at Philadelphia, *"Him that overcometh will I make a pillar in the temple of my God, and he shall go no more out: and I will write upon him the name of my God, and the name of the city of my God, which is new Jerusalem, which cometh down out of heaven from my God: and I will write upon him my new name."*

Therefore, when Revelation 21:22 says, *"And I saw no temple therein,"* it is not saying that there is no temple at all in the eternal state. It says that there is no temple therein—that is, inside of the new Jerusalem—because the new Jerusalem itself is the temple. Notice Revelation 21:3. *"I heard a great voice out of heaven saying, Behold, the tabernacle of God is with men, and he will dwell with them, and they shall be his people, and God himself shall be with them, and be their God."*

Three times God emphasizes the truth that He will be with them. What *"with them"* means is that when they dwell on the new earth, they will not have to go someplace to find the special personal presence of God. Instead, the special personal presence of God will surround them wherever they are on the new earth.

Speaking prophetically of the new Jerusalem that is in the new earth, Zechariah 2:1–5 says, *"I lifted up mine eyes again, and looked, and behold a man with a measuring line in his hand."* Recall that in Revelation 21:15 there was an angel with a measuring rod in his hand.

"2 Then said I, Whither goest thou? And he said unto me, To measure Jerusalem" (the new Jerusalem) *"to see what is the breadth thereof, and what is the length thereof."* When it was measured, it

was twelve thousand furlongs by twelve thousand furlongs by twelve thousand furlongs. "[3] *And, behold, the angel that talked with me went forth, and another angel went out to meet him,* [4] *And said unto him, Run, speak to this young man"* (to Zechariah), *"saying, Jerusalem shall be inhabited as towns without walls for the multitude of men and cattle therein."*

When you have a great multitude which no man can number, of every kindred, tongue, tribe, and nation in the new earth, you do not build a literal physical wall around it. You cannot contain that many people within a wall. But notice what the wall of protection will be, verse 5: *"For I, saith the LORD, will be unto her a wall of fire round about, and will be the glory in the midst of her."*

God says, "I am the wall of protection around this city, and within this wall of My protection will be My glorious presence. My glory will permeate, saturate, and completely envelop everyone in this new Jerusalem." God will be with those in the new Jerusalem, and what this means is that His unveiled glory will be manifested among them everywhere within new Jerusalem.

In Jeremiah 3, Jeremiah is prophesying about the new heavens and the new earth as well. Notice what he says about them in verses 16 and 17: *"And it shall come to pass, when ye be multiplied and increased in the land, in those days, saith the LORD, they shall say no more, The ark of the covenant of the LORD: neither shall it come to mind: neither shall they remember it; neither shall they visit it; neither shall that be done any more.* [17] *At that time they shall call Jerusalem the throne of the LORD; and all the nations shall be gathered unto it, to the name of the LORD, to Jerusalem: neither shall they walk any more after the imagination of their evil heart."* Verse 17 is speaking about the new Jerusalem that is in heaven.

Therefore, when verse 16 says the ark will not be there anymore, we must understand that he is talking to Old Covenant believers who understood the ark to be the focus of their temple and the central object in the worship conducted there. The ark was in the Holy of Holies where the Shekinah glory of God dwelled, and it was a revolutionary thought to the Jews that a day would come when the ark was done away with. Jeremiah 3:16–17 describes the new earth, the holy city of the new Jerusalem, and the fact that there will be no more temple to visit and no more ark to be seen in that day because the whole city—that is, the whole earth—will be the temple of God.

In the new earth, you cannot visit a temple. You cannot travel to a temple because you are already living inside the temple, and everywhere is the temple. There will be no need to go to church because you will be living within the church all day, every day, for eternity. This is why those who despise the church and want nothing to do with the church, and who never attend church even when they could, will not be in the new earth.

If you want nothing to do with the temple of God on this present earth once a week, how could you bear to live within the temple of God all day, every day, for eternity? If you avoid the worship of God now, how could you endure worshiping God as your primary activity for all eternity? If you are glad to avoid the special presence of God now in the local church by absenting yourself from meeting with the saints there, then how will you bear being in the special presence of God every moment forever and ever?

To be sure, there are people who are providentially hindered from attending a local church by age or illness or distance. You may be providentially hindered from going to church, but if you could be there, you would be there. These remarks are not directed at such people. But know this, that if you want nothing to do with attending a biblically functioning church now, do not think you will be received into heaven as part of the church then. If you want nothing to do with the temple of God now, you will certainly not be living in it in the new earth.

A Christ-centered Christian is a church-centered Christian because Christ loved the church, Christ died for the church, Christ is building the church, and Christ indwells the church with His special personal presence. Those who love Christ love what He loves, and since Christ loves the church, so do they. Those who love the temple of God here on this earth are those who will live in the temple of God there in the new earth.

The Illumination of the Temple

The illumination of the temple is described in verse 23. *"And the city had no need of the sun, neither of the moon, to shine in it: for the glory of God did lighten it, and the Lamb is the light thereof."* Verse 23 tells us that the new Jerusalem, which has no temple because it is the temple, is filled with the light of the glory of God.

Isaiah 60 prophesies that this would be the nature of the temple in the new earth. Isaiah 60 has numerous parallels with Revelation 21, and a great deal of what is spoken of in Revelation 21 is a fulfillment of the prophecies in Isaiah 60. The entire sixtieth chapter of Isaiah predicts the blessedness of the new earth and the new Jerusalem.

Notice Isaiah 60:19–21. It says regarding the new Jerusalem, "*The sun shall be no more thy light by day; neither for brightness shall the moon give light unto thee: but the* LORD *shall be unto thee an everlasting light, and thy God thy glory.* [20] *Thy sun shall no more go down; neither shall thy moon withdraw itself: for the* LORD *shall be thine everlasting light, and the days of thy mourning shall be ended.* [21] *Thy people also shall be all righteous: they shall inherit the land for ever, the branch of my planting, the work of my hands, that I may be glorified.*"

In verses 19 and 20, the Lord is twice said to be the everlasting light of the new earth, and we are told the sun and the moon will not be needed to illuminate the earth. I am not suggesting there will be no sun or moon, but they will become irrelevant as the source of light in the new Jerusalem and on the new earth. It will be light all day, every day, for eternity. Isaiah is saying that the light in the new Jerusalem will be like the sun that never goes down. That is the consistency and the continuous nature of this light. It is a light that proceeds from the Lord Himself.

In Isaiah 24:23 it says, "*Then the moon shall be confounded, and the sun ashamed, when the* LORD *of hosts shall reign in mount Zion, and in Jerusalem, and before his ancients gloriously.*" The amount of light that the sun and the moon put out is going to be like a tiny spark in comparison to the brilliance of the light of the glory of God. The light from the sun and the moon will be utterly irrelevant in comparison with the brilliance of the glory of God that is going to continuously fill the new earth in every place for all eternity without remission.

God's glory will provide constant light to the new earth, so there shall never be any period of darkness or nighttime ever again. Just as God's universal presence removes any need for a localized temple in the new earth, God's universal presence also removes the need for a localized source of light in the new earth. Since His presence illuminates everything, everywhere, all the time, there are not going to be any dark spots into which you are going to need to shine a flashlight.

Here will be the ultimate fulfillment of Psalm 139. This is the psalm that exalts the omnipresence of God. Verses 7–12 say: "*Whither shall I go from thy spirit? or whither shall I flee from thy presence?* [8] *If I ascend up into heaven, thou art there: if I make my bed in hell, behold, thou art there.* [9] *If I take the wings of the morning, and dwell in the uttermost parts of the sea;* [10] *Even there shall thy hand lead me, and thy right hand shall hold me.* [11] *If I say, Surely the darkness shall cover me; even the night shall be light about me.* [12] *Yea, the darkness hideth not from thee; but the night shineth as the day: the darkness and the light are both alike to thee.*"

There is a great deal of application in these verses to our personal lives right now, but there is an ultimate application of them in the new earth, in that, wherever we are, God's presence and God's light exist. Never again will there be any darkness, and never again will we be able to go away from the presence of God. On earth, you can go away from the special presence of God. Just stay out of church. But in the new heavens, every place will be the church, and there will be no place to go to be away from the special presence of God.

The psalmist is saying, in effect, "It is a huge comfort to me now that everywhere I go, there I experience the presence of God and the light of God, and it does not matter how high I go up, or how low I go down, or how far to the east or to the west, wherever I go, You are there with Your presence and with Your light." But the ultimate fulfillment of that comfort is going to be in the new earth.

Revelation 21:23 makes it clear that both the Lord God Almighty and the Lamb share an equal glory because both of Them are an equal source of this universal light of glory in the new earth. Notice verse 23: "*And the city had no need of the sun, neither of the moon to shine in it: for the glory of God did lighten it, and the Lamb is the light thereof.*"

Both the Lord God Almighty and the Lamb shine out an equal glory because both of Them are the source of this universal light in the earth. The reason They shine out an equal light of glory is that They share an equal essence. Both of Them are fully God.

Revelation 5:13 describes the throne room of heaven and the gathered saints in the presence of the enthroned God and His Son Jesus Christ, who has taken the book out of His hand. Notice the praise and worship that flows. "*And every creature which is in heaven, and on the earth, and under the earth, and such as are in the sea, and all that are in them, heard I saying, Blessing, and honour, and glory, and power, be unto him that sitteth upon the throne, and unto the Lamb for ever and ever."*

In other words, the Lamb receives the same praise and worship the Father on the throne receives. When John fell down to worship the angel, the angel said, "Do not do that! Worship God!" Here the whole host of heaven is worshiping Jesus Christ. Not only are they not rebuked, as if Jesus is something less than God, but they are commended for the worship and praise they offer to Jesus, because Jesus Christ is God.

Jesus said of Himself in John 8:12, *"I am the light of the world."* This is spiritually true now, but it will also be physically true in the new earth.

This is spoken of in Luke 1:76–79 when Jesus was born. Zacharias, John the Baptist's father, is prophesying and says in verse 76: *"And thou, child"* (John the Baptist), *"shalt be called the prophet of the Highest"* (God the Father): *"for thou shalt go before the face of the Lord"* (Jesus Christ) *"to prepare his ways; 77 To give knowledge of salvation unto his people by the remission of their sins, 78 Through the tender mercy of our God; whereby the dayspring from on high hath visited us, 79 To give light to them that sit in darkness and in the shadow of death, to guide our feet into the way of peace."*

When Jesus said, *"I am the light of the world,"* this is what was being spoken of. He brought the spiritual light of the truth of the gospel to the world that was in the darkness of sin and damnation and depravity, and ultimately, along with that spiritual light, He will bring physical light to fill the new Jerusalem and the new earth.

Without the light of God's presence, the Holy of Holies in the Old Covenant tabernacle would have been totally dark. The lampstand was out in the Holy Place, but the Holy of Holies had no source of light. But when the high priest entered, it was not dark, because it was illuminated with the Shekinah glory of God.

In the same way, the entire new earth will be filled with the light of God's glory as well. *"God is light, and in him is no darkness at all"*; and therefore, there will be no darkness at all in the earth, either spiritually or physically.

On the Mount of Transfiguration in Matthew 17 when Jesus was transfigured, the brilliance of His face shined like the sun, and His clothing was as white as the light. He shined with the Glory of God.

We will live forever not only in the presence of that pure, beautiful, spiritual light, but also in the presence of that pure, beautiful, physical light of His blessed presence and His infinite love forever and ever.

I have to ask: What is your attitude toward that light? In John 3:17–21 Jesus says, *"For God sent not his Son into the world to condemn the world; but that the world through him might be saved.* [18] *He that believeth on him is not condemned: but he that believeth not is condemned already, because he hath not believed in the name of the only begotten Son of God.* [19] *And this is the condemnation, that light is come into the world, and men loved darkness rather than light, because their deeds were evil.* [20] *For every one that doeth evil hateth the light, neither cometh to the light, lest his deeds should be reproved.* [21] *But he that doeth truth cometh to the light, that his deeds may be made manifest, that they are wrought in God."*

If we flee from the spiritual light that Jesus brings now, we will never dwell in the physical light He provides later. Those who love darkness now—those who flee from the light of the truth of the gospel—would never be able to bear the light of God's presence and God's truth in the new earth. Those who prefer darkness now will live in outer darkness forever, where there will be weeping and wailing and gnashing of teeth. When the light of the gospel comes to you, if you embrace it, you may expect to enjoy this blessed light of the new earth and dwell in it. But if you hate the light now, you will really hate the light then. It is the nature of the damned and the depraved that they prefer darkness over light.

How can you tell if somebody is going to wind up in the new earth? Ask yourself: Do they love the place of God's special presence here on this earth? Do they love the spiritual light of Christ's teaching here on this earth? If they love God's temple here, and if they love God's light here, they will dwell in God's temple there, and they will dwell in God's light there. Heaven is just a continuation and perfection of the trajectory that we have begun here on earth. Do not think that you can live like hell on earth, and wind up with God in heaven.

The Occupants of the Temple

The occupants of the temple are described in verses 24 to 27 which says: *"And the nations of them which are saved shall walk in the light of it: and the kings of the earth do bring their glory and honour into it.* [25] *And the gates of it shall not be shut at all by day: for there shall be no night there.* [26] *And they shall bring the glory and honour of the nations into it.* [27] *And there shall in no wise enter into it anything that defileth, neither whatsoever worketh abomination, or maketh a lie: but they which are written in the Lamb's book of life."*

In verses 24 to 27, we are told who will be included and who will be excluded from the temple of the presence of God in the new earth. Notice first of all, that those who are included in the temple of the presence of God in the new Jerusalem are the saved of all the nations. Verse 24: *"And the nations of them which are saved shall walk in the light of it."*

Those who are saved are those who dwell on the new earth. They are the ones whose names *"are written in the Lamb's book of life."* God's saving purposes are not small, they are not narrow, and they are certainly not confined to one ethnic group or one nationality of people. God promised Abraham in Genesis 17 that he would be the father of many nations. In the new Jerusalem in the new earth, we see the fulfillment of that promise when it says, *"And the nations of them which are saved shall walk in the light of it."*

God has saved a multitude of people no man can number out of the nations of the earth: from the north, south, east, and west. That is why this city is symbolically pictured as a square with those orientations. These people who are saved through faith in Jesus Christ are gathered together in the presence of God to live with Him forever.

In Isaiah 60:1–5 we see that those being gathered into the new Jerusalem are the nations of the earth. God is not going to save just the Jews; He is going to save people of every class and category, and of every nationality and race.

Notice verses 1–5: *"Arise, shine; for thy light is come, and the glory of the* L*ORD is risen upon thee."* This is the light of God in the new earth. "[2] *For, behold, the darkness shall cover the earth, and gross darkness the people"* (what we have now): *"but the* L*ORD shall arise upon thee, and his glory shall be seen upon thee.* [3] *And the Gentiles shall come to thy light, and kings to the brightness of thy rising.* [4] *Lift up thine eyes round about, and see: all they gather themselves together, they come to thee: thy sons shall come from far, and thy daughters shall be nursed at thy side.* [5] *Then thou shalt see, and flow together, and thine heart shall fear, and be enlarged; because the abundance of the sea shall be converted unto thee, the forces of the Gentiles shall* *come unto thee."* The sea symbolically represents the unsaved Gentile nations, and this is why it says in Revelation 21:1 that there shall be no more sea. It means there will be no more seething mass of unsaved Gentile nations in the new earth.

This is what is described in Revelation 21:24: *"The Gentiles shall come to thy light."* The light they come to is the light of salvation that Christ brought at His first coming; and it is also the light of the blessedness of living in the eternal temple in the new earth, which is full of the light of the glory of God.

When it says in verse 24, *"And the nations of them which are saved shall walk in the light of it: and the kings of the earth do bring their glory and honour into it,"* and in verse 26, *"And they shall bring the glory and honour of the nations into it,"* this is exactly what Isaiah is talking about when he says, *"And the Gentiles shall come to thy light, and kings to the brightness of thy rising."* Jew and Gentile will, as it says in Isaiah 60:5, flow together into one people who are the citizens of the kingdom worshiping God forever and ever. This salvation of the nations occurred in a very small and limited fashion prior to the coming of Christ. We see Ruth the Moabitess saved, we see some people from Nineveh saved, and we see some Babylonians saved, but it was a small and limited number of people.

But the salvation of the nations exploded on the day of Pentecost, in which representatives of a multitude of nations listed in Acts 2 heard the gospel, which then spread rapidly to the uttermost parts of the earth in the following centuries. Hundreds of millions of people from all the nations of the earth, and the kings of many kingdoms, have been saved by Jesus Christ and will inhabit the temple of the new earth.

In Revelation 7, we had a very brief summary of Revelation 21. Because the book of Revelation is written in a cyclical fashion, we are brought time and again to the eternal state as we proceed through this book. Revelation 7:9–10 says, *"After this I beheld, and, lo, a great multitude, which no man could number, of all nations, and kindreds, and people, and tongues, stood before the throne, and before the Lamb, clothed with white robes, and palms in their hands;* [10] *And cried with a loud voice, saying, Salvation to our God which sitteth upon the throne, and unto the Lamb."*

These kings of the earth mentioned in Revelation 21:24 followed the counsel of Psalm 2:10–12 where it says, *"Be wise now therefore, O ye kings: be instructed, ye judges of the earth.* [11] *Serve the LORD with fear, and rejoice with trembling.* [12] *Kiss the Son, lest he be angry, and ye perish from the way, when his wrath is kindled but a little. Blessed are all they that put their trust in him."* The kings of the earth who followed this counsel will bring the homage of their glory and honor and lay it before the enthroned Christ in humility and worship, and the people of the nations will do so as well. As it says in Revelation 21:26, *"And they shall bring the glory and honour of the nations into it."*

Who is going to be in heaven? All the people who are saved. Is it just going to be Jews? No, it is going to be all the kings of the earth and all the nations of the earth who repented of their sins and received Jesus Christ as Lord and Savior. They will be those who inhabit the new Jerusalem on the new earth, who live in the temple of God, and who live in the light of illumination provided by the glory of God.

There is an interesting statement in verse 25. Notice it says, *"And the gates of it,"* (the gates of the new Jerusalem) *"shall not be shut at all by day: for there shall be no night there."* That is a significant statement: earthly gates of earthly cities were always shut at night because night was a time of vulnerability and danger from enemies. But in the new earth, there will be no night. In the new earth, there will be no enemies because they have all been cast into the lake of fire. There will be no need to shut the gate because those who live on the new earth dwell in perfect security and total safety.

It would be like going to bed and leaving your doors and windows wide open all night long. Have you ever done that? You would not think of it! You shut those gates by night because you are afraid of who is out there, and who might come in to harm you.

But in the new heavens, we will have such perfect safety and such total security that we will have no fear of anything harming us ever again. We can be entirely unconcerned about our safety because there is no danger. All the enemies of the people of God have been vanquished and cast into the lake of fire, so it is impossible that the city could or would ever be assaulted at any time by anyone for any reason.

Notice Isaiah 60:11: *"Therefore thy gates shall be open continually; they shall not be shut day nor night; that men may bring unto thee the forces"* (or wealth), *"of the Gentiles, and that their kings may be brought."* There is coming a day, Isaiah says, when you will not even need to shut the gates of Jerusalem. All the Gentiles are going to come, not to attack you, but to bring themselves and their treasures to lay them down in homage at your feet.

The idea behind Isaiah's prophecy is that the Gentile nations will bring their strength. That is why it is translated *"forces."* The question is, what kind of strength is it? Is it military strength, or is it economic strength? It could be either, and that is why some translations translate it "wealth" instead of forces. But whatever power the nations have, be it economic, military, personal, or political, they are going to bring it all and lay it down at the feet of Jesus.

The kings from the East who came and brought their gifts to Jesus and laid them down at His feet were a foreshadowing of how the nations of the earth are going to bring all they have and all they are and lay it down at the feet of Jesus. The elect of the nations of the earth have already been doing that for the last 2,000 years. They will do it to the fullest extent in the new earth. It says in Psalm 86:9, *"All nations whom thou hast made shall come and worship before thee, O Lord; and shall glorify thy name."*

This is the description of the occupants of the temple. They consist of the nations which are saved.

But notice secondly, those who are excluded from the temple of the presence of God in the new earth. Verse 27 says, *"And there shall in no wise enter into it anything that defileth, neither whatsoever worketh abomination, or maketh a lie: but they which are written in the Lamb's book of life."* Here is a description of the character traits of those who are not saved, and the behavior they practiced during this life.

They are those who practice morally defiling behavior, they are those who practice the abomination of idolatry and the worship of false gods, and they are those who practice deceit and dishonesty and embrace and teach lies that are contrary to God's truth. Such people will not enter into the new Jerusalem, the new earth, or the presence of God. Jesus said in Matthew 7:21, *"Not every one that saith unto me, Lord, Lord, shall enter into the kingdom of heaven; but he that doeth the will of my Father which is in heaven."*

Three vices are mentioned in verse 27. One cannot practice immorality, one cannot practice idolatry, and one cannot practice deceit and be a saved person. Saved people repent of such behavior, saved people depart from such behavior, and saved people do not practice it or defend it or persist in it. A believer may fall into such sins, but he does not continue in them, and he does not defend them or justify them. He repents of them, and they do not characterize his life.

This is the nature of the temple: it involves the entire world as being a place where the special presence of God dwells. This is the illumination of the temple: the light of the glory of God is the light of this new earth. These are the occupants of the temple: those who are saved from sin, but not those who practice and justify sin.

Being in the temple of God's special personal presence for all eternity is the greatest blessing that salvation brings to us. There is no higher blessing than that. This is what every believer has always aspired to. It is not health and wealth. It is drawing near to God and being in the presence of God and having nothing standing between our souls and God. That is what we long for.

David says in Psalm 27:4–6, *"One thing have I desired of the LORD, that will I seek after; that I may dwell in the house of the LORD all the days of my life, to behold the beauty of the LORD, and to enquire in his temple. [5] For in the time of trouble he shall hide me in his pavilion: in the secret of his tabernacle shall he hide me; he shall set me up upon a rock. [6] And now shall mine head be lifted up above mine enemies round about me: therefore will I offer in his tabernacle sacrifices of joy; I will sing, yea, I will sing praises unto the LORD."*

If that does not resonate with your heart at the deepest level, it is doubtful that you are a saved person. The heart of every saved person is that *"I would dwell in the house of the LORD all the days of my life, to behold the beauty of the LORD, and to enquire in his temple."*

That is what we are going to be doing for eternity. We are going to be in His house, we are going to be in His presence, we are going to be looking upon the wonder of His person, and we are going to be conversing with Him and inquiring of Him all the things we ever wanted to know regarding Him and His works and His glorious person. We shall see Him, and He will talk with us.

Communion with Christ in the new earth is the pinnacle of the blessing of salvation. That is where we are headed, and the destiny to which Christ is bringing us. The heartbeat of every believer in Jesus Christ is to be with Him and love Him and follow Him, and to never have anything stand between us and Him. May the Lord cause us to have such a heart, and to seek Him with all of our heart.

66

Eden Restored, Revelation 22:1–7

> "[1] *And he shewed me a pure river of water of life, clear as crystal, proceeding out of the throne of God and of the Lamb.* [2] *In the midst of the street of it, and on either side of the river, was there the tree of life, which bare twelve manner of fruits, and yielded her fruit every month: and the leaves of the tree were for the healing of the nations.* [3] *And there shall be no more curse: but the throne of God and of the Lamb shall be in it; and his servants shall serve him:* [4] *And they shall see his face; and his name shall be in their foreheads.* [5] *And there shall be no night there; and they need no candle, neither light of the sun; for the Lord God giveth them light: and they shall reign for ever and ever.* [6] *And he said unto me, These sayings are faithful and true: and the Lord God of the holy prophets sent his angel to shew unto his servants the things which must shortly be done.* [7] *Behold, I come quickly: blessed is he that keepeth the sayings of the prophecy of this book.*"

The Bible traces human history from beginning to end. It opens with Adam and Eve being created and placed into the paradise God had made for them. All God did in creation was very good.

But sadly, as a result of Satan's temptation, mankind fell into sin against God and became subject to defilement, depravity, and death. Paradise itself became cursed and corrupted, and mankind was driven out of Eden.

But God was determined to redeem mankind from sin, restore the fallen creation, and destroy all the works the devil had achieved. That restoring and redeeming work was accomplished by Jesus Christ when He came to save His people from their sins and destroy the works of the devil. By making atonement for sin, Jesus removed the effects of sin and provided the basis for the restoration of both mankind and the original creation.

The history of humanity that began in Genesis 1 is coming to a conclusion in Revelation 22. As we move from Genesis 1 to Revelation 22, history has come full circle. In chapter 22, mankind is now redeemed from sin and has been given a perfect and permanent righteousness. The works of the devil have been destroyed. The devil himself has been cast into the lake of fire so he can never trouble us again.

In chapter 22, we see that the creation has been released from the curse, and paradise has been restored and perfected in both its function and its beauty. And most wonderful of all, mankind now dwells in the presence of God, is surrounded with the glory of God, and enjoys perfect fellowship with God. In chapter 22, we see paradise restored and elevated to all it could have become had Adam not sinned, and had he exercised proper dominion over it. The good news of the Scriptures is that Jesus Christ, who is the last Adam, has done all that the first Adam failed to do. Jesus has not only restored the garden of Eden; He has cultivated and kept it in such a way that it has reached perfection, and has now covered the whole earth.

Jesus has not only forgiven our sins; He has provided us with a perfect and permanent righteousness.

Jesus has not only saved us from death and from hell; He has placed us into the paradise of God.

Jesus has not only restored us to life; He has perfected our bodies and our souls so they are holy and sinless and incorruptible forever.

Jesus has not only delivered us from the wrath of God; He has made us holy and unblameable and unreproveable in His sight, and has presented us faultless before His presence so we may see God's face without shame or guilt or dread.

The conclusion of human history is a conclusion of triumph and victory. It is a conclusion that achieves the perfection of the natural creation and the human creation. Once again, God is able to look upon all things and say of them: *"Behold, it [is] very good."*

In our previous studies of Revelation 21, we have seen the perfection of the church in the new earth, in verses 9 to 21. We then saw the habitation of God in the new earth, in verses 22 to 27. Now we will see the restoration of paradise in the new earth, in 22:1–7. Revelation 22:1–7 really belongs to chapter 21, because it extends and concludes the description of the eternal state we will enjoy on the new earth which began to be described in 21:1.

John provided us with a summary description of our eternal state in Revelation 21:1–8. He then provided us with an expanded explanation of our eternal state in 21:9 through 22:7, in which he supplied many additional details about our eternal home and the blessedness we will enjoy there.

The perfection of the church, the habitation of God, and the restoration of paradise are the three great themes which were expanded on after they were all introduced to us in Revelation 21:1–8.

The Source of Life in the New Earth

The source of life in the new earth is spoken of in verses 1 and 2. Notice the allusions to the garden of Eden restored. *And he shewed me a pure river of water of life, clear as crystal, proceeding out of the throne of God and of the Lamb.* [2] *In the midst of the street of it, and on either side of the river, was there the tree of life, which bare twelve manner of fruits, and yielded her fruit every month: and the leaves of the tree were for the healing of the nations."*

Here we have the river of life and the tree of life.

First of all, consider the river of life spoken of in verse 1. *"And he shewed me a pure river of water of life."* Water in the Scriptures has long been a symbol of life, both literally and spiritually. Literally and physically, all living things need water for life. Plants and animals and people cannot live without it. This was true from the very beginning of creation.

At the center of the garden of Eden was a river that ran through it to provide water for the garden. The mist that went up from the earth and watered the whole face of the ground was not sufficient to meet the needs of the animals and of the people. Therefore, God provided them with a life-giving river, whose supply was abundant and whose source was God Himself. God supplied the water out of the earth for the river in the garden of Eden, just like He supplied the water out of the rock which Moses smote so Israel could survive when she was in the wilderness. This river God provided not only flowed through the garden, but it also divided into four rivers that ran in various directions to water the whole earth.

But as we know, mankind fell and was driven out of the garden; and eventually, the flood came and covered the earth and dramatically changed the geography of the world. The result is that Eden was obliterated, the geography of the earth was tremendously altered, and this river and its distributaries were lost. Eden and the rivers that flowed out of it, and the lands Genesis 2 describe they flowed into, can no longer be identified with any geographical place on earth.

The source of water out of Eden was removed, and the source of the rivers on earth are now supplied by the normal hydrological cycle of rainfall and runoff. But this cycle of rainfall and runoff is seriously defective due to the fall and the curse, resulting in horrible floods in some areas, and terrible droughts in other areas. Large areas of the earth consist of uninhabitable deserts or swamps.

But what was lost in Eden due to the fall will be restored in the new earth. This was an especially precious promise to the people of Israel because they lived in a dry and thirsty land, and the failure of the water supply due to drought caused many Israelites to die of thirst or starvation due to crop failure.

But in the new earth, the river of God will be restored, and what was lost in the fall will be regained, so that the river of God will once again water the whole earth, and drought and desert will disappear forever. Paradise will be physically restored in all the original beauty and balance and abundance it possessed in the garden of Eden before the fall. Never again will we live in a dry and thirsty land.

But there is not only a literal and physical significance of this river described in verse 1; there is also a symbolic and spiritual significance that is even more profound and compelling. In the Scriptures, water and rivers are symbols of blessing, of eternal life, and of the Holy Spirit.

First of all, water is a symbol of blessing. Notice Psalm 1. It opens with these words, "[1] *Blessed is the man that walketh not in the counsel of the ungodly, nor standeth in the way of sinners, nor sitteth in the seat of the scornful.* [2] *But his delight is in the law of the* L*ORD*; *and in his law doth he meditate day and night.* [3] *And he shall be like a tree planted by the rivers of water, that bringeth forth his fruit in his season; his leaf also shall not wither; and whatsoever he doeth shall prosper.*"

Here a river of water is symbolically pictured: one that is pure, abundant, free-flowing, and life-giving. This water symbolizes the blessing of God on the life of the man who rejects the wicked ways of the world's conduct and thought, and who embraces God's righteous ways of conduct and thought revealed in the Scripture.

The blessing of God symbolized by this river brings the man of God a life of spiritual productivity—one *"that bringeth forth his fruit in his season."* It brings him a life of spiritual preservation: *"his leaf also shall not wither."* It brings him a life of spiritual prosperity: *"whatsoever he doeth shall prosper."* Clearly, the river is the symbol of the blessing of God in the life of a man who walks with God.

Secondly, water is a symbol of eternal life. Notice John 4. Here we see Jesus talking with the woman at the well, and He asks her for a drink of water. They have a discussion, and as this discussion develops, Jesus says to her in verses 10–14, *"If thou knewest the gift of God, and who it is that saith to thee, Give me to drink; thou wouldest have asked of him, and he would have given thee living water.* 11 *The woman saith unto him, Sir, thou hast nothing to draw with, and the well is deep: from whence then hast thou that living water?* 12 *Art thou greater than our father Jacob, which gave us the well, and drank thereof himself, and his children, and his cattle?* 13 *Jesus answered and said unto her, Whosoever drinketh of this water shall thirst again:*
14 *But whosoever drinketh of the water that I shall give him shall never thirst; but the water that I shall give him shall be in him a well of water springing up into everlasting life."*

Here, water is a symbol of eternal life. In fact, three times—in Revelation 21:6, 22:1, and 22:17—water is called *"the water of life."* In the context in which it is spoken, it is speaking about eternal life. Therefore, water is not only a symbol of God's blessing, but also a symbol of eternal life.

Thirdly, water is a symbol of the Holy Spirit. In John 7:37–39, Jesus was at the Feast of Tabernacles, and said in verse 37, *"In the last day, that great day of the feast, Jesus stood and cried, saying, If any man thirst, let him come unto me, and drink.* 38 *He that believeth on me, as the scripture hath said, out of his belly shall flow rivers of living water."* The interpretation of what that means is in verse 39: "39*(But this spake he of the Spirit, which they that believe on him should receive: for the Holy Ghost was not yet given; because that Jesus was not yet glorified.)"* The Holy Spirit is likened to a river of life-giving water that brings life to the sinner and produces life in the believer and then flows out of him to extend life to those around him.

What do we have in Revelation 22:1 when we are told that *"a pure river of water of life, clear as crystal,"* proceeds out of the throne of God and of the Lamb? This rich symbolic metaphor tells us that, in the new earth, God's blessing will be on His people, as described in Psalm 1. It tells us that God's eternal life will be given to His people, as described in John 4. Finally, it tells us that God's Holy Spirit will be filling His people, as described in John 7.

But what is even more amazing is that this flow of God's goodness to His people will be constantly increasing throughout all eternity. You will think when you get to heaven and are first there that you have immense benefits. You have God's blessing, you have eternal life, you have the indwelling operation of the Holy Spirit; does it get any better than that? Yes, it does! It gets better, and better, and better, because those things will increase more and more as eternity progresses.

Ezekiel 47:1–12 provides a vision of this ever-increasing blessing in the form of an ever-increasing river. In chapters 40–48 Ezekiel has a vision of an immense temple. This is a symbolic temple and not a literal one, for all the reasons stated in Appendix 3.

The church is the temple of God under the New Covenant. This temple in Ezekiel is a visual symbolic image of the size to which the church will grow under the New Covenant as the New Covenant temple of God. Therefore, Ezekiel's temple is not a picture of a literal temple in a future literal Millennium. It is a picture of the New Covenant church in this age.

Ezekiel's temple is also a symbolic image of the church as it will exist in the new earth. The perfection, beauty, and balance of this magnificent temple is an Old Testament picture of the new Jerusalem described in Revelation 21. Therefore, this temple is a picture of both the church in this age, and also in the age to come.

Ezekiel brings to our attention a life-giving river that flows out from under this temple he describes. Notice Ezekiel 47:1–12: "*Afterward he brought me again unto the door of the house; and, behold, waters issued out from under the threshold of the house eastward: for the forefront of the house stood toward the east, and the waters came down from under from the right side of the house, at the south side of the altar.* [2] *Then brought he me out of the way of the gate northward, and led me about the way without unto the utter gate by the way that looketh eastward; and, behold, there ran out waters on the right side.* [3] *And when the man that had the line in his hand went forth eastward, he measured a thousand cubits, and he brought me through the waters; the waters were to the ankles.* [4] *Again he measured a thousand, and brought me through the waters; the waters were to the knees. Again he measured a thousand, and brought me through; the waters were to the loins"* (or the waist.) "[5] *Afterward he measured a thousand; and it was a river that I could not pass over: for the waters were risen, waters to swim in, a river that could not be passed over.* [6] *And he said unto me, Son of man, hast thou seen this? Then he brought me, and caused me to return to the brink of the river.* [7] *Now when I had returned, behold, at the bank of the river were very many trees on the one side and on the other.* [8] *Then said he unto me, These waters issue out toward the east country, and go down into the desert, and go into the sea:"* (Jerusalem was to the west of the Dead Sea, so these waters are pictured as flowing out of Jerusalem eastward and down into the Dead Sea) *"which being brought forth into the sea, the waters shall be healed."*

The Dead Sea is dead. Nothing lives in it. It is six times as salty as the ocean. It is where Sodom and Gomorrah were destroyed. It is very, very dead. These waters flowing out of Ezekiel's temple are getting deeper and larger as they flow, and they are flowing into the Dead Sea.

Verse 9: *"And it shall come to pass, that every thing that liveth, which moveth, whithersoever the rivers shall come, shall live: and there shall be a very great multitude of fish, because these waters shall come thither: for they shall be healed; and every thing shall live whither the river cometh.* [10] *And it shall come to pass, that the fishers shall stand upon it"* (on the shore) *"from En-gedi even unto En-eglaim; they shall be a place to spread forth nets; their fish shall be according to their kinds, as the fish of the great sea, exceeding many."* The Dead Sea is going to be full of fish, fishermen are going to stand on the shore of the Dead Sea with their nets, they are going to fish in it, and they are going to get as many fish out of it as they get out of the Mediterranean Sea.

Verse 11: *"But the miry places thereof and the marshes thereof shall not be healed; they shall be given to salt."* Salt is a necessity of life, and we need some salt available. "[12]*And by the river upon the bank thereof, on this side and on that side, shall grow all trees for meat,"* (or food) *"whose leaf shall not fade, neither shall the fruit thereof be consumed: it shall bring forth new fruit according to his months, because their waters they issued out of the sanctuary: and the fruit thereof shall be for meat, and the leaf thereof for medicine."*

Ezekiel 47:1–12 is a visual symbolic image of increasing abundance, increasing provision, and increasing blessing that completely overwhelms us. When Ezekiel begins describing his vision, the blessings are to his ankles, and then they are to his knees, and then they are to his waist; and finally, they are so great he is overwhelmed by this river of blessing. Life flourishes where the river flows, and it flows in ever-increasing amounts of volume of blessing.

In Revelation 22, John is using the imagery of Ezekiel 47. Therefore, the blessings of Eden symbolized by the river, both the physical blessings and the spiritual blessings, will all be restored in the new earth, and they will be increasing more and more throughout eternity. The river of blessing gets greater and greater in volume as eternity unfolds.

John tells us two more things about this river. He says in verse 1, *"And he shewed me a pure river of water of life, clear as crystal, proceeding out of the throne of God and of the Lamb."* This river is said to flow out of the throne of God and the Lamb. This tells us that God is the source of this river and all it represents, and it is His sovereign grace that has given us the eternal life it symbolizes, the blessings it conveys, and the Spirit it bestows.

Furthermore, it tells us this river is pure. It is as clear as crystal. This tells us that there will be no sin in heaven and no impurity to deface and pollute the good we will enjoy there. As it says in Proverbs 10:22, *"The blessing of the Lord, it maketh rich, and he addeth no sorrow with it."* His blessings are pure. They are as clear as crystal, and there is nothing that pollutes them.

Numerous other passages from the Old Testament speak of the blessedness of the river that is in the new earth. Notable among those passages are Psalm 46:1–11, which describes the new earth, as well as Isaiah 35:6–10, Joel 3:16–18, and Zechariah 14:8–9. Those are just the major passages. There are many others as well. This theme of the river of God's blessing in the new earth is a prominent one in the Old Testament.

Having seen the river of life; secondly, notice the tree of life in verse 2. *"In the midst of the street of it, and on either side of the river, was there the tree of life, which bare twelve manner of fruits, and yielded her fruit every month: and the leaves of the tree were for the healing of the nations."*

As we consider how paradise is restored in the new earth, not only does God tell us about the restoration of the river of life, but He now tells us about the restoration of the tree of life. The tree of life played a prominent role in the garden of Eden. According to Genesis 3:22, to eat of the tree of life would result in living forever. To consume it was to obtain eternal life. Once Adam sinned by eating the tree of the knowledge of good and evil, he was cast out of the garden and was prevented by sword-bearing angels from ever approaching the tree of life again. The point is that man would never be able to obtain eternal life for himself from this point forward. Once he had sinned, there was no possibility of him doing something to obtain eternal life. The only thing he could have done was to eat of the tree of life, and the way to the tree of life was barred; and in the flood, it was obliterated.

But God planted another tree of life on Mount Calvary, upon which Jesus died and shed His blood. Galatians 3:13 says that *"Christ hath redeemed us from the curse of the law, being made a curse for us: for it is written, Cursed is every one that hangeth on a tree."* First Peter 2:24 says that Jesus Christ *"his own self bare our sins in his own body on the tree, that we, being dead to sins, should live unto righteousness: by whose stripes ye were healed."*

Jesus was cursed on that tree so we might be justified from our sins and have our record cleansed. Jesus bore our sins in His own body on the tree so that we might be sanctified from our sins, and have our person cleansed and our behavior transformed.

In Galatians 3:13, His death accomplished our deliverance from the curse our sins brought upon us; and in 1 Peter 2:24, His death accomplished our deliverance from the power and the practice of sin in our lives.

Because Christ, by His death on the tree, has justified us and cleansed our record; and because Christ, by His death on the tree, has sanctified us and cleansed our persons, we now once again have access to the tree of life.

Just like the river of life continues to flow, forever providing endless blessings, so the tree of life continues to bear fruit and leaves for the healing of the nations. This healing is from all the effects and consequences of sin. It imparts ongoing life and health to all who are in the new earth. The tree will not be there to look at. The tree will be there to eat of, to enjoy, and to receive healing from. This promise of eating of the tree of life was first given to us in Revelation 2:7, when Jesus said to the church at Ephesus, *"To him that overcometh will I give to eat of the tree of life, which is in the midst of the paradise of God."*

The tree of life will be food and medicine for both body and soul to provide us with perfect physical and spiritual health. We read of this previously in Ezekiel 47. Ezekiel 47:12 said, *"And by the river upon the bank thereof, on this side and on that side, shall grow all trees for meat, whose leaf shall not fade, neither shall the fruit thereof be consumed: it shall bring forth new fruit according to his months, because their waters they issued out of the sanctuary: and the fruit thereof shall be for meat, and the leaf thereof for medicine."*

Ezekiel envisions this tree of life under the imagery of a multitude of trees, growing on the banks of the river. Whether there will be one tree of life or a multitude of identical trees of life, the point is this: the tree of life bears twelve kinds of fruit, and it bears them twelve months out of the year. The reason why the number twelve is used is because twelve symbolizes the people of God. The point is that every need of all of the people of God, whether physical or spiritual, whether for body or soul, will be fully met by the supply of God in the new, restored Eden in the new earth.

Revelation 7:16–17 speaks of this in summary form when it says regarding those in the new earth that *"They shall hunger no more, neither thirst any more; neither shall the sun light on them, nor any heat. [17] For the Lamb which is in the midst of the throne shall feed them, and shall lead them unto living fountains of waters: and God shall wipe away all tears from their eyes."* This tree is how they eat, and this river is how they drink. This is the source of life in the new earth: the river of life, and the tree of life.

The Nature of Life in the New Earth

The nature of life in the new earth is found in verses 3 to 5. *"And there shall be no more curse: but the throne of God and of the Lamb shall be in it; and his servants shall serve him: [4] And they shall see his face; and his name shall be in their foreheads. [5] And there shall be no night there; and they need no candle, neither light of the sun; for the Lord God giveth them light: and they shall reign for ever and ever."*

Notice first of all what is missing from the new earth and from the restored garden of Eden. It says in verse 3 that in this restored garden of Eden, *"there shall be no more curse."* That is what is missing, thank God! There was no curse upon the first garden of Eden until Adam sinned. Originally, everything there was very good. But with sin came the curse, and that curse was exceedingly dreadful and painful.

That curse is described in Genesis 3:16–19: *"Unto the woman he said, I will greatly multiply thy sorrow and thy conception; in sorrow thou shalt bring forth children; and thy desire shall be to thy husband, and he shall rule over thee.* [17] *And unto Adam he said, Because thou hast hearkened unto the voice of thy wife, and hast eaten of the tree, of which I commanded thee, saying, Thou shalt not eat of it: cursed is the ground for thy sake; in sorrow shalt thou eat of it all the days of thy life;* [18] *Thorns also and thistles shall it bring forth to thee; and thou shalt eat the herb of the field;* [19] *In the sweat of thy face shalt thou eat bread, till thou return unto the ground; for out of it wast thou taken: for dust thou art, and unto dust shalt thou return."*

God cursed mankind and the creation because of Adam's sin. For the woman, she was to have sorrow in childbirth and be in subjection to a fallen husband. For the man, he was to have a stubborn earth requiring arduous labor to make a living from it. And for both of them, there would be death and decay of the body in the ground.

In a word, sorrow, hardship, suffering, and death are the result of the curse. The curse brought about loss and misery and ruin; and after that, eternal damnation in hell under the wrath of God. The curse is the explanation for all human suffering and heartaches that exist. Every sorrow, every pain, every misery, every hardship, every loss that you experience is the result of the curse of God on the earth and on humanity.

But this curse is completely done away with in the new earth. Because Jesus atoned for sin, the curse which was caused by sin can no longer exist. The curse is the effect of sin, and when sin is eradicated by the work of Christ, the curse has no more basis for existence. Never again will we experience sorrow, hardship, suffering, or death. Never again will we experience loss and misery and ruin. Never again will we experience pain and the displeasure and punishment of God.

But the new earth is not just noted for what is missing from it. Secondly, the new earth is also noted for what is present in it. He mentions three things that are present. What is present is intimate personal face-to-face fellowship with God, the soul-satisfying work of serving God, and the intellectual joy of having our minds filled with the thoughts of God. Life in the new earth will be a delightfully positive experience.

People often think of Christianity in terms of what you cannot do and what you cannot have. But God's prohibitions in this life are very small and narrow, and only consist of things that will hurt us. His permissions are very wide and generous, and only consist of things that will bless us. In the new earth, the only thing we are going to be without is all that which causes us misery, heartache, pain, damnation, and death. What we will have are those things that give us life, joy, peace, fulfillment, and pleasure.

First of all, we will have intimate, personal, face-to-face fellowship with God. We will be in the direct presence of the Father and the Son as They rule and reign over the universe, and we will see Their face. It says in verses 3–4, *"but the throne of God and of the Lamb shall be in it; and his servants shall serve him:* [4] *And they shall see his face."* Prior to this time, seeing the face of God has been impossible. God said to Moses in Exodus 33:20, *"Thou cannot see my face: for there shall no man see me, and live."* First Timothy 6:16 says, *"God dwells in light that no man can approach unto; whom no man has seen, nor can see."* Jesus said in John 1:18, *"No man has seen God at any time."* John the apostle echoes that same statement in 1 John 4:12 when he says, *"No man has seen God at any time."*

Sinful men cannot see the sinless God and live. The burning holiness of God would consume the sinner in an instant. But the wonderful work of Christ and the wonderful promise of the gospel is this: By believing in Christ, we can be made completely pure before God, and thereby be able to see the face of God and live.

It says in Matthew 5:8, *"Blessed are the pure in heart: for they shall see God."* Christ purifies our hearts by faith and presents us faultless before His Father; and because He does, we can see God. To be able to see God and behold Him and to gaze on His face is the greatest blessedness that any human could ever know. David said in Psalm 27:4, *"One thing have I desired of the Lord, that will I seek after; that I may dwell in the house of the Lord all the days of my life, to behold the beauty of the Lord, and to enquire in his temple."* In the new earth, we will be in the direct presence of the Father and the Son as They rule and reign over the universe, and we will behold the beauty of the Lord, and we will see His face.

Secondly, we will enjoy the soul-satisfying work of serving God. It says here, *"His servants shall serve him."* Much of the work that we do now is onerous because of the curse. It is wearisome because of our physical weaknesses. It is pointless because much of it has no lasting value. Our greatest works disappear into the dust of time; and from that perspective, the author of the book of Ecclesiastes said regarding our work, "*Vanity of vanities; all is vanity.*"

But in the new earth, serving God will be a pleasure. Serving God will energize us, not drain us. Serving God will have eternal significance and value. The meaning and value of the work we do will never pass away. When we have served God, we will have a sense of fulfillment and accomplishment that will fill us with delight and give us a satisfaction we have never known on earth. We will finally feel we have found our calling and purpose. In the new earth, we will enjoy the soul-satisfying work of serving God.

Thirdly, in the new earth we will have the intellectual joy of having our minds filled with the thoughts of God. It says here in verse 4 that "*his name shall be in their foreheads.*" This is not some kind of a literal tattoo of God's actual name displayed on our foreheads. This is the same symbolic concept we previously looked at in Revelation 7:3, where it says God sealed His servants with His seal in their foreheads.

The name of God in the forehead is symbolic of the fact that God is at the forefront of His servant's mind at all times, and that thoughts about God have the place of highest prominence in his life. The forehead is at the forefront of the mind; it is at the highest place of the body; and therefore, what is being said is that thoughts of God in heaven are always going to be at the forefront of our mind, and they are always going to have the highest place in our thinking.

In this world, our minds are often a jumbled mess, and our thoughts are occupied with the mundane, the ridiculous, and the sinful. Often our thinking is confused and darkened and distracted. We focus on the wrong thing; we focus on even good things in the wrong way; and we often come to wrong conclusions. Our mental health on this earth is very, very poor. The more we look at the Internet, the worse it gets. The more we play on our phones, the less we think the thoughts of God.

But in the new earth—with perfected bodies and souls, and with all sinful impediments removed—the clarity of our thinking, the focus of our thinking, and the wisdom of our thinking will be perfect. Our thinking will dwell without distraction on the most satisfying object conceivable, and that is the person and the work of God. That is what we will be thinking about all of the time; it will be at the forefront of our mind and have the highest place of prominence in our thoughts. His name—that is, all He is and all He has done—will occupy our thoughts. No higher object and no better object could fill our minds for all eternity than the person and the work of God.

But heaven is also noted, not only for what is missing, no curse; not only what is present, being able to see His face, being able to serve Him, and being able to think about Him; thirdly, heaven is also noted for what is restored. Notice verse 5: *"And there shall be no night there; and they need no candle, neither light of the sun; for the Lord God giveth them light: and they shall reign for ever and ever."*

When it says there shall be no night there, and the Lord God gives them light, it repeats and reinforces what we studied at length in Revelation 21:23–25. The special presence of God, here represented by this continuous and pervasive light which is so universal and brilliant that it renders all other sources of light irrelevant, insignificant, and unnecessary, is the light and environment and atmosphere in which we dwell.

Right now, we do not have the light of God's special personal presence to this degree. He is there in heaven, and we are here on earth. But someday, we will dwell in His presence without any barrier, without any limitation, and without any distance. Wherever we may go, whenever it may be, and whatever we are doing, we will always be dwelling in the immediate special personal presence of God. Never will there be any physical or spiritual distance between God and ourselves. We will be enveloped in the light of His presence.

Not only is the light of God's special personal presence restored to us, but the dominion over the earth is also restored to us. Notice the last phrase of verse 5. It says, *"And they shall reign for ever and ever."* This is the final step in the restoration of Eden, in which the dominion over the earth we once had, which was forfeited to Satan in the fall so that he became the god of this world, is once again restored to us.

Once again, we will have dominion over the fish of the sea, and over the fowl of the air, and over every living thing that moves upon the earth. Once again, we will subdue the earth under our rule and reign, and manage the Eden that has been restored to us. God will make us once again the lords of the earth.

Thus, Eden is fully restored. All we lost has not only been regained, but it has also been brought to its highest level of conceivable perfection, so that we enjoy what Adam would have had if he had passed the test. But, thank God, Jesus did pass the test. When Satan came to tempt Him, He resisted him, He rejected him, and He won for us the restoration of Eden. He wrested Eden out of the hand of Satan, and by His saving work, He gives it back to His people completely perfected.

Notice the conclusion in verses 6 and 7: *"And he said unto me, These sayings are faithful and true."* All we have read in chapters 21 and 22 seems far too wonderful for us to believe. Therefore, the angel reinforces the truthfulness of his testimony and the visions of John in verse 6 when he says, *"These sayings are faithful and true."* In other words, this is what is going to happen. This is not a fantasy, this is not a fairy tale, and this is not somebody's dream. This is exactly what is going to happen, this is exactly how it is going to be, and this is exactly what you are going to experience. Everything represented here is faithful and true.

He goes on to say in verse 6, *"And the Lord God of the holy prophets sent his angel to shew unto his servants the things which must shortly be done."* The reason why he said this *"must shortly be done"* is because all that is said in the book of Revelation was beginning to be fulfilled even in John's day. We saw this when we first began the exposition of the book. In Revelation 1:1, He said He was going to show John things that must shortly come to pass.

All that is in the book of Revelation began to occur in John's day. It has been occurring for the last 2,000 years, and it will continue to occur into eternity in its completion and fulfillment. The book of Revelation is not a book for some day in the future when the rapture finally occurs and the tribulation begins. The book of Revelation is a book for right now. It has been coming to pass in terms of the spiritual conflict it describes and the outcome it proclaims for the last 2,000 years.

Now notice verse 7. Jesus says, *"Behold, I come quickly: blessed is he that keepeth the sayings of the prophecy of this book."* Verse 7a tells us that the second coming of Christ will occur quickly in relationship to the length of time it took for His first coming to occur.

We need to understand that "quick" is a relative term. Sometimes quick is two minutes and sometimes quick is two weeks, depending on what you are talking about. When Jesus says He will come quickly, we have to ask this question: "Quickly with reference to what?" He can only mean quickly in reference to His first coming, which took place at least 4,000 years from the promises of Genesis 3:15 until Matthew 1, when Jesus was born. It has only been 2,000 years now. I do not know how long it will be and I do not set dates, but it will not be as long as it took for Him to come the first time. He will come quickly in relation to that.

But however long it takes for Christ to come the second time, understand that He is going to come quickly for you as an individual. How long do you have to live? Well, as far as you know, not another second. Jesus could come very quickly for you individually in just a moment or two. But at the most, you might live for sixty, seventy, eighty, or ninety years, possibly even a hundred years, which would be very unusual. It is a very short period of time. Jesus is coming very quickly for you. Are you ready for His coming? He has told us in this book all that His coming involves, and we need to be prepared by repentance and faith.

Jesus says in verse 7, *"Behold, I come quickly: blessed is he that keepeth the sayings of the prophecy of this book."* Jesus is telling us to take this book seriously—to trust its promises, believe its warnings, act on its commands, and find comfort and peace in its explanation as to why things happen the way they do.

In a word: Use this manual of spiritual warfare to live by. This book reveals what spiritual warfare will look like between the first and second coming of Christ, why things occur as they do, and how you should respond to it all.

Jesus is saying this to us: "Live by this book and its teachings, keep your focus on what it declares, and most of all, keep your focus on the person it reveals, for it is the revelation of Jesus Christ." Learn about Him and what He has done and what He is doing and what He will do, by learning this book. He says in verse 7 that you are blessed if you do.

May God help us as we approach the end of this book not to set it aside and forget it. May we live in it and all it teaches about what spiritual warfare looks like; about what building the kingdom of God consists of; about what the outcome is going to be; about the conflict we are going to have until we get there; and about the perseverance we need to engage in while we are in the midst of the battle. May God help us to be people who not only understand the book but who live by this book and personally keep its sayings.

67

The Conclusion to Revelation, Revelation 22:8–21

“[8] *And I John saw these things, and heard them. And when I had heard and seen, I fell down to worship before the feet of the angel which shewed me these things.* [9] *Then saith he unto me, See thou do it not: for I am thy fellowservant, and of thy brethren the prophets, and of them which keep the sayings of this book: worship God.* [10] *And he saith unto me, Seal not the sayings of the prophecy of this book: for the time is at hand.* [11] *He that is unjust, let him be unjust still: and he which is filthy, let him be filthy still: and he that is righteous, let him be righteous still: and he that is holy, let him be holy still.* [12] *And, behold, I come quickly; and my reward is with me, to give every man according as his work shall be.* [13] *I am Alpha and Omega, the beginning and the end, the first and the last.* [14] *Blessed are they that do his commandments, that they may have right to the tree of life, and may enter in through the gates into the city.* [15] *For without are dogs, and sorcerers, and whoremongers, and murderers, and idolaters, and whosoever loveth and maketh a lie.* [16] *I Jesus have sent mine angel to testify unto you these things in the churches. I am the root and the offspring of David, and the bright and morning star.* [17] *And the Spirit and the bride say, Come. And let him that heareth say, Come. And let him that is athirst come. And whosoever will, let him take the water of life freely.* [18] *For I testify unto every man that heareth the words of the prophecy of this book, If any man shall add unto these things, God shall add unto him the plagues that are written in this book:* [19] *And if any man shall take away from the words of the book of this prophecy, God shall take away his part out of the book of life, and out of the holy city, and from the things which are written in this*

> *book.* [20] *He which testifieth these things saith, Surely I come quickly. Amen. Even so, come, Lord Jesus.* [21] *The grace of our Lord Jesus Christ be with you all. Amen."*

In the last chapter, we completed the exposition of the message of Revelation. There we saw Christ bring the full application of His saving work to completion with the restoration of the garden of Eden in the new earth. We saw that the works of the devil had been totally destroyed, and Satan and his helpers have been cast into the lake of fire, never to harm us again. All that God originally intended to achieve in the first creation has been brought to fulfillment by Jesus Christ in the final creation. Once again, all things are very good, and they will remain that way for all eternity.

In Revelation we have seen all that Jesus has done in implementing His saving work and in destroying the works of the devil. What the devil began in the garden of Eden has now been completely dismantled and destroyed by Christ.

Revelation has set before us the nature of spiritual warfare we experience in this present age, and what we might expect as we fight it. This book tells us why this spiritual warfare is happening, and what its outcome will be.

After the study of this book, we understand the parties at war, how they behave, and who is going to triumph in the end. We are now better equipped to understand why things happen the way they do, and how we should respond to them. We now understand how everything is going to turn out, and where we will spend eternity.

Most of all, after we study this book we should be filled with gratitude to the Lord Jesus for saving us, preserving us, and presenting us faultless before His Father, so we can live with Him in the new earth for all eternity. This book has been a glorious book to study, because it has provided us with understanding and encouragement regarding our present experiences, it has filled us with hope and confidence regarding the future, and it has done so in a way that no other book of the Bible does.

We have now arrived at the conclusion of this book in Revelation 22:8–21. The purpose of this conclusion is to confirm that all this book contains is true and trustworthy, and what has been said is exactly how things are going to turn out in the end. There is no delusion or deception in this book. It is not a record of someone's dream or fantasy or his guess about what the future may contain. Rather, these words are faithful and true. This book accurately tells us what will come to pass. Jesus said in Revelation 21:5, "*Write: for these words are true and faithful*"; and then in Revelation 22:6, "*And he said unto me, These sayings are faithful and true.*" The book of Revelation is going to come to pass exactly as it is written.

Furthermore, the purpose of this conclusion is to confirm that Christ is coming quickly; and therefore, we should always be ready, and be resolute in refusing to embrace the beast or Babylon. We must not set our hearts on this world, because this world will soon come to an end.

Finally, the purpose of this conclusion is to remind the readers they need to take heed to the warnings it gives. They need to take heed to the invitations that it extends. They need to take heed to the comforts that it offers. They need to take heed to the encouragements it provides. They need to take heed to the exhortations it issues.

This book is not a book you learn about and then forget about. Rather, this book is something you live out and live by every day of your life in the spiritual warfare you experience. The practical and personal help the book of Revelation provides is irreplaceable in the Christian life. We should live with this book at our elbow, and we should reflect on it often as we engage in the spiritual warfare it describes that will characterize every generation until Jesus returns.

This is the burden and message of the conclusion to this book. Let us consider it together, and as we do so, we see two parties speaking to us. We see the angel addressing us in verses 8 to 11, and then we see Jesus addressing us in verses 12 to 21.

The Exhortation of the Angel

The exhortation of the angel is found in verses 8 through 11. Notice verse 8: "*And I John saw these things, and heard them. And when I had heard and seen, I fell down to worship before the feet of the angel which shewed me these things.*"

When John says, "*And I John saw these things, and heard them,*" he is referring to all he has previously seen from Revelation 1:1 through 22:7. He is saying that his record of what he saw and heard was true and faithful. He did not add anything to it, nor did he omit anything from it. What he wrote is exactly what he saw and heard, no more and no less.

Having now heard and seen the whole revelation, John is overwhelmed with amazement and gratitude for what he has seen. He is so awe-struck by the things the angel has revealed to him that he falls down at the feet of the angel to worship the one who provided him with such a wonderful understanding of all God is doing in the world and all God is going to do in the future.

The angel immediately puts a stop to this. Notice verse 9: "*Then saith he unto me, See thou do it not: for I am thy fellowservant, and of thy brethren the prophets, and of them which keep the sayings of this book: worship God.*"

Often, we feel a profound debt of gratitude to those who have opened and explained the word of God to us. God has used them to reveal tremendous amounts of truth to us. They have conveyed the unsearchable riches of Christ to us. Through these teachers, we have become saved from sin and matured in our understanding of the word of God.

But we must never confuse the messenger with the message, and think the one who tells us the wonderful news of salvation and redemption is somehow the source of the message, the supplier of its truth, or the accomplisher of its work. Teachers of the word of God are instruments in the hand of God to convey the truth of God, but we must never confuse them with God, or give them the esteem that belongs to God. Thank God for the teachers He supplied to you, thank God for the teaching they conveyed to you, and thank God for the truth you learned and the blessing you received through them. But always remember that God is the source and supplier of it all.

Teachers are stewards of the truth and dispensers of the truth, but they are not the source of the truth. As the angel says, teachers are our fellow-servants. Teachers have to keep the truth and obey the truth just as much as those they teach have to keep it and obey it. Teachers and students alike are both under the authority of the word of God, and both are to worship the God who is revealed in that word, and no one else.

It is important for you to understand that you must never substitute a visible man for the invisible God in your affections, in your loyalty, or in your worship. Worship belongs to God alone, and never to any man, no matter how much blessing that man has brought into your life through the enablement of God. This is what the angel is saying to John: "Yes, I have shown you all these things, but do not worship me for having done so. Worship the God who has provided these things and accomplished these things."

Notice verse 10: *"And he saith unto me, Seal not the sayings of the prophecy of this book: for the time is at hand."* Here the angel tells John, in effect, "Do not seal up the content of the teachings of this book. Do not conceal or hide this manuscript. Publish it far and wide, because it is relevant right now in this first century, and it will continue to be relevant until the second coming of Christ."

In Daniel 12:4, God told Daniel, "Seal up the sayings of this book, for the time is not at hand." But now God is saying to John, "Do not seal this up. The time is at hand. These things are going to start being fulfilled right now." This is what the angel means when he says, *"The time is at hand."* Notice Revelation 22:6: *"And he"* (the angel) *"said unto me, These sayings are faithful and true: and the Lord God of the holy prophets sent his angel to shew unto his servants the things which must shortly be done."*

What the angel is saying in verse 6 and verse 10 is that the time is at hand; in other words, the time for the usefulness of the book of Revelation begins right now. Since this book describes the nature, the principles, and the participants of the spiritual warfare that will occur during the entire period between the first and the second coming of Christ, it has been intensely relevant in every century, and for every people, wherever they live on the earth. The time to use this book, and use all of it, is right now. It is not for some period in the distant future.

This book is a field manual for the spiritual warfare of every generation between the first and second coming of Christ; and therefore, the time to publish it, the time to understand it, and the time to implement it is right now in John's day, during John's time, because all this book contains was just as relevant in the first century as it is in the twenty-first century. It is not to be sealed up for later use centuries from now.

Notice verse 11: *"He that is unjust, let him be unjust still: and he which is filthy, let him be filthy still: and he that is righteous, let him be righteous still: and he that is holy, let him be holy still."* Not only is now the time to publish this book; now is the time to obey this book, because the trajectory we are living on in this life is the trajectory we will remain on for the rest of eternity. That is such an important point it bears repeating: The trajectory we are living on in this life is the trajectory we will remain on for the rest of eternity.

Character is destiny. Whatever a man sows, that will he also reap. If you live a life of injustice now, if your behavior toward others is one of violating their God-given rights detailed in the second half of the Ten Commandments, then you will be confirmed on the Day of Judgment as being an unjust person forever, and you will be punished in hell accordingly. If you live a life of moral filthiness now, then you will be confirmed on the Day of Judgment as being a morally filthy person forever, and you will be punished in hell accordingly.

On the other hand, if you live a life of righteousness now—that is, you engage in positive acts of obedience to God's law as the dominating characteristic of your life; and if you live a life of holiness now; that is, you abstain from violating the prohibitions contained in God's commands as the dominating characteristic of your life; in a word, if you live a life devoted to God—then you will be confirmed on the Day of Judgment as being a holy and righteous person forever, and you will be rewarded in the new earth accordingly.

The point in verse 11 is that the dominating characteristic of your life determines your destiny, because the dominating characteristic of your life displays whether you are regenerate or not, and whether you actually believed in Christ as your Lord and Savior or not.

Therefore, do not trifle with the teachings of this book and the warnings and exhortations it gives. Believe what it says about the coming Day of Judgment, and flee from the wrath to come by fleeing to Christ for forgiveness and eternal life. The decisions and the choices you make now about who you trust—and therefore, about how you live—will be set in stone for all eternity on the Day of Judgment. Choose wisely and choose well, because the trajectory you set yourself on in this life is the one you will remain on forever.

That is why you need to repent of your sins and believe in Christ as your Savior and Lord today. You need to start following Him and live a life of righteousness and holiness and obedience to Him, not to earn your salvation, but because you are saved. As you demonstrate that salvation, it will be said by God on the Day of Judgment that this is who you are; and therefore, this is who you will be forever.

The Proclamation of Christ

The proclamation of Christ is in verses 12 to 21. The speaker now shifts from being the angel in verses 8 to 11, to the person of Christ in verses 12 to 21.

The first thing Jesus does is make a proclamation regarding the final judgment. This is in verses 12 to 17. Notice in verse 12, Jesus is speaking in the first person and says, *"And, behold, I come quickly."*

Jesus repeatedly stresses this point about coming quickly. Notice Revelation 22:7, *"Behold, I come quickly."* Then in 22:12, *"And, behold, I come quickly."* Finally, in 22:20, *"He which testifieth these things saith, Surely I come quickly."* Three times in one chapter Jesus says that He is coming quickly. He wants us to get the point.

We previously discussed what this meant when we explained Revelation 22:7, where this phrase was first introduced in this chapter. There we said that the word *"quickly"* was a relative term. You would be very quick if you ran a mile in four minutes, but you would be very slow if you tied your shoes in four minutes. The word "quick" is a relative term. We might ask, "Quick in relationship to what?"

When Jesus says, *"Behold, I come quickly,"* He is saying He will come quickly in relationship to His first coming, which took at least 4,000 years. Jesus was promised to come in Genesis 3:15. He would be the seed of the woman that would crush the head of the serpent. How long did it take for Him to come the first time? At least 4,000 years. Now if Jesus came back in the next century or two, He would come back in half the time it took Him to come the first time. It would be quickly compared to how long His first coming took.

When Jesus said to John in John's day, "I am coming quickly," He was saying to John, "I am coming quickly in relationship to the length of time it took Me to come the first time." How quick is that? John did not know how quick it was going to be. It could have been 100 years; it could have been 1,000 years. It has now been 2,000 years. But if He came back today, it would still be quickly in relationship to the time it took for Him to come the first time.

But in any event, Jesus will quickly come for each one of us individually, because in just a few years we will all meet our appointment with death, and then He will return for us and receive us individually into heaven, there to await His second coming at the end of the age.

So for each of us individually, the coming of Christ is imminent, and it could happen at any moment.

But the second coming of Christ at the end of this age is not imminent, because before His second coming occurs, the signs of that coming must take place. There must be the loosing of Satan; there must be the great apostasy of the Christian church; there must be the appearance of the Antichrist and his one-world government; there must be the rise of the transnational persecution of believers that results in only a tiny remnant of them being left alive on the earth; and there must be the disruption of the heavens. Only after the fulfillment of all of these signs will Jesus come back at the end of this age.

He may come back for you at any moment. He will come at the end of this age after these signs are fulfilled. When they are being fulfilled, we will know the age is quickly coming to an end. Jesus will be coming. He will be coming quickly, once Satan is loosed.

When Jesus does come the second time, He will come in judgment. Notice verse 12b. He says, *"Behold, I come quickly; and my reward is with me, to give every man according as his work shall be."*

This reflects and reinforces what verse 11 stated: *"He that is unjust, let him be unjust still: and he which is filthy, let him be filthy still: and he that is righteous, let him be righteous still: and he that is holy, let him be holy still."* Our life, our character, and our conduct infallibly reveal our faith in Christ as our Lord and Savior; or else, they infallibly reveal our rejection of Christ as Lord and Savior.

Jesus says, "I am coming back, I am going to pass judgment, and I am going to reward people according to the life they lived here on earth." They will reap what they have sown. How people lived their lives will prove whether they trusted in Christ as Lord and Savior, or whether they did not.

Notice verses 13 to 15. He says, *"I am Alpha and Omega, the beginning and the end, the first and the last.* [14] *Blessed are they that do his commandments, that they may have right to the tree of life, and may enter in through the gates into the city.* [15] *For without are dogs, and sorcerers, and whoremongers, and murderers, and idolaters, and whosoever loveth and maketh a lie."* In verses 13 to 15, we first see the qualifications of the judge; and secondly, we see the two categories of people who are judged.

Notice the qualifications of the judge in verse 13. *"I am Alpha and Omega, the beginning and the end, the first and the last."* These three terms used to describe Christ were first introduced to us in Revelation 1, and what they collectively tell us is that Christ constitutes the bookends of human history. Since He stands at the start of history and at the end of history, He is therefore sovereign over all that happens within that history and He sits as judge upon that history. These terms describing Christ tell us that Christ is inescapable. Everything starts with Him, and everything ends with Him. Everything begins with Him, and everything finishes with Him. No one is outside the scope of His authority or His judgment at any point from start to finish.

Notice the first category of those who are judged in verse 14: *"Blessed are they that do his commandments, that they may have right to the tree of life, and may enter in through the gates into the city."* Those whose conduct and character demonstrated their genuine faith in Christ as Lord and Savior will have access to all the blessings of paradise restored. True faith in Christ results in a love for Christ that longs to keep the commandments of Christ, and actually does keep His commandments as the dominating characteristic of their lives. Jesus only has to look at someone's conduct to determine the presence or the absence of true faith in Him as Lord and Savior. Those who do His commandments will have the right to enter into the new Jerusalem and to eat of the tree of life.

Notice the second category of those who are judged in verse 15: *"For without are dogs, and sorcerers, and whoremongers, and murderers, and idolaters, and whosoever loveth and maketh a lie."* Here are those who do not have faith in Christ, as demonstrated by their conduct. Jesus said: *"Ye shall know them by their fruits."* You know the saved by the fruits of how they live, and you know the lost by the fruits of how they live. How they live does not determine their salvation, but how they live does demonstrate their salvation, or the lack of it.

The term *"dogs"* here is used metaphorically to refer to those who have no care or concern for what is holy and good. On the contrary, these are people who treat every good and holy thing with contempt, and they defile whatever they are involved in with their impurity and their wickedness. The other terms in the list are easily understood: sorcerers, whoremongers, murderers, idolaters, and whoever loves and makes a lie. The point is that those who practice such things will not inherit the kingdom of God.

This is the third time in these last two chapters we have been given similar lists like this. There was one in 21:8: *"But the fearful, and unbelieving, and the abominable, and murderers, and whoremongers, and sorcerers, and idolaters, and all liars, shall have their part in the lake which burneth with fire and brimstone: which is the second death."* There was one in 21:27: *"And there shall in no wise enter into it any thing that defileth, neither whatsoever worketh abomination, or maketh a lie: but they which are written in the Lamb's book of life."* There is one in our passage in 22:15: *"For without are dogs, and sorcerers, and whoremongers, and murderers, and idolaters, and whosoever loveth and maketh a lie."*

The point is, you cannot live for the devil and be received by Christ into the new earth just because you prayed the sinner's prayer at some point in your past. A lot of people think like this: "I came forward in church to an altar call or I prayed and asked Jesus to save me." But there is no change in their behavior, there is no difference in their life between how they live and how the wicked of the world live. But they prayed the prayer, so they think they are right with God.

The Bible makes it clear that a faith in Christ that does not transform the behavior is not genuine faith at all. The faith that saves arises out of a regeneration that is wrought by God which takes out the old nature that loves sin, and gives us a new nature that loves righteousness. And while we still have the flesh pulling us and drawing us into sin, in our heart of hearts we want to serve the Lord, we strive to serve the Lord, and we do serve the Lord all the days of our life.

Those who have true saving faith in Christ delight in His commandments and live according to them as the dominating characteristic of their lives. Nothing less than a life of living for Christ will be evidence of saving faith in Christ on the Day of Judgment. You must live what you say you believe or else you do not believe it. This is not a hard and onerous burden to place on a genuine Christian. He delights in the law of God after the inward man. It says in 1 John 5:3 that God's commandments are not grievous to the believer. The only thing that grieves him is that he does not keep them better.

Therefore, the Christian strives to keep God's commandments in every circumstance all the days of his life. And when he does not, he does not justify himself or defend himself. He condemns himself, he confesses what he did was wrong, he changes his behavior, and he starts doing the right thing again. It is those with such a heart that issues forth in such behavior who enjoy the paradise of God.

Notice verse 16: *"I Jesus have sent mine angel to testify unto you these things in the churches. I am the root and the offspring of David, and the bright and morning star."* The book of Revelation began with these words in 1:4: *"John to the seven churches which are in Asia."* Now we see how the book of Revelation closes: *"I Jesus have sent mine angel to testify unto you these things in the churches."*

Revelation is a church epistle. It was written to the church so the church could understand how to carry out spiritual warfare in this age. This is the manual for spiritual warfare for the local church. It is not something that has already been largely fulfilled in AD 70; it is not something that is going to largely be fulfilled only in the last seven years before Jesus comes; it is something that is being lived out in all it teaches every day throughout the centuries by all the churches all across the world.

Jesus declares Himself in verse 16 to be *"the root and the offspring of David."* That is a very interesting phrase when you think about it. He is the root of David in that He is the God who gave David his life. He is David's God, the source of David's life. Clearly, a plant grows out of the root, and David came from Christ. But He is also the offspring of David in that He is a physical descendant of David. He is David's son who sits on David's throne. By this phrase, Jesus declares Himself to be the God-man. He is David's God and He is David's son all at the same time because He is the God-man, Jesus Christ.

Jesus also declares Himself to be *"the bright and morning star"* in verse 16. One morning I got up pretty early and was sitting on my couch looking out through my window to the east. As the sun started to come up, all the stars disappeared but one. There was a brilliant star sitting just above the horizon. It was the only star in the sky, and it was very bright. It was saying by its appearance: "Daytime is coming." The morning star is the herald of the dawn, and in a few minutes, the sun came up over the horizon and a new day was born.

Jesus declares Himself to be the bright and morning star who heralds the dawn of a new everlasting day in which there will never be night again. Time and again we are told this in these last two chapters. For example, in 22:4–5 we are told, *"And they shall see his face; and his name shall be in their foreheads.* [5] *And there shall be no night there; and they need no candle, neither light of the sun; for the Lord God giveth them light: and they shall reign for ever and ever."*

This proclamation of Jesus regarding Himself is a proclamation of His identity. He is the Lord of the churches, sending this message to His churches regarding how they are to conduct their spiritual warfare. He is the God-man who is both David's God and David's son. He is the herald of the everlasting day that is coming in which there will never be night again. Never again will there be the darkness of sin and ignorance. There will only be the light of truth and holiness for all eternity.

This proclamation regarding this final judgment closes with a free and gracious invitation. Notice verse 17: *"And the Spirit and the bride say, Come. And let him that heareth say, Come. And let him that is athirst come. And whosoever will, let him take the water of life freely."*

Both the Spirit of God who works in the heart, and the church of God who preaches to the ear have the same message to the lost. The message of the Spirit and the message of the church to the lost is this: Come to Christ. Satisfy the spiritual thirst of your soul by receiving Christ as your Lord and Savior from your sins. Take of the water of life freely! Salvation is free. It is provided by Christ at no cost to you, though at great cost to Him.

He will give it to you freely, but you have to take it. He says, *"Let him take."* That is, you must repent and you must believe. You must receive this salvation from Christ as an act and choice of your will, saying, "I am wicked, I am guilty, I am under the wrath of God, and I need forgiveness and cleansing and redemption. Lord Jesus, save me from my sins! I have nothing to offer You by way of payment, but You have said that You will give it freely. Lord Jesus, bestow the free gift of forgiveness and salvation and eternal life upon me!"

That is how you take the water of life that is freely offered to you. You can do nothing to earn the forgiveness of God for your sins. You can only accept it as a gift which is bestowed as an act of the mercy and grace of God. There is no reason for any person to remain outside the paradise of God. The only thing that will keep you out is your rebellion and your impenitence.

Come to Christ now. Come to Christ today, just as you are, with all of your sins, and ask Christ to forgive you and save you from those sins—and He will. The final judgment does not have to be a day of terror that leads to an eternity of suffering in hell. The final judgment can be a day of joy that leads to an eternity of happiness in the new earth. The difference between those two outcomes depends on whether you have come to Christ in repentance and faith and received the salvation He offers you in the gospel, or whether you have not. Believe on the Lord Jesus Christ, and you will be saved.

This is the first proclamation that Christ has made in this conclusion of the book. But not only does Christ make a proclamation regarding the final judgment; secondly, He also makes a proclamation regarding the sanctity of this book. Notice what He says in verses 18 and 19. *"For I testify unto every man that heareth the words of the prophecy of this book, If any man shall add unto these things, God shall add unto him the plagues that are written in this book:* [19] *And if any man shall take away from the words of the book of this prophecy, God shall take away his part out of the book of life, and out of the holy city, and from the things which are written in this book."*

Jesus issues a severe warning against adding anything to this book by way of supposed additional revelation, or taking anything away from this book by removing any part of it because it seems uninspired or unnecessary. This warning was written primarily to the transcriptionists who were going to be making copies of this book. He is saying to those who make copies of this book for distribution, "As you are reading it, do not think this part is implausible, and leave it out because you do not understand the symbolism it contains; and neither should you think that no one will understand another part, and therefore add some additional explanatory material so it will be more clear."

The point is that you do not alter God's inspired revelation in any way, for any reason, at any time. Nothing more than what has been written is needed, and nothing less than what has been written is sufficient. And what is true of the book of Revelation is true of the entire Bible as well. Nothing is to be added to it and nothing is to be taken away from it.

Those who think the Bible is inadequate, and therefore feel the need to supply additional books to it like the Koran or the Book of Mormon or any other writings that claim to be equal in authority with it, will come under the judgments of this book. On the other hand, those who dismiss any part of the Scriptures as uninspired or unnecessary or irrelevant, who cut out parts of it as being superfluous and unimportant, will be deprived of any possibility of being in the new earth, the new Jerusalem, or in the book of life.

To add to the word of God is to say that God was inadequate in His communication. To subtract from the word of God is to say that God was excessive in His communication. To say that God is either inadequate or excessive in His communication is to blaspheme God.

Jesus then concludes with these words: "[20] *He which testifieth these things saith, Surely I come quickly. Amen. Even so, come, Lord Jesus.* [21] *The grace of our Lord Jesus Christ be with you all. Amen.*"

Jesus has repeatedly stated in this last section that people's deeds will be brought to account, either to their blessing or to their condemnation. To remind them of this fact and to reinforce the certainty of it, Jesus says a third time, "*Surely I come quickly.*" For the believer, that promise makes his heart leap with joy, and he responds: "*Amen. Even so, come, Lord Jesus.*"

That is the heart of every Christian who has truly believed in Christ, and because of that belief, is seeking to honestly live for Christ. He looks forward to the Day of Judgment with anticipation because that is the day of graduation—that is the day of liberation—the day in which all of Christ's salvation is fully applied and fully experienced in his heart and life in the new earth for eternity.

Christians do not look forward to the Day of Judgment with any dread at all. All of our sins have been paid for by Christ. Our need for righteousness has been supplied by Christ. All of our good deeds are going to be rewarded by Christ. We will enter into all of the blessings of Christ. The Day of Judgment is the day we long for. It is the wicked who tremble and try to hide in the caves and the rocks and cry out to them in these words: "Hide us from the face of the wrath of the Lamb, for who shall be able to stand before Him?"

You do not want to be in that position when Jesus returns. Therefore, come to Christ and believe in Him. Live for Christ and follow Him. And on that great day, He will say to you, "*Well done, thou good and faithful servant. . .enter thou into the joy of thy Lord.*"

You may ask, "How will I be able to make it into the new earth? How can I persevere in following Christ?" You can do it because of what it says in verse 21: "*The grace of our Lord Jesus Christ be with you all.*" That is how you will make it: on the basis of grace. The grace of Christ will be with you and it will sustain you, strengthen you, and preserve you. There is no better security than that.

I can leave you with no better words than the words that John closes with: "*The grace of our Lord Jesus Christ be with you all. Amen.*"

Our Father, how thankful we are for this blessed book, for the wonderful lessons it has taught us, for the heights to which it has lifted us, and for the encouragements it has given us. To be able to see the things above, to be able to see down through the corridors of eternity, and to grasp a little of the wonder and grandeur and glory of the things Christ has laid up for those who love Him, is blessing beyond words to express.

May we live every day inspired and strengthened by this book as we fight against the beast, and Babylon, and the false prophet, and those with the mark of the beast, who think and act according to Satan's will and direction.

Father, we pray that we might be faithful to death so we might have a crown of life, be given the right to eat of the tree of life, to drink of the river of life, to see the face of Christ, and to be with Him and serve Him forever. Father, how we long for that day and look forward to it. Bring us to that day we ask, in Jesus' name. Amen.

Appendices

Appendix 1
The Exposition of Matthew 24

A proper understanding and interpretation of Matthew 24 is critical to a proper understanding and interpretation of the book of Revelation, and the book of Revelation also helps us understand Matthew 24. These two major prophetic passages are interdependent and complementary in their teaching, so that each provides teaching that is critical to the understanding of the other. The misunderstanding of the teaching in Matthew 24 has led to major errors in the eschatology of many prophetic teachers and many prophetic schemes. It is for this reason I have provided an exposition of Matthew 24 in this appendix.

The Characteristics of the Current Age
Matthew 24:1–8
Chapter 1

> "1 *And Jesus went out, and departed from the temple: and his*
> *disciples came to him for to shew him the buildings of the*
> *temple.* 2 *And Jesus said unto them, See ye not all these things?*
> *verily I say unto you, There shall not be left here one stone*
> *upon another, that shall not be thrown down.* 3 *And as he sat*
> *upon the mount of Olives, the disciples came unto him pri-*
> *vately, saying, Tell us, when shall these things be? and what*
> *shall be the sign of thy coming, and of the end of the world?*
> 4 *And Jesus answered and said unto them, Take heed that no*
> *man deceive you.* 5 *For many shall come in my name, saying, I*
> *am Christ; and shall deceive many.* 6 *And ye shall hear of wars*
> *and rumours of wars: see that ye be not troubled: for all these*
> *things must come to pass, but the end is not yet.* 7 *For nation*
> *shall rise against nation, and kingdom against kingdom: and*
> *there shall be famines, and pestilences, and earthquakes, in*
> *divers places.* 8 *All these are the beginning of sorrows.*"

In Matthew 24, Jesus is privately instructing His disciples on eschatology. His teaching covers the whole period of time between the first and second coming of Christ. The main emphasis of Matthew 24 is on the necessity of being faithful to Christ in the face of persecution and tribulation.

This chapter tells us there will be many difficulties in the days ahead, both from deceivers and persecutors. It emphasizes that we must remain loyal to Christ until the end if we would be owned by Christ on the Day of Judgment as being one of His children. Because of the intensity of the coming persecution that Jesus speaks of, many people will fall away from the faith and from Christ. They will begin to follow false teachers and false Christs, and ultimately, they will follow the Antichrist himself. Then they will begin to betray the true Christians. These are apostates from the Christian faith, and we must not be among them. When Jesus returns, He should find us faithful and busy in the work of His kingdom.

This is the big picture we need to keep in mind as we study the details of this difficult time Jesus describes in this chapter. Jesus reveals these prophecies so we will not be surprised or offended or fall into deception when they come. When Jesus returns, blessed is that servant that shall be found still loyal to Christ, still loving Christ, and still serving Christ in spite of the persecution and the tribulation he is going to experience.

Although it is certainly a desirable goal to pursue, understanding every detail of every prophetic text is not what matters in the end. What matters is that we understand the big picture of prophetic truth, and because of that understanding, we remain faithful to Christ to the end of our lives.

Matthew 24 is designed to prepare us for the tribulation that lies ahead of us, and to encourage us to persevere in our faith in Christ and in our faithfulness to Christ in the face of rampant deception and persecution. We must maintain our loyalty to Christ to the end if we are to be saved on the Day of Judgment. This is the message of the passage.

The Occasion of the Discourse

The occasion of this discourse is found in verses 1 to 3. "*And Jesus went out, and departed from the temple: and his disciples came to him for to shew him the buildings of the temple.* [2] *And Jesus said unto them, See ye not all these things? verily I say unto you, There shall not be left here one stone upon another, that shall not be thrown down.* [3] *And as he sat upon the mount of Olives, the disciples came unto him privately, saying, Tell us, when shall these things be? and what shall be the sign of thy coming, and of the end of the world?*"

These three verses provide the occasion for the entire discourse in chapter 24.

In Matthew 23, Jesus had pronounced woe on Israel for her hypocrisy and her hatred of Christ and His people. Jesus declared in Matthew 23:38 that Israel's house would be left desolate.

This pronouncement must have amazed the disciples. They could not imagine such a magnificent and important building being deserted and abandoned. They began to point out the marvelous nature of the temple and the buildings around it to Jesus, and draw His attention to its magnificence. Verse 1 records that "*his disciples came to him for to show Him the buildings of the temple."* No doubt they were saying, "Look at this magnificent structure and these giant blocks of marble of which it is made. Look at its beauty and strength!" Their implied question was, "How could this be made desolate? How could this be destroyed?"

Jesus was completely unmoved by considerations of the magnificence, beauty, and strength of the temple and the buildings around it. He repeated and reinforced what He said in Matthew 23 about the desolation of Israel's house. Jesus said in verse 2, "Do you see this temple and these buildings? They will be decimated, leveled, and reduced to rubble. It will all be completely thrown down to the point that no part of any wall will be left. There will not be left one stone on top of another."

This statement Jesus made in verse 2 amazed the disciples. It seemed incomprehensible to them that this temple and the buildings around it would be leveled to the ground and reduced to rubble. They were dumbstruck.

Jesus walked out of the temple, and the disciples followed Him. They left the temple and the city, and went out the eastern gate of the city. They went down the hill to the bottom of the Kidron valley, and up the western side of the Mount of Olives, and they sat down somewhere on the mountain.

In verses 1 and 2, they were at the temple. In verse 3, it says Jesus sat down in the Mount of Olives. There is a considerable break in time between verses 2 and 3. This was a journey of about a half a mile, and it would have taken about a half-hour to make as they wound down the steep slope to the bottom of the Kidron valley, crossed the Kidron brook, and wound their way up the side of the mount of Olives and sat down.

Along this journey, the disciples must have digested the dreadful pronouncement Jesus had made, and questions now began to arise in their minds and spilled out of their mouths as they sat on the mountain.

Notice verse 3. *"And as he sat upon the mount of Olives, the disciples came unto him privately, saying, Tell us, when shall these things be? and what shall be the sign of thy coming, and of the end of the world?"* In verse 3 the disciples asked regarding Jesus' previous statements, "When will this happen—that is, when will this great judgment occur that will leave the house of Israel desolate and destroyed?"

If this is all they wished to know, and if they had asked this single question, Jesus might have said, "It will happen in about thirty-seven years (AD 70), and Jerusalem and the temple will be destroyed by Rome." But that is not all they asked. They did not just ask when the temple was going to be leveled. They asked two more questions in verse 3—questions that completely overshadowed in importance that first question—and which became the primary subject of Jesus' answer in this chapter.

The two additional questions they asked were stated in verse 3: (1) "What shall be the sign of Your coming?" and (2) "What shall be the sign of the end of the world?" Perhaps they thought all three of these events would occur at the same time, so they asked these three questions together. It seems they thought the destruction of the temple in Jerusalem would certainly mean the end of the world and bring about the second coming of Christ. They appeared to think it would all happen at once.

But they were mistaken about this. The fall of the temple and the fall of Jerusalem would not occur at the same time as the second coming of Christ and the end of the world. Jesus corrected their error by telling them in the subsequent discourse that a lengthy period of time would intervene between the fall of Jerusalem and His second coming at the end of the world.

This does not mean there was no connection between the fall of Jerusalem and the end of the world. There was indeed a connection between the judgment to be executed on the Jewish nation and the second coming of Christ and the end of the world, and the connection is this: The city of Jerusalem's approaching catastrophe was going to be a type and a foreshadow of the great tribulation that would occur just before the second coming and the end of the world.

As Jesus describes the great tribulation later in this chapter, He describes it in the language of the destruction of Jerusalem by the Romans, and the flight from that destruction the Christians engage in when it occurs in AD 70. The fall of Jerusalem and the desolation of the temple is alluded to by Christ in His answer in Matthew 24, but only by way of: (1) warning the Christians how to avoid it when it comes in AD 70, and (2) by way of setting it forth as a foreshadow of a far greater tribulation that would occur at the end of the age.

The destruction of Jerusalem and the temple is not the main subject of Christ's discourse or even the subject of very much of it at all. The destruction of Jerusalem and the temple is merely a background issue in this discourse. The primary subject of His discourse is the answer to those two last questions: *"What shall be the sign of thy coming, and of the end of the world?"* The answer to those two questions is at the forefront of all Jesus says in this discourse. As we shall see, His second coming and the end of the world occur together, because the second coming of Christ causes the end of the world and brings it to pass.

Jesus says in Matthew 23 that the temple and Jerusalem are going to be left desolate. The disciples ask these questions in Matthew 24: Have you seen the temple? Did you notice how well it is built? Jesus replies, answering that it is going to be leveled. Then they ask Jesus when that is going to happen, and what is the sign of His coming and of the end of the world, thinking all those events would happen together.

Jesus then says—and I am paraphrasing His words here—"I will tell you about My coming, and the end of the world. Yes, the destruction of the temple is going to happen, and here is what you need to do when it does: You need to run away. But this is really just a foreshadowing of a far greater tribulation, one that will be so much greater than the destruction of Jerusalem and the temple, that there has never been another tribulation like it before, and there will never be another tribulation like it afterward. The fall of Jerusalem just foreshadows that great tribulation to come at the end of this age. Let Me tell you about that greater tribulation, and how that tribulation will lead to My second coming and the destruction of the world and the bringing in of the new heaven and the new earth."

That is the thrust of the passage. Jesus is answering those last two questions—What will be the sign of Your coming, and the end of the world? He deals with the destruction of Jerusalem, but it is not the primary subject of the passage. His statement regarding the destruction of Jerusalem is provided for two reasons: (1) Here is what you need to do to escape; and (2) This is a picture of what is coming in the end.

The Characteristics of This Age

The characteristics of this age between the first and second coming of Christ are set out in verses 4 to 8. There are three characteristics of this age that are going to be manifest throughout this age, prior to the final events that will conclude this age.

The first characteristic of this age is that there will be great religious deception.

Notice verses 4 and 5. Answering this question, "*What shall be the sign of thy coming and the end of the world?* [4] *Jesus answered and said unto them, Take heed that no man deceive you.* [5] *For many shall come in my name, saying, I am Christ; and shall deceive many.*" Jesus begins to describe the period from the time He was sitting with them until the great tribulation begins, and He sets forth the characteristics of that time frame.

During this time, there will be great religious deception. Jesus opens His discourse with a warning against being deceived. He says in verse 4, "*Take heed that no man deceive you,*" and then He repeats this warning in verse 5 when He says, "*Many shall come in my name, saying, I am Christ, and shall deceive many.*" There will be much deception regarding many matters, but in particular, there will be many individuals who will claim to be Jesus Christ on earth.

This is something that has occurred repeatedly during the last 2,000 years since Jesus uttered these words. Numerous individuals have claimed to be Christ on earth including mental institution inmates, Eastern religion gurus, Roman Catholic popes, and doomsday cult leaders. At numerous points in past history, religious deception and religious deceivers have led many to think the coming of Christ was imminent, or that Christ had already come to this earth and was personified in this individual or that individual—when clearly that was not the case.

There has been, there are now, and there will be in the future many religious impostors, religious date-setters, and religious apocalyptic cults leading people into false beliefs about the second coming of Christ and the end of the world. Jesus told us beforehand about such people and warned us against falling into their deception. One of the characteristics of the age we are currently living in is that there will be great religious deception.

The second characteristic of the age in which we are living is that there will be great political turmoil.

Notice verse 6–7a: "*And ye shall hear of wars and rumours of wars: see that ye be not troubled: for all these things must come to pass, but the end is not yet.* [7] *For nation shall rise against nation, and kingdom against kingdom.*"

These verses describe the great political turmoil that is going to take place in this age. In the last 2,000 years, there have been countless wars, some of them involving the whole world. Nations have risen against nations, and kingdoms have risen against kingdoms, and they do so to this very day. There has never been a point in history since the time Christ uttered these words that there have not been multiple conflicts going on across the globe. Some of these wars have been so great, like World War I and World War II, that many people thought Armageddon was upon us and the end had come—but they were wrong.

Jesus said in verse 6: Do not let these wars—even those that may involve most of the nations of the world at the same time—trouble you to the point that you think this must be the end. These things must come to pass. They are manifestations of human depravity, but they are not signs of the end. Political turmoil is no sign of the end times. World War I and World War II were not signs of the end times. All the wars in the Middle East are not signs of the end times. Great political turmoil characterizes the present age in which we live.

The third characteristic of this age in which we are living is that there will be tremendous natural disasters.

Notice verses 7b to 8. "*. . .and there shall be famines, and pestilences, and earthquakes, in divers places.* [8] *All these are the beginning of sorrows.*"

Throughout this present age, there will be great convulsions in nature. There will be droughts and outbreaks of insects that will destroy crops and bring about mass starvation in various places in the world. Great famines will occur. There will be pestilences and outbreaks of disease that will cause millions to die, things like the Bubonic Plague, the influenza outbreak of 1913, Ebola, and many other contagious diseases that have arisen throughout the last 2,000 years. Millions of people have died from these things in very short periods of time.

There will not only be famines and pestilences, but there will also be massive earthquakes—earthquakes in which tens of thousands, and sometimes hundreds of thousands of people die all over the globe. For example, in 2004 we experienced the Indian Ocean 9.2 magnitude earthquake and tsunami that resulted in over 200,000 people dying in one day.

Great religious deception, great political turmoil, and tremendous natural disasters have characterized the world for the last 2,000 years. However, none of them is a sign of the end or of the coming of Christ.

When these things occur, *"the end is not yet."* They are only *"the beginning of sorrows."* The real sorrows are later, after these events. These sorrows described in verses 4 to 7 are nothing compared with the sorrows that will occur when the end times start and are finally upon us.

What we have in verses 4 to 8 is a description of what has been going on for the last 2,000 years and will continue to go on until the end times begin with the loosing of Satan. When Satan is loosed, that is when the end times begin. But until Satan is loosed, the events of verses 4 to 8 will continue to be the norm from this point forward, just like they have been the norm for the last 2,000 years.

Where are we in the prophetic time clock? We are in verses 4 to 8, a long period of great religious deception, great political turmoil, and great natural disasters, none of which is a sign of the second coming. There are signs of the second coming, and we will identify what those signs are when we get to them in our text, but Jesus specifically warns us not to view anything mentioned in verses 4 to 8 as a sign of the second coming. They are merely the norm for this present period and will be the norm until Satan is loosed for his little season. That begins in verse 9, which we will examine in the next chapter. The lesson of this passage is this: Do not be deceived into thinking that because the things described in verses 4 to 8 are happening, the second coming is somehow imminent.

The second coming of Jesus is not imminent. There will be definite signs that will occur before He comes back. We will be able to see and discern those signs, and that day will not overtake us without warning. The second coming will not surprise us like a thief in the night. It will surprise the ungodly, but it will not surprise us. We know what the actual signs are that tell us when Christ's coming is imminent.

We will see the fig tree budding—that is, we will see the signs that tell us when it is near. We will identify them in the next chapter. However, none of those signs exists yet. Therefore, we need to continue to engage in spiritual warfare in these three areas. We must fight religious deception by preaching the truth. We must encourage peacemaking when strife and wars occur. We must seek to relieve those who are affected by great convulsions of nature. There is much to occupy us in ministry until the signs of the second coming appear. Let us be busy in the work of the kingdom until they do.

Signs of the End Times
Matthew 24:9–14
Chapter 2

> "[9] *Then shall they deliver you up to be afflicted, and shall kill you: and ye shall be hated of all nations for my name's sake.* [10] *And then shall many be offended, and shall betray one another, and shall hate one another.* [11] *And many false prophets shall rise, and shall deceive many.* [12] *And because iniquity shall abound, the love of many shall wax cold.* [13] *But he that shall endure unto the end, the same shall be saved.* [14] *And this gospel of the kingdom shall be preached in all the world for a witness unto all nations; and then shall the end come.*"

We began our exposition of Matthew 24 by considering verses 1 through 8. This extended discourse on eschatology was provoked by Jesus stating that the temple at Jerusalem would be leveled to the ground as an act of God's judgment on Israel for her rejection and crucifixion of Jesus Christ. Jesus stated that the temple would be destroyed when He said, "*There shall not be left here one stone upon another, that shall not be thrown down.*"

This statement Jesus made about the destruction of the temple amazed the disciples and provoked them to ask the question "*When shall these things be?*" In other words, when will the temple be leveled? But that is not all they asked. They asked at the same time two additional questions—questions that completely overshadowed the importance of the first question. Notice verse 3: "*And as he sat upon the mount of Olives, the disciples came unto him privately, saying, Tell us, when shall these things be?*" That is, when will the temple be leveled? Then they asked two additional questions: ". . .*what shall be the sign of thy coming, and of the end of the world?*" Those two questions overshadow the first question, and the answer to them is the primary focus in the remainder of this chapter and the next. Jesus does answer their first question "When will the temple be leveled?" later in chapter 24; but He handles it incidentally, and He handles it in relation to these two primary questions.

Jesus addresses these last two questions in verses 4 through 14. It is the answer to these last two questions—"What shall be the sign of Your coming?" and "What shall be the sign of the end of the world?"—that is at the forefront of all that Jesus says in this discourse. This discourse is primarily about the sign of the second coming and the end of the world, not about the leveling of the temple.

Jesus begins in verses 4 to 14 to address the question: What shall be the sign of the end of the world? He begins to answer that question by telling us about the things that are not the sign of the end of the world in verses 4 to 8. He states that from this day; that is, from the day they were sitting there talking until the end times begin, that there will be three elements that will characterize that entire period.

This period between the time of Jesus and the start of the end times that leads to the end of the world will be characterized by three things. It will be characterized by great religious deception, verse 5: "*Many shall come in my name, saying, I am Christ; and shall deceive many.*" It will be characterized by great political turmoil, verses 6 and 7: "*And ye shall hear of wars and rumours of wars. . .nation shall rise against nation, and kingdom against kingdom.*" Finally, it will be characterized by great natural disasters, verse 7b to verse 8: "*. . .there shall be famines, and pestilences, and earthquakes, in divers places.*"

However, none of these things is a sign of the end times, for in verse 6 Jesus says, "*See that ye be not troubled: for all these things must come to pass, but the end is not yet.*" And in verse 8 He says, "*All these are the beginning of sorrows*"—that is, these are just the preliminary sorrows prior to the end times.

Great religious deception in verse 5, great political turmoil in verses 6 and 7, and great natural disasters in verses 7 through 8 are the things that have been continuously going on for the last 2,000 years all across the world. Those things will continue to go on until the end times begin. They could continue to go on for a very long time yet.

The point is that these things are not (and never have been) signs of the end. They have been the norm, they are the norm now, and they will continue to be the norm until the end times begin. Therefore, what is described in verses 4 to 8 is the time period we have been living in for the last 2,000 years, and continue to live in at the present moment. The question then arises: When will the end times actually begin? When will the norm of great religious deception and great political turmoil and great natural disasters end, and the end times actually begin? What will the trigger be that will set the end times in motion?

The event that triggers the beginning of the end times is the decision on the part of God to loose Satan from the bondage and restraint he is currently under. When Satan is loosed, the end times begin. We will not see him loosed because he is a spirit, and we cannot see those things. But what we will see are the effects of him having been loosed, and they will be very visible.

The passage before us now sets forth the effects of Satan being loosed, and the things we will experience that will make it clear to us that he has been loosed. When we see the events in verses 9 to 14 begin to take place, then we know that the end is near. But until they take place, it is not near. Let us consider our passage together.

The Concept of the Binding and Loosing of Satan

Before we approach verse 9 and the following verses, we have to establish some background from other passages that will help us understand verses 9 to 14. Crucial to our understanding of verses 9 to 14 is an understanding of the concept of Satan being bound and Satan being loosed.

The central passage that addresses the issue of Satan being bound and loosed is Revelation 20:1–10. *"And I saw an angel come down from heaven, having the key of the bottomless pit and a great chain in his hand.* [2] *And he laid hold on the dragon, that old serpent, which is the Devil, and Satan, and bound him a thousand years,* [3] *And cast him into the bottomless pit, and shut him up, and set a seal upon him, that he should deceive the nations no more, till the thousand years should be fulfilled: and after that he must be loosed a little season."* Notice the binding and the loosing of Satan taking place in verses 2 and 3.

Now the scene shifts to heaven: "[4] *And I saw thrones, and they sat upon them, and judgment was given unto them: and I saw the souls of them that were beheaded for the witness of Jesus, and for the word of God, and which had not worshipped the beast, neither his image, neither had received his mark upon their foreheads, or in their hands; and they lived and reigned with Christ a thousand years."* They are living and reigning with Him in heaven. "[5] *But the rest of the dead lived not again until the thousand years were finished. This is the first resurrection.* [6] *Blessed and holy is he that hath part in the first resurrection: on such the second death hath no power, but they shall be priests of God and of Christ, and shall reign with him a thousand years."*

Now the scene shifts back to earth in verse 7. *"And when the thousand years are expired, Satan shall be loosed out of his prison"* (notice the loosing here), "[8] *And shall go out to deceive the nations which are in the four quarters of the earth"*—that is, north, south, east and west—"*Gog and Magog, to gather them together to battle: the number of whom is as the sand of the sea.* [9] *And they went up on the breadth of the earth, and compassed [surrounded] the camp of the saints about, and the beloved city: and fire came down from God out of heaven, and devoured them.* [10] *And the devil that deceived them was cast into the lake of fire and brimstone, where the beast and the false prophet are, and shall be tormented day and night for ever and ever."*

In this chapter and in the entire book of Revelation we have what is called "apocalyptic literature." Apocalyptic literature is different from ordinary literature, in that apocalyptic literature is written in highly symbolic and dramatically figurative language, largely couched in metaphor, allegory, and similes. In many respects, apocalyptic literature is to be interpreted like parables are to be interpreted. When Jesus gave a parable, nobody thought it was literal; they recognized it was a story He was telling, and each of the events in the story was a symbol of something else. This is how apocalyptic literature is written. It is a genre of literature that is predominantly symbolic. Notice verse 1 opens with the words *"And I saw."* By using this phrase, *"And I saw,"* John is informing us of the visionary and thus the symbolic and figurative nature of this passage. He is having a vision.

This passage was never meant to be taken literally. It has many symbolic and figurative elements in it, so it is to be interpreted in light of how the symbols and analogies it contains are used in other passages in the Bible. We must ask the question: Is there anywhere else in the Bible where Satan being bound is spoken of? If so, then those passages will be able to shed light on this one.

Notice the alternating structure of this section in Revelation 20. In verses 1 to 3, we have a description of the millennial reign on earth and a description of Satan and the nations. In verse 3, Satan is cast into the bottomless pit and *"the seal is set on him that he should deceive the nations no more, till the thousand years should be fulfilled: and after that he must be loosed a little season."* Verses 1–3 deal with what God is doing in relationship to Satan and the nations here on earth.

In verses 4 to 6, we have a description of the millennial reign in heaven. The scene shifts to heaven, and we have a description of the souls who were beheaded and are reigning with Christ. Beheaded people do not live on earth. People who are on earth do not sit on thrones in heaven. These are people who have died during this millennial period. They have been beheaded for the cause of Christ, they are martyrs, and they are in heaven with the Lord.

Having seen that verses 1 to 3 talk about the millennial reign on earth and Satan and the nations—and that verses 4 to 6 talk about the millennial reign in heaven and souls who are reigning with Christ there—verses 7 to 10 then switch back to the millennial reign on earth and Satan and the nations once again. Notice verse 7: *"And when the thousand years are expired, Satan shall be loosed out of his prison,*
8 *And shall go out to deceive the nations which are in the four quarters of the earth."*

Verses 1 to 3 and 7 to 10 deal with Satan and the nations on earth during the Millennium. We see Satan being bound, and we have to ask ourselves the twofold question: When was Satan bound, and why was Satan bound? This is where other passages shed light on Revelation 20, since they use the same metaphors Revelation 20 uses.

Notice Matthew 12:22–29: *"Then was brought unto [Jesus] one possessed with a devil, blind, and dumb: and [Jesus] healed him, insomuch that the blind and dumb both spake and saw.* 23 *And all the people were amazed, and said, Is not this the son of David?* 24 *But when the Pharisees heard it, they said, This fellow doth not cast out devils, but by Beelzebub the prince of the devils.* 25 *And Jesus knew their thoughts, and said unto them, Every kingdom divided against itself is brought to desolation; and every city or house divided against itself shall not stand:* 26 *And if Satan cast out Satan, he is divided against himself; how shall then his kingdom stand?* 27 *And if I by Beelzebub cast out devils, by whom do your children cast them out? therefore they shall be your judges.* 28 *But if I cast out devils by the Spirit of God, then the kingdom of God is come unto you.* 29 *Or else"* (notice the metaphors here) *"how can one enter into a strong man's house, and spoil his goods, except he first bind the strong man? and then he will spoil his house."*

The context of Jesus' statement in verse 29 is the binding of satanic forces. He is casting out a demon. He is taking control of Satan and his demons. The binding of the strong man in verse 29 pictures this act of binding Satan, which is something Jesus says He is doing in establishing His kingdom at His first advent. Notice He says in verse 28: *"But if I cast out devils by the Spirit of God, then the kingdom of God is come unto you."*

When Jesus established the kingdom of God at His first coming, He bound the strongman, namely Satan, so that Jesus could then enter his house—that is, enter his kingdom, and then ravage it. Having bound Satan, Jesus is going into Satan's kingdom and taking his citizens captive and bringing them into His kingdom through conversion. He transfers them out of the kingdom of darkness and into the kingdom of light by saving them. In this manner, He spoils (ravages) Satan's house and kingdom.

When Jesus began His kingdom, He was a King, but He had no subjects. He is now bringing subjects into His kingdom, but where does He get them? He gets them out of the kingdom of Satan. Why does Satan let that happen? Because he cannot stop it. Jesus has tied him up. Jesus can now pillage Satan's house as He pleases. By way of illustration, if I broke into your house, I would have to deal with you before I could take your possessions. But if I tied you up, I could walk around in your house, look through all your things, and take whatever I wanted. You are tied up, and therefore you cannot stop me. That is the picture here. Jesus has bound Satan, and now He is moving through Satan's house and taking his people for Himself.

It is clear that the binding of Satan is associated with the establishment of Christ's kingdom at His first advent. In Matthew 12:29, it says, *"How can one enter into a strong man's house, and spoil his goods, except he first bind the strong man?"* That word "bind" is the same Greek word used in Revelation 20:2 when it says that Satan was bound for a thousand years. Satan was bound by the events of Christ's first advent and at the time when Christ first came. To answer our twofold question: When was Satan bound? He was bound at the first coming of Christ, through the ministry of Christ in defeating Satan. Why was Satan bound? He was bound so Christ might ravage his kingdom.

Now the third question is: How long is Satan bound? Our text in Revelation 20 is very clear. It says he is bound a thousand years. It says it twice. He is bound, verse 3, for a thousand years: *"till the thousand years should be fulfilled."* And then in verse 7: *"And when the thousand years are expired, Satan shall be loosed out of his prison."*

The question we have to ask ourselves is this: Are the thousand years literal or figurative? It must be one or the other because there are no other options.

When we look at Revelation 20:1–3, we see there a chain, a key, a lock, and a pit. All of these are employed in the binding of Satan. Now obviously, Satan is a spirit. He does not have a physical body. You cannot use a literal chain, a literal key, a literal lock, and a literal pit to bind a spirit, because spirits cannot be bound with physical objects. Clearly, the chain, the key, the lock, and the pit are all symbolic. Now if the prison itself, and everything associated with it, is symbolic, then by what rationale is the prison sentence literal? If the prison in which Satan is bound is symbolic, why would the prison sentence not also be symbolic? The point is, we must not do what the Dispensationalists insist on and literalize this symbolic language. The number one thousand is used symbolically here. It represents an age-long, but definitely limited period of time.

When the various covenants were given, like the Davidic Covenant, we did not know how long it was going to be until it was fulfilled. It was an age before it was finally fulfilled. It was a long time—centuries and centuries. It was the same way with the Abrahamic Covenant.

The New Covenant era is also a long time. It covers an entire age. The number one thousand refers to an age-long period that is definitely limited. The number conveys the idea that there is a fixed length to it, but the size of the number conveys the idea that it is a very long time. When was Satan bound? At the first coming of Jesus Christ. Why was he bound? So Jesus might ravage his kingdom. For how long is he bound? For an entire age, until that age reaches the perfect length that God has established for it.

Ten is the number that symbolizes perfection, and when multiplied by itself three times to equal one thousand, it represents an intensification of the concept of perfection to the highest degree. The age of salvation is an age of perfect length to accomplish the calling and redemption of all of God's elect.

There is a fourth question: In what respect was Satan bound, and in regard to what matters or activities? We must understand that Satan was not bound to total inactivity. For example, in 1 Peter 5:8 we are told that Satan walks about as a roaring lion, seeking whom he may devour. We read in 2 Corinthians 4:4 that the god of this world has blinded the minds of those that believe not, lest the light of the glorious gospel should come unto them, and they should be saved. We read about quite a bit of satanic activity still going on after the death and resurrection and ascension of Jesus in the book of Acts.

Plainly, Satan was not bound to total and complete inactivity. Satan was bound with respect to the fact that he cannot deceive the nations. Notice it says in verse 3: *"and cast him into the bottomless pit, and shut him up, and set a seal upon him, that he should deceive the nations no more."* Verse 7: *"And when the thousand years are expired, Satan shall be loosed out of his prison,* [8] *And shall go out to deceive the nations."*

Satan was bound not with reference to everything he does, but with reference to deceiving the nations. In other words, he was bound so he cannot deceive the nations into making an intense, unified, prolonged, and comprehensive effort to destroy Christianity from the world; because, when he is loosed, that is exactly what he attempts to do. He gathers together all the nations of the whole earth to go to war against the Christians, here called *"the camp of the saints"* and *"the beloved city."* The city of God is the New Jerusalem described in Revelation 21, which is the whole body of the redeemed.

Notice Revelation 20:7–10: *"And when the thousand years are expired, Satan shall be loosed out of his prison,* [8] *And shall go out to deceive the nations which are in the four quarters of the earth"* (north, south, east, west), *"Gog and Magog, to gather them together to battle: the number of whom"* (take notice) *"is as the sand of the sea."* This language describes all of earth's population minus the Christians.

Verse 9: *"And they went up on the breadth of the earth"*—that is, they covered the whole earth—*"and [surrounded] the camp of the saints about, and the beloved city"* (the camp of the saints and the beloved city are two metaphors for the people of God), *"and fire came down from God out of heaven, and devoured them."* That fire proceeds from Jesus at His second coming. Satan and his people will be destroyed with the brightness of Christ's coming.

In verses 7 to 10, Satan is loosed, and the time period for which he is loosed is *"a little season."* Verse 3 says: *"and after that he must be loosed a little season."* So for a short time—that is, short in comparison to the millennial period, which is a very long time—Satan is loosed in order that he may do what he has been restrained from doing for the last 2,000 years, which is uniting all the nations of the world in a determined effort to attack the Christian church. When

Satan is loosed, all nations are deceived and all nations are brought together in a transnational coalition to attack the Christians everywhere on the earth at the same time, so they are surrounded and there is no place for them to flee for refuge.

Historically, believers have always had places to flee for refuge. For example, when believers were persecuted in England, they sailed across the ocean to America. There has always been a place to flee from religious persecution; but in this day, there will be no place to flee in order to escape persecution.

Revelation 20:1–10 describes a long period of protection, here called the thousand years; followed by a short period of intense, worldwide, transnational persecution, here called a little season; which will be ended by the second coming of Christ.

In 2 Thessalonians 2, we have a parallel passage describing the end times and what is going to occur during them. This passage also addresses the binding and loosing of Satan. Notice 2 Thessalonians 2:1: *"Now we beseech you, brethren, by the coming of our Lord Jesus Christ, and by our gathering together unto him. . . ."* This is a reference to the second coming and the rapture. When Jesus comes and we are gathered to Him, that occurs in the end times. With reference to that end-time event he says in verse 2, I do not want you to be *"shaken in mind, or be troubled, neither by spirit"*—that is, by somebody saying he has a revelation—*"nor by word,"* by somebody's teaching—*"nor by letter,"* as if we wrote it, *"as [though it is] from us, as that the day of Christ"*—that is, the second coming—*"is at hand."* Paul says the second coming is not at hand.

Clearly, the second coming is not at hand. It is not imminent. Paul did not preach that Jesus can come back at any second. It is true that He can come back at any second for you individually. If you died right now, He would be coming back for you personally. Christ's coming for you is imminent at any moment. This is why you need to be ready to die every moment of your life. But Paul is talking about Jesus coming back to the world at His second coming. His second coming to the world is not imminent. The day of Christ is not at hand.

Verse 3: *"Let no man deceive you by any means"* (and there are plenty of people who want to deceive you), *"for that day shall not come, except there come a falling away first"*—that is, a great apostasy in the Christian church. Secondly, that day will not come except the *"man of sin be revealed, the son of perdition"*—this is the Antichrist.

Verse 4: "*Who opposeth and exalteth himself above all that is called God, or that is worshipped; so that he as God sitteth in the temple of God, shewing himself that he is God.*"

The day of Christ—that is, the day of the second coming—is not going to happen until there is a falling away into great apostasy, and until the Antichrist, the man of sin, is revealed on the world's stage. He says in verse 5, "*Remember ye not, that, when I was yet with you, I told you these things?*" He asks, "Why are you doubting them now? Have you forgotten what I taught you when I was with you?" Verse 6: "*And now ye know what withholdeth [or restrains] that he*" (Antichrist) "*might be revealed in his time.*" Something is restraining the advent of Antichrist.

Verse 7: "*For the mystery of iniquity doth already work*" (it is presently in process) "*only he who now [restrains] will [continue to restrain], until he be taken out of the way.* [8] *And then shall that Wicked [One] be revealed, whom the Lord shall consume with the spirit of His mouth, and shall destroy with the brightness of His coming,*"

Verse 9: "*Even him, whose coming is after the working of Satan with all power and signs and lying wonders,* [10] *And with all deceivableness of unrighteousness in them that perish; because they received not the love of the truth, that they might be saved.* [11] *And for this cause God shall send them strong delusion, that they should believe a lie:* [12] *That they all might be damned who believed not the truth, but had pleasure in unrighteousness.*"

Notice the parallels between this passage and Revelation 20. In Revelation 20:1–3, we see Satan bound by a chain and an angel. In 2 Thessalonians 2:6–7, he talks about Satan being restrained. In verse 6, he talks about "*what*" he is restrained with—namely, the chain. In verse 7 it talks about "*he*" who is doing the restraining—namely, the angel.

So "*what*" is doing the restraining in verse 6 is the chain, and "*he*" who is doing the restraining in verse 7 is the angel. When the chain and the angel are taken away, what happens? Satan is loosed. There is going to be this short time of loosing, it says in Revelation 20:3, after this long period of protection, this metaphorical thousand-year period. After Satan is loosed, what happens to the nations? They are deceived.

In 2 Thessalonians 2, when the restraint and the restrainer are taken out of the way, and the man of sin is revealed, the nations are deceived. Verse 3: There is going to come a great falling away; people are going to depart from Christianity and follow Antichrist. Why are they going to do this? Notice verse 9: *"Even him, whose coming is after the working of Satan with all power and signs and lying wonders."* When Satan is loosed, he is going to raise up this Antichrist, this man of sin.

This man of sin is going to be able to do fantastic miracles. He is going to deceive the vast majority of the Christian church, who will apostatize and start to follow him, and who will be deceived, as verse 10 says, *"with all deceivableness of unrighteousness in them that perish; because they received not the love of the truth, that they might be saved."* They went to church. They heard the truth, but they never really believed it. They never really embraced it. Therefore, when the deception came, they abandoned the truth. Why? Because they loved their sin more than they loved the truth. They *"had pleasure in unrighteousness."*

God sent them the strong delusion of the Antichrist, that they would believe his lie, because they believed not the truth, but had pleasure in unrighteousness, verses 11–12. They would never embrace God's truth, because they loved their sin more than they loved the truth, and they were willing to abandon the truth in order to keep their sin. Antichrist says to them, "You can keep your sin. As your god, I have the right to give you permission to sin all you want."

The flesh would rejoice if it had a god who said you may indulge the pleasures of the flesh. You would no longer have a battle in your heart. You would not have to repent of anything. This is what the false god Allah is like. He says to the Muslims that they can kill, lie, and steal like their prophet Mohammed did, and Allah will reward them if they do. They will have seventy-two virgins in heaven to defile. Allah is in the mold of Antichrist.

But leaving Islam aside, notice that both Satan and the nations are destroyed in Revelation 20:9–10. Fire comes down from heaven and consumes them as they are surrounding the camp of the saints and trying to destroy them. What happens in 2 Thessalonians 2? The man of sin and those who follow him are judged by Christ, verse 8: *"And then shall that Wicked [One] be revealed, whom the Lord shall consume with the spirit of his mouth, and shall destroy with the brightness of his coming."* The brightness of his coming is the fire of Revelation 20:9–10: *"and fire came down from God out of heaven, and devoured them,"* and they are *"cast into the lake of fire."* Second

Thessalonians 2:12: *"that they all might be damned who believed not the truth, but had pleasure in unrighteousness."*

We see these exact same parallel teachings: in Revelation 20:1–3, Satan is bound by a chain and an angel; in 2 Thessalonians 2:6–7, there is an item that restrains Satan and there is an individual that restrains Satan, which are the chain and the angel.

There is going to be a short time of loosing of Satan after the Millennium in Revelation 20:3, 7–10. During this period, the nations are deceived. In 2 Thessalonians 2:3–7, 9–11, the restrainer is taken out of the way, the man of sin is revealed, the deception occurs, and the people all believe the lie.

In Revelation 20:9–19, Satan and the nations that persecute the Christians are judged and destroyed and damned by Christ. In 2 Thessalonians 2:8, 12, the man of sin and those who follow him are judged and destroyed and damned by Christ. The two passages are parallel and contain the same events.

Let us summarize. At the end of the thousand years—that is, at the end of the church age, this long period of protection—we have:

1. Intensified activity of Satan. He is loosed. He is now doing more than he did before. (Revelation 20:3b, 7a)
2. The appearance of Antichrist and great apostasy of the Christians. (2 Thessalonians 2:3)
3. The worldwide persecution of the church; all nations are now against Christians, and are united as a matter of national policy and national cooperation in their persecution. We are going to have a United Nations of persecution of Christians. (Revelation 20:8–9a)
4. The preservation of the church from that determination to destroy it by Christ's second coming, which instead destroys Antichrist and all the wicked. (2 Thessalonians 2:8, Revelation 20:9b–10)

These things are the teaching of Revelation 20 and 2 Thessalonians 2.

We are now ready to examine Matthew 24:9–14. Having seen the background concept of the binding and the loosing of Satan in Revelation 20 and in 2 Thessalonians 2, let us now consider together Matthew 24:9–14.

The Explanation of Matthew 24:9–14

Verses 4 to 8 describe what has been going on during this millennial period, this long period of protection. There is great religious deception, verses 4 and 5; there is great political turmoil, verses 6 and 7; and there are great natural disasters, verses 7 and 8. These things are the characteristics of this age. They have been going on for 2,000 years as we have been spreading the gospel throughout the world.

But notice the very first word in verse 9, "*Then. . .*" The word "*Then*" in verse 9 introduces a transition from what was described in verses 4 to 8. It tells us of a change, of a new and different situation which will arise subsequent to the period described in verses 4 to 8. It says, "*Then shall they deliver you up to be afflicted, and shall kill you, and*" (notice) "*ye shall be hated of all nations for my name's sake.*"

It has not been the case up to this point in time that Christians have been hated of all nations. There have always been nations that were receptive or at least not hostile to Christians and Christianity. America is a classic example. There have always been nations into which persecuted believers could flee and find refuge and peace to practice their religion. It has not yet been the case in the history of the world that Christians have been hated of all nations, but "*then*" it will be the case.

The loosing of Satan will cause this change in the attitude of the nations toward Christians. When he is loosed, he will go out and deceive all nations to surround the saints in such a way that there is no place on earth for them to flee to. Right now, if believers want to flee persecution, there is a place to go. There will not be any place to go in that day.

Verse 9 says, "*Then,*" when Satan is loosed, "*Then shall they deliver you up to be afflicted, and shall kill you: and ye shall be hated of all nations for my name's sake.*" That is what is being described in Revelation 20:9 when it says, "*And they went up on the breadth of the earth, and compassed the camp of the saints about,*" with the purpose of destroying them.

Notice verses 10 and 11. "*And then shall many be offended, and shall betray one another, and shall hate one another.* 11 *And many false prophets shall rise, and shall deceive many.*" Verse 10 describes the great apostasy spoken of in 2 Thessalonians 2:3, and verse 11 describes the great deception spoken of in 2 Thessalonians 2:9–12. Verse

10 describes the great apostasy of professing Christians in falling away from Christ in order to worship the man of sin. As a result of their apostasy, they will become persecutors and haters of true believers. It says in verse 10, *"And then shall many be offended"* when they realize they must suffer for Christ. They are offended at Christ, and will not suffer persecution for His name's sake, and therefore they switch their allegiance to the Antichrist to escape it. As a result, they are going to *"betray one another."* They are going to point out Christians to these persecuting governments. They will know who we are because they used to dwell among us. *"And shall hate one another."* That is, these apostates will hate the Christians, when previously, they were part of them. First John 2:18–19 says that they went out from us, because they were not of us.

Verse 11 describes the great deception. *"And many false prophets shall rise, and shall deceive many."* In 2 Thessalonians 2:9–10 it says the Antichrist is able to do signs and lying wonders with all deceivableness. Not only is Antichrist able to do these miracles, but he is also going to send out his false prophets to preach his message to the nations of the world in order to bring them under his authority. The false prophets will also go out to the Christian churches and say, "Turn away from Jesus and follow Antichrist, this man of sin, this son of perdition. He is your God." He is going to sit in the temple of God, showing himself that *"he is God."* Through the deceptions of these false prophets, people are going to be led to switch allegiance from Jesus to this man who claims to be God on earth.

This phrase in verse 12, *"And because iniquity shall abound,"* tells us these people plunged into sinful practices. They loved unrighteousness and they had pleasure in unrighteousness. *"And because iniquity shall abound, the love of many shall wax cold."* As they follow the man of sin and have pleasure in unrighteousness, their love for Christ will become cold, their love for the true believers will become cold, and they will become offended at Christ and His people. They will hate the believers and betray them into the hands of these persecuting governments. Sadly, many Christians will be afflicted and killed by these governments.

This is the great tribulation that will occur when Satan is loosed. This great tribulation is going to be described in more detail in Matthew 24:15–22, when we see how the destruction of the temple in Jerusalem foreshadows it. What we have in verses 9–12 is a summary of what it will be like during the great tribulation after Antichrist arises. Verses 15–22 are an expansion of that summary.

Verse 13: "*But*," in contrast to those people described in verses 10 to 12, *"he that shall endure unto the end, the same shall be saved."* Here is the mark of the true believer: he endures. He does not fall away. He does not participate in the great apostasy. His love for God and his love for people does not grow cold. He does not become offended at God for the suffering he must endure from these persecutors. He does not betray or hate his fellow believers. He is not deceived by the false prophets and the signs and lying wonders of the wicked one. In a word, he is not a rocky-ground hearer. He endures in his faith in Christ and he endures in his faithfulness to Christ, until either the end of his life or the end of this world, whichever comes first. He never apostatizes.

Verse 14: *"And this gospel of the kingdom shall be preached in all the world for a witness unto all nations; and then shall the end come."* We have now come in our text to the end of the world: *"then shall the end come."*

The gospel witness of the believers will not be extinguished by the man of sin. They will not shut their mouths just because there is persecution. They are going to keep preaching. We see this in Revelation 11 with the two witnesses. Even though there is massive hatred against them, they go out and preach. And, yes, they are finally slaughtered when their testimony is finished. But it has never been the case that persecution has shut the mouths of true Christians. They just keep preaching. The message of the martyrs is going to be spread throughout the whole world. The gospel will reach all nations, the gospel will penetrate deeply within those nations; and when it has, then the end will come.

So back to the question the disciples ask in verse 3: *"What shall be the sign. . .of the end of the world?"* The sign of the end of the world is the start of the great tribulation brought about by Satan being loosed, the great apostasy of professing Christians taking place, the revelation of the man of sin (the Antichrist) occurring along with his deceptive false prophets, Christians being hated of all nations, and the gospel being preached by fearless Christians in the whole world; when all these things come to pass, then the end will come. Those are the signs of the end of the world. The sign of the end of the world is Satan being loosed and all the things that flow out of that loosing described in Revelation 20:1–10, in 2 Thessalonians 2:1–12, and in Matthew 24:9–14.

Now you know when the end of the world will come, in the sense that you know the signs that will tell you when it is near. Later in Matthew 24, Jesus talks about the budding of the fig tree. He says that when you see the fig tree budding, you know summer is near. Likewise, when you see all these things, you know the coming of the Son of man is near.

While we do not know the day or the hour of the second coming, we do know the general time it will occur, because we will see the signs of the times that tell us that the time is short until Jesus returns. When those things occur, Jesus is coming back right away. Until those things happen, the day of Christ is not at hand, as 2 Thessalonians 2:2 plainly states.

So to recap: Matthew 24:4–8 is what is going on right now; Matthew 24:9–14 is what is going to happen in the end times. The key word that marks the transition from the present times to the end times is the word *"Then"* in verse 9.

The purpose of this teaching is to tell us two things. First, God is in control. He knows exactly what is going to happen. Therefore, we do not need to fear the future. Secondly, we need to always be on guard against apostasy in our own lives. We must be on guard against being deceived by others about who Christ is, when Christ is coming, and into following false Christs. The lesson of eschatology is this: Do not fear the future, and do not fall into the deception that is coming in the future.

Details of the Great Tribulation
Matthew 24:15–22
Chapter 3

"[15] *When ye therefore shall see the abomination of desolation, spoken of by Daniel the prophet, stand in the holy place, (whoso readeth, let him understand:)* [16] *Then let them which be in Judea flee into the mountains:* [17] *Let him which is on the housetop not come down to take any thing out of his house:* [18] *Neither let him which is in the field return back to take his clothes.* [19] *And woe unto them that are with child, and to them that give suck in those days!* [20] *But pray ye that your flight be not in the winter, neither on the sabbath day:* [21] *For then shall be great tribulation, such as was not since the beginning of the world to this time, no, nor ever shall be.* [22] *And except those days should be shortened, there should no flesh be saved: but for the elect's sake those days shall be shortened.*"

Jesus predicted the destruction of the temple at Jerusalem in Matthew 24:1–2. This prediction was very shocking to the disciples, and so they asked Him three questions in verse 3: When will the temple be destroyed? What will be the sign of Your coming? And what will be the sign of the end of the world? Jesus took up this last question, and answered it first in verses 4 to 14. In those verses, He provided a description of the entire period from His first coming to the end of the world. In these verses, Jesus tells the disciples what the sign of the end of the world will be.

In this section of Mathew 24:4–14, we have two subsections.

The first subsection in verses 4 to 8 is a description of the characteristics of the vast majority of the coming period of time. It will be a period of great religious deception, in verses 4 and 5. It will be a period of great political turmoil, in verses 6 to 7a. It will be a period of great natural disasters, in verses 7b to 8. These things will characterize the time to come; however, none of these things is a sign of the end of the world. These things have been going on for the last 2,000 years and they will continue to go on until the end times arrive. Great religious deception, great political turmoil, and great natural disasters are the norm for the vast majority of the time between the first coming of Christ and the end of the world. These things are the preliminary sorrows that are the prelude to the great sorrows of the end times.

In the second subsection in verses 9 to 14, just before the end of the world occurs, there will be a *"little season,"* a short period of time, in which there will be great sorrows and great tribulation. This short season is what is referred to as the "end times."

After the long period described in verses 4 to 8, there will be the short period described in verses 9 to 14. This period in verses 9 to 14 is introduced in verse 9 with the word, "*Then.*" *Then*, after the events in verses 4 to 8 have gone on for a long time, *then* the end times come; *then* will occur the hatred and murder of Christians by all the nations of the world under the leadership of Antichrist; *then* there will be a severe intensification of apostasy and deception; *then* iniquity will abound so the false Christians lose all love for the true Christians; *then* will the gospel have been preached in all nations; and *"then shall the end come."*

The event that will trigger the beginning of this final end-times period is the loosing of Satan, described in Revelation 20:3, 7–9. We are told that, when Satan is loosed for a little while, he will deceive the nations and gather them from the four corners of the earth into a transnational coalition to persecute the believers.

Satan will raise up the Antichrist, and through him deceive the whole world into a united worship of the Antichrist and a united persecution and murder of Christians in an attempt to eradicate them from the earth. All this is described in Matthew 24:9–14, which flows out of and follows the loosing of Satan.

However, despite this great falling away of professing Christians to follow Antichrist and betray their former fellow Christians, the gospel continues to go forth to all nations. The Christians do not stop preaching the gospel in spite of martyrdom. When the gospel shall have been preached in all the world for a witness to all nations, then the end of the world will occur.

To summarize: Matthew 24:4–8 describes the long period of relative protection that believers enjoy because Satan is bound. There will be sorrows during that time, but they are small compared to the tribulation to come. Verses 9 to 14 describe the short period of great tribulation that believers will go through because Satan is loosed. *"Then"* there will be a united, worldwide, transnational effort to wipe the Christians off the face of the earth under the leadership of the Antichrist; but the Christians will continue and complete their witness to all nations, and then the end will come.

This brings us to Matthew 24:15–22. When Jesus predicted the destruction of the temple in verses 1 and 2, the disciples asked in verse 3, "*. . .when shall these things be?*" In other words, "When will the temple be leveled to the ground so one stone is not lying on top of another?"

In verses 15 to 22, Jesus answers that question. He tells the disciples it will happen when they *"see the abomination of desolation, spoken of by Daniel the prophet, stand in the holy place."* Now *"the holy place"* was the holy land, the holy city, and the holy temple. All of them are *"the holy place."* When the abomination of desolation stands in the holy place is when Jerusalem and the temple will be destroyed. But this destruction of the temple, as terrible as it is, cannot possibly be the complete fulfillment of all Jesus says in verses 15 to 22, not only because of what those verses themselves contain, but also because of what the subsequent verses say regarding the second coming of Jesus.

There is an important principle we must understand in the construction of many of the passages in the Bible, and the principle is this: Very often, the Scripture will set forth a succinct chronological summary of an event, and then it will go back and fill in additional detail by way of a recapitulation of that event. The classic example of this recapitulation to fill in additional detail is that of Genesis 1 and 2.

Genesis 1 sets forth a chronological summary of the creation account, and chapter 2 goes back and fills in some of the additional details revolving around the creation of animals and man on the sixth day. We have this same construction in Matthew 24.

Matthew 24:4–14 sets forth the chronology of the last days, much like Genesis 1 sets forth a chronology of the first days. Matthew 24:4–14 sets forth the chronology of the last days, which extends from the first coming of Christ to the end of the world. At Matthew 24:14, the world ends. But then Matthew 24:15–22 goes back and fills in the details of the second subsection (verses 9–14) which describes the great tribulation.

The fact that there is a double reference in verses 15 to 22 to both the destruction of Jerusalem in AD 70 and also to the great tribulation that will occur at the end of the world seems very clear. The destruction of Jerusalem and the temple—which did occur in AD 70, and was predicted in Matthew 24:15–22—is a foreshadowing of the even greater tribulation and defilement of God's temple and assault upon God's people that will occur in the end times with the loosing of Satan.

The Destruction of the Temple in AD 70 Is Taught in Matthew 24:15–22

"15 *When ye therefore shall see the abomination of desolation, spoken of by Daniel the prophet, stand in the holy place, (whoso readeth, let him understand:)* 16 *Then let them which be in Judea flee into the mountains:* 17 *Let him which is on the housetop not come down to take any thing out of his house:* 18 *Neither let him which is in the field return back to take his clothes.* 19 *And woe unto them that are with child, and to them that [are nursing] in those days!* 20 *But pray ye that your flight be not in the winter, neither on the sabbath day:* 21 *For then shall be great tribulation, such as was not since the beginning of the world to this time, no, nor ever shall be.* 22 *And except those days should be shortened, there should no flesh be saved: but for the elect's sake those days shall be shortened.*"

First of all, notice the sign that Jesus provides.

The sign that Jesus provides as to when the temple is going to be leveled is in verse 15. "*When ye therefore shall see the abomination of desolation, spoken of by Daniel the prophet, stand in the holy place,*" that is when it is going to happen.

The sole sign that Jesus gives to His disciples as to when the temple is going to be destroyed is set forth. Notice that Jesus does not supply a date. Instead, He gives a sign. Jesus is not a date-setter. He says, "I will give you a sign, and the sign will tell you when it is imminent." The disciples did not know if this was going to happen in five years, ten years, or twenty years. As it turned out it was thirty-seven years later, but they did not know that. Jesus did not tell them. He says, "Here is the sign. When this sign is seen, then you will know that the destruction of the temple is imminent."

What is the sign that Jesus speaks of? Verse 15 tells us. It is "*the abomination of desolation, spoken of by Daniel the prophet.*" Daniel spoke of this abomination of desolation at least four times in his book. He spoke of it in Daniel 8:13 and 9:27. Even more explicitly, he spoke of it in Daniel 11:31. Finally, he spoke of it in Daniel 12:11.

The abomination of desolation is a major theme in the book of Daniel. But what is it? A survey of its usage tells us that the abomination of desolation consisted of the defilement of God's temple by ungodly men.

There are going to be two subsequent fulfillments of these prophecies of Daniel about the abomination of desolation that is coming. Daniel does not say it is going to happen twice, but, in fact, that is what the Bible reveals. There is going to be a double fulfillment of this prophecy.

The first fulfillment occurred a couple of centuries after Daniel prophesied. After Israel's seventy-year captivity in Babylon ended, she returned to the land and rebuilt the temple. About 240 years later, during the intertestamental period, during the time of the Maccabees, Antiochus Epiphanes invaded Israel and performed the first abomination of desolation when he offered a pig on the altar in the temple in Jerusalem.

Josephus and the Book of Maccabees both record this abomination of desolation taking place in the temple. Daniel 11 gives a detailed prophecy of this military campaign that takes place between the southern Roman kingdom and the northern Roman kingdom. They went back and forth through the Holy Land, and, in one of those excursions, Antiochus Epiphanes offered a pig on the altar, defiled the temple, and performed the abomination of desolation. This is the first fulfillment of the prophecy.

The second fulfillment is the appearance of the pagan Romans with their idolatrous images of Caesar worship who entered the temple in AD 70 and destroyed it. Jesus is telling His disciples in Matthew 24:15 that the Roman defilement and destruction of the temple is also going to be a fulfillment of Daniel's prediction of the abomination of desolation in the holy place. Just as in the past the holy place of the Lord had been defiled by ungodly men, Jesus says it will happen again in the future.

Jesus Himself authorizes us to see a double fulfillment of Daniel's prophecy. It was already fulfilled in the intertestamental period, and Jesus is saying there is still yet another fulfillment that lies ahead, which was the Romans bringing their images of Caesar worship into the temple, and then burning the temple and tearing it down. Since

Daniel's time, this was the second time God's temple had been defiled by ungodly men. This is the sign that Jesus provides.

Secondly, notice the counsel Jesus gives, in verses 16 to 22. The counsel Jesus gives to the Christians is this: When they see the Roman army approaching for the purpose of defiling and destroying the temple, they must, with great urgency, flee out of Jerusalem and into the hills, lest they be trapped in Jerusalem by the surrounding Roman armies and be slaughtered along with the unbelieving Jews by the victorious Roman legions.

They are not to worry about their possessions; they must only worry about preserving their own lives and getting away before they are surrounded and destroyed.

Verses 16 through 18: "*Then let them which be in Judea flee into the mountains:* [17] *Let him which is on the housetop not come down to take any thing out of his house:* [18] *Neither let him which is in the field return back to take his clothes.*" When they see the Roman armies coming on the plain, they are just to drop everything and run, because the Roman army will come so rapidly that if they took the time to pack a suitcase or two, the city would be surrounded and they would not be able to escape. If they are working out in the field and they look up and see the Romans coming, they are to drop their tools and run. If someone had a tunic just fifty yards away, he was just to leave it there and run.

They are not to be concerned about their possessions; they are only to be concerned with preserving their own lives. Any impediment to their flight could be fatal. Notice verse 19: "*And woe unto them that are with child, and to them that give suck in those days!*" When a woman is pregnant or has a nursing child, she cannot run very fast. It will make it far more difficult to escape.

He says in verse 20: "*But pray ye that your flight be not in the winter*" because it is much harder to travel rapidly in the winter, or "*on the sabbath day*" because it is much harder to get provisions and things you need to facilitate your escape as you go. If you are traveling on the sabbath day, modes of transportation are not available, the whole country is shut down, and you cannot buy at the market. Any impediment to flight from the city could be fatal.

He says in verses 21 and 22 that the city and the temple will be leveled, and terrible things will be done by the Romans. "*For then shall be great tribulation, such as was not since the beginning of the world to this time, no, nor ever shall be.* [22] *And except those days should be shortened, there should no flesh be saved: but for the elect's sake those days shall be shortened."* When the Romans came to take over Jerusalem, there would be terrible cruelty and mayhem and slaughter. And in fact, that is what happened. Josephus records this in graphic detail in his writings, and it is horrifying to read.

Jesus is very clear in verses 15 to 22. He is saying that Israel will not win this war. Jerusalem and the temple will not be delivered. The Jewish people in Jerusalem will not survive.

The Great Tribulation That Will Occur in the End Times Is Taught in Matthew 24:15–22

While Jesus certainly felt a concern and responsibility to warn His disciples about the coming destruction of Jerusalem and the temple so they would not be slaughtered along with the unbelieving Jews, this was not His primary emphasis or concern in His prophecies about the destruction of the temple. Jesus knew that some of these people He was talking to were going to be alive in AD 70. He did not want them to get caught by the Romans and slaughtered. So He told them: "Here is the sign, and this is when it is time to go." But His major concern and primary emphasis were on something else.

Jesus saw the destruction of the temple and the abomination of desolation that stood in the holy place in AD 70 as a foreshadowing of the appearance of the Antichrist in the New Covenant temple, which is the church, and of the destruction he would bring upon the people of God in the end times. Here is where His primary emphasis and concern lay.

There are two reasons why this is true, and we will first summarize them and then develop them. The reason why Jesus saw the destruction of the temple and the abomination of desolation in AD 70 as a foreshadowing of the behavior of the Antichrist in the end times is first of all because of the language that is used in verses 21 and 22; and secondly, because immediately after the great tribulation described in verses 21 and 22, Jesus comes back, as stated in verses 29 to 31. Let us examine those two reasons in more detail.

First of all, notice the language in verses 21 to 22. *"For then shall be great tribulation, such as was not since the beginning of the world to this time, no, nor ever shall be.* [22] *And except those days should be shortened, there should no flesh be saved: but for the elect's sake those days shall be shortened."*

Verse 21 says, *"For then shall be great tribulation, such as was not since the beginning of the world to this time."* Verse 21 cannot possibly be describing what happened in Jerusalem in AD 70. Now granted, what happened in AD 70 was bad, but it was no different and it was no worse than what happened when Nebuchadnezzar destroyed Jerusalem and Solomon's Temple and took Israel captive in 586 BC. What happened in AD 70 was just a repeat of something that had already happened before.

Solomon built the temple, but Israel was wicked, the kingdom was divided, and ultimately, Nebuchadnezzar came and surrounded Jerusalem, destroyed the city, defiled and destroyed the temple, slaughtered many Jews, and dragged the rest off to another nation. This is exactly what the Romans did in AD 70. They came, they surrounded Jerusalem, destroyed the city, defiled and destroyed the temple, slaughtered many Jews, and scattered the rest to other nations. What happened in AD 70 was no different and no worse than what happened when Nebuchadnezzar destroyed Jerusalem and Solomon's Temple and took Israel captive in 586 B.C.

In contrast to this, the tribulation described in verse 21 is entirely unique. It has no parallel in any previous historical event, from the day of creation until the time of the end. It is *"great tribulation, such as was not since the beginning of the world to this time."* This tribulation spoken of in verse 21 will be a singular event that is far beyond anything that has ever occurred, and to which nothing else can be compared. This will be a tribulation like the world has never seen before. But the tribulation that occurred in AD 70 had been seen before, in almost identical form, in 586 BC.

The point is this: the tribulation of AD 70 is simply not severe enough to fulfill the language contained in verse 21. This tribulation described in verse 21 is so great that it will completely overshadow and eclipse any previous tribulation by far. Therefore, the calamity described in verses 15–22 must also refer to something far greater and far worse than the destruction of Jerusalem and the temple in AD 70.

Furthermore, notice verse 22. *"And except those days should be shortened, there should no flesh be saved: but for the elect's sake those days shall be shortened."* What is in view is the total eradication of all of the saved; that is, all of God's elect, by means of a violent death if the effort of the Antichrist to kill them all is not cut short.

Notice the words *"except those days should be shortened, there should no flesh be saved."* The salvation spoken of here is that of being saved from physical death. Unless the time of the great tribulation (that is designed to wipe the Christians from off the earth) is cut short, no saved person would be left alive on the earth, *"but for the elect's sake those days shall be shortened."* The elect are those who, in this context, are already saved. Therefore, the salvation spoken of in verse 22a is referring to physical salvation—that is, physical deliverance from this great persecution of the killing of the elect.

The massacre the Romans carried out in AD 70 foreshadowed the killing that the Antichrist and the nations will carry out in the end times. What kind of killing did the Romans do? They killed people physically.

So the salvation that is being spoken of in verse 22a is salvation from physical slaughter, and what is being said is that for the sake of the elect, in order to prevent them from all being physically slaughtered, God is going to shorten the reign of this persecuting Antichrist.

In verse 22, the total eradication of all of the saved (all of God's elect) by means of a violent death is what is in view. This was something the fall of Jerusalem and the temple could never begin to accomplish since that was merely a local event, and by this time, the elect were scattered all over the world. By AD 70, Paul had already been on his missionary journeys and spread the gospel across the Roman Empire. Since the believers were not even going to be in the city and temple anyway, having fled to the hills because of the warning of Jesus, then verse 22 could not be referring to the events of AD 70.

The events of AD 70 couldn't physically wipe out all of the saved people in the entire world (or even in Jerusalem for that matter) unless it was cut short, because it was a local event, and because the Christians were not even there. They had fled because of Jesus' instruction to do so. But a unified, transnational, worldwide persecution of believers by all nations could fulfill verse 22 and could eradicate all of the elect by a violent death if that unified, transnational, worldwide persecution of believers was allowed to go on long enough.

But it will not be allowed to go on long enough. Though the political powers of the earth surround the believers on every side to destroy them as Revelation 20:9 says, Jesus will return in time to prevent such eradication. It says that Antichrist and the nations will surround the camp of the saints, just like the Romans surrounded Jerusalem, but before they can actually crush the believers, Jesus comes back and destroys them with the brightness of His coming.

This is the first reason why we say that the section in verses 15 to 22 cannot just refer to the destruction of Jerusalem in AD 70, and that it has to refer to the great tribulation that occurs in the end times just before the second coming, because the language in verse 21 and 22 cannot possibly be describing and be exhausted by what happened in AD 70. What happened in AD 70 was no greater tribulation than what happened in past history, and what happened in AD 70 could not possibly physically wipe the elect off the face of the earth through a violent death.

But there is a second reason why what is said in verses 15 to 22 is not just fulfilled in AD 70, but is a reference to what is going to happen in the end times, because immediately after the great tribulation described in verses 21 and 22, Jesus returns in verse 29 to 30.

Verses 23 to 28 do not advance the chronology of the passage. They are descriptive of the false Christs and the deceptions that surround them which will occur throughout the great tribulation period described in verses 9–14. Verses 23 to 28 are merely an expansion of verse 11. In verses 23 to 28, there is some discussion about false Christs, and people saying, "Christ is over here or Christ is over there, or Christ is in some other place." Jesus said, in effect, "Ignore all that talk. When I return, there will not be any question about where I am." This is what is discussed in verses 23 to 28, and it is not relevant to the sequence of events.

What is relevant to the sequence of events is the language of verse 21 which says, "*For then shall be great tribulation,*" and verse 22, "*those days*" of great tribulation "*shall be shortened.*" Then the same language is used in verse 29: "*Immediately after the tribulation of those days shall the sun be darkened, and the moon shall not give her light, and the stars shall fall from heaven, and the powers of the heavens shall be shaken.*" Verse 30: "*And then shall appear the sign of the Son of man in heaven: and then shall all the tribes of the earth mourn, and they shall see the Son of man coming in the clouds of heaven with power and great glory.*" Verse 31: "*And he shall send his angels with a great sound of a trumpet*" (this is the trumpet at the rapture) "*and they shall gather together his elect*" (they will be caught up to be with Jesus) "*from one end of heaven to the other.*" What follows is the final judgment, which is described in Matthew 25.

We have in verses 21 and 22 a description of the great tribulation of the end times, far greater than what happened in AD 70. Immediately after this great tribulation described in verses 21 and 22 Jesus returns in verses 29–30, showing that the events of verse 15 to 22 cannot only be referring to the fall of Jerusalem and the temple in AD 70, because clearly, Jesus did not return then. The heavens were not disrupted, Jesus was not seen, the trumpet did not sound, and the angels did not gather the elect from off the entire earth.

If the events of verses 15 to 22 are immediately followed by the return of Jesus Christ (and they are), then the events of verses 15 to 22 must be referring to things that occur in the end times, after the loosing of Satan, and not just to the events of AD 70, though they do refer to them as well.

Now we will expound verses 15 to 22. Consider how the events of verses 15 to 22 not only refer to the fall of Jerusalem and the temple in AD 70, which we have already explained, but now consider how the events of verses 15 to 22 refer to the time of great tribulation spoken of in verses 9 to 14 of this chapter after Satan is loosed for his little season.

We will use the same subheadings.

First of all, notice the sign that Jesus provides. The sign Jesus provides is in verse 15. *"When ye therefore shall see the abomination of desolation, spoken of by Daniel the prophet, stand in the holy place."* What is this referring to, with reference to the end times? We saw what it was referring to with reference to AD 70. It was talking about the Romans showing up and defiling God's temple. This sign is now talking about the Antichrist showing up and defiling God's temple.

Verse 15 is referring to what is described in 2 Thessalonians 2:3–4. Paul says in verse 2 that the day of Christ is not at hand, meaning the second coming is not at hand; it is not imminent. He tells us why in verse 3. He says, *"Let no man deceive you by any means: for that day shall not come"*—that is, the second coming spoken of in verse 1 will not happen—*"except,"* or until, *"there come a falling away first"* (that is the great apostasy of the professing church) *"and that man of sin be revealed, the son of perdition"*—that is, the Antichrist.

Notice what Antichrist does: "[4] *Who opposeth and exalteth himself above all that is called God, or that is worshipped; so that he as God sitteth in the temple of God, shewing himself that he is God."*

He is the abomination of desolation that sits in the temple during the end times. Now, what temple is this? What New Covenant temple do we have? The New Covenant temple is the church. The church collectively is the temple of God, as we are told in 1 Corinthians 3:16–17, Ephesians 2:20–22, and 1 Peter 2:5

This man of sin, this Antichrist, enters into the church and is an abomination of desolation in that church, because he is set up as the god of the Christian church, defiling that church, and declaring himself to be the head of the church. Who fits that description better than the Pope of Rome? This is why the London Baptist Confession of 1689 in 26:4 calls the Pope the Antichrist.

First John 3:18 says there have been many antichrists, but there is going to be The Antichrist who is going to be someone who claims to be a Christian, who claims to stand at the head of the church, and who in fact is an abomination of desolation because he is saying, "I am God on earth. Worship me." We already see that in incipient form in Roman Catholicism, and it is going to take place in explicit form in the last day.

The Antichrist is not going to be a Muslim sitting in a mosque. The Antichrist is going to be someone who is enthroned as the head of the worldwide Christian church. The false Christians are going to fall away and go after him. They are going to be caught up in the deception because they love their iniquity, and he will justify them in it. The true believers will not be caught up in this deception. This apostate church will then turn on the true believers at the direction of Antichrist, and begin to hate them and persecute them and kill them. Antichrist will rally all the nations of the world around himself and unify them in the hatred and persecution of the true Christians. He will be both a political leader and a religious figure in one person.

The sign Jesus provides in verse 15 is that of the Antichrist stepping into the New Covenant temple, declaring himself to be God, demanding to be worshipped, and then destroying the true believers because they will not worship him. What is restraining that from happening now? Satan is still bound. But when he is loosed, it will happen. When you see the great apostasy, and when you see the Pope standing as the head of the church universal, demanding to be worshiped as God, then you know that the end is near. You know the day of Christ is at hand. Until then, it is going to be more of Matthew 24:4–8.

Notice, secondly, the counsel Jesus gives. The counsel Jesus gives is in verses 16 to 20: *"Then let them which be in Judea flee into the mountains:* [17] *Let him which is on the housetop not come down to take any thing out of his house:* [18] *Neither let him which is in the field return back to take his clothes.* [19] *And woe unto them that are with child, and to them that give suck in those days!* [20] *But pray ye that your flight be not in the winter, neither on the sabbath day."*

When Antichrist is enthroned in the church, the New Covenant temple, and he begins to launch his transnational worldwide persecution of the believers, the Christians are going to have to flee with great urgency to wherever they can to avoid the persecution which the Antichrist and his united nations will unleash on them. This persecution is that which is spoken of in verses 9 and 10 of this chapter: *"Then shall they deliver you up to be afflicted, and shall kill you: and ye shall be hated of all nations for my name's sake.* [10] *And then shall many be offended, and shall betray one another, and shall hate one another."*

When that occurs, you have to run. When you do, you are going to lose your possessions. You are going to have to leave them behind. Many will lose their lives, and great difficulties and impediments will hinder the flight from the persecutors. You think it is tough to flee when you are pregnant or have a nursing baby, or there is snow on the ground, or it is the Sabbath day; think of how hard it will be to flee when there is electronic surveillance and infrared tracking. It is going to be very hard to flee.

Verse 21: *"For then shall be great tribulation, such as was not since the beginning of the world to this time, no, nor ever shall be."* The Christians will be persecuted in a way and to a degree they have never experienced since the foundation of the world. Have Christians been martyred or persecuted in the past? Yes, but they will be martyred and persecuted to a degree they have never known when Antichrist arises and begins to direct the united nations against the believers. Verse 22: *"And except those days should be shortened, there should no flesh be saved"* (there would be no one that would not be slaughtered), *"but for the elect's sake those days shall be shortened,"* so they cannot fully carry out their intention to its conclusion and totally eradicate every single believer from the earth.

Revelation 20:7–11 says: *"And when the thousand years are expired, Satan shall be loosed out of his prison,* [8] *And shall go out to deceive the nations which are in the four quarters of the earth, Gog and Magog, to gather them together to battle: the number of whom is as the sand of the sea."* Who are they going to fight? Verse 9a: *"And they went up on the breadth of the earth, and compassed [surrounded] the camp of the saints."* They are not going to be fighting each other. They are all going to be united. They are going to be fighting us. They are going to surround us. Wherever we are, we are going to be surrounded. All across the face of the globe, we are going to be surrounded. Perhaps we will flee into little groups, and they will surround us.

But notice verse 9b–11, ". . .*and fire came down from God out of heaven, and devoured them.* [10] *And the devil that deceived them"*—that is, all the nations that united against the Christians—*"was cast into the lake of fire and brimstone, where the beast and the false prophet are, and shall be tormented day and night for ever and ever.* [11] *And I saw a great white throne. . . ."*

God will mercifully bring this great tribulation to an end before the church is wiped off the face of the earth. He will bring it to an end by the return of Jesus. Matthew 24:30, *"And then shall appear the sign of the Son of man in heaven: and then shall all the tribes of the earth mourn."* They will go from triumphalism—"We are finally going to wipe out these Christians!"—to a soul crushing mourning. They will cry out in terror. Revelation 6:12–17 expands and explains the terror of Antichrist and his people at the second coming of Christ.

All of this is also portrayed in Revelation 11, where the two witnesses represent the church. They will preach the gospel to the whole world for a witness to all nations. When their testimony is finished, they will be attacked and overcome, but they will rise from the grave when Jesus comes back. The gospel witness is going to go out to all nations; but in the end, it will seem like the Antichrist and his united nations have triumphed over the gospel. But then they will have their "uh-oh" moment when it becomes obvious they have not, because Christ comes back, and the kingdoms of this world become the kingdoms of our God and of His Christ, and He shall reign forever and ever, and they will all be cast into the lake of fire.

The True Nature of Christ's Second Coming
Matthew 24:23–31
Chapter 4

"23 Then if any man shall say unto you, Lo, here is Christ, or there; believe it not. 24 For there shall arise false Christs, and false prophets, and shall shew great signs and wonders; insomuch that, if it were possible, they shall deceive the very elect.
25 Behold, I have told you before. 26 Wherefore if they shall say unto you, Behold, he is in the desert; go not forth: behold, he is in the secret chambers; believe it not. 27 For as the lightning cometh out of the east, and shineth even unto the west; so shall also the coming of the Son of man be. 28 For wheresoever the carcass is, there will the eagles be gathered together. 29 Immediately after the tribulation of those days shall the sun be darkened, and the moon shall not give her light, and the stars shall fall from heaven, and the powers of the heavens shall be shaken: 30 And then shall appear the sign of the Son of man in heaven: and then shall all the tribes of the earth mourn, and they shall see the Son of man coming in the clouds of heaven with power and great glory. 31 And he shall send his angels with a great sound of a trumpet, and they shall gather together his elect from the four winds, from one end of heaven to the other."

In our previous studies of Matthew 24, we have seen that Jesus predicted the destruction of Jerusalem and the temple, and this provoked three questions from the disciples: When will the temple be destroyed? What will be the sign of Your coming? What will be the sign of the end of the world?

Jesus answered the last question first: What will be the sign of the end of the world? Jesus told His disciples in verses 4 to 8 what would not be the sign of the end of the world. He told them there would be a long period of great religious deception, great political turmoil, and great natural disasters. These things would be the norm for the vast majority of the age to come, and none of them were signs of the end of the world.

Jesus then told His disciples in verses 9 to 14 what the signs of the end of the world would be. There would be a much shorter period in the end time in which Satan would be loosed. This loosing of Satan would begin the great tribulation and cause several events to be set into motion. Antichrist would arise and deceive many through his false prophets. This would result in a great apostasy from the Christian faith by those who claimed to be Christians, but who really were not. They would then begin to hate and betray the faithful Christians, and would lose any love they ever had for them.

The Antichrist will raise up a coordinated, unified, transnational program of persecution and murder of the faithful believers. They will be hated by all nations. In spite of this, they will still continue to preach the gospel in all the world until they are martyred or until Jesus comes. Just when it seems that all the believers are going to be wiped off the face of the earth by the Antichrist, and this transnational persecution of the believers is going to succeed, then the end of the world will come.

In the last chapter, we looked at verses 15 to 22, where Jesus answered the first question that was asked in verse 3: When will the temple be destroyed? He told them in verse 15 the sign they were to look for would be the abomination of desolation coming and standing in the holy place. This abomination of desolation would occur when ungodly men come to defile the temple.

This prophetic statement of Jesus in verse 15 about the coming abomination of desolation standing in the temple was fulfilled in the desecration of the temple in AD 70 by the Roman legions. This statement of Jesus was also a foreshadowing of the desecration of the New Covenant temple (the church) by the Antichrist in the end times. The Antichrist is the abomination of desolation that will stand in the church, claiming to be God, demanding to be worshiped as God, and thereby defiling the church.

In verses 15 to 22, we have a description of both the events of AD 70 and the events of the end times. The events of AD 70 simply foreshadow the events of the end times. When the Antichrist sits as the head of the Christian church around the world, proclaiming himself to be God and demanding to be worshiped as God as 2 Thessalonians 2:4 says, he will institute the severest persecution the world has ever known against the Christians who refuse to give him the worship he demands. If that persecution the Antichrist perpetrates against the true believers were allowed to go on for very long, all of God's elect all over the world would be killed. But God will not allow that, and He will cut off that persecution by the second coming of Jesus Christ.

This brings us to verses 23 to 31, in which Jesus addresses and answers the second question the disciples ask in verse 3, which is this: What will be the sign of Your coming? In verses 4 to 14, He answered the question "What will be the sign of the end of the world?" In verses 15 to 22, He answered the question "What will be the sign of the destruction of the temple?" Now in verses 23 to 31, He is going to answer the question "What will be the sign of Your second coming?"

The Warning Against False Understandings Regarding the Second Coming

These warnings that Jesus gives against false understandings regarding the second coming are found in verses 23 to 28. *"Then if any man shall say unto you, Lo, here is Christ, or there; believe it not.*
24 For there shall arise false Christs, and false prophets, and shall shew great signs and wonders; insomuch that, if it were possible, they shall deceive the very elect. *25 Behold, I have told you before"* (ahead of time is the idea). *"26 Wherefore if they shall say unto you, Behold, he is in the desert; go not forth: behold, he is in the secret chambers; believe it not.* *27 For as the lightning cometh out of the east, and shineth even unto the west; so shall also the coming of the Son of man be.* *28 For wheresoever the carcass is, there will the eagles be gathered together."* Jesus is saying, "Let no man deceive you about the nature of My second coming." Deceptions regarding the second coming will be rampant, and Jesus warns the disciples against those deceptions.

To combat those deceptions, let us review and summarize the true nature of the second coming for a moment.

The background to the second coming is the great tribulation. Recall verses 21 and 22: *"For then shall be great tribulation, such as was not since the beginning of the world to this time, no, nor ever shall be.*
22 And except those days should be shortened, there should no flesh be saved: but for the elect's sake those days shall be shortened."

These verses speak of horrific and unprecedented persecution and killing of Christians, at a level and to a degree the world has never seen since the day of creation. That is why it is called the *"great trib-*

ulation," because it is greater than any tribulation that believers have ever experienced prior to this time.

This great persecution against believers will be perpetrated by the Antichrist, who is the abomination of desolation standing at the head of the professing Christian church. He will be coordinating the united nations of the world in a transnational assault against the Christians. This assault against the Christians coordinated by the Antichrist will be so well executed, so unified, and so comprehensive that verse 22 says that if it were allowed to go on very long, then no saved person—that is, none of God's elect—would be saved alive.

However, that effort to kill all the Christians will be cut off and cut short by the second coming of Christ, so that Antichrist will not achieve his goal of total eradication of true Christians from the face of the earth. We saw this in Revelation 20. At the end of this long period of protection described in Matthew 24:4–8 when Satan is bound, Satan is then loosed.

In Revelation 20:7–9 it says: *"And when the thousand years are expired, Satan shall be loosed out of his prison, [8] And shall go out to deceive the nations which are in the four quarters of the earth, Gog and Magog, to gather them together to battle: the number of whom is as the sand of the sea. [9] And they went up on the breadth of the earth, and compassed [surrounded] the camp of the saints."* For what purpose? In order to kill them.

But notice what happens, verse 9: *"And fire came down from God out of heaven, and devoured them."* This is the cutting short that Matthew 24:22 is talking about: *"Except those days should be shortened, there should no flesh be saved: but for the elect's sake those days shall be shortened,"* or ended, or cut off. And what is going to cut them off? The fire that comes down out of heaven is going to destroy Antichrist and all of his followers. What is this fire? It is Christ returning in time to prevent the eradication of all the believers from the earth. Notice several passages that describe the second coming of Christ with fire.

In 2 Thessalonians 1, notice verses 7 and 8: *"And to you who are troubled rest with us, when the Lord Jesus shall be revealed from heaven with his mighty angels"*—here it is—*"[8] In flaming fire taking vengeance on them that know not God, and that obey not the gospel of our Lord Jesus Christ."* That is the fire of Revelation 20:9. Second Thessalonians 1:9 says, *"Who shall be punished with everlasting de-*

struction from the presence of the Lord, and from the glory of his power." This is what Revelation 20:10 is speaking of when it says they will all be cast into the lake of fire. Notice also 2 Thessalonians 2:8. *"And then shall that Wicked [One] be revealed"*—that is, the Antichrist—*"whom the Lord shall consume with the spirit of his mouth, and shall destroy with the brightness of his coming."*

So we have this language of Christ coming with fire and brightness and all of His glory in 2 Thessalonians 1 and 2, in Revelation 20, and in Matthew 24, demonstrating that all of these passages are speaking about the same event.

The cutting short of the great tribulation described in Matthew 24:21 is brought to pass by the second coming of Christ with His flaming fire that is going to burn up these people who have surrounded the believers in order to finish their slaughter.

Notice Matthew 24:29–30: *"Immediately after the tribulation of those days."* Tribulation of what days? The tribulation of verse 21–22. Verse 21–22 states that there shall be great tribulation, and those days will be cut short. How will they be cut short? Verse 29 states: *"Immediately after the tribulation of those days shall the sun be darkened, and the moon shall not give her light, and the stars shall fall from heaven, and the powers of the heavens shall be shaken: [30] And then shall appear the sign of the Son of man in heaven: and then shall all the tribes of the earth mourn, and they shall see the Son of man coming in the clouds of heaven with power and great glory."*

At the end of the tribulation, when the time comes to cut it short, Jesus is going to return. The believers in that day who are going through this great tribulation are going to understand the sequence of events we are talking about. They will know they are in the great tribulation because they will see the Antichrist. They will see and experience the great apostasy of those that they thought were their brethren, and they will experience the coordinated transnational persecution of Christians over the whole world from all nations.

Therefore, they will be looking for and expecting the second coming. The signs of the second coming will all be present for those that are in the great tribulation, and therefore they will know that the second coming of Christ is imminent. The second coming of Christ is not imminent today. We are not in the great tribulation. Antichrist has not been revealed. The great apostasy has not happened. The coordinated worldwide persecution of Christians among all nations has not occurred. Therefore, we know Jesus is not coming yet. But when all those things do happen and all those signs do occur, then they will know He is coming. Then, He could return any second.

However, there will be a great danger to the believers at that point in time. Believers will desperately long to see Christ return to deliver them from this terrible persecution they are under during the great tribulation. They rightly understand He could return at any moment. The false prophets will take advantage of this desire believers have to see Christ's return, and try to lead them into believing that someone other than Christ is in fact Christ, and that Christ has already returned, when in fact, the true Christ has not yet returned.

This review brings us back to our text in Matthew 24:23–28.

Notice verse 23: *"Then. . ."* Here you are. You are in the great tribulation, and it looks like all the Christians are going to be martyred. Then people are going to appear who say, "Jesus has come back!" Verse 23: *"Then if any man shall say unto you, Lo, here is Christ, or there; believe it not."* During the great tribulation, there will be those who say Christ has recently returned, His return is secret, and He is located in this or that place. Jesus says, "Do not believe those deceivers."

Notice verse 24: *"For there shall arise false Christs, and false prophets, and shall shew great signs and wonders; insomuch that, if it were possible, they shall deceive the very elect."* Some of these deceivers will claim to be Christ, some will claim to be prophets of these false Christs, and these false Christs and these false prophets will be able to do tremendous signs and wonders—amazing miracles done by the power of Satan to attempt to validate their claims. They will be like Pharaoh's magicians in Exodus 7 and 8 who were able to do miracles to attempt to deceive Pharaoh into believing they were the true prophets of God, and not Moses.

These amazing miracles and signs and wonders done by these false Christs and false prophets will be so powerful and persuasive and convincing that they would deceive even the elect, if that were possible. But it is not possible. Verse 24 states: *"For there shall arise false Christs, and false prophets, and shall shew great signs and wonders; insomuch that, if it were possible"* (and the clear implication is that it is not possible), they could *"deceive the. . .elect,"* who have continued to remain faithful, and have not yet gone after Antichrist.

The problem is that when people say that Jesus Christ has come back, and they are in the midst of tribulation, they are going to want to believe it, because they are getting hammered so hard with persecution while they are waiting for His coming. Therefore, when somebody says, "Christ is over here," he is going to want to run there. Jesus said, "No, that is a false Christ, that is a false understanding of the nature of My second coming and the revelation I will make of Myself when I do come."

Philippians 1:6 states how we are *"confident of this very thing, that he which hath begun a good work in you will perform it until the day of Jesus Christ."* Therefore, Jesus is not going to lose any of His disciples to the deception of these false prophets, even though these false prophets are going to be very persuasive. They are going to be able to do incredible miracles, real ones, just like Pharaoh's magicians did real miracles by the power of Satan. Jesus says that they are going to be so good, and so real, and so convincing, that if it were possible, the elect will be deceived. But they will not be deceived, because they cannot be deceived. Jesus will preserve them from deception by His grace and by giving them perception and discernment about the true nature of these miracles. What an incredible comfort that is to us, to know that God will preserve us from this final deception.

Satan loses his people to Christ, but Christ never loses any of His people to Satan. It says in John 10:4–5, 27–29, *"And when He putteth forth his own sheep, He goeth before them, and the sheep follow Him: for they know His voice. [5]And a stranger will they not follow, but will flee from him, for they know not the voice of strangers. [27]My sheep hear my voice, and I know them, and they follow me: [28]And I give unto them eternal life; and they shall never perish, neither shall any man pluck them out of my hand. [29]My Father, which gave them me, is greater than all; and no man is able to pluck them out of my Father's hand."*

It is not possible that any saved person would ever be deceived into following a false Christ, irrespective of the degree of persuasiveness of the messenger, because Jesus is not going to let him go; and we are not going to hear that voice, because it does not sound like the voice of Jesus.

True Christians always listen to the voice of Scripture over the voice of signs and wonders.

Matthew 24:25: *"Behold, I have told you before"*—that is, "ahead of time." Jesus warns of these false prophets and these false Christs ahead of time so that disciples would be forewarned. Jesus was always doing this for His disciples. In John 13:19, He says, *"Now I tell you before it come, that, when it is come to pass, ye may believe that I am he."* He is telling them ahead of time about Judas's betrayal. In John 14:29, Jesus says, *"And now I have told you before it come to pass, that, when it is come to pass, ye might believe."* In John 16:4, He says, *"But these things have I told you, that when the time shall come, ye may remember that I told you of them."*

Jesus is saying, "This is what the future holds. I do not want you to be deceived, so that when it happens, you will remember that I forewarned you and told you this was going to occur. When you remember that, then you will believe that I really am the true Messiah. Your faith will be strengthened all over again."

When those who are going through the great tribulation are getting persecuted by Antichrist and his people, and these false prophets are pointing to these false Christs and doing miracles, the people of God are going to say, "Jesus warned us about this. We are not going to believe it, and the fact that Jesus warned us about this, and told us that this is exactly the way it was going to occur, just reaffirms our faith in Him even more."

Instead of these false prophets pulling these people away from Christ, they actually make them believe in Christ even more. That is why we do not have to worry about false prophets, even today. They never draw away true believers. It is not possible to deceive them. All it does is strengthen the real believers to investigate their faith a little more and become even more solidified in it. The wicked only drive the righteous closer to Christ. That is why they are on the losing team, and all their efforts are counterproductive to their cause.

When the deception arises, the disciples going through the great tribulation are forewarned and forearmed, and therefore they will not be seduced. Notice verse 26: *"Wherefore if they shall say unto you, Behold, he is in the desert; go not forth: behold, he is in the secret chambers; believe it not."* Jesus will not be found—not in some desert wilderness, nor will He be hidden in some room in a city somewhere; rather, verse 27 says, *"For as the lightning cometh out of the east, and shineth even unto the west; so shall also the coming of the Son of man be."* Jesus tells them in verse 27 that not only will you not have to go somewhere to find Christ, but that Christ will come in such a fashion that you cannot possibly avoid

Him. You do not need to go find Him; He will find you.

Revelation 1:7 says, *"Every eye shall see him."* If you have ever been in a lightning storm, even if you have your eyes closed, when the lightning bolt goes off, it shines right through your eyelids. You cannot help but see it, even if you do not want to see it. When it goes off and flashes across the sky, everyone under that sky sees it. No one says, "I did not see that." Everybody says, "Oh, look at the lightning!"

That is how Jesus is going to come. Jesus is going to come in such a dramatic fashion that every single person, without exception, will know this is Jesus, and that He has come. He will come with all the subtlety of a lightning bolt.

Notice verse 28: *"For wheresoever the carcass is, there will the eagles be gathered together."* Just as carrion-eating birds gather to consume the dead and corrupt animals, so God's wrath is going to fall upon this spiritually dead and corrupt world. God's wrath, personified by these vultures, is going to come upon this spiritually dead and corrupt world and consume it and destroy it.

There is an expanded description of this event in Revelation 19:11–21. *"And I saw heaven opened, and behold a white horse; and he that sat upon him was called Faithful and True, and in righteousness he doth judge and make war."* This is the second coming of Jesus. Notice verse 17: *"And I saw an angel standing in the sun; and he cried with a loud voice, saying to all the fowls that fly in the midst of heaven, Come and gather yourselves together unto the supper of the great God;* 18 *That ye may eat the flesh of kings, and the flesh of captains, and the flesh of mighty men, and the flesh of horses, and of them that sit on them, and the flesh of all men, both free and bond, both small and great.* 19 *And I saw the beast, and the kings of the earth, and their armies, gathered together to make war against him that sat on the horse, and against his army."* They are all gathered together against the Christians, Jesus comes back, and they think they are going to fight with Jesus. 20 *And the beast was taken, and with him the false prophet that wrought miracles before him, with which he deceived them that had received the mark of the beast, and them that worshipped his image. These both were cast alive into a lake of fire burning with brimstone."* (Revelation 20:10 records the same event.) "21 *And the remnant were slain with the sword of him that sat upon the horse, which sword proceeded out of his mouth: and all the fowls were filled with their flesh."*

This is the extended description of Matthew 24:28. When Jesus comes back, there is going to be a huge slaughter, He is going to destroy them with fire, and the vultures are going to devour the wicked. We are told in the Old Testament that when the iniquity of the Amorites was finally full, God sent Israel to wipe them out. In the same way, when the iniquity of this world finally becomes full by the unified persecution of Christians by its people, God is going to come and wipe them out.

The Declaration of the True Nature of the Second Coming

Jesus has just warned His disciples about false notions regarding His second coming, and now He talks about the true nature of the second coming in verses 29 to 31. Notice verse 29a: *"Immediately after the tribulation of those days"* Jesus is coming back.

The timing of the second coming is clear. It occurs at the end of the great tribulation. When the earth is drenched with the blood of the saints in the most terrible tribulation and persecution of all time, then Christ will come. Notice He does not give us a date, He gives us a sign. We do not know when that sign is going to happen, but when it does, we know that Christ's coming is very, very near.

Notice the sign that is going to attend the second coming, verse 29. *"Immediately after the tribulation of those days,"* the stellar heavens are going to be dismantled and destroyed. Notice: *"Immediately after the tribulation of those days shall the sun be darkened, and the moon shall not give her light, and the stars shall fall from heaven, and the powers of the heavens shall be shaken."*

When it is time for Jesus to come back, the universe starts literally physically falling apart. The sun goes out, the moon goes out, and stars start collapsing and falling. The constellations are not there anymore. This is clearly spoken of in 2 Peter 3:3–13. Peter says: *"Knowing this first, that there shall come in the last days scoffers, walking after their own lusts,* [4] *And saying, Where is the promise of his coming?"*—the coming of Christ—*"for since the fathers fell asleep, all things continue as they were from the beginning of the creation* [5] *For this they willingly are ignorant of, that by the word of God the heavens were of old, and the earth standing out of the water and in the water:* [6] *Whereby the world that then was, being overflowed with water, perished."*

In other words, there has been a worldwide judgment before. It used to be that the land stood out of the water, and the water stayed in the oceans. But then there was a worldwide catastrophe. It was the flood. The whole world overflowed with water. Therefore, there is a precedent for the world being destroyed a second time, because the world had already been destroyed the first time by the flood. It was not destroyed in the sense that it was annihilated, but in the sense that it was completely ruined, and then reemerged after the flood in a different form than it had before in terms of its geography and climate.

Verses 6–7: *"Whereby the world that then was, being overflowed with water, perished:* [7] *But the heavens and the earth, which are now, by the same word are kept in store, reserved unto fire against the day of judgment and perdition of ungodly men."* The first time the world was destroyed by water, but the second time it will be destroyed by fire.

Verse 8: *"But, beloved, be not ignorant of this one thing, that one day is with the Lord as a thousand years, and a thousand years as one day."* In other words, this millennial period we are in now is relative; it is not absolute. It is a fixed period, but it cannot be measured literally. Second Peter 3:8 is the one other place beside Revelation 20 that the millennium is described by the symbolic term *"a thousand years."*

Verse 9: *"The Lord is not slack concerning his promise"* (to return), *"as some men count slackness; but is longsuffering toward us, not willing that any"* (of us; that is, any of us elect) *"should perish, but that all"* (of us) *"should come to repentance."* In other words, why has Jesus not come back for 2,000 years? Because He is saving His elect. It is not that He is slack concerning His promise about coming back. We are now in this period of Matthew 24:4–8, in which He is saving His elect. He has Satan bound. The gospel is spreading throughout the world. The church is being built. This metaphorical thousand-year period will continue until all of God's elect are saved, so that none of them perish.

Verse 10: *"But the day of the Lord will come as a thief in the night."* It will come as a thief in the night to the unsaved, but not to us. We will know when it is coming, but they will not know. The reason we will know is that we know the signs of His coming, but they do not. It says in 1 Thessalonians 5:1–4 that the day of Christ's return will not overtake you as a thief. It will overtake the world as a thief, but it will not overtake you that way. You will know. We will see this as we progress further through Matthew 24.

He says in verse 10, *"But the day of the Lord will come as a thief in the night;"* (to the wicked) *"in the which the heavens shall pass away with a great noise"* (Matthew 24:29), *"and the elements shall melt with fervent heat, the earth also and the works that are therein shall be burned up."* Jesus is coming back with flaming fire to take vengeance on those who do not obey the gospel.

Verse 11, *"Seeing then that all these things shall be dissolved"* (described in Matthew 24:29), *"what manner of persons ought ye to be in all holy conversation and godliness,* 12 *Looking for and hasting unto the coming of the day of God, wherein the heavens being on fire shall be dissolved, and the elements shall melt with fervent heat?* 13 *Nevertheless we, according to his promise, look for new heavens and a new earth, wherein dwelleth righteousness."*

When Jesus comes back, He is going to dismantle the stellar heavens, He is going to burn up the earth, and then He is going to recreate them both, and there is going to be a new heaven and a new earth. It is all going to happen at the second coming. There is no place for a literal thousand-year period after the second coming. When the second coming occurs, everything is wrecked, everything is rebuilt, and we are in the eternal state of the new heavens and the new earth. When is the thousand years spoken of taking place? It is taking place when the period of salvation is going on. A thousand years is as a day, and a day as a thousand years, but when is that spoken of? It is spoken of before the day of the Lord when Jesus returns. The symbolic thousand years is a time period during which God is patiently putting up with the wickedness of the world in order to save His elect.

In Matthew 24:29 it says: *"Immediately after the tribulation of those days shall the sun be darkened, and the moon shall not give her light, and the stars shall fall from heaven, and the powers of the heavens shall be shaken:"* (described in 2 Peter 3:3–13). Notice the second thing that is going to happen, verse 30: *"And then shall appear the sign of the Son of man in heaven: and then shall all the tribes of the earth mourn, and they shall see the Son of man coming in the clouds of heaven with power and great glory."*

The sign of the Son of man in heaven is simply the brilliant self-manifestation of Christ Himself in His unveiled glory, coming in the clouds of heaven with power and great glory, as described in Revelation 19 and other passages. When Jesus was here, His glory was veiled. But when He was on the Mount of Transfiguration, His face shone like the sun, and the disciples had to fall on their faces. The Mount of Transfiguration is a preview of the second coming and the kingdom of God. Who was there? Moses and Elijah. Moses pictured those who died while they were on earth; Elijah pictured those who were caught up alive from the earth at the rapture. Each represented one of two groups: those in Christ who had died, and those in Christ who did not die but were instantly transformed and caught up to heaven.

Christ's brilliant self-manifestation in the sky will be the sign He is about to descend to meet His people, who arise to meet Him in the air. All who oppose Christ will see Him like a flash of lightning across the heaven, and knowing what is going to happen to them, they will start weeping and wailing. Notice it says in verse 30, *"and then shall all the tribes of the earth mourn"* when *"they shall see the Son of man coming in the clouds of heaven with power and great glory."*

Revelation 6:12–17 expands on this as well. *"And I beheld when he had opened the sixth seal, and, lo, there was a great earthquake; and the sun became black as sackcloth of hair, and the moon became as blood.* [13] *And the stars of heaven fell unto the earth, even as a fig tree casteth her untimely figs, when she is shaken of a mighty wind.* [14] *And the heaven departed as a scroll when it is rolled together; and every mountain and island were moved out of their places."* This is Matthew 24:29. "[15] *And the kings of the earth, and the great men, and the rich men, and the chief captains, and the mighty men, and every bondman, and every free man"* (these are all the people who are gathered together to persecute the believers) *"hid themselves in the dens and in the rocks of the mountains;* [16] *And said to the mountains and rocks, Fall on us, and hide us from the face of him that sitteth on the throne, and from the wrath of the Lamb:* [17] *For the great day of his wrath is come; and who shall be able to stand?"* That describes the mourning that Matthew 24:30 is speaking of: *"and then shall all the tribes of the earth mourn, and they shall see the Son of man coming in the clouds."* Revelation 6:15–17 describes that mourning.

Now verse 31: *"And he shall send his angels with a great sound of a trumpet, and they shall gather together his elect from the four winds, from one end of heaven to the other."*

The rapture will be accomplished by means of angelic activity. The angels are going to come and lay hold of the believers and take them up. The angels will carry us up to meet the Savior in the air when the trumpet sounds.

The second coming of Christ will not only be seen as this brilliant display in the heavens, but it will also be heard. There will be the blast of a great trumpet. The sound is like the blast of the military trumpet. In the military, when the time came to charge, they would blow the trumpet and all the troops would charge into battle. This trumpet sound mentioned in verse 31 is the battle blast of Jesus coming to do His work of conquering and defeating Satan, the Antichrist, the False Prophet, and all their followers.

When you hear the blast, Jesus is coming! He is bringing His angels. The world is done. The few remaining believers are being assaulted by the nations, and then, suddenly, Jesus and His angels appear to rescue the believers and crush their persecutors.

What is described in Matthew 24:31 is also described in two other passages as well. First Thessalonians 4:13–17 is the famous rapture passage. "*But I would not have you to be ignorant, brethren, concerning them which are asleep, that ye sorrow not, even as others which have no hope.* [14] *For if we believe that Jesus died and rose again, even so them also which sleep in Jesus will God bring with him.*" Those are our brethren who have died. They are already in heaven with Jesus. He is bringing them back with Him.

"[15] *For this we say unto you by the word of the Lord, that we which are alive and remain unto the coming of the Lord shall not prevent [precede, go ahead of] them which are asleep.*" We who have lived through that great tribulation shall not go to heaven ahead of those who have previously died. "[16] *For the Lord himself shall descend from heaven with a shout, with the voice of the archangel, and with the trump of God:*" (here is the trumpet of Matthew 24:31) "*and the dead in Christ shall rise first:* [17] *Then we which are alive and remain shall be caught up together with them in the clouds, to meet the Lord in the air: and so shall we ever be with the Lord.*" Once again, this catching up will be done by the angels.

The trumpet is going to sound, and the souls that have previously gone to heaven at their death are going to come back from heaven with Jesus. Their bodies are going to rise from the grave, their souls will inhabit their resurrected bodies, and then we who are alive and remain will be transformed in body and soul as they are, and then together, as glorified people, we will all be caught up by the angels to be with Jesus and accompany Him as He comes in His great cavalry charge to conquer the world.

This sounding of the trumpet is also spoken of in 1 Corinthians 15:51–54. Paul says in verse 51, *"Behold, I shew you a mystery; We shall not all sleep,"* (we are not all going to die) *"but we shall all be changed"* (transformed). Verse 52: *"In a moment, in the twinkling of an eye,"* (notice) *"at the last trump: for the trumpet shall sound, and the dead shall be raised incorruptible, and we shall be changed.* [53] *For this corruptible must put on incorruption, and this mortal must put on immortality.* [54] *So when this corruptible shall have put on incorruption, and this mortal shall have put on immortality, then shall be brought to pass the saying that is written, Death is swallowed up in victory."*

Death is going to be swallowed up in victory at the second coming. Right now, death still has victory over the bodies of the saved. They are still lying in the grave. But death is going to be defeated, those bodies are going to rise, and victory over death will be fully realized and experienced. Victory over death has been fully procured at the cross, but it will be fully applied when Jesus returns.

Notice 2 Thessalonians 2:1, *"Now we beseech you, brethren, by the coming of our Lord Jesus Christ"* (Matthew 24:30) *"and by our gathering together unto him"* (Matthew 24:31). The sequence is the same: Christ comes back, and then we go to meet Him. There is no trumpet in this text, but there is a trumpet in Matthew 24:31, there is a trumpet in 1 Thessalonians 4:13 to 17, and there is a trumpet in 1 Corinthians 15:51 to 54.

Clearly, all of these passages are talking about the same event. There is going to be a long period of protection while Satan is bound. In the end times, he is going to be loosed, Antichrist is going to rise, he is going to gather the nations and all the apostate believers, and they are going to go to war against the Christians. But when it looks like they are going to completely wipe them out, Jesus will come back to rescue them and destroy their enemies.

When He comes back, there is going to be this disruption of the universe; there is going to be an appearance of Christ in heaven that no one will be able to deny. The people on the earth are going to go into mourning and try to hide from the face of the Lamb who is coming back. The angels are going to come and pick up the glorified believers, and then Christ will take vengeance on the wicked with flaming fire. We read in Revelation 20:9 that they shall be destroyed with fire from heaven.

The question is this: Are you ready to meet Jesus when He comes back? He is coming back at the end of the age as we have described, but He is also coming back for every person when he dies, and each person will either meet Him as a Savior or as a Judge.

It is imperative for us that we are faithful under persecution now because the persecution we receive now is light affliction. It is just the beginning of sorrows. The real persecution is coming when Satan is loosed and Antichrist appears. Could that happen in our lifetime? Yes. Satan could be loosed today. Antichrist could show up tomorrow. The great tribulation could start next month. Or, all of this could be centuries down the road. No one knows for sure when it will happen.

You could be in the great tribulation. You could be alive when Jesus comes. Some things have to happen before that is a possibility, but it could happen in your lifetime. Are you ready? Are you enduring persecution now instead of compromising, so that when the real persecution comes, you are not going to fall away? If we cannot stand the little bit of persecution we are getting now, how are we going to stand the tremendous persecution we are going to get then?

Stand firm for Christ now. When you are persecuted now, do not let it change you, do not let it defeat you, do not let it discourage you, do not give up and quit in the midst of it. Stand up, press forward, and fight on. As Paul says to Timothy, *"Endure hardness as a good soldier of Jesus Christ,"* because the hardness we have now is nothing compared to what it is going to be.

The good news is that when the real hardness comes, when the great tribulation does occur, God will be there to give us the grace and strength to go through it. Not one of us will be lost in it if we are truly saved people. Do you know how to find out who the truly saved people are? Watch them under severe persecution, and you will find out those who are going to turn back and turn away; and those who are going to lay down their life for Him, who laid down His life for them.

Let us understand these things and prepare our hearts for them so that if and when they occur in our lifetimes, we will be ready. When it comes, it is going to unfold quickly. We do not know how long it is going to last, but certainly not more than a generation. Jesus says the generation that sees these signs of the great tribulation will not pass before He comes back. So whether it is going to be a few years, or whether it is going to be twenty years, we do not know. But it will certainly be less than a generation from start to finish. A generation in the Bible is forty years. Whether it lasts that long, we do not know. Jesus says He is going to cut it short. We pray that He will cut it very short, but that is up to Him.

The Generation Who Sees the Second Coming
Matthew 24:32–41
Chapter 5

> "32 *Now learn a parable of the fig tree; When his branch is yet tender, and putteth forth leaves, ye know that summer is [near]:* 33 *So likewise ye, when ye shall see all these things, know that it is near, even at the doors.* 34 *Verily I say unto you, This generation shall not pass, till all these things be fulfilled.* 35 *Heaven and earth shall pass away, but my words shall not pass away.* 36 *But of that day and hour knoweth no man, no, not the angels of heaven, but my Father only.* 37 *But as the days of Noah were, so shall also the coming of the Son of man be.* 38 *For as in the days that were before the flood they were eating and drinking, marrying and giving in marriage, until the day that Noah entered into the ark,* 39 *And knew not until the flood came, and took them all away; so shall also the coming of the Son of man be.* 40 *Then shall two be in the field; the one shall be taken, and the other left.* 41 *Two women shall be grinding at the mill; the one shall be taken, and the other left."*

Jesus told His disciples about the impending destruction of the temple in Jerusalem in verses 1 and 2, in which He said there would not be one stone left on top of another. This startling prediction on the part of Jesus provoked three questions from His disciples. When will the temple be destroyed? What will be the sign of Your coming? What will be the sign of the end of the world? Jesus answered these three questions in His subsequent discourse in verses 4 to 31, but He did not answer them in the order in which they were asked.

In verses 4 to14, Jesus first answered the third question—What shall be the sign of the end of the world? In verses 4 to 8, Jesus said that there would be a long period of great religious deception, great political turmoil, and great natural disasters, but none of those things were the signs of the end.

However, in verses 9 to 14, Jesus did describe the signs of the end. He said that the great tribulation would immediately precede the end of the world. He said it would be marked by worldwide transnational persecution of Christians led by the Antichrist, and by a tremendous apostasy of professing Christians who would be deceived by false prophets, who would practice iniquity, and who would cease to have any love for the true believers. However, this persecution by the nations and this betrayal by their fellow Christians would not silence the witness of the believers. They would endure in faithfulness to Christ until the end, and they would continue to preach the gospel to the whole world. Once these things were accomplished, verse 14 tells us that the end would come.

Jesus then proceeded in verses 15 to 22 to answer the first question—When will the temple be destroyed? Jesus does not give them a date for the destruction of the temple. Instead, He gives them a sign—verse 15. Jesus tells them the sign of the imminent destruction of the temple is the abomination of desolation spoken of by Daniel the prophet, when evil men will come into the land in order to enter the temple and defile it. Jesus goes on in verses 16 to 22 to tell them the danger and the difficulty those days will entail, and how they could escape from this great tribulation.

The words of Jesus in verses 15 to 22 had a double reference. They were fulfilled in AD 70, when Rome came and destroyed the temple and scattered the Jews. But that fulfillment was also a foreshadow of the time when Antichrist will enter the temple of the church and defile it by setting himself up as God in it. Therefore, verses 15 to 22 also describe the great tribulation during the end times that was first explained in verses 9 to 14.

Jesus then proceeded in verses 23 to 31 to answer the second question—What will be the sign of Your coming? Jesus made it clear in verses 23 to 31 what would not be the sign of His second coming, when He told them in verses 23 to 26 that His coming would not be secret, hidden, or clandestine. Instead, He said His coming will be as obvious and as universally known by all men as a bolt of lightning is obvious and universally seen by all who are witness to a thunderstorm.

Furthermore, not only will His second coming be universally obvious to everyone on the face of the earth, but verse 29 tells us that it will occur immediately after the great tribulation described in verses 15 to 22. The signs of Christ's coming are set forth in verses 29–31. We are told that the heavens will be shaken, the sun and the stars will be darkened and removed, and then Jesus will visibly appear in the heavens, the trumpet of God will sound, the angels will gather God's elect from off the whole earth and bring them up to Christ, and they will return with Him in victory and triumph to the earth. All the people of the earth who have rebelled against Him and persecuted His people will be seized with terror, and all of them will be destroyed in flaming fire.

This concludes Christ's answers to the disciples' three questions that they ask in verse 3. Question number three—What will be the sign of the end of the world?—was answered in verses 4 to 14. Question number one—What will be the sign of the destruction of the temple?—was answered in verses 15 to 22. Question number two—What will be the sign of Your second coming?—was answered in verses 23 to 31.

But Jesus is not done yet. In verses 32 to 41, He wants to further clarify two matters, one of which is the indicators of His second coming, and the second of which is the order in which He will deal with the wicked and the righteous when He returns.

Believers Will Be Anticipating the Second Coming of Christ

Verse 32: "*Now learn a parable of the fig tree; When his branch is yet tender, and putteth forth leaves, ye know that summer is nigh:* [33] *So likewise ye, when ye shall see all these things, know that it is near, even at the doors.* [34] *Verily I say unto you, This generation shall not pass, till all these things be fulfilled.* [35] *Heaven and earth shall pass away, but my words shall not pass away.* [36] *But of that day and hour knoweth no man, no, not the angels of heaven, but my Father only.*"

One of the constant problems that have plagued the Christian church is that of the errors regarding both the nature of the second coming and the timing of the second coming. There are two particular errors that are current in our day regarding the nature and timing of the second coming, and both of these grow out of Dispensationalism.

The first error is that the second coming of Christ is imminent—that is, the second coming of Christ could occur at any moment. The rapture is said to be possible in the next split second; nothing needs to be fulfilled before it could occur.

A second error is that the coming of Christ will be like a thief in the night—that is, it will take us completely by surprise because we will have no indication before it occurs. Believers will be as surprised as anyone else when the rapture occurs.

There is also a third error that has plagued the church for centuries not related to Dispensationalism, which is declaring that upon some particular date, Jesus will come again. This error is not one that is peculiar to our day, but it is certainly present in our day. Date setting is something that people never seem to learn not to do.

Verses 32 to 36 address these three errors. In these verses, Jesus makes it clear that we know some things, and the things we know prevent us from thinking that the second coming is imminent, they prevent us from thinking that it will be a surprise when it occurs, and they prevent us from thinking that we would ever possibly know the date.

In the first place, notice the illustration given. There is an illustration given in verse 32 when Jesus says, *"Now learn a parable of the fig tree; When his branch is yet tender, and putteth forth leaves, ye know that summer is nigh."*

There are some things we can know for sure. We all know that trees bud in the spring as winter ends and as summer approaches. It can be cold and raining in the spring and the wind can be blowing, but if you see the buds on the trees start to swell up and prepare to burst and bring forth leaves, then you know something. You know that summer is imminent. It is just around the corner. It will come really soon. You may not know the exact date that the weather turns and summer actually arrives, but you do know one thing: you know it is close, and you know it is very close. That is the illustration given in verse 32.

Secondly, notice the explanation given in verse 33. *"So likewise"* (in the same manner), *"ye, when ye shall see all these things,"* you will *"know."* You will *"know that it is near, even at the doors."* When you see all of the signs He has been talking about in the previous 31 verses (*"all these things"*), you *"know"* that the second coming is imminent. In verses 4 to 31, Jesus has given us numerous signs as to when the second coming is going to occur. What are those signs? We know what they are not. They are not the things mentioned in verses 4 to 8. Great religious deception, great political turmoil, and great natural disasters are not the signs of the second coming. Those have been going on for the last 2,000 years, and verses 6 and 8 tell us they provide no indication of the end.

Jesus tells us what the signs of the second coming in fact are. Notice verses 9 to 14. *"Then shall they deliver you up to be afflicted, and*

shall kill you: and ye shall be hated of all nations for my name's sake.
[10] *And then shall many be offended, and shall betray one another, and shall hate one another.* [11] *And many false prophets shall rise, and shall deceive many.* [12] *And because iniquity shall abound, the love of many shall wax cold.* [13] *But he that shall endure unto the end, the same shall be saved.* [14] *And this gospel of the kingdom shall be preached in all the world for a witness unto all nations; and then shall the end come."* What is contained in verses 9 to 14 are signs of the end. Transnational worldwide persecution led by the Antichrist and his false prophets, worldwide apostasy in which false Christians betray the true Christians to their persecutors, and worldwide evangelism are signs of the end.

Notice verse 15: *"When ye therefore shall see the abomination of desolation, spoken of by Daniel the prophet, stand in the holy place,"* verse 21, *"then shall be great tribulation, such as was not since the beginning of the world to this time, no, nor ever shall be."* When that level of defilement of God's temple (the church) occurs, and that level of tribulation comes to the earth, that is a sign of the end. Notice verse 24: *"For there shall arise false Christs, and false prophets, and shall shew great signs and wonders; insomuch that, if it were possible, they shall deceive the very elect."* When powerful false miracle workers appear, that is a sign of the end.

There has been great religious deception going on for centuries, but this is something that is in a completely different category of deception, in that these people will actually be able to do great signs and wonders. They will be able to do miracles like Pharaoh's magicians were able to do miracles when Moses appeared before Pharaoh.

Notice verse 29: *"Immediately after the tribulation of those days shall the sun be darkened, and the moon shall not give her light, and the stars shall fall from heaven, and the powers of the heavens shall be shaken."* That is a sign of the end. Verse 30: *"And then"* (after all these signs) *"shall appear the sign of the Son of man in heaven"*; that is, the Son of man Himself appearing there. All these signs lead up to the ultimate sign, which is Jesus appearing in the upper heavens, *"and then shall all the tribes of the earth mourn, and they shall see the Son of man coming in the clouds of heaven with power and great glory."*

The end times begin when Satan is loosed, and the loosing of Satan produces these signs we just described. The Antichrist appears, claiming to be God on earth. He is *"the abomination of desolation."* The worldwide, transnational universal persecution of Christians by all nations occurs: *"Ye shall be hated of all nations for my name's sake."*

This will bring about the great apostasy of professing Christians, in which they will betray their fellow believers and betray Jesus Christ. They will not endure to the end, verses 10, 13. Their iniquities shall begin to abound, verse 12. They will be offended over the persecution that Christians receive, and will abandon their allegiance to Christ. They will begin betraying other Christians and hating them. There will be this great deception by powerful, miracle-working, false prophets, verse 11.

Great tribulation will occur that seeks to kill all Christians everywhere on the earth, and nearly succeeds in doing so. Except those days would be shortened, no Christian would be saved alive, verses 21–22. Then the heavens will begin to shake and be disrupted, and the sun will go dark and the moon will go dark, and the stars will start to fall, verse 29. Those are the signs. When you see those things, then you know the end is near, even at the door. Then you know the second coming of Christ is imminent. But until you see those things, it is not. If you go out and look at the tree and the buds are not swelling, then summer is not close. But if later you look at the tree and the buds are swollen up and just about ready to break out, then summer is near!

Likewise, when you see these signs, these things that are described in verses 9 to 29, you know that the second coming is now imminent. You know that it is near, even at the door. Verse 33, *"So likewise ye, when ye shall see all these things,"* (all these signs) *"know that it is near, even at the doors."* When someone is at the door, he is very close to coming into the house. When these signs occur, Jesus is very close to coming into this world.

Thirdly, notice the assurance given in verses 34 and 35: *"Verily I say unto you, This generation shall not pass, till all these things be fulfilled. 35 Heaven and earth shall pass away, but my words shall not pass away."* When Jesus says in verse 34, *"This generation shall not pass,"* what generation is He talking about? He is talking about the generation that sees the signs of verses 9 through 29. The generation that sees these signs, the generation that, as it were, sees the buds of the tree swell up, *"this generation shall not pass, till all these things be fulfilled."*

We should notice something very carefully. Jesus is talking to His disciples, and He does not say, "Your generation will not pass away till all these things be fulfilled." He says: "*This*" generation. What generation? The generation that witnesses the signs: that generation will not pass until all these things are fulfilled. In other words, when Satan is loosed, and Antichrist appears, and the great apostasy occurs, and the great tribulation starts—it will end within one generation. The generation that sees those things will not die off before the second coming occurs.

We know the great tribulation is going to be short in comparison to the period from verses 4 to 8, which has been going on for 2,000 years now. The great tribulation, when it starts, will end within one generation. It will not last longer. Indeed, we are told it will be cut shorter in verse 22, lest all the remaining believers are killed in the persecution that arises during that time of great tribulation.

These promises and predictions Christ makes about all of this are more solid and certain than even the universe itself. Notice verse 35: "*Heaven and earth shall pass away,*" (When is it passing away? Verse 29: Just before the second coming). "*Heaven and earth shall pass away, but*" Jesus says, "*my words shall not pass away.*" This passing away of the heavens and the earth is not only described in verse 29, but also in 2 Peter 3:10–13.

Second Peter 3:10–13 says: "*But the day of the Lord will come as a thief in the night; in the which the heavens shall pass away with a great noise, and the elements shall melt with fervent heat, the earth also and the works that are therein shall be burned up.* [11] *Seeing then that all these things shall be dissolved, what manner of persons ought ye to be in all holy conversation and godliness,* [12] *Looking for and hasting unto the coming of the day of God, wherein the heavens being on fire shall be dissolved, and the elements shall melt with fervent heat?* [13] *Nevertheless we, according to his promise, look for new heavens and a new earth, wherein dwelleth righteousness.*"

We know that heaven and earth are going to pass away, but the promises and predictions that Christ made in this passage will not pass away until every single one of them is completely and fully fulfilled just as they are stated.

Fourthly, notice the warning given. The warning is in verse 36. He says, "*But of that day and hour knoweth no man, no, not the angels of heaven, but my Father only.*" Jesus warns us not to start trying to set dates. Jesus gives us signs, but He does not give us dates. We can know when the second coming is near, but we cannot know the day or the hour when it will actually occur, even after the signs appear.

What is going to trigger the beginning of the end times is the loosing of Satan. We do not know when that will occur. What we do have are certain signs that will tell us when it has occurred. They will be so clear that we will know he has been loosed. Then we know that within a generation it is going to be over. Therefore, do not get involved in date setting, and do not believe those who set dates. In fact, Jesus was so adamant about date setting that He repeated Himself in Matthew 25:13, *"Watch therefore, for ye know neither the day nor the hour wherein the Son of man cometh,"* which is a virtual quotation of Matthew 24:36 when He says, *"But of that day and hour knoweth no man, no, not the angels of heaven, but my Father only."*

Is the second coming imminent? The second coming is not imminent. Not until the tree buds is it imminent; that is, not until the signs occur that are contained in verses 9 to 29. Only when those signs occur is the second coming imminent.

Will the second coming take believers by surprise? We will not be surprised. Verse 33 says, *"So likewise ye, when ye shall see all these things, [you] know that it is near, even at the doors."* When it gets close, we will know. When the tree buds, we know summer is near. When these signs occur, we will know the second coming is right around the corner. It will not happen to us by surprise.

Will believers know the date of the second coming? We will not know the date. The loosing of Satan, which sets all of this in motion, could occur tomorrow, or it could occur centuries from now. We have no idea of the date when the swelling of the bud will begin, or when the signs will start to appear. We know what the signs are, but we do not know when those signs will first begin to swell and show. Even after the signs appear, we will still not know the day or hour of Christ's coming. We will only know that it is very soon, in less than a generation.

There are two parallel passages that further illuminate these matters. The first one is 1 Thessalonians 4:13 to 5:4. *"But I would not have you to be ignorant, brethren, concerning them which are asleep"* (those who have died), *"that ye sorrow not, even as others which have no hope.* 14 *For if we believe that Jesus died and rose again, even so them also which sleep in Jesus will God bring with him.* 15 *For this we say unto you by the word of the Lord, that we which are alive and remain unto the coming of the Lord shall not prevent [precede] them which are asleep.* [16] *For the Lord himself shall descend from heaven with a shout, with the voice of the archangel, and with the trump of God:"* (this is exactly the event that is described in Matthew 24:30–31) *"and the dead in Christ shall rise first:* [17] *Then we which are alive and remain shall be caught up together with them in the clouds, to meet the Lord in the air: and so shall we ever be with the Lord.* [18] *Wherefore comfort one another with these words.*

Chapter 5: "[1] *But of the times and the seasons, brethren, ye have no need that I write unto you.*" That is, regarding the times and the seasons for the second coming and the rapture and the resurrection you have no need for me to write to you, because you already know these things. Verse 2: *"For yourselves know perfectly that the day of the Lord so cometh as a thief in the night."* A thief in the night for whom? For the people mentioned in the next verse: "[3] *For when they*" not us, but they—that is, the unsaved *"shall say, Peace and safety; then sudden destruction cometh upon them, as travail upon a woman with child; and they shall not escape.* [4] *But ye, brethren, are not in darkness, that that day should overtake you as a thief."*

Clearly, Jesus is going to come as a thief for the ungodly, but not for the godly. He is going to come as a thief for "them" in verse 3, not for "you" who are spoken of in verse 1 and verse 4. Verse 1: *"But of the times and the seasons, brethren, ye have no need that I write unto you,"* Verse 4: *"But ye, brethren, are not in darkness, that that day should overtake you as a thief."* You know the times and the seasons. I have already told you about them. What are the times and the seasons? They are those signs that are mentioned in Matthew 24:9–29.

When the fig tree starts to bud, it is like a pregnant woman. She knows she is going to have a baby for sure within about nine months. In the same way, when the fig tree starts to bud, you know summer is going to come in two or three months. The point is, when you see these signs, you know Jesus is going to come in just a little while, in less than a generation.

But these unsaved people do not recognize this pregnant period, this budding period. They are going on as though nothing is going to happen and then suddenly, summer arrives, and the baby comes—that is, Jesus comes back. They are taken by surprise, even though all the signs were there. If the husband of a pregnant woman was shocked that a baby showed up, we would ask questions like: "Were you not paying attention? Did you not see the changes in her body? Were you not observing? You are taken by surprise that your wife had a baby?" We might say the same thing to the ungodly: "You are surprised that Jesus came back? All the signs were there!"

The rapture is not a secret event where we are just snatched away suddenly while nobody saw it coming. You are going to see all the signs, after which Jesus is going to come, and every eye is going to see Him; and then, as stated in Matthew 24:31, the rapture occurs, as the angels gather the elect and bring them up to Christ. There is nothing secret about the rapture. It is going to happen after everybody sees Jesus in verse 30, and then the rapture occurs in verse 31. There is no secret rapture.

The second passage is 2 Thessalonians 2:1–4: *"Now we beseech you, brethren, by the coming of our Lord Jesus Christ, and by our gathering together unto him, [2] That ye be not soon shaken in mind, or be troubled, neither by spirit, nor by word, nor by letter as from us, as that the day of Christ is at hand."*

People were saying, "The second coming is imminent! It is at hand! He is standing right outside the door!" Paul says, "No, it is not." He says in verse 3: *"Let no man deceive you by any means: for that day shall not come, except"* the fig tree bud; except the signs of pregnancy start to manifest themselves; except the signs appear. And what are the signs? *"A falling away first"*—that is, the great apostasy of the Christian church—and *"that man of sin be revealed."* That is the appearance of Antichrist, committing the abomination of desolation, sitting in the temple of the church universal, declaring himself to be God: *"[4] Who opposeth and exalteth himself above all that is called God"* (the God of the Bible) *"or that is worshipped; so that he as God sitteth in the temple of God, shewing himself that he is God."*

Is the second coming imminent? Paul says, "No, it is not imminent. The great apostasy has to occur and the antichrist has to appear first. After those two things occur, then and only then will the coming of Christ to gather us together to Himself take place."

This is parallel with what Jesus is saying in Matthew 24. There He says His coming is not imminent until these signs show up. When these signs do show up, that generation will not pass until He returns. But until those signs show up, His coming is not imminent.

The believers understand the nature of the second coming. It is not going to be imminent, it is not going to be a surprise, and they do not know the date. Jesus made that clear. When the signs occur, then it will be imminent, and because they see the signs, the believers will not be surprised. They will not know the day or the hour, because it will be within a generation, and that is a long time—about forty years. They should not even be date setting during the time when they are seeing the signs. All they should be saying is, "The signs are here. He is at the door. It is going to come in just a little while, maybe a few years, maybe a decade, but it is coming soon. It is at the door." We cannot say that now, because none of the signs of the loosing of Satan has yet occurred.

The Ungodly Will Be Surprised by the Second Coming of Christ

We will not be surprised by the second coming of Christ, but the ungodly will. Notice Matthew 24:37–41. Jesus is not talking about the believers now, but about the ungodly. In verse 37, He says, "*But as the days of Noah were, so shall also the coming of the Son of man be.*
[38] *For as in the days that were before the flood they were eating and drinking, marrying and giving in marriage, until the day that Noah entered into the ark,* [39] *And knew not.*" Take note: "*And knew not.*"

Notice the contrast between the phrase in verse 32 and the phrase in verse 39. "*Now learn a parable of the fig tree; When his branch is yet tender, and putteth forth leaves, ye know. . .*" Verse 39: They "*knew not.*" Believers know; unbelievers do not know. It is not that the unbelievers are not warned. Noah warned the people in his day, but they just ignored it, refused to believe it, and mocked it.

It says in verse 39, they "*knew not until the flood came, and took them all away; so shall also the coming of the Son of man be.*" The unsaved knew not because they chose to ignore the warnings. "[40] *Then shall two be in the field; the one shall be taken, and the other left.*
[41] *Two women shall be grinding at the mill; the one shall be taken, and the other left.*"

We have already seen in 1 Thessalonians 5:2–3 that the ungodly will be clueless about the second coming. They will not notice that their wives are pregnant. They will not notice the trees are budding. They will not notice the signs of the second coming. They will not notice that Noah is building an ark! They will dismiss all of those things as being meaningless and irrelevant. They will think that because the Christians are about to be wiped out, and because there is now a one-world ruler and a one-world religion and a one-world god over the whole church, that all will very soon be peace and safety.

Is this not what the globalists are promising us? If we just get rid of all national boundaries and all religious differences, the whole world can live in peace and unity. They have been promising that forever. They will think they have achieved it when Antichrist rallies them around himself. They could not be more mistaken. The moment of their greatest security and self-confidence is the moment of their greatest danger and their imminent ruin. In verse 39 it says, *"They knew not."* The ungodly will be marked by complacency, security, confidence, and a mockery of the warnings of impending judgment, just as they were in Noah's day.

What happened before the flood, with reference to the ungodly, is exactly what is going to happen before the second coming of Christ. They will be utterly surprised by the second coming, just like a homeowner sleeping in his house is utterly surprised by a thief showing up in the night. He did not expect him to come.

I want you to notice the order of judgment and the sequence in which it will occur. Going back to verse 37, *"But as the days of Noah were, so shall also the coming of the Son of man be.* 38 *For as in the days that were before the flood they were eating and drinking, marrying and giving in marriage, until the day that Noah entered into the ark,* 39 *And knew not until the flood came, and took them all away."*

Who was taken away? Clearly, all of the people outside the ark. Who were they? They were the ungodly. The ungodly are those who are taken away. They were taken away after Noah and his family were removed from the earth in the ark. The ungodly were all drowned. Noah and his people were lifted up above the wrath that was falling on those below.

Notice verse 40: *"Then shall two be in the field; the one shall be taken."* Who was taken in verse 39? The ungodly people. So who is taken in verse 40? The ungodly one. So two shall be in the field, and one shall be taken and the other left. The one that is left is like Noah. He was left. Everyone else was taken to judgment except Noah and his family. Verse 41: *"Two women shall be grinding at the mill; the one shall be taken, and the other left."* In verses 39, 40, and 41, this taking is the taking of the unsaved to judgment by God to be objects of His wrath.

The parallelism of verses 39, 40, and 41 tells us that the ones taken are the ungodly, and therefore those verses could not possibly be a reference to the rapture; because in the rapture, it is the godly who are taken, as 1 Thessalonians 4:13–18 makes clear.

In Matthew 13:24–30, we have the parable of the sowing of the tares in the field of wheat. *"Another parable put he forth unto them, saying, The kingdom of heaven is likened unto a man which sowed good seed in his field:* [25] *But while men slept, his enemy came and sowed tares among the wheat, and went his way.* [26] *But when the blade was sprung up, and brought forth fruit, then appeared the tares also.* [27] *So the servants of the householder came and said unto him, Sir, didst not thou sow good seed in thy field? from whence then hath it tares?* [28] *He said unto them, An enemy hath done this. The servants said unto him, Wilt thou then that we go and gather them up?* [29] *But he said, Nay; lest while ye gather up the tares, ye root up also the wheat with them.* [30] *Let both grow together until the harvest: and in the time of harvest I will say to the reapers, Gather ye together first the tares, and bind them in bundles to burn them:"* take the tares for destruction, but *"gather the wheat into my barn."*

Notice Matthew 13:36: *"Then Jesus sent the multitude away, and went into the house: and his disciples came unto him, saying, Declare unto us the parable of the tares of the field.* [37] *He answered and said unto them, He that soweth the good seed is the Son of man;* [38] *The field is the world; the good seed are the children of the kingdom; but the tares are the children of the wicked one; the enemy that sowed them is the devil; the harvest is the end of the world; and the reapers are the angels."* There we have the meaning of the symbols declared.

Here is the interpretation, verse 40: *"As therefore the tares are gathered and burned in the fire; so shall it be in the end of this world."* Now we are going to get the description of the disposition of each. Verse 41: *"The Son of man shall send forth his angels, and they shall gather out of his kingdom all things that offend, and them which do iniquity;* [42] *And shall cast them into a furnace of fire: there shall be wailing and gnashing of teeth.* [43] *Then shall the righteous shine forth as the sun in the kingdom of their Father. Who hath ears to hear, let him hear."* Two outcomes are set forth: the wicked are taken and burned, and the righteous are revealed and glorified.

Notice 2 Thessalonians 1:6–10. The Thessalonians are being persecuted, and Paul offers them the comfort of the second coming and how Jesus is going to deal with their persecutors at that time. He says in 2 Thessalonians 1:6: *"Seeing it is a righteous thing with God to recompense tribulation to them that trouble you;* [7] *And to you who are troubled rest with us, when the Lord Jesus shall be revealed from heaven with his mighty angels,* [8] *In flaming fire taking vengeance on them that know not God, and that obey not the gospel of our Lord Jesus Christ:* [9] *Who shall be punished with everlasting destruction from the presence of the Lord, and from the glory of his power;* [10] *When he shall come to be glorified in his saints, and to be admired in all them that believe (because our testimony among you was believed) in that day."*

At Christ's second coming, the righteous will find rest from their persecutors when the rapture occurs, verse 7, and then the flaming fire is going to come and take away all the wicked, verses 8 and 9. The righteous are going to glorify and admire the Lord Jesus as they see the wicked taken away in flaming fire, verse 10.

Notice Revelation 20:7–9: *"And when the thousand years are expired, Satan shall be loosed out of his prison"* (this is the beginning of the great tribulation, Matthew 24:9–29), *"*[8] *And shall go out to deceive the nations which are in the four quarters of the earth, Gog and Magog, to gather them together to battle:"* (against the Christians) *"the number of whom is as the sand of the sea.* [9] *And they went up on the breadth of the earth, and compassed the camp of the saints about, and the beloved city:"* At this point, the rapture occurs. This is how Jesus saves His people from imminent destruction, and once they are safely removed from the scene, then *"fire came down from God out of heaven, and devoured them."*

When Jesus returns, the angels will gather the resurrected righteous dead together with the living believers who have been instantly glorified, and bring them to meet Jesus in the air. Immediately, one hundred percent of the wicked will be killed by the flaming fire of Jesus Christ. The believers will then come back with Jesus to the earth. The wicked will then be resurrected, there will be the final judgment, and then the new heavens and the new earth will be inaugurated. There is no place in any of that for a literal thousand-year Millennium. This is why we know the Millennium began at the cross, because that is when Satan was bound. Jesus bound the strong man at His first coming, as Matthew 12:29 tells us.

Matthew 24:30–31 sets forth this same order. *"And then shall appear the sign of the Son of man in heaven: and then shall all the tribes of the earth mourn, and they shall see the Son of man coming in the clouds of heaven with power and great glory."* They mourn because they see the judgment coming. Then the rapture occurs, verse 31: *"And he shall send his angels with a great sound of a trumpet, and they shall gather together his elect from the four winds, from one end of heaven to the other."* Jesus then comes in flaming fire and takes vengeance on the wicked, and they are done.

Therefore, when we come to verses 40 and 41 and they say, *"Then shall two be in the field; the one shall be taken, and the other left.* [41] *Two women shall be grinding at the mill; the one shall be taken, and the other left,"* the one that is taken is the one that is taken in judgment when the fire falls and consumes that person and takes that person away. The ones that are left are the believers, whom the angels have caught up to be with Jesus in the rapture, and who shall ever be with the Lord.

The believers will be anticipating the second coming. They will see the signs, they will be following the signs, they will know that the second coming is very close, and they will not be surprised at all when it occurs. They will not know the exact day or the hour, but they will see the signs and will know it is right at the door. Jesus will not come as a thief in the night for them. They will not be surprised. The ungodly will be surprised. They will not see it coming, and when it happens, they are going to mourn, and then they are going to be burned up in the fire of the wrath of Jesus.

It is clear from 2 Thessalonians 1:7–9 and Revelation 20:9 that the fire is going to come and take them away. Therefore, people are in error when they try to use verses 40 and 41 to describe the rapture. Those verses are really describing the judgment when the tares are gathered (*"taken"*) and burned. Over and over again, Jesus says He is going to burn them. We are told that the wicked are going to be burned in Matthew 13 under the symbolism of the tares, in 2 Thessalonians 1:7–9 they are going to be burned in flaming fire, and in Revelation 20:9 they are going to be burned in fire from heaven. This is how they will be taken away. That is the sequence of events, and that is how it is going to unfold.

Christ wins and His people win, and the wicked are destroyed at the very brink of their triumph. They are destroyed by Christ, and thus His triumph is magnified and His people are magnified in that triumph.

Therefore, when things are going bad, and we are getting Supreme Court rulings that go against us, we should not be alarmed. The highest Supreme Court is showing up, and His name is Jesus. When He shows up, all those rulings are going to be overturned. We do not have to worry about the ungodly and their apparent successes. The ungodly are going to have a lot more success during the great tribulation than they are having even now. They are going to look like they have totally won. There is going to be just a little remnant of believers left, and then there will be such a reversal that it will be unimaginable. How many people were killed in the flood, and how many people were saved? In the same way, when Jesus comes back, there is going to be a tiny number of people still alive and who will be saved physically, and there are going to be billions that will be taken away in the flood of fire that is going to come down from God out of heaven.

Appendix 2
An Explanation Regarding Daniel 9:24–27

In the process of writing this commentary on Revelation, I was repeatedly asked by numerous people: What about Daniel 9? Many people recognize that Daniel 9 is pivotal to the Dispensational interpretation of Revelation, and they were curious as to how I was going to deal with it.

My initial response was that I was not going to deal with it at all, since Daniel 9 is never quoted or alluded to in the entire book of Revelation even once. It would seem that if Daniel 9 had any importance at all to the meaning and message of Revelation, it would make some reference to it, but it does not. This is doubly strange because Revelation is saturated with Old Testament references. Revelation is not shy about using Old Testament passages to convey its meaning and message. Revelation has more references to the Old Testament than the entire rest of the New Testament put together, and it is very telling that it omits Daniel 9 as a part of those references.

The reason for this omission is that Daniel 9 deals with the first coming of Christ, and it was a prophecy of that event. It covers the time frame from the decree to rebuild Jerusalem after the captivity until the time of the Messiah and the events surrounding His first coming. Its statement about the abomination of desolation was fulfilled in the destruction of the temple in AD 70, and that is the extent of its prophetic scope.

Daniel 9 was relevant when Jesus was still alive and teaching in Matthew 24 before the destruction of Jerusalem; and therefore, He quoted it in Matthew 24:15 concerning that event, but once Jerusalem was destroyed, Daniel 9 had been completely fulfilled. Because of this, it plays no part in the book of Revelation.

Revelation was written in AD 95, and by that time Daniel's prophecy was in the rearview mirror in terms of its fulfillment. This is why it is not spoken of in Revelation. It had already been fulfilled.

But in spite of this explanation, many people were insistent that I include an exposition of Daniel 9 in an appendix because it is so widely used as an interpretive framework for Revelation by the dominant dispensational school of thought. I have yielded to that request.

It is important to understand that this passage is widely disputed as to its interpretation, and it bristles with difficulties. Every phrase is argued as to its meaning. It is not my intention to deal with all of the various possible interpretations that have been advanced regarding it. To adequately do so would require a book in itself, and would be far beyond the scope of this appendix.

But since it is so widely disputed as to its meaning, it seems very strange that some teachers of prophecy would use Daniel 9 to provide the primary framework for their eschatological teachings. Surely less-controversial passages should be used to provide the framework for eschatology, and an extremely difficult passage such as this one should be interpreted in light of those clearer passages, and not vice-versa. Therefore, Daniel 9 must be understood as it fits into passages of plainer and less-controversial meaning. Eschatology should not start with Daniel 9; it should end with Daniel 9, after all of the plain prose passages in the New Testament have been exegeted and integrated with one another.

After careful reading of authors on this passage from all of the various perspectives, it seems that the simplest and best explanation as to the true meaning of this passage is as follows.

The Introduction to the Passage

There are one of two fundamental errors that virtually all the interpreters of Daniel make. Some of them make both errors.

The first error that one group of interpreters makes is that of making the numbers in this passage to be equivalent to a fixed number of literal years. They suppose that each week spoken of in this passage is equivalent to seven years, so that it covers a time frame of 490 years, broken up into three periods of 49 years (seven weeks), 434 years (sixty-two weeks), and 7 years (one week).

The problem with literalizing these numbers is that there is no way to make the events that are described in verses 24–27 fit into any kind of a 490-year time frame, no matter when one thinks the commandment went forth to restore and build Jerusalem. Pick any one of the four decrees you wish regarding the restoration of the temple or the restoration of Jerusalem (Ezra 1:1–4, 6:6–12, 7:11–26, or Nehemiah 2:1–8), the math does not and cannot work out to cover in 490 years all the events that are clearly said to occur in this passage.

Here is the heart of the matter: The numbers used in this passage are very vague in the way they are stated. The word "years" is never mentioned in this passage. The idea that the "seventy sevens" (the literal translation of "seventy weeks" in verse 24) must have the meaning that it refers to "seventy weeks of years" must be imported into it from other passages by the interpreter, because it is absent from the passage itself. Various justifications are offered for importing the idea of "years" into this passage, but all of them are questionable.

But suppose that importing the idea of "years" into the passage is wrong. Suppose further that it lies at the very heart of why this passage is so frustrating to deal with by interpreters. It is beyond dispute that "seven" is used symbolically in apocalyptic literature, a category into which Daniel certainly falls. Seventy sevens is used symbolically in this passage just like seven and multiples of seven are also used symbolically in Revelation. We will return to this concept shortly.

The second error that another group of interpreters makes is that of separating the seventieth week from the sixty-nine weeks that precede it with some kind of a time gap, usually making that time gap large enough so that the last week includes the actions of the Antichrist just before the second coming. Some interpreters literalize the seventy weeks as being weeks of years (Walvoord) and some of them view the seventy weeks as symbolic (Leupold), but all of them posit a gap between the sixty-ninth week and the seventieth week, and apply the seventieth week to the time immediately preceding the second coming.

But this is without warrant, because no one posits a gap between the "seven weeks" and the "sixty-two weeks" of verse 25. What then is the justification for doing so between the sixty-ninth week and the seventieth week? There is nothing in the passage that suggests that there is a gap. The only reason a gap is suggested is because the interpreter decides that there must be one, based on the meaning he determines verse 27 must have. But the meaning supplied to verse 27, that it applies to the Antichrist, is in error as we will demonstrate, and therefore no gap is needed or required.

I would suggest a third path to properly interpret this passage, one that solves the vexing problems that attend the standard approaches to it.

First, recognize that *the language used in this passage to describe the time frame* (seventy sevens, seven sevens, sixty-two sevens, and one seven) *is very vague and indefinite*, and is therefore symbolic, as numbers used in apocalyptic literature almost always are. No adjectives are used to assign any definite meaning to these numbers; are they weeks of days, weeks of months, or weeks of years? There is no need to supply an answer to that question. The passage does not require it. The numbers stand for themselves as symbolic time periods of completion, because seven is the number of completion. (The proof for the number seven symbolizing completion is set forth in chapter 5 of volume 1.)

Second, recognize that *the events that are described in this passage are very specific and definite* as to their identity, and therefore they determine the literal time frame this passage covers. The language used to describe the events that take place in this passage is plain enough to be without any real doubt as to its meaning.

Everyone agrees (other than liberals) that this passage includes three events. It includes the command to restore and build Jerusalem during Ezra and Nehemiah's time, the coming and atoning death of Messiah the Prince who is Jesus Christ, and the destruction of Jerusalem in AD 70. These are very definite historical events.

Therefore, this time frame begins with the decree to restore and build Jerusalem (at the earliest in 538 BC with the decree of Cyrus in Ezra 1:1–4, or at the latest in 445 BC with the decree of Artaxerxes in Nehemiah 2:1–8) as described in Daniel 9:25. This time frame includes the coming and substitutionary atoning death of Jesus Christ as described in Daniel 9:25–26. This time frame ends in AD 70 with the destruction of Jerusalem and the temple as described in Daniel 9:26–27. At the minimum, this period of history lasts for at least 515 years. These three events are the true time markers of the passage.

The point is this: Do not fit the events into the seventy-week time frame; fit the time frame of the seventy weeks into the events. The events are clear and certain; the time frame is vague and unclear. We should start with the clear, and interpret the unclear in light of the clear. Therefore, the events dictate the meaning of the time frame, and the events dictate to us that the time frame must be symbolic. Whatever these seventy weeks are, they have to cover these three events. Furthermore, this symbolic time frame continues without separation between its stated segments. There is no indication in this passage that the seventy weeks are anything other than contiguous.

There are three major events in this passage: The rebuilding of Jerusalem, the coming and work of Messiah the Prince, and the destruction of Jerusalem. Likewise, there are three major symbolic periods for the completion of those three events: seven sevens, sixty-two sevens, and one seven.

The Exposition of the Passage

First of all, we have the general outline of the future provided in verse 24.

"*Seventy weeks*" in the Hebrew is literally "seventy sevens." And while the Hebrew word translated "weeks" can certainly be translated that way, if it is understood literally, then it would mean ordinary weeks made up of days, and this would result in a 490-day time period, which would be too short to mean anything. If it is used as weeks of years, it is still too short to encompass the destruction of Jerusalem in AD 70, which is plainly referred to in this passage. Therefore, it must be understood symbolically. What we have is seven times ten times seven, which, according to the symbolic meaning of those numbers, is completion times perfection times completion, indicating that this time period of "seventy sevens" is the perfect amount of time needed to complete all the events that are subsequently described.

The next phrase "*are determined upon thy people and upon thy holy city,*" is critically important to the interpretation of this entire passage. This phrase sets forth the objects of the prophecy—that is, whom this prophecy is about and whom it concerns. It concerns the Jewish nation, and it concerns the Jewish capital. The angel is speaking to Daniel, and speaks to him about "*thy people*" and "*thy holy city.*" Who are Daniel's people but the Jewish nation, and what is Daniel's city but Jerusalem? The critical point is this: the whole prophecy is about them, and them alone. Therefore, whatever follows is about God's dealing with them, and with no one else. All subsequent phrases must be interpreted in light of the angel's declaration about the objects of this prophecy. This prophecy is about the Jewish nation and the Jewish city.

The angel tells Daniel that God is going "*to finish the transgression, and to make an end of sins*" of the Jewish nation and the Jewish city. The Jews were currently in the seventy-year captivity due to their sins, and their holy city was in ruins as a result of them. And while they were going to shortly be restored back to their land and were going to rebuild their city as verse 25 says, yet they were going to fall into even worse sins than previously, by crucifying the Messiah their Prince. The result would be that God would end His covenantal relationship with both the Jewish people and their city, and He would make a New Covenant with a new Israel who would ultimately inhabit a New Jerusalem.

Jesus declared the end of His relationship with the Old Israel in Matthew 21:43, and He declared the end of His care for Jerusalem in Matthew 23:37–24:2. Both the Nation and the City would no longer represent Him, and their sins and transgressions would no longer continue as a reproach to His Name, because they would cease to exist as the earthly expression and representative of the kingdom of God. The days of their transgressions were sealed and shut and ended as a collective representation of the kingdom of God. Never again could this Nation and City sin and transgress against God, because they ceased to have any existence as a covenant Nation and City. They ceased to exist in that regard, and that which does not exist cannot sin or transgress anymore. As a result, their transgressions and sins were finished and ended.

But the future would not only hold a rejection of Israel and Jerusalem; it would also hold a redemption for God's elect from within them. Previously, no adequate atonement for sin had been achieved through the animal sacrifices, nor had any means of obtaining righteousness been provided. But the good news was that Messiah the Prince would come *"to make reconciliation for iniquity, and to bring in everlasting righteousness."* Salvation would come within this "seventy sevens" of time that would both atone for sin and provide a righteousness to all who trusted in Messiah the Prince to provide it.

These "seventy sevens" would bring a final fulfillment and end to all of God's prophecies regarding national Israel. It would *"seal up the vision and prophecy"* regarding the Jewish nation. Everything God has to say about Old Israel would be completed at the end of the "seventy sevens," and everything He said regarding her would be fulfilled. Prophecy regarding Old Israel would be sealed, shut, and finished. Never again would any vision or prophecy be given regarding Old Israel or Old Jerusalem after the "seventy sevens" were ended. That aspect of divine revelation ended when the "seventy sevens" ended, because Old Israel ended.

During these "seventy sevens" God will *"anoint the most Holy,"* who is Jesus Christ. This anointing took place at His baptism when He was anointed with the Holy Spirit who descended on Him in the form of a dove, Matthew 3:13–17, Luke 4:18, Acts 10:38. There He was publicly commissioned to do His work of ministry and redemption. He is the Messiah, the anointed one, as verses 25 and 26 state. He is *"most Holy"* because He is sinless.

Secondly, we have the specific details of the future explained in verses 25–27.

"Know therefore and understand, that from the going forth of the commandment to restore and to build Jerusalem unto the Messiah the Prince shall be seven weeks, and threescore and two weeks: the street shall be built again, and the wall, even in troublous times."

The first historical event the angel says will take place at the beginning of this "seventy sevens" is *"the commandment"* by the Persian king for the Jews to be released from their seventy-year captivity (as Jeremiah prophesied) and return to the land of Israel *"to restore and to build Jerusalem"*—that is, to restore and rebuild the temple and the city that contained it. *"The street shall be built again, and the wall, even in troublous times,"* and all of this rebuilding and the trouble that attended it is recorded in Ezra and Nehemiah.

The second historical event the angel says would occur would be the coming of *"Messiah the Prince."* This is clearly a reference to Jesus Christ. The time frame between *"the going forth of the commandment to restore and to build Jerusalem unto the Messiah the Prince"* is set forth in two segments of "seven sevens" and "sixty-two sevens," totaling "sixty-nine sevens." The first period of "seven sevens" is the period between *"the commandment to restore and to build Jerusalem"* and the time it took to complete that task. In other words, the first time period of "seven sevens" is the time period between the command to rebuild Jerusalem and the time it was completed.

Immediately upon the completion of the rebuilding of Jerusalem, the second time period of "sixty-two sevens" began, and it went on until Messiah the prince came. So, the first time frame encompassed the period it took to rebuild Jerusalem, and the second timeframe encompassed the period it took from the completion of Jerusalem until Jesus came.

"[26]*And after threescore and two weeks shall Messiah be cut off, but not for himself: and the people of the prince that shall come shall destroy the city and the sanctuary; and the end thereof shall be with a flood, and unto the end of the war desolations are determined."*

Verse 26 takes up the second time frame of "sixty-two sevens" that was mentioned in verse 25, and states that *"after"* that time frame is completed, *"Messiah [shall] be cut off, but not for himself."* The work of Messiah takes place *"after"* the second time frame of "sixty-two sevens," making it clear that the work of Messiah began in the final seven, the last of the "seventy sevens" this passage began with in verse 24. *"Messiah [shall] be cut off, but not for himself"*—that is, His death was for others, it was not for Himself or as a result of His own transgressions. He died for others, not Himself, 1 Peter 2:22–24. He was *"cut off"* from life by the Jews.

He was put to death by the Jews in the most evil and wicked act that has ever been committed by humanity, Acts 2:23. As a result, *"the people of the prince that shall come shall destroy the city and the sanctuary; and the end thereof shall be with a flood, and unto the end of the war desolations are determined."* God sent the Roman army under the leadership of Titus to destroy Jerusalem and the temple, and to dismantle and scatter the Jewish nation and people across the earth. A flood of Roman soldiers came and wrought desolation on the land and the people. This is described in great detail by Josephus.

"[27]*And he shall confirm the covenant with many for one week: and in the midst of the week he shall cause the sacrifice and the oblation to cease, and for the overspreading of abominations he shall make it desolate, even until the consummation, and that determined shall be poured upon the desolate."*

Here the angel returns his focus to Messiah, and says of Him that *"he shall confirm the covenant with many for one week: and in the midst of the week he shall cause the sacrifice and the oblation to cease."* During this period of the "final seven" in which Messiah is doing His work, He will make and *"confirm"* with His blood *"the [new] covenant"* with His people, the New Israel, made up of *"many"* peoples. As a result of His perfect sacrifice on the cross, *"he shall cause the sacrifice and the oblation"* of the Jewish ordinances and animal sacrifices to *"cease"* because they are no longer valid, nor do they have any benefit.

This will occur in the middle of this "last seven" time frame, *"in the midst of the week."* If the "sixty-two sevens" period ended and the "last seven" period began at the birth of Christ, then the *"midst of the week"* when "the covenant was confirmed" would be after 33 years had passed. It would then be 37 more years until the destruction of Jerusalem in AD 70, thus making the new covenant occur virtually in *"the midst of the week"* that defines this time period.

The focus in the last half of the verse once again turns to the destruction of Jerusalem. Titus and the Roman legions will spread their abominations over the city and temple like a predatory bird spreads his wings over its prey once it is captured. This is *"the overspreading of abominations"* by which *"he shall make it desolate, even until the consummation, and that determined shall be poured upon the desolate."* God has determined to make Jerusalem desolate for crucifying His Son, and He will use the Roman army as His sword to do it, Isaiah 10:5–6. The abomination of desolation will take place: God's temple will be defiled by ungodly men, the temple will be destroyed, and the nation will become desolate, dispersed, and dismantled.

Both verse 26 and verse 27 have the same parallel structure: the first half of each verse deals with the work of the Messiah, and the second half of each verse deals with the destruction of Jerusalem. Each conveys the message that Messiah does His work, Jerusalem rejects His work, and Jerusalem is destroyed as a result.

Conclusion

Seven is the number of completion. In the seven sevens, the rebuilding of Jerusalem was completed. In the sixty-two sevens, the time between the finishing of Jerusalem and the coming of Jesus was completed. And in the final seven, the ministry of Jesus in providing atonement, instituting the New Covenant, and implementing His wrath on Jerusalem and the Jews was completed. Here the prophecy and the passage end. It has nothing to do with the end times or the second coming of Jesus. This is why it has nothing to do with the book of Revelation or its interpretation.

Appendix 3
An Explanation of Ezekiel's Temple in Ezekiel 40–43

When the errors of dispensationalism are addressed, the issue of Ezekiel's temple is often brought up to defend the necessity of a future millennium. The question is asked: Without a millennial kingdom, how and when and where will Ezekiel's temple be built?

This of course assumes that Ezekiel's temple must be built at all. The necessity of such a temple being literally built as Ezekiel describes it is highly questionable for several reasons.

First, given the final, finished, and perfect sacrifice of Christ, which renders any further animal sacrifice for sin blasphemous, it is inconceivable that a temple would be built in the future to offer such sacrifices. Hebrews 9–10 make this abundantly clear. But priests in Ezekiel's temple are commanded to make animal sacrifices as sin offerings in 40:39, 42:13, and 43:18–27. Hebrews 10:1–18 makes it clear that it would be an insult and a rejection of Christ's once-for-all sacrifice for sin to either now or in the future make any further animal sacrifices for sin.

Dispensationalists insist that animal sacrifices in this temple during the Millennium will be memorial in nature. The text plainly says they will be for sin. The only way they can arrive at the conclusion that these sacrifices will be memorial in nature is to abandon their commitment to literal interpretation at this point and spiritualize these sacrifices.

Second, Jesus abrogated worship in a physical temple in John 4:19–24 as a result of His life and death. This abrogation was implemented when the veil in the temple was rent from top to bottom when He died, rendering access to God through a physical temple no longer legitimate and no longer necessary. The way into the holiest presence of God is now made possible in a new and living way through the sacrifice of Jesus' blood and body on the cross, in which we come to God by faith and worship Him in spirit and in truth, as Hebrews 10:19–22 teaches us.

Third, building Ezekiel's temple is unnecessary, since the physical temple of the Old Covenant has been replaced with the spiritual temple of the New Covenant, which is the church, 1 Peter 2:1–5. The New Covenant priesthood made up of all believers offers, in the New Covenant temple, the verbal sacrifice of thanksgiving and praise, as Hebrews 13:15 states, rendering any physical animal sacrifice of thanksgiving both unnecessary and inappropriate, and therefore any physical temple pointless and useless.

Fourth, we are in the Millennium right now. The proof of this is in chapter 57 of this book. There is no future Millennium in which to build Ezekiel's temple; there is only the present Millennium, and it is agreed by all that it would be inappropriate to build a Jewish temple in this present age. Dispensationalists all state that it would only be built after Christ's second coming, and it would be out of place in the "church age" in which we are now living. But the age we are now living in is also the Millennium of Revelation 20, and after Christ's second coming we enter the New Heaven and New Earth where there is no physical temple, as Revelation 21:22 says. This leaves no time and no place for Ezekiel's temple to be built.

Fifth, Ezekiel's temple supposedly needs to be built for a revived and restored Jewish nation that had been "set aside" during the "church age" in order for them to offer sacrifices of thanksgiving to their formerly rejected and crucified Messiah. But this fails to understand that the church is the New Israel with whom the New Covenant was made, and that all Christians are spiritual descendants of Abraham; and therefore, they are the true Jews, as Galatians 3:29 and Romans 2:28–29 makes so clear. There will be no "revived Jewish nation" made up of ethnic Jews. As for the ethnic Jews, Matthew 21:43 says of them that the kingdom of God has been taken away from them and given to a nation that will bring forth the fruits thereof. That new Jewish nation is the Christian church, as 1 Peter 2:9–10 says. It is to them that all the promises made to Israel apply.

Some have suggested that Ezekiel's temple was built by the Jews as described in Ezra. It is clear that Ezra's temple does not match the description of Ezekiel's temple, even after being upgraded during Herod's reign. Ezekiel's temple is far greater in magnitude than even Solomon's temple.

This leads us to a consideration of Ezekiel's temple itself. Is it meant to be taken as a literal temple that was going to be literally built to its literal dimensions?

The answer is plainly no, for all the reasons stated above. But it is also unreasonable for this temple to be built because of its literal dimensions. Let us examine Ezekiel 40–43.

The temple was measured by Ezekiel with a reed (rod) that was six cubits in length. These cubits were long cubits (a cubit and a handspan, see also 41:8), about two feet in length. This means that the reed was about 12 feet long. This is all set forth in 40:5.

The temple court is 500 reeds long and 500 reeds wide (42:15–20), which means the temple covered an area 1.14 miles wide by 1.14 miles long. This is larger than the entire city of Jerusalem; in fact, this temple could not even be contained on Mount Zion itself.

It was unthinkable to a Jew that the temple would not be built inside of Jerusalem. But this temple is so large that it would obliterate Jerusalem and the entire mountain on which it was built. Building it was a physical impossibility for the returning Jews. They never thought they should build it, though they knew all about it because this vision was given decades before the return from the captivity.

If Ezekiel was not describing a literal temple that was to actually be built, then what was he describing? To answer that question, we must understand an important principle of biblical interpretation, and it is this: New Covenant blessings and promises are often conveyed in Old Covenant imagery and language of physical, material, and earthly blessings. The future spiritual prosperity of God's people was described in terms that Old Covenant believers could relate to and understand, and which made sense to them in their world at their point in history.

Notice several points about the New Covenant blessings that are conveyed by this Old Covenant imagery.

First, Ezekiel's temple, which was immensely larger than even Solomon's temple, is a symbolic picture of the New Covenant temple, the church. The church is immensely larger than national Israel ever was, both in terms of the number of people it contained, and in terms of the geographical area it covered. Israel had a couple of million people in it at most; the church has hundreds of millions of people in it. Israel covered a few hundred square miles, but the church covers the whole earth. This extraordinarily large temple spoke of the extraordinarily large size and reach of the temple to come, which is the church of Jesus Christ, Ephesians 2:19–22.

Therefore, we see that the size of this temple was conveying a message about the size of the New Covenant temple in the future, the immense area it would cover, and the immense reach it would have.

Second, we see that the detail with which this temple is described and measured indicates the detailed concern and attention Christ has for every member of His temple and for every aspect of its work. Everything is measured; that is, it is marked out for His protection, as explained in chapter 32, and every part of it is noticed; that is, no part of it is overlooked or forgotten. This indicates that every person is protected by Christ, and every person is seen by Christ, and every person is the object of His attention and concern. Every part of the church is seen and protected by Christ, and no part of it is overlooked or unnoticed. Every part of the church, wherever it is in the world, is a part of the glorious temple of the church universal that Christ said He would build in Matthew 16:18, and it constantly receives both His protection and His attention.

Third, the glory of God filled this temple (43:1–5), indicating that the presence and glory of God will fill and indwell His church in time, as we are told in Matthew 18:20, and in eternity, as we are told in Revelation 21:2–3.

Fourth, we observe that a life-giving river ran out from under this temple in 47:1–12, which is clearly not a literal river in the way it flows or a normal river in the effects it produces. It is a picture of the life-giving gospel that flows out of the witness of the church. Jesus spoke of this life-giving river in John 8:38. The Spirit of God empowering the word of God as it flows out of the temple of God gives life to the world. It finds its final expression in Revelation 22:1–2 as the river of life in the New Earth. See chapter 66 for a detailed explanation of this river.

This entire last section of Ezekiel 40–48 is a picture of the church as a temple, believers as priests, and the division of their respective areas of work and responsibility in the land of the whole earth.

Ezekiel begins his book with a highly symbolic visual image of the throne of God in the opening chapter, and it ends with a highly symbolic visual image of the temple of God in the closing chapters.

Ezekiel's temple will never be literally built, but what it foreshadows and pictures is already being built as the New Covenant temple, the church.

Appendix 4
The Source and Nature of Civil Government

In Revelation 13 we are taught that all civil government derives its power, its position, and its great authority from the Dragon, that is, from Satan. With temporary exceptions when the head of the Beast is wounded, civil government is characterized by blasphemy of God and by persecution of the people of God. Civil government is a minister of Satan.

The reader may be confused by this teaching, because he has been taught to view civil government not from the perspective of Revelation 13, but from the perspective of Romans 13.

Romans 13 seems to set forth the opposite perspective of Revelation 13. Romans 13 states that civil government derives its authority from God, and that civil government is a minister of God.

What view shall we take of civil government? Is it a minister of Satan or a minister of God? Does it derive its authority from Satan or from God?

The answer to this apparent conflict is not to see these passages as contradictory, but as complementary to each other. We must not take a simplistic view of the complex subject of the source and nature and function of civil government.

This complexity of the interaction between God and Satan and the impact it has on the human experience and in human institutions can be seen in the story of Job. God's works in providence provide us with some indication of how God works in civil government.

From one perspective, all that happened to Job was the work of God. God gave direction for what was to happen to Job, and when it was over, Job recognized God's management of it and control over it. He said, "*. . .the* L*ORD gave, and the* L*ORD hath taken away; blessed be the name of the* L*ORD.*" He went on to say, "*. . .shall we receive good at the hand of God, and shall we not receive evil?*"

Job saw the Sabeans and the lightning from heaven and the Chaldeans and the tornado as instruments of God. He accepted them as deriving their authority and ability to do what they did from God. He was right to do so. If you will, this is the Romans 13 view of providence. God worked them all together for good to Job.

But from another perspective, all that happened to Job was the work of Satan. As *"the god of this world,"* Satan gave these agents the authority and power and direction to do the evil that was done. Satan sent them as his ministers to produce blasphemy against God and to persecute the people of God. Satan was permitted to work within God's authority and power to exercise his authority and power for evil. We can rightly say that Satan controlled providential events for evil in Job's life. If you will, this is a Revelation 13 view of providence. Satan worked them all together for evil to Job.

This story of Job makes it clear that both God and Satan operate in the realm of providence at the same time and through the same instruments, but each has different goals and purposes. Satan's work is meant for evil, but God's work is meant for good. Satan's work ultimately fails, and God's work ultimately succeeds. The hierarchy is clear: God's authority is supreme; however, Satan's delegated authority is both real and powerful.

These same principles operate in civil government. Civil government exists by the authority and power of God as Romans 13 teaches. It is supposed to reward good and punish evil as God's law defines those terms. When it does so, we are to submit to it, respect it, yield obedience to it, support it with taxes, and see it as a blessing from God. Civil government in fact does operate in this fashion whenever God sees fit to wound the head of its blasphemy to the point of death.

But civil government also exists by the delegated authority and power of Satan, as Revelation 13 teaches. Governments derive their authority and power from Satan. The kingdoms and governments of this world belong to Satan because Adam forfeited them to him in the fall when Adam lost dominion over the earth. It is these kingdoms that Satan offered to Christ in the temptation if Christ would only worship Satan. Christ did not dispute that all the kingdoms of the world belonged to Satan, but He refused to obtain them by that means. Instead, He would obtain them by defeating Satan at the cross and at the second coming.

When Jesus returns, then *"the kingdoms of this world [will] become the kingdoms of our Lord and of his Christ,"* showing they are not currently the kingdoms of Christ. He will take possession of them all when He returns; but until then, they are still the kingdoms of Satan. Within the limits placed on Satan by God, Satan controls their governments in this age so that they blaspheme God and continue to persecute Christians. They will do so with great intensity after Satan is loosed.

Therefore, it follows that both God and Satan operate in the realm of civil government at the same time and through the same instruments, but each has different goals and purposes. Satan's work is meant for evil but God's work is meant for good. Satan's work ultimately fails and God's work ultimately succeeds.

God has final control over civil governments. The king's heart is in the hand of the Lord, and He turns it wherever He wills, but Satan is given a large liberty and a wide authority to use civil government for evil, and evil predominates in the actions of civil governments as a result.

By the mercy of God, the blasphemy and Satanic power of civil government is often moderated to a degree so that in some ways it does punish evil and reward good, but its natural direction is always away from good and toward greater measures of evil, because the god of this world is driving it in that direction.

When Satan is loosed at the end of this age, civil government will become an instrument of pure evil. But until then, as much as we are able, let us encourage our civil authorities to be ministers of God and not ministers of Satan. But let us never labor under the delusion that civil government is only a minister of God and that all it does is only from God. It is the Beast out of the sea, and it needs to be seen from that perspective.

Select Bibliography

The following books were consulted in the preparation of these messages, as well as many others not listed here. These are the most helpful in assisting the reader in his understanding of Revelation, and will richly repay any effort expended in reading them.

G. K. Beale and David H. Campbell. *Revelation, a Shorter Commentary*. Grand Rapids: Eerdmans Publishing Company, 2015.

Gary B. Ferngren. *The Book of Revelation*. Unpublished lectures, Corvallis Oregon, 2009.

Steve Gregg. *Revelation, Four views: a Parallel Commentary*. Nashville: Thomas Nelson, 1997.

William Hendriksen. *More Than Conquerors: An Interpretation of the Book of Revelation*. Grand Rapids: Baker, 1962.

Leon Morris. *Revelation (Tyndale New Testament Commentaries)*. Downers Grove: InterVarsity, 1987.

Derek Thomas. *Let's Study Revelation*. Edinburgh: Banner of Truth Trust, 2003.

Samuel E. Waldron. *The End Times Made Simple: How Could Everyone Be So Wrong About Biblical Prophecy?* Amityville: Calvary Press, 2003.

Michael Wilcock. *I Saw Heaven Opened: The Message of Revelation*. Downers Grove: InterVarsity, 1975.

Geoffrey B. Wilson. *New Testament Commentaries, Volume Two, Philippians to Hebrews and Revelation*. Edinburgh: Banner of Truth Trust, 2005.